GENERALFELDMARSCHALL
FEDOR VON BOCK
THE WAR DIARY 1939-1945

GENERALFELDMARSCHALL
FEDOR VON BOCK

THE WAR DIARY
1939-1945

Edited by Klaus Gerbet
Translated from the German
by David Johnston

Schiffer Military History
Atglen, PA

Book Design by Robert Biondi.
Translated from the German by David Johnston.

This book was originally published under the title,
Generalfeldmarschall Fedor von Bock: Zwischen Plicht und Verweigerung,
Das Kriegstagebuch,
by F.A. Herbig Verlagsbuchhandlung GmbH, Munich-Berlin.

Printed in the United States of America.
ISBN: 0-7643-0075-X

We are interested in hearing from authors with book ideas on related topics.

Published by Schiffer Publishing Ltd.
77 Lower Valley Road
Atglen, PA 19310
Please write for a free catalog.
This book may be purchased from the publisher.
Please include $2.95 postage.
Try your bookstore first.

CONTENTS

THE WAR DIARY: May 1939 to July 1942

FOREWORD

As probably the last surviving member of the staff of Feldmarschall von Bock (General Staff Officer in the Army Group's Tactical Group) during the campaigns in Poland and France and the preparation and execution of the war against Russia, I would like to write a brief foreword for the field marshall's war diary.

I admired him very much; he was a fascinating person, a gentleman in the best sense of the word and a great expert in his field. Very self-assured, he was definitely neither a "comfortable" subordinate nor a superior, as the conflicts with Feldmarschall von Kluge and Generaloberst Guderian described in the diary reveal.

The diaries offer the interested reader, especially the historian, a wealth of information about the events in the years 1939 to 1942. This is particular relevant to the evaluation of three decisive phases:

– The shifting of the point of main effort from Army Group B to Army Group A before the start of the campaign against France and the halting of the attack before Dunkirk,

– the abandonment of the decisive attack on Moscow in 1941 in favor of Army Group A (Battle of Kiev),

– and the winter crisis before Moscow, which I experienced firsthand as Ia of a division in front of Moscow.

Peter von der Groeben
Lieutenant-General (Rtd.)
May 1995

NOTES FROM THE EDITOR

The original of the von Bock diary was in the possession of the Historical Division, Washington. The reworked copies of the diary notes – including the appendices – of Generalfeldmarschall Fedor von Bock were kept by the Federal Archive-Military Archive Freiburg. The source material which was used here, however, was written by Bock on the spot as the war unfolded and is in the possession of his stepson Kurt-Adalbert und Dinnies von der Osten. It is therefore of significance in two respects; first it contains no dubious "improvements" or "corrections"; second it is an outstanding replacement for the war diaries of the army groups commanded by Bock in the Polish and Western Campaigns, which were burned in 1942 (Bock diary from 23/6/42). Bock gave one copy to Generaloberst von Salmuth, whose son in turn passed the copy over to Bock's stepson. The diary notes, as they were designated by Bock himself, were made primarily for:

– the writing of history,
– the personal vindication of Bock with respect to decisions made by him which had a bearing on the course of the war and which often conflicted with the orders of his superiors
– the realization of his testamentary will, given to his stepson Dinnies, to have them published.

Fedor von Bock subdivided his writings, which represent a unique historical source, into:

– Diary notes from the Polish Campaign May/June 1939 to 3 October 1939
– Diary notes from the preparation for the Western Campaign 4 October 1939 to 9 May 1940
– Diary notes from the Western Campaign (offensive and occupation period) 10 may 1940 to 11 September 1940
– Diary notes from the Eastern Campaign
Part 1 from 20 September 1940 to 21 June 1941 (preparation)
Part 2 from 22 June 1941 to 15 July 1942
Part 3 from 16 January 1942 to 2 May 1945 (Ex post)

The diary notes after Bock's dismissal as Commander-in-Chief of Army Group B are not presented strictly chronologically, rather as they relate to problem areas, in order to more clearly illustrate Bock's thinking in the period leading up to his tragic death in May 1945.

The authenticity of the diary notes is beyond doubt; they were obviously recorded daily or even immediately after important events (conferences, important telephone calls, changes in personnel, significant changes in the military situation, etc.) and stylistically improved, dictated to his stenographer, Feldwebel Jüngling.

According to statements by Fedor von Bock's stepson, in many places he edited his diary notes immediately after they were written in order to neutralize or even omit compromising comments or emotional accounts which might endanger his person. This is doubtless typical behavior for that time; compare the appraisals of those historians who have published the diary notes of Generalfeldmarschall Ritter von Leeb, Generaloberst von Halder and others.

"Field Marshall von Bock's diary reflects the reporting style of a highly-gifted pupil of the traditional school of the Royal Prussian General Staff. Even where Bock's opinion differs from that of the OKH, he shows himself to be a superior mind, a military leader of substance." (Görlitz, Walter. "Paulus, Ich stehe hier auf Befehl!": Frankfurt am Main, 1960, PP 175.)

Errors were quietly corrected. These resulted from the immediacy of the dictation and the frequent inability to check the style of writing. Because of the dynamics and the workload of the staff personnel, the diary notes obviously remain largely as they were written. The abbreviations for military ranks were eliminated or adapted to match conventional forms. Notes by the editor were noted and placed in italics or in square brackets - [.....] - in the original text of the diary.

This diary provides a vivid impression of the great authority which Fedor von Bock enjoyed, no matter where and when it was felt, which was due to his extraordinary military capabilities, his personal magnetism, his constructive critical thinking – which also brought him within a certain proximity of the Stauffenberg circle – his ties with the troops, and his concern for the soldiers as well as for the civilian population in enemy countries.

To better understand the diary notes of Fedor von Bock I also drew upon works based on political and military files, like the War Diary of the Wehrmacht High Command (Wehrmacht Operations Staff) 1940-1945, introduced by H. Greiner and P.E. Schramm. Volume I: 1 August 1940 to 31 December 1941, compiled and explained by H.-A. Jacobsen, Frankfurt am Main 1965 and The Secret Daily Reports of the German Armed Forces Command in the Second World War, by von Mehner, Kurt, Vol.2, Osnabrück 1993, Vol. 3, Osnabrück 1992, Vol. 4, Osnabrück 1992.

The statements concerning Fedor von Bock and the military actions of his army group made at the Nuremberg Trial after the end of the Second World War are irrelevant, insofar as the defendants there could easily blame some-one who was no longer alive – Fedor von Bock died on 4 May 1945 as a result of injuries suffered the day before as a result of a strafing attack by English aircraft. If one considers that the statements made by the witnesses or ac-cused who were questioned there were largely of a procedural-tactical nature anyway, their greatly reduced value as historical sources is obvious (See the Nuremberg Trial against the main war criminals before the International Mili-tary Court, Nuremberg, 14 November 1945 - 1 October 1946, France – CIC A.Grp.B, Vol. VII, PP 297; Conspiracy of Generals, Vol. XII, PP 254, Vol. XV, PP 339; Group of Generals Vol. IV, PP 453, Vol. XXII, PP 319; USSR "Barbarossa" Conference 9/6/41, Vol. IX, PP 259; Commissar Order (Rejec-tion), Vol. IX, PP 211, Vol. XVII, PP 337, Vol. XX, PP 635; CIC A.Grp.C, Vol. IV, PP 530, Vol. XXI, PP 58, Nuremberg 1947-49).

My special thanks go to Herren Dinnies and Kurt-Adalbert von der Osten, the Field Marshall's stepsons, who not only made preparation of this publica-tion possible, but as well contributed to the diary being made accessible to the public in this form with photographs and documents. As the film's author, I also wish to thank them for their great commitment in preparing and making the television documentary "Zwischen Pflicht und Verweigerung" (first broadcast on Ia on 28 April 1995). In doing so they made a very significant contribution to disproving or correcting all the distorted accounts concerning the person of Generalfeldmarschall von Bock.

GENERALFELDMARSCHALL
FEDOR VON BOCK:
Biographical Notes

Fedor von Bock, one of the most capable German field marshals of our century, was born in Küstrin on 3 December 1880. The old city on the Oder had been founded in the year 1235 and its walls formed one of Germany's strongest fortresses until 1918. Together with Berlin-Spandau and Peitz, Küstrin was one of the three Prussian fortress cities which Elector Johann V built.

It is obvious that Prussia's defensive character was embedded in the personality of the future field marshall and found expression in his desire to serve and his military-strategic philosophy.

His father, Moritz Karl Albert von Bock, was born in Koblenz on 15 January 1828. He rose to the rank of Major-General. On 19 January 1873 he was elevated to the nobility, because on 19 January 1871, while serving as a major and commander of Infantry Regiment No. 44, he had refused to give up his command though severely wounded in the Battle at St. Quentin. Instead he remained with his regiment until the battle was over and led it from his field hospital.

On 18 January 1871 General August von Goeben assembled his army around St. Quentin, which was defended by the two Faidherbes Corps; finally General von Goeben's force, advancing by way of Vermaud led by the 44th Fusiliers, forced the French back through Holnon to Selency. The 44th advanced on Fayet. This severely threatened the line of retreat of the French in the north and as a result there was costly fighting. The bloody victory cost the Germans 96 officers and 2,304 men; the French admitted losing more than 10,000 men.

For his action, Bock was recommended for the award of the Order *Pour le Mérite* by his superior, the brilliant general August von Goeben. However, in 1873 Kaiser Wilhelm I instead decided instead to award him a title. Von Bock ultimately became a major-general and commander of Torgau. Both his sons would later receive the highest Prussian award for valor, the future field marshall and his older brother Fedor Franz Karl, an outstanding general staff officer who received the decoration while Chief of Staff of III Army Corps.

Moritz Karl Albert died on 16 April 1897 in Berlin-Charlottenburg. He was buried at the Invaliden Cemetery in Berlin on 19 April.

Bock's mother, Olga Helene Franziska von Falkenhayn, who likewise came from the nobility – a sister of Prussian Minister of War and later Chief of Staff of the Field Army Erich von Falkenhayn – was born on 4 March 1851 in Burg Belchau, Graudenz District. She died on 14 December 1919 and was also buried in the Invaliden Cemetery. Fedor von Bock's grandfather was Friedrich Wilhelm Bock, Major and deputy commandant of Magdeburg. Born on 25 May 1780 in Ohlau, he died in Magdeburg on 1 February 1838. His wife was Albertine von Hautcharmoy, born 16 June 1800, died in Teplitz 11 January 1876.

Military Career Before, During and After
The First World War

After attending school in Wiesbaden and Berlin, Bock joined the 7th Company of the Royal Prussian Cadet Institute at Groß-Lichterfelde. The cadets called him *"Böckchen"* on account of his friendly nature. Bock was universally respected for his outstanding achievements. He "was very good in such academic subjects as modern languages, mathematics and history. He spoke fluent French and very good English and Russian." (Turney, Alfred W.: *Die Katastrophe vor Moskau – Die Feldzüge von Bocks 1941-1942*, PP 4.)

"Under the influence of his father, even in his early years he was filled with the idea of unconditional loyalty to the state and set his mind on a career in the military. The new German Reich was the product of a series of victorious wars. Bock was taught that it was his life's duty as a career military man to contribute to the further glorification of Prussian Germany. These early teachings were to stay with Bock throughout his life. They also served to close his thoughts to all other considerations and direct them solely to the immediate consequences of his status as a soldier in the service of the Fatherland." (Turney, PP 4.)

After serving as a senior non-commissioned officer, on 17 March 1898, at the age of 18, he passed the selection board and began his service as a second-lieutenant (commission: 15/3/1898) with the 5th Foot Guards Regiment in Berlin-Spandau. Now he developed "those physical and mental qualities which later took him to the top of the German military hierarchy. He was tall and slim, had narrow shoulders and a posture straight as a ramrod. His sharp features, piercing green eyes and narrow lips made him look emaciated, indeed almost starved." (Turney, PP 5.) The same year, on 9 October, he married Mally von Reichenbach, who died at an early age in 1910. In 1907 Bock became regimental adjutant.

Effective 10 September 1908 he was promoted to *Oberleutnant* (commission: 10.9.1908 Z 2 z). From 1910 to 1912 Bock, who had not attended staff college, was sent to the Grand General Staff for general staff training and was promoted to *Hauptmann* on 22 March 1912. He subsequently joined the Army General Staff and was transferred from the Grand General Staff to the General Staff of the Guards Corps (commission: 22.3.1912 R 2 r). In 1913 he first became 2nd then 1st General Staff Officer of the Guards Corps. In this period he joined the Army League, where he met Walther von Brauchitsch, Franz Halder and Gerd von Rundstedt.

After the outbreak of the First World War Bock took part in the fighting in the west (Namur, St. Quentin, Arras, Ypres, Artois). In 1915 he became a battalion commander in the 4th Foot Guards Regiment. Effective 28 December 1916 he became a *Major* in the General Staff of the Grand General Staff (commission: 28.12.1916 U u). Bock subsequently joined the 200th Infantry Division as general staff officer; this unit saw action in the mountain war in the Carpathians and took part in the defensive battles against the Russian "Brusilov offensive" of 1916.

In 1917 and 1918 Bock served as 2nd then 1st General Staff Officer in the staff of the German Crown Prince's Army Group. There he won the friendship of his Commander-in-Chief and he remained faithful to him and the House of Hohenzollern – even after the abdication of the Royal Family.

In his book *Erinnerungen aus Deutschlands Heldenkampf,* the Crown Prince of the German Reich and of Prussia, Wilhelm, wrote of Bock:

"Through his inexhaustible vigour, this highly-gifted officer was a never-wavering support to me and my chief of staff in times of the hardest and most demanding work."

For his military accomplishments Bock was awarded the Iron Crosses First and Second Class, the Order of the House of Hohenzollern and in April 1918 the Order Pour le Mérite. In 1919 he served as a member of the army peace committee.

Bock's services in the initial phase of the "great battle in France" were generally acknowledged; like Majors Beck and Freiherr von Fritsch, he was one of the "farsighted men with the highest culture and education." (von Thaer, Albrecht: *Generalstabsdienst an der Front und in der O.H.L.,* Göttingen, 1958, PP 278).

As 1st General Staff Officer with the Chief of Staff of Lüttwitz (Reichswehr Army Group Headquarters 1), *General* von Oldershausen, he flatly refused to take part in the Kapp Putsch.

As Chief of Staff of Military Area Headquarters III (Berlin), on 1 October 1920 he was entrusted with, among other things, the formation and liquidation of the Black Reichswehr.

On 1 October 1920 Bock became Chief of Staff of the 3rd Division (commander was *Generalleutnant* Rumschötter) in Berlin (RDA: 1.10. 1920-140) and on 25 December he was promoted to *Oberstleutnant.*

In 1924 he became commanding officer of II Light Infantry Battalion of the 4th Infantry Regiment (4th Prussian Infantry Regiment) in Kolberg. On 20 May of the following year he was promoted to *Oberst* while serving with the 4th Infantry Regiment (RDA: 1.5.25) and on 10 June 1926 was appointed commander of the regiment. On account of his services in times of war and peace, on 6 February 1929 Bock was promoted to *Generalmajor* (RDA: 1.2.1929-8-).

"In the late twenties and early thirties, when Bock was one of the highest officers in the Reichswehr, he was now and then invited to talk to graduates of his alma mater. He spoke passionately, and his theme was always that the highest honor for a German soldier was to die for the Fatherland on the battlefield. Because of this passionate, fanatical encouragement von Bock received the title 'the holy fire of Küstrin'." (Turney, PP 6)

On 14 September 1929 Bock was named commanding officer of the 1st Cavalry Division (Frankfurt/Oder) effective 1 December; under the division's command were six cavalry regiments stationed in East Prussia, Pomerania and Brandenburg. On 7 February 1931 he was promoted to *Generalleutnant* (RDA: 1.2.1931-2-).

On 14 September 1931 Bock was named commanding officer of the 2nd Infantry Division as well as Commander Military Area II (Stettin), whose units were stationed in Pomerania, Mecklenburg and Schleswig-Holstein. His promotion to *General der Infanterie* and simultaneous appointment to Commander-in-Chief of the Army Office Berlin, the later Army Group 3 (Dresden; Bock at first lived in the Taschenberg Palace, later Heidepark-Str. 8) – which was subdivided into IV, VII and XIII Army Corps – followed on 1 March 1935. Bock expressed his satisfaction with his new function in a letter to Hardenberg on 31/5/1935. (See Agde, Günter: *Carl-Hans Graf von Hardenberg...*, Berlin 1994, PP 140.)

Fedor von Bock married Wilhelmine Gottliebe Jenny, nee von Boddien (1893-1945), in Berlin on 20 October 1936.

Army Commander in the Second World War

Three years later, in March 1938, Bock was named Commander-in-Chief of the newly-formed 8th Army. The 105,000 men of the German 8th Army faced the 100,000-man Austrian Federal Army with its very up to date armaments. The 8th Army consisted of the VII Army Corps, Headquarters XIII Corps, the 2nd Panzer Corps, Army office 10 for the occupation of Tirol and the 97th reserve Division. There were elements of the Luftwaffe as well, including three army cooperation squadrons, three bomber wings and the Aiblingen Fighter Group as well as anti-aircraft forces (according to the report submitted by Bock on the action in Austria dated 18/7/1938; BA-MA WF-03/16719, PP 247). Bock assumed in his plans that "there is little likelihood of coordinated resistance by the Austrian Army," rather he reckoned on "active and passive resistance by the indoctrinated workers in the industrial areas" (BA-

MA, WF-03/16719, PP 252). The march into Austria ultimately turned out to be an unopposed occupation of the alpine republic, but it bore features of later *blitzkrieg* actions. How did Bock assess the attitude of the neighbor states? While he assumed that "no trouble was to be expected from Yugoslavia and Hungary and that Italy was expected to remain neutral" when the Germans marched into Austria, only three days before the troops moved he asked the OKH to clarify whether Czechoslovakian troops and aircraft entering into Austrian territory were to be treated as "hostile." In keeping with the answer that followed promptly, Bock instructed his generals that: "...Czechoslovakian troops on Austrian soil are to be treated as hostile." The 8th Army marched into Austria on 13 March 1938; the Austrian Federal Army was incorporated into the Wehrmacht. During the night of 15/3/1938 "*General* Bock, the Commander-in-Chief of the 8th Army, swore in Under-Secretary of State Angelis and Field Marshall Lieutenant Bayer... Simultaneously, the Commander-in-Chief of the 8th Army, *General der Infanterie* von Bock, issued the following order of the day: 'The *Führer* and Supreme Commander has placed me in command of the entire German Armed Forces within the national borders of Austria...'" (*Dresdner Neueste Nachrichten*, 15/3/38, PP 4). On the same day Hitler promoted *General der Infanterie* von Rundstedt and *General der Infanterie* von Bock to *Generaloberst*. "The *Führer* personally announced the latter's promotion shortly before the big parade in Vienna and had especially appreciative words for the actions of the troops under his command." (*Dresdner Neueste Nachrichten*, 16/3/38, PP 4).

The incorporation of the Austrian Federal Army into the Wehrmacht was completed on 1 April. Army Group Headquarters 5 was formed in Vienna. "His mission complete, *Generaloberst* von Bock, the former Commander-in-Chief of the 8th Army, returned to his peacetime post of Commander-in-Chief of Army Group Headquarters 3 in Dresden." (*Dresdner Neueste Nachrichten*, 30/3/38, PP 1.)

In the autumn of the same year Bock's troops participated in the occupation of the Sudetenland. The Czechoslovakian frontier region was occupied in stages between 1st and 10th October according to the provisions of the Munich Agreement. The commanders of the participating army groups exercised full authority until 20 October 1938 (see Appendix 1). On 6/10/38 Hitler and Bock

– then still the Commander-in-Chief of Army Group 3 – drove together into Zone II (see Munich Agreement), whose troops were under Bock's command.

Bock's military accomplishments were highly appreciated by the Army Command. On 22 October 1938 Bock received the following letter from Brauchitsch, Commander-in-Chief of the Army:

"Generaloberst!

After the conclusion of your activity as army commander in this historically so significant time for Germany I wish to express my special gratitude for the outstanding work you have done for the Reich and its armed forces. I am aware that the superb preparation and smooth conduct of the entry into the sector under your command was thanks to you, which I acknowledge with special gratitude.

It would be a special pleasure, Generaloberst, if you continue to offer your proven work and your vast experience in the service of the army and assist us in the planned revision of the fundamental command manuals which is to take place in the near future." [BA-MA NF-1/20].

Soon afterward, on 10 November, Bock was named Commander-in-Chief of Army Group 1 (Berlin).

Under the command of Army group 1 were I, II, III and VIII Army Corps (Königsberg, Stettin, Berlin and Breslau).

Bock's first protest against National Socialism, involving the case of *Generaloberst* Freiherr von Fritsch (March 1938) is significant. Canaris and Hoß characterized the stand taken by *Generaloberst* von Bock as "very significant" (document in: Müller, Klaus-Jürgen: *Das Heer und Hitler*, 1969, PP 639. Responsibility for excesses against the Jews in the so-called Night of Broken Glass in November 1938 was not placed on Hitler, rather on the radical elements of the National-Socialist movement, "like Goebbels, whom *Generaloberst* and later *Feldmarschall* von Bock would most dearly loved to have strung up." (Rauh, Manfred: *Geschichte des Zweiten Weltkriegs*, Duncker & Humboldt, Berlin, PP 310). During a meeting of commanders an agitated Bock asked whether they couldn't "hang this swine Goebbels." (Krausnick, Helmut: *Vorgeschichte und Beginn des militärischen Widerstandes gegen Hitler* in: *Vollmacht des Gewissens* by European Publications, Vol. I, Berlin/Frankfurt a. M., 1960, PP 373).

Having played a leading role in the strategic planning preceding the attack on Poland, on 26 August 1939 Bock was appointed Commander-in-Chief of Army Group North (Polish Campaign), made up of two armies. In the Polish Campaign Bock – as his diary shows – Bock was responsible for directing significant operations. His army group attacked on 1 September 1939, and by 4th September it had destroyed the Polish army in the corridor in the Tucheler Heath, taken Graudenz and was marching toward Modlin and Warsaw. East of Warsaw the army group's left wing drove across the Narew and Bug Rivers to Brest-Litovsk; there it linked up with the panzer corps of Army Group South. The heroically-fighting Polish units were encircled. On 16 September the enemy forces between the Vistula and the Bzura, surrounded by elements of the 4th Army and the 10th Army, the latter part of Army Group South, were forced to lay down their arms.

Warsaw fell on 27 September, Modlin, the last Polish bastion, three days later.

Bock was awarded the Knight's Cross for his military accomplishments.

In October 1939 Bock was transferred to the Western Front (northern wing) as Commander-in-Chief of Army Group B; under his command were the 6th Army under *Generaloberst* von Reichenau, the 18th Army under *General* von Küchler, and the 4th Army under *General* von Kluge.

Bock was promoted to the rank of *Generalfeldmarschall* on 19 July 1940 (RDA: 19.7.40-4-). Barely a year later, on 22nd June, he became Commander-in-Chief of Army Group North and led it to victor in the battles at Bialystok and Minsk, Roslavl, Smolensk, Gomel, Kiev, Vyazma and Bryansk. He demonstrated his command skills in Russia, especially in the breakthrough battles of Minsk and Vyazma.

Between Subordination and Insubordination

At no time was Bock a National-Socialist. On the contrary: "There are indications that he had scant regard for nazi pomp. He was of the opinion that he stood above the raw political and propaganda intrigues of the nazis. The story is told that during an official reception at the Reich Chancellery in 1938, Hermann Göring, like Bock a wearer of the *Pour le Mérite*, approached him and said that as wearers of Germany's highest military honor they could actually be good friends. Bock answered with an icy stare and told Göring in no uncertain terms that the medal at their throats did not place them on the same social level.

On the other hand Bock regarded Hitler as head of state and supreme commander of the armed forces and in his diary refers to him almost reverentially. As a high-ranking commander during the Third Reich's early victories in the Second World War, Bock usually concluded his orders of the day with 'long live the *Führer*,' not 'hail to the *Führer*' as the commanders who were adherents of national-socialism did." (Turney, PP 5).

Also noteworthy is the clear position Bock took in the case of the Commanding General of XXXXII Army Corps, *Generalleutnant* Graf von Sponeck. At the end of December 1941 Sponeck, who was responsible for defending the Kerch Peninsula, faced a major Soviet offensive with just the 46th Infantry Division. Acting on his own initiative he ordered his troops to withdraw to the Parpatsch Line. This resulted in a court martial at *Führer* Headquarters presided over by Göring. The result of the brief trial was a death sentence against Sponeck, which Hitler reduced to imprisonment. As his superior, Manstein, "on learning of the judgement immediately submitted a report to the Commander-in-Chief of the army group [Center, Bock]... took Graf Sponeck's side and demanded that the case should be heard again. *Generalfeldmarschall* von Bock agreed with this position entirely. The result was a reply from Keitel in which he rejected the idea in what was to my mind an unjustifiably rude way" (Erich von Manstein, *Soldat im 20. Jahrhundert*, produced by Rüdiger von Manstein and Theodor Fuchs, Bernard & Graefe Verlag, Bonn, 1994, PP 151). Not only were subsequent attempts to affect a complete rehabilitation of Sponeck unsuccessful, but he was shot three days after the attempt on Hitler's life (20 July 1944).

Against an Attack on Moscow before Winter

It was Bock, not the German General Staff, who had been the chief proponent of a concentrated and quick attack on Moscow since mid-July 1941 (Reinhardt, Klaus: *Die Wende vor Moskau*, Stuttgart, 1972, *Beiträge zur Militär- und Kriegsgeschichte*, Vol. 13). However, by December 1941 he was warning emphatically against the attack that had been ordered on Moscow. He pointed out in his memo:

"I am unaware of the command's intentions. But if the army group is to ride out the winter on the defensive, it can only do so in its present general disposition if sufficiently strong reserves are brought in to allow it to deal with incursions and to allow for the temporary relief of the exhausted divisions in the fighting front so that they can rest and recuperate. 12 divisions will be needed for this. I do not know if they are available and can be brought in in the foreseeable future. Another essential condition is order and dependability in the running of the trains and with it the possibility for well-regulated supply and stockpiling. If both conditions cannot be completely met, an abbreviated position for the eastern army in the rear suitable for defense must be chosen without delay and all suitable personnel assigned to set up quarters, supply dumps and defensive positions, so that it can be occupied within a short time of the order being given." (Bock, Fedor, diary entry 1/12/41).

Army Group Center attacked on 2nd October. Following considerable initial success – Guderian reached Tula – the decisive turn of events took place. The crisis Bock had predicted had arrived. In spite of his largely accurate assessment of the situation and his military success, on 19 December 1941, at his own request – but mainly on account of serious quarrels with Hitler – Bock was transferred to the OKH's officer reserve in Berlin. The subsequent catastrophic course of military events proved Bock's exact and real powers of judgement.

It was just this course of events he had wanted to avoid.

His Attitude Towards the Liquidation of Jews, Soviet Commissars and Prisoners of War

Hans Laternser, who defended the "General Staff and the OKW," said in his closing remarks:

"When in March 1941 Hitler first verbally issued this order, which was planned solely by him (the commissar order), it immediately met with strong resistance from all the generals present on moral and military grounds. When all the attempts by the OKH and OKW to prevent Hitler from publishing the order had no success and some time later the commissar order was issued in written form, the commanders of the army groups and armies either simply refused to pass this order on to their troops or took measures on their own to circumvent it. They did so with full knowledge of the danger of being severely punished for disobeying an order from the supreme commander in wartime." (IMG, XXII, PP 91).

There is also a record of a protest by Bock against the order on the maintenance of discipline issued by the Commander-in-Chief of the Army together with the commissar order. When he learned of the Barbarossa decree with disciplinary order on 4 June 1941, Bock noted indignantly that the order gave "every soldier the right...to shoot at any Russian he considered – or claimed to consider – a bandit, from in front or behind." Bock instructed his Chief of Staff, *General* von Greiffenberg, to inform Brauchitsch that this order had to be changed immediately. When there was no noticeable reaction, Bock intervened personally! He won the concession that punishable acts by soldiers against Soviet civilians should be investigated as usual by courts martial and punished. These deviations from orders were only granted to Bock. "The course of the intervention by Bock shows..., what a commander could achieve if he came forward with confidence." (Streit, Christian. *Keine Kamaraden, Die Wehrmacht und die sowjetischen Kriegsgefangenen 1941-1945*: Verlag J.H.W. Dietz, Bonn, 1991, P 44.) Ultimately this order had to be rescinded!

Furthermore Bock took the position, "that members of the police should decide over life and death of prisoners of war in military camps" (Bock, diary entry 9/11/41) but not military personnel.

Instead Bock was interested "in an improvement of the situation in the prisoner camps – but only if it came about through help from above." (Streit, Christian. *Keine Kamaraden...*: PP 157.) He was aware of the inhuman conditions, especially in the prisoner of war camps. A few prisoners, driven by hunger, resorted to cannibalism; six "cannibals" had already been shot, five more had just been seized and "will be bumped off tomorrow." (Prisoner of War District Commander J, report dated 14/11/41 RH 22/v. 220)

Bock stepped in energetically against mistreatment of prisoners of war by the soldiers under his command. He noted: "Acts of brutality have occurred while prisoners of war are being shipped to the rear: I have objected strongly in a toughly-worded letter to the armies. With the exhausted state of the prisoners and the impossibility of feeding them properly during long marches through vast, uninhabited regions, their removal remains an especially difficult problem." (Bock: diary entry 22/8/41.) Historian Christian Streit also emphasized: "Generals like Bock...tried through orders to prevent mistreatment and willful shooting of prisoners" (Streit, Christian. *Keine Kamaraden...*: PP 169), however as reports on such shootings from Rear Army Area Center, *General* von Schenckendorf responsible, show, this did not succeed.

Bock also rejected the actions against the Jews as "the biological root of bolshevism," even though not with the required resolution, as demanded by officers of his staff.

(Gerbet, Klaus. *Carl-Hans Graf von Hardenberg. Ein preußischer Konservativer in Deutschland*: Edition Hentrich, Berlin, 1993.)

Worthy of note are his efforts to "limit claims to power by party functionaries." (Stahl, Friedrich-Christian. *Ostdeutsche Gedenktage 1995, Persönlichkeiten und historische Ereignisse, Kulturstiftung des deutschen Vertriebenen*, PP 131.)

The analysis of Bock's basic ideological-political attitude by creditable historians annuls such a generalizing opinion as: "Bock's differences with the supreme command were not political but purely of a military-professional nature and never went beyond these professional boundaries." (Dr. Bernd Wegner, historian, Military-Historical Research Office, Potsdam. TV documentary by Ia *Zwischen Pflicht und Verweigerung – Generalfeldmarschall Fedor von Bock*: broadcast on 28/4/95.) The statements by Dr. Horst Mühleisen, that Bock "was one of Hitler's paladins, whose orders, no matter what their nature, he never criticized" (Mühleisen, Horst. *Patrioten im Widerstand, Carl-Hans Graf von Hardenbergs Erlebnisbericht*: in The Quarterly for Contemporary History, 3/1993, PP 425) are quite obviously contradicted by Bock's diary entries, especially when one bears in mind that military orders and directives issued by the supreme military institutions came either directly or indirectly from Hitler. In this context it is significant and historically relevant that this diary documents the permanent and escalating protest against cardinal military orders and directives which were of Hitlerian origin! Instead Bock's "loyalty to Hitler" can best be explained by his monarchist background and his history of service to the most senior representatives of the state, whether the King, the Reich President or the *Führer*.

The Last Months at the Front

On 20 January 1942, following the death of Reichenau, Bock was made Commander-in-Chief of Army Group South. *Generaloberst* von Salmuth assessed his activities there: "He mastered every crisis there, in fact in May 1942 he smashed powerful enemy forces which had broken through south of Kharkov."

In June 1942 the army group was divided; Bock assumed command of the newly-formed Army Group B. But then on 15 July 1942 he was sent back to the OKH (Berlin) Officer Reserve.

"It was a serious blow to this great soldier" (von Salmuth). Bock did not receive another command for the rest of the war.

"Fedor von Bock was possibly the most conservative of the career soldiers of the Second World War. His character was dominated by a mixture of national pride, political disinterest, patriotic devotion, and a proud awareness of his high military position. The latter character trait manifested itself in his stubborn striving to act independently and without regard to moderating factors from above or below, which could have distracted him from fulfilling his duty as a Prussian-German soldier.

In contrast to many other German generals also from the Prussian aristocracy, Bock was insensitive to inconveniences and used to them. His own lifestyle was austere, and he expected austerity from others. He sympathized with the suffering and distress of his soldiers on the battlefield only insofar as these things hindered them in fulfilling their mission. There never appears to have been a case of Bock's orders not being followed. When there were military operations to be carried out, Bock appears to have been a man who could put aside the usual human impulses. Statements by subordinate commanders, according to whom it was difficult to serve under Bock, and nicknames like 'holy fire' and 'pusher' confirm this." (Turney. Introduction, PP XVI.)

Bock's military accomplishments in the Second World War were acknowledged with the Bars to the Iron Crosses, First and Second Class (22/9/39), the Knight's Cross of the Iron Cross (30/9/1939), the Order of the Yugoslavian Crown 1st Class (1/6/1939), the Grand Cross of the Order of the Crown of Italy (27/8/1940), the Order "Michael the Brave" 3rd and 2nd Class (29/7/1942), the Grand Cross of the Hungarian War Service Order with Swords (27/11/1942), and the Order "Michael the Brave" 1st Class (1/12/1942).

Final Activities Before Germany's Surrender and His Death

After July 1942 Bock spent most of his time at the Grodtken Estate, was active in his Berlin office (Kaiserallee), and occasionally visited his adjutant, Graf von Hardenburg, in Neuhardenberg.

On 18 January 1945 Bock, together with his wife, left the Grodtken Estate in East Prussia. [Note: Their driver was *Feldwebel* Martin Kallinich, procured by Bodo von der Marwitz for Carl-Hans Graf von Hardenberg; Bock's manageress Gertrud Kieslich accompanied them.]

The next day he reached Schötzow near Kolberg (Pomerania); on 1 February 1945 Bock drove to his quarters on Helfferichstraße in Berlin. On 15 April he left there together with his stepson Dinnies von der Osten and the rest of his party to drive to Ludwigslust via Neuruppin, Wittstock and Parchim. From that day he lived in the castle of the Grand Duke of Mecklenburg. Arriving in Petersdorf (near Lensahn, Holstein) on 23rd April, he and his party were given shelter by the Ludowig family in their farmhouse; there Bock met Karin von der Osten and he friend Ingrid Jahr.

The day after, *Generalfeldmarschall* von Manstein, who was staying with

Count and Countess Platin at Gut Weißenhaus (East Holstein), contacted Bock. Both "sought, as far as was possible – for example through contact with the Commander-in-Chief of the remnants of the German Army facing west in Northern Germany, *Generalfeldmarschall* Busch – to use their influence to see to it that everything was done to save the troops fighting in the east and the civilian population there." (Manstein, Rüdiger von/Fuchs, Theodor. *Manstein – Soldat im 20. Jahrhundert*: PP 213.) On 28 April 1945 both field marshals called on *Großadmiral* Dönitz at his headquarters in Plön, totally unaware that he was to be Hitler's successor. As a result of their discussions they agreed to save "the largest possible segment of the population from being cut off by the Russians" (Bock diary entry 28/4/45). On the basis of the "shocking" (*ibidem*) military situation Bock considered any resistance futile. Resignedly he summed up: "German resistance is collapsing everywhere, in Berlin, at the mouth of the Vistula, in West Pomerania, Mecklenburg and Brandenburg, in Bohemia and Southern Germany, and in Italy (*ibidem*)." Since Bock did not learn that Dönitz had been named Hitler's "deputy or successor" until 1st May, any official advisory function in Dönitz's staff by him, as has been uncritically taken from Soviet sources, is out of the question (Mühleisen, Horst).

Dönitz wrote: "Field Marshals Bock and von Manstein were with me in the last days of April. We discussed the military situation. Manstein in particular stressed the need to gradually withdraw the armies of the Eastern Front, in order to bring them near to the American and English fronts. This coincided with my view entirely. On 1st May I therefore instructed that Manstein be contacted. I wanted to ask him to take over the Armed Forces High Command in place of Keitel. However we were unable to contact Manstein."

(Dönitz, Karl, *Großadmiral. Zehn Jahre und Zwanzig Tage*: Bonn, 1958, PP 447.)

On 2 May 1945 Bock visited *Generalfeldmarschall* von Manstein at the liaison headquarters of the Army High Command, then *General* Kinzel, *Großadmiral* Dönitz's Chief of Staff since 22 April 1945 and soon afterward liaison officer to Field Marshall Montgomery.

Bock intended to visit Manstein in Weißenhaus again on 3rd may to discuss their policy toward the English after the surrender, which was imminent. Early in the afternoon he left the farm in Petersdorf with his wife, stepdaughter Karin von der Osten and her friend Ingrid Jahr, and driver *Feldwebel* Martin Kallinich. On the road to Oldenburg, about two kilometers north of Lensahn, the car was strafed by low-flying English aircraft and set on fire. Only Bock, severely injured, was able to escape the vehicle; all the others were killed instantly. A Wehrmacht patrol took Bock to the navy hospital in Oldenburg, where his 16-year-old stepson Dinnies von der Osten and *Generalfeldmarschall* Manstein were able to speak to him. The *Generalfeldmarschall* died on 4 May 1945. It was his wish that Manstein should take care of his stepson Dinnies, which he did until he was taken prisoner. His last words were: "Manstein, save Germany." (Manstein, Rüdiger von/Fuchs, Theodor: PP 215.)

The dead were buried in Lensahn cemetery; as well as Pastor Otto Jensen, Manstein spoke at the grave:

"Militarily, von Bock was an especially gifted leader, one of our best. He looked splendid and was very charming by nature, even when he stated his opinions energetically. He was far above average, both as a leader of great military operations and as a trainer of the forces and an educator of the officer corps. He was one of the best among his contemporaries!"

(Schröter, Bernhard. *Der Soldatentod des Generalfeldmarschall Fedor von Bock bei Lensahn*. In: *Jahrbuch für Heimatkunde im Kreis Oldenburg-Holstein*, Vol. 10, PP 167.)

With English approval the dead Field Marshall was given a guard of honor by a German panzer company.

MAY/JUNE 1939 to 3 OCTOBER 1939
(POLISH CAMPAIGN)
Commander-in-Chief Army Group North

I n keeping with the plan for the invasion of Poland (Case "White"), Germany's army, air force and navy had been secretly mobilized and deployed for the start of the campaign against Poland. Troops had been moved into East Prussia on the pretext of ceremonies marking the twenty-fifth anniversary of the Imperial Army's victory over the Russians in August-September 1914 (the Battle of Tannenberg). Divisions were transferred to Pomerania and Silesia, ostensibly to work on entrenchments. Tank and motorized units were assembled in central Germany for maneuvers, in order to allow them to quickly reach the concentration areas before the invasion of Poland.

In his directive, *Generaloberst* Walther von Brauchitsch, Commander-in-Chief of the Army, called upon the army to "open the war with surprising, heavy blows and to achieve rapid successes." The military doctrine called for "a surprise drive into Polish territory" in order "to forestall the orderly mobilization and organization of the Polish Army," and concentric attacks from Silesia and Pomerania-East Prussia "to smash the main forces of the Polish Army west of the Vistula and the Narew."

The German plan of operations was based on the concept of a strategic operation to deeply outflank, encircle and destroy the main forces of the Polish Army. The armored forces and the Luftwaffe were given a decisive role to play in the realization of this goal. Two army groups were given the task of carrying out the strategic attack operation: Army Group South under *Generaloberst* Gerd von Rundstedt and Army Group North under *General-oberst* Fedor von Bock.

Army Group North had under its command the 3rd (East Prussian) and the 4th (Pomeranian) Armies, which on 1 September 1939 consisted of a total of 21 divisions, including two panzer and 1 motorized infantry divisions. Its orders were to drive in the general direction of Warsaw from East Prussia and Pomerania and in cooperation with the units of Army Group South attack the Polish forces in a southeasterly direction toward Warsaw. The 4th Army (Kluge) was to launch its assault from Pomerania, drive north of the Narew and then advance on Warsaw and Siedlce. In *Generaloberst* von Bock's reserve were another 3 infantry divisions. Army Group North's operations were supported by the air forces of Air Fleet 1 under *General der Flieger* Albert Kesselring.

The force committed by Germany in the war against Poland comprised almost 63 divisions, including 7 armored and 4 light divisions as well as 4 motorized infantry divisions, with more than 2,800 tanks. Not counting the forces under the fortress commanders and frontier sector commands, on 1 September 1939 the German military command had 54 divisions on the Polish border with which to initiate hostilities.

May-June 1939

The "Draft Plan for Strategic Concentration" in case of a war with Poland reached the army group on 1st May.

General von Stülpnagel (Deputy Chief of the General Staff, Operations) [hereafter referred to as OQu I] held a briefing at which he discussed Commander-in-Chief of the Army Brauchitsch's plan to launch an attack from Southeast Prussia in the direction of Warsaw simultaneous with the attack on the corridor and Graudenz. I took the view that at least three divisions were necessary for the attack on Graudenz and into the Kulmer Land. This attack, which I considered especially important in the interest of a rapid capture of the corridor, was not contemplated by the Commander-in-Chief of the Army [Brauchitsch] to begin with and he had to be convinced. But if three divisions were used for this attack, only four divisions would be left for the drive toward Warsaw! That would not do. Stülpnagel asked me how many more divisions I thought were necessary in East Prussia from the beginning, in order to achieve a quick and decisive success in the direction of Warsaw. I answered: five divisions, so that a total of twelve divisions – not including garrison troops – are ready in East Prussia when the war begins, namely: three for the attack into the Kulmer Land, eight for the attack in the direction of Warsaw and one in reserve. Stülpnagel expressed doubts as to whether that could be made possible.

The Army Command later decided to transfer one division from 4th Army [Kluge], the Pomeranian Army, to East Prussia by sea before the outbreak of war. I wasn't happy about this, for it seriously weakened 4th Army without sufficiently reinforcing the 3rd Army [Küchler].

The Army Group and the Army High Command agreed that the attack by 4th Army had to be made through the southern part of the corridor. In the north weak forces would be committed to first cut off and later capture Gdynia. The 4th Army (Kluge) did not have overly strong forces with which to break through the corridor, on which everything depended. As early as the beginning of May, therefore, the army group began looking at the idea of using border guards, security forces and frontier troops to reinforce the army, and it requested the Army Command to arm and equip them for use as mobile forces, even beyond our borders. At the end of May the request was broadened to make mobile the frontier troops in the Küstrin sector as the "Küstrin Frontier Division" and to put them into the line as quickly as possible. The Army Command at first rejected this request and it was not until June and July that we got our way: the Küstrin Frontier Division was formed as the "50th Division" [Sorsche]. In spite of many shortcomings which were inherent in this improvisation, it was a welcome addition to our strength.

According to the "draft" of the directives for the strategic concentration, there was to be no opposition to the occupation of Danzig by the Poles. In fact we were in favor of the Poles tying down strong forces in the northern part of the corridor; they were lost as soon as the 4th Army's attack in the south of the corridor reached the Vistula [Wisla]. But I was worried that I would be ordered to recapture Danzig if the attack through the corridor did not proceed quickly and the enemy then occupied the city. I would then be forced to take forces from the 3rd (East Prussian) or 4th (Pomeranian) Armies in order to carry that out. That could not be done without endangering my primary mission. Since our information told us that there were about 10,000 trained soldiers of all age classes in Danzig, on 27 May I proposed to the Army Command the immediate formation and arming in secret of a combat unit under military command in Danzig. If the Poles did attack Danzig, the resistance of this "combat unit" would either force them to commit stronger forces – we could only hope for that – or abandon the attack. If they then recognized the danger of being cut off, they would have to retire with the "combat unit" at their backs. If the Poles did not attack Danzig, the "combat unit" could do valuable service in the attack on Gdynia. Formation of "Combat Unit Danzig" was authorized in mid-June after a talk with the *Führer*; when the attack began it would be placed under the command of the army group.

Establish "contact with East Prussia by taking the corridor!"

"The Taking of the Corridor"

14/6/39

Following the final meeting of my trip to see the *Führer* at Bad Salzbrunn, which dealt with Army Group North's probable objectives in a war against Poland, *General* Halder (Chief of the Army General Staff) discussed with me a new version of the strategic concentration directive. Salmuth [Chief of the General Staff of Army Group North] was present. The text of the strategic concentration directive drafted by the general staff struck me as too one-sided, calling for the bulk of the 4th Army [Kluge] to be moved forward across the Drweca after gaining the Vistula River line. I took the position that an operation with the main weight of the attack from Southeast Prussia across the Narew then past Warsaw to the east, behind the Vistula, would undoubtedly be more effective than a frontal attack across the Drweca. Perhaps forces will also have to attack there to prevent the enemy from disengaging; but the army group must subsequently always strive to keep its eastern wing strong! That is a difficult operation, for the necessary forces can only be taken from the 4th (Pomeranian) Army, after that army has established contact with East Prussia by taking the corridor. When and to what extent elements of this army can be sent to Southeast Prussia behind the fighting 3rd Army [Küchler] is impossible to predict at this time. After hearing these arguments Halder changed the wording of several parts of the strategic concentration directive. He emphasized that he agreed with my point of view and that freedom of action for the army group, which was to be unrestricted, was contained in the sentence:

"According to the directives of the Army Group!"

I said: "You needn't worry. I won't make a horizon crawl!"

To this Halder replied, laughing:

"That's fine then!"

They had apparently been worried about that after I had stressed several times the necessity of a strong east wing.

First: "Capture of the corridor" – then – "Attack in the direction of Warsaw."

End of July 1939

Discussion with Halder in the presence of Salmuth. I pointed out that the plan of "forestalling the enemy" expressed in the strategic concentration directive, according to which the attack was to be based on the element of surprise, has been overtaken by events. I called his attention to the fact that intelligence reports issued by the General Staff indicate that the Poles have strong forces – about 7 divisions – in the corridor and about 5 divisions in the area of Mlawa. If, as ordered, Army Group North attacks these forces simultaneously from Pomerania with only 4, near Graudenz with only 2, and near Mlawa with only 5 divisions, there is an obvious danger that it might be too weak everywhere and achieve success nowhere. The first and most urgent mission is the capture of the corridor. I therefore returned to my old proposal, to conduct the attack on Graudenz and into the Kulmer Land, which is so important to this capture, east of the Vistula with stronger forces and to delay the decisive blow near Mlawa in the direction of Warsaw until sufficient forces are assembled in East Prussia! The sooner the corridor is taken, the sooner this will be the case. I also consider a strengthening of the 4th Pomeranian Army to be undesirable; they must consider whether the planned transport of the 12th Divison [Leyen] to East Prussia should go ahead under these conditions or if in this situation it would be better to leave the division with the 4th Army. Halder agreed that the possibility of surprise no longer exists. He also characterized the capture of the corridor as the most vital task! He does not believe in the strong Polish forces reported in the corridor, rather he expects to find the enemy in a broad, thinner formation on the border. I stressed that they should assume the most difficult case in order to assure quick success and once again proposed making the capture of the corridor "Priority 1" and the decisive attack in the direction of Warsaw "Priority 2." Obviously, in this event an attack would also have to be made in the general direction of Mlawa beginning on the first day, but only to the extent required to guard the east flank of the attack on Graudenz and tie up enemy forces. Halder promised to consider the idea, which would be fully justified should the presence of strong Polish forces in the corridor be confirmed. When asked how long I would need to make the necessary changes to my orders, I replied, "Two hours, but I Army Corps will need several days, because it will have to rework its entire buildup."

Halder didn't think he could endorse leaving the 12th Division [Leyen] in Pomerania, as having it transported to East Prussia had been "too hard won."

17/8/39

Conference of the Commander-in-Chief of the Army [Brauchitsch] with the army commanders and the commanding generals of II [Strauss], III [Küchler], and XXI [Falkenhorst] Army Corps in the Kaisersallee in Berlin. The proceedings are recorded in the files of the army group headquarters. The Commander-in-Chief of the Army declared that the attack would proceed as originally ordered by him. I once again stated that, according to the intelligence on the enemy, we did not have superiority at any of the army group's three attack fronts and again requested that the 23rd [Brockdorff-Ahlefeldt], 50th [Sorsche] and 20th Divisions [Wiktorin] be sent to the 4th Army [Kluge] as quickly as possible rather than later as planned. If they could take part in our attack on the first day we would at least have a favorable ratio of forces in one place.

Furthermore, I again pointed out that XXI Army Corps [Falkenhorst] lacked suitable heavy artillery with which to engage the defensive works at Graudenz. The Commander-in-Chief of the Army once again promised to give the matter consideration.

The General Staff very soon declared that moving in the 23rd and 50th Divisions sooner was impossible. The 20th Division would come somewhat sooner; a battery of heavy howitzers was promised for Graudenz.

19/8/39

Further deliberations under way by the Army High Command regarding my proposal. I wrote to the Chief of the General Staff [Halder] to once again present my point of view. (Draft in the Army Group's files.)

21/8/39

Halder phoned and informed me that the Commander-in-Chief of the Army had stuck to his decision after my letter was read. The validity of my ideas was fully acknowledged; they are fully aware that the disposition of forces ordered by the Commander-in-Chief of the Army might initially result in the army group "stalling" in one or even every place. This was "consciously accepted." But the Commander-in-Chief of the Army stuck to his answer, that it was necessary as a counterpart to the missions of Army Group South [Rundstedt].

Halder offered to give me this decision in writing as well; it might be of value for the later writing of history.

"In a Terrific Speech the *Führer* Explained..."

22/8/39

Discussions with the *Führer* on the Obersalzburg. All army commanders and so on were present. In a terrific speech the *Führer* explained the political situation, the just-concluded pact with Russia, and its possible consequences. Militarily, he said that the most important objective was to quickly establish contact with East Prussia and from there make a rapid advance toward and across the Narew. He demanded fast, hard blows. The military operations were to be conducted independent of all political considerations such as future borders, for example, with the sole object of destroying the enemy's armed forces.

Before Hitler's speech Brauchitsch spoke to me about my letter to Halder and said that he had to stick to his decision for the well-known reasons; I replied that I had considered it my duty to explain my point of view once again.

I pointed out forcefully to both of my army commanders the necessity of concentrating their forces, especially the artillery, precisely at the decisive points. I told them once again that at no time and nowhere was this to be an advance in stages or an attack with limited objectives, rather that we must advance vigorously everywhere!

Postscript to 22/8/39

Later it was claimed that the *Führer* had expected that the English would not intervene in the war. I don't believe that was the case, for at the conference on 22 August 1939 he said:

"I don't know whether the English will enter the war against us or not."

Commander-in-Chief of Army Group North

24/8/39

Left Berlin; I arrived in Polczyn [in German Polzin, HQ Army Group North] at about 10:00. At noon I assumed command of Army Group North.

25/8/39

Maps and orientations concerning its plan of attack have not yet arrived from the 3rd (East Prussian) Army. I have the feeling that the army is not looking forward to the offensive with an overflowing heart. Right from its very first proposals I had the impression that it would like to proceed with caution everywhere. Several days ago it decided not to move its sole reserve up to the attack front but to hold it back near Allenstein; after some urging it was finally moved forward as far as Hohenstein. Even moving the wartime garrison of Lötzen up to the border required some gentle pressure. The army headquarters is worried about the gap between the attack group near Graudenz and the one near Neidenburg. In spite of the distance involved, I feel that my unusual step of designating the 206th Division [Höfl] in Northeast Prussia as army corps reserve was correct, because it was the only way I could do anything to counter a dispersal of the forces in East Prussia, which I feared. I ordered the division to "stand ready for transport." Böckmann, head of the General Staff of the 3rd Army said today:

"Just don't move it out too soon, otherwise it won't be ready to entrain."

Concern over a Polish advance from Suwalki probably has something to do with this!

I was on the road all day and spoke to Guderian (XIX Army Corps), Geyr [Geyer in original; Geyr von Schweppenburg, 3rd Panzer Division], Kluge (Headquarters, 4th Army), Strauss (II Army Corps), and Gablenz, who commands a battalion of border guards and the hard-won Küstrin Frontier Division (the 50th Division). All are well-informed, calm and clear. Everywhere I went I emphasized once again that only a vigorous advance could achieve success with the unfavorable ratio of forces. Kluge [4th Army] calmly accepted the possible threat to both of his flanks, especially the southern flank.

The expected note from the Chief of the General Staff [Halder] arrived in the evening; he acknowledged my proposal and confirmed the negative decision by the Commander-in-Chief of the Army. The note stated that the difficulties pointed out by me had been acknowledged but that they were being consciously accepted. It is interesting that the note also mentioned a later strengthening of the 3rd Army's eastern group of forces. Previously all the talk was about the Drweca, but that was the western group! Even though it was stated at the [Bad] Salzbrunner conference that I would have freedom to act according to the situation, it seems to me that only now is the idea that a strong east wing is desirable gradually sinking in "up above!"

The mobilization order came in the evening. According to the order it starts tomorrow!

An hour later Salmuth (Chief of Staff, Army Group North) informed me of the ban on initiating hostilities. I was thunderstruck! As I thought it might be a mistake, I contacted Halder. He confirmed the order. I said:

"Everything is moving! Of course everything possible will be done to halt the troops; but I can't guarantee that there won't still be exchanges of fire." Halder understood. I asked what was supposed to happen now; whether we should retire from the border again – and how far?

Halder answered:

"Far enough so that what was intended for the 26th [August] can be carried out on the 27th if the order is given."

I pointed out that they should be under no illusions as to the effect the order to withdraw will have on the troops. Halder was clear on this. When I asked if he might tell me the reason for it, he explained:

"The English-Polish agreement was ratified today – and a negative reply has come 'from the south' (Italy)!!!"

Neither surprised me; I saw the first as a certainty sooner or later and the Italians are no strangers to us.

What now? Under the first depressing impression the consequences of the attack order appeared to me to be grim. If only they would now wait until the 4th Army's rear divisions arrived.

In the evening Polish Radio reported that an NCO from the 2nd Cavalry Regiment had been shot near Ostroleka when he and his patrol crossed the border.

36/8/39

The report of the death of the NCO was confirmed.

Drove to Headquarters, 4th Army; Kluge was beside himself over the order to withdraw the troops but arranged everything in an orderly, rational manner.

Drove to the frontier guard in Preussenfeld and to the customs post at the border; all quiet.

Also nothing out of the ordinary in *Oberst* Büchs' frontier guard sector [subsequently the 2nd Frontier Guard Detachment from 1 September to 24 October 1939] in Krajenke.

In the evening a telex arrived from the Army Command asking how we envisioned the operation if it was to be carried out on the sixth day of mobilization at the earliest.

The diplomats are negotiating – but with warm cannon! The English fleet is in blockade positions in the North Sea.

The first good joke has happened: inmates of the Kaiserbad Sanatorium, my quarters [HQ Army Group North], suspect a spy in every harmless passer-by. Today four sanitorium patients fell upon a man messing about in the garden, took him into custody in spite of his loud protests, and locked him up. The alleged "spy" turned out to be a plainclothesman from my headquarters!

27/8/39

At midmorning Brauchitsch called and expressed his appreciation to the troops for the movements carried out to date. He asked if I thought the sixth day of mobilization was right for the day of the attack. I replied:

"Based on the previous considerations yes; but before I give a definitive answer I would like to speak to the army commanders again."

Brauchitsch said that the English ambassador [Sir Nevile Henderson] was on his way to Berlin; no clarification of the situation was yet possible. France has ordered "Tension Level IV." Belgium is about to mobilize and has declared that it will consider anyone who sets foot on Belgian territory to be the enemy.

Consultation with Kluge in Polczyn [HQ Army Group North] as to how to carry out the attack if it should be ordered for the sixth day of mobilization. Full agreement after quick clarification of intentions. Salmuth discussed the same with Böckmann [Chief of Staff, 3rd Army], where no change is planned.

Appropriate report sent to the Commander-in-Chief of the Army (in the files of the Army Group).

In the afternoon drove to the 20th [Wiktorin] and 2nd [Bader] Divisions, spoke with several battalion and regimental commanders. Everything in order. Impression of the troops very good.

I asked what the reaction had been when the order came to withdraw from the frontier. One battalion commander's reply was typical:

"It was a shame, for our people were really ready to go. They complained mightily when the order came. But then one of them said, 'It's probably for political reasons'." The good mood soon returned and everything is in order. That's how it is everywhere and at home they tell me that the morale of the troops is low!

I instructed the commanders to keep an especially firm hand on their units in this difficult situation and to train them; some diversionary measures were also ordered.

28/8/39

Kluge came in the morning and discussed details of the attack with me. [The] Army High Command gave a verbal promise to finally send additional forces to 4th Army [Kluge]. That is also necessary.

Drove to the 32nd Division [Boehme], 4th Infantry Regiment, the 3rd Division [Lichel], Reconnaissance Instruction Battalion. Everything in order and in good shape.

In the evening the Commander-in-Chief of the Army announced that he was coming early on the 29th [of August].

29/8/39

Brauchitsch cancelled at the last minute. A great pity, for I wanted to discuss my growing East Prussian worries with him. More can undoubtedly be brought out of East Prussia. Wedel, the army group's liaison officer with Headquarters, 3rd Army [Küchler], is to fly here today to answer various questions in this regard.

I asked Halder:

"How is the Lithuanian mobilization being interpreted?"

Answer:

"It's not against us in any case."

I went on:

"The situation in East Prussia is such that the 206th Division [Höfl] cannot be left standing near Goldap much longer; I must move it nearer. Headquarters, 3rd Army is full of worries about the province." I said that was understandable due to the burden of responsibility. I had earlier explained to *General* von Küchler that responsibility for the province was not just his but in particular mine as well.

I told him that he was responsible for the operation given him. I would now instruct that the most useful elements of the replacement formations and whatever else could be scraped together be assembled into units and made ready to take over guarding the flanks east and northeast of the lakes in an emergency – ignoring regulations which read somewhat differently. Halder agreed, and by the way has the same impression of East Prussia as I. I went on to say that my assumption that the Poles will fight in the corridor had lost none of its probability. The enemy is entrenching there in three lines; after all they now have time to dig in.

Drove to Frontier Sector Detachment 1 [Kaupisch] in Stolp and to the 207th Reserve Division [Tiedemann]. According to the commanding officer the reserve division's materiel mobilization was not in order, Headquarters, 4th Army is to help.

Wedel arrived from East Prussia toward evening. He had an extremely good impression of the command there. I was very glad of that, for Wedel's opinions are reliable. Army High Command [Brauchitsch] only today ordered the formation of the Replacement Army. I don't know if my talk with Halder was the reason behind it. I sent orders to East Prussia for the creation of a mixed formation – as talked about yesterday – which is to be scraped together from everything that is available. This is certainly contrary to every regulation, but there's nothing I can do for I simply don't have enough soldiers.

One has the feeling that the political situation is coming to a head and that the war is unavoidable. England is apparently not giving in.

30/8/39

Brauchitsch came with Halder in the morning. From his statements it might appear that a basis for negotiation with England has been found. The Poles are to go to Berlin today for negotiations. The question is whether they will accept the basis of negotiations for themselves; I don't believe they will.

Militarily nothing significant. My misgivings about the shape of the attack from East Prussia were discussed again, but the matter is settled. My order for the formation of the "Temporary Unit" in East Prussia was approved. Brauchitsch declared that in the later course of operations emphasis would have to be put on the eastern wing! I explained that I had never been in doubt about that! In the afternoon drove to Headquarters, III Army Corps [Haase], and to the 50th [Sorsche] and 23rd [Brockdorff-Ahlefeldt] Divisions. Haase [appears as Hasse in the original; however the latter was Ia of Army Group North] is sad that he has none of his lovely divisions under him, instead just reserve units and fortress garrisons. The 50th Division doesn't appear to be as good as we thought; it supposedly has 10% untrained and many very old replacements. The 23rd Division is in tip-top shape all around.

An advance warning for the attack came in the evening. So, the day after tomorrow! East Prussia suddenly began pressing for the rapid transport of the 206th Division toward Allenstein.

31/8/39

Kluge [4th Army] came in the morning and proposed that the attack by the 207th Division [Tiedemann] be made somewhat farther south and, on account of the necessary movements, a day later than originally planned. He suggested strengthening the assault by committing the 10th Panzer Division [Schaal], the army group's reserve. I agreed to the new direction of attack and the delay in launching of the attack until the 2nd [of September], but not to the use of the 10th Panzer Division. I need it as a strong, mobile reserve for the decision. I have reservations about delaying the attack by the 207th Division. I therefore agreed on the 2nd as the day of attack – another 24 hours are required for the division to assemble – only under the force of circumstances.

On the Ratio of Forces in the "Corridor"

Orders went to East Prussia to move up the 106th Division [Höfl]. All available reports indicate that the Poles still have strong forces in the corridor. "Slipping through" will thus be out of the question; there will be a fight there. Up till now the army command hasn't wanted to believe it.

In the afternoon the order arrived that the attack is to begin tomorrow at 04:45.

Drove to the 10th Panzer Division [Schaal] and its Reconnaissance Battalion. The division comes from the Protectorate; apparently there was little to commend its stay there on account of the sullen attitude of the populace.

The commander of the 208th Reserve Division [Andreas] reported the detraining of his division. In his opinion it is fully equal to the demands to be placed on a reserve division.

Summary of the Military Operations Commanded by Generaloberst von Bock as Commander-in-Chief of Army Group North

Battle in West Prussia	1/9/39 – 5/9/39
1. Battle of the Brahe	1/9/39 – 2/9/39
2. Fighting in the Tucheler Heath	2/9/39 – 5/9/39
3. Storming of Fortress Graudenz	1/9/39 – 3/9/39

Pursuit toward Warsaw on both Sides of the Vistula
Breakthrough Battles in the Mlawa – Chorzele area.

Battle of the Narew Crossings	
1. Fighting for Pultusk	6/9/39 – 7/9/39
2. Fighting for Rozan	5/9/39 – 7/9/39
3. Storming of the Nowogrod fortifications	9/9/39 – 10/9/39
4. Fighting for Lomza	7/9/39 – 11/9/39
5. Piercing of the fortifications east of Wizna	8/9/39 – 10/9/39
6. Capture of Ossowiec	13/9/39

Battle of the Bug Crossings	
1. Fighting for Wyszkow	8/9/39 – 10/9/39
2. Fighting for Brok	8/9/39 – 10/9/39

Pursuit in Eastern Poland	11/9/39 – 21/9/39

1. Fighting south of Zambrow	11/9/39 – 13/9/39
2. Fighting in the area around Kaluszyn –	
Siedlce – Garwolin – Minsk, Maz – Otwock	12/9/39 – 21/9/39
3. Battles of Bialystok	15/9/39 – 18/9/39
4. Capture of Fortress Brest	14/9/39 – 17/9/39
5. Fighting at Zabinka-Kobryn	14/9/39 – 18/9/39

6. Fighting at and south of Wlodawa   17/9/39 – 19/9/39

Battles in Front of Modlin and Praga
until the Surrender   10/9/39 – 28/9/39

1. Battles in Front of Modlin   10/9/39 – 28/9/39
2. Battles in Front of Praga   13/9/39 – 27/9/39

Battles for the Polish Coastal Fortifications   1/9/39 – 1/10/39
1. Battle for the Westerplatte   1/9/39 – 7/9/39
2. Capture of Gdynia and the Oxhöft Warrior   8/9/39 – 19/9/39
3. Capture of Hela   8/9/39 – 1/10/39

The Attack

1/9/39

Morning report says: "Attack has begun according to plan. Luftwaffe failed to take off on planned major strike due to fog!" Like 1918!

I drove to the front. My old light infantry battalion in a fabulous mood. Then to the 3rd Panzer Division, which has already taken casualties. Command of the division [Geyr von Schweppenburg] good and firm. No need for me to encourage, for the division commander himself said:

"I'm going as far today as I can."

Contrary to all earlier reports by the intelligence service, the enemy has withdrawn from the southern part of the corridor, leaving only weak rear guards behind; but there may be more in the northern part.

No significant letup in the fighting against initially weak enemy forces. Things would move even faster if everyone would move up and concentrate their artillery and employ it quickly.

Progress in the attack on Graudenz slow, which is to be expected given the distribution of forces. Also very slow at Mlawa of course.

Unable to prevent destruction of the Dirschau Bridge; unfortunately that too was to be foreseen! On the other hand we did succeed in establishing a bridgehead near Dirschau, so the enemy can't be strong there.

The planned capture of the Westerplatte by the Navy failed. German population in the corridor nice; so far road demolitions noticeably limited.

2/9/39

3rd Panzer Division [Geyr von Schweppenburg] made good progress
during the night and in the morning.

Brauchitsch spoke to me by telephone; positions in agreement: "Fast forces
to East Prussia, then strong eastern wing!" At last they have made up their
minds.

England and France continue to threaten.

We contemplate quickly sending forces to East Prussia. Order to 3rd Army
[Küchler] to construct as quickly as possible a bridge near Mewe from the
material stockpiled in East Prussia for that purpose. The second heavy bridge
equipage is to be towed via Marienburg as far as possible toward the Nogat;
the third is on the rails ready to be moved.

Order from above: Only attack the Westerplatte again when outlook for
success is certain! – Good!

Drove to II Army Corps [Strauss], to the 32nd Division [Boehme] and to
the 69th Infantry Regiment. Splendid march performances by the troops on
the worst roads. Morale outstanding; warm welcome.

32nd and 3rd [Lichel] Divisions must break resistance in well-built field
and bunker positions in the lake sector west of the Brahe. So there's still something left in the corridor. The II Corps is supposed to reach the Vistula sometime today with reconnaissance forces, which Strauss cheerfully promises.
Fighting right and left of II Army Corps; roads clogged by terrible traffic
jams!

In the evening I directed the 4th Army to move its right wing right up to
the Vistula in the direction of Schwetz, guarding its flank in the direction of
Bromberg. I am sending the 10th Panzer Division [Schaal] behind the north
wing, with the intention of getting it to East Prussia as quickly as possible.

The frontier guard is to move up on the wings of the army – south across
the Netze and in the north toward Gdynia.

Chapter 1: May/June 1939 to 3 October 1939

England and France Declare War

3/9/1939

Drove to Headquarters, 4th Army. A report came that the east bank of the Vistula was free near Kulm. Issued orders for II Army Corps [Strauss] to establish a bridgehead near Kulm; bridge equipage up to enable a crossing near Kulm. I briefed Kluge on my intention to send the bulk of the 4th Army and Army Headquarters to East Prussia as soon as possible.

Fighting on the 4th Army's entire front, especially at the edges of the Tucheler Heath and north of Bromberg, where there is said to be a well-fortified bridgehead. Increase in road and rail demolitions beyond the Vistula. Some progress near Graudenz, but counterattacks against the east wing of the XXI Army Corps [Falkenhorst]; the reserve army "yielded somewhat there," but a few fresh troops quickly put things back in order. Good progress on the eastern wing of the 3rd Army; not near Mlawa.

Not until the evening did I learn that the 3rd Army was turning the its left-wing corps to the southwest in order to take the enemy at Mlawa in the rear. An error, because this must cause our forward movement to stop. I intervened immediately and instructed Küchler to advance on Rozan with his left wing as per his orders. Hopefully it will still work out. But time has been lost!

England and France declare war!

The *Führer* is coming tonight at 01:00.

Hitler: "What This Means to Me"

4/9/39

Reported to the *Führer* in his train in the morning, then drove to Headquarters, 4th Army [Kluge], IInd Army Corps [Strauss], 3rd Division [Lichel]. The *Führer* went to the hill near Topolno as the 3rd Division was crossing the Vistula. Overwhelming impression on the *Führer*; Kulm, Schwetz, the Vistula in bright sunshine. The *Führer* said to me:

"What this means to me!"

Pride and jubilation among the troops.

Graudenz has been taken!

The surrounded elements in the corridor still fight on. Difficulty in convincing the 4th Army that "apprehending" these forces is of secondary importance and that strong mobile forces will have to be freed up for the drive to East Prussia.

Difficult decision, whether the entire II Army Corps [Strauss] should cross the Vistula near Kulm. Yes! For that is the shortest way. If the enemy has already evacuated the Kulmer Land, then I can quickly move the corps up to the railroad and transport it to the eastern wing.

When the *Führer* set out for the front there came a report that a Polish company that had fought its way through was still in the corridor east of Krone, thus right in the *Führer*'s path. The fellows are bold! They have ambushed various rear elements and have already shot 18 of our people. The *Führer* is taking another route, which in my view is also not quite kosher. Suddenly small arms fire! It turns out that a German formation is firing at the *Storch* that is escorting the *Führer*'s column at low level; stupidly it has no insignia. Never before have I seen a pilot land so quickly!

On the way back a Polish flyer dropped bombs near Krone; but the *Führer* had already passed through.

In the evening I decided to form a strong east wing near Johannisburg from part of the forces sent to East Prussia and from forces which had been freed up there, in order to attack toward Lomza.

5/9/39

30 English planes have attacked Wilhelmshaven and hit nothing, 10 were shot down. In the west nothing but a propaganda war so far. The French are said to have hung signs in their front lines which say: "We won't shoot if you don't shoot!"

Morning conversation with Brauchitsch. When I told him that I was going to advance on Lomza with my strong east wing, he issued an order for the 4th Army to advance on Ostrow – Maz with its left wing. The objective of the Army Group (North) Warsaw. Reason: the Poles are by and large no longer capable of operations. Of course things will move quickly that way, but why commit an entire army in a purely frontal way? This comes as all the more of a surprise, when last night the Army Command still agreed with me that we had to advance toward and through Lomza. I summoned Kluge [4th Army] and discussed the new situation with Küchler [3rd Army] by phone. I am making the 4th Army weak and hope, by moving it around behind the 3rd Army, to yet be able to scrape together a strong wing.

I briefed Halder on my plan. He was not entirely in agreement with my desire to make the drive on Lomza so "strong." I told him that, for example, it would take the 23rd Division, which is earmarked for this wing, only one hour longer to drive there than behind the center and that the Komza-Ostrow-Malkinia direction of attack was of vital importance for the later crossing of the Bug.

Kluge's aircraft struck a tree on takeoff; he has been injured and taken to hospital. Strauss has temporarily assumed command of the 4th Army. I urge him to make the drive on Lomza quick and not to waste time on elaborate planning. It is a risk, but of great importance if it succeeds. Salmuth [Chief of Staff, Army Group North] drove to Headquarters, 4th Army to brief Strauss on the new assignment and to press him to finish things in the corridor, pull out the motorized divisions and prepare them to depart for East Prussia.

Toward evening Headquarters, 3rd Army [Küchler] reported that the Falkenhorst Group [XXI Army Corps] has completed its preparations and can attack toward Lomza on the 8th. Subsequent order to HQ, 3rd Army to assemble a mixed detachment from elements of the 21st Division [Both] and the 10th Panzer Division [Schaal] so as to be ready to advance on Lomza on the morning of 7 September if the order to attack is issued early on the 6th [September].

6/9/39

Drove to the new headquarters in Allenstein, through the corridor and over the military bridge near Kulm. Awful scene near Schwetz, where everything was shot up following a futile attempt by the Poles to escape the corridor by taking the Vistula ferries near Kulm. Hundreds of riderless horses of the Polish cavalry and supply trains.

"The Westerplatte Has Been Taken"

7/9/39

Drove to 3rd Army Headquarters in Neidenburg. Then to Falkenhorst's corps headquarters [XXI A.C.] and to the 10th Panzer Division. The desolate steppe near Prasznycz was depressing. On the way met elements of the 21st Division, which had fought at Graudenz. His eyes sparkling, a company commander whose unit had lost 4 killed and 12 wounded there praised his people, especially the NCOs.

Brauchitsch was worried that I was swinging too far to the east, Halder too. As I couldn't convince them I reassured them. My eastern wing is to advance on Ostrow! That's far too narrow thinking! But I was ordered to do it. If I take all my forces behind the east wing, especially the fast reserves, it will still be reasonable in the end.

The booty from the battle in the corridor is considerable; 15,000 prisoners, 90 guns and much equipment reported so far.

The Westerplatte has been taken.

8/9/39

Brauchitsch came this morning. Discussed the situation. I protested against locking my east wing into the advance on Ostrow and argued that, apart from operational concerns, between the Narew and Ostrow was no place at all for the forces of the 3rd Army. Gradually, with the assistance of Salmuth, I was able to convince him to at least allow the wing to go toward Siedlce. I don't understand why they gave me no freedom of action. Regrouping the army group in a few days was no simple matter, standing ready as it is, with strong motorized reserves behind the east wing, for the last decisive thrust into the deep flank of the Polish Army.

Why do they want to squeeze these tremendous forces together and take away their freedom of movement? We will not achieve the destruction of the enemy with restricted operations. Schlieffen would turn in his grave!

I informed Brauchitsch that my Reserve Army divisions are not yet ready to be used against a serious opponent; officers and training not up to the task. Experience from the fighting: artillery far to the front, then concentrated fire.

The Poles can't bear that. Infantry good; march performances outstanding; but too timid in their first engagement! "That comes from years of being trained to be cautious, which I always opposed!" Its better that the infantry get its feet wet straightaway.

"Sharp Objection"

After sending a written report yesterday or the day before, I filed a sharp objection with the Commander-in-Chief of the Army against the unmilitary style of the radio propaganda and army communiques ("notorious Pomorska Brigade," horror stories, "dashing attack.")

Drove to command post of the 21st Division north of Nowogrod. The Division is good, but tired. The enemy sitting in concrete bunkers near Nowogrod; our own heavy artillery has not yet arrived; nothing more will happen today.

Indescribable road conditions; unbelievable delays and traffic jams!

I was able to present the first Iron Cross of this war to a Private First Class of the 94th Regiment who acted bravely at Graudenz. The young man beamed; too beautiful these lads!

"Frightful Misery, But What Can I Do...?"

9/9/39

Drove through Pultusk to the Ist Army Corps [Petzel] and to the command post of the 61st Division [Haenicke], which was engaged in the first fighting for the Bug crossings near Wyszkow. The enemy has little artillery. The worst are the road conditions, here and especially on the left wing of the 3rd Army. There are stops at every one of the many blown bridges, which have received only hurried, makeshift repairs. In many places the vehicles have to be sent through one at a time. Thousands of refugees with children, cattle and wagons stream back from the Bug on the road to Pultusk. Frightful misery, but what can I do, I must have the roads clear. Traffic control is miserable in spite of all my exhortations and suggestions. Issued a sharply-worded order on traffic discipline. Unless we get some discipline we'll never get the motorized corps with its four divisions through and to the front.

There finally appears to be some progress at Nowogrod, also at Wizna. Probing at Lomza. In the evening an order arrived from Army Command finally giving the left wing of the Army Group freedom to advance east of the Bug as well. Quite incredible that they're only now seeing things my way.

Chaos has been avoided, because tomorrow I will have freedom to act at Nowogrod and Wizna.

Guderian [XIX Army Corps] came in the evening. I ordered him to attack across the Wizna with the 10th Panzer Division [Schaal] and the 20th Motorized Division [Wiktorin] – under the direct command of the Army Group – on the left of the 3rd Army and advance across the Bug. He was happy to receive this choice assignment.

An inquiry was followed by the order to release the 23rd Division [Brockdorff-Ahlefeldt] and the 3rd Division [Lichel] to the Supreme Army Command. I had no objections.

10/9/39

Things finally began to break loose at Nowogrod and Wizna. Armored fortifications had to be taken at both crossings. Guderian bravely led the 10th Panzer Division forward. Now, finally, I have freedom of movement for my motorized forces. Seeing this thing through was a test of nerve – but not with the enemy!

Drove to 3rd Panzer Division [Geyr von Schweppenburg] at Arys; unit discipline and morale exemplary, looking forward to new deeds.

600 Kilometers a Day "By Road"

As of yesterday evening I have driven 6,000 km since the start of the war.

The situation facing the Polish Command is difficult. I assume that they will try to halt the remains of their army in the general line Brest-Bug to Kamionka-lake sector west of Lemberg (Lvov)-upper course of the Dniestr. Therefore my intended drive on Brest is correct! The Poles will leave screening forces in the line Slonim-Brest to guard the Brest-Baranowicze rail line.

The Lötzen Reserve Brigade received orders to take Bialystok so that the motorized corps need not worry about its left flank while advancing on Brest.

Court Martial Against Those Responsible For Killing Jews

I learned that members of the SS artillery have rounded up and murdered Jews; the 3rd Army [Küchler] has convened a court martial.

(Küchler requested that the SS units under his command be transferred elsewhere on account of their murdering of Jews, calling them "a disgrace to the army." Müller, Klaus-Jürgen, on the events preceding and the contents of Himmler's speech to the senior German generals on 13 March 1940 in Koblenz, VfZ 18 (1970), PP 95-120.)

11/9/39

Lomza has been taken by the Lötzen Reserve Brigade, the bridge is under construction. This evening two bridges between Nowogrod and Wizna; the possible for the advance and supply of the motorized corps [XIX] has thus been done.

In the morning Salmuth's Department I called and advised that the line Warsaw (excl.)-Wlodawa was planned as the new boundary between Army Groups North and South. I had him state that at the moment the army group [North] was on a frontal advance straight toward this boundary and then had him ask what sort of order the army group was to receive then.

Swing 90 degrees to the east?

Then I spoke with Halder myself and asked for orders, as I had to rework the movements intended for the next day in the event that such a directive was planned. I set forth my objections and proposed allowing the right wing of the Army Group to continue advancing on Lublin and the left on Brest, and that the elements of Army Group South which were "supposed" to cross the Vistula at Gora Kalwaria be placed under my command. In return III Army Corps [Haase], which was now fighting south of the Vistula together with the 8th Army [Blaskowitz], would be placed under the command of Army Group

South. I wanted Headquarters, 4th Army [Kluge] to go to the left wing, because command there by the army group was too difficult. Halder had all sorts of objections, none of which was sound. The decision will be made this evening. My faith in clear, open-handed solutions has been shaken. After numerous telephone calls back and forth, in the evening came the order to turn toward the line Kowel-Slonim! None of my other wishes was granted. Once again the Army Command waited for events to force its hand. That might work against the Poles!

"Distress Call from Army Command: "Counterattacks!"

12/9/39

3rd Army [Küchler] reached the Warsaw-Siedlce road, taking several thousand prisoners in the process, a battery as well. Drove to XXXI Army Corps [Falkenhorst], to the Lötzen Brigade and the 2nd Motorized Division [Bader]. The Army Command now decided to place the elements of the 4th Army [Kluge] near Kutno, namely III Corps, under the command of the 8th Army [Blaskowitz] which was fighting there and to release Headquarters, 4th Army for use on the east wing.

The 3rd Division also joined the 8th Army. There you are! The other will yet come and the curious operation ordered yesterday will correct itself.

In the evening a distress call from the Army Command. Things look serious near Kutno; the enemy is counterattacking and attacking west from Warsaw. We wanted to keep an eye our right flank near Warsaw and seal it off there. I confirmed with Halder that this was alright and told him that I had ordered the 3rd Army to clear the area between the Narew and the Vistula and bar the Warsaw crossings and initially not to advance beyond the line Garwolin-Siedlce in order to prevent the army from becoming strung out. This also means a halt to the 3rd Army's advance to the southeast. The motorized corps is carrying on toward Brest. The left wing of the army is wheeling toward Bialystok. Halder is in full agreement.

The Polish 18th [Infantry] Division [Podhorski] was encircled south of Zambrow [according to Piekalkiewicz, J: *Der Zweite Weltkrieg*, PP 98, the 18th Infantry Division was smashed on 10 September], more than 1,000 prisoners and many guns captured so far; more prisoners, about 3,000, taken on the 3rd Army's southern front by the Wodrig Corps [XXVI Army Corps]. The misery of those fleeing the war is terrible.

In the west the French appear to be ranging in their guns and have moved into observation and jump-off positions for an attack. We are not allowed to fire on French territory, so that the French can do what they like undisturbed.

13/9/39

The history of the war will not forget that during its advance, made unbelievably hard by the enemy and the terrain, the army group has so far voluntarily released to the Army Command: the 73rd [Rabenau], 50th [Sorsche], 208th [Andreas, appears as 108th in the original] and 218th Divisions, [Battle] Group Netze [Gablenz], Headquarters, III Army Corps [Haase] and several battalions of heavy artillery!

Drove to Headquarters, 3rd Army in Prasznycz. I ordered I Army Corps [Petzel] to take possession of the Warsaw bridges as fast as possible and remove the explosive charges, but not to allow itself to become involved in house fighting in Warsaw west of the Vistula. If all goes smoothly, then it is planned to later split off the Ist Army Corps to the south again while keeping a firm hold on the bridges.

Heavy Fighting with Polish Divisions

14/9/39

Drove to Headquarters, I Army Corps [Petzel] (east of Warsaw) and to Headquarters, 3rd Army [Küchler] in Ostrow. Dreadful trip; 16 hours on hair-raising roads. Refugees, enemy stragglers who fire at our people from the woods. The car became stuck in one lonely forest nest; peasants pulled it out with horses. Two hours later we were stuck in a ford, and so on.

I Army Corps is not tackling Warsaw sharply enough, it is tired. I lit a fire under them! The army was reminded that there are many Polish soldiers – entirely or partly dressed in civilian clothes – mixed in with the refugee columns and elsewhere in the rear. The countermeasures are simple if they are applied quickly by barring the few bridges over the Bug and the Narew.

Heavy fighting by the 1st Division [Kortzfleisch] against elements of various Polish divisions seeking to break out to the east; 2,000 prisoners. The Poles are very clever and daring in night combat.

During the night consultation with Salmuth from Army Headquarters over the continuation of operations.

Except for the citadel, Brest has been taken by the XIX Motorized Corps [Guderian].

15/9/39

New operations began in the morning. Army stood guard at Wyszogrod and Modlin, took the east bank of the Vistula near Warsaw, turned left wing and sent it to Lulow-Miedzyrzec. XIX Motorized Corps [Guderian] advancing on Kowel with one armored and one motorized division, standing guard toward Wlodawa. The corps' other two divisions, one motorized and one armored, are later to be placed under the command of the 4th Army [Kluge], which today assumes command of the northern wing. The next objective of the 4th Army is Pruzana-Wolkowysk-Grodno.

I informed Brauchitsch that I had ordered this, he is in full agreement.

The 3rd Army wants nothing to do with the turning of the Wodrig Corps [XXVI Army Corps] toward Lukow-Miedzyrzec. I also find it awkward, but I must think of the continuation of the operation, free the motorized corps at Brest and take a firm hold on Brest so that the motorized corps can advance without worrying, for half of it is later to advance on Kowel, the other half on Slonim. Infantry divisions would need at least eight days to reach the objectives assigned by me. If we have Kowel and Brest, than we need nothing for the marshes themselves.

16/9/39

1st Division [Kortzfleisch] was still fighting yesterday. Many prisoners and guns, much equipment captured.

Army Group South's battle at Kutno still getting nowhere! The Army Command believes it has indications that the enemy forces fighting there intend to break out to the north through Modlin. I ordered 3rd Army to scrape together whatever could be scraped together there; there isn't much. The army has unfortunately already sent the bulk of the 228th Division [Suttner] across the Bug. When I told Halder about three days ago that I didn't believe that the battle at Kutno would be over in less than two days, he said:

"We think it will take less!"

The Army Command's order assigned to the army group [North] as its objective the line Kowel-Slonim, therefore with its front facing east-south-east; it has now turned out that the army group's point of main effort was near Warsaw, in the west! Even though this isn't dangerous given the state of the enemy, it's still an uncomfortable situation.

In the evening a motorcyclist drove into the car at full speed. The poor fellow fortunately escaped with a broken leg.

During the night an Army Command order announced that on the 16th [of September] a representative of the 3rd Army is to request the surrender of Warsaw and inform the Poles that in the event of a defense of the city all means will have to be used to force its surrender. Since I consider it a mistake to request the surrender of a defender who is a long way from giving up and who has so far demonstrated a very active will to defend and who will interpret any negotiation as weakness, I had Salmuth warn against these things. But also, and most of all, because the attack by the 3rd Army, which I have been pushing so hard, will now have to be stopped again for the negotiations! My people must think me mad if I drive them today and stop them tomorrow! But there's nothing I can do; the order is coming. I spoke with Küchler, including about how we can make ourselves stronger opposite Modlin. He is scraping something together – then I spoke with Brauchitsch, who confirmed the Army Command's view that the enemy will try to break out of the Kutno battle through Modlin. I then said that I am too weak there to face an attack by strong forces and asked that all or at least elements of the Eberhardt Brigade (Danzig) be placed under my command. It is currently engaged in rear-area duties, which is unfortunate. Brauchitsch asked how I intended to get it here; I replied solemnly that that was my affair, whereupon I was promised a reinforced regiment from the brigade. Furthermore, I flew two machine-gun companies of the 4th Army, which is now facing only weak enemy forces, to the area north of Modlin. In the late morning Küchler reported that the Wodrig

Corps [XXVI Army Corps] would attack from the west, southwest of Siedlce. There is a bridge over the Vistula near Gora Kalwaria, but he thinks it in Polish hands; he also definitely believes that the Poles are using the bridge, for resistance is stiffening in front of the Wodrig Corps. He requested that Wodrig, contrary to previous orders, be allowed to attack west. I told him that according to all the reports so far from the Army Command, the bridge near Gora Kalwaria had been built by the 1st Panzer Division, which had sent some elements across. The situation he described was thus new to me. But now he was of course completely free to have Wodrig attack west, for the matter there first had to be cleared up and brought to a conclusion. As of last night Wodrig reported 12,000 prisoners, about 100 artillery pieces and much booty.

Briefed the Army Command, with a request that Halder be informed that 3rd Army had, under the force of events, now redirected its front to face the Vistula with all units.

At 01:00 3rd Army reported that the emissary was back from Warsaw. He had sat blindfolded for 1/2 an hour before a Polish regimental commander, who advised him that the commander of Warsaw [J. Ròmmel] refused to see him. He asked the Polish officer if the letter could be passed on to the commander and this, too, was rejected. That was to be expected! I asked Halder to release the 23rd Division, which had been placed at the disposal of the Army Command, as the forces of the 4th Army were too weak for its mission – all the more so since there were supposedly two Polish reserve divisions in the Bialowice Forest. The 4th Army intended to send two divisions into the Bialowice Heath and continue in the direction of Grodno with just the Brand Group [78th Inf.Div.]. I intervened and instructed the army that the point of main effort would lay in its assigned main direction of attack Grodno-Wolkowysk and that the bulk of its forces were to be sent there. It was to guard against any threat from the heath; clearing it would have to wait until one of the motorized divisions was freed up at Brest so that it could lend a hand from the rear, from the approximate area of Pruzana. At 21:00 inquiry to the Commander-in-Chief of the Army asking if and when the leaflets prepared by the Army Command, giving the civilian populace 12 hours to withdraw through my front lines, are being dropped. It turned out that they had already been dropped at 16:30 and that as the result of an oversight the Army

Group had not been informed. Very stupid, for the 3rd Army's artillery was laying continuous fire on the Praga exits; not exactly encouraging for the civilian population, coming out there, and fine propaganda for the enemy. But how could they think of allowing the civilian population to stream through our lines at night? A perfect opportunity for a determined enemy to sally forth. I ordered the 3rd Army to have forward outposts halt any refugee columns before they reached our lines; they are not to be let through until daylight and are to be searched. I doubt that this order can now be carried out in the middle of the night, but there's no other choice.

17/9/39

Argument over the question of emissaries, who don't come! Now Praga is not to be attacked for the time being. I am betting that the order to take it will come before long. Then it will be more difficult! The citadel at Brest has been taken by the XIX Motorized Army Corps [Guderian].

The Russians are moving into Poland. By way of greeting a Russian bomber bombed our 23rd Division [Brockdorff-Ahlefeldt].

18/9/39

Drove to 228th Division [Suttner], which is in front of Modlin and Nowy Dwor; command post of an artillery battalion and an infantry regiment. My fear that nothing would come of its attack on Nowy Dwor was justified. Apart from the fact that the reserve division lacked the strength and the ability to take the defensive works, the entire affair was insufficiently prepared. To continue the attack in this way serves no purpose, therefore it is being stopped. I personally wouldn't have attacked Nowy Dwor, but Modlin. But there is no possibility of a timely intervention now, because I didn't learn of the error until the 228th Division had already crossed the Bug. Since the 3rd Army [Küchler] called the attack promising, I let it run.

When I returned home in the evening the order for the attack on Warsaw was there! The 3rd Army wishes to regroup and proposes the 21st [September] as the attack date. I asked that they reconsider the deadline, for I have the impression that the planned regrouping cannot be carried out by the 21st. 4th

Army [Kluge] will send the 3rd Army [Küchler] heavy artillery, engineers and tanks, which will help and be of some use to it.

The Demarcation Line

A demarcation line has been established between the Russians and us. Beginning tomorrow 4th Army will pull back behind this line.

19/9/39

After determining the position of the Warsaw Waterworks, the Luftwaffe was sent against the main waterworks; two smaller waterworks lie within range of our artillery.

A definitive demarcation line between us and the Russians, west of the first line and running roughly along the San-Vistula-Narew river line, has been declared. Asked Army Command not to evacuate the areas east of this line too quickly, because there are large quantities of supplies and booty there and a great deal of bridge equipment.

23rd Division [Brockdorff-Ahlefeldt] is to be transferred to the west; I offered a motorized and later a panzer division as well. In the evening I discussed the attack on Praga in detail with Böckmann. Asked if the army needed anything else, answer no.

20/9/39

Determination of the demarcation line with the Russians is unclear. The Russians dropped leaflets over Bialystok, which is occupied by us, requesting the Polish troops to surrender. I spoke with Halder: "What about the uncertainties about the demarcation line and what about Warsaw?"

Answer:

"The Army Command has itself only just learned of the definitive demarcation line: Uszok Pass-Przemysl-San-Vistula-Narew-Pissa. First serious incidents due to the lack of clarity have taken place near Lvov. We must make preparations to possibly withdraw behind the demarcation line relatively quickly. No more German blood is to be spilled east of it."

I:

"And the attack on Praga?"

Answer:

"Still unclear, but I hope to be able to give a definite answer tonight."

I:

"I wish to point out that the Poles are attempting to break out to the southeast from Praga. There's fighting there! We can't simply pull back. Also the majority of the 3rd Army's rear communications run through the area on the enemy side of the final demarcation line!"

Halder:

"I know that. But perhaps you can send what is not needed for the attack from in front of Praga across the Narew to the northeast??!"

Discussed with Salmuth directives for the 4th Army which are to prepare a more rapid withdrawal across the demarcation line and avoid collisions with the Russians. Sent a Brandt telegram to the Army High Command [Brauchitsch] with the suggestion that we not give up the attack on Warsaw! In the meantime the order arrives that Praga is not to be attacked! No more German blood is to flow east of the Vistula! How do they think that? The Poles are making forays and counterattacks from Praga! Are we supposed to withdraw? I had Stuka dive-bombers attack Warsaw's main waterworks. 3rd Army [Küchler] was instructed to intensify its artillery fire.

Continued back and forth with emissaries and now also with the departure of the neutral diplomats from Warsaw. Salmuth attempted to talk the Army Command into a slower evacuation, because the one previously ordered is scarcely feasible, and inevitably the booty as well as much of our own supplies will have to be left behind in this hasty withdrawal.

21/9/39

Küchler [3rd Army] arrived. He asked that the attack not be made before the 24th [September], in particular he has not yet received the heavy artillery from the 4th Army. I therefore gave orders that the attack not be made on the 22nd; Salmuth got on the telephone and tried to find out if the Army Command was going to order it for the 24th but was told: "That all depends on the negotiations taking place in Moscow this afternoon!" Attack and evacuation have just been closely amalgamated. Küchler [3rd Army] requests 9 days for complete evacuation, beginning with the conclusion of the attack. This was reported to the Army Command. Today 800 members of the Diplomatic Corps are to be allowed out of Warsaw.

Note: A Polish-German agreement guaranteed that the foreigners still in Warsaw, 178 diplomats and ambassadors as well as 1,200 foreign nationals, could leave the burning city. They were received by officers of the German 3rd Army.

The commander of Warsaw [J. Ròmmel] is leading us around by the nose; through these tricks he obtains several hours each day in which he can move forces, stock up on ammunition and do whatever else he wants.

The daily activities of the emissaries, together with orders which declare the campaign in Poland over, have depressed the offensive spirit of the forces in the field.

Stülpnagel [OQu I] told Salmuth that the *Führer* and Brauchitsch agree with my point of view in regard to the attack on Warsaw, but everything is linked to the evacuation deadlines. Obviously! The order concerning the evacuation arrived in the evening, bringing only limited improvements; still no decision on the attack on Warsaw. The political reason is said to be a meeting of Congress in America! The diplomats from Warsaw came out. I am anxious to see what new back doors the Poles will find.

I'm pessimistic about 3rd Army's attack on Warsaw. One can't attack well while looking over his shoulder; but if it is to attack, then let it be very soon!

Principles of Military Doctrine

Infantry must have their heavy weapons when they attack, but then they must advance quickly and without pause. Artillery and heavy weapons must be kept close at hand. Even during an advance they belong far to the front, especially since moving the artillery past a march column is often impossible. The old catchphrase, "the infantry must wait until the artillery arrives," is wrong! It should say, "the artillery may not keep the infantry waiting!" Anything else makes good decisions impracticable, causes many opportunities to be missed. The artillery must also be kept close during the attack. It is not enough if the infantry regimental commander is standing next to the artillery battalion commander, contact must first and foremost be sought up front. In the attack individual batteries belong far to the front, in the midst of the infantry.

Where these principles are followed, as for example by the II Army Corps [Strauss], all resistance is bowled over; where they are ignored weak enemy forces have often held us up for too long. Our combat manuals should be shortened by half. They should contain a few clear principles. Then we can demand that everyone master them.

Today I once again took the opportunity to speak to the army commanders and to the officers of I Army Corps [Petzel] gathered in Glinki about training the field forces to seize the initiative.

23/9/39

The 4th Army [Kluge] is slowly withdrawing behind the demarcation line, 3rd Army [Küchler] has also begun the evacuation, as far as it is compatible with the encirclement of Praga. The units still needed for the attack on Modlin [32nd Division, Boehme, and heavy artillery] are being pulled out of the line at Praga. Conversation by Salmuth with Böckmann [Chief of Staff, 3rd Army] in the evening, in order to put more vigor and more order into affairs in front of Praga. Böckmann is reasonable and rather despairing, fearing that we can get nowhere against the passivity of the middle level of command. The back and forth with "attack" and "no attack" on Praga and the awareness that everything is pulling back behind the army, that the campaign there is over, has taken the vigor out of the already tired field forces.

Reports from Warsaw indicate that the population is being left in the dark concerning the fact that the Polish field army no longer exists; the people are also being told of the great successes by the English and French as well as the lie that the Germans are killing all prisoners. No one is touching our leaflets because they are supposedly poisoned. The Army Command wants to slip Polish POWs into Warsaw to spread the truth.

I instructed that all East Prussians over 45 years of age are to be released from the construction and labor units and immediately sent on leave to help with the harvest and plowing. They're more important there than in the unfamiliar work on road construction and so on where they are achieving nothing. A similar order arrived from Berlin later in the day, which calls for the release of the oldest age classes, even among the field forces.

24/9/39

Letter to Strauss [II Army Corps], who is to direct the attack on Modlin. In it I described the state of the field forces in front of Praga, the inadequate concentration of effect of the heavy artillery firing on Warsaw, and gave suggestions for the conduct of the attack and the employment of the artillery.

After weeks of driving and fighting, the panzer divisions and their tanks are worn out and require a thorough overhaul and rest. In a conversation with Halder, I described to him my impression of our infantry, but pointed out that the constant forest fighting had played on the nerves of my troops and that my assessment might not apply generally.

Now 60 Russians are to be let out of Warsaw. I am curious to see what happens tomorrow!

25/9/39

They say that there are currents in the Army Command which also don't want the attack on Warsaw from the west; one hopes that it turns out that way.

To Salmuth, Bieler [Chief of Staff II Army Corps] described the attack on Modlin ordered by me as difficult. I don't believe it, rather I am of the opinion that it will not be difficult to take if it is done correctly. Salmuth will therefore drive to II Army Corps tomorrow.

26/9/39

A Polish emissary delivered a letter to Ist Army Corps [Petzel] signed by the commander of Warsaw, General Ròmmel, which contained the following:

"1. Request 24-hour halt in firing to spare the civilian population.
2. A Polish officer will arrive for surrender negotiations."

Point 1 was rejected. No pause in firing may take place, apart from a brief local pause to enable the Polish officer to be sent. Or else exactly the opposite, an increase in the rate of fire!

Point 2 is to be accepted, in case the city and garrison is surrendered unconditionally.

I informed Brauchitsch of these events at 18:40. Brauchitsch said that he was considering whether an orderly retreat with the honors of war (for the Poles), after first disarming them naturally, should be allowed and whether the captured officers should keep their sabers. I asked if I was really supposed to tell the army this, Brauchitsch answered that he would therefore call again. At 18:50 conversation with *Oberst* von Greiffenberg of the Army High Command [Chief of the OpA OKW]; I proposed that the garrison of Warsaw become prisoners of war. No objection to the commander retaining his saber. I asked him to think about whether to allow the other officers to keep their swords. Just no unmotivated generosity which might be taken as a sign of softness or stupidity on our part! No question of marching off the entire garrison east in the direction of Siedlce. Once disarmed, half the garrison is to be sent west to the 8th Army [Blaskowitz], the other half to the 3rd Army [Küchler]. I think it important that half the garrison marches to the 3rd Army, in order to show the field units what a large role they played in the fall of Warsaw. Bridges and military installations are to be handed over by the enemy in their present condition by officers on the spot. The civilians can be allowed to leave to the east, then we're rid of them! There is to be a pause of 24 hours between the departure of the garrison and the marching off of the population.

At 20:00 my Ia, *Oberst* Hasse, had a conversation with Greiffenberg, according to which the surrender negotiations with Warsaw are to be conducted by Headquarters, 8th Army [Blaskowitz]. Part of Army Group South [Rundstedt], 8th Army has been advancing on Warsaw from the west, thus on the other side of the Vistula, since a few days ago. We have no contact with it. Hasse raised objections at once. At 21:50 I called Halder and told him: the Polish commander [Ròmmel] is apparently unaware of the Army Command order that surrender negotiations are to be conducted with the 8th Army. In any case, up until now he had contacted the 3rd Army. As the next emissary is once again expected at the 3rd Army, I request orders as to what to tell him.

Halder replied that the surrender negotiations were to be carried out by the 8th Army, with which he presently had no contact! I answered:

"Yes, then where is the emissary supposed to be sent!"

However we couldn't put on the show of not knowing what we were supposed to do. I didn't understand at all why they couldn't leave the negotiations to Headquarters, 3rd Army, to where the emissary was now coming, it could conduct them just as well as 8th Army. Halder replied that sending out the emissary was due to the effect of the 8th Army on the western part of the city. I rejected that and said that the hundred batteries of the 3rd Army, which had been firing on Warsaw for nearly eight days, surely had the same share in wrecking the city as 8th Army, which began attacking yesterday. When Halder objected that it had only fired on the eastern part, I declared:

"On the contrary, fire was concentrated directly on the western part of the city, in the presence of the *Führer*, for example."

I expressed my regret over the hurtful impression that must arise among the 3rd Army, if – as planned – it was shoved aside now, at the moment of the city's surrender! Halder replied that the 3rd Army's contribution was fully acknowledged; he could only attribute this sensitivity to a nervousness born of the high tension of recent days. I answered:

"Not a man is nervous here!" and asked, as the emissary might come back at any time, for an order as to what to say to him. The Chief of the General Staff replied:

"That I can't tell you, for the instructions to be given haven't been worked out, and I can't reach the 8th Army."

I subsequently spoke with the 3rd Army's Chief of Staff [Böckmann]. He expected the emissary to return at about 20:00; he considered sending the man somewhere else without instructions impossible. At about 20:00 I learned that yesterday, probably on orders from the Army Command, a leaflet had been dropped over Warsaw promising the garrison facilities during the handover.

27/9/39

The representative of the defenders of Warsaw, the Polish General Rommel, arrived today at Headquarters, I Corps [Petzel] – thus once again with 3rd Army – to offer the unconditional surrender of the city. All firing ceased; leaflets were dropped urging Modlin to surrender.

I reported the situation to Brauchitsch. In doing so I briefed him on yesterday's conversation with Halder. He said that, according to discussions the *Führer* had with Headquarters, 8th Army on the occasion of a visit there, that the 8th Army must be "in charge" of the surrender negotiations. The 3rd Army was to accept the surrender, which had already happened, and discuss all details with Headquarters, 8th Army, for the surrender must of course be conducted uniformly. I replied that I understood. If it had been explained to me thus yesterday I would have complied. But that had not been the case. On the contrary, I had received no answer when I inquired what 3rd Army was to say when the emissary returned. Brauchitsch said that he didn't know that. He was well aware of the 3rd Army's contributions, including to the fall of Warsaw, but all eyes were now on the 8th Army's path from the Battle of Kutno to Warsaw. I replied, "That may be."

But I couldn't take it upon myself to silently allow the 3rd Army to be put out of action in the fall of Warsaw after I had flogged it on to the suburbs of the city! Brauchitsch agreed.

Drove to 1st [Kortzfleisch] and 12th [Leyen] Divisions. Troops I met on the way gave a very fresh impression; the horses, too, look quite good after four weeks of a war of movement. *General* von Kortzfleisch has a very favorable opinion of the field forces! Very encouraging, for Kortzfleisch is dependable and knows what's going on. He strongly underlined the view that speed and boldness of action are vital in a war of movement. There can be no stopping while on the attack! He has a high opinion of heavy infantry weapons; especially the MG 34 machine-gun. His 1st Division's attack against a fortified field position (four enemy batteries, individual bunkers) proceeded as if on the training grounds. Two kilometers in three hours with the entire division! Regimental and battalion command should be better. To this end Kortzfleisch asked for more unit exercises in peacetime, similar to the situation before the World War. Quite correct!

According to 8th Army intelligence, the reason for the fall of Warsaw was not the pressure starting to be exerted by the 8th Army, as stated in the army communique and believed by Halder, rather the water shortage of the past five days! But the destruction of the waterworks was achieved by the 3rd [Küchler] and not the 8th Army [Blaskowitz].

Halder called in the evening and in a gracious and comradely way expressed his regret over yesterday's misunderstanding.

28/9/39

During the night an emissary was sent from Warsaw to Modlin with a Polish staff officer. Things are different now than before in front of Warsaw! In the morning Modlin surrendered unconditionally. Reason for surrender: the fall of both forts which were attacked and a shortage of water as a result of the destruction of the water supply! Vigorous action has paid off.

The campaign began four weeks ago, today the last Polish resistance was broken! I presented Salmuth [Chief of Staff, Army Group North] the well-deserved bar to the Iron Cross, First Class.

Relayed a proposal to the Army High Command [Brauchitsch] that the labor service formations, which are scratching about relatively unproductively on the roads, be disbanded. They are more important at home, whether helping out with the harvest or being trained as recruits.

Army Group North is gradually dispersing. Headquarters, 4th Army [Kluge] goes west tomorrow. 21st Division [Both] and the motorized corps [XIX] are being kept in East Prussia by the Army Command until the situation in the border states is clear; their days as independent states are probably numbered.

An announcement came from Berlin in the evening, according to which the demarcation line with the Russians is to be pushed farther forward again. Downright uncomfortable, after half of the army group [North] has just moved behind the former demarcation line and the entire supply system was reorganized for the short supply distances!

29/9/39

In Modlin nearly 25,000 men, including 1,200 officers, and 100 artillery pieces.

The new treaty with Russia is revealed.

Drove to the Brand Group [78th Inf.Div.] in Lötzen; many colds among the "old gentlemen," morale good. I warned against too close contact with the Russians! No fraternization, contact by officers only.

Impression of the Russians according to available reports: officers mostly reserved, political commissars overbearing, in some cases hostile; enlisted men poor in dress and deportment; equipment mediocre.

Tomorrow I am to go to Berlin with the army commanders to see the *Führer.*

30/9/39

Drove to Berlin.

The *Führer* expressed his thanks to the army group and army commanders. He declared that if the war could not be ended by diplomatic means, he must and would force a decision. A compromise is out of the question.

Brauchitsch [Commander-in-Chief of the Army] and Halder [Chief of the General Staff] spoke to me briefly about my new assignment. I am to relinquish command in the east as soon as possible and go to Berlin. My staff is coming with me. Good, for it is, with a few exceptions, outstanding.

1/10/39

Drove back to Allenstein (Belchau!).

2/10/39

I relinquished command. Küchler and Headquarters, 3rd Army took command in the former area of Army Group North. My report on the campaign to the Army High Command. Farewell order to the troops of the army group:

"Army Group North is leaving the ranks of the Eastern Army as of today. The accomplishments of the army and units of the Luftwaffe under my command in the Polish Campaign are a part of history. You defeated the enemy in four weeks! You retook the old West Prussia and Fortress Graudenz, destroyed the Polish army in the corridor, reunited Danzig and East Prussia with the Reich! You stormed the fortifications at Mlawa and on the Narew; in difficult marches and battles you drove the enemy across the Bug and delivered the fatal blow against the rear of the Polish army fighting in the bend of the Vistula, thus sealing its fate and the fall of Warsaw! You took the fortresses of Modlin and Brest! Troops of the army group fought gloriously at Plock and Gdynia, at Bialystok and Wlodowa.

True to the traditions of the old army, true to old German military obligation, in you the new German Army has passed its baptism of fire magnificently! You have done your duty and I am certain that you will gladly fulfill all further tasks which the *Führer* gives you."

3/10/39

Travelled to Berlin.

Inaccurate depictions of the fall of Warsaw are circulating in word and picture on the radio and in the press. Why? Army High Command and Armed Forces High Command now know how it really was. Salmuth recently wrote to Wedel of the Armed Forces High Command again for this reason. As conclusion of the campaign in Poland I received a letter from *General* Kaupisch, who had the job of taking Gdynia with the Pomeranian Frontier Guard and the 207th Reserve Division, later bolstered by the addition of the Eberhardt Brigade [Combat Unit Danzig]:

"Zoppot, 1/10/39
Kurhaus

Generaloberst!

I have just concluded surrender negotiations with the empowered Chief of Staff of Admiral von Unruh [referring to Rear Admiral Unrug, Josef, commander of the Polish Fleet]. Garrison of Hela laid down its weapons at 10:00 on 2/10 [the unconditional surrender took place on 1/10]. 250 officers, more than 4,000 men... Ca. 350 officers and more than 13,000 men in the battles for Gdynia and Oxhöfter Warrior; thus ca. 600 officers and more than 17,000 [16,000 in the original] men.

The assignment you gave me is thus completed. Thank you once again for this excellent assignment..."

4 OCTOBER 1939 to 9 MAY 1940
(PREPARATIONS FOR THE OFFENSIVE IN THE WEST)

Commander-in-Chief Army Group B

I n spring 1940 the main forces of the armies of the warring states of Europe faced each other across the French-German border, along which defensive fortifications had been built: the French Maginot Line and the German *Westwall* (Siegfried Line). The *Westwall*, which consisted of fixed defensive installations and tank and infantry barriers, extended from Aachen to Basel.

The German High Command decided to strike a concentrated blow against the center of the enemy army's concentration area, split the Allied front, force the northern group of enemy forces back to the Pas de Calais and the English Channel, and destroy it. The main thrust would be made through the Ardennes to the mouth of the River Somme, or north of the Maginot Line and south of the concentration area of the Anglo-French forces scheduled to advance into Belgium.

By the beginning of May 1940 the German armed forces on the Western Front had completed their strategic concentration and deployment. On their northern wing, from the North Sea Coast to Aachen, were two armies of Army Group B under *Generaloberst* von Bock. With the support of *Luftflotte* (Air Fleet) 2 their to objective was to take the Netherlands, break through the defensive positions of the Anglo-French troops at the Belgian border, and drive them back beyond the line Antwerp-Namur.

4/10/39

Berlin. Suspense whether England will come round; the population gives a very calm, almost disinterested impression. More impetus will be needed to survive the difficult battle against England – if comes to that.

9/10/39

Meeting with Brauchitsch, who briefed me on the overall situation. I am to assume command in the northern sector of the Western Front on the evening of 10 October. I am to submit my opinion in writing concerning the possibilities of an offensive from my sector as soon as possible. Brauchitsch views these possibilities with skepticism. The necessity of better protection of the Ruhr against air attack plays a role in the question of the attack – they would like to gain more depth for an "early warning" of the industrial region; there is also a desire to move our own air bases closer to England. And finally they hope to bring the Anglo-French army into an open field battle through an offensive through Holland and Belgium and smash it – if this is not the primary motivation. If we don't attack, so the argument goes, then one fine day the enemy will be standing at the Belgian-German border, which will pose an unbearable threat to the industrial area of Northwest Germany.

Commander-in-Chief of Army Group B

10/10/39

Drove to Godesberg [HQ Army Group B]. Stopped in Frankfurt am Main on the way; conferred with Leeb [CIC Army Group C], the former Commander-in-Chief of the Western Front. He and his Chief of Staff [Sodenstern] both flatly reject the question of a German offensive at present.

11/10/39

In the morning conference with army commanders Kluge [4th Army] and Reichenau [6th Army; from 25 August to 10 October 1939 Reichenau was Commander-in-Chief of the 10th Army, which was renamed the 6th Army on

10 October] concerning general matters and the question of the attack. Both against it at present. Both also against attacking if the enemy should move into Belgium.

12/10/39

Sent my opinion concerning an attack on the Western Front to the Commander-in-Chief of the Army [Brauchitsch] (original in the files of the army group).

17/10/39

Early conference with Halder in the headquarters at Zossen. He was visibly depressed after difficult negotiations with the political leadership. He is faced with the question, what should he and the Commander-in-Chief of the Army do if the *Führer* persists in totally rejecting the military proposals. Brauchitsch is also suffering from these battles. He is wrestling with himself as to what he should do personally and also wanted to know my opinion on the subject. I said that I couldn't give an answer to such an important question "off the cuff," but promised a reply in the very near future. Brauchitsch said that he knew that Reichenau [6th Army] had spoken out against an attack; but he didn't want to give the impression that he was using Reichenau to support his – Brauchitsch's – position.

Returned to Godesberg [HQ Army Group B].

Rundstedt, former Commander-in-Chief in the east is coming to the west [with his new army group headquarters].

18/10/39

Meeting with Reichenau.

At noon dispatched my answer to Brauchitsch's questions by plane. We have time to work ourselves into the large general framework, because basic orders for subsequent plans aren't supposed to arrive until tomorrow or the day after.

19/10/39

Haase [Commanding General III Army Corps] arrived in the morning; I presented him with the Iron Cross, Ist Class.

The 8th Army [Blaskowitz] apparently forgot to do so!

In the evening orders arrived for the reorganization of the Western Front. I urged Brauchitsch to publish the orders for the attack preparations as early as possible so that we might go to work.

The radio announced a treaty between England, France and Turkey!

20/10/39

The order for the strategic concentration for the attack arrived in the evening [this "Strategic Concentration Order Yellow" of 19 October was re-worded on 29 October 1939].

21/10/39

Meeting with *General* Brand (Army High Command) [artillery general with the Commander-in-Chief] over the question of the role and employment of the artillery.

Reichenau [6th Army], Weichs [2nd Army] and Kluge [4th Army], my three army commanders, came and were briefed on the working process of the coming days: first they are to envisage how they propose to direct the attack and report as soon as possible; further they are to consider the details of conducting the buildup, so that the Army Group might have information with which to determine how and when the troops are to be moved into position.

A spy reports that a German plan of attack which coincides rather precisely with the plans of the Army Command has been leaked and is the topic of the day among French and Belgian officers. Even if it wasn't betrayed, it wouldn't be hard to construe.

In recent days the French have carried out a planned evacuation of the approaches to the Maginot Line between the Rhine and Luxembourg, which they had earlier fought to win. Army Group Leeb [CIC Army Group C] has pressed ahead to the border of the Reich against rearguard actions. My assessment of this is that the French are withdrawing to their fortress front, in order to mobilize the forces thereby released to meet the threat of a German attack.

In the evening an order from Berlin that the *Führer* wishes to speak with Reichenau at the beginning of next week.

22/10/39

Drove into 6th Army's sector of the front and to the 253rd Division [Kühne]. Together with Reichenau, Kluge and I are to go to see the *Führer* on the 25th [October].

23/10/39

General von Stülpnagel of the Army High Command came in the late morning and briefed me on the questions to be discussed on the 25th.

In the afternoon discussions with Kluge and Reichenau, who laid out their plans concerning conduct of the attack. From Headquarters, 2nd Army only the Chief of Staff, Felber, was present, but he as yet had no clear picture as to how the army will carry out its mission.

24/10/39

Drove to Berlin.

Hitler's Defensive Motivation

Meeting with Hitler [Supreme Commander of the Armed Forces]. The *Führer* described the general political situation and justified the need for the attack. If the enemy arrives at the Belgian-German border first, the situation for us – he said – will be untenable, for the threat to the Rhine industrial region, shipping traffic on the Rhine and to the Ruhr would paralyze the production potential in the heart of our armaments industry. We cannot wait! Our situation is favorable, the situation "over there" is not. But in time the others will become stronger than we can. As well there is the risk that one fine day we will wake up to the news that the enemy is standing at the Belgian-German frontier!

Concerning the conduct of the operations, the *Führer* stressed that we must not fall back on the tactics of the linear battles of the World War; we must strike quickly and vigorously and employ rapid advances by motorized and armored units to force the enemy to operate and act quickly, which is beyond the ability of the systematic French and the clumsy English.

I was able to state that I could make allowances for these ideas by bolstering the 6th Army [Reichenau] with a third panzer division and readying a strong motorized reserve behind it. I went on to say:

"The French are already on the Maas near Givet, the Belgians have six to eight divisions around Brussels and Antwerp, the English will probably move as soon as they learn that we have attacked; they can therefore reach Antwerp sooner and with stronger forces than can we. If they succeed in this, the result will be a frontal battle which will bog down by the general line Antwerp-Namur-Maas at the latest. Our northernmost army, the 2nd [Weichs], cannot have an effect on the situation at Antwerp until days later if the Dutch put their flooding plans into effect, or probably too late. After the recent rains many of the Dutch lowlands are already under water! The only means of delaying the enemy's advance, especially of his motorized forces, is a maximum effort by air power against this advance. But now the weather, as it usually is here in late autumn, is so unsettled that the potential for use of the Luftwaffe is very limited and difficult to predict in advance. In any case it is dangerous to base everything on it alone." The *Führer* agreed with me.

Reichenau described the difficulties posed by the Dutch lowlands and expressed doubts about an attack at this time of year. While discussing the possibilities of a postponement talk turned to the political sphere. Reichenau fought bravely for his view.

Finally I intervened, turning attention back to the operation itself, which the *Führer* immediately picked up on. I once again alluded to the threat that the enemy could be in Antwerp sooner and with stronger forces than we. Once again the *Führer* agreed. The *Führer* proposed various and innovative possibilities for Luftwaffe participation. I stated that I had too little understanding of the technical details to have an opinion, but pointed out that experience showed that at present there were all too often weather conditions which made any air operations impossible. Within the overall framework of the attack, therefore, it was impossible to make decisively important matters, for example the time of the attack, solely dependent on the success of such air operations; if they succeed they are a welcome plus! The use of the Luftwaffe to delay the enemy advance on Antwerp could be decisive, but whether it is even possible in this weather situation is questionable.

The *Führer* raised various objections against the Army High Command's plan of attack. Finally, in response to a question from Brauchitsch, he said that from the beginning he had the desire and ideas of making the main attack south of the Maas – perhaps with a secondary operation against Liège – in order to advance west and then northwest and cut off and destroy the enemy forces in and moving into Belgium. Brauchitsch and Halder were apparently taken completely by surprise and there ensued a "lively" exchange about these ideas. I could only declare that in my area, including south of the Maas, all roads were already full, so that inserting further forces there was not easily possible.

The conference, which began at noon, concluded at 19:00 with the Army High Command being instructed to assess the new ideas.

Attack on Holland – "Water Pantomime"

26/10/39

Returned to Godesberg.

It is becoming ever clearer to me that the *Führer* is not going to be talked out of the idea of the attack. He considers it necessary politically and militarily. But perhaps he will yet realize that a postponement of the date is necessary. I believe that the northern wing of the attack, apart from "Water Pantomine" [the attack on Holland] must stay where it is, because the area between the Maginot Line and the right wing of the 6th Army must inevitably be fully exploited if we are to be able to bring the forces into action at all. The right wing of the assault still points toward Antwerp. Thus the danger remains that the enemy will get there before we do – and with it also that of bogging down into a purely frontal battle, for given the weather situation in this region in fall and winter the effective employment of the Luftwaffe is a very uncertain matter. The *Führer* has acknowledged this danger. Therefore if the Army High Command considers putting off the attack until spring to be correct, it has the possibility of further defending this point of view.

27/10/39

I spoke with Stülpnagel by telephone about the ideas described above. Intelligence suggests that the French are shifting forces to their northern wing. The English are said to be staying in the area of Lille.

"The Senior Staffs Are Too Big..."

28/10/39

Paris radio reports that the German headquarters is located at Bad Godesberg [HQ Army Group B; Headquarters, Army Group A was located in Koblenz]. Pleasant prospects!

Bringing the divisions coming from the east up to strength in men and materiel is taking unusually long. We have therefore already pressed them several times. I brought up the matter again in Berlin on the 25th [October]. Why things are still not in order, four weeks after the conclusion of the Polish Campaign, is difficult to understand. The senior staffs – including mine – are too big. Consequently too much is written and too little done! I therefore spoke with Brauchitsch once again. He informed me that the "final" decision had been made today and that issuance of the orders was being expedited.

In the evening a visit from Dr. Ley [leader of the German Labor Front]. I told him of some difficulties that had arisen with the civilian workers on the *Westwall* which affected their morale. Ley was in the picture and said that corrective measures were being implemented. He had come from a trip through the industrial region on the Lower Rhine and was pleased by the determined mood and the "enthusiasm" of the workers.

30/10/39

In the morning an amendment to the concentration directive came. Plenty of dreams of the future, but otherwise largely as expected. Several things impractical, they will simply be changed. "Water Pantomine" was dropped.

Afternoon drove to see Rundstedt [Army Group A] in Koblenz. He has the same opinions as we concerning the great unsettled questions.

Brauchitsch is coming on the 2nd [November].

I spoke by telephone with *General* Roese [Inspector of Infantry, Replacement Army], who is working on the replacement component of the infantry and told him that the poor quality of the replacements for the infantry – officers and men – cannot go on. Declarations that those "above" were aware of that too are of no use; something has to happen! Strauss [Commanding General II Army Corps] and Both [Commanding General I Army Corps] came to see me. Both agree completely with my point of view in the matter of replacements for the infantry and several of the tactical questions of the conduct of the battle discussed by me.

Officers are constantly on the go checking up on the condition of the divisions. It was again reported today that replacement of materiel is far from adequate. I called Fromm [Commander-in-Chief of the Replacement Army]; he "hopes" to put things in order in time.

31/10/39

Morning meeting with the army commanders [Weichs, Kluge, Reichenau] concerning their plans. All is not yet quite set; but on the whole there is unanimity.

Stülpnagel [OQu I, OKH] came but brought nothing new. Rundstedt [Army Group A] has officially expressed views similar to mine on the question of the attack. Reichenau [6th Army] is driving to Berlin again today to speak to the *Führer* about the attack.

"Unsatisfactory State of the Field Forces"

1/11/39

Brennecke, the Chief of Staff of the 4th Army, came in the evening and outlined the army's plans. According to these the army will commit everything against the sector of the Meuse south of Namur and forego the crossing at Huy. I spoke out against the idea; the army must try to seize the crossing at Huy – and quickly! On the one hand because the forcing of the section of the Meuse between Namur and Givet will be eased if simultaneous pressure is applied north of Namur, and on the other because the army must stretch itself farther to the north in order to achieve a more effective close cooperation with the 6th Army [Reichenau] should it run into difficulties in its initial attacks, which might very well happen to its southern wing at the Maastricht river crossings.

Reichenau's meetings in Berlin were fruitless; the *Führer* is sticking to his decision.

Brauchitsch came to Düsseldorf and Cologne to discuss the plans proposed by the 6th and 4th Armies. The presentation by Kluge – the 4th Army – ignored the conversation I had with his Chief of Staff [Brennecke] yesterday. Not until Brauchitsch echoed my position concerning the crossing at Huy did he fall into line. Unfortunately, the unsatisfactory state of the field forces in terms of personnel and equipment was not expressed as clearly in the commanding generals' statements as it should have been. It took several questions from me to give a clear picture, that at present another fourteen days were needed even for good divisions, for example those of II Army Corps [Strauss], in order to make them really capable of attacking.

According to the descriptions by the Quartermaster-General's Chief of Staff, on the whole the ammunition situation does not appear to be adequately assured for decisive battles.

Long, very serious talk with Brauchitsch on the train during the trip from Düsseldorf to Cologne.

3/11/39

Today the 4th Army reported that its divisions are nowhere near up to strength or ready for operations! Why not yesterday?

4/11/39

Reichenau is on his way to Berlin again; the *Führer* wishes to speak with him again.

5/11/39

Drove to the 8th [Koch-Erpach] and 28th [Obstfelder] Divisions, both of which are still having problems with replacements. What will happen if there is heavy fighting?

In the evening came the order from the Army Command: "A-Day is the 12th of November."

6/11/39

As both army commanders were away, I spoke with the army chiefs of staff about the need to maintain strict discipline behind the front, especially in the large cities, at train stations and in the streets. I demanded that there be action instead of more warnings. I gave similar instructions to the acting commander of the corps headquarters in Münster, which is not under my command – but after all one is allowed to clean up even in strange rooms.

Several units have received back their requests for replacements submitted some time ago, while still in Poland, with the comment that the requests were to be submitted as per another "regulation" model! That is unheard of! I called the Chief of the Army General Staff [Halder] and told him. Halder took the opportunity to tell me that there had been a decisive discussion concerning the matter of the attack yesterday and that the *Führer* was sticking to his orders.

The A-movements began this evening according to plan.

The Quartermaster-General [Stülpnagel] arrived in the morning. Salmuth discussed with him the failures in replacement of men and materiel, and I resisted the unrequested and unnecessary enlargement of my staff.

Late morning meeting in Düsseldorf with *General* Hoepner [XVI Army Corps] and the Chief of Staff of the 6th Army [Paulus] concerning their plans. After hearing once more about the miserable replacement situation, especially in the panzer divisions, it was learned that the heavy howitzer batteries have only 600-800 rounds of ammunition altogether.

The army has prepared well everything that is in its power. I learned that orders have been issued from Berlin for employment of the Luftwaffe and for the carrying out of certain air operations in the A-Case. As well Reichenau has just reported from Berlin that the launching of the attack is being determined by the requirements of the Luftwaffe; so it is going to happen on a clear day. My suggestion not to make the starting date of the operation solely dependent on these operations has not sunk in.

In the afternoon came orders to halt the A-movement begun yesterday, initially for 24 hours. Soon afterward it was announced that the order to continue the movement is not to be expected before the 9th [November]. I learned from Stülpnagel that the reason is the weather situation! How can they know today what the weather will be on the 12th?

In the evening English radio announced that Belgium and Holland have offered to act as peace intermediaries. What might it mean? Is it just a chess move aimed at branding as bandits anyone who attacks these nations while they are trying to mediate peace? In any case it's probably not a friendly stance toward us, especially since the Belgian Army is formed up with its front facing Germany.

8/11/39

The leader of the "military civilian administration" planned for Case A reported to me in the presence of representatives of the Ministry of the Interior and of the Quartermaster-General. I used the opportunity to point out several unclear areas in the basic directive and as well requested that it be organized in such a way that it might assemble and go to work quickly when Case A comes.

Unpleasant exchange of telegrams with the Army High Command. There is no point in recording details.

9/11/39

In the morning news of an attempt on Hitler's life in Munich; the *Führer* is unhurt. Before noon I drove to Koblenz to see Rundstedt. Later in the day I learned by telephone that A-Day is being further postponed. It will be bad for the field forces if the matter isn't cleared up soon, for constant march readiness prevents the time won from being used for training and refurbishing the units, which is needed. I sent a telegram to the Army High Command, once again reporting the poor replacement situation. My outlook is pessimistic if the makeup of the replacement organization – personnel as well as materiel – is not thoroughly reorganized.

10/11/39

During the night orders came to postpone A-Day, "not before the 19th." Drove to the 251st [Kratzert], 225th [Schaumburg], 269th [Hell], and 61st [Haenicke] Divisions. Very good impression, but almost everywhere the same major problems with supply, especially of motor vehicle equipment.

All intelligence suggests that the Belgians are placing maximum emphasis on improving their defensive measures against Germany, in contrast to the front facing France, where there as good as no Belgian troops any more. English and French radio speak openly of the imminent German attack on Holland and Belgium. The "peace offer" is characterized by the Allies as an "emergency measure" against the German threat and hopeless.

Several days ago the Army Command took away one of the two panzer divisions from the army corps reserve and now today they demanded the other and last one. The point of main effort of the attack is being constantly watered down. I reported by telegraph that the missions assigned to me can no longer be accomplished with the forces of the army group alone.

11/11/39

Reichenau arrived at midmorning; he confirmed that the *Führer* is sticking to his decision in every detail.

The Army Command claims that the removal of the panzer divisions was due to the personal intervention of the *Führer*. If that is true then the mainspring is uppermost in his mind: main thrust south of the Meuse! But if that is true, they should clearly express this change of plan. The gradual watering down of the previous basic concept will lead to blurred interpretations and confused orders; and the ultimate result will be that in striving to be strong everywhere, we will really be strong nowhere!

Drove to the 4th [Hansen] and 11th [Böckmann] Divisions; many shortages, but both commanders are trying to help themselves as best they can.

12/11/39

Drove to Headquarters, II Army Corps [Strauss] and the 12th [Leyen] and 32nd [Gablenz] Divisions. In a telephone conversation with Salmuth, regarding my telegram of the 10th on account of the removal of the two panzer divisions, Halder took the position that he agreed with me, but that the order had come from the *Führer* himself; Brauchitsch expressed a similar view. According to a telegram which arrived later, on the *Führer*'s order a motorized corps is now also to be formed by Army Group Rundstedt [Army Group A], with very far-reaching plans for its use. This dispersal of forces can lead to no good and I can't understand why the military command does not establish a clearer point of main effort.

Toward evening I was visited by Tresckow. He had apparently heard somewhere that I had changed my opinion on the planned operations. I telephoned Brauchitsch and asked him if he knew about the rumor and whether he was in doubt about my position. He declared that he knew nothing of the rumor and had no doubts whatsoever. It was nothing but "demigod gossip." *General* Busch [VIII Army Corps] has been summoned by the *Führer* to describe the method of attack in his sector!?

I telegraphed a brief, succinct picture of the state of the field forces to the Army High Command; the assessment culminated with:

"Capable of a brief offensive; major operations only when timely replacement of everything, especially motor vehicles, is assured. Additional training time desirable in any event."

13/11/39

Drove to the 18th [Cranz], 35th [Reinhard] and 253rd [Kühne] Divisions. Toward evening order arrived postponing A-Day by three more days!

15/11/39

Today, not surprisingly, the order came that the attack by the northern wing was now to be extended as far as the northern part of Holland!

"Water Pantomine" has come to life again in expanded form! The justification is incomprehensible. It states that there is a danger that the English might set foot in Fortress Holland and establish a base there for its air force. But since the same order states that Fortress Holland is not to be taken, I don't know how this attack is supposed to prevent the English from gaining a foothold in the fortress with their air force. I discussed this curious affair with Halder; he agreed with me. The order came from above! I suggested – if this operation was now to be carried out – that the airborne division might be more suitable there than for the other operations for which it is being considered. Halder said that he too was looking into this matter.

Falkenhorst [Commanding General XXI Army Corps] visited me. He too is of the view that we should not attack in the west at this time. Significantly, in addition to their military reservations, all the generals are loath to injure the often-assured neutrality of two nations.

16/11/39

Two interesting reports from spies: one says that on 13 November the members of the American Consulate General in Cologne received instructions to burn all their files as a German invasion of Belgium and Holland was imminent, which would result in America intervening on the side of the western powers. The other says that extensive arrangements exist between England and Holland for the eventuality of a German invasion and that England desires this invasion!

After England and France have stuck to their previous conditions in replying to the Belgian-Dutch peace move, Germany has now in a brusque way characterized the mediation attempt as "finished."

Afternoon visit from Hansen, the Commanding General of the X Army Corps; I discussed with him his new assignment, the occupation of northern and northwestern Holland.

Telegram from the Army High Command stating that the decision on A-Day has been postponed by another four days. That is the fourth change! The front-line divisions of the field forces have now been ten days in quarters that were originally considered only interim quarters, scarcely bearable in the long run. Cramped quarters, no chance to train, some of the horses in the open – and today pouring rain. With the busy border traffic this "blitz buildup" naturally cannot be kept secret. My officers say that that is not so bad, for in time the Belgians will take this kind of buildup for a bluff!

I learned via Paris radio that I have been sacked "on account of monarchistic intrigues."

17/11/39

Drove to the 7th Division [Ott].

18/11/39

Visit from Reichenau [6th Army] in the late morning; he has been ordered to Berlin again on the 20th [November]. It's probably just about details of the attack and not about the big question itself.

I called the Chief of the Army High Command [Halder] and once again made him aware of the attack's lack of depth (see also my telegram of 10 November). Reichenau's Army [6th] has just enough reserves, be it to replace the panzer divisions which advance far ahead or those stuck in the attack front. The reserves of the army group, whose attack front is now 200 km wide, consist of a total of just seven divisions. That is not nearly enough to sustain the battle. Halder said that he had just spoken to Brauchitsch about it, both agree with me; but I know the *Führer*'s chief desire, which keeps drawing him south! Originally the point of main effort was supposed to lie with me, now there are three attack spearheads! I was right about my concern over the blurring of the point of main effort. The Army High Command would attempt to accommodate further requests for shifts to the south only in the rear, or among the reserves, anything else wouldn't work. They would also only take place if the ability to commit them where the situation demands is fully preserved. To this I replied:

"But for heaven's sake don't softly and gradually wash out the point of main effort. Better to make a clear start!"

It had been clear by mid-September that the Polish Campaign was rapidly nearing an end. Had the Army High Command made a clear proposal for the continuation of the war in the west to the supreme authority or not? If not, then no one can be surprised if now the supreme authority comes up with its own ideas – and with different ones than the military command desires!

19/11/39

Orders came during the night that we were to make preparations to occupy the West Friesian Islands with weak forces together with the Navy in order to obtain a forward base for the air warning service. That would be a fine job for the Luftwaffe itself, in which case the Navy wouldn't be needed at all!

The 29th Motorized Division [Lemelsen] has been taken away from the Army Group [B] and designated Army High Command reserve. The three points of main effort remain! One by the 4th [Kluge], one by the 6th Army [Reichenau], and one by Army Group Rundstedt [Army Group A] – and not really strong anywhere!

Travelled to Berlin.

Chapter 2: 4 October 1939 to 9 May 1940

Rejection of the "Colonization" of the East

20/11/39

In Berlin I learned that A-Day has been postponed – for the fifth time! The weather is said to be the reason. The Army High Command has concerns that I have overestimated the forces required to take northeastern Holland. It is my view that this secondary operation should be brought to an end as swiftly and surely as possible. In turn this would free the bulk of the forces used equally quickly. I won't change my mind.

Night trip to Koblenz in the train of the Commander-in-Chief of the Army [Brauchitsch]. There I heard stories about the "colonization" of the east, which shocked me deeply. If they continue to act this way there, these methods will one day turn against us!

21/11/39

Conference of the Commander-in-Chief of the Army and the army group and army commanders in Koblenz. Details of Case-A were examined thoroughly. I got my way with my position concerning the occupation of northern Holland. Still doubt on the northern wing of the 6th Army; the northern wing has to be strong and deep and reach the general area of Breda as quickly as possible. Whether it would go better and more quickly if two divisions initially advance one after another on the former northern wing of the army, the first going toward Tournhout and the second later being diverted through Tilburg – or if from the start we send one division across the Maas in the area of Gennep and then past Hertogenbosch past Breda to the south, is still being examined.

Another panzer division is being taken from the 6th Army's front, leaving just two in the front lines; in the past it was repeatedly stressed that we should concentrate all our motorized forces at the front. Now it's different and I have nothing against it, for here, with our nose on the Maas and the canals, I would rather have this panzer division in reserve than at the front.

In the evening came the surprise order that the *Führer* wishes to speak to all commanders-in-chief and commanding generals in Berlin on the 23rd [November].

22/11/39

Travelled to Berlin.

23/11/39

The *Führer* once again expressed to all the commanding generals of the Armed Forces "his unbending will" to see the war through to total victory. Once again he justified the compelling necessity to attack soon with the need for greater security for the Ruhr Region, with the necessity for better air and U-boat bases, and finally with the necessity to defeat the enemy and thus assure a lengthy peace for Germany.

"One cannot achieve victory by waiting!"

"At last we are in the position we have longed for for sixty years, not to have to fight a war on two fronts," he said, "it would thus be a great mistake not to take advantage of this favorable moment, for no man can say how long it will last!"

The *Führer* took a firm position against any defeatism. He refused to accept the idea that our infantry was not as good as in 1914. The possibility of a revolution he rejected completely:

"There will be no revolution!"

A certain ill feeling toward the commander of the army was obvious in all his remarks. The Navy and Air Force were depicted as models of initiative. The reason is clear: the *Führer* knows that the bulk of the generals do not believe that attacking now will produce a decisive success. This is regrettable after the sacrifices and successes in Poland, for the army bore almost the entire burden of the campaign, because there was neither a Polish navy worthy of note nor a Polish Air Force to be taken seriously.

There had been a serious disagreement between the *Führer* and Brauchitsch before the conference; the latter has nevertheless stayed on, and thus apparently intends to bear the responsibility for the planned operation!

25/11/39

Return trip to Godesberg.

26/11/39

The Army Command has meanwhile taken away the Army Group's [B] last motorized reserves and placed them under its command. By doing so it wishes to keep open the possibility of committing its reserves where a success appears likely. That is a compromise, but no "solution." My reserves have thus been reduced to a minimum. I am trying to help myself by making the employment of the motorized division and the freed-up panzer division there subject to my authorization. If I openly declare them "army group reserve," the Army Command will take them away too!

27/11/39

The sixth postponement of A-Day has been ordered! Here and there one hears that the weather is just an excuse for the postponements. What is the real reason then? I don't believe there will be any fundamental changes in the political line.

The armies have been directed to use the time gained by the latest postponement for intensive training, as far as the cramped quarters permit.

The 6th Army [Reichenau] has made a decision about its northern wing: it will send one division through Gennep toward Tilburg-Breda from the beginning; only if the crossing near Gennep should fail will this division to be sent in behind the former northern wing in the second line and redirected north during the course of the advance.

28/11/39

Wietersheim [Commanding General XIV Army Corps] came in the late morning, Brand [Inspector of Artillery] in the afternoon.

A Luftwaffe order was revealed, according to which the flak corps is to be employed "primarily" in a ground role. We would be happy if the flak corps fulfilled its mission of keeping the enemy air force out of our hair! If we need anti-aircraft guns in the ground war we'll help ourselves!

29/11/39

A tooth and jaw problem that has been bothering me for weeks has resulted in the situation where I have been unable to visit the troops for some time. That is bad, for it is especially important right now; equipment, training and morale must all be promoted and brought forward.

I spoke to the Commanders-in-Chief of the 2nd [Weichs] and 18th [Küchler] Armies and asked them to use all available means to thoroughly familiarize themselves with Liège and Antwerp, as both corps headquarters might be considered to command the attack on these fortresses.

Sharp Protest against Three Points of Main Effort

30/11/39

Reichenau [6th Army] has requested leave in Berlin. He wants to speak to the *Führer* in order to try to explain the army's views and line of reasoning and give him a better understanding of them.

Brauchitsch announced a meeting to be held the day after tomorrow.

Russia has opened hostilities against Finland.

Justification for the war has been very clumsily prepared: Finland is alleged to have fired at Russian troops across the border with artillery – which no one believes. The whole world comes out against Russia; of course we can't do that now.

Salmuth [Chief of Staff Army Group B] brought news from Berlin that now the Army Command is worried because there are now only very weak reserves behind my front! I have had these concerns since the moment the Army Command began taking away my reserves.

2/12/39

Meeting with Brauchitsch at Godesberg. Many details. When asked I once again explained my position on the advance by the 6th Army's right wing: as per orders, the division on the right wing is to advance through Breda in order to occupy the land as far as the coast. In the center XXII (Motorized) Army Corps has to go toward Tournhout, for in Antwerp is a foe which cannot simply be bypassed. Redirecting XXII Army Corps to the southwest, past Antwerp, can only be considered if conditions there are relatively clear. The 6th Army has orders to send reserves behind its northern wing so that the strongest possible forces are available or can be freed quickly for the southwestward advance. I am also going to send two reserve divisions there, in order to later relieve active divisions which might become bogged down in front of Antwerp with reserve divisions. The active divisions of the Army Group reserve are to be used to sustain and promote the drive south of Antwerp, be it by the 6th [Reichenau] or the 4th [Kluge] Army.

Talk once again turned to the need for the 4th Army to also provide forces for Huy; here our views coincided.

Paulus, Chief of Staff of the 6th Army, brought up the fact that the order which arrived yesterday concerning the use of gliders and other special formations to support the 6th Army's attack had been changed again. The matter is to be clarified. I spoke further about the difficulties of the present uncertain state of suspense, which is beginning to affect morale; it is absolutely necessary that we once again gain a firm grip on the field forces and train them more thoroughly. I said that if the attack is further postponed, then they should do it in one large jump instead of "in sips," so that the field forces can really make something of it. I am going to submit an appropriate proposal by telegraph.

4/12/39

Today in response to my proposal of yesterday came the seventh postponement of A-Day, this time by two days! Serious flooding in the lowlands of the Lower Rhine is making troop movements off the roads impossible.

6/12/39

And now the eighth postponement! The new decision is to be made on 12 December.

At noon Minister Goebbels and *Gauleiters* Terboven and Grohè had lunch with us.

7/12/39

Drove to the 30th [Briesen] and 216th [Boettcher] Divisions. The 30th is back in shape again after its heavy losses in the east; Briesen, the commanding officer, is still troubled by his wound. I encouraged him to take a rest and go on leave. The reserve division is – not without justification – in a bad mood because the older soldiers have not been released yet, while in Germany many "young snot-noses" are running around without being drafted.

8/12/39

Drove to Berlin to take a rest after my jaw episode.

12/12/39

Returned to Godesberg. There I was met by news of the "ninth" postponement. But finally it is envisaged for somewhat longer – the next decision is not to be made before 27 December. We immediately set about trying to ease the accommodations situation, as far as this is possible given what is still a short period of time, in order to create better opportunities for quarters and training.

13/12/39

In the morning near Cologne a demonstration of a mine-detector designed by a pioneer officer with the help of the Aachen Technical School; it is simple and practical, so we ordered 300. Visit by the Luftwaffe Chief of Staff [Jeschonnek] and the commanders of Air Fleets 2 [Kesselring] and 3 [Sperrle]. The uncertainty about the focal point of the attack – or more accurately "the game with the points of main effort" – had also resulted in difficulties for the Luftwaffe. The Luftwaffe Chief of Staff said that all attempts to achieve clarity had failed; the army must press for clarity on its own accord. I promised that I would – as I had so often – again push in this direction. Conversation revealed that the Armed Forces High Command was considering moving the point of main effort on the first day of the attack if the Maastricht bridges were not taken intact. I pointed out the dangers of such ideas and all three

Luftwaffe generals were in agreement. There was also agreement on the impossibility of moving the flak corps, which was to be massed near the front, at right angles to the direction of attack in the event of a change in the point of main effort. I also pointed out that, in spite of the total lack of certainty as to where it was actually to take place, the planned airborne operation is drawing attention and forces to the Luftwaffe – be it for its preparation or for guarding and watching over it – so that the main objective, namely supporting the attack by the armies, has receded into the background! Jeschonnek, Luftwaffe Chief of Staff, admitted that this was the inevitable result of the entire plan.

I sent a written report on this meeting to the Army High Command and warned against rashly shifting the point of main effort; I also once again proposed using the airborne troops in close cooperation with the planned operation – thus at the point of main effort of my Army Group B.

Kluge [4th Army] brought proposals for a considerable shortening of the pre-attack buildup, in order to at least improve somewhat our chances of surprising the enemy. We have also given thought to this idea.

14/12/39

Drove to Headquarters, 6th Army and to the 31st [Kaempfe] and 207th [Tiedemann] Divisions.

The question of shortening the preparation period was discussed with HQ, 6th Army.

15/12/39

Drove to Headquarters, V Corps [Ruoff] and to the 211th Division [Renner].

In the evening Miss von Hüllessem of the Army Group's base detachment called from Berlin to say that according to the Hotel Fürstenhof a man was staying there who claimed to be my personal adjutant. The hotel was suspicious and asking for confirmation. The fellow was arrested under the most delicate conditions the same evening; a large number of phoney identity cards were found on him.

16/12/39

Drove to the 27th Division [Bergmann].

Quite independent of our deliberations, yesterday Stülpnagel of the Army High Command asked Hasse [Ia of Army Group North] whether we consider a shortening of the preparation period to be possible. This is the case under certain conditions and these conditions are possible with the help of the Army High Command. A telegram with appropriate proposals went to Berlin.

Propaganda "At the Cost of Trust"

18/12/39

News release that the battle cruiser *Graf Spee* has scuttled herself after an engagement with English cruisers in order to avoid being interned.

But why did our propaganda speak of a great "victory at sea" instead of preparing the public for the almost inevitable from the beginning? This was done at the cost of trust! It is embarrassing that the English *Royal Oak*, which our propaganda has several times reported torpedoed, took part in the hunt for the *Graf Spee* and in doing so showed itself in a neutral port! The English lie too, of course!

On the night of 12-13 December 1939 the battle cruiser *Graf Spee* was off the mouth of the River Platte, where it encountered Force G of the Royal Navy, consisting of the heavy cruiser Exeter and the light cruisers *Ajax* and *Achilles*. After a heavy exchange of fire with his ship badly damaged, *Kapitän zur See* Langdorff of the *Graf Spee* decided to sail to Montevideo as he was of the opinion that the damage could be repaired using the ship's own resources. In Montevideo the ship was given 72 hours to make itself seaworthy again. At the same time an intensive propaganda effort by the enemy convinced the *Graf Spee*'s captain that the area was surrounded by strong fleet units of the Royal Navy; Langdorff decided to scuttle his ship, which took place on the evening of 17 December 1939. The captain shot himself immediately after-ward. In the course of its sortie into the South Atlantic and the Indian Ocean, which lasted from 2 September until 13 December 1939, the *Graf Spee* had sunk 9 merchant vessels totalling more than 50,000 tonnes.

20/12/39

Intelligence confirms that the enemy's intelligence service is very well informed about everything we are doing. Replacement of units in the 4th Army's front was reported 24 hours later by the Belgian press and radio. How do they plan to keep secret a buildup lasting several days? As well a steady flow of reports that the Belgians and Dutch are stepping up the blocking all approach roads; in the Ardennes the roads are said to be barricaded in great depth.

21/12/39

I heard about a talk by the Commander East [Blaskowitz] with the Commander-in-Chief of the Army [Brauchitsch] about the serious situation in the east in the internal-political field.

22/12/39

The Commander-in-Chief of the Army [Brauchitsch] rejected the army group's proposals for a shortening of the preparation period. No reasons given. We therefore tried again, this time in a letter from Salmuth to the Army Chief of Staff [Halder]. The letter summarized the thinking on which our proposals were based. At the same time it pointed out that the increased barricading of the Ardennes roads made hopeless the employment of massed panzer divisions there on the first day of the attack; we proposed bolstering the "attack spearheads" there with weak armored forces and then only commit the bulk of the panzer divisions when room had been made for them. We were thus back to our initial proposal. I telephoned Halder to tell him about Salmuth's letter and advised him that I agreed completely with its contents. By the way, the Army Group appears to have made a similar proposal for shortening the buildup, for a similarly worded letter from the Commander-in-Chief of the Army rejecting the idea was also sent there.

23/12/39

Travelled to Berlin.

28/12/39

Returned to Godesberg.

The decision on A-Day has been put off again; there has been severe cold for days. What sort of weather are they expecting?

The Army High Command has approved our proposal to move the panzer divisions behind our front, east of the Rhine. Concentrating our forces will thus be simpler and, if those above should yet decide on a shortening of the buildup time, it will now be very easy for us to carry out.

Apart from one minor exception, the Army High Command did not agree to our proposal to move weak elements of the armored divisions, which we would like up front as soon as possible to reinforce our "attack spearheads," across the Rhine now. Still no response to our concerns about employing entire armored divisions in the front line in the Ardennes on the first day of the attack.

31/12/39

A letter from the Armed Forces High Command concerned itself with the "possible" A-Date. The question of the time of the attack was also touched upon once again. The letter admits that the attack has no initial point of main effort, but states that it is to be created based on initial successes! The letter stressed that this fixing of the point of main effort cannot be based solely on the success of the planned surprise attack by the 6th Army in the early hours! Our warning of 13 December was at least useful in this point.

On 22 December the Army High Command sent a study for the attack on Holland as a proposal and to stimulate debate as to whether stronger forces will eventually have to be committed against Holland in order to reach certain objectives there, for example the capture of the Zuider Zee dam. Surprising, for previously they were of the opinion that I had deployed too strong a force against the north of Holland!

5/1/40

Conference with the army commanders about reexamining the attack preparations by corps and divisions, the difficulty of employing armored divisions in the front line if we attack under the present conditions, and so on.

Kluge [4th Army] and Reichenau [6th Army] once again advocated a shortening of the buildup time. I am of the same view and will once again try to push it through. Kluge brought up the conditions in the east, of which he has naturally also heard. Here on the Western Front we have learned about briefing notes from the Commander-in-Chief East [Blaskowitz] to the Commander-in-Chief of the Army which contain hair-raising descriptions of the conditions in the east. Serious encroachments by police authorities etc. against the armed forces are mentioned, apparently without the guilty parties being called to account. I promised Kluge that I would try to clear up what the report was about and whether anything has come of it. By the way I take the following point of view, which I made clear to the army commanders:

"If the brazen encroachments by any organizations against the armed forces really are true, the affected officers and Wehrmacht offices are not to be exonerated. In any case, I will not tolerate in my area of command any officer who allows insults to the Wehrmacht or his person to go unpunished! And I expect superiors to stand up for and support every subordinate to the extent possible in the protection of the honor and reputation of the Armed Forces!"

General von Weichs, 2nd Army, gave a presentation on the possible methods of attack on Liège worked out by Headquarters, 2nd Army.

Visit by a representative of the chemical industry. Major expansion program which should not only help us out of our present troubles, but also gain a lead over the enemy states in the chemical field, which the industry sees as attainable – provided America, with its "unlimited means and possibilities," does not join the side of our enemies. All very lovely, but why are they just starting with it now? They have known for long that this struggle for existence was coming.

6/1/40

Meeting with Halder in Cologne: shortening the preparation period is apparently running into difficulties in the Army Command, mainly of a railway-technical nature.

Halder declared that shortening the period by one or two days could not relieve the political leadership of making the decision to attack as early as before. The matter would be looked into further however. The matter of using the tanks resolved itself surprisingly easily; as to my statements, Halder said that he had no objections if the panzer divisions were not committed en masse in the front line until there were prospects of them making real progress – but then immediately! At last!

Halder believes that he can promise two of the divisions from the Army Command Reserve that I requested for Liège – in the event that the Belgians hold Liège. I expressed concern that the enemy had learned the prospective attack date, for the third time! There must be a leak somewhere, where these things seep through with surprising speed.

There has apparently been an interim ruling on the eastern question as the Commander East [Blaskowitz] has talked these matters over with his civilian governor and hopefully the discussion will result in a cessation of the encroachments or at least an improvement.

7/1/40

Sponeck, commander of the 22nd (Airborne) Division, poured out his heart to me about the recklessness with which a possible employment of his division was "worked out"; allegedly he was himself totally ignored during the preliminary planning. Right after him came *General* Speidel, the Chief of Staff of Air Fleet 2, who informed me that the entire air landing operation was now finally under the command of Air Fleet 2; with the condition, however, that the *Führer* reserves to himself the decision as to if, where and when one of the two prepared operations – Ghent or Namur – is carried out. I set forth my reservations against both operations. Speidel shares them. To Speidel's question, when the 4th Army was likely to reach the Meuse (Maas) south of Namur, I replied:

"I can't promise it before the fourth day! It is possible that it might go faster under very favorable circumstances, but I can't guarantee it."

Speidel then observed that the entire operation would thus probably be voided; he was therefore going to fly to Berlin and report that. I am very much in agreement, for I don't believe in operations of this sort.

Kluge [4th Army] called in the afternoon, having also spoken with Speidel in the meantime, and asked me to request that the Namur airborne landing not be scheduled for the first day, as he could not guarantee that he would reach the Meuse in time to prevent the airborne forces from being destroyed. The timing of the operation should instead be adapted to suit the course of the land battle.

8/1/40

Drove to the 267th Division [Fessmann].

I had Salmuth ask Halder if I should write to Keitel on account of the airborne operations; but I only wanted to do so if I was doing the Army Command a favor in the process. Halder was unenthusiastic about this idea, so I'm letting it be. During the conversation we discussed what I had said yesterday to Speidel about the chances of the 4th Army's arrival. The Army Command apparently doesn't think this is right, because it believes that Göring will use it to say: "The Army just can't handle it!" On the one hand such a manner of speaking would be very easy to retort, while on the other it's not enough to cause me to paint things prettier than they really are.

9/1/40

In a letter to Halder I argued point by point why I can't promise any effect by the 4th Army at the Meuse before the fourth day of the attack. I stated that in my opinion the root of all evil lies in the fact that both airborne operations being considered lie too far outside the scope of the ground operation. I can only promise success from operations of this type if they are prepared in such a way that they can be effective as close as possible to the point of main effort of the ground operation and then at the proper time. If this cannot be done then they should try their luck with these things in Holland; they can take greater risks there.

A decision on the day of the attack, which was actually supposed to have been made today, has been postponed until tomorrow.

10/1/40

Hansen, the Commanding General of X Corps, which is to lead the way in Holland, came before noon. He stated that a report by the Naval Intelligence Station in Wilhelmshaven says that the West Friesians are guarded by anti-aircraft guns and infantry and that the garrison has been beefed up recently. As the navy and the air force reject any support in the attack on the islands, which is solely in the interests of the Luftwaffe, I hold out no hope for it. Sending infantry against the occupied islands in unprotected boats with no support must lead to failure. If it turns out in the course of the operation that the Dutch are not going to fight or at best halfheartedly, then perhaps that's something else. The Army Command was informed accordingly. Toward evening received advance notice of the date of the attack by telephone; it may not be passed on yet; the ultimate order is promised tomorrow.

11/1/40

Discussed details of the attack near Maastricht and the plans for the capture of the bridges there and those over the canals west of Maastricht with the commanding officer of the 4th Panzer Division [Reinhardt].

12/1/40

The attack order came for the 17th of January.

The Army Command advised that a German aircraft with two Luftwaffe staff officers has made an emergency landing on Belgian soil; the officers had Air Fleet 2's general orders for the attack with them. These orders not only reveal the strength, organization, and bases of our air force, but the planned ground operation as well. The officers allegedly failed to destroy the orders! Not until evening did we receive the reassuring news that they apparently did succeed in destroying the papers.

Marcks, commander of the 18th Army, gave a speech on the possible methods of attack on Antwerp which he had worked out. Discussed with Brennecke, 4th Army Chief of Staff, the fact that I consider rapid initial success by the 4th Army very possible. But the army mustn't allow itself to depict the chance of such success more optimistically than it really is in discussions with the Army Command. Therein lies the great danger, that in overestimating an initial success the Army Command will decide prematurely to shift the 4th Army's operational point of main effort. If the 4th Army then meets strong resistance at the Meuse between Namur and Givet, which has to be broken by a planned attack probably entailing a considerable loss of time, the result could be that strong motorized forces sent to 4th Army prematurely may end up sitting uselessly on the narrow Ardennes roads. Then if a real decision becomes imminent somewhere else we will be unable to extract these divisions in time. In any case, if such talks are held with the Army Command the Army Group [B] must be informed of their content immediately. In this context I once again pointed out to Brennecke the significance that a crossing near Huy could have for the army as well as for the entire operation.

13/1/40

Still very cold. The roads are ice-covered and slippery. One panzer division driving 120 km to new quarters left 60, another 69 tanks (of a total of 329), stranded. How can they think of an armored attack over frozen plowed fields? And where are the replacements for the losses which are certain to come in battle to come from? A check of the reserve stocks sitting in the army parks reveals a sad picture; at least there are some complete artillery pieces, machine-guns, etc, but there is a catastrophic shortage of replacement parts. I told the Quartermaster General [Stülpnagel], who came today, that the materiel replacement situation was my greatest worry, but I did not get an impression of great sympathy.

Drove to XXII (Motorized) Corps at Rheinberg. When I returned I was greeted by the news that "the movements ordered yesterday are not to commence!"

Air Fleet 3 [Sperrle] advised of the intention to strike the French air fleet at its bases with strong forces tomorrow. This operation, too, was postponed.

14/1/40

General der Flieger Kesselring came by in the morning and informed me that he had taken over Air Fleet 2, with which the Army Group [B] has to work; a pleasant surprise, for we worked together well in the Polish campaign.

The Ic reported to me the unconfirmed rumor that the Belgians have ordered general mobilization. It is certain that Belgium and Holland began a further strengthening of their defensive measures several days ago.

15/1/40

Travelled to Berlin.

16/1/40

Meeting with the Commander-in-Chief of the Army [Brauchitsch] in the presence of Halder [Army Chief of Staff]: I warned once again, quite generally, against a premature shifting of the point of main effort of the overall operation on the basis of optimistic reports from somewhere and then described the situation of the 4th Army in particular. They agreed with me; however, it is their view that whether the whole operation stands or falls depends on the 4th Army crossing the Meuse between Namur and Givet and taking possession of the high ground to the west. I once again made reference to the difficulties that forcing a crossing of the Meuse at the likely well-manned front between Namur and Givet will offer, and that an advance by Army Group A [Rundstedt] through Sedan cannot open the named sector of the Meuse until a sweeping success by Army Group A leads into the deep southern flank of the specified sector. But I don't believe in this possibility, because the bulk of the French reserves have to be expected in front of and in the southern flank of the attack by Panzer Division A [Rundstedt]. Brauchitsch and Halder agreed with this assessment and the *Führer* too is said to hold the same view. I went on to say that the Meuse line will probably be forced quickest if the 4th Army sends its northern wing through Huy and then north past Namur to the west, while at the same time the 6th Army [Reichenau] is driven forward sharply, as soon as possible. True they have concerns that this operation is too narrow, but there is no other choice! The airborne operation was discussed once again. The plan involving Ghent and Namur is apparently dead for good. Instead consideration is now being given to a "Holland Plan," but not as we desired near Utrecht, where there is supposed to be nowhere to land, rather farther away in the area of Rotterdam. When I objected that the 6th Army probably can't arrive there in time to support and relieve the airborne troops I was promised a motorized division. Whether and how quickly this can get past and through the numerous reported barricades and floodings is an open question, but I was naturally happy to accept it. When I said that the motorized forces suited me particularly well, even in the event that I was ordered to take Walcheren Island after reaching Breda, I was told that this was already being considered.

I took the opportunity to once again point out that we have to reckon with the possibility of meeting perhaps superior English forces and armor northeast of Antwerp.

Now that it has been confirmed that the West Friesian Islands have been occupied by Dutch troops, I consider their capture possible only with the strong support of the Luftwaffe. So far this support has been refused, however I have found understanding in Kesselring [Commander Air Fleet 2]. But the icing conditions up there are so changeable that the operation can't be carried out until there is precise reconnaissance on the spot; its conduct cannot therefore be reckoned on until this reconnaissance is completed. They agreed with my view.

The inadequate supply situation in weapon replacement parts was once again brought up by me.

In conclusion I reported the flat rejection of the "Stab in the Back Order" by the officer corps and pointed out that it was an attack on the foundations of the army. Brauchitsch declared that he will never allow these foundations to be shaken.

17/1/40

Telephone conversation with Halder, who raised the question whether we will have to consider a shifting of the 6th Army's point of main effort from IV Army Corps [Schwedler] farther north in view of the new defensive measures by the Dutch and Belgians. I promised to examine the idea. Halder said that the question of shifting the point of main effort to the north was under discussion at present anyway; unfortunately there wasn't time for a thorough discussion of this point on the phone.

The order expected yesterday or today has not arrived.

Bitter cold, icy roads.

18/1/40

Returned to Godesberg.

19/1/40

A lengthier postponement of the attack date appears to be in the offing; Army High Command issued orders for the large-scale release of personnel for new formations and training courses.

20/1/40

The removal of two divisions from the front was ordered; they are to be sent to troop training grounds for training; relief of one began today – as well today French radio promptly reported that "two German divisions are being regrouped on the Belgian-Dutch front!"

23/1/40

Hasse [Ia Army group B], who was ordered to Berlin, returned with surprising news:

(1) The Army Command is demanding a thorough shortening of the buildup time and to this end now intends to move the bulk of the panzer divisions to the left bank of the Rhine.

(2) The airborne landing is now being considered for Holland. The Army Group's [B] mission is being broadened, as all of Holland is now to be occupied. The only reinforcements the army group will receive is the already announced motorized SS division; but the Army Command suggested to the

army group that the 254th Division [Koch, F.], which was previously supposed to attack toward Antwerp on the northern wing of the 6th Army, and the 8th Panzer Division [Kuntzen] be committed from the army group reserve for the attack on Holland. The Army High Command released Headquarters, 18th Army [Küchler] for the unified command of operations in Holland.

(3) The Army High Command proposes removing three divisions from the 6th Army's front, one division from the 4th Army – also for the attack.

Bock's Critical Opinion of Demands by the Army Command

(Re. 1) The shortening of the buildup time is in keeping with our oft-expressed wishes. Whether or not the premature moving of the bulk of the panzer divisions across the Rhine is really necessary and desirable is being considered.

(Re. 2) Back when the army group proposed conquering Holland with two reserve divisions and a cavalry brigade, that was too much in the opinion of the Army Command. Now three divisions, a motorized division, a panzer division, a cavalry division and an airborne division, or seven divisions all told, are to attack there! But with expanded objectives, for in the meantime even those "above" have come to realize that we can't sit still in front of Fortress Holland if we wish to stop the enemy from putting his air force there.

(Re. 3) Is being checked; I consider the substantial weakening of the 6th Army's front to be wrong.

24/1/40

Meeting with the Commanders-in-Chief of the armies. Shortening of the attack time is feasible. Reichenau [6th Army] and Kluge [4th Army] declared themselves in favor of the early moving forward of the panzer divisions.

Employment and probable objectives of the 18th Army [Küchler] were discussed. Definition of the 18th Army's objectives was discussed. The harmonization of objectives for the 18th [Küchler] and 6th [Reichenau] Armies will not be easy, as the appearance of strong English forces must be reckoned with at the "seam" between the two armies; but a shifting of the "seam" is impossible in the interest of a unified battle command in Holland.

25/1/40

Meeting with Brauchitsch and Halder in the presence of the Commanders-in-Chief and their Chiefs of Staff at Godesberg to clarify the questions raised on the 23rd [January].

Chances of abbreviating the concentration of forces were discussed, its immediate and accelerated implementation was ordered by the Commander-in-Chief of the Army.

Of the four divisions that the Army Command wants to withdraw from the front, I can release only one, from the 4th Army; the divisions of the 6th Army must remain; otherwise the army will be inadmissibly weakened right at its point of main effort. In my view solving the problem presents no difficulties, for the acceleration of the buildup – which is what it is all about – will scarcely be affected.

I gave a brief report on the entry into Holland; in it I expressed the opinion that the left wing of the 18th Army had to reckon on encountering English-Belgian forces northeast of Antwerp. On news of the German invasion of Holland the English will probably not content themselves with the occupation of Antwerp; rather they will then strive to take possession of a land link with Holland and at least parts of the Dutch coastal region, because they know what a threat the occupation of this coast by German forces would pose to England. They will reckon on a delaying of the German advance by Dutch troops and the serious natural obstacles and will try to quickly take possession of the bridges over the Hollandsch-Diep. But we need these bridges in order to carry out our mission of occupying Holland and to link up with the airborne troops in time. Because no delay in the English advance by hostile Dutch action is to be anticipated, there will probably be a fight for the bridges in question. The German forces committed to this battle have to so strong that the bridges come into our hands with certainty, or, if we should reach the bridges before the English, remain in their hands. But beyond that, the southern wing of the 18th Army has to have the necessary forces at its disposal in order to, by advancing north over the bridges, bring about the fall of "Fortress

Holland" together with the divisions advancing north of the Vaal. Since, as I have said, strong English forces can appear on the southern wing of the 18th Army early on, it will not be enough if, as previously intended, only one army corps (an infantry division, a motorized division, a panzer division) is sent ahead there, and all the less so if the northern wing of the 6th Army, weakened by the loss of the 254th Division [Koch, F.], then has to advance toward Tournhout to keep the attack by 6th Army from coming apart. Moving a strong army corps to the seam between the 18th and 6th Armies as the Army Corps [B] reserve is also something that cannot be avoided. Taking this corps from the existing army group reserves is not possible! Every man of the army corps reserve is needed at the point of main effort, and the point of main effort will lie in the center and the left wing of the 6th Army and later probably on the right wing of the 4th Army! And it must remain there, for a serious weakening or even the destruction of the English army can only be achieved if we succeed in breaking through the enemy far south of Antwerp and so pinch off and smash the elements of the enemy army fighting near and north of Antwerp. So, as things stand, I would therefore strongly advise against shifting the army group's point of main effort. As well I can scarcely imagine another point of main effort for the western army's overall operation. Where should it be? In the north the attack will run into Fortress Antwerp at the start; in the south, Army Group A's advance, narrowed by the Maginot Line, leads into the midst of strong French reserves; one can scarcely reckon on it gaining ground quickly so as to open the Namur-Givet line from the south. If it does not and then the 4th Army becomes hung up on this part of the Meuse, its opening can only be achieved from the north, by the right wing of the 4th Army advancing through Huy and then on to the west in conjunction with a brisk advance by the 6th Army. If we succeed in breaking through the Antwerp-Namur line, the 6th Army will need strong forces to smash the English, while the 4th Army will have to fight for possession of the high ground south of Charleroi. Accomplishing these missions will require all the reserves of the Army Group [B], to the last man, and even further forces. I therefore request that the corps I need for the seam between the 18th and 6th Armies be made available from the Commander-in-Chief of the Army's reserves. – Commander-in-Chief of the Army and Halder agreed, quite emphatically in the matter of the army group's point of main effort. The question of the point of main effort of the overall operation is being glided over. The requested corps is being promised. The Army High Command intends to issue the new objectives in writing.

In the foreword to this publication Peter von der Groeben quite appropriately made reference to the cardinal discussion about the formation of the point of main effort of this overall operation. This opened differences of opinion, especially between Halder and Bock. Adolf Heusinger, a general staff officer in the Operations Department since 1930, summed the situation up as follows:

"In February 1940 Halder and the Operations Department were still wrestling with the question of whether they should assign the point of main effort to Army Group A from the beginning, or whether they should reserve decision on the formation of the point of main effort and the direction of attack, each according to the progress of operations. Manstein, on the other hand, had already decided in favor of a clear-cut assigning of the point of main effort to Army Group A. He presented this proposal directly to Hitler. His ideas then formed the basis of Hitler's map entries, of which Halder also spoke. Many parties therefore struggled over the decision. But Halder's most significant service was his determined holding on to this hard-won decision in the months March to May 1940 against all entreaties, especially on the part of Bock and also Guderian." (Countess Schall-Riaucour H., Aufstand und Gehorsam, Wiesbaden 1972, PP 72

The transport situation remains poor. Even outside observers could see this misfortune coming in peacetime; in terms of punctuality and reliability the German rail system was already poor. The main reasons are probably as follows: years of delays in the replacement and expansion program; too much emphasis on speed and load factors in the schedules, resulting in overworked personnel and finally a delay in reducing civilian traffic when war came. And now there is the constant cold, which increases all the operating difficulties ad infinitum.

29/1/40

Drove to training course for company commanders in Wahn and to Headquarters, 4th Army.

30/1/40

Drove to the 14th [Weyer] and 19th [Schwantes] Divisions.

31/1/40

Conference with Küchler [Headquarters, 18th Army] concerning the conduct of operations by the 18th Army.

The Army Command's new attack order has arrived. It contains the shortening of buildup times, otherwise nothing that wasn't known from the meeting of 25th January.

1/2/40

Conference with the Chiefs of Staff of V [Allmendinger] and VIII
[Steinmetz] Army Corps concerning their attack preparations.

Toward evening *General* von Manstein, Chief of Staff of Army Group A,
arrived. Among other things the talk turned to the operations, whereupon
Manstein expressed the opinion that the operation's point of main effort should
be moved to Army Group A, because only thus would it be possible to really
smash the Anglo-French army. His ideas are undoubtedly bold, but I don't
know if the Army Command has the forces necessary to cope with this huge
task at the same time; if it doesn't have the forces, I am of the view that they
have to smash the nearby English and then the French. The English have to
make a stand when we go into Belgium; otherwise they will be giving away
the country and its coast – and they won't do that without a fight! Hopefully
the expected counterattack by the French against Army Group A [Rundstedt]
will cost them more blood than us and will be a good prelude to the later
attack on the French.

2/2/40

Report by the commander of the 7th Panzer Division [Stumme].

All recent intelligence makes it increasingly clear that the German air officers who crash-landed in Belgian in January did not succeed in destroying the papers they had with them.

5/2/40

Conference with the Chiefs of Staff of XXVII [Zorn] and IV [Beutler] Army Corps concerning their attack plans.

6/2/40

Lengthy meeting with *General* Kesselring, commander of Air Fleet 2, his Chief of Staff, a general staff officer from the 7th Air Division, and *General* Count Sponeck, the commander of the airborne division [22nd Div.] Topic: the airborne landing in Holland.

I made it clear that strong English forces could be in position in and northeast of Antwerp within a day of the start of our attack; the 18th Army must therefore reckon on the possibility of meeting enemy forces as early as the general area of Tilburg-Breda; this places in doubt its rapid breakthrough to the bridge at Moerdijk and with it a timely linking up with the airborne troops. The army group has done everything in its power to strengthen the 18th Army for this mission. A request will have to be made of the Luftwaffe to delay for as long as possible the approach of English motorized units expected from Northern France. Kesselring promised this.

Furthermore it was specified that the airborne troops would come under the command of the 18th Army from the moment first contact was established with the ground forces. The question was raised of direct Luftwaffe support for the 18th Army and, going beyond the previous plans, also the center and right wing of the 6th Army. The Luftwaffe hopes to be able to make additional forces available for this. In this context I listed the most important missions to be support for the 6th Army near the mouth of the Roer, then the 18th Army near Gennep, and finally the 4th [Army; 6th in the original] near Venlo.

Recommendations for More Effective Propaganda

In the afternoon I was visited by *Oberstleutnant* Hesse, who has been tasked by the Commander-in-Chief of the Army [Brauchitsch] with "winding up" the propaganda for the army. In general I agree with his ideas. But in my opinion everything depends on making the propaganda more active and livelier, otherwise nobody will bother with it and it will remain ineffective. I proposed setting forth openly and unmistakably the great ethical foundations on which the Prussian-German Army was built and on which it must remain if it is not to fall. One must of course realize that the enemy will call these foundations into action! But that is just what we desire, for then life will come to the propaganda. But on the other hand there will be a visible sigh of relief and cheerful approval. My only fear is that the Army High Command lacks the power to put such a propaganda program on its feet if it doesn't suit the Ministry of Propaganda; and feeble struggling attempts by the Army High Command will change nothing.

Chief of Chaplains Dohrmann

Evening visit from the Protestant Chief of Chaplains Dohrmann. He is having a tough fight and his influence on spiritual guidance in the army has been as good as eliminated. The reasons are apparently only partly of a factual nature. I don't understand why the Army Command doesn't clear up the matter – one way or another – for this state of affairs is unworthy.

7/2/40

Meeting with Halder in Godesberg. I told him that the 18th Army's southern wing is too weak to fulfill its mission with any degree of certainty, and that reinforcement of this wing is pointless, if, as previously planned, it is not to be made available until five days or even more after the start of the attack. Halder agrees and will send a division to the 18th Army now.

I went on to once again speak about the objectives of the 4th Army and explained why it was necessary to point out in the Army Group's [B] reworded order that the army's first objective is not reaching the Ourthe but opening the crossings over the Ourthe. My order to the army, to cross the Meuse "in force" on both sides of Namur, raised concerns in Halder that the 4th Army's southern wing might become separated from the northern wing of Army Group A. I replied that that was not what I had in mind and that the army's objectives and boundaries are specified clearly in the order. Opinions in the 4th Army as to whether or not they should commit elements through Huy have swung to such a degree that, as I consider this crossing very important to opening the Namur-Givet section of the Meuse, I now wish to make it absolutely clear that it is to be taken. My explicit question to Halder, whether he was of another opinion in the matter, was answered with a definite no!

He is not wrong to fear that the 4th Army could become separated from Panzer Division A [Rundstedt]. If the army advances on both sides of Namur – and that is what the Army Command's order calls for – in the best case it will be left with two armored and four infantry divisions for the Meuse front between Namur and Givet, or much too little to fill up the entire area between it and Panzer Division A. If one commits two army groups to attack eccentrically, as the Army Command has done, a gap must inevitably be created as they advance! The fundamental error is and remains that the Army Command has not clearly expressed itself as to where the point of main effort of the overall operation is to be.

8/2/40

General Sperrle, commander of Air Fleet 3, came to Godesberg for a brief meeting.

9/2/40

Meeting with Kluge [4th Army]. Subject Huy. I held to my view that we absolutely must make the attempt to go across at Huy. I went on to say that an equal effort has to be made to seize the Meuse crossings between Namur and Givet with mobile forces as long as there is a chance of success; this is being emphatically demanded by the Army Command. Since Kluge felt restricted by the wording "in force on both sides of Namur" in my order, I had the words "in force" deleted. Technically it changes almost nothing. *General* Kienitz, Commanding General of XVII Corps [in original XIX Corps], came. Since Headquarters, 2nd Army [Weichs] has to be handed over to Army Group A, Kienitz was given the task of familiarizing himself with the preliminary work on the attack on Liège done by Headquarters, 2nd Army.

Meeting with the head of the civilian administration, *Gauleiter* Terboven, at Godesberg.

11/2/40

Drove to Berlin for a brief period of leave.

18/2/40

Returned to Godesberg.

The Army Command has meanwhile provided the division promised for the 18th Army.

23/2/40

Drove to Berlin.

Army Group B's Mission Remains...

24/2/40

Meeting of the Commander-in-Chief of the Army [Brauchitsch] with the army group and army commanders of the Western Front.

Brauchitsch said:

The situation on the Western Front has changed radically! English and French have readied strong forces to defend against a German attack through Belgium. Documents were probably lost in the ominous crash-landing in Belgian which largely revealed then current German plans. He has therefore decided to establish a concentrated point of main effort, by Army Group A, instead of the three spearheads previously planned. In order to ensure uniformity of action in the point of main effort, he has been forced to move 4th Army [Kluge] from Army Group B [Bock] to Army Group A [Rundstedt]. Army Group B retains the objective of occupying Holland, breaking through the Belgian border fortifications, and drawing the strongest possible enemy forces to it.

This is finally a complete decision, even if at the cost of my army group. We were confronted with a fait accompli; the concentration directives were issued to the Ia's during our meeting. I could only point out again that the French could be at the Meuse between Namur and Givet with strong forces the morning after our first attack. Brauchitsch admitted this, but naturally it didn't change anything. I can't warm to this operation, because it has to bog down if the French haven't taken leave of their senses. As well much seems not yet quite clear. Since I am supposed to give up a panzer division, two infantry divisions, heavy artillery, engineers and bridging equipment, in addition to the 4th Army, the army group will be too weak to carry out the missions left to it – all the more so, as the new directives widen the 6th Army's attack area considerably and the potential support from 4th Army for its attack on Huy is gone. Army Group B has to reckon on the entire Dutch armed forces, with the overwhelming mass of the Belgian and certainly also the English army as opponents and probably also French forces. The focal point of its attack has to lie at and north of Maastricht. First this will have the effect of widening Army Group A's breakthrough front decisively, for a breakthrough near Maastricht will bring about the fall of all the Belgian fortifications to its north, namely the Maas and Albert Canal fronts. Moreover the thrust will lead the 6th Army in the for the army group decisive general direction of the weakest part of the rear Belgian defenses between Havre and Namur. But the operational exploitation of the breakthrough will only be possible if sufficient reserves can be sent through the gap created – and they are no longer there!

The army group has the further task of taking Holland – and taking it quickly. If the English oppose this plan, which must well be expected, and advance through Antwerp, situations can result which also require the employment of stronger forces there than appear desirable in light of the overall situation – for we must hold near Antwerp until link-up with the airborne troops south of Rotterdam and the fall of Holland is settled.

Unless it receives new reserves the army group will be unable to accomplish its missions.

25/2/40

I discussed my concerns with Halder once more.

Most of all I would like another motorized division. Halder wants to position one at the seam between the two army groups so that it can be employed by both [Army Groups] A and B. He hopes to be able to give two active divisions I am asking for as reserves. He cannot grant my request not to weaken me in engineers, bridging equipment and heavy artillery.

26/2/40

Returned to Godesberg.

27/2/40

Reichenau [6th Army] arrived. We agreed in our views on the 6th Army's new missions. If it succeeds in crossing near Maastricht, the army must immediately be sent forces strong enough to quickly expand the bridgehead and hold it, even against an attack by much superior forces, until sufficient of our forces arrive to continue the attack. To this end I am placing a division at the disposal of the army. Furthermore the sole motorized division of the army group reserve will be moved close enough so that it can be sent through Maastricht as soon as the opportunity to do so arises.

The necessity of sending a division behind the right wing of the army also remains. Reichenau [6th Army] is worried that the 18th Army [Küchler] might have its eyes too much on the north, so that the enemy in Antwerp gets a free hand against the northern wing of the 6th Army; most of all he would like to assume command over everything that takes place south of the Vaal. That won't work, for Operation Holland has to remain in one hand. Furthermore, events will force the 18th Army to advance on Antwerp with its left wing.

28/2/40

Drove to the 18th Army's war game in Wesel. The exercise confirmed my view of the Holland situation. In my conference I instructed the assembled commanders on the vital importance of speed in carrying out the operation: "We have to race forward!"

1/3/40

Marcks, Chief of Staff of the 18th Army, arrived with several concerns. I was able to relieve his greatest worry by promising that I would send two divisions as close as physically possible behind the left wing of the army's attack, therefore to the XXVI Army Corps [Wodrig].

The Army Command made available two divisions requested by me and urgently needed for the 6th Army's missions; one of them is again a reserve division, but I am grateful for every man.

2/3/40

General Kienitz [XVII Army Corps], which is first to be placed under the command of the Army Group [B] for the capture of Liège, gave a brief talk on his mission. His plans correspond to the preliminary work already done by Weichs [2nd Army].

4/3/40

Kesselring [Air Fleet 2] arrived. He is unhappy that I cannot be at the Moerdijk bridge, even in the most favorable case, before the third evening of the attack if there is Dutch resistance; he fears that his airborne troops will be killed by then. I agreed that this danger exists, but I had to stick to my position that it cannot go any faster and that I cannot promise an earlier arrival. Since there is a meeting of the commanders of the three branches of the armed forces with the *Führer* tomorrow and Kesselring is to see Göring beforehand, the subject will probably come up.

6/3/40

Unavoidable but downright unpleasant situation, as new missions are assigned to the artillery, engineers and armored units daily.

8/3/40

I presented a memo to the Commander-in-Chief of the Army with my assessment of the Army Group's [B] situation within the framework of the planned overall operation. [Original in the files of the army group.]

9/3/40

Drove to Headquarters, IVth Army Corps, *General* von Schwedler, and to the 4th Panzer Division [Stever]. The latter still has serious shortcomings in materiel, which are difficult to overcome because of a shortage of replacement parts.

12/3/40

Drove to the 3rd Panzer Division [Stumpff]. There, too, there are still significant shortcomings in materiel. Both panzer divisions urgently require training, because they cannot leave the roads in the partly highly-cultivated, partly marshy terrain. I will apply to have at least the armored units of this division sent to troop training grounds one battalion at a time.

I have been ordered to Berlin with my army commanders on the 16th [March].

13/3/40

Peace has been reached between Russia and Finland.

Afternoon conference of the Commander-in-Chief of the Army with the commanders of the army groups and armies in Koblenz [HQ, Army Group A]: the Commander-in-Chief of the Army once again briefly explained the reasons which led him to transfer the operation's point of main effort to Army Group A [Rundstedt]. On one hand his change of mind was caused by the

difficult water conditions in Holland and the fact that the Belgian border fortifications are being steadily reinforced in conjunction with the "Antwerp-
Liège-Namur triangle of fortifications" (?!), while on the other it was partly
due to purely tactical reasons:

A breakthrough by Army Group B [Bock] cannot take place on a broad
front as by Army Group A [Rundstedt]; like in 1914, the operation as originally planned could have led to a pivoting about the left wing and then to a
frontal attack. If strategic surprise is still at all possible, it is only by moving
the point of main effort to Army Group A. If the attack succeeds, we can hope
to split the English and French and subsequently deliver a crushing blow to
the English. It is assumed that the English will move forces forward to Antwerp
early on, but they attribute the English and the French with so little initiative
that they don't believe that they would attack across the line Namur-Antwerp.

Army Group B has to complete its mission alone, as difficult as it is, but
can achieve decisive importance. Command has to be very flexible. Since all
available forces must now be concentrated in the point of main effort, a substantial weakening of Army Group B cannot be avoided. The northern wing of
Army Group A – the 4th Army [Kluge] – now has to cover its flank itself. To
my question whether the army group could then also not reckon on additional
forces being sent if it succeeded in quickly taking possession of the crossings
at Maastricht, I was told that that depended on how the overall situation developed; in any case the Army Group [B] could not count on it.

Liège is to be sealed off under the unified command of *General* Kienitz
[XVII Army Corps], overall command there by Army Group B.

I reported that the state of the 3rd [Stumpff] and 4th [Stever] Panzer Divisions in regard to training and materiel was serious. I could not characterize
the 4th Panzer Division as fully attack capable as it did not have a single
serviceable command vehicle and all requests for additional vehicles and spare
parts had come to nothing. Many of the panzer division's junior company
commanders could never lead their companies in practice, because there is no
way to train at the front. Training opportunities absolutely have to be provided. I also brought up the total lack of flak cover in IX [Geyer] and X [Hansen]
Army Corps. A reexamination as to whether help can be provided in all these
areas was promised.

The Army Command then proposed various changes in preparation for the meeting with the *Führer* scheduled for the 16th [March]; they concerned themselves largely with trivialities, for example:

Whether it is really necessary to deploy the *Leibstandarte* to Deventer or if they would rather send a regiment [21st Cav. Rgt., Broich] of the 1st Cavalry Division [Feldt] there; whether the SS Motorized Division [Hausser] could not be moved forward immediately to the Rhine in the event of Case-A, whether a strengthening of the motorized forces south of the Vaal can be achieved without weakening the motorized forces north of the Vaal; whether the 227th Division [Zickwolff] could not now be pushed together more to its left wing?

My argument, that I could guarantee that the SS Division could also arrive on time from its presently-planned formation, in order to be sent forward quickly beside or behind the panzer division – based on the number of available crossings – apparently wasn't enough. My suggestion that a dangerous crowding would take place in the corner around Wesel, in which one hindered the other and thus achieved the opposite of the speed of forward movement we were striving for, was not well received. I therefore promised to reexamine the questions raised – but I was so annoyed that I first had to take a half-hour drive in the open air to regain my composure.

In the evening *Reichsführer* Himmler spoke about the eastern problem and the measures planned to resolve it.

14/3/40

Morning meeting with Küchler and Marcks [HQ, 18th Army] about the requests made yesterday by the Army Command. Most took care of themselves, because they often involved matters that had already been thought out and needed no further changes; the requested move forward of the SS Motorized Division was done; the only advantage it will bring is that they will now leave us alone. Brief telephone conversation with Halder about it. When I asked if my memo about the situation had arrived, Halder said:

"Yesterday's statements by the Commander-in-Chief of the Army should be your answer"; I hadn't realized that!

Cooperation with the Luftwaffe

Meeting with *General der Flieger* Kesselring [Air Fleet 2] and *General-leutnants* Student [Inspector of Parachute and Airborne Troops and CO 7th Air Division] and Count Sponeck [22nd Infantry (Airborne) Division] at Godesberg about our cooperation with the Luftwaffe, especially with the air-borne troops during the invasion of Holland. The most important result was the need to maintain continuous, close communications, first by radio, then by visual signals – not just between the command centers, but especially with the most forward troops.

15/3/40

Travelled to Berlin. Headquarters moved to Düsseldorf.

16/3/40

Breakfast and conference with the *Führer*. I briefly outlined the army group's situation and plans and pointed out that – provided that the break-through at Maastricht succeeds – the left wing of the 6th Army [Reichenau] cannot achieve major successes, because it is too weak in fast forces and can no longer reckon on any support from Huy by the 4th Army [Kluge].

Reichenau [6th Army] presented his plans so optimistically that when he arrived at and beyond Namur – simultaneous with the end of his presentation – I poured some water into his wine and said:

"With three divisions!"

In his subsequent remarks the *Führer* once again emphasized the neces-sity of attacking soon. Following the official discussions, Schmundt, the *Führer*'s adjutant, offered me the chance to see the *Führer* alone, in order to present my divergent opinion concerning the operations. Much to my regret, I had to decline, because I cannot and do not wish to be disloyal to the Com-mander-in-Chief of the Army [Brauchitsch].

18/3/40

Drove to Düsseldorf [HQ Army Group B]. I hear that on the evening of the 16th [March] the *Führer* returned to my remarks, especially my doubts on regarding the further advance by the southern wing of the 6th Army, and has instructed the Army High Command to reexamine this question. Visited the civilian offices in Düsseldorf.

19/3/40

Drove to the 256th [Kauffmann] and 254th [Koch, F.] Divisions to discuss their roles in the presence of the commanding general of XXVI Army Corps [*General* Wodrig].

20/3/40

Drove to the 207th Division [Tiedemann], the motorized *SS-Standarte "Der Führer"* [Dietrich], and to the 9th Panzer Division [Ritter von Hubicki].

21/3/40

Drove to the 227th Division [Zickwolff], meeting there also with the commanding officer of the 1st Cavalry Division [Feldt] and with *SS-Obergruppenführer* Dietrich, commander of the *SS-Leibstandarte* ["*Adolf Hitler*"].

I urged my headquarters staff to find ways and means now to relieve a division of XXVII Army Corps on the eastern front of Liège with frontier guards and other scraped-together units immediately after a successful breakthrough near Maastricht, in order to be able to send it to the left wing of the 6th Army; I just have to help myself as best I can, for if the breakthrough succeeds we simply can't be too strong there!

27/3/40

Returned to Düsseldorf.

Repercussions from the meetings of 13th March in Koblenz [HQ Army Group A] and of 16th March in Berlin becoming evident. Individual flak battalions and the equipment of several bridging columns will be transferred to the Army Group; beginning on the fourth day of the attack, two divisions are to be transported by rail to the area of Viersen-Aachen – initially as reserves of the Army Command: not much, but better than nothing! A motorized SS Division is to be placed at the seam between the two army groups so that it can be employed by Army Group A as well as by me.

We are finally able to transfer individual panzer battalions to Camp Senne for training, as well as several regiments of divisions which especially require it.

28/3/40

Drove to the 56th Division [Kriebel], also there the Commanding General of the IX Army Corps, *General* Geyer.

Fighting Spirit Good – Combat Worth "Mediocre"

29/3/40

Military attaches arrive from Brussels and The Hague. They bring nothing new of significance: the internal attitude of the Dutch and the Belgians is against Germany; they rate the combat worth of the Dutch and Belgian Armies as mediocre, but the fighting spirit of both, especially the Dutch, is entirely good.

30/3/40

Drove to Headquarters, XI Army Corps [*General* Leeb]. [According to *Organization and Command Positions "Case Yellow", as of 1/5/40*, and Mehner, Kortzfleisch became the Commanding General of this corps on 1/3/40.]

31/3/40

Visited the 20th Motorized Division [Wiktorin].

1/4/40

Drove to the 253rd Division [Kühne] and discussed its missions in the presence of the Commanding General of the XXVII Army Corps, *General* Wäger [Waeger in original]. Good morale among the officers, especially nice with the regimental commander of the frontier guard. A clear, broad view of the difficult terrain over which the division has to attack from a tower in the Aachen city forest; the enemy positions in the approaches to Liège lie on commanding hills before the front; all that matters is who will be sitting in them afterwards! The division's attack can become uncomfortable if the enemy has strong artillery there. The Belgians are busy putting up barbed wire around their border positions right in front of our noses, but the Belgian frontier troops do not make a fearsome impression.

I spoke with the Commanding General about my plan to take away a division of his corps from the western or northwestern front of Liège and send it to the left wing of the 6th Army as soon as the advance near Maastricht begins. He was very understanding.

Conditions for Promotion

2/4/40

Drove to an exercise by the 31st Division [Kaempfe] in the presence of the Commander-in-Chief of the Army [Brauchitsch]. The exercise showed that the field forces are not as well prepared as required for their initial missions.

I discussed with the Commander-in-Chief of the Army the impossibly limited training possibilities caused by the restrictions in the supplying of fuel and the excessive zeal in the promotion of NCOs to officers.

Whether he can help in the first matter is questionable; on the second he agrees with me: if a man from the non-commissioned officer ranks becomes an officer, it is a reward for outstanding merit and performance. Bravery in the face of the enemy alone is not enough!

Character, attitude, leadership qualities and leadership ability are prerequisites for promotion.

The army's sole infantry school at Döberitz was nowhere near able to meet the front's tremendously-increased demand for new infantry officers. Anticipating brief, victorious campaigns, the OKH decided to close the army's five officer candidate schools, including the one at Dresden, when mobilization was implemented in August 1939, in order to use the numerous instructional personnel as cadres for new divisions; this was now to prove a serious mistake.

The commanding officers are absolutely responsible for the people suggested (for promotion) by them. Brauchitsch spoke with me about possible developments in the near future.

Düsseldorf

4/4/40

Meeting with the army commanders and commanding generals in Düsseldorf [HQ Army Group B].

Topic:

(1) Completion and conclusion of attack preparations, especially for the advance detachments. I called attention to the discovered shortcomings and once again stressed that we have to be aggressive everywhere if the attack across the waterways is to succeed. That (one or the other) gets his nose burned in such a process has to be accepted in the interest of the whole. I repeatedly pointed out that it all depends on thorough preparation and rapid execution and on determined exploitation of every success. Nothing that can be prepared may be left to chance!

(2) Officer replacement, whereby the question of the promotion of non-commissioned officers to officers was dealt with in keeping with my discus-

sion of yesterday with the Commander-in-Chief of the Army. (Minutes in the files of the army group.)

Münster

5/4/40

Drove to Münster to a war game by the motorized SS-Division.

Afterward, at the invitation of the *Gauleiter* and Senior President Meyer, I visited the lovely old "Peace Hall" in the town hall.

6/4/40

Drove to the 35th Division [Reinhard], discussed its missions in the presence of the Commanding General of IV Army Corps [Schwedler].

7/4/40

I don't quite understand 6th Army's plans for its extreme southern wing. If the attack at Maastricht succeeds, the army plans to move the strongest possible elements of the 269th Division [Hell], the right-wing division of XXVII Army Corps [Wäger], across the Maas. I have doubts if that will succeed under the fire from Liège. But on the other hand I consider it absolutely imperative to free up a division of the XXVII Army Corps on the east bank as soon as possible, in order to send it across the Maas behind or alongside the breakthrough troops if the crossing at Maastricht is a success. Therefore, in spite of gentle passive resistance in my headquarters [Düsseldorf], I requested in writing that the 6th Army keep me informed about the deliberations it is making in this direction.

8/4/40

Drove to the 18th [Cranz] and 7th [Gablenz] Divisions. Both commanders are well in the picture.

Greiffenberg, Head of the Operations Department [OKW], came in the afternoon and advised me that Denmark and Norway are to be occupied tomorrow morning. As it is not out of the question that the English and French might subsequently march into Belgium and Holland, the preparations made for an immediate entry into these areas are to be reexamined. That has taken place. I would be uncomfortable with the "immediate case," because the enemy would thereby have the lead and gain an advantage; also we can then not choose the timing that appears best to us for the commitment of the Luftwaffe. The safest countermeasure would be to attack ourselves; but apparently they are unwilling to consider this until the situation in Scandinavia is cleared up to some degree.

Conferred with the Ia of the 6th Army [Reichenau], *Oberstleutnant* von Bechtoldsheim, about the questions raised by me yesterday; we agreed for the most part.

9/4/40

Took part in an exercise by the 14th Division [Weyer]. There, as recently in the 31st Division [Kaempfe], the clear shortcomings of the lower level of command were apparent. Everything took too long, no one took charge, mental dexterity and initiative could not be compared to what was demanded and achieved in peacetime. That is no wonder, for the good core of the junior officer corps has been dispersed for new formations, and the large-scale training of our reserve officers could only be started a few years ago.

Apart from some insignificant exchanges of fire, the occupation of Denmark went smoothly; the Danish government surrendered! Norway put up a fight, but resistance was broken at the most important points before the day was over; parachute and airborne troops were committed in places. The fleet which put to sea to watch over the operation was engaged near Oslo by Norwegian coastal batteries and – off the west coast of Norway – by heavy English ships; French naval forces are en route there. That will cost plenty! Hopefully our weak fleet will succeed in escaping the much superior enemy and make its way through after completing its mission.

10/4/40

Drove to the 225th [Wetzel] and 223rd [Körner] Divisions.

Reports coming from Scandinavia are sporadic and contradictory. Foreign radio stations claim that an English expeditionary corps is on its way to Norway. The battles by the fleet are still in progress; it undoubtedly has suffered heavy losses. The English fleet has allegedly also lost much of its fighting strength to attacks by our air force. Holland is on a state of alert.

Repeat the Mistakes of 1918!

From the Commander-in-Chief of the Army [Brauchitsch] comes an order, according to which he intends to send liaison officers to the armies, but not to the army groups, when hostilities begin. This is a repetition of a mistake of 1918! I wrote to Brauchitsch immediately and asked him to oblige the liaison officers "not to bypass the army group" in their reporting. [See: 18/4]

11/4/40

The foreign radio stations are saying everything imaginable about Scandinavia in order to depict our situation as critical. One is especially inclined to be taken in by every bit of bad news since all is apparently not going quite smoothly.

That is dangerous – and also contrary to the lessons of war, which teaches that in critical situations "the other side" is at least as frightened as oneself!

Kesselring, Air Fleet 2, arrived at noon for a meeting.

12/4/40

Drove to an exercise by the army group's signals regiment and to watch firing by heavy tanks of the 4th Panzer Division [Stever].

The Allies are trying to convince Belgium and Holland to ask for their help now, therefore before the Germans invade. Belgium has declined for the moment; it has even withdrawn several divisions from its eastern front to face France. Holland too is beginning to guard its coast more strongly.

In addition to military resistance, in Norway passive resistance by the population appears to be causing difficulties.

13/4/40

Drove to the 208th (Motorized) Division [Andreas] and to the 9th Panzer Division [Ritter von Hubicki].

In order to promote the training of the SS Motorized Division in cooperation with the 9th panzer Division, I order a war game to be led by the Commanding General [Hoepner] of XVI (Motorized) Army Corps [Panzer Corps].

The English have occupied one or two islands off the northwest coast of Norway. For all I care! The English fleet is reported on its way to Narvik with transports. Happily our heavy ships are back at home.

15/4/40

French warships and transports are allegedly also en route to Norway.

About the "Sense of this War"

16/4/40

Speech by *Reichsleiter* Rosenberg about "the sense of this war" to officers in Düsseldorf; afterwards breakfast with me. Rosenberg spoke of "securing German living space," which made necessary the occupation of Denmark and Norway, of a situation which must in the end lead to the absorption of the smaller states by the larger, and finally about a "great German Reich including the northern germanic peoples."

I don't know if he has found the right tone for the front. This interpretation of "securing German living space" is new to the majority of the men; the old "we have to defend ourselves, because otherwise Germany will go under," was simple and clear and was closer to the view of the soldier.

17/4/40

Took part in an exercise by the 11th Division [Böckmann]. The impression was good, the unit's war experience is obvious.

18/4/40

The Commander-in-Chief of the Army answered my letter about the liaison officers; he insists that they will be sent, but their list of instructions will take my wishes into account.

19/4/40

Exercise by elements of the 9th Panzer Division with a regiment of the SS Motorized Division at Senne; afterward dropped in on the training course for company commanders in the camp. Combat training of the NCOs and enlisted men of the SS is insufficient; that will cost much blood! A pity – such magnificent manpower!

20/4/40

As far as things in Norway can be assessed from the sparse reports, it appears that we may be able to bring stronger Norwegian forces to battle before significant English forces arrive. That would be good, for we have to free our hands against the Allies, who are said to have since landed in three places: north of Narvik, near Namsos and near Aandalsnes. (*The Allied landing operations on 14/4 and 17/4/40, whose objective was to attack Trondheim in a pincer movement, failed because of German air superiority; see Ottmer, Hans-Martin, Weserübung, produced by the Military-Historical Research Office, Volume 1, R. Oldenbourg Verlag, Munich, 1994.*)

It is good that England is finally forced to really commit her fleet, for it gives us the opportunity to strike the British at their most sensitive spot with our air force. England has weakened her Mediterranean Fleet as a result of the events in Norway and the losses in ships suffered there – and officially Italy speaks ever louder of entering the war! I don't believe Italy will strike until it is completely sure of its position – and we haven't reached that stage yet!

My head of the civilian administration, *Gauleiter* Terboven, is going to Norway as Reich Governor [Terboven's mainstay there was Vidkun Quisling's *Nasjonal Samling*]. Government President Roeder of Düsseldorf is taking over his affairs until further notice. Roeder was chosen as my head of administration for the occupied territories in the offensive and as such has worked well with us for a long time.

22/4/40

Bridge-building exercise by the 6th Army's combat engineers, in the afternoon a war game involving the motorized units of the army group under the direction of the Commanding General of the XVI Motorized Army Corps [Hoepner].

English troops have joined the fighting north of Oslo. They have thus established contact with the main Norwegian forces remarkably quickly, even though with only weak forces at first.

23/4/40

For several days a wrestling match has been going on between Hasse, my Ia, and the Army Command as to whether we can still allow troops who desperately need it to spend several days at training grounds, or whether A-Day is so near that that no longer goes. Army Command has apparently not been informed of the plans, not even for the next few days, for the orders as to whether the troops can stay at the training grounds swing back and forth.

In the evening *Oberst* Matzky, the military attache in Tokyo, paid us a visit.

25/4/40

Drove to an exercise by panzer companies at Wahn.

26/4/40

Took part in an exercise by the 1st Division [Kleffel]. The fuel situation is allegedly be so tight that the motorized divisions aren't receiving enough fuel to train their drivers.

27/4/40

My Ic, *Major* Mantey, who flew to Oslo the day before yesterday to examine the situation there for us, has returned. Falkenhorst [Commander-in-Chief, Operations Group Denmark and Norway] takes a calm and optimistic view of the situation there.

The surprise landing near Oslo was less than a complete success, because the night before the landing a German transport beached off Kristiansand. The Norwegians identified the ship as a German troop transport. Thus warned, they manned their coastal batteries and the King and government were able to flee. Hopes of occupying the country without fighting were thus dashed. This probably also explains why reinforcements for the German forces in Norway came gradually and in "penny packets." Disorganization in cooperation among the three branches of the armed forces, which were instructed to do so there extensively, is frightful. If Falkenhorst wants something from the Luftwaffe, he has to turn – from Oslo! – to the air base at Hamburg, if he wants something from the Navy, he has to turn to the Admiralty in Berlin!

29/4/40

Exercise by a company of armored combat engineers of the 3rd Panzer Division.

30/4/40

Rhine crossing exercise by the 6th Army.

Late in the evening a brief meeting with Hess, the *Führer*'s deputy, in Düsseldorf.

2/5/40

Berlin. Good progress in Norway; nevertheless the English succeed in getting away from the southern part of Norway, though with the loss of some materiel. The situation in the northern sector, at Narvik, looks serious. Our weak forces are facing a far superior opponent there. Supply must be extraordinarily difficult there. Freedom of movement is limited by the English Fleet at sea on the one hand and by the Swedish border on the other. The air fleet claims to have sunk a British battle cruiser by bombing.

Criticism of the Military Administration Apparatus

7/5/40

Visited the army group's long-range reconnaissance squadron.

In a telephone conversation I proposed to the Quartermaster General [Stülpnagel] that the personnel of the Army Group's Quartermaster, who have done all the preliminary work, assume responsibility for administering the territories to be occupied. Reasons:

(1) The occupied area must be administered uniformly; running of the administration by two administrative heads contradicts this principle.

(2) Party Offices – the Lorenz Organization and Party training courses – are, despite an order to the contrary from the *Führer*, preparing to act in the occupied area. This must lead to conflicts which the army group, if it is in battle, will have neither the time nor means to settle.

(3) The administration apparatus built up in six months has gradually swelled to such an extent that it can no longer satisfy the basic requirement of military administration, to work simply and quickly, because of its own corpulence. An army of people and agencies has been created. This huge apparatus is being expanded by the Quartermaster General through the continued assignment of new officers, whose purpose is in some cases unclear even to him. If things ever become serous, the practical work must become bogged down in paper. This apparatus is no longer a sharp instrument which willingly follows the gentle pressure of the hand of the military commander; it has lost the character of a military administration through its over-organization. Its really effective utilization will only be possible through strict leadership from

one agency. I therefore propose that the Army Command take over the entire administration apparatus.

In the evening the same proposal in a somewhat toned-down form followed by letter. I have the impression that they think I'm mad, because I say that the family's favorite baby smells bad.

Indications are that A-Day is near. We are not allowed to send any more units back to the training grounds; otherwise the field units are unaware of the growing tension. But the Dutch have suddenly cancelled all leave again. Where are they getting their intelligence?

8/5/40

Bridge-building exercise by the 254th Division [Behschnitt] with equipment which the unit assembled and in part designed itself.

9/5/40

Visited a battery of 420-mm heavy howitzers; the senior officer commanded a similar battery in the World War; now he is a *Hauptmann* of the Reserve. His observation officer of 1914 is today a *Leutnant* again and back in the same position in his battery.

The attack order arrived at noon!

I drove to Headquarters, IVth Army Corps [Schwedler] and to the 4th Panzer Division. I told Stever, the division commander, that he has to advance unconcerned if we take possession of one of the bridges west of Maastricht; 3rd Panzer Division and 20th Motorized Division will be sent after him at once if that is the case; Headquarters, XVI Army Corps [Hoepner] would probably then very soon assume command of all these motorized units.

CHAPTER THREE

10 MAY 1940 to
11 SEPTEMBER 1940
(OFFENSIVE IN THE WEST
AND OCCUPATION PERIOD)

Commander-in-Chief Army Group B

"I pushed where and however I could..."

10/5/40

The attack begins [18th Army: direction of attack Holland; 6th Army: direction of attack north of Liège, Maas crossing].

Reports about the success of our airborne landings in Holland are unclear, they apparently have not been a complete success; but two parachute battalions have succeeded in seizing the Moerdijk bridge; that is the main thing for the moment.

The Dutch have blown all the Maas bridges, only the railway bridge at Gennep fell into our hands intact. The Maas bridges were blown up right under the nose of the 4th Panzer Division, whose advance was seriously delayed by obstacles. Nevertheless, parachute and glider troops which landed at the destroyed bridges at Veldwezelt and Vronhoefen succeeded in linking up and established bridgeheads there. Fort Eben-Emael is silent! The airborne landing there was therefore a success!

I drove to the IV Army Corps [Schwedler] and then to Maastricht, where I found the commander of the 4th Panzer Division, *General* Stever, at the bridge. The crossing was proceeding slowly as bridge equipage had not arrived yet. I pushed where and however I could, for I have to have the 4th Panzer Division across the Maas and the Albert Canal tonight so that the enemy does not recover. The Maas, and in places the Maas-Schelde Canal, have been crossed on the rest of the army group's front; a crossing of the Ijssel has also been forced at two places. It is going well!

3rd Panzer Division [Stumpff] and 20th Motorized Infantry Division [Wiktorin] were sent ahead as far as possible in the direction of Maastricht; all reserves are moving up. From my reserves I placed the 225th [Schaumburg] and 223rd [Körner] Divisions, both moved up by rail, at the disposal of the armies, so that they will have the necessary depth for the subsequent advance from the outset.

I pointed out to Reichenau [6th Army] the necessity of getting the entire 4th Panzer Division across the river lines this night! I asked Küchler [18th Army] to push his motorized forces forward as quickly and as far as possible through Gennep. This gentle pressure was unnecessary, for both knew what was at stake – but I cannot allow any opportunity to whip the matter forward to pass by.

The Dutch fought poorly at the frontier. The Dutch population is friendly and nice, the prisoners of war appear satisfied with their lot. Curious, so far there has been no sign of the Belgians. Toward evening incoming reports suggest that the airborne landing in Holland has cost considerable losses and that the airborne troops are having a hard time of it. The English are intervening in the fighting from the sea.

11/5/40

Drove to the headquarters of the 256th Division [Kauffmann] in Mill, found it in the Peel Position which was taken just before. Frightful crowding on the bridges at Gennep, which is especially dangerous as the 9th Panzer Division has to cross there. Luckily there was no sign of enemy aircraft! On the way back I met the Commanding General of the XXVI Corps, Wodrig, in Gennep; I spoke with him about the necessity of clearing the bridge. In Gennep a report reached me that six motorized march columns were advancing through Antwerp to the northeast! So the rascals really are coming!

The only way to yet reach the Moerdijk Bridge is to drive forward the southern wing of the 18th Army. Perhaps it will then succeed in overrunning the fronts of the enemy columns. I drove on to Wesel to Headquarters, 18th Army and discussed the situation with the Chief of Staff, *General* Marcks. We agreed that the 9th Panzer Division has to get across the Zuid-Wilhelms-Vaart tonight.

Spoke with Reichenau in the evening in order to urge the 4th Panzer Division forward.

I then briefed Brauchitsch as follows:

"Leading elements of the 1st Cavalry Division have reached the Zuider Zee and are scouting potential crossing sites. Apparently there are small Dutch warships on the Zuider Zee.

Foremost elements of X Army Corps [Hansen] have reached the Grebbe Line; it intends to attack Grebbe Hill, its southern wing advancing west of Wagedingen. Impression that the Dutch intend to hold the Grebbe Line, for resistance there is stiffening.

XXVI Army Corps [Wodrig] advancing briskly, leading elements of the 9th Panzer Division crossed the Sprang-Tilburg road this morning.

254th Division [Behschnitt] nearing Hertogenbosch, 256th Division [Kaufmann] keeping pace on its left.

Leading elements of the SS Division [Hausser] are said to be north of Eindhoven already, but this has not yet been confirmed.

IX Army Corps [Geyer] advancing toward the road leading south from Eindhoven.

Forward elements of the XI Army Corps [Kortzfleisch] have crossed the Hechtel-Hasselt road.

IV Army Corps [Schwedtler] at the Albert Canal with its right-wing division; I do not yet know if elements are across.

Leading elements of the 18th [Cranz] and 35th [Reinhard] Divisions have crossed the Albert Canal and are continuing to advance.

This morning the 4th Panzer Division [Stever] had its command post in St. Remy. Since the division was short of fuel and deliveries across the Maas and the Albert Canal are impossible, I had 20,000 liters delivered by aircraft to the St. Remy area.

The bulk of the 3rd Panzer Division [Stumpff] is apparently across at Maastricht.

The 20th Motorized Infantry Division [Wiktorin] is closing ranks behind the 3rd Panzer Division and is to cross after it.

As no more bridging equipment was available, the 269th Division of the XXVII Army Corps [Wäger] faced extreme difficulty in crossing, nevertheless some elements are already across. The right wing of the 253rd Division [Kühne] is also in the process of crossing, and I can place the entire XVII Army Corps at the army's disposal for use west of the Maas. The 223rd Division [Körner] is detraining in the rear. I have the impression that the enemy is not defending stubbornly in the outer ring of forts at Liège; it is too early to say whether he intends to do so in the inner. The forts themselves are firing. Fort Neufchateau is surrounded, some of our people are "said" to have been seen on the fort. I have pulled the [SS] *Leibstandarte* out of the line because it became bogged down. For now it will remain with the 18th Army, especially since I can't get it across at Maastricht in the foreseeable future."

It is strange that the Dutch have so far failed to show any artillery worthy of mention!

March performances by the troops, especially those of the 207th [Tiedemann] and 227th [Wachter] Reserve Divisions, as well as the 256th Division [Kauffmann], outstanding. To my relief two bridges were found undamaged at the Zuid-Wilhelms-Vaard.

Yesterday, as the day before, very considerable difficulties due to the advance of the flak corps [Desslach], which, as expected, hopelessly clogged the roads with thousands of vehicles. I asked that the corps be placed under my command for its march movements, otherwise I cannot accept responsibility for the forward progress of my troops. Air Fleet reports state that there is movement toward the rear in the direction of Antwerp and Brussels along the entire front between Vaal and the Maas. Rail transports are also said to be steaming west from Namur; but they could be empty transports.

I reported the army group's plan as: "Push forward hard with the southern wing of the 18th Army, in order to establish contact with the airborne troops.

Push forward very hard with the southern wing of the 6th Army, in order to pierce the Namur-Löwen line as quickly as possible and break through there. The army group's reserves have been allotted accordingly: elements behind the southern wing of the 18th Army, main body behind the southern wing of the 6th Army." – After this conversation I asked the Commander-in-Chief of the Army:

"Is the 4th Army now going to take possession of Huy? Among my worries is that the garrison of Liège will simply march off between the 6th and the 4th Armies west into the Maas Valley."

Answer:

"No! The 4th Army's point of main effort is in the south. Its panzer divisions are also there."

No then!

12/5/40

Drove to the 3rd Panzer Division and to LVI Motorized Army Corps in the area of Tongern. Hoepner had assumed command over the 3rd and 4th Panzer Divisions and over the 20th Motorized Infantry Division. The 4th Panzer Division was engaged with French tanks; Hoepner wanted to wait, as the division was low on fuel and the 3rd Panzer Division had not yet arrived.

Conditions at the bridges at Maastricht are still very difficult, greatly delaying and making difficult the assembly and supply of the panzer corps and the Army Command's stripping me to the skin of bridging columns is having an impact. Nevertheless, I continued to press, stressing to Hoepner that a rapid breakthrough toward and through Gembloux by the panzer corps is of tremendous importance. I knew that I wasn't making myself popular – and Hoepner greeted me with the words:

"You don't need to push me!"

But I had to demand the utmost.

In the afternoon the air fleet dropped fuel for the tanks.

In the evening an exhaustive conversation with Reichenau.

"There is not a single report," I said, "that the main body of the Anglo-French army has crossed the French-Belgian border. The French and English now facing us are advance elements. If we act quickly there is a possibility that we may be able to smash these elements and break into the Dyle Position between Löwen and Namur before the main body of the French Army arrives.

This must be attempted in any case! All minor adversities which the panzer corps will doubtless face have to be overcome toward this objective."

Hopefully I convinced Reichenau!

In the evening came the very encouraging news that the 18th Army's 9th Panzer Division had succeeded in establishing contact with the parachute troops at the undamaged Moerdijk Bridge! An outstanding feat in view of the enormous difficulties presented by the terrain. So I have been able to keep my word!

Pointed out to the 18th Army the necessity of a rapid occupation of Rotterdam – while keeping an eye on Antwerp.

13/5/40

18th Army reports that it intends to employ the corps headquarters [Rudolf, XXXIX Panzer Corps], for which I had asked for months and which was finally placed at its disposal yesterday, to take "Fortress Holland," while the task of screening toward Antwerp is to fall to the XXVI Motorized Army Corps. The army wants to make the main direction of advance toward Utrecht. I am of a different opinion and spoke to the Ia of the army [Schmidt, Arthur], the only one I could reach: "Amsterdam" is the decisive direction. Salmuth drove to see Küchler [18th Army] to talk him into the same thing.

Liège is slowly collapsing. Some of the forts are still firing to the east; two northern forts have been taken, a Lieutenant raised the Reich War Flag on the citadel.

6th Army reports that the XVI Motorized Army Corps does not want to attack until 12:00. That can't be changed now; but I spoke with Reichenau again to press him, for I am altogether against the delay. At 11:00 the first rail transports, soon afterward numerous motorized march columns, reported advancing toward the French-Belgian border! Now they're coming! French have arrived near Vlissingen.

The picture has become clear; guarded by his vanguard of motorized divisions, the enemy is massing in the line Antwerp-Löwen-Namur and perhaps will go to the attack across this line. His feeble attempt to establish land contact with the Dutch Army via Antwerp has been smashed by the rapid advance of the southern wing of the 18th Army. I have the impression that we will succeed in driving back the enemy fighting near Tilburg and Breda – apparently just two French divisions. The 18th Army has taken the Grebbe Hill and thus the commanding bastion of the Grebbe Position.

I continued my efforts to drive forward the southern wing of the 6th Army.

Concerning Army Group A, the 4th Army has succeeded in crossing the Meuse near Yvoir and Dinant and has established bridgeheads there. The French really do appear to have taken leave of their senses, otherwise they could and must prevent it. The elements of Army Group A attacking toward Sedan now have their front facing almost south, while the 4th Army is going west. Was it really right to take the army away from Army Group B, likewise striving toward the west?

Battles "Not Easy"

14/5/40

Drove to Headquarters, 6th Army [Reichenau], to Headquarters, XVI Army Corps [Hoepner], and to the command post of the 4th Panzer Division [Stever]. The panzer divisions' battles with the French tanks thrown against them in the area of Hannut were not easy. The Luftwaffe provided outstanding support. Many shot-up, but even more undamaged French tanks lie about; unable to withstand the enormous moral effect of the combined panzer and Stuka attacks, their crews "bailed out." In spite of many crises during the tank battle, our own losses were moderate.

Drove to Headquarters, XXVII Corps [Wäger]. Apart from Eben Emael, only two forts have fallen so far at Liège. The others can hold out until the last day as long as they don't bar the crossing over the Maas [Meuse] in Liège. For the time being all the bridges there have been blown; I drove into Liège and ensured that work on their restoration was tackled energetically. The mayor, too, is to lend his complete support "in the express interests of the population." The march performances of the XXVII Army Corps are outstanding; how the corps actually got across the Maas remains a mystery, for it had no bridging equipment.

Dutch radio broadcast an appeal by the Dutch Commander-in-Chief [Winkelmann], in which he called for resistance to cease. Only in Zeeland, where the French have arrived, is fighting to continue. I reported this to Brauchitsch, who acknowledged this not unimportant occurrence with "*Ja.*" He urged me to free up forces in Holland, especially motorized forces, soon.

An order from the Army Command that arrived shortly before this conversation called for a swing to the northwest by the Army Group [B], with instructions for its left wing to advance along the line Charleroi-Tournai. Furthermore the army group received orders to build a bridge near Huy, in order to facilitate the delivery of reserves to Army Group A; the close inner connection between the 6th and 4th Armies is becoming ever more apparent!

Brauchitsch explained this move by stating that he suspected there to be 40 enemy divisions in northwest Belgium, which I – given the numerical weakness of the Army Group [B] – could not simply bypass. He hopes that by applying sharp pressure from the south, we might yet cut off the enemy in northwest Belgium. Unfortunately, in the process the army group is temporarily being relegated to a secondary role. I don't yet believe that it will happen that way (!), even though today the XVI Motorized Army Corps is stalled. On the other front we did not break into the Dyle Position today; however, pilots are reporting withdrawal movements behind this front. The Army Command raised the idea of pulling XVI Motorized Army Corps out of the line. It turns out that Brauchitsch gave the 6th Army orders not to continue the attack until the 16th [May] after completing its buildup. He said "that it would suit him quite fine" if the army did not now go so far forward! I could not follow this, to my way of thinking, artificial idea, and instructed 6th Army that it was definitely to continue attacking the enemy, that it had to pursue immediately if the enemy in front of it gave way. If that happens, the XVI Motorized Army Corps must naturally advance and all thoughts of pulling the corps out will then have to be dropped.

15/5/40

At 11:45 Küchler [18th Army] and the Dutch General Winkelmann signed the capitulation of the Dutch Army in a small village between Dordrecht and Rotterdam. I arrived just as the unhappy Dutchman left the house after the surrender.

In Rotterdam I found the headquarters of the 9th Panzer Division [Ritter von Hubicki] and was able to thank him for his division's rapid advance. – Following bombing raids carried out to relieve the airborne troops, the inner city of Rotterdam has been turned into one great pile of smoking rubble – a dreadful scene! [Military Science Review, May 1958, PP 257.]

From there I drove straight through the Dutch Army, whose sentries presented arms, to Utrecht. There I encountered elements of the SS-*Standarte "Adolf Hitler"* [in the original *"Der Führer"*] and the 208th Division. Both had experienced heavy fighting in the storming of the Grebbe Hill, evidence of which was still visible.

Drove back past Doorn. The Kaiser indignantly rejected a British offer to flee which was passed on by the Dutch Queen (Wilhelmina). In Doorn there was a guard from the 208th Division commanded by an officer. I was forbidden to see the Kaiser.

In the evening I spoke to Halder about my plans, which include the continuation of the attack by XVI Motorized Army Corps. He agreed!

16/5/40

Move by the army group to Aachen.

Drove to Headquarters, 6th Army [Reichenau]. – The enemy is on the retreat near Wavre and to the south! My orders: the army is to go on striking at the enemy – also and especially the XVI Motorized Army Corps! There is no other solution!

When I returned to Aachen I found *Generaloberst* Keitel [Head of the OKW] there. He pressed for the withdrawal of all motorized units, which the *Führer* wishes to use to reinforce the main thrust by Army Group A [Rundstedt]. Correct! He is also to get all of the 18th Army's motorized units. But under the conditions that arose today I cannot release the XVI Motorized Army Corps. Hopefully it will advance so far that later, west of Charleroi, it will be able to attempt and achieve link-up with the motorized elements of the 4th Army. All that can be expected of a zigzag march by the 4th Army is a considerable loss of time. In the evening I discussed this topic once more with Halder; and Salmuth did the same with Jodl, both are in agreement. Then in the evening I learned that the XVI Army Corps has not attacked. That is very bad!

The 18th Army was instructed to leave no stone unturned in order to overrun Antwerp if such an opportunity should present itself.

Spoke with Keitel on the topic of the military administration in the occupied areas, from which I gathered that the notion of a permanent military administration has already been abandoned. The head of the civil administration for Holland, Seyß-Inquart, has been chosen. While all this was going on, the designated military commander for Holland, *General* von Falkenhausen, arrived in Aachen and was placed under my command.

17/5/40

The enemy in front of the 6th Army is giving ground! The battles of recent days by XVI Motorized Army Corps were extremely hard, as is reflected in the casualties – Army Group A is making very good progress.

I briefed Brauchitsch. Everyone is seeking to solve the mystery as to what the enemy's actual intentions are. Perhaps he will try to hold Antwerp, the *"Reduit National"* around Ghent-Brugge, and the Dendre Line against me; but the latest air reconnaissance reports also make that appear questionable. At noon came the report that the 56th Divison [Kriebel, 6th Army] had seized Antwerp's Fort Lierre in a *coup de main*. If Antwerp really is now tottering, it would be a tremendous relief to me! An English counterattack against my right wing would then, if at all, only be possible within very narrow limits. I again urged the 18th Army to strike hard at Antwerp.

During the night, however, came the order to pull out XVI Motorized Corps and give it to Army Group A. I am still against it, because the corps is of more use, including to the 4th Army, if it advances straight ahead, than if it makes a "left face" and marches off across the Sambre, where the bridges first have to be built! In this way days will be lost! A frightful argument developed over this question. I spoke with the Army Command, the Armed Forces High Command, and – bypassing the Army Command and Army Group – to the 6th Army, so that finally no one knew what was going on. I therefore asked Halder to clear up the matter once and for all.

In order to allay the 6th Army's worries about Liège, deep in its rear, the troops still there were brought together under the command of the 223rd Division and placed under the direct command of the army group.

Different Socio-Political Ideas About Holland than Hitler

The representative of the Military Administration of Holland, *General* von Falkenhausen, Government President Roeder, and Senior Government Advisor von Kraushaar arrived and had the following to say: for Holland a military administration is the only right one. Dutch State secretaries are ready to cooperate; they are concerned about the Jewish question and hope that the German authorities will abide by the Hague Land Warfare Convention and would like to recognize this as binding. The Dutch people have expressed a high degree of trust in the German soldier. The actions of the military administration have to be made in the long view; its replacement after a short time by a civil administration would have a miserable effect. – I am of the same opinion, even though after my talk with Keitel I know that the *Führer* has other ideas – therefore it will turn out differently [see 31/5/40]. But I called Brauchitsch and proposed that we listen to the gentlemen, which he promised to do.

Himmler paid me a visit. Nothing of consequence was discussed.

The following order was sent to Küchler: "Victory is within reach!"

"In 5 days the 18th Army has forced the brave Dutch Army to lay down its arms, smashed English and French reinforcements rushing to the front, occupied the Netherlands, and cut off Antwerp.

The unprecedented use of airborne troops, the first in history, has contributed to this success of German arms. The air units of the Luftwaffe stand at our side with their usual comradeship and willingness to sacrifice. Victory is within reach! We owe this to your proven officers, the understanding actions of your NCOs, the tireless drive to advance and outstanding bravery of your troops. To the 18th Army – all of its officers and men – I express my full appreciation."

18/5/40

The ultimate order to release the XVI Motorized Army Corps came during the night. Wrong – but this straining back and forth could not go on.

The 18th Army has now also broken through the outermost front line of Antwerp.

Drove to the IV Army Corps. On the way I met elements of the 7th and 31st Divisions and the 9th Panzer Divisions. Detours and awful loss of time because almost every bridge we came to had been blown. Returned through Brussels, just occupied by us.

The 223rd Division has taken Forts Barchon and Pontisse at Liège with support from the Stukas; Fort Fleron surrendered without being attacked.

A new directive from the Army Command arrived in the evening: now I have to give up the I Army Corps as well. My direction of advance remains as ordered. I am to assume full responsibility for Liège, thus the southern front, formerly allocated to [Army Group] A. The troops which [Army Group] A previously had there are going away. We now have practice in carrying out or assignments almost without soldiers.

19/5/40

I briefed Brauchitsch on the situation: the 18th Army, which has forced its way across the Schelde near Antwerp, has orders to advance toward Ghent at a fast pace. 6th Army continues to advance briskly, IV Army Corps [Schwedler] toward Tiurnai; XXVII Army Corps [Wäger] is lagging behind somewhat as a result of the regroupings.

The southward movement of numerous motorized units, at right angles to the forward movement of the army group, is causing considerable delays and traffic jams; everything possible is being done to deal with these. I therefore asked him once again to consider whether the marching-off to the left of the I Army Corps, just like that of the XVI Motorized Army Corps, will not result in more delays, in particular for the operational potential of the I Army Corps, and thus do more harm than good! Brauchitsch said:

"No! All forces must go south. The 4th Army will eventually swing northwest and will then be placed under the army group's command. In any case the enemy probably has no more than 20 divisions in reserve."

Brauchitsch went on to inform me that a civil administration was later to take over in Belgium and Holland. I told Brauchitsch that I intend to put Salmuth [Chief of Staff, Army Group B] up for the Knight's Cross; he agreed.

Fort Marchevolette near Namur has been taken.

The 18th Army has established a bridgehead across the Schelde near Antwerp – all the more noteworthy since there is no bridge and the river is very wide there. Most of the Schelde Tunnel, designed for motor vehicle traffic, is blocked up, perhaps has even been blown; the pedestrian tunnel is passable by infantry.

Drove to the 223rd Division at Fort Pontisse, which was taken yesterday. The effect of the Stuka attacks was devastating; the heavy armored cupolas were simply overturned.

Meanwhile Keitel [Head of the OKW] has spoken with Salmuth: near Valenciennes and Mons heavy counterattacks are under way against the northern wing of the 4th Army, in part from the north! When then would the XVI Motorized Army Corps arrive!?

Where these heavy attacks are supposed to have come from is not clear to me; probably by French units jammed between my southern wing and the northern wing of the 4th Army, now trying to break out. Even if they are locally and temporarily uncomfortable, these attacks can have no strategic significance.

But all my efforts to have the XVI and I Army Corps left with me were in vain! How nice it would have been if the XVI Motorized Army Corps hadn't been pulled out and was now positioned north of Mons, in the rear of this supposedly so threatening enemy!

As for the rest of Army Group B everything is moving forward. The only remaining resistance is west and southwest of Antwerp. Will the Belgian Army really allow itself to separate from the English and turn back to the *Reduit National* near Ghent? Are there really still serious English and French forces opposite my front? I can't truly believe that there are, for why then don't they fight to the finish – or, if they no longer intend or want to after our success against the Belgian Army and that of Army Group A, why don't they withdraw further in big steps?

The order was finally issued for the military administration to take over in Holland and Belgium. But the same evening the radio announced the appointment of Seyß-Inquart as Reich Commissar for Holland!! I called Keitel, who explained that the appointment had been signed, but was not to take effect until about the beginning of June!

What Is To Become of the Dutch Army?

20/5/40

I discussed these matters with Brauchitsch once again. He said that orders were coming to set up the military administration for the time being. The *Führer* is reserving to himself the decision as to when the civil administration will take over. The most important thing at present is clearing up the question of what is to become of the Dutch Army; I am against shipping it to Germany; we already have to transport more than 100,000 men there and feed them. As the mood of the Dutch Army is peaceful and in general nothing is being done against us, I propose demobilizing the army and discharging the men, in order to restore and maintain the agricultural and food industries and other vital things. If the rumor that parts of the Dutch Army are ready to fight against England are true, then this question too can be cleared up after demobilization.

Drove to the XI Army Corps. Once, when I stopped beside our march column, the soldiers immediately surrounded my car and jumped onto the running boards and were cheerful and pleasant in spite of all the hardships of recent days.

Leading elements of the 6th Army have reached the Schelde almost everywhere; only its left wing is lagging, naturally, due to the cross-marches by LVI and I Army Corps. Advancing through Antwerp, the northern wing of the 18th Army has got as far as St. Nikolas, its left wing is attacking the occupied bunker line south of Ghent from the southeast. Crossing the Schelde at Antwerp is proving extraordinarily difficult, because ebb and flood are making bridge building difficult. An attack on Fort Neufchateau near Liège by the 223rd Division failed, because it was flanked from Fort Battice. That was unnecessary! The Headquarters of the Army Group [B] is going to Brussels.

Brussels

21/5/40

Drove to Antwerp to the 18th Army. Tremendous stocks of all sorts in the harbor. Before they left the English set a number of oil tank farms on fire.

They are said to have rendered the large stocks of gasoline useless by adding something to them. From the pier a wonderful martial scene of the 18th Army crossing the broad Schelde by bridge and ferry.

At 18th Army Headquarters news reached me that strong elements of the army group's motorized corps had reached Abbeville and Arras and were swinging north, deep into the enemy's rear.

I immediately drove back to Brussels. There the 6th Army reported strong resistance opposite its front at the Schelde, and that in contrast to yesterday the enemy was employing heavy and very heavy artillery.

The individual advances undertaken at various places on the army's front had not led to success. According to reports from spies, the English headquarters is in Lille. The army proposed shifting its main effort to the right wing. I had the following teletype sent to the Army Command:

"Enemy resistance has increased opposite the army group's front. Counterattacks by tanks southeast of Ghent. As well determined resistance opposite the entire front of the 6th Army, which so far has only won insignificant bridgeheads across the Schelde, with the use of heavy and very heavy guns. English and French identified opposite 6th Army's front. – Army Group intends to transfer point of main effort to the right wing of the 6th and to the 18th Army. This joint effort should enable us to push a strong wing of the army group along the coast. Precondition for this is that the Army Command plans to attack in a northerly direction across the line Valenciennes-Arras-Abbeville with strong forces. Request decision soon on the Army Command's intent."

"Can't Understand for the Life of Me!"

The following telegram arrived from the Army Command in reply:

"The following is the position of the Army High Command: intent of the Army High Command unchanged. Army Group B is to attack and pin down the enemy in its sector. By attacking through Arras in the direction of Calais, Army Group A will block the enemy's retreat to the Lower Somme. Attack to the northwest by Army Group A is possible only after the high ground northwest of Arras has been taken by infantry divisions."

I can't understand that for the life of me! The fourth sentence says exactly the opposite of the third; the whole thing is so unclear that I can't get involved without endangering the affair. I therefore gave the 6th Army my agreement to its proposal to attack with a strong right wing. Then, during the night, a second order arrived from the Army Command:

"The Commander-in-Chief of the Army has declared in passing that he places particular value on a rapid advance by the left wing of the 6th Army, in order to support the decisively important advance by the 4th Army."

I telephoned Halder and told him that I couldn't change anything now. As well, the 6th Army was of course attacking on its southern wing. Halder in agreement. Talk turned once again to the allegedly heavy attacks against the northern flank of the VIII Army Corps, the northern wing of the 4th Army, in the area of Valenciennes. That's rubbish! I therefore said to Halder:

"The attack can't be very heavy, for the area between the 6th and 4th Armies would be much too confined for the deployment of an attack by stronger forces! Where is the depth for such a strong attack supposed to come from?"

Halder replied:

"Twelve kilometers at least!"

They can't go on talking like that. Soon afterward I learned that elements of the XXVII Army Corps were standing undisturbed in the area from which the enemy was supposed to be attacking the northern wing of the 4th Army! I informed Halder, who now declared that an attack of strategic significance was naturally out of the question. But then I don't know why the Army Command wasted any time at all over this trifle!

Fort Neufchateau has been taken. In order to spare blood, I ordered that both forts at Liège still holding out, Battice and Tancremont, be requested to surrender voluntarily.

22/5/40

Fort Battice surrendered; now hopefully Tancremont will fall so that I can get free the 223rd Division. Now that they have taken the XVI and I Army Corps away from me, I need every man at the front.

Drove to Headquarters, IV Corps and XXVII Corps and to the 18th Division, which experienced heavy fighting yesterday. Morale is exemplary everywhere.

I learned from *Hauptmann* Naudè, whom I had sent to the VIII Army Corps, and by other means, that the supposedly heavy attacks from the area of Mons were pure rubbish! The situation there is exactly as it appeared to us and just as I described it to *General* Keitel and the Army High Command. The whole stupid fuss was unnecessary! Salmuth briefed Halder, I briefed Brauchitsch. The latter said that Army Group A and the 4th Army had just described VIII Army Corps' situation differently. I replied:

"Then both of them are just not in the picture!"

Why did they take the 4th Army from me? Why the XVI Motorized Army Corps? Why the I Army Corps? I repeatedly asked that they cease the flanking march by these corps and instead send both by the shortest route where they should go, namely via Mons toward Valenciennes! Command of both corps was child's play if they stayed in the hands of Army Group B. The drive through Valenciennes belongs in one hand, the northern wing of the 4th Army belongs, to Army Group B!

The way the attack near Valenciennes is now being carried out, it can and will lead to nothing!

Strong German armored forces are driving through Arras toward St. Omer and Calais! Yesterday's reply from the Army Command is becoming ever more inexplicable!

The attack by 6th Army's XI Corps – the right wing of the army – has crossed the Schelde in heavy fighting with the English. The army has the impression that it is going well. The left wing of the 18th Army [IX Army Corps] has broken into the bunker line southeast of Ghent.

Visit from the Italian ambassador [Attolico].

23/5/40

In the morning a new order from the Army Command, turning the army group's southern wing sharply to the northwest in the direction of St. Amand-Carvin-Fournes [southwest of Lille].

Drove to Headquarters, 6th Army [Reichenau] to discuss the measures necessary to carry out this order; encouraging agreement.

The enemy is withdrawing toward the Lys before the XI and IV Army Corps! IX Army Corps broke through the bunker line southeast of Ghent in several places and entered Ghent in the evening.

While visiting 6th Army I learned from an VIII Corps radio message to the army's left-wing corps, that the 1st Machine-Gun Battalion and *Leibstandarte* – both elements of the northern wing of the 4th Army – "have gone over to the defensive east and southeast of Valenciennes!"

I asked Salmuth to inform the Army Command of this. In the evening I was visited by our former ambassador in Warsaw, Herr von Moltke.

Brauchitsch: "...often hostile Resistance"

24/5/40

During the night received an order placing the elements of the 4th Army that had been redirected north – and its southwest-facing front between Abbeville and Amiens under Army Group B. Thus the direction of the battle has finally been placed in one hand. A shame that it didn't happen earlier, much lost time would have been avoided.

Brauchitsch arrived in the morning. We agreed on a vigorous advance to the north-northwest at the boundary between the 6th and 4th Armies, and that the main body of the armored units in the enemy's rear must continue to attack. In parting, he said to me that "the heads of the army group (!)" are resisting the demands of the Army Command in an often hostile way. Not entirely without reason! But I promised to remedy this "grievance."

I was told of the new operation planned after the conclusion of the battle in progress. Once again the army group received a secondary role. Who knows whether things will again develop differently than the Army Command believes it sees them.

Brauchitsch had just driven off, when I learned from Groeben, who had been sent to establish contact with the 4th Army, that serious attacks by the British and French were under way on the Somme near and southeast of Amiens, and that Kluge, the Commander-in-Chief of the 4th Army, had had to divert three of the divisions assigned to the battle in the north by Army Command there, or to the south. Furthermore, the 4th Army had received an order from the *Führer*, according to which the armored units were to advance no farther! He probably wishes to preserve them for future missions.

That can have very unpleasant consequences for the outcome of the battle I am fighting! I briefed Brauchitsch by telephone. He agreed with the diversion of the three divisions; unfortunately, where the armored units are concerned, for now we have to content ourselves with them establishing bridgeheads in the line Gravelines-Aire-Bethune.

Two hours later, when the basis for the assumption of command was clear and all the orders ready, orders came from Brauchitsch that I was now "not yet" to assume command over the 4th Army today; he reserves decision on the timing of transfer of command! I do not know the reason why.

25/5/40

Orders came that the decreed assumption of command over the 4th Army has not just been postponed, but cancelled. I did not learn the reason why today either!

Yesterday we succeeded in crossing the Lys at two places, the 18th Army with initially weak elements, on the northern wing of the 6th Army with stronger forces.

Reichenau thinks it possible that IV Army Corps' drive may collapse the enemy front, as elements are withdrawing in a great arc around Ypres-Ostend, others to the west and southwest. As I have only very weak reserves left, that wouldn't be at all as comfortable to me as it looks.

Drove to the headquarters of IX and XI Army Corps. IX Corps did not advance at all today, the XI only a little. Consequently the more effective attack by IV Army Corps was flanked from the north. – Drove to Courtrai to the 54th Infantry Regiment, which was just crossing the Lys. The regiment was in a fabulous mood.

The attack on the left wing of the 6th Army got nowhere, the army wanted to repeat it in the evening. As I saw it, its only hope was that the French might perhaps pull out under the pressure from all sides. In any case, it no longer served any purpose to continue the attack with the point of main effort there.

I therefore moved it to IV Army Corps, which was advancing well, and to the left wing of the 18th Army – which was in keeping with my original plan. I made a report to the Army Command.

26/5/40

In the morning I telephoned Brauchitsch and asked what orders he had had for me yesterday, as I had been called several times during my absence. He asked about the situation. I told him that a gradual tiring of the troops was starting to become apparent, that the 56th and 269th Divisions would soon be exhausted, but that morale was nevertheless outstanding. Brauchitsch observed that the troops probably had to have a rest. I stated that that was out of the question now. What I strongly desired was the continuation of the army group's heavy, purely frontal attack, and that II Corps [4th Army] and the armored units continue attacking in the direction in which they had been committed! Brauchitsch replied:

"Unfortunately the panzer units have been halted for today!" I then said that I considered the capture of Dunkirk to be absolutely necessary, otherwise the English might transport what they wanted out of Dunkirk under our noses. Brauchitsch promised that he would try to get the armored units included in the attack on Dunkirk.

I repeated that that was urgently desired. They mustn't deceive themselves about the ferocity of the army group's attack, losses were serious in places. The Commander-in-Chief of the Army now agreed with my intent to place the point of main effort on the inner wing of the army and to continue the attack on the southern wing of the 6th Army without employing many men, taking individual fortifications one at a time. Regarding the cancellation of the order which was to have placed the entire attack front under me, Brauchitsch stated that as far as he was concerned he still stood by his order, "but that there was no way around these changes!"

I declared that I deeply regretted that in the interest of the matter at hand!

Drove to Headquarters, IV and XI Army Corps, to the command post of the 216th Divison, to Headquarters, IX Army Corps, Headquarters, 18th Army and to the command post of the 208th Division. Everything is in order with the IV Army Corps. All is not well in the command of the 216th Division, the effect of which is noticeable in the unit. I spoke a few friendly words to elements of the division I met on the march and they were well received. A gradual but definite slackening of the enemy artillery fire is apparent on the entire long front that I drove down. Together with the rapid advance by the IV Army Corps, which has reached the Channel south of Ypres, the advance on the right north of Ghent will surely bear fruit tomorrow.

A new order came in the evening: the tanks were finally allowed to attack again. Their central assault group, which was assigned the general direction of Ypres, is to come under my command as soon as I establish working contact with it. Curiously, the northern group again is not! It is not to take Dunkirk, but rather just surround it! That is a very serious mistake – and they're probably worried that I would correct it if they placed the group under my command!

The drive by the IV Army Corps has resulted in the formation of two pockets:

In the north the Belgians and elements of the French and English who failed to get away from Dunkirk, and around Lille the bulk of he French facing me.

In a conversation between my Ia [Hasse] and the 4th Army [Kluge], the latter adopted a half-hearted attitude toward being placed under my command. Since Kluge is not stupid, and as our previous marriage [the 4th Army was under the command of Army Group B until mid-February 1940] was quite happy, this is quite difficult to understand.

Endless columns of refugees are making their way toward Brussels on all the roads. Today it was obvious that there were a number of Belgian soldiers in civilian clothes among them.

Franc-Tireur Psychosis

On the way I experienced a classic example of how the *franc-tireur* [guerilla] psychosis arises: I saw a German soldier lying at the side of the road who had just had a wound dressed. I got out and asked what was going on. The fellow had been riding with his rifle strapped to his bicycle – safety off; his leg had touched the rifle and the resulting shot passed through his leg.

When I returned to my car, my driver told me that other soldiers had just come over to him and excitedly told him that "snipers are firing from these houses – that man over there was hit!"

16 Straight Days of Fighting

27/5/40

I requested thc 4th Army to deploy Armored Groups Center and North toward Ypres with the right wing and Dixmuden with the left, which it promised to do.

There is forward progress on the entire attack front! I'd like to see anyone match the performance of our field forces! 16 straight days of fighting and marching – on very thin, broad fronts – against an enemy fighting for his life!

Drove to IV Army Corps and the command post of the 255th Division. At Thielt there was a mixup and an hour-long stop because the armies deviated from their assigned combat sectors and "agreed" on a boundary which differed from the one in their orders.

On my return came the report that a Belgian general [Major-General Derousseaux, Deputy Head of the Belgian General Staff] had arrived at XI Army Corps in the name of the king to request terms for the surrender of the Belgian Army. After conferring with the Army High Command, unconditional surrender was demanded.

I am worried that the unavoidable negotiations with the Belgians will result in a halt of our forward movement which, abetted by the resulting tangle of German and Belgian troops, the English will be able to exploit for themselves. The Belgians were therefore told to stay off the roads in complete units under their officers until further orders came.

I set the boundary between the two armies at Dixmuden so that both could simply proceed straight ahead and create the minimum possible friction and delay.

The panzer corps attacking toward Dunkirk from the west is bogged down near Cassel against heavy resistance; the English thus have time to position themselves opposite me at the Yser Canal and can continue to evacuate what they can from Dunkirk by ship.

On the Fate of the Belgian King

I asked the Army High Command where the Belgian king [Leopold III], who had remained with his troops to the bitter end, was to go.

Answer:

"Either Germany, if he comes alone – or to a suitable residence in Belgium, away from the larger cities, if he comes as a general with his army."

In the evening Hasse, who had been at the Army Command, brought directives for the conduct of subsequent operations.

28/5/40

Worry that the surrender of the Belgians will stop the advance of my armies won't let go of me. I therefore issued orders for motorized battalions to be driven forward toward the Yser Canal between Nieuport and Ypres as powerfully and quickly as possible.

At 10:10 I telephoned Brauchitsch and informed him that the authorized Belgian general had signed the unconditional surrender of the army. The king surrendered with his army. When asked if he had any personal request the king had answered "no." Brauchitsch replied:

"Thank you! Please carry out the orders I have given you."

I:

"I will have the king brought to Château Laeken near Brussels. It is isolated, the king enjoyed a previous stay there, and it is easy to watch over."

Brauchitsch:

"Very well."

I therefore had it suggested to the king that he go to Laeken. Everything was quickly put in order there; we provided provisions and a guard was installed. – Two enemy armies defeated and taken prisoner in 18 days!

The English and French trapped at Dunkirk and Lille are putting up a bitter fight. Pressure from the west from our panzer corps is and remains weak. The corps is making slow progress against apparently strong resistance. My southern wing, which yesterday broke through the French bunker line, has wheeled through Orchies and is fighting in Lille; II Army Corps [Strauß], which unfortunately still belongs to the 4th Army, is fighting to the west, apparently at the same level. The VIII [Heitz] and I [Both] Army Corps, both of the 4th Army, which had stalled for days in the Valenciennes area, have now suddenly smashed their way out! The result of this strange disunity of command, maintained with great energy in the very focus of the battle, is that everything now rests on my exhausted, weak units and that the English continue to get away from Dunkirk. The Luftwaffe's attacks are also failing to hinder them from doing so.

29/5/40

Drove to Charleville. I spent a long time there in the World War. It looks bad now, bombs and artillery have smashed the town; the population, with few exceptions, has fled.

In Charleville there was a meeting of the Commander-in-Chief of the Army with the army group and army commanders. Placed or left under my command were: 4th Army [Kluge], 6th Army [Reichenau], 9th Army [Strauß] and the Kleist Armored Corps.

When I returned I learned that the 18th Army had taken Furnes and the 6th Army the Kemmel, the latter in the face of weak enemy resistance. Very well done! Reichenau is waging something of a special war. He has once again veered north into the sectors of the 18th Army [Küchler]. The latter is furious, because this is the third time and each occasion results in confusion and lost time. Reichenau was with the king of the Belgians in Brugge this afternoon instead of with his army where a firm hand was needed, especially in the center and on the southern wing on account of the steadily shrinking pocket. He is and remains a "big kid." I tried to unravel the situation by halting both wings of the assault group from Reichenau's army that had turned northwest and ordering that all elements of that army which had crossed the boundary with the 18th Army were from that moment under the command of Headquarters, 18th Army.

A comment by Rundstedt in Charleville made it clear to me why the armored units near Dunkirk were not more active. Rundstedt said:

"I was worried that Kleist's weak forces would be overrun by the fleeing English!"

I had no worries of this sort whatsoever; if they were ever at all justified, they have become completely invalid ever since the 18th and the 6th Armies got the English by the throat, making them happy just to escape with their lives. But why wasn't I told this before? Then I could have dispelled these concerns and the English wouldn't have gotten away. In this connection, a call for sharper pressure from my northern wing by an officer of the Operations Department caused much amusement.

Still on the 21st [May], contrary to my suggestion the Army High Command ordered a strengthening of my southern wing!

When I returned home toward evening, I learned that the Belgian King was still sitting in Brugge and didn't want to go to Laeken, but instead to a private villa in Quatre Bras. First of all I don't know whether the villa there is still standing or if it meets our requirements as to location and security possibilities, and second the *Führer* eventually wants to speak to the King in Laeken tomorrow. The lines to Brugge have been cut. I therefore sent my air general Bieneck to Brugge and had him ask the King to come to Laeken this evening, as it is in his best interests. There we would gladly discuss and consider his wishes. Bieneck returned late in the evening with news that the King was coming.

30/5/40

The English continue their evacuation from Dunkirk, even from the open beaches! By the time we finally get there they will be gone! The halting of the panzer units by the Supreme Command is proving to be a serious mistake!

We continue to attack. The fight is hard, the English are as tough as leather, and my divisions are exhausted. On the right wing, the 18th Army, there is no progress; the northernmost attack wing is taking fire from the English fleet. Contrary to previous reports, Bergues, possession of which is of importance to the capture of Dunkirk, has not yet been taken. The X Army Corps is being sent to the attack along the Poperinghe-Bergues road.

Now, finally, the XIV Motorized Army Corps [Wietersheim] is being placed under my command, but with the announcement that it has to be released again as soon as possible. The secondment is now not of much practical use. Six days ago it would have been of decisive importance. Today the corps merely interferes with the movements of the X Army Corps.

In the morning I drove to Laeken as I had promised to ask the King about his wishes. The Adjutant-General [van Overstraeten], a Walloon, gave me a cool reception for a well-educated man in this situation. He asked if I wished to make "my visit" with the King, to which I replied that I did. But first I wanted to discuss several matters with him, the adjutant, so that the King was not caught unprepared:

(1) I had to insist yesterday that the King go to Laeken, because his safety did not appear to be assured in Brugge, especially as there were still English and French at large there.

(2) The matter of the eventual move by the King to the Villa Les Bouleaux.

(3) The question of relocating the Queen Mother.

The adjutant disappeared to, I supposed, brief the King. After a few minutes he returned and relayed a request by the King that the officers of his entourage, for whom there was no room at Les Bouleaux, might live in Brussels, from where they would come each day to the villa to carry out their duties. I declared that I saw difficulties with this solution, but that an answer would be found. When the discussion was over I waited a moment, but the invitation to see the King was not forthcoming. When I was about to leave, one of my officers asked if I didn't want to see the King. In the presence of the adjutant I said that the King could have had me told that. I had the impression that the adjutant had sabotaged the talk with the King; not clever, because I was ready to make things as easy for him as possible.

I briefed Brauchitsch on the factual part of the conversation and told him that I did not consider having the King's adjutants living in the city acceptable; any control over who saw the King would become impossible, especially since there were still numerous "neutral" diplomats in Brussels. I proposed that Envoy Kiewitz, whom the *Führer* had sent to serve with the King, should clarify this and all other questions that arose directly with the *Führer* train, so that I would be relieved of this burden. Brauchitsch agreed; I briefed Kiewitz, who arrived in the afternoon.

When I set out for the front at noon, I met thousands of unguarded Belgian soldiers, streaming into Brussels on foot and on horseback, in wagons, on bicycles and in cars. Neither the Belgian command or our armies were able to prevent it. This posed a huge danger! If these people should reach their destroyed villages there would be an outbreak of distress and hunger, then heaven knows what would happen. I took rigorous action.

In the evening the "Deputy *Führer*," Hess, arrived; he wants to go to the front.

31/5/40

In the morning orders were issued for the regrouping in preparation for the new operations. I drove to the headquarters of the 18th Army, to the headquarters of the VXII, IX and X Corps, and to the 56th Division at Westend. At Dunkirk progress is hesitant in bitter fighting; near Nieuport the right wing too is making only negligible progress, the left wing is lagging behind for reasons which are well known. Between Ostend and Westend a British cruiser exchanged fire with one of our field batteries – a battle which inflicted no damage on either party; the English vessel eventually sailed away. – In Lille the fighting in the streets is still not over; Reichenau attributes this to a rather half-hearted effort by the tired units, which he is personally urging forward from the front lines. A French division commander was captured; the French army commander, allegedly still in Lille, wants to parlay. So far 20,000 prisoners have been taken in and around Lille, mainly French. Late in the evening 6th Army reported that the rest – 4 generals and another 6,000 men – had surrendered.

An intercepted English radio message revealed that the last English troops, 5,000 strong, are to be evacuated from Dunkirk tonight. I spoke with the 18th Army and Air Fleet 2, in order to intensify artillery fire and bombing attacks on the embarkation points.

Today my travels took me through the battlefields of Ypres and Langemarck. The sight of the huge graveyards of the World War is moving and the heavy battles fought by the Guard in autumn 1914 come before my eyes again in all their harshness.

In the evening Minister Meißner dined with me. He spoke with the King of the Belgians on behalf of the *Führer*; it is possible that he will be taken to Germany. According to what Meißner had to say, two possibilities are being considered for the future of Belgium: if the King is reasonable and is ready to go along with Germany, then the Kingdom of Belgium will continue to exist, closely allied to Germany; in the other case there are plans for the creation of a *"Gau Flandern"* [District of Flanders]. – Holland is apparently to become a German district.

The Final Tally of a Battle

1/6/40

The enemy is yielding at Dunkirk – whether for good or whether he is retiring to a smaller bridgehead front is still not clear. In any case the battle is coming to an end. The Army Group [B] crossed the frontier with 32 divisions; in the course of the campaign it gave up 11 divisions to other army groups and fought against 11 Dutch, 22 Belgian, 25 French, and elements of 14 to 15 English divisions – an opposing force with a more than two-fold superiority in numbers. More than half of these divisions were captured, the rest smashed with heavy losses.

Hitler in Brussels

At 11:00 the *Führer* arrived from Brussels. My army commanders were on hand. I gave a brief summary of the situation, development and state of affairs at Dunkirk. The *Führer* thanked us and set forth his thoughts on the overall war situation and the new operations. He informed us that Italy's entry into the war was imminent. He is worried about Paris, from which he expects French counterattacks. Afterwards the *Führer* drove with me through the city; only a few people recognized him and they appeared shocked. Incidentally, he knew his way around Brussels much better than I, probably from the World War.

In the evening another English radio communication was intercepted; it said that the last English troops were to be evacuated from Dunkirk during the night by means of numerous motorboats.

2/6/40

Drove to a regimental command post on the Dunkirk Front, to the head-quarters of the X Corps, and to the command post of the famous 18th Division, which was just attacking Bergues. Dunkirk had been fortified more heavily in peacetime than we knew; several rings of defensive lines with heavy wire obstacles in places and a number of concrete bunkers. The scene on the roads used by the English retreat was indescribable. Huge quantities of motor vehicles, guns, combat vehicles, and army equipment were crammed into a very small area and driven together. The English had tried to burn everything, but in their haste they succeeded only here and there. There lies the materiel of an army whose completeness of equipment we poor wretches can only gaze at with envy.

Preparations for New Operations

My headquarters moved to Château Havrincourt, where I arrived at about 19:00. Waiting for me there to discuss the new operation were the army commanders. We discussed the following points:

(a) Timing of the start of operations.

The bulk of the 4th Army is already in the new front and is essentially ready. On 4 June, the day before the general attack, Kluge wants to expand a bridgehead won by the army near Abbeville on 4 June; on the one hand because the Bavarian reserve division in the bridgehead [57th Division, Blümm] is beginning to "waver" after repeated attacks by enemy tanks, and also to obtain another jump-off point.

Reichenau declared that that he could be ready by the deadline specified by the Army Command only under certain conditions and even then only provisionally on the 5th of June. Strauß [9th Army, 8th Army in the original] still has no clear idea when his artillery and combat engineer formations will arrive.

That is all not very good, for the *Führer* is insisting on the 5th [June] as the attack date.

(b) Conduct of the Operation.

Everyone agreed with my plans. I discussed the possibilities that might arise in the course of the advance, especially from Paris, and stressed that I could not give from my army group reserve as long as the overall situation was unclear. The armies would have to help themselves for that long.

Salmuth spoke with the Army High Command concerning conditions for the timely start of the attack. Halder agreed to an early start by the 4th Army; he also said:

"A postponement of the attack is out of the question!"

At the request of the 9th Army [8th in the original], a request was made to the Army Command that the right wing of Army Group A, which unfortunately is not supposed to attack until several days later, at least participate in the first attack on the 5th [June] to gain a bridgehead at Bourg et Comin, because otherwise the left wing of the 9th Army [8th Army in the original] will have to put up with flanking attacks from the southeast. The Army Command reserved decision.

The 18th Division took Bergues in the evening. Under its splendid commander, *General* Cranz, this division truly did everything one asked of it.

6th Army reported the final tally of the booty taken at Lille: 7 generals, 350 officers, 34,600 enlisted men, 300 guns, 100 armored vehicles!

Accommodations in Brussels' Hotel Metropole were excellent. It was surely uncomfortable for the owner, having a headquarters in his usually well-cared-for house with all the inevitable disturbances, guards, telephones, etc. I expressed my regrets to the cultivated, unfailingly courteous man and I was pleased to be able to arrange some preferential treatment for him in the future assignment of quarters. Before we left, I had special instructions issued to the men staying in the hotel that they were to leave their quarters in spotless condition and that they might take nothing, not even small items, with them. When I arrived in Havrincourt, I discovered that my batman had draped all the walls of my room with my things, hung neatly on coat hangers. But on closer inspection it unfortunately turned out that all the hangars belonged to the Hotel Metropole! I was thus probably the only one who had misappropriated anything there! The mishap was corrected as quickly as possible.

3/6/40

The business at Dunkirk is finally drawing to an end! We could have achieved that eight days earlier if a unified command had been created there sooner. It was the same at Lille. Why?

In the morning I drove to see Reichenau to congratulate him on the successes at Lille. – Kesselring [Air Fleet 2] arrived in the afternoon, then Kleist [XXII Motorized Army Corps]. The latter requested that the most thorough possible preparations be made now for the planned combining of the two panzer corps [XIV, XVI] as *"Gruppe Kleist"* [XXII Motorized Army Corps, also designated *Panzergruppe Kleist*], and that he and his staff be closely involved in these preparations with regards to supply, liaison, cooperation with the Luftwaffe and so on; I agreed to that. Right afterward came Brauchitsch, who had been approached by Kleist in a similar vein. I was able to reassure him and determine that all our plans were in complete agreement. There was a brief discussion as to whether it was more practical to have both panzer corps attack together from the Amiens bridgehead or commit them separately by way of Amiens and Peronne. I declared that both had advantages and disadvantages; the army, which knows the local conditions extremely well, was very much in favor of attacking separately and linking up later in the advance, and it would be hard to change now. As soon as Brauchitsch left Reichenau arrived. He termed an attack by all the armored forces together from the narrow gap near Amiens "sheer madness."

Regarding Kleist's involvement in the preparations for the later formation of the panzer corps, he [Reichenau] said that everything had been discussed with Kleist and initiated along the lines that Kleist and I were thinking.

The 4th Army dropped the premature attack to expand the Abbeville bridgehead, for which I was quite glad. On the other hand the Army Command insists on sticking to the attack deadline. I fear that it will become a rushed affair. If it were up to me, I would wait twenty-four hours, for we are short on things everywhere. But apparently there are such compelling reasons against it that it has to proceed as planned. They just have to be clear that carrying out this attack "off the cuff" with untested divisions is a brash thing to do!

4/6/40

French and English tanks again attacked the Abbeville bridgehead.

Dunkirk has fallen! According to 18th Army's report 30,000 to 40,000 prisoners, mainly French, and very much materiel. The English are gone!

Drove to Combles, where I gave the commanding generals of the 6th Army assembled by Reichenau a few brief instructions for the attack. Then drove to the headquarters of the XXXVIII [Manstein] and II [Stülpnagel] Corps.

The 4th Army [Kluge] is essentially ready, the 6th [Reichenau] and 9th [Strauß] still have a long way to go.

In the afternoon I made a brief detour to the coast near Etaples. The restaurants were closed in the resort town of Le Touquet, but there was plenty of activity on the beach; French vacationers, cut off there by our rapid advance, mingled freely with our soldiers. I also saw some French officers and soldiers, who saluted very politely.

Impressions gained from the past few days forced me to issue a sharply-worded order to restore order behind the front.

The Attack

5/6/40

All three armies of the army group began the attack, Army Group A unfortunately not yet.

Drove to Headquarters, 4th Army, to *Gruppe* Kleist [XXII Motorized Army Corps], and to the command post of the 9th Panzer Division south of Amiens, where I found Wietersheim, commanding general of the XIV Motorized Army Corps. Amiens cathedral is undamaged, but most of the city center has been totally destroyed by bombing.

The French are defending themselves stubbornly. Their tactic in the face of our panzer attacks is to establish themselves in towns and forests, placing the main weight of their defense in "tank-proof" terrain. This has caused some local discomfort; however, since they are leaving the intervening spaces between strongpoints free, this tactic will do them little good in the long run. For the moment, however, it provides them with an advantage, for while near

Amiens and Peronne the panzer divisions can advance between the occupied towns, their riflemen are unable to follow under the effects of flanking fire from the towns. Consequently, moving the motorized divisions forward today was not yet possible.

In the afternoon drove to the 9th Army and to the headquarters of the XXXXIV [Koch, F.] and V [Ruoff] Corps. The consequences of the overly-hasty attack are especially evident in the V Corps; the concentration of fire of the artillery, some of which only reached their firing positions during the night, was not good, and after moderate initial success the attack got no farther.

Only the first day and already Reichenau was demanding a division from my reserve. It was given, so as not to deny him anything that might drive the attack forward.

6/6/40

Difficult, crisis-filled day! It appears as if we are pinned down! I once again drove to the XIV Motorized Army Corps and to the 9th Panzer Division to get a clear picture of what was happening and sent Salmuth to the other panzer corps, to the XVI. At noon, when we were all back, Reichenau arrived. I was of the opinion that if the enemy continued to hold, as it presently appeared likely, only by vigorously forming a point of main effort could anything be made out of the thin soup of the 6th Army. Things look more promising for the XVI Motorized Army Corps than for the bottled-up XIV Motorized Army Corps, which furthermore has reported a new, almost unbroken fortified line opposite its front. With a heavy heart, I therefore decided to withdraw the XIV Motorized Army Corps south of Amiens and deploy it behind the XVI Motorized Army Corps near Peronne so as to break through in the direction of Creil-Compiègne with a strong armored spearhead. Kleist is to take command of both panzer corps. VIII Army Corps is to be committed east of Amiens. The resulting quite strong attack force should get the army moving forward between Amiens and Peronne. Reichenau, who had a different opinion earlier, now agrees.

In the afternoon, just as the orders for the regrouping were being issued, there came news that the enemy in front of the 4th Army was yielding and that on the left wing of the 6th and in front of the 9th Armies the enemy defense of the Chemin des Dames had collapsed under the attack of the 1st Mountain Infantry Division and the 25th Division! That changed the situation completely! Pulling the XIV Motorized Army Corps out at this moment and allowing it to go pleasure driving behind the front would have been a mistake, for the enemy in the arc Noyon-La Fère-Amiens cannot now hold out for long. Now everything must be hurled at the enemy. I spoke with Reichenau, who agreed. The VIII Army Corps is being moved forward as planned, for it will thus be in the right place for any eventuality. Everything else is proceeding straight ahead as originally planned. As originally foreseen, assembly of [*Panzer*]-*Gruppe* Kleist cannot take place until we are moving forward and in front of the armies' front. I have placed a division from my reserve at the disposal of the 4th Army, because as it advances it is becoming too broad and therefore has to guard both of its wings itself.

7/6/40

Drove to various sectors of the front.

The Hoth Panzer Corps [XV Motorized Army Corps], part of the 4th Army, has won some breathing room and has driven deep through the enemy as far as the Forges les Eaux area. Behind it the divisions of the 4th Army are attacking the enemy still clinging grimly to towns and forests. The 4th Army is thus beginning to advance, only opposite its right wing, on the Bresle, is the enemy still holding firm. Opposite the 6th Army he is only yielding in places; progress by both panzer corps is also minor. But left of the Oise things are going well for the eastern wing of the 6th Army and the 9th Army. The enemy has been driven across the Oise on almost the entire front and several bridgeheads have been established on the south bank. Frequent telephone conversations with Brauchitsch and Halder about the operation, especially over the future direction of advance of the Hoth Corps. I am in favor of driving the corps on as far as the Seine, in order to exploit the favorable situation there. If the corps reaches the Seine near Rouen, we will have complete freedom to then use it as we wish. I think it premature to turn the corps in a generally easterly direction, roughly toward Beauvais. I therefore ordered the XV Motorized Army Corps [Hoth] to carry on to Rouen and reconnoiter immediately toward Tilly-Beauvais. Motorized forces which are now or become free will be sent after the XV Motorized Army Corps, to enable the 4th Army to hold the Seine at Rouen while turning the Hoth Panzer Corps to the east should the enemy still wish to fight forward of the Seine.

I subsequently made Halder aware that as long as Army Group A does not attack, the enemy will be able to throw in reserves opposite my front; the probable result will be that nothing will come of the planned "leap forward" by [*Panzer*]-*Gruppe* Kleist [XXII Motorized Army Corps]! It almost looks as if they – why I don't know – want to avoid a decision on the army's right wing. That won't stop me from using everything within my limited power to force one.

8/6/40

In the morning it seemed clear that the 6th Army was still bogged down west of the Oise, while the 4th Army was making good progress by exploiting yesterday's success by the XV Motorized Army Corps. The English have landed troops at Le Havre, the French are moving reinforcements to their western wing. Everything suggests that the enemy intends to fight forward of the Seine. I therefore ordered the 4th Army to first take Rouen with the panzer corps, in order to attack across the general line Gournay-Marseille-Crevecoeur le Grand with the main body of the army while holding the Seine at Rouen. To this end I subordinated the I Army Corps [Both] to the army from my reserve and expanded the army's sector to the east somewhat. The 6th Army is to maintain contact with the enemy in the center, but continue attacking with its left wing – left of the Oise. The 9th Army also continues to attack across the Aisne. I drove to see Kluge in order to discuss with him the basic ideas behind these plans.

At about five in the afternoon came the news that the enemy was retreating in front of the XIV Motorized Army Corps and that the corps had advanced to the area of Breteuil, while reconnaissance forces had reached the area north of St. Just! An intercepted radio message from the French 7th Army, which is opposite me, promised: "*Solution immèdiate!*" Suddenly the situation was clear! The enemy was giving up the fight. The orders issued this morning when the circumstances were different were therefore rescinded before they were carried out; everyone retained his original missions. The 4th Army was instructed to send strong forces behind its left wing, in order to once again throw them against the enemy making a stand in the area of Beauvais.

The 9th Army won bridgeheads across the Aisne everywhere. I briefed Halder on the situation and my intentions; he is in agreement. The Supreme Command is worried about the 4th Army's right wing, where the enemy is still holding at the Bresle. I do not share this concern! If the enemy continues to hold there he may regret it.

Within two days I have twice had to decide to drastically modify orders already issued. In both cases the change proved itself to be inappropriate and I was able to correct it in time. Naturally we asked ourselves whether we had acted rashly, particularly in the second case, on the 8th [June]. Appearances suggested that we had. But detailed examination of the information led to the realization that the amended orders were correct had the enemy stuck to the plan that had to be accepted as given. It was completely within the realm of possibility that the enemy might still fight forward of the Seine in spite of his difficult situation. If he did not, he gave up a decisive battle as lost before it was fought. But if he intended to fight it out, and that had to be assumed based on the available reports, it was vital for the Army Group [B] to exploit every opportunity to initiate the destructive blow against the enemy holding forward of the Seine. Of course, seen theoretically it would have been more effective to direct the main body of the 4th Army across the Seine on either side of Rouen deep into the rear of the French Army, instead of turning it against the west flank of the enemy holding north of the Seine, while keeping a firm hold on the Seine north of the river. But the forces available to the Army Group [B] were nowhere near sufficient to carry out such a wide-ranging operation. Should the 4th Army cross the Seine, its eastern wing would have to guard against the French Army elements holding there, while simultaneously driving back the French holding on its western wing at the Bresle. What was left for the Seine crossing and the drive into the depth of enemy territory would undoubtedly be insufficient to bring about the decisive decision. I therefore believe that the rapid overturning of the decisions was justified.

Assessment of the Overall Situation

9/6/40

Opposite the right wing of the Army Group [B] the enemy is pulling back from the Bresle behind the Bethune. As well, the 4th Army is standing close to Rouen. The enemy is also yielding before the 6th Army. The Aisne has been crossed.

As I see the situation, the enemy will try to hold the Seine-Marne line. He will probably make a stand in front of Paris in the "Paris Defense Position" [hills of Luzarches and Dammartin]; this position runs roughly along the Oise between Pontoise and Beaumont, then further over the hills of Luzarches and Dammartin, and then bends back toward the Marne in the general direction of the Meaux area. If the enemy does not hold this position he gives up Paris. In spite of all the tirades on French radio, I consider it quite unlikely that the French will allow it to come to street fighting in their capital. But if they want to preserve the city, they have no other choice but to withdraw so far beyond Paris to the south that the city is removed from the artillery battle. That means that they are then forced to leave us a wide bridgehead over the Seine, thus endangering the defense of the Lower Seine as well. They will therefore once again make a stand in the "Defense Position!"

The Army Command wants the XIV Motorized Army Corps [Panzer Corps Wietersheim] pulled out and directed around behind, or via Noyon, to the XVI Motorized Army Corps [Panzer Corps Hoepner], in order to then employ the assembled *Panzergruppe* Kleist to drive through Soissons-Château-Thierry. That is not possible at present, for the XIV Motorized Army Corps is engaged against the French streaming back toward the Oise in front of the right half of the 6th Army. But I consider it wrong in itself to direct the corps, which is later to be committed forward of the Oise and the Aisne, around through Noyon, then to send it forward over the two rivers on the few, clogged roads, instead of sending it in its previous direction behind the retreating enemy through Creil and Verberie and in this way catching him just beyond the Aisne. Salmuth also tried to bring *General* Mieht of the Army High Command around to this way of thinking.

Army Group A has finally joined the attack. But we must fight the major battle alone.

Drove to the Headquarters of the V [Ruoff] and XXXXIV [Koch, F.] Army Corps.

10/6/40

4th Army has reached the Seine, has taken the part of Rouen lying north of the river, and established a bridgehead near Andelys. The army intends to try and catch the English and French still holding on the Bethune by turning the panzer corps to the north.

6th Army is pressing forward on the entire front and its left wing has reached the Marne with advance detachments, as has the 9th Army.

Brauchitsch called in the morning: the XIV Motorized Army Corps is to be pulled out and sent through Noyon; as well, elements are eventually to link up with the XVI Motorized Army Corps by way of Compiègne. I had to point out that given the very difficult road and bridge conditions and the overcrowding of the roads, subsequent forward movement by the corps will take a long time. Brauchitsch was impatient and said that Reichenau had already twice caused difficulties, this was the third time! But in fact Reichenau was right and the mistake lay with the party which now for the second time was pulling the panzer corps out at the moment when the fruits of a protracted battle were finally beginning to ripen.

Asked for my assessment of the overall situation opposite the army group's front, I outlined what I wrote yesterday. I added:

"Whether I receive orders to take Paris or not, I have to take the group of hills at Luzarches and Dammartin, because it is impossible to march past this commanding position and because it is just as impossible to take Paris from the north or west without these hills in our hands. Also I'll never know what is going on behind the line of hills if I never stand on them myself."

Brauchitsch said that he "had nothing against it!"

Then the possibility of employing Headquarters, 18th Army, which had meanwhile become superfluous up north, was discussed briefly. To Brauchitsch's question, how I explained the rapid withdrawal by the French who had previously fought with such determination, I replied that in the days to come the enemy would fight much harder and more decisively than it perhaps at first appeared.

I am very glad that they didn't restrain me in taking the "Paris Defense Position," for I apparently rate the purely military, the operational significance of Paris much higher than does the Army Command. Should the enemy abandon the city after the loss of the "Defense Position," I will pursue quickly and strongly – using the numerous bridges over the Seine in Paris – and soon the Lower Seine too will be untenable for the enemy – and thus his last connection with the "Channel" will be lost to him!

Drove to the command posts of the 98th [Schroeck] and 62nd [Keiner] Divisions, which are engaged east of the Compiègne Forest south of the Aisne. The 62nd Division was taking flanking fire from the Compiègne Forest; but I didn't get the impression that the enemy there was determined to fight to the finish. Instead heat and unbearable dust are making life difficult for the field units.

Orders came in the afternoon that Headquarters, 18th Army is to be inserted between the 4th and 6th Armies. The order also spoke of consideration being given to exploiting 4th Army's success for a further advance across the Seine. I telephoned Halder and told him that according to air and signals reconnaissance the enemy was moving what appeared to be strong forces out of the Le Mans area to the northeast. Whether he merely intended to shore up his badly-battered troops on the Seine and near Paris, or whether he still had the courage and strength for wide-ranging ideas, I did not know. In any case, I had to consider very carefully whether a lone advance across the Seine by the 4th Army was yet justified. As the army has meanwhile won several bridgeheads across the river, it can enlarge them so that it can resume the offensive without loss of time as soon as the moment to do so arrives. Halder agreed with every point.

Italy has declared war on the western powers!

11/6/40

Drove to Caulaincourt to see Reichenau and discussed with him the insertion of Headquarters, 18th Army. Naturally he is saddened that at the very moment when, after heavy crises and battles, Paris has come within sight of his army, another is being deployed against it, and with troops most of whom were formerly under Reichenau's command. He was nevertheless friendly and courteous at that moment, for which I thought highly of him.

In the afternoon the Commander-in-Chief of the 18th Army [Küchler] arrived; we discussed the employment and objectives of his army; he assumes command tonight.

The 9th Army's 25th Division [Clößner, XVIII Army Corps] has won a bridgehead across the Marne west of Château-Thierry. I at once dispatched the XVI [Panzer] Corps there and sent *General* von Kleist [XXII Motorized Army Corps] to the XVIII Army Corps by the quickest route to prepare for the employment of the panzer corps. Hasse was sent here by aircraft with orders for all participants, so that – without losing a moment – the XVI Motorized Army Corps, with the XIV Motorized Army Corps positioned close behind it, can attack south from the bridgehead.

It is becoming ever clearer that the battle at the Somme is a very heavy defeat for the French. The number of prisoners has surpassed 60,000 and, like the number of captured guns, is steadily growing. The enemy's losses in personnel have been very heavy, especially southwest of Noyon, where his retreat stalled at the blown Oise bridges and was taken in the flank by the pursuing XIV Motorized Army Corps.

"If I Had a Free Hand..."

In my frequent conversations with the Army Command I brought up the subject of whether, in view of these facts, I should really be seeking the enemy in the direction of attack assigned to me, namely in the southeast, or if we should not take into consideration his turn back to the southwest beyond the Seine. If I had a free hand I would first of all go straight south in order to completely smash the enemy by the shortest route and then turn to where the main body of forces left to him are. Opposite my front I suspect that these forces are regrouping beyond the Seine. These considerations are acute, because the direction of attack for the Kleist Corps [XXII Motorized Army Corps] depends on them.

12/6/40

The right wing of the 4th Army has succeeded in encircling the enemy between Bethune and the Seine. A French commanding general, three French and one English division commanders and about 26,000 men have been captured. Here too the English have once again saved themselves, but were caught by Stukas while being evacuated from the coast.

Further bridgeheads have been established across the Marne on the army group's left wing.

I drove to Headquarters, XVIII Corps [Speck, from 5 May to 15 June 1940] and to the Marne bridge at St. Pere, where I found elements of the 4th Panzer Division busily crossing a military bridge erected during the night. Happily the division commander, Stever, was back up front again. On the way I met the commanding general of the XXVIII Army Corps, *General* von Speck, then drove to the headquarters of the 25th Division [Clößner], to congratulate the unit on its successes of recent days. Subsequently to Kleist, who was very happy about his mission and full of confidence.

The roads between the few repaired bridges over the Aisne and the Marne are so hopelessly clogged that it is hard to understand how the XVI Motorized Army Corps managed to get through and how the XIV Motorized Army Corps is to get through!

In the evening I once again spoke with Halder about the Kleist Group's direction of attack. Personally he shares my view that Kleist has to go after them beyond the Seine from the start and thus should be committed toward Romilly. But Brauchitsch wants the direction to be toward Sezanne, because he hopes to catch even stronger French elements now retreating before Army Group A. I wriggled out of it by ordering Kleist to first take Sezanne, but then to advance across the line Nogent sur Seine-Romilly sur Seine and west – or to the south!

Paris Falls

13/6/40

Drove to Headquarters, 18th Army at Fitz James near Clermont. When I arrived news came that the enemy had abandoned the Paris Defense Position after a short, sharp battle! The attack by the VIII Army Corps across the Oise against the position's western cornerpost and by the 62nd Divison against the northeast corner made this decision easier for the French. An ambitious anti-tank battalion is already in Le Bourget! I ordered 18th Army to follow up at once and take possession of the general line Meuland-south of Versailles-ponds near Vigeneux-Brie Comte Robert-Fontenoy. The most vital parts of Paris are to be occupied by just one division at first. I called special attention to the rigorous sealing off and monitoring of through roads, so that no man lags behind in Paris and the march through the city results in no delaying of the general movement. I called Salmuth [Chief of Staff, Army Group B] and asked him to advise the Army Command of my orders. Like the surrender of the Dutch and the Belgian Armies, today I did not get the impression that the Army Command was especially happy about the fall of Paris. Even those "up above" are now thinking about turning southwest. At first the Army Com-mand specified the direction of attack for the Army Group [B] as south in a verbal directive; the idea of later turning to the southwest was expressed, and in conjunction with this 4th Army was given authorization to strike out across the Seine. I immediately sent the I [Both] and X [Hansen] Army Corps, alto-gether five divisions, to the [4th] Army. Two of these I subordinated to the army so that it now had – apart from its fast forces – nine divisions at its disposal, followed by three more as my reserve. The result was an army right wing strong enough for any eventuality.

14/6/40

In the morning to Le Bourget, where I greeted the leading elements of the 9th Division [9th Rifle Brigade, Apell], then into Paris to the Place de la Concorde; there a march past by elements of the 9th Division. The French "acting" commander of Paris, a general, found his way to me with his adju-tant. I told him that I assumed that he would see to the maintenance of vital services and order in the interests of the population of Paris until the German authorities took over.

The French historian Herbert R. Lottman wrote in his publication "The Fall of Paris 1940":

14/6/40... On this day Oberst Hans Speidel was sent into the city by General Fedor von Bock to set up the military administration. He soon decided that the Parisians were relieved by the sight of the Germans, for their presence meant that they would not destroy the city." (Lottman, Herbert R., "The Fall of Paris 1940," Piper, Munich/Zurich, 1994, PP 425)

He said that was the reason why he had stayed on. He went on to express his astonishment at our entry, having had no idea that it was so imminent! Reviewed troops of the 8th [Koch-Erpach] and 28th [Sinnhuber] Divisions as they marched past the Arc de Triumphe. Afterward I then drove to see Napoleon's tomb in the Invalide Cathedral then had a very good breakfast at the Ritz.

Paris is rather empty; apparently only the poorer elements of the population stayed there. They stand around curiously by the roads leading into the city and voluntarily provide information when asked. The reception from and behavior of the police is also courteous.

Compiègne

The Headquarters of the Army Group [B] has meanwhile relocated to Compiègne. There I found a new directive from the Army Command; Army Group B is to drive the enemy across the Loire and force him away from the coast – left wing from Provins toward Gien. Army Group A [Rundstedt] is also to send its right wing toward Gien and with its left wing destroy the enemy forces in eastern France. The 9th Army [Strauß] is to be transferred from me to Army Group A.

15/6/40

The enemy is retreating on the army group's entire front; I don't think he will make another stand before the Loire. Advance forces are staying on his heels; Army Group B, spread apart by unbroken fighting and marching, is closing ranks at the Seine and, east of Paris, at the Marne. Even Kluge, who previously pressed forward vigorously, now says that he can not now "dash off that way."

At my request I was relieved of guarding the coast, at least as far as the mouth of the Somme. There was still no one in Abbeville when, in the afternoon, a report was received from Air Fleet 2 that the English were landing there. I didn't believe it and it would be all the better if it were true. 4th Army was informed just in case and the air fleet was asked to verify the report.

Drove to Headquarters, 4th Army, where I discussed the operation against the Loire with the Chief of Staff [Brennecke].

Meanwhile Salmuth had telephoned the army and informed it that the Army Command was demanding the occupation of all the seaports in Brittany by motorized troops and had changed 4th Army's direction of advance to Le Mans! Correct! I considered the previously-given direction toward Blois to be in error.

In the evening I drove to the cease-fire memorial of 1918 in the forest of Compiègne and was disgusted by the lack of dignity of the inscription.

16/6/40

Drove to see the military commander of Paris, *General* von Bockelberg. There I spoke with Reichenau [6th Army] about the continuation of operations.

Unfortunately the 30th Division [Briesen], which was to follow behind the seam between the 4th and 18th Armies as my reserve, has been halted at Paris on orders of the Army Command, probably for "parade reasons."

I spoke with Halder about operations by the 4th Army. We agreed on the direction of its main body, but things were hazy regarding the panzer corps. If the panzer corps is split up to "speedily" occupy six different ports, nothing will be left of it. In my opinion we first have to reach the Loire, and as quickly as possible. As far as I am concerned, the important port of Cherbourg can be taken as soon as we're standing at the Loire. As well, by then it will have become apparent what is happening with the seaports and how they are to be assessed.

The Army Command is already worrying about my right flank again! There can only be two or three enemy divisions hidden in the hills around

Flers. So what! And anyway I consider that to be out of the question. What is true, unfortunately, is that 4th Army has taken the cavalry divisions from the wrong, meaning its eastern, wing and can't be talked out of it; I therefore had to apply gentle pressure to correct this.

In the afternoon an advance detachment of the 33rd Division under the command of the division commander [Sintzenich] reached Orleans and found an intact bridge there. Verdun has fallen to Army Group A; the Maginot Line was breached near Saarbrücken, the Rhine crossed at Colmar.

17/6/40

The French government has fallen; a new one has been formed by Marshall Petain. It is seeking to contact the German government by way of Spain in order to negotiate a cease-fire. – Several years before the war the Chief of the German General Staff, *General* Beck, visited Paris and called on Marshall Petain; the gist of what he said to him was: You will see much here that you don't like. But that is not France. The real France is different!

Forward elements have reached the Loire on the left half of the 18th Army and the entire front of the 6th Army. The 4th Army, quite naturally, is lagging a day's march behind.

The tremendous march performances of the past weeks can only be explained by the fact that the divisions have greatly increased their mobility through the maximum use of bicycles and captured vehicles of every type. Nevertheless, the "advance detachments" often display very moderate fighting strength; their successes are attributable to their speed and the vigorous actions of their leaders together with the rapidly dwindling fighting morale of the French.

In the afternoon came an order from the *Führer* to continue the pursuit with all vigor; it also stated that the occupation of Cherbourg and Brest were "obligations of honor" to the army. Half of the Hoth Panzer Corps [XV Motorized Army Corps], which has just gained ground in front of the 4th Army, will therefore be sent toward Cherbourg and half toward Brest.

In the evening Halder, when asked, revealed that in the subsequent course of operations the left wing of the Army Group [B] is to turn sharply southwest toward Rochefort by way of Issodun!

18/6/40

18th and 6th Armies have reached the Loire everywhere, elements of the 18th Army are already across. 4th Army is still lagging behind; as per orders the Hoth Panzer Corps has wheeled toward Cherbourg and Brest. Isolated French divisions continue to defend themselves bravely, others throw their weapons away and declare a cease-fire.

I drove to Orleans to the 33rd Division and there was able to congratulate its commanding officer on his success of the previous day. Scenes of chaos between Paris and Orleans; an endless line of French troop trains with entrained batteries, munitions and rations trains, loaded and unloaded, all jammed together. On the roads long columns of prisoners, refugees and returnees, some in pitiable condition; a picture of total collapse!

In the evening I learned that *General* von Speck, Commanding General of XVIII Army Corps, was killed on 15 June [successor: Boehme]. The death of this brave soldier is a heavy loss.

The Headquarters of Army Group B has moved to Versailles. We have taken up residence in the Hotel Trianon, which was where the German delegation stayed during the peace negotiations in 1919. The offices are in the prefecture, the German "Grand Headquarters" of 1870-71.

The *Führer* is meeting with Mussolini today.

19/6/40

The Army Group [B] has continued to advance toward and across the Loire. 7th Panzer Division [Rommel] has taken Cherbourg after a fight; about 20,000 prisoners. The number of prisoners taken by the army group usually exceeds the attackers by a factor of more than two!

20/6/40

Brest has been taken by elements of the Hoth Panzer Corps [XV Motorized Army Corps].

During the night orders came that the Army Group [B] is to take and hold a narrow corridor to the Spanish coast "immediately." To this end Kleist [XXII

Motorized Army Corps] was sent to me again with two panzer and two motorized SS divisions. The 6th Army is to stand fast at the Cher.

The French cease-fire commission was supposed to passed through the lines near Tours in the afternoon and be sent on to Paris. It had not appeared by evening; on the contrary, the French fired at our officers who stood by with white flags to receive the commission.

21/6/40

The commission passed through our lines during the night.

The movements ordered yesterday have begun. The enemy is still defending himself in places on the Loire and the Lower Cher. The bridgeheads across the Loire were expanded; the 18th Army reached the Vienne, the 6th Army is holding its position as per orders.

The 4th Army has taken Lorient. The number of prisoners and amount of booty continue to grow, at Cherbourg it has climbed to 30,000 men. The 6th Army found 700 brand-new French tanks in a factory.

The plight of the refugees is worsening. The French government did its people a great disservice when it not only allowed the mass flight of the population, but abetted it with horror stories.

22/6/40

A demarcation line has been laid down. Movements toward this line by the 4th and 18th Armies continue as planned, isolated pockets of French resistance here and there.

The French delegates have signed the cease-fire terms at Compiègne. Suspension of hostilities is not to take effect until six hours after the Italian terms are also accepted. The French are said to have expected and also acknowledged tough terms, because the German Armed Forces have honorably won the right to impose them. But as soon as talk turned to the Italians, they are said to have openly displayed anger and disgust.

23/6/40

My most forward unit, the 1st Motorized Reconnaissance Battalion, has reached the provisional demarcation line Rozan-Angoulême.

24/6/40

The Kleist Corps [XXII Motorized Army Corps] also reached the demarcation line today; there was no resistance. All remaining forces closed ranks and rested.

The "Commanding Admiral France" [Schuster] arrived to establish contact with me. So far his forces consist of his and several other headquarters.

The End of the French Campaign

25/6/40

The French have signed the Italian terms. Hostilities cease at 01:35 tonight.

I issued the following order to my armies:

"The war with France is over!

In 44 days the Army Group has overrun the Dutch and Belgian land fortifications, forced the armies of both states to surrender after a tough struggle, and in a bloody battle inflicted a destructive defeat on the Anglo-French armies hastening to the scene; Paris and the coasts of France are in our hands.

The number of prisoners taken on the army group's front has exceeded 1 1/2 million men. The booty in tanks, guns and weapons of all kinds is huge.

Shoulder to shoulder with the Luftwaffe, we have won a victory whose beauty and scope is unsurpassed in history.

The young German Army has passed its severest test before the whole world, before history and before itself. The distress and disgrace that descended over our people after the World War has been blotted out by your loyalty and bravery!

The main burden of bloody sacrifice was borne by the German Army. We will bear it proudly and willingly in firm belief in ultimate and total victory! Long live the *Führer*!"

26/6/40

Orders came to occupy the strip of coast south of Gironde to the Spanish border. At the request of the French government, Bordeaux is to remain free until 1 June so that it can move from there to Clermont-Ferrand in some peace.

Regrouping of the Army

Yesterday evening the Army Command released orders for the armed forces to face England, for the regrouping of the Western Army for this task, and for the occupation of French territory. The 6th Army is to move to Army Group A [Rundstedt]. Army Group B has been left with the inglorious task of occupying an unfortunate land. Salmuth drove to see Halder in hopes of getting us included in any action against England. Unfortunately the talk led only to disagreements instead of practical results!

28/6/40

Russia has occupied Bessarabia and a part of the Bukovina.

The English have dropped bombs on German territory in scattered raids with the obvious purpose of making the population nervous, and they succeeded in the hardest-hit areas, such as on the Rhine. True we have attacked England from the air here and there, but never with concentrated force; the reorganization of the Luftwaffe has not yet reached that stage. The *Führer* is "said" to have made a generous peace offer to England.

Orders arrived for reorganization of the army. Fifteen divisions are going to Eastern Germany to show to Russia in a friendly way that we are still there; several divisions are to be disbanded; the number of armored and motorized divisions is going to be increased considerably. The rest of the army is to remain in France – I am to keep watch on the Atlantic between Brest and the Spanish border with two weak armies and see to it that the coast isn't carried away and the demarcation line isn't stolen!

End of June 1940 – Beginning of July 1940

The Army Group [B] is regrouping itself according to orders from the Army Command. Much is still unclear, such as regulation of the defense of the coast, conditions of command on the coast, conduct at the demarcation line and more. Discussions with the Army Command and with *Admiral* Schuster go back and forth.

The English Channel Islands of Guernsey and Jersey were occupied by a battalion of the 216th Division; it arrived by air and met no resistance.

The French government is going to Vichy. One repeatedly hears rumors of peace discussions with England. – All does not appear to be proceeding as desired with the civilian administration in Holland; demonstrations are said to have taken place there; a division of the SS is being sent to Holland.

3/7/40

The English and French are clashing over the French Fleet. The English have demanded that the French scuttle those of their ships that are outside the British sphere of influence and threaten to shoot if the French do not go along. The French have refused outright; there has been fighting between elements of the English and French fleets at Oran.

In the evening my former army commanders ate with me along with their chiefs of staff and those of the army group's commanding generals who could attend. After dark there was a big tatoo in front of Versailles Palace. The troops approached doing the parade step; the tattoo began with "Now All Give Thanks To God"; three Prussian marches followed; concluded with taps and prayer. To me, and probably to many others, this was the most beautiful and solemn military ceremony of my life.

Refugee and Feeding Problems

4/7/40

Talk with Halder concerning worries about refugees and feeding the people. I pointed out that the harvest was at the point of ripening in France. Some of the forage crop had already been lost. There was now no time for any large-scale organization, because the practical effect would last too long. I therefore proposed that we no longer interfere with the streams of returnees, but instead let them carry on. Experience had shown that everyone would get back to where they belonged much more quickly this way. The farmer's first concern on returning home is seeing to it that he and his children do not go hungry, which means getting the harvest in. To what degree the former regulation of refugees had affected the political question of the population I could not say. But I believe that the question of feeding the population has to take precedence over everything else at the moment. – Halder replied: he has also been giving thought to this problem. One problem is that the most difficult areas to feed, the large cities, have in many cases suffered such destruction that the population cannot be allowed in until the supply of water and food at least have been assured at least in broad outlines. I replied that that applied here and there in my area of jurisdiction, with the exception of Paris which of course played a special role, but not to the extent that could change the basic lines of my proposal.

Halder promised to reexamine the matter once again and hoped to be able to bring about a decision that would give the army groups more of a free hand in these matters than before.

I characterized the second question, that of the speedy release of skilled agricultural workers in particular, to return to Germany, as especially urgent. I proposed ordering that they be sent on leave immediately. Halder answered that the urgency of the matter was clear to him. Such an extensive leave program was above all a problem of transport. I replied that I would take it upon myself to solve the transportation problem in the area of my army group if I was assured that the Quartermaster-General would not deny me the fuel necessary for the trucks with which to transport the men going on leave.

Halder promised to look at this question too and would also try to obtain a free hand for the army groups in this regard.

5/7/40

I am driving almost daily to one of the divisions which is leaving my area of command as a result of the reorganization of the army.

France has broken off relations with England; she has ordered her fleet to consider all English ships as hostile. The government of France has asked its German counterpart to temporarily ignore the paragraph of the cease-fire agreement which requires France to disarm her fleet and to allow French ships to pass through the Strait of Gibraltar. Both were agreed to.

Furthermore the French government has announced that it intends to constitute itself on authoritarian, social and "anti-plutocratic" bases!

7/7/40

Aircraft of "unknown nationality" have bombed Gibraltar!

Halder informed me that the blockade on returnees at the Loire has been lifted and that it will be lifted at the Seine in a few days. I spoke to the armies and called attention to the direct interest that we have in getting in the French harvest; we may not wait for a "big organization" from the Quartermaster-General to bring in the harvest; the field forces have to help wherever necessary. All that counts for all harvest measures is common sense.

9/7/40

Drove to Berlin.

Promoted to Field Marshall

19/7/40

Reichstag, with a major speech by the *Führer*, in which he once again extended a hand to England. In the second part of his speech the *Führer* warmly thanked the Armed Forces. The Army received its full due in this undoubtedly well-considered speech. Göring was named "*Reichsmarschall*" and the commanders in chief of the army groups and the two western air fleets were promoted to Field Marshall to loud applause from the house.

On 27 July 1940 the German Crown Prince congratulated von Bock on his promotion to the rank of Field Marshall. (See Jonas, Klaus W.: Der Kronprinz Wilhelm, Frankfurt am Main, 1942, PP 265.)

21/7/40

Returned as far as Paris.

22/7/40

Drove to Château Serrant near Angers, to where the Headquarters of my Army Group [B] had relocated. Salmuth had drawn up a company from my old regiment, a company of the Army Signals Regiment and the Headquarters Staff and welcomed me with a very warm speech. In my reply I was at last able to present him with the Knight's Cross before the assembled troops.

Received the first orders in preparation for the attack on England.

The 6th Army [Reichenau] was returned to Army Group B, so that I now have under my command the 6th, 4th [Kluge] and 7th [Dollmann] Armies.

28/7/40

Drove to the 44th Division [Siebert] at La Rochelle.

30/7/40

From the Army High Command came further directives for the England operation.

Drove to Headquarters, 4th Army at La Baule.

2/8/40

Drove to Dinard to Headquarters, 6th Army; I subsequently visited St. Malo and the wonderful Mont St. Michel on the Brittany Coast.

6/8/40

Drove to the 46th Division [Kriebel] at Tours and the demarcation line. Things have practically reached the point there where we are not deciding who crosses, but what the French are doing. There is in fact no control over who goes in and out there. It could only be done effectively if it were done at the demarcation line itself and if all the checkpoints were manned by people – with sufficient assistants – who were in a position to check people passing through and their reasons for doing so. The Military Administration of France, in whose hands these things lie, is not in a position to provide the necessary personnel – neither according to number or to suitability.

8/8/40

I have issued instructions that the maximum possible number of the divisions not earmarked for England also receive training for the crossing.

9/8/40 – 11/8/40

Drove to Headquarters, 7th Army in Bordeaux, Headquarters, XXXI Army Corps in Cognac, to Headquarters, I Army Corps and the 1st Division in Biarritz and to the 11th Division at Hossegort. Also part of the trip was a brief excursion to Spain – Irun and St. Sebastian.

12/8/40 – 13/8/40

The *Führer* presented us with our Field Marshall's batons in the Reich Chancellery. He gave a short speech, in which he thanked us for what we had achieved. He stressed the importance of the continued unity of the German people and how inevitable it is that the German Armed Forces, too, declare themselves fully in favor of the National-Socialist ideal.

After the breakfast that followed, the *Führer* gave a very thorough and clear talk on the situation and the possible developments in the east and west. He is considering a landing in England only as a last resort, if all other means of persuasion fail. Italy and Japan are firmly allied with us. America's attitude does not frighten him; it will be a long time before its aid to England can make itself felt. Russia had once shown a tendency to go beyond the agreements with us, however at the moment she is loyal. But should she prepare to crush Finland or attack Romania we would be forced to intervene. Russia must not be allowed to become the sole master of the Eastern Baltic and we need the

Romanian oil. But perhaps sending a German General with a "provocative" name to the east would be enough to keep Russia quiet.

17/8/40 – 18/8/40

Returned to Brussels via Serrant.

24/8/40

Took part in a landing exercise by the 31st Division [Kalmukoff] at Cancale [east of St. Malo] and drove to the 12th Reconnaissance Battalion at Carentan.

27/8/40

The chain of command in case of an attempted landing in England is so unclear that things cannot stay as they are. The Army, Navy and Air Force are all running things on the coast at the same time. The Navy has deployed 17 entire batteries on my area's more than 1,000 kilometers of coastline. Therefore, on my own responsibility I have ordered that as soon as army troops are committed to meet an enemy attack the responsible army commander is to assume command of all elements of the armed forces deployed in the affected sector.

28/8/40

Drove to the 255th Division at St. Gilles.

"To The East"

31/8/40

In the evening orders came that the Headquarters of the Army Group is going to the east. Headquarters, 4th Army [Kluge], several corps headquarters and divisions are going with it. What else will come under my command there and what my mission is I do not yet know. To begin with my role over there is probably nothing more than to act as a scarecrow against any sort of Russian ambition.

1/9/40

I met Brauchitsch at the Headquarters of the 4th Army in La Baule. As yet he has go directives of any sort for the east. It appears that he, too, hasn't a clear picture of the overall situation and plans, perhaps the decisions by the political leadership are not firm yet. – I have the impression that our air attacks on England have only begun to really "go" in recent days. Before the Luftwaffe was hampered by the weather. But if a profound effect is achieved against the Royal Air Force and its production sites, it can only be of decisive importance if it is exploited before the English have recovered with American help. So that means: this autumn! But will the weather hold that long? Will the Navy, which began its preparations so late, be ready in time?

It is becoming ever more obvious that the Americans want to "get into" the war against us. This is stiffening the backbone of the English, so that I don't believe there will be any backing down until England is finished. Whether this end can be achieved by air, submarine and mine warfare alone I cannot estimate, because I lack the necessary information.

The first orders for departure for the east have arrived. Army Group C is taking over my former area of command.

Brauchitsch has said that the military administration is to remain in place in the east. That means that neither I nor the commanders of the armies are to receive "executive authority." I find that entirely correct in itself. It is disquieting, however, that this ruling might lead to a foggy chain of command; since at present the military administration and the Commander of the Replacement Army have certain command rights over the military area headquarters and replacement troops which will be part of my area of command, I have requested in writing that the chain of command be put in order so that there can be no confusion and that powers be clearly defined; I enclosed a positive proposal.

11/9/40

Army Group C, *Generalfeldmarschall* von Leeb, assumed command in my former area.

Left for Berlin via Brussels. Accommodations in Posen pose problems as the city is swamped with troops and agencies. Headquarters going to Berlin until everything is clear over there.

CHAPTER FOUR

20 SEPTEMBER 1940 to 21 JUNE 1941
(PREPARATIONS FOR THE OFFENSIVE IN THE EAST)

Commander-in-Chief Army Group B

The German Reich and its European allies mustered a tremendous military potential in well-armed and technically well-equipped troops for the invasion of the USSR. 153 German divisions, 33 of them armored or motorized, were mobilized in accordance with the "Barbarossa" plan; apart from 24 German divisions which formed the OKH reserve, these were concentrated along the western border of the USSR.

There were three main assault groups arrayed from the Baltic Sea to the Carpathians; this area formed 40 percent of the Soviet land border in the west and contained 70 percent of all the country's divisions, 75 percent of its artillery and mortars, and 90 percent of its tanks and combat aircraft. The military aims were to smash the main forces of the Soviet frontier districts in the territory extending to the Dvina and the Dniepr as quickly as possible and pave the way for the advance by German forces into the depth of Soviet territory to the nation's political and economic centers of Moscow, Leningrad, and the Donets Basin.

Army Group North, commanded by Generalfeldmarschall Wilhelm Ritter von Leeb, concentrated in the direction of Leningrad, was ordered to destroy the Soviet forces in the Baltic States and deprive the Soviet Baltic Fleet of its bases by capturing the Baltic ports, including Kronstadt and Leningrad.

The objective of the strongest grouping, Army Group Center under Generalfeldmarschall Fedor von Bock, was to smash the Soviet forces in Byelorussia and subsequently continue to attack in the direction of Smolensk and Moscow.

Army Group South under Generalfeldmarschall Gerd von Rundstedt was to attack in the direction of Kiev with the objective of destroying the Soviet forces in the Western Ukraine, take possession of the Dniepr crossings in the area of Kiev and to its south and pave the way for an attack east of the Dniepr.

The invasion of the USSR was planned as a "blitz" campaign of the most extreme harshness. The destruction of the Soviet Union was to have been completed by the start of the winter of 1941-42.

20/9/40

Army Group Headquarters has assumed command in the east but for the time being is remaining in Berlin, mainly because installation of the essential telephone lines to and from Posen is not finished yet.

22/9/40

I have to go to bed on account of an old stomach problem, which has become downright uncomfortable, but for now I am continuing to run things.

21/10/40

My illness has taken such a turn for the worse that I have had to hand over command of the army group to a temporary replacement, *Generalfeldmarschall* List. The Headquarters is now moving to Posen [HQ Army Group Center].

Halder Diary, 26/10/40, PP 151: "Von Bock sent on sick leave until the beginning of December."

1. This villa at Heideparkstraße 8, Dresden housed Fedor von Bock's office from 1 March 1938 until 10 November 1939 (photo taken sometime in 1938).

2. Generalleutnant von Bock, his wife, two stepdaughters Annemarie and Karin and his stepson Dinnies von der Osten in the garden of his villa in Dresden.

3. Central German motor-transport exercise at the Grafenwöhr Troop Training Grounds (Upper Pfalz, July 1935). From left to right: von Blomberg, Hitler, Beck, von Bock.

4. On the occasion of the 224th birthday of Frederick the Great, creator of the Order Pour le Mérite, the Knights of the Order lay wreaths at the monument and memorial to the former Kaiser. Generalfeldmarschall von Mackensen (center left) and General der Infanterie von Bock (to his right) make their way to the memorial after laying a wreath at the monument to Frederick the Great (24 January 1938).

5. Fedor von Bock in Vienna after the entry into Austria in March 1938; his promotion to Generaloberst followed on 15 March 1938; at that time the Pour le Mérite was the only decoration worn at his throat.

6. Hitler takes the report from Generaloberst Fedor von Bock during the 8th Army's big parade in Heroes Square in Vienna, 16 March 1938.

7. *The 8th Army parades past Hitler in Heroes Square in Vienna; next to him on his left is Generaloberst von Bock (18 March 1938).*

8. *On 27 March 1938 Generalfeldmarschall Göring honored the dead of the old Austrian Army by laying a wreath at the memorial in Heroes Square in Vienna. Afterward he took the march past of the Wehrmacht Honor Guard in the Burghof; standing to the right of Göring are the Commander-in-Chief of the 8th Army, Generaloberst Fedor von Bock and Reich Administrator Seyß-Inquart.*

9. *Modern international pentathlon for officers in Dresden (1938); when the winners were announced the leader of the Swedish team, Captain Thofeldt, stepped forward and on behalf of Gustav Adolf of Sweden handed a silver goblet for the best pentathlete to Generaloberst Fedor von Bock for presentation to Oberleutnant Lemp.*

10. *Retired Generalleutnant Heß (left) and Generaloberst Fedor von Bock (10 August 1938).*

11. Generaloberst Fedor von Bock, Commander-in-Chief of the German troops that marched into the Sudetenland, in the marketplace of Schluckenau (2 October 1938).

12. Generaloberst Fedor von Bock (center) is welcomed by Lord Mayor Rohn (left) on the steps of Reichenberg city hall (9 October 1938).

13. *Generaloberst Fedor von Bock, Commander-in-Chief of Army Group 1 (17 January 1939).*

14. *Led by Generaloberst von Bock and General der Infanterie von Comta, Knights of the Pour le Mérite make their way to the monument to Frederick the Great (24 January 1939).*

15. *Former Chief of the Army Command Generaloberst Heye celebrates his 70th birthday on 31 January 1939; Generaloberst Fedor von Bock offers congratulations on behalf of the armed forces.*

16. *Prince Regent Paul of Yugoslavia reviews the Wehrmacht Honor Battalion; beside him to the left Generaloberst von Bock and Generalleutnant Seifert (2 June 1939).*

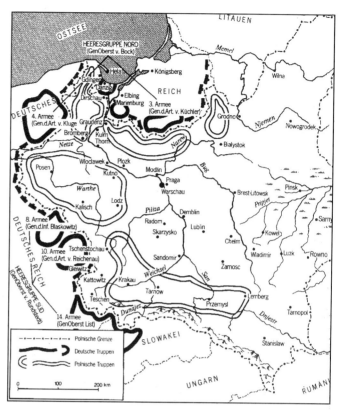

17. End of August 1939, strategic concentration of the German armies against Poland.

18. Hitler in conversation with Generaloberst von Bock, the Commander-in-Chief of Army Group North, which was formed for operations in Poland (25 September 1939).

19. Prior to the campaign against France Josef Goebbels (2nd from left) greets Generaloberst Fedor von Bock at the Hotel Dreesen in Bad Godesberg.

20. Generaloberst Fedor von Bock in his office (6 April 1940).

21. *Generaloberst Fedor von Bock and General der Artillerie Georg von Küchler arrived in The Hague for the surrender negotiations (May 1940).*

22. *Generaloberst Fedor von Bock (right) with Hitler and Generaloberst von Brauchitsch in Brussels (1 June 1940).*

23. Generaloberst Fedor von Bock with senior staff officers crossing the Marne at Chateau-Thiery (12 June 1940).

24. Generaloberst Fedor von Bock (center) in conversation with French Generals in Paris in June 1940; also present are General der Infanterie Hans Salmuth (2nd from right) and Oberleutnant Heinrich Graf Lehndorff-Steinort (3rd from right).

25. *Generaloberst Fedor von Bock (left) with his adjutant Oberleutnant Heinrich Graf Lehndorff-Steinort (mid-June 1940).*

26. *The tricolore is passed to Generaloberst Fedor von Bock in Paris; left Oberleutnant Heinrich Graf von lehndorff-Steinort (mid-June 1940).*

Facing page:
27. Generaloberst Fedor von Bock (2nd from right) at the Arc de Triumphe (mid-June 1940).

28. Bicycle unit during a march past by Generaloberst Fedor von Bock (2nd from right) at the Arc de Triumphe; 2nd from right General der Artillerie Georg von Küchler (mid-June 1940).

29. Generaloberst Fedor von Bock (center), General der Artillery Georg von Küchler (2nd from left), General Staff Officer Hans Speidel (right; later a general in the Bundeswehr), Feldwebel Wolf (driver) seen leaving the Notre Dame Cathedral in Paris (June 1940).

30. Generaloberst Fedor von Bock (4th from left) at the Place de la Concorde in Paris; march past by elements of the 9th Division (14 June 1940); postcard to his stepson Dinnies von der Osten.

*31. Generalfeld-
marschall Fedor von
Bock (June 1941).*

*32. After the campaign
in France: promotions to
Generalfeldmarschall in
the Reich Chancellery in
Berlin (19 June 1940).
Keitel, von Rundstedt,
von Bock, Göring, Hitler
von Brauchitsch, von
Leeb, List, von Kluge,
von Witzleben and von
Reichenau (from left to
right).*

Hitler Visits Bock

11/11/40

The *Führer* visited me [Berlin, Helfferichstraße], sat by my bed for a good half hour, and was very kind and concerned. We discussed the overall situation at length. He is beside himself about the Italian escapade into Greece; the Italians not only concealed it from us but even denied it when questioned. The *Führer*'s trip to Florence to attempt to prevent the disaster or at least postpone it until we could provide effective help was in vain; Mussolini declared that the action was under way and could not be halted. The immediate, most uncomfortable consequence is the threat to the Romanian oil fields posed by the Royal Air Force from Salonika. This danger is such that it might force us to take countermeasures. The *Führer*'s position on a landing in England is unchanged. – He would like to take Gibraltar; but apparently there are serious obstacles, founded partly on considerable difficulties associated with preparation and transport and partly on internal conditions in Spain. What is to happen in the east is still an open question; conditions might force us to intervene in order to head off a more dangerous development.

21/11/40

Not only has the Italian attack bogged down in Greece, but they are taking a considerable beating as well! The entire affair makes no sense politically – quite apart from the fact that it presents the English with the long-desired opportunity to occupy Crete. But even militarily I can see no advantage in their excursion to Epirus. On top of this the operation was begun without adequate preparation, with inadequate forces, based on a false assessment of the mood of the Albanian-Greek border population, and with less than brilliant planning. This recklessness may force us to commit forces in directions which are undesirable and dangerous. Greece is now open to the English.

3/12/40

The *Führer* visited me again in Berlin to wish me a happy 60th birthday. He sees the bright and dark sides of the big picture calmly and clearly. His assessment of the Greek affair has not changed. Many factors stand in the way of our intervening in the Balkans; road and rail conditions are poor, crossing the Danube will be difficult. Romania is now with us; Bulgaria is probably for us in spirit, but not solidly; Yugoslavia is allegedly afraid of Germany. – Spain has folded on the Gibraltar question! Franco has internal difficulties; apparently the Italian failure has heightened his apprehension. – The assessment of the English situation is unchanged; a landing appears to have been shelved for now. The Luftwaffe and the submarine arm, whose activities are to be stepped up considerably in the new year, are to shoulder the main burden of the war against England. – The eastern question is becoming acute. There are said to be contacts between Russia and America; a Russia-England link is therefore also likely. To wait for the outcome of such a development is dangerous. But if the Russians were eliminated, England would have no hope left of defeating us on the continent, especially since an effective intervention by America would be complicated by Japan, which would keep our rear free.

10/12/40

My former Ia, Hasse, is being transferred to the 18th Army as Chief of Staff; his successor is *Oberstleutnant* von Tresckow.

12/12/40

Now the Italians are taking a beating in Libya! I don't know if a larger offensive from Egypt into Libya is possible, if seasonal and ground conditions allow it. If that is the case, and the successful advance by the English near Sidi Barani is the prelude to it, then as I see it things look black. If the English have further success there, it is not out of the question that the French colonial army might then come to life and take the opportunity, perhaps with the urging of the "rebel" General de Gaulle, to join with the English to go after the hated Italians in Africa; they have sufficient forces in Africa to do so.

The idea of striking "the Axis" at its weakest point – Italy – and forcing that country to conclude a separate peace is certainly not a bad one. But even if England is not thinking that far ahead yet, they do know that the cheap success in Africa is raising England's sunken prestige in the world, and that the English situation in the Mediterranean becomes firmer with every step the Italians lose. No matter how the new Italian failure might turn out, it will prolong the war in any case.

"How France Lost the War"

14/12/40

In a series of articles in the *New Zurich Times* entitled "How France Lost the War," French journalist Maurois has expressed the opinion that the well-known crash-landing by the two German air officers in Belgium in the winter of 1939-40 was a stratagem. M[aurois] wrote:

"They apparently tried to burn their documents, but saw to it that they did not succeed!"

The consequence of the fabricated German attack orders was that the western powers carried out the countermeasures planned in the event of a German attack – under the watchful eye of German reconnaissance aircraft! A pity that the reality was so different!

I found Maurois' view of the fall of Paris [See: Lottmann, Herbert R., *Der Fall von Paris 1940*, Piper, Munich, 1994, PP 213, 263, 291, 429] especially interesting. He wrote:

"At that moment it was clear to me that it was all over. After the loss of Paris France had to become a body without a head. The war was lost!"

19/12/40

List called to say goodbye; he is first going to Vienna, then is to be employed in the Balkans. *Generalfeldmarschall* Kluge is taking over as my acting replacement.

21/12/40

The Berliners are "griping" – especially about the English air raids, which are of course uncomfortable but so far no more than pinpricks. It is sad and dangerous that this grumbling is also going on in educated circles. These people are always on about Old Fritz [Frederick the Great], but spiritually they are miles away from him!

Salmuth's Operational Proposal

2/1/41

Salmuth informed me that on orders from the Chief of Staff of the Army [Halder] the Chiefs of Staff of the army groups have prepared an operational study in case of a war with Russia. He outlined his operational proposal, which has apparently received the approval of Army Command, for on 24 December the OKH ordered preparations for a buildup which corresponds in general to this proposal.

5/1/41

The English are continuing to attack in Libya.

31/1/41

The Italians have taken a bad beating in Africa. – For the first time in four months I returned to duty and took part in a meeting of the Commander-in-Chief of the Army [Brauchitsch] with the Commanders-in-Chief of the army groups [Participants: Halder as Chief of Staff of the Army, Rundstedt, Witzleben, Leeb, Bock]. Brauchitsch gave a description of the situation that I did not like. He declared that the attack on England was not going to take place in the fall, because the Armed Forces High Command and the Navy began preparing for this task too late and too slowly and because the success of the air attacks on England was considerably less than the expectations of the Luftwaffe High Command. He confirmed that Italy had surprised us with its attack on Greece. Brauchitsch's proposals to take Gibraltar and intervene in Libya had unfortunately been rejected, and his suggestion to reach an amicable agreement with Greece, for which that country was surely ready, was also rejected. They have failed to reach an understanding with Spain about Gibraltar.

Tensions have arisen with France, heightened by the booting out of Minister Laval. Political intrigues have caused further problems; they very skillfully talked the Frenchman into believing that the Germans intended to use the transfer of the bones of the Duke of Reichstadt to Paris to lure Marshall Petain there and then to lock him up! – The position of the French colonies, those in the hands of the government, is unclear; Weygand is no friend of Germany, but one assumes that he follows Petain's instructions.

Brauchitsch subsequently stated that the order would be given to prepare for the struggle against Russia. The general outlines of the proposed operations were given. The OKH is proceeding from the assumption that the Russians will fight in front of the Dvina-Dniepr line. When I asked Halder whether he had information that the enemy would take a stand in front of the rivers, he said "that it might well happen otherwise."

In the afternoon the gala first screening of the film "Victory in the West," which in no way justified the money spent on it.

Hitler's Assessment of the Situation

1/2/41

I was ordered to report to the *Führer*, who received me very warmly. He once again spoke at length on the overall situation. The effects of the Italian failure are still so minor that it is difficult at the moment to base major decisions on this shaky foundation. When I asked whether there wasn't a danger that Weygand might join with the English to drive the Italians out of Africa, the *Führer* replied that it was doubtful, for Weygand is surely aware that our response would be the immediate occupation of unoccupied France. Conditions in France urgently require clarification; it is too early to say whether that can be achieved without an occupation of the rest of France. – England continues to be stubborn. The landing was not talked about. – The *Führer* justified the need to prepare for the struggle against Russia by stating that this great event would very quickly divert the world from events in Africa and present it with a new situation. "The gentlemen in England are not stupid; they just act that way" and "they will come to realize that a continuation of the war will be pointless for them if Russia too is now beaten and eliminated."

The implications for Japan and America he assessed as on 3 December [1940]. – I said that we would defeat the Russians if they stood and fought; but I raised the question of whether it would also be possible to force them to make peace. The *Führer* replied that if the occupation of the Ukraine and the fall of Leningrad and Moscow did not bring about peace, than we would just have to carry on, at least with mobile forces, and advance to Yekaterinburg.

"In any case I am glad," he said, "that we have continued to arm to the point where we are ready for anything. Materially we are well off and already have to think about a conversion of some factories. In terms of personnel the armed forces are better off than at the start of the war; economically we are absolutely solid."

The *Führer* sharply rejected any idea of backing down – without my having suggested it to him. "I will fight" and: "I am convinced that our attack will sweep over them like a hailstorm."

3/2/41

Drove to Posen, where I took over. Big reception at the station from the Commanding General, *Gauleiter*, Lord Mayor and an honor guard – which I unfortunately was unable to do anything to prevent.

The OKH's fundamental orders for the planned operations arrived.

Coup d'état with Bock?

4/2/41

Oberstleutnant Rathke of the OKH arrived to tell me about a very foolish affair:

A Staff *Oberstleutnant* appeared at the Reich Chancellery and there broached the subject that, according to his former superior, *Oberst* von C., there was great dissatisfaction with the government in the army right up to the top. For example, they had approached me with the request to change things by force! But I had refused! The whole thing is absolute rubbish!

6/2/41

Reich Governor Greisser briefed me on the situation in the Warthe District and his plans. He sees things with eyes open and his ideas are sober and clear. What he says about settlement, the Polish question, and about the desired healthy mix of large estates and small farms, makes sense.

Benghazi has been taken by the English; they claim to have taken far more than 100,000 prisoners since the start of their Libyan offensive and a huge booty in materiel. I believe that! English gains are also reported from Abyssinia and in Greece things are definitely not going the way the Italians would like.

10/2/41

Intelligence from Russia might suggest that the Russians are withdrawing forces from the frontier behind the Dvina and Dniepr. But this is in no way certain and requires continued, closer observation.

In the evening received a visit from Gienanth, commander in the Government-General [occupied Poland].

13/2/41

Generaloberst Guderian, Commander-in-Chief of Panzer Group 2, came to Posen and briefed me on a war game that he was to direct; also discussed operational questions. *General* Henrici [Waldemar, Dr.], commander of the 258th Division, reported for duty.

14/2/41

Exercise by a rocket battalion at Schrimm, where I met several of the army group's commanding generals and division commanders.

21/2/41

First meeting with the Ia of the 9th Army [Blaurock] concerning its objectives. Called attention to the necessity of attacking quickly and with surprise at Grodno and in the bend of the Narew near the frontier. – Brief meeting with the General in Charge of Rocket Troops from the OKH.

24/2/41

Tresckow returned from Berlin, after being summoned by Halder to discuss details of the army group's role in the planned operation. Apparently there are no major differences in opinion concerning the conduct of the initial operation [see also 27th March].

I welcome a possible minor broadening of my northern army, the 9th [Strauß], to the north. There is unanimity that the swamp fortress front is not to be attacked, but Halder is alone in believing that the extreme southern wing of this front can also be left alone. That will work of course; only they must be prepared to sit by and watch themselves be outflanked in their fortress front.

25/2/41

Kluge [4th Army] came. He was informed that the northern wing of his army is being extended as far as Ostroleka and that the army will be receiving one more division. The orders for the northern wing of the 4th Army are being written in such a way that the army only has to guard against the swamp fortress front, which will also not be attacked seriously by the 9th Army. The main weight of the army's attack remains on the southern wing! This does nothing to change the requirement to send in an echelon behind the northern wing, so that the army's advance is delayed as little as possible by fortress garrisons breaking out.

Kluge suggested committing Panzer Group Guderian in the initial attack, because, as Guderian also feels, it will move faster that way. Guderian is to command all agencies and troops at the panzer group's operational front, naturally under the high command of the army. Guderian has thus had a wish fulfilled. Kluge voiced concern about enemy counterattacks from the Pinsk area and proposed sending the [1st] Cavalry Division [Feldt] toward Pinsk. I am of the same view.

26/2/41

War game under Guderian's direction at Posen; theme: command of armored units.

The day before yesterday the first German troops in Libya engaged the English in combat.

27/2/41

Continuation of the war game; subsequent discussion of the planned operation. Present were the 4th Army Chief of Staff [Blumentritt], *Generaloberst* Strauß, commander 9th Army, with his Chief of Staff [Weckmann], the commanders of the two armored groups [Panzer Groups Guderian, Hoth], and the Chief of Staff of Air Fleet 2. Hoth, commander of Panzer Group 2, made difficulties, because he doesn't want infantry divisions in either his buildup area or in his attack sector. In contrast to Guderian he sees this as a complication. I could not agree with him and had to insist that three infantry divisions advance simultaneously with the panzers between and beside the armored divisions. These infantry divisions are initially to be subordinated to Hoth, so that he has the right to move them off the roads wherever they are supposed to be holding up the panzers. If I gave in to Hoth's demand, the leading infantry might not cross the border until four to five days after the tanks in Panzer Group 3's attack area, meaning the entire northern sector of the 9th Army.

28/2/41

Salmuth [Chief of Staff Army Group B] went on extended convalescent leave.

2/3/41

Today German troops marched into Bulgaria, following yesterday's official entry into the Three-Power Pact by Bulgaria.

7/3/41 - 10/3/41

Weekend in Berlin.

11/3/41

Obernitz, commander of the 293rd Division, reported to me.

Reports from spies in Lithuania speak of major Russian maneuvers in the Baltic States and claim that these maneuvers are part of a secret concentration of forces against Germany. Unbelievable! But it is certain that the Russians know of our buildup and are taking countermeasures.

12/3/41

In America the "Aid for England Law" takes effect; this means that England and her allies will be backed by all the resources of America; only the American armed forces remain to be committed.

15/3/41

Intelligence concerning Russian military measures at the border is growing stronger.

Evening of 15/3/41 - afternoon of 17/3/41

Weekend in Berlin.

Talks with Goebbels

18/3/41

Ceremonial reopening of the theater in Posen. Minister Goebbels [Reich Minister for Enlightenment of the People and Propaganda] spoke with me about the difficulties facing the propaganda program. He has realized that, in contrast to experience with the French populace, it is extraordinarily difficult to get the phlegmatic English to listen to propaganda; he also knows that Churchill is altogether popular in England and that the image of him we portray – portly, brazen and with the omnipresent cigar – is especially loved by the English.

The Italians are trying to go over to the attack in Albania, but they are so hopelessly bogged down that they don't even mention their offensive in the army report.

German officers back from Libya are dismayed at the indifference and passivity of many senior Italian officers. – The initial deployment of Panzer Group 3 for the attack is difficult. Hoth is casting his eyes beyond the Dniepr and Dvina from the very outset and is paying scant attention to the possibility of attacking and defeating enemy forces which stand and fight somewhat farther forward. But since the Army Command considers the latter likely and in its directives is demanding that the panzer groups assist in the destruction of the enemy forces in the frontier zone, I will have to reject Hoth's solution, even though there is much to be said in its favor. That won't happen without a lot of sparring. Tresckow therefore drove to Berlin to ascertain in advance whether the Army Command intends to stick to its guns.

20/3/41

Vietinghoff, Commanding General of the XXXXVI Motorized Corps [appears as XXXIX in the original], reported for duty; he raised the topic of the far from complete state of equipment of the new motorized divisions; it is so inadequate that training is suffering badly as a result.

25/3/41

Feldmarschall Kesselring, commander of Air Fleet 2, which is once again to work with the army group in the coming operations, came for the meeting. Subsequent brief talk with the Chief of Staff of the 4th Army, Blumentritt.

26/3/41

Yugoslavia joined the Three-Power Pact yesterday.
Drove to Berlin.

*Not until 1993 was the Soviet General Staff's complete war plan of 1941
against the German Reich revealed to the public in articles by Russian Colonel Valery Danilov in the Austrian Military News, No. 1/1993! The document
"Reflections on the Plan of Strategic Concentration by the Armed Forces of
the Soviet Union in Case of War with Germany and its Allies" (May 1941)
demands a historical reevaluation of the notion of aggressive-preventive war.*

*Beyond that, it must be assumed that the Soviet troop movements men-
tioned by Bock were following the intentions of this plan.*

This historically very significant document states:

*"II. The initial strategic objective of the troops of the Red Army is to
destroy the main forces of the German Army massed south of Demblin and by
the 30th day of the operation achieve a general front line of Ostroleka, Narew
River, Kreuzburg, Oppeln and Olmütz, in order to:*

*(a) Conduct the main assault with the forces of the southwestern front in
the direction of Cracow-Kattowitz and completely cut off Germany from her
southern allies;*

*(b) conduct the secondary assault with the left wing of the western front
in the direction of Siedlce-Demblin, in order to tie down the grouping of forces
around Warsaw and support the southwestern front in the destruction of the
enemy groupings of forces;*

*(c) conduct a mobile defense against Finland, East Prussia, Hungary
and Romania, in order to be ready to carry out a strike against Romania when
the situation is favorable...*

*The following measures must be implemented in a timely fashion in order
to assure the implementation of the plans outlined above, without which the
conduct of a surprise attack on the enemy from the air as well as on the main-
land is impossible...*

The People's Commissar for the Defense of the USSR
Marshall of the Soviet Union
S Timoshenko

The Chief of the General Staff of the Red Army
G. Zhukov"

[Danilov, Valery: *Did the General Staff of the Red Army Prepare a Preventive Strike against Germany?* Austrian Military Magazine, No. 1/1993, PP 43; Hoffmann, Joachim: *Stalin's War of Destruction 1941-1945*, Munich 1995, Military Science Publishers Munich.]

This is in stark contrast to the German Command's assessment of the potential of the Red Army to achieve these military-strategic objectives (See: Schulze-Wegner, Guntram: "The Red Army as Assessed by the German Command before Operation Barbarossa" in: Historical Reports, Vol. I/94, PP 102.)

27/3/41

Meeting at the OKH about the operation against Russia. Nothing but minor details! When I mentioned the matter of the linking up both of my panzer groups in the Minsk area and the difficulties of their subsequent advance from there, I received no clear statement on it, the same sort of answer Tresckow had received in Berlin recently. The question is important, for between Minsk and the "gateway to Smolensk" – the land bridge between the Dniepr and the Dvina – lie the marshes from which the Beresina springs; massing armored forces near Minsk would therefore be very detrimental to their further forward movement. – No decision yet on the Army Group's request for orders to hold the frontier in case of a Russian attack and for permission to move the necessary forces closer to the frontier. Even if there is still little to suggest the probability of a Russian attack, we can't allow ourselves to be complacent, for any advance across the frontier threatens the vast quantities of ammunition, rations and equipment stockpiled there for the offensive. As well the Luftwaffe has doubts about installing itself near the frontier if their installations there will not be secure.

Trouble in the Balkans

Military coup in Yugoslavia! The government and the regent (I had been sent to Berlin to join his entourage) have been overthrown; there have been anti-German demonstrations in Belgrade. The English have apparently spent a great deal!

Hopefully the big operation will not be delayed by the necessary clearing up of the Balkans.

28/3/41

Breakfast with the *Führer* in honor of the Japanese Foreign Minister.

Hitler On the Necessity of "Bring Down Russia"

30/3/41

The *Führer* gave a speech in the Reich Chancellery to the future army group and army commanders of the Eastern Front.

The question of a landing in England was not raised. On the other hand an English landing on the continent is not considered possible at present, primarily on account of the great shortage in shipping space. – The situation in France was characterized as still somewhat hazy; they have had to make concessions in order to prevent North Africa from breaking with the Petain government.

The *Führer* said nothing about Yugoslavia and the imminent attack on Greece, but he did speak about the "source of all evil," the failed Italian attack in Albania. He also assessed the other Italian defeats, all of which are in part the result of the Albanian operation. Nothing was said of the possibility that Italy might be forced into a separate peace. Japan was not mentioned. The possibilities of effective American support for England are not considered decisive at present. American production cannot keep pace with our growing rearmament, specifically in the area of the Luftwaffe, but also in submarines and tanks, for a long time. The *Führer* gave a detailed explanation of why we must bring Russia down; constant threat to our rear, constant threat of communism, possibility of England and America establishing a new front against us in Russia.

"The possibility now exists to strike down Russia with our own back free; such an opportunity will not soon come again. It would be a crime against the future of the German people if I did not seize the opportunity!"

The objective is the demolishing of the Russian armed forces, the destruction of Russian industry, if necessary including that in the Urals, and the severing of the Russian empire from the Baltic and the Ukraine. – The pact concluded with Russia at the start of the war cannot justify moral reservations against the attack. Stalin had entered into it voluntarily in the hope of enticing Germany into the war, so that when it was at the point of being bled dry he could fall upon it with bolshevism. In spite of numerous grounds to do so, as long as we were tied down in the west he, the *Führer*, had avoided anything that might have led to friction with Russia. But this has in no way reduced the irreconcilable differences between us and bolshevism. (Harsh action. Commissars.) All in all plans and goals which the *Führer* himself describes as gigantic.

The objections raised by Bock at this time are sometimes not clearly depicted in the relevant literature.

Hans-Adolf Jacobsen wrote in his publication "From the Strategy of Power to the Politics of Securing the Peace. Essays on the History of Germany in the Twentieth Century" that "it cannot be ascertained with certainty whether, for example, the objections raised by Generalfeldmarschall von Bock were not directed primarily against the decree issued at the same time limiting the power of courts martial in regard to 'Case Barbarossa'...which has been claimed with some justification.

Hitler's main justification for ideologizing the conduct of the war was the fact that the Soviet Union was not a signatory of the Geneva Convention (1929); from this he drew the conclusion that German prisoners of war would surely not be treated according to its provisions, and this view was supported by the behavior of the Red Army and the commissars in Poland, in the war against Finland, in the Baltic States, and in Romania.

"...Fortunately It Is also Not My Affair!"

Not having all the facts, I am not fully convinced that an Anglo-American landing is impossible. Spain, for example, is incapable of offering any sort of resistance and, as it is starving, could easily be won over with bread.

The country is an easy mark for an English or an American landing, and what is more bringing over the French colonial army from Africa would pose no great problems. I do not know whether, with our main forces occupied in the east, our weak units in France would be sufficient to prevent a landing army from linking up with unoccupied France – fortunately it is also not my affair!

In the afternoon a talk with the *Führer* over the planned Russian operation. The *Führer* went on to comment that my armored groups in particular might become decisively important in the later course of an advance on Leningrad, in order to encircle and destroy the Russian forces fighting in the Baltic region. I once again spoke of the difficulties facing a subsequent advance by the tanks out of the area assigned to me at Minsk. Brauchitsch interjected that "link-up at Minsk" was intended to mean the general area of Minsk. As I left I said to Halder:

"You have issued written orders that the panzer groups are to advance "in close contact," whereupon Halder replied with a laugh: "Spiritual contact is what we meant!" That clarified nothing.

Once again the *Führer* appeared very cordial and concerned about my health.

31/3/41

Returned to Posen.

1/4/41

General Harpe, commander of the 12th Panzer Division, reported to me. In the evening I was joined by *Gauleiter* Greisser.

Entry in Halder's diary, dated 2/4/41, PP 341: "Call from Field Marshall von Bock: Gienanth has exhausted every possible avenue in efforts to influence the SS in the Government-General. Requests intervention by the OKH in order to get his way in the question of evacuating quarters."

6/4/41

The German attack on Yugoslavia and Greece has begun. The OKH has gone to the southeastern theater in order to direct the operation itself.

7/4/41

Large-scale "smoke exercise" [cover designation for rocket units] at the Warthelager practice grounds in the presence of numerous generals from the entire army.

9-10/4/41

War game under my direction with the Commanders-in-Chief of the 4th [Kluge] and 9th [Strauß] Armies, the leaders of the panzer groups [Guderian, Hoth] and the Commanding Generals of the corps which are to take part in the operation as part of the army group.

Very nice successes in Serbia and Greece, and surprising success by our weak units in Africa.

The English have become very bold in the air; in recent days they have twice attacked Kiel and yesterday Berlin successfully with a large number of aircraft. In spite of assurances to the contrary, our defenses don't seem to be much to write home about; in any case the numbers of enemy aircraft shot down are quite modest.

11/4/41 - 15/4/41

Easter leave in Berlin.

17/4/41

Generalmajor Zorn, the commander of the 20th Motorized Division, reported the arrival of his division; coming from France, it drove into the Vienna area and there prepared for action in Serbia. The total collapse of the Serbs made the deployment of his division unnecessary; it was therefore diverted to the Eastern Front.

18/4/41

The night before last an anti-aircraft shell exploded in front of our apartment during an English air raid on Berlin. The garden fence and several windows are gone, otherwise there was no damage.

23/4/41

Surrender of the Greek Epirus Army – more than 20 divisions – was announced. The Greek King [George II] is said to have gone to Crete, "in order to continue the war from there!" The English transport fleet was effectively caught by the Luftwaffe while evacuating the English troops from Greece. – I once again raised my concern about the northern wing of the 4th Army. True, it is not decisive if this wing is held up for a short time by escaping fortress garrisons; but time will be lost, and forces may have to be diverted from the center of the army to the struggle in the north. The OKH has therefore agreed that, beginning on the first day of the attack, one of the divisions from its reserve is to be detrained behind the 4th Army's northern wing. If it really arrives as planned, it will have to do, for I would like to avoid moving the army group's reserves to the north; the main effort definitely belongs on the right, meaning the southern wing. The XIII Corps [Felber] therefore will only form up behind the center of the 4th Army in order to keep it away from the roads on the right wing overburdened by the panzers and their supply units. It is to be sent through Bielsk, because in all probability it will arrive behind the right wing of the army group quicker that way.

25/4/41

Generalleutnant Heinemann, the army group's artillery advisor, returned from a trip to the 9th Army [Strauß]. Conditions there are difficult for artillery observation, especially in the wooded terrain near Augustov, where support for the attack will be possible by individual guns only, which will probably become stuck in the marshy woods. This reinforced my view that the main thrust by the XX Corps [Materna] will have to be made not at Augustov, but better farther east, where artillery support is possible and where the path to cutting off the Russian route of retreat from Augustov to Grodno is shorter –

thus in the area northwest of Lipsk. This will also establish a connection between XX Corps' attack and that of the VIII Corps, which now will not have to worry about its right wing. The operational effect of the attack by the right wing of the 9th Army will thus be increased. Further, these ideas will probably lead to a tighter concentration of the XX Corps by the 9th Army, so that the feint attack toward Ossowiec will only require quite weak infantry with strong artillery.

1/5/41

After scouting his panzer group's attack sector, Guderian came for a brief talk, which produced nothing new of importance.

2/5/41

Salmuth, my proven Chief of Staff in peace and war, has been named Commanding General of the XXX Corps. After such a long time as a chief of staff and after having held the rank of *General der Infanterie* for three-quarters of a year, it is good to see him going to an independent position. Halder asked me if I agreed with *General* von Greiffenberg [Chief of the OP Dept. OKW, then Chief of Staff of the 12th Army] as his successor; I asked for time to think it over. He was appointed without waiting for my answer.

Unfortunately two more of the army headquarters' general staff officers are going at the same time: the fabulous Groeben and Manthey, our Ic, who in the interests of their continued training as general staff officers are being assigned to divisions.

Halder's diary, 2/5/41: "FM von Bock called on account of the Salmuth/ von Greiffenberg change. Salmuth is still going to take over the XXX Army Corps. Greiffenberg's successor is Foertsch."

4/5/41

The *Führer* lauded the accomplishments of the command and the field units in the Balkans Campaign. I took the opportunity to ask Halder to place another division at my disposal in order to more tightly concentrate the attack by the right wing of the 9th Army and at the same time be able to "tackle" the Bob front.

Halder's diary, 5/5/41: "Evening 20:00-21:00 hours discussion with the Army CIC... open question Barbarossa. Talk with Bock, Reichenau and Kleist."

8/5/41

Drove to Warthelager to the 4th Panzer Division [Freiherr von Langermann und Erlenkamp].

9/5/41

Drove to the 293rd Division [Obernitz], which I saw on the march.

In the evening a farewell dinner for Salmuth, Manthey and Groeben. English bombs on Posen during the night.

Evening of 10/5/41 to evening of 12/5/41

In the evening it was announced that Hess, the *"Führer*'s Deputy," has disappeared in an aircraft and apparently landed in England. A mysterious story! The surrounding circumstances make it seem very unlikely that Hess was on a mission. Unfortunately, it is typical that no one I spoke to believes the official version!

Rudolf Hess flew to England on 10 May 1941, hoping to initiate German-English peace negotiations before the offensive in the east began. Hitler knew nothing of this action.

13/5/41

Greiffenberg took over his offices.

Evening of 14/5/41 to the evening of 16/5/41

Travelled by train to the frontier in the 4th Army's sector; on the way discussions concerning the coming missions with the Commanding Generals of the XII [Schroth], XXXIX, IX [Geyer], and VII Corps, the commanders of the 7th [Gablenz], 31st [Kaempfe], 131st [Meyer-Bürdorf], 252nd [Boehm-Bezing], 258th [Henrici], 268th [Straube] and 292nd [Dehmel] Divisions and the 1st Cavalry Division [Feldt], and with several regimental commanders. Visited several troop quartering areas. Everywhere I went the troops made a fresh, cheerful impression; when I asked about their rations the answer was the same everywhere:

"Good, but there could be more!"

And as of 1 June the meat portion is to be reduced!

While passing through Warsaw I spoke to Kluge, told him what I had seen, and talked over with him the points that Brauchitsch, who was in Posen on the 15th [May], wanted to discuss with him today:

(1) Consideration is to be given as to whether infantry from the army and army group reserves might not be committed with Panzer Group 2 for the first attack in order to save the rifle brigades of the panzer divisions for their later missions. Guderian had so far spoken out harshly against splitting up the units of the panzer divisions in the first attack. I am also not happy about the idea, for artillery and combat engineers of the reserve are already being committed in the first attack; if they are now joined by the infantry, there will be practically nothing left of the reserves.

Kluge spoke out against any change; but I asked him to ask Guderian once again.

(2) Brauchitsch thinks the reserves are too far behind the army's right wing. The same dictate as the year before at Wesel, where they forced me to move them closer! That led to dangerous traffic jams, which were overcome only with great difficulty. It will be exactly the same here, for days will pass before Panzer Group 2 departs and before the XII Corps is across the Bug, in which the reserves can close ranks calmly. Kluge is also against moving the reserves even closer.

(3) Brauchitsch is once again proposing that the divisions of the XIII Corps, which are initially to follow behind the center of the 4th Army as its reserve, also be moved behind the right wing immediately. This case has al-

ready been considered several times and the point was put forward that any further accumulation there will inevitably lead to traffic jams, and that as it is now to be deployed, the XIII Corps will move forward faster and reach the right wing by shorter routes than if it too is packed in behind. Kluge shares my view.

(4) In Brauchitsch's view at least one, perhaps even two divisions should be removed from the VII Corps [Fahrmbacher] and positioned behind as an echelon.

Removing one is correct. The division in question was crammed in by the 4th Army against my wishes on the occasion of the conference at the OKH on 27 March – thus in Brauchitsch's presence – and is now absent from behind the army's left wing – I have already voiced my concerns in that area.

I don't agree with taking two divisions. With no rivers standing in its way, the attack by the VII Corps has to be made quickly and powerfully in the first days, in order to ease the task of the other corps of the 4th Army, which have to cross the Bug in their initial attacks. Kluge will think the matter over.

When we returned Tresckow reported that he had once again raised the question with Brauchitsch on my behalf as to how we are supposed to interpret the rather foggy order concerning the link-up of the two panzer groups in the Minsk area. Brauchitsch replied that what in fact was meant was the area near Minsk, and that furthermore strong elements of Panzer Group 3 will have to be moved forward over the Molodechno land bridge towards Minsk. The subsequent forward movement of Panzer Group 3 is planned north around the Beresina marshes. So finally all is now clear and there is nothing left for the army group to change in its directives.

Evening of 17/5/41 – evening of 19/5/41

Weekend in Berlin.

On the evening of 19 May I presented Greiffenberg with the Knight's Cross he had earned as Chief of Staff of Army List [1 January to 10 May 1941) in the Balkans.

The OKH has made available to the army group the division requested on 4 May, so that it is now possible to more tightly concentrate the assault wing of the 9th Army and at the same time manifest on the Bob front.

The facts of the Hess case are said to match the official version. It was an independent act by Hess aimed at moving England toward peace!

21/5/41

Yesterday evening the English reported that German parachute troops have landed on Crete. According to available reports, all seems to be going well. After the Italians got us into the Greek adventure the occupation of Crete was probably unavoidable. It can also have a positive effect on conditions in Libya and at the Suez Canal, but it contains the danger of dissipation, for out of their fear for the canal the English will see to it that significant forces are tied up there for a long time. Since we deployed air forces to Iraq, the Luftwaffe is strewn between the Atlantic and the Tigris! But on the other hand our attack on Crete will force the English to commit their fleet – just as before in Norway – which hopefully will cost them dearly.

Greiffenberg has cleared up the question of the attack by the 9th Army's right wing with its Chief of Staff, in that the attack will now be carried out as I wish, meaning with the main effort at Lipsk. The matter of the army's subsequent advance after crossing the Neman was also clarified once again; a maximum effort has to be made to bring at least the leading elements of all four corps into the front line side by side. According to the army's existing plans the rearward arrangement of the right-wing corps, caused by the course of the frontier, is to be retained in the subsequent advance. This will result in an enormously-broad front line for the corps, which I do not consider acceptable.

Bock - Kluge

Greiffenberg, who visited the 4th Army yesterday, advised me that Kluge is coming and that he plans to ask me to give the 4th Army a freer hand than before; he feels that he is on too tight a rope! The impetus behind this request was my last trip, during which I saw and talked a great deal, something the army had never seen before. For example, Kluge named other army group commanders who never visited the divisions! I was aware of my former Chief of Staff's ego, and so far I had scrupulously avoided anything that might have injured it. My concern went so far that I recently left an exercise before the concluding conference in order to allow Kluge to speak alone. Before the war game in Posen I told him that I would direct all important questions during the game to "the 4th Army"; it was thus left to him in every case to decide whether to answer himself or allow his chief of staff to reply. The result of all this was that at the conclusion of the exercise he took over and gave an unsolicited speech about the employment of panzer units, in which "he no doubt possessed the greatest experience!"

I swallowed this for the sake of peace. Perhaps Kluge saw that as weakness – then I will have to disappoint him.

I therefore asked Greiffenberg to inform him that I was ready to confer at any time, but that he [Greiffenberg] might not propose seeking such a discussion, for I would surely adhere strongly to the limits imposed on me, but I would never allow the most minor restriction to be placed on my duties and rights.

24/5/41 - evening 26/5/41

Berlin.

Initial losses apparently high in Crete, among the parachute troops and during the improvised sea transport; but on the whole it seems to be going well. The English have committed their fleet and have taken heavy losses in ships.

27/5/41 noon - 30/5/41 morning

Trip to the 9th Army at Suwalki Point. Briefing in the marshalling area with Headquarters, XX Corps [Materna] and the 256th Division [Kauffmann], with Headquarters VII Corps [Fahrmbacher] and the 8th [Hoehne], 28th [Sinnhuber] and 161st [Wilck] Divisions, Headquarters, V Corps [Ruoff] with the 5th [Allmendinger] and 35th [Fischer von Weikersthal] Divisions, Headquarters, VI Corps [Förster] and the 6th [Auleb] and 26th [Weiß] Divisions, and with Headquarters, LVII Panzer Corps [Motorized Army Corps; 15 Feb. 41 to 21 June 1942, Kuntzen; renamed LVII Panzer Corps], whose commanders outlined their missions and plans. Panzer Group 3's Ia took part in the trip.

In general everything appears to be on the right path, still some details to improve. Impressions of the field units, as far as I saw, good. Countryside and population of Suwalki Point look wretched; the area appears to be dirt poor and without any culture, only the forest is good in places. – En route came news of the sinking of the battle-cruiser *Bismarck*, which, after sinking the *Hood*, apparently fell prey to a superior English force with her entire crew. – The situation in America is becoming more critical. – It is going well in Crete; now the Italians too have landed on the east part of the island – unopposed.

A rumor is circulating at the front and at home that the Russians have made such generous offers to the *Führer* that there will be no war with Russia. On the 29th the Commanding General of V Corps, Ruoff, reported that Russian soldiers had approached the border in his sector, waved over civilians and told them that there would be no war because Stalin and the *Führer* had agreed on everything!

Unbelievable!

31/5/41 evening - 3/6/41

Pentecost leave in Berlin.

OKW Order "Unacceptable in this Form"

4/6/41

The Armed Forces High Command has issued an order governing the conduct of the field forces toward the Russian civilian population. It is so worded that it virtually gives every soldier the right to shoot at from in front or behind any Russian he takes to be – or claims that he takes to be – a guerrilla. The order rules out any constraint towards punishment of any offenses in this regard, even "if a military crime or offense is involved." Brauchitsch issued a supplement to this order which was undoubtedly intended to weaken it but which only partly succeeded. A telegram arrived at the same time with instructions to halt the order already in the hands of the army until specific regulations arrived. I gave Greiffenberg, who was at the OKH just then, the task of determining from Halder whether the announced regulations contained any significant changes to the order. If that was not the case, Greiffenberg was to report to the Commander-in-Chief of the Army that in this form the order was unacceptable and was not compatible with discipline.

Kluge Arrives

Kluge came and discussed, in a very friendly way, the complaints about infringements of his rights which he recently expressed to Greiffenberg. The only remaining evil was that, in Kluge's view, I spent to much time with the troops, which was the place of the army commander. I had done too much of that in the Battle of the Corridor and so on. I offered a few polite phrases and asked that he bring to my attention any encroachments that might come from my staff; I promised to intervene immediately, especially since I allowed no interference in my own area of work. – Thus nothing came of this unnecessary conversation; it did nothing to weaken my feeling that I spend too little time with the field forces. – The OKH continues to press for the deployment of the infantry of other divisions with Panzer Group Guderian in the initial attack instead of the rifle brigades of the panzer divisions. That is possible only if I move forward two of my three reserve divisions positioned behind the 4th Army. If Guderian agrees and the OKH orders it I will have no other choice.

5/6/41

Greisser and Himmler came. The latter described the objective of the campaign in the east as the splitting up of Russia into small individual states and extension of Germany's sphere of influence well beyond the Urals.

Doubt in Victory

6/6/41

Greiffenberg brought news from Berlin that they are sticking to the planned date of the attack. Concerning the overall situation, he reports that the affair begun in Iraq with no involvement on the part of Germany is over and has been "written off." They are also not happy about the situation in Libya. What is to happen after the Russian campaign is uncertain – perhaps Suez, perhaps West Africa. Following America's energetic participation, they no longer seem to believe that England is being defeated in the "Battle of the Atlantic." Our food situation is difficult where fats and meat are concerned; a further reduction in the meat ration is expected for the winter.

Can this war be won with weapons alone? – Even if we don't go for England's throat, that is to say attack on the island itself?

"...Not Meddle in Political Matters"

7/6/41

Since as of today I had received no reply to my attack of 4 June against the order concerning the treatment of the Russian civilian population, I telephoned Brauchitsch and made a positive proposal as to how they can put the order in a form which the field officers can understand and which is acceptable to the army. Br[auchitsch] called back an hour later and said that what I wanted might be read into the order, and that it was intended as I wished to interpret it – which meant: nothing has changed for the field units in dealing with punishable acts against civilian persons! The officers of the court will decide whether an action is to be punished by the court or not; the maintenance of discipline is to play a deciding role in their decision! Now I am in agreement!

Br[auchitsch] thinks it important that trials be processed quickly, even while the fighting is in progress, so as to avoid subsequent paperwork.

Guderian has apparently relented in his direct negotiations with the OKH on the employment of infantry in the panzers' attack sector and the OKH has now ordered the commitment there of two infantry divisions from my reserve.

An underground radio transmitter, probably communist, has brought up my name, linking me with a Herr von Braunschweig, who its says is in prison. When I was commanding general in Stettin Braunschweig was one of a small circle of ultra-right people in East Pomerania, whose politics were driven solely by their hearts. My sole contact with one of Braunschweig's brothers occurred during this period in Stettin; though we had never met, Braunschweig, who already feared arrest, came to me asking that the Wehrmacht protect him. I had to tell the sorely worried man that I could not meddle in political matters.

7/6/41 - 9/6/41 evening

Weekend in Berlin.

On the way home visited the 3rd Panzer Division at Pinne.

English and "Free French" – General de Gaulle – have moved into Syria.

Against Unnecessary Losses

12/6/41

Meeting with Headquarters, 4th Army [Kluge] in Warsaw concerning details of the attack in the presence of the Commander-in-Chief of the Army [Brauchitsch]. In the matter of the employment of infantry within the framework of the panzer divisions, Guderian has now come up with a compromise which does not please the Commander-in-Chief of the Army but which he does not wish to change now. I too can see no advantage to this newest solution. Guderian now happily commands elements of 15 divisions! And up front is a huge mass of infantry, which can easily lead to large and unnecessary losses. Behind it all is the failure of those in charge to clearly and in good time order what they wanted; that would have eliminated all discussions and compromises.

With the *Führer*

14/6/41

The *Führer* discussed the coming operation with the army group and army commanders in the Reich Chancellery. Nothing new for my army group.

After dinner the *Führer* spoke about the situation: the more he had thought about the decision to attack Russia during the months, the more determined he became. Russia posed a grave threat to Germany's back and we now have to have our back free; as soon as she is cast down England will have no ally left to win over on the continent, and Germany can only be beaten on the continent. If following the victory over Russia we are able to at least feed the elements of the armed forces which will remain there – all told about 65 to 75 divisions – off the land, Germany's food and raw material needs will be guaranteed indefinitely. Furthermore, after the conclusion of operations in the east a large number of divisions can be disbanded and returned to industry, which can then reduce its armaments work and increasingly turn to other tasks. England will see all this, and it is to be assumed that it will then abandon the hopeless struggle. The *Führer* hopes that this will come to pass in the first months after the end of the eastern operation. He had posed the question to Russia some time ago, whether she was ready to make common cause with Germany. Russia had responded with evasive counterquestions which showed clearly that it was only intent on increasing its power.

See Hoffmann, Joachim, "Stalin's War of Destruction 1941-1945", Military Science Publishers, Munich, 1995.

Hoffmann wrote: "On 6 November 1941 Stalin called for a war of destruction, not against the so-called fascists, but for a war of destruction against the Germans, which in reality had been going on since 22 June 1941... There is not the slightest shadow of a doubt today that Hitler's attack forestalled a prepared attack with overwhelming forces on the part of Stalin by only a short time. The treasure trove of files I discovered, supplemented by important material from Russia, leave not the slightest doubt in this regard." New Freedom, No. 17/95, of 28/4/95).

See also Danilov, Valery, "Did the General Staff of the Red Army Prepare a Preventive Strike against Germany" in Austrian Military Magazine, No. 1/ 1993, PP 43.

Furthermore experience has shown that Russia becomes bold as soon as it knows that Germany is occupied elsewhere, as for example in the autumn of 39, when it claimed Lithuania contrary to every agreement. Whether and which territories Germany would take over after victory was considered; it is clear that Russian influence has to be expelled from the Baltic Sea and that Germany has to secure for itself decisive influence in the Black Sea, for there lie interests vital to our survival, for example oil. British shipping losses are high; the *Führer* hopes that these can be maintained with our growing number of submarines. Together with the Luftwaffe's success against British shipping, this would stimulate England's desire for peace. America's help is coming too late; it will not really make itself felt until summer at the earliest. The downfall of Russia would of course not be without influence on Japan; however active assistance on the part of Japan when Germany attacks is not yet to be expected. Turkey too will eventually have to show its colors. But it has not reached that point yet. The situation in Libya, where there are only quite weak German forces, is difficult. Some relief, even if only a threat from Turkey or Syria, is therefore desirable. It is expected that Sweden will align herself with German politics after the victory over Russia. Spain: the capture of Gibraltar and the passage of German troops was clear and agreed upon with Franco in February when the Italian defeats began. Understandably Franco subsequently backed out. The idea has in no way been given up, for the capture of Gibraltar would make the situation in the Mediterranean look very different. The successes in Greece and Crete had an encouraging effect on morale in Spain; a victory over Russia would do the same to a greater degree. Curiously the *Führer* said nothing about France.

20/6/41

After Brauchitsch recently told me the planned time of attack in Berlin, the OKH is now suddenly refusing to order it uniformly. In vain I expressed my concerns regarding the timing of the attack on the ground, but especially from the air. Agreement with Rundstedt was easy. But Leeb absolutely wants to begin ten minutes earlier. So I'm the one who has to suffer and have to attack with my right wing at Rundstedt's time and with my left wing at Leeb's time. The damage will be minimized if the time separation is placed at the boundary between my two armies, as their inner wings will not be attacking.

A Mr. H., who just returned from Moscow, visited me and described the conditions on the other side of the border. He says that the leading people in Russia have no doubts that the war is coming. He believes that they are also sure that Russia will be defeated militarily. But perhaps Stalin does not altogether mind if he is defeated in European Russia; then he would withdraw beyond the Urals and wait until Germany eventually succumbed to the united democracies. He could all the more easily do this, as the worry of feeding European Russia with its millions of people and all the prisoners of war would now be Germany's affair. Stalin would find sufficient people and raw materials to defend the country east of the Urals should Germany launch such a wide-ranging offensive. The temporary destruction of the Russian state apparatus would play no decisive role given the prevailing conditions in Russia. Today my Polish cleaning lady proved how hard it is to keep something secret in wartime; she asked me to see to it that she kept her position as I was after all going away!

21/6/41

Change of position to Rembertow near Warsaw. We attack in the morning! Kesselring – friendly and ready to help as always – came in the evening to once again discuss our cooperation.

CHAPTER FIVE

22 JUNE 1941 to
5 JANUARY 1942
(EASTERN FRONT)
Commander-in-Chief Army Group Center

22/6/41

Everything began according to plan. Strangely the Russians didn't blow a single one of the existing Bug bridges.

Citadel Brest (Litovsk)

Drove to Brest. Not until noon was there a bridge, the railroad bridge, usable for crossing there; all military bridges are still under construction.

Then drove to XII Corps, to the Guderian Group and to Panzer Corps Lemelsen [XXXXVII Motorized Army Corps, later renamed XXXXVII Panzer Corps]. While everything else was going smoothly, Lemelsen was having difficulties crossing the Bug, because the approach roads to the military bridges were sinking into the swamp.

Enemy resistance appeared at first to be only moderately strong.

The question as to whether the Russians are conducting a planned withdrawal cannot yet be answered; at the moment there is just as much evidence for as against it. It is striking that nowhere have they shown noteworthy artillery, apart from northwest of Grodno against VIII Army Corps.

Our air force is apparently far superior to the Russian's.

"The Russians Are Defending Themselves Stubbornly..."

23/6/41

We are moving ahead, best of all Panzer Group Hoth [PzGr 3], which in the evening came under the direct command of the army group. Things are not going quite as smoothly with Panzer Group Guderian [PzGr 2]. Difficulties in crossing at Brest, similar to those of the Lemelsen Corps, have impeded the delivery of fuel.

The enemy is still holding out in the citadel of Brest-Litovsk. I drove to the 19th [Panzer] Division, where from a company command post I watched as the last bunker still being defended by the enemy in his border position was taken out. The most dangerous thing in this operation was our own artillery!

Lack of culture and the state of the roads are indescribable.

The Russians are defending themselves stubbornly. Women have often been seen in combat. According to statements made by prisoners, political commissars are spurring maximum resistance by reporting that we kill all prisoners! Here and there Russian officers have shot themselves to avoid being captured.

The deep advance by Panzer Group Hoth gives urgency to the question whether Hoth should go into the area north of Minsk as originally ordered by the Army Command or strike out at once in the direction of Vitebsk-Polotsk. I am for the latter, because I doubt that a closing of the "pocket" at Minsk will lead to decisive successes; I fear the enemy will already have withdrawn strong elements from there. By turning the panzer group toward Minsk time will be lost, which the enemy can use to establish a new defense behind the Dvina and Dniepr. After Greiffenberg and Halder failed to get anywhere in this direction, I telephoned Brauchitsch, for this old point of contention had to be resolved now! Brauchitsch said that the enemy in front of Army Group North was retreating behind the Dvina and that there were considerable enemy tank forces up there. Under the conditions he thought it dangerous to allow weak Panzer Group Hoth to advance to and beyond the Dvina alone. Therefore, it is to link up with Panzer Group Guderian near Minsk as per orders, and then the two are to advance together to and across the Dniepr-Dvina line. I then pointed out that after it had turned toward Minsk, the roads to the Dniepr-Dvina sector would later force Panzer Group 3 to veer back to the northeast again. Moreover, on turning toward Minsk Hoth would show his flank and back to the expected Russian tank forces, and therefore would have to send a strong screening force toward Vitebsk-Polotsk. Brauchitsch confirmed that this screening force was necessary, but refused to change the existing orders.

I therefore issued the following order to Hoth:

"Further advance toward Minsk and north, with continued deployment of powerful screening force toward the upper Dvina between Vitebsk and Polotsk. Army Group will issue the necessary orders on timely basis if – after taking the land bridge southeast of Molodechno – the situation calls for the entire panzer group to wheel toward Vitebsk-Polotsk."

In this way I hoped to lay the groundwork for the Hoth Group's later departure toward the Vitebsk-Polotsk line, which would yet become necessary.

The Luftwaffe reported devastating effects from its attacks on the Russian columns flooding toward Minsk.

24/6/41

At midmorning came Gienanth [Military Commander High Command East, later Government General] and Kesselring [Air Fleet 2].

Further discussions between Greiffenberg and the Army High Command about the direction of advance of the panzer groups; no change in position of Army High Command.

The Russians are defending desperately; heavy counterattacks near Grodno against the VIII [Heitz] and XX [Materna] Army Corps; Panzer Group Guderian is also being held up near Slonim by enemy counterattacks.

25/6/41

Only now has the citadel at Brest fallen after very heavy fighting.

In the morning Schmundt [the *Führer*'s Chief Army Adjutant] arrived and told us that the *Führer* is debating whether, as a result of sending the panzer groups to Minsk, the encircled area will be so large that our forces will be insufficient to destroy the trapped Russians or force them to surrender. The

Führer will decide this afternoon whether the pocket should not be closed at Novogrudok. Schmundt is going to pass on my views to *General* Jodl of the Armed Forces High Command.

I then telephoned Panzer Group 3's Chief of Staff [von Hünersdorff] and informed him that the drive to the Dvina was now of secondary importance; now the most important thing was to conclude the battle currently in progress, completely encircle the Russians between Bialystok and Minsk and destroy them. A speedy arrival in the Minsk area by Panzer Group 3 was a prerequisite for this. Screening the group's eastern flank and rear near Borisov and toward the upper Dvina were especially important. Hünersdorff agreed at once, but pointed out that the roads were frightful!

I briefed Strauß [9th Army] on the situation and my thoughts about the subsequent conduct of the battle and told him his army would probably be turned toward the encircled Russians – while screening to the east.

I told the Chief of Staff of 4th Army [Blumentritt] that the left wing of the 4th Army, too, had to advance smartly to relieve the right wing of the 9th Army.

At about 15:00 came news that the Army High Command considers an even tighter limiting of the desired encirclement of the enemy to be correct, as everyone had earlier planned! Halder visualizes the southern arm of the pincer advancing toward Zelva and Volkovysk and consequently a tighter concentration of the main forces of the 9th Army which are to complete the encirclement. I am furious, for here we are unnecessarily throwing away a major success!

In the meantime a written order for the further employment of the panzer groups arrived, which sends them toward Minsk and there, after closing ranks and taking on additional fuel, readies them for a further advance to the east.

I called Strauß [9th Army] again and told him that our discussion had been overtaken by a new order which was just being sent to him. The order significantly narrowed the army's attack area. Strauß expressed his thanks, obviously relieved. He had no idea how little I deserved his thanks, since in spite of the severe crises facing the XX and VIII Army Corps I was for keeping our nerve for the big solution.

Panzer Group Guderian has overcome its difficulties near Slonim; in the afternoon its left column reached Baranovichi and the right also continues to advance.

Using Russian equipment, today the railroads are already running again as far as 80 km east of Brest – a very important relief for the overcrowded supply roads to Panzer Group Guderian.

26/6/41

Brauchitsch arrived in the morning. I was still so annoyed by the order to close the pocket prematurely, that when he congratulated me I replied gruffly, "I doubt there's anything left inside now!"

When I expressed doubts whether 4th Army would succeed in closing the eastern front of the "pocket" near Zelva, which had been ordered so suddenly, Brauchitsch suggested committing the 29th Motorized Division [Boltenstern]. That is not what I would like, but unfortunately it cannot be avoided; the division was temporarily placed at the disposal of the 4th Army.

The Army High Command intends to unite the two panzer groups near Minsk under the command of Kluge, to whom the infantry divisions released from the battle are to be subordinated at the same time. *Generaloberst* von Weichs [2nd Army] is to assume command over all the troops involved in the "pocket." I consider this solution to be unfortunate and I spoke out against it yesterday. The "pocket" can best be taken care of by the two armies that created it and that is how I am going to do it.

Weichs will therefore replace Kluge in command of the 4th Army if Kluge is now to assume command of the two panzer groups [Kluge was Commander-in-Chief of the 4th Army until 18 December 1941].

Twelve-hour drive in great heat, awful dust and terrible roads to XIII and VII Army Corps, to the 19th [Panzer] and 197th Divisions. The Commanding General of VII Army Corps [Fahrmbacher] reported that the enemy was showing clear signs of disintegration. The troops made a good impression everywhere.

Greiffenberg has flown to the 9th Army to harmonize our views. It turned out there that the situation with XX Corps on the army's right wing is completely secure and that the corps has certainly not been "reduced to cinders" as was said yesterday, rather it is fully combat ready. It is understandable that the enemy is trying to break out of "the pocket."

All parts of the citadel at Brest have still not fallen. The report of the 25th [June] was incorrect. Unfortunately casualties there are high. The enemy is also holding out in other, smaller groups of fortifications far behind the front. Guderian is still getting nowhere at Baranovichi; his right wing has got some breathing room, however, and is advancing briskly toward Slutsk.

"Indications of 'Standing Still' Apparent..."

27/6/41

I gave orders for a further reduction of the "pocket," especially by the 4th Army and the right wing of the 9th Army. Indications of "standing still" are becoming apparent; 4th Army conceals this by saying that it wants to build a "battle front." The Russians are making repeated attempts to break out where pressure from the pincer is greatest, leading to serious crises at various spots, in particular on the right wing of the 4th Army [XXXXIII Army Corps, Heinrici]. Guderian is finally also moving at Baranovichi! It's about time, since at Minsk Hoth has had to withstand considerable counterattacks by enemy tanks. If all goes well the larger pocket will now yet be closed, even if somewhat flimsily. That would be undeserved luck! I removed the Guderian Group from the 4th Army and placed it under the direct command of the army group as of midnight.

The Army High Command is worried about Guderian's right column, which I have ordered to occupy Bobruisk and which is on its way there. Since the Army Command itself ordered the deployment of screening forces as far as the Dniepr, this concern can only be based on the fact that Guderian's forces are rather weak to close the southeast front of the larger pocket from Slonim to Minsk. I consider it necessary that we at least take the Beresina bridges, so as to be able to conclude the current battle undisturbed and because we will need them later.

Weichs [2nd Army] came at noon with his Chief of Staff [*Oberstleutnant*] Witzleben; in the afternoon *General der Artillerie* Brand of the Army High Command, who described to me details of the attack on the citadel at Brest.

I briefed Brauchitsch on the situation and told him that the Russians were naturally trying to prevent the two pincers from closing and had themselves gone on the offensive at the two main pressure points. The right pressure point lies with XXXXIII Corps [Heinrici], where 4th Army also had to commit XII Corps [Schroth]; I urged in vain that this be done by giving the corps an offensive mission. The second pressure point lies with the 9th Army, mainly the 28th Division [Sinnhuber]. On its left the 161st Division [Wilck] is battling a strong enemy force for possession of Lida. If the enemy pressure against these divisions becomes stronger or the army fails to close the gap at the Zelwianka, the commitment of V Corps [Ruoff] as well, with its general front to the south, will be unavoidable. VI Army Corps [Förster], which arrived southwest of Vilna today, will still be at our disposal. Vilna itself is to be occupied by the 900th Motorized Brigade. – Brauchitsch agreed.

In the evening it was learned that XXXXIII Army Corps has slackened its effort considerably – only very well-trained ears could interpret that from Kluge's midmorning briefing. But this will be headed off. The main area of concern for me is the east side of the pocket, which is being closed at the Zelwianka River line by just the 29th (Motorized) Division. It is certain that the enemy will attempt to break out there. If that happens, the only possible means of support for the 29th Division would be to commit units of Panzer Corps Vietinghoff [XXXXVI Panzer Corps], Guderian's reserve corps, which is just now advancing through Slonim toward Minsk. I would prefer not to divert this corps as it is of course also needed up front at Minsk. But I may be forced to do so, because as the battle has now developed I must not allow the enemy out.

Late in the evening came the news that XXXXIII Corps' situation is apparently even more difficult than we supposed. Contact has been broken between it and IX Corps in the Bialowice Heath and – the enemy is attacking at the Zelwianka.

"...The Garrisons Refuse to Surrender"

28/6/41

Panzer Group Hoth has taken Minsk, still heavy fighting there. The group's right flank is also coming under repeated attack from the pocket.

Lida has been taken by the 9th Army, whose entire front is moving toward and over the Neman, eastern wing toward Zdoiedciot.

The inner wings of both armies are nearing each other east of Bialystok, while the 4th Army has still not succeeded in closing the gap on the eastern front of the "pocket," at the Zelwianka. When in the morning, with a very heavy heart, I placed the 10th Panzer Division at Kluge's disposal in order that we might reach a quicker conclusion there, he replied:

"I haven't been able to make up my mind to do so yet."

When he finally did decide, it was too late to effect an attack on this day.

The 1st Cavalry Division [Feldt], which hitherto was subordinated to Guderian, is said to be at Pinsk; as it is out of the Panzer Group's reach there, I subordinated it to the 4th Army.

In the evening I spoke with the Chief of Staff of the 9th Army, Weckmann, about the situation and told him that after the battle was concluded the army would probably advance across the general line Molodechno-Hoducisky to the east. From this point of view, the army should now move forward its reserves and forces freed up in the front. The 4th Army was similarly briefed on its later direction of march.

Our losses are not inconsiderable. Thousands of Russian soldiers are sitting in the forests, far behind our front, some in civilian clothes. They will eventually come out when they get hungry. But catching them all is impossible given the tremendous size of the area. 100 km behind the front, at Siemiatycze, the 293rd Division is still fighting for a row of strongly-fortified bunkers, which have to be taken one at a time. In spite of the heaviest fire and the employment of every means the crews refuse to give up. Each fellow has to be killed one at a time.

"That Is the Curse of an Evil Deed!"

29/6/41

Reports vary widely, which is understandable given the difficult terrain. Today the 1st Cavalry Division was determined to be 100 kilometers north of the place it was reported yesterday. As it is now in the panzer group's area, I gave it back to it.

Conditions on the right wing of the 4th Army are unclear. The units have become badly mixed together there. The Russians are trickling through here and there. According to army reports, XII Corps was supposed to attack yesterday evening to close the Zelwianka River line. Then the attack was to take place today at dawn. That too was not the case. It has supposedly been under way since 11:00.

I am not happy with the employment of forces there. Apart from the mixing of units, the fact that strong elements of Panzer Group Guderian – the 29th Motorized Infantry Division and elements of the 10th Panzer Division – are pinned down there will have a negative effect. On the other hand the attempt has to be made to finally shut the door. If that doesn't succeed this evening, elements of the panzer group will have to be pulled out and once again placed at Guderian's disposal. Otherwise he will neither be in a position to establish contact with Hoth near Minsk nor even partially seal off the southern front of the "pocket" between the Schara and Minsk. I therefore issued orders for the withdrawal of these elements to begin.

Since the terrible swampy terrain has prevented the 9th Army from getting through from Dworek to the Schara bridge, I still haven't completely closed the "small" pocket! But now Guderian, too, has finally reached Minsk and thus the bigger ring is closed! Both were reminded that the order to send reconnaissance and screening forces across the Beresina to the Dniepr is to be executed to the extent possible, but that the "primary mission" for the time being is the closing of the "pocket."

That is the curse of the evil deed! If we turn in near Minsk, there will inevitably be a stop there until the entire Bialystok-Minsk pocket has largely been cleared. I wanted to take possession of the Dniepr or at least the Beresina bridges quickly, so as not to have to fight for them later – which unfortunately will now be the case! The pocket should be closed in the east by sealing off these few crossings and not near Zelva or near Minsk!

In the evening I spoke with Guderian again, because I am concerned about the front between Stolpce and Slonim. Guderian replied that this concern is unfounded. I nevertheless asked him to take the matter seriously, for the probable direction of a Russian breakout will lie in the southeast, because they have already burned their noses in the northeast and the east – at Lida and Minsk – and then because strategically southeast is the right direction for them.

Guderian's right column has reached Bobruisk, where it established a bridgehead across the Beresina.

I had Hoth told once again that Borisov has to be taken, as least insofar as it ties in with his primary mission.

30/6/41

Drove through Bialystok, where stores had just been captured, to Headquarters, VII Corps and to the 23rd Division [Hellmich], parts of which I met on the march. The people are fresh, the horses are tired out – with these roads they should receive much more oats.

The Bialystok-Volkovysk road is a scene of desolation; the picture of destruction is complete. Hundreds of tanks, guns of all calibers and vehicles of every kind lie there in a tremendous jumble. The Luftwaffe did a good job of catching the fleeing columns. The enemy has been hit very hard.

The troop commanders report that the Russian ruse of pretending to surrender and then opening fire again has so infuriated our people that they kill everyone who crosses their path. But there are also reports of mutilation of German wounded.

When I returned home in the evening I found that the business on the right wing of the 4th Army between Zelwianka and Schara was still not in order!

1/7/41

First thing in the morning I was informed that Kluge had set out for XII Corps and had not arrived all day. Almost every corps of the 4th Army has a different front. The difficult terrain – the Bialowice Heath lies inside the pocket – and the dogged resistance of the Russians, elements of whom repeatedly break out and rip gaps in our thin front which have to be closed, are the main reasons for this confusion and the widespread mingling of the units. For today 4th Army sent elements of IX Corps [Geber] to the attack across the Zelva to the northeast, to clear the area between Zelwianka and Schara, which has now at last succeeded. The "small" pocket is thus, by and large, finished. Numbers of prisoners and captured equipment are said to be very considerable.

Now it is the turn of the eastern pocket, which I suspect does not hold as much and whose clearance I expect will be easier, because the enemy's ability to resist has to have fallen by now due to lack of supplies.

The Army High Command has ordered a division sent forward to Pinsk to screen toward the swampy region.

In the afternoon the army group issued an order which governed the sorting out of the pocket front and initiated the new operations.

The next objective is the high ground due east of Smolensk. The panzer groups pressed for an early start, which I would like just as much, but all that can be done for the 2nd [July] is to allow them to strengthen the reconnaissance forces they have sent east across the Beresina and toward the Dniepr, while maintaining the containment of the eastern pocket. A combined attack by the panzer groups is not called for until the 3rd. Kluge is to assume command of the panzer groups, Weichs of 4th Army, which from then on will be called the 2nd Army, at midnight of the 2nd-3rd [July]. The panzer groups were just as much against this ruling as I.

In the afternoon I drove to see the commander of the rear army area, General von Schenckendorff, at Constanczin near Warsaw, in order to discuss the takeover of his area, which I proposed to the Army Command for the 3rd [July].

2/7/41

Brauchitsch telephoned in the morning and had me brief him on the army group's intentions. Three points caused him concern: one was whether the panzer groups already had sufficient forces in place so that they could really attack tomorrow; the second, whether their attack was adequately prepared in terms of supply, and the third, which preyed on him most, whether the containment of the eastern pocket by the remaining elements of the panzer divisions was and would remain firm enough. I was able to reassure him, even though I had to tell him where supplies were concerned the attack by the panzer groups was of course a "flying start" – for naturally completion of a supply base at Minsk was still out of the question, and that the containment of the pocket was hardly hermetic and as well cannot be. I went on to inform him that the panzer groups were continuing to reconnoiter east as per orders, strengthening their patrols and closing ranks to the east, because we must not lose any time. Brauchitsch agreed.

All intelligence reports indicate that the enemy is establishing a new defensive front at the Dniepr and the "Gateway to Smolensk" [Orsha-Vitebsk]. Voroshilov [member of the State Defense Committee] and Timoshenko [People's Commissar for Defense of the USSR, also responsible for the "Western Front" as Commander-in-Chief of the Army] were knocking about there yesterday; my fear that it will come to serious fighting there appears to be proving to be true.

In the afternoon Halder telephoned Greiffenberg. The high command is still worried as to whether the Novgorod, meaning the eastern, pocket is contained firmly enough. They are even toying with the idea of halting the panzer groups. If the latter happens, they will have failed to exploit the bloodily-won success of the battle now winding down; they are committing a major error if they give the Russians time to establish a defensive front at the Dniepr and the Orsha-Vitebsk land bridge! In my opinion we have already waited too long.

I called Halder, who told me that he needed to know my position before going to see the *Führer*. I informed him that, first, the armored groups might not take away a single man from the elements deployed against the pocket without my permission, second that the pocket was being reduced automatically by the forward pressure of the infantry divisions and that the danger of a breakthrough was growing smaller every minute, third that I was moving the 900th Motorized Brigade [900th Instruction Brigade, Krause] behind the pocket's northeastern front, in order to further bolster the front there and later relieve elements of Panzer Group Hoth, fourth that the 4th Army had moved advance elements of the infantry corps ahead through Slonim to reinforce the encircling ring there, fifth that I had implemented the Army High Command's suggestion regarding the armored groups, ordering them to advance with their inner wings from Minsk west to the Naliboki Forest, provided the situation, which I cannot watch over there, permits it.

Hitler: "Where Are the Prisoners Then?"

So far the situation in the eastern pocket has been very different than in the western one. The enemy remnants still inside have made no serious, coordinated attempts to break out. One can hope that they will also lack the strength to do so in the future. In any case it is possible that Russians are trickling through, especially through the thin southeastern front; there is no way whatsoever to prevent it. I then described my personal impressions from having been on the spot, which are that the enemy has suffered a very serious defeat.

Halder also confirmed that as his view and observed that he thought that as a result of this success the enemy would be unable to again establish an orderly front. The *Führer* was skeptical and asked:

"Where are the prisoners then?" whereupon I replied: "100,000 isn't chicken feed, furthermore there are more every day. Hadn't the huge quantities of materiel been reported to the *Führer*? The figures in today's armed forces communique are far less than half the army group's numbers!"

I asked Halder, who shared my opinion in everything, to once again press not to have the panzer divisions halted. When asked by Halder if this halt was even technically still possible, I answered, "No!" The OKH's order, "thrust an entire corps into the swamps..."

Today the Army High Command issued orders for an entire corps to be thrust through Pinsk to David-Gorodok into the swamps, in order to eliminate a threat to the inner flanks of Army Groups South and Center from the swamps. Who knows when I will see the corps again.

3/7/41

The panzer groups have set off. Guderian has crossed the Beresina at various places and his right wing has reached the Dniepr near Rogachev. Hoth's left wing has arrived at the Dvina near Dzisna on terrible roads. The enemy occupies the opposite banks of the Dniepr and Dvina.

There is still shooting everywhere in the rear. Today the Russians tried to break through on the southern front of the pocket.

I called both armies and asked them to relieve the elements of the panzer divisions still deployed on the pocket front as soon as possible.

The Problem of the Railway Gauges!

The railroad is keeping up surprisingly well. We are already running as far as Baranovichi on German gauge tracks. The day after tomorrow the trains are to be running to Minsk – on Russian gauge. Talked the chief of field transport [Gercke] into converting the tracks from Baranovichi to Minsk to the German gauge, as we haven't captured any Russian tank cars and fuel can only be transported to the front in large quantities in German tank cars. Behind the 9th Army a shuttle service has been started between Grodno and Molodechno. The bridge at Grodno is supposed to be finished on the 7th or 8th, then we will be able to steam through from the German border to Molodechno on the Russian gauge.

4/7/41

Drove via Brest-Litovsk to Baranovichi. Brest citadel looks devastated.

En route I spoke to the commander of the 293rd Division [Obernitz] and to the Commander-in-Chief of the 2nd Army, *Generaloberst* von Weichs. All movements proceeding according to plan. Panzer Group 2 has arrived at the Beresina at Bobruisk and at two other places and has reached Rogachev and Bykov on the Dniepr.

Resistance in the eastern pocket is becoming weaker. Near Minsk 50,000 men surrendered to the 12th Panzer Division. Feeding them and transporting them to the rear is an unsolved problem for the armored groups far to the front.

5/7/41

Brauchitsch arrived in the morning and spoke very amicably about the successful operations.

Concerning the coming operations he spoke of the three suggested possibilities, namely that after reaching the area east of Smolensk the panzer army [since Panzer Group 2 had been subordinated to HQ, 4th Army, Bock referred to Panzer Group 2 and the 4th Army as the "Panzer Army"] will either advance straight toward Moscow or will be turned right or left depending on how the situation presents itself. For now the specified objective remains the same: the high ground on either side of Yarzevo.

Brauchitsch agrees with my plan regarding the deployment of the Kaempfe Corps [XXXV Senior Detachment(Special Purpose)] with the 45th [Schlieper] and 293rd [Obernitz] Divisions) in the direction of Gomel and north.

Everything going according to plan with the 2nd and 9th Armies. No substantive reports from the panzer groups as of the evening. The enemy has occupied the Dniepr-Dvina crossings and the Orsha-Vitebsk land bridges with forces, some from the rear, some from the south; in part they are units which were already shattered opposite my front.

Only on the extreme wings – near Rogachev and Dzisna – have the panzer groups succeeded in establishing their bridgeheads across the Dniepr and the Dvina. Casualties have in places been serious. Equipment, too, has suffered considerably from the uninterrupted fighting and the hair-raising roads. Among the infantry divisions it is the heavy horses which are suffering the worst.

I drove to IX [Geyer] and XII [Schroth] Corps and met elements of various divisions on the march, which is made especially strenuous by the dust and heat and the frightful roads. March order varies greatly and in some cases is not too good. XII Corps' casualties, which, based on the descriptions of the fighting, I assumed were especially high, have fortunately been light. The Commanding General, Schroth, asked me whether such a premature turning inward to close the pocket had really been necessary! My self-control was not sufficient to answer "yes." When I asked him if it had not been possible to commit his corps to attack north along the Zelwianka with both divisions side by side instead of splitting it apart defensively behind the Zelwianka, Schroth answered that he had requested such an order several times in vain. My worries about this part of the battlefield were therefore justified.

There is visible dissatisfaction in Panzer Group 2 with being under the command of Headquarters, 4th Army [Kluge].

"...Scattered over a Wide Area..."

6/7/41

Everything going "according to plan" with the 2nd [Weichs] and 9th [Strauß] Armies. The 4th [Panzer] Army [this was not formed until 1 January 1942; what is meant is the 4th Army under Kluge and its attached panzer forces; see 1 July 1941] reported the same, which does not mean too much, for nowhere has it made any significant progress. I tried to take precautions against its apparent tendency to rip units apart by temporarily placing the 900th Brigade at its disposal. At present the army is scattered over a wide area, which is natural after the earlier development; but now "a fist has to be made" somewhere. I therefore directed a written inquiry to the army, asking what plans it has for the continuation of the attack and how it thinks it can build the required depth at the point of main effort chosen by it.

As the day went on resistance stiffened opposite Guderian's front at the Dniepr. Here and there the enemy launched counterattacks, which were carried out on the extreme southern wing near Zhlobin and even on the west bank of the Dniepr. Enemy forces were suddenly reported again far to the rear in the area north of the Beresina. It is not clear if they are parachute troops. Aerial reconnaissance reports large enemy concentrations around Gomel.

Hoth has apparently gained some breathing space. Kluge probably has it in mind to sit still, for he has expressed the desire to be allowed to turn Panzer Group Hoepner [PzGr 4], which is advancing toward Leningrad, south, in order to gain a breathing space for his army. Late in the evening I telephoned the army, where once again the only one I could reach was the Chief of Staff; I informed him that this idea was unrealistic and the opposite of the intentions of the Army Command. Then I asked what ideas the army had come up with for the continuation of the attack. Blumentritt said that his Commander-in-Chief was away, but that based on available reports he was of the opinion that the main thrust had to be carried out on Guderian's northern wing and by Panzer Group Hoth. I told him that – seen purely from the map – that this was also my view. The most important thing was that the army, which was now scattered widely, be concentrated for a sharp thrust at the place chosen by it for the continuation of the attack. I told him that he might inform his commander in chief of that.

Minsk

If Hoth fails to advance, we will find the panzer army sitting still at first – the natural result of the premature turning inward toward Minsk and the timid detaining of panzer forces to close the Minsk pocket beyond the time required. The battle is coming to an end in this pocket, after a Russian general, who was in command of the remaining wreckage there, was taken prisoner yesterday with a few thousand men.

I am nervous as to whether the enemy can really still manage to mass serious forces near Gomel, in order to strike out from there against my southern wing or against Rundstedt's northern wing. But if he does! That would give us the opportunity to inflict another major defeat on him!

At Minsk things are said to look awful. The large city is a pile of rubble in which the population is stumbling about without food. An officer of my staff related that he had met many thousands of Russian soldiers, unarmed true, but also unsupervised, who were moving down the road from Minsk t Slutsk, hungry and exhausted. I directed 2nd Army to intercept this stream if possible. Even partly clearing the huge regions behind the front with their large forests is impossible. I am convinced that there are still thousands of Russian soldiers hanging around there. We have no choice but to leave divisions behind to clear and watch over the rear area. Apart from the three security divisions [213th, 286th and 403rd Security Divisions], two active divisions were initially selected for these duties in the army group's area.

A so-called "Rosenberg Staff" [Rosenberg was designated to handle matters concerning the Eastern European territories] is intended for the civilian administration of the occupied regions, and it has sent a liaison man to the commander of the rear area of the army group [Center]. His mission will be a difficult one. The region is barren in places. Its yields will scarcely suffice to feed the civilian population.

The communist system with its central control of all farms and the economic system is shattered, there are as good as no private shops, so that I don't know how they intend to solve the problem of feeding the people.

Drove to the right wing, where I saw elements of the 52nd [Rendulic] and 17th [Loch] Divisions on the march.

7/7/41

In the morning came news that the enemy had been driven back across the Dniepr near Zhlobin on the right wing of Panzer Group Guderian. Transport movements continue around Gomel, but in the Luftwaffe's opinion they are of no strategic importance. Since by late morning there was still no word from 4th Army on its intentions, I sent my Chief of Staff [Greiffenberg] and Ia [Tresckow] to the front by aircraft to sit in on a conference being held by the panzer army for its Chiefs of Staff.

Major von Grolmann of the Army Command came to be briefed on the panzer army's situation. I outlined my view and the difficulties that had arisen – above and below – from the use of the Headquarters of the 4th Army to command the panzer groups.

When he returned from Borisov, Greiffenberg related to me the 4th Army's situation and intentions. It turned out that there were still enemy forces west of the Dniepr opposite XXXXVI [Motorized, Vietinghoff] Corps's front as well as that of XXXXVII [Motorized] Army Corps [Lemelsen]. Under these circumstances my original plan, to shift XXXVI [Motorized] Army Corps to the north and to continue the 4th Army's attack with a pronounced point of main effort by Panzer Group Hoth and on the northern wing of Guderian's group, is no longer feasible, the necessary regroupings would not be possible until the west bank of the Dniepr is in our hands on the entire front. To avoid losing time, therefore, I gave in to 4th Army's proposal. It will halt the advance by the Guderian group on the southern wing and, after driving the enemy back across the Dniepr, force a crossing at two places, near Stary Bykhov with limited forces and with a pronounced point of main effort near Shklov. The Hoth Group is to continue its attack, bringing up all of its forces now freed at Minsk.

The 2nd and 9th Armies are now receiving orders to accelerate the release of all elements of the Panzer Army still in the army's rear area and furthermore to provide the Panzer Army with everything available in heavy artillery, assault artillery, combat engineers and bridging columns. If this attempt by the strengthened panzer groups to advance does not achieve success, the attack across the rivers will have to wait for the arrival of the 2nd and 9th Armies.

I called Brauchitsch and briefed him; he concurred. Soon afterward Kluge, who had received a gentle prod from Greiffenberg, called and briefed me in the same way Greiffenberg had already done.

I discussed with Kesselring the employment of the Luftwaffe in support of the 4th Army; we agreed that the resources of the entire air fleet are to be committed at one place where the situation makes it appear possible and advantageous. Details are to be worked out with the air fleet by 4th Army directly.

It has been raining on the 4th Panzer Army for two days. This has made the conditions of the roads frightful and placed an unusually heavy strain on men and materiel.

8/7/41

I was surprised to learn from the morning report that Panzer Group Guderian had given up the bridgehead across the Dniepr at Rogachev! Whether voluntarily or involuntarily is not clear. I discussed with Strauß by phone the possible employment of his army when it arrives at the Dniepr. First to arrive will be XXIII Corps on the northern wing; it may very well happen that the corps will then have to be temporarily subordinated to Panzer Group Hoth; the same may become of VI Corps, which will reach the Dniepr immediately afterwards. If I get the impression that the tanks are stalled and can go no further on their own, then the 9th Army will have to force the crossing. Then I would be in favor of Panzer Group Hoth being subordinated to the 9th Army for the initial assault, just as at the start of the offensive. Such a ruling would be simple, clear and natural. Headquarters, 4th Army [Kluge] would then become superfluous.

In the afternoon I flew to the command post of Panzer Group 3 at Lepel, where I spoke with Hoth, Richthofen [VIII Air Corps] and also Weckmann, the Chief of Staff of the 9th Army.

Hoth is quite clear. He knows that his attack represents our last opportunity to overrun the enemy elements pulled together at the Dvina and break through toward Smolensk. If it fails, we will have to wait for the 9th Army. Hoth is worried that his group could be turned south after a successful attack in order to help Guderian's group advance. I told him that I was not considering such action. His cooperation with Richthofen and with 9th Army is outstanding. Strong advance detachments of the 9th Army began arriving today and came under the command of the panzer group. I advised Hoth that XXIII Corps, which had about a day's lead on the main body of the 9th Army, would presumably be subordinated to him when it arrived, which he welcomed warmly.

Heavy enemy counterattacks against the bridgehead at Dzisna, where elements of the Kuntzen Corps [LVII Motorized Army Corps] are across the Dvina; the Russians stormed the position in several waves one behind the other, their people having linked arms. The attacks were repulsed.

With the fighting near Minsk over, I issued the following order of the day:

"The double battle of Bialystok and Minsk is over. The army group faced four Russian armies with approximate strengths of 32 rifle divisions, 8 tank divisions, 6 motorized-mechanized brigades and 3 cavalry divisions. Of these were destroyed: 22 rifle divisions, 7 tank divisions, 6 motorized-mechanized brigades and 3 cavalry divisions. The remaining units which succeeded in escaping the encirclement also suffered a reduction in their fighting strength.

The enemy's casualties are very high. As of yesterday the count in prisoners and booty stood at:

287,704 prisoners, including several corps and divisional commanders, 2,585 tanks destroyed or captured, including vehicles of the heaviest type, 1,449 guns and 246 aircraft captured.

As well there are vast quantities of small arms, ammunition and vehicles of all types, as well as numerous rations and fuel dumps.

Our own casualties were no higher than a brave unit is ready to bear.

This huge success, against a powerful enemy often fighting to the last man, is due to your loyalty and bravery!

I express my wholehearted appreciation to all troops and command agencies, as well as to the army group's supply units and labor formations, for their tireless fulfillment of duty and their outstanding achievements. The Luftwaffe, which repeatedly proved itself in willing comradeship, is deserving of our special thanks.

We must now exploit this victory! I know that the army group will continue to do its utmost; there can be no rest until total victory has been won!

Long live the *Führer*!"

The figures for prisoners of war given above have since increased to far more than 300,000.

9/7/41

Panzer Group Hoth has successfully crossed the Dvina at several places and has reached Vitebsk.

I immediately asked the Chief of Staff of Air Fleet 2 [Seidemann] to commit the strongest possible forces in support of the panzer group. This was the only, but very pronounced, request that I made of the air fleet today.

On the basis of this welcome news I placed XXIII Corps [Schubert] and the 900th Motorized Brigade [Krause] at the disposal of 4th Army "for use on its northern wing." I also passed on to the 4th Army the proposal that fast forces of Panzer Group 2's rear wave now also be shifted to Hoth, in order to exploit this success as powerfully as possible. The 4th Army's Chief of Staff replied that there was much to be said against this, first and foremost on "psychological grounds!" That meant that he was hesitant to give Guderian such an order. Kluge was temporarily confined to bed with an illness. It certainly is no easy task for the Chief of Staff to deal with the two strong men, Guderian and Hoth. Headquarters, 4th Army called again later and claimed that the condition of the roads made the proposed shift to the northern wing impossible – but within Panzer Group 2 considerable troop movements are going ahead!

When, in the evening, the news arrived that Hoth had taken Vitebsk and with air reconnaissance reporting rearward movements by road and rail from the Orsha-Vitebsk land bridge to the east, 4th Army was ordered to take advantage of any weakening of enemy resistance to advance sharply on its northern wing in conjunction with the advance by the Hoth Group. I consider Panzer Group 2's adherence to the planned attack across the Dniepr near Stary Bykhov and Shklov to be unfortunate. Days will be lost in preparation and it is possible that the moment in which Panzer Group Hoth's success can be exploited strategically will be missed. So far no good has come from inserting an army headquarters between the Army High Command and the panzer groups!

10/7/41

In the morning 4th Army went to the attack south of Mogilev with relatively weak forces and at the same time gave the army group's high command a tranquilizer; it informed us that it would step in on the northern wing of the Guderian Group at once should the enemy gave any indication whatever of yielding. Furthermore it expressed the view that the enemy is apparently about to withdraw. Regrettably there was also an incautious comment about this in the army group's daily reports, which I hadn't seen. This is just what gives me headaches: is the enemy still fighting at the Dniepr or is he retreating? He can only do the former with success until my infantry divisions arrive, and the latter he can unfortunately do as he wishes.

Spoke on the telephone with Halder, whom I briefed on the situation. He, too, is unhappy about the 4th Army's piecemeal approach.

In the evening I discussed with Strauß the possible developments and the necessity of subordinating XXIII Corps to the Hoth Group.

Unfortunately the Army High Command ordered that XXIV Motorized Army Corps [Geyr von Schweppenburg] be sent into the swamps via David-Gorodok further to the east.

"At Only One Place on the Eastern Front..."

11/7/41

Drove through destroyed Minsk, where I visited the Headquarters of 2nd Army [Weichs] and Air Fleet 2 [Kesselring], to Borisov [Novy Borisov near Smolensk, the new headquarters of Army Group Center]. The new quarters are situated right beside an airfield; the staff was greeted by bombs. Our accommodations are in a sanatorium and are distinguished by having one wash basin for every twenty rooms!

The impression of today's success by the 4th Panzer Army is not excessive. Here and there it has gained a little breathing space. The extreme northern wing is still stuck fast. In the evening I sent Greiffenberg to Kluge and had him present three questions:

1. Is it advantageous to halt the attack, in order not to use up the precious panzer troops in a hopeless battle?

Answer: No, the enemy is seeking to withdraw everywhere. It is important that we push ahead everywhere.

(Unfortunately, so far I can't see anything of the retreat!)

2. The attack front is 250 km wide. Is it not yet possible to form a clear point of main effort somewhere?

Answer: No, that is not possible on account of the road conditions.

3. Should VI Army Corps [Förster], which is approaching in the direction of Polotsk, be subordinated to Panzer Group Hoth?

Kluge attaches no great importance to that.

12/7/41

A captured order has revealed that the Russians have brought up a new army with six divisions, including armored units, and thrown it into the battle near Vitebsk. They therefore appear intent on fighting at the Dniepr; a captured Russian flying officer confirmed this.

13/7/41

Greiffenberg related a conversation with Halder, according to which the Army High Command is considering the idea of turning into the rear of the Russians fighting in the Ukraine after resting for a few days once we reach Smolensk. On the other hand, elements of Panzer Group Hoth are to be turned sharply to the north in order to surround and trap powerful enemy forces still holding in front of the southern wing of Army Group North [Leeb]. Other elements of the Hoth Panzer Corps are to be left in the former direction of advance to the east.

I drove to Kluge, briefed him and took the following position:

The enemy is only really beaten at one place on the Eastern Front – opposite Army Group Center. If the armored groups now fly apart to the south, east and north, it means foregoing the exploitation of our success. The enemy brought fresh forces up to the Dniepr. These were caught by the panzer army's attack while massing and have been hit hard frontally. What matters now is to completely smash this foe and make it impossible for him to establish another new front before Moscow. To do so it is necessary to tightly concentrate all armored forces and with them drive quickly to the east until I can report that the enemy is offering no more resistance in front of Moscow! I consider diverting elements of Panzer Group Hoth to the north while elements continue to march east to be futile. Because of the tremendous wear and tear on their equipment, the panzer groups are only still an effective striking force if employed in unison. I consider employing individual panzer corps to operate alone pointless, their fighting strength has become too low.

If the army group carries out the tasks outlined, it will – in whole or elements of it – be completely available for further use.

Kluge agreed with my ideas; Schmundt [Hitler's chief Army adjutant] was present at our discussion. I had Greiffenberg brief Halder on my intentions and as well followed it up with a similarly-worded telegram to the Army Command.

Later in the day came the report that the enemy is introducing new forces into the battle between Vitebsk and Orsha. He is therefore far from throwing in the towel and the numerous reports that the enemy was in retreat appear premature.

Toward evening came orders from the Army Command to turn elements of Panzer Group Hoth to the north "in the course of its forward movement," in order to encircle the enemy there together with the right wing of Army Group North! The order is so loosely worded that one can almost read into it what he wants. The only thing that it changes at the moment is that I reserve it to myself to order the next objective for the northernmost element of Panzer group 3, the Kuntzen Corps, as soon as it reaches Nevel. Impossible to say when that is possible, for the enemy stands between Kuntzen and this town.

14/7/41

In the morning I talked with Strauß, who apparently intends to commit overly-strong forces for the capture of Polotsk. I warned against it. If Polotsk is not overrun in the first assault, it will have to be sealed off with weaker forces and taken slowly, bunker by bunker, while everything else continues to advance past to the east. Strauß agreed with me.

The following written directive was sent to the armies:

Panzer Army forward to the line Yelnya-Vop River line – Beloye; Kuntzen Group initially to Nevel, reconnaissance toward Velikiye Luki. 2nd and 9th Armies forward in their sectors initially as far as the line Roslavl-Smolensk-Bayevo.

I drove to the headquarters of the 4th Army, where I discussed the new directive and the possible northward diversion of elements of the Hoth Group with Kluge, then to the 17th Panzer Division, which had got its nose burned the day before yesterday but was in good spirits again already, and subsequently to Panzer Group Guderian. When I returned Halder had already "been at it" again on account of the turn to the north! In the evening there arrived an officer from Army Group North, whom we had invited to discuss our possible assistance. We came to total agreement: for a first, small pocket in front of Army Group North's southern wing, it would suffice if the Kuntzen Corps reached Nevel, blocked the lake sector north of Nevel, and linked up there with the 12th Reconnaissance Battalion of II Corps [Brockdorff-Ahlefeldt]. I cannot promise stronger support for a larger pocket which might form later until my battle here is over.

15/7/41

Strauß has gone ahead and committed four or five divisions against Polotsk. I called him again and told him the same as yesterday. He didn't back down quite as far. I therefore had to tell him that if the attack today did not succeed, he might only keep one division at Polotsk and everything else had to move past to the east; the objective of the left wing is Nevel. This is necessary because I have to move forward and also help the Kuntzen Corps, which is being attacked in its northern flank while marching north. But this corps has to go forward so that it can help Army Group North. To be on the safe side I asked Greiffenberg to once again talk over the subject of Polotsk with the Chief of Staff of the 9th Army, which proved necessary, for Weckmann, too, was trying to get around the solution I was demanding. So he said:

"So the Field Marshall is demanding that Polotsk be taken today!"

That was never talked about! Or he said:

"We can't advance past Polotsk because the enemy is attacking too strongly from there."

But according to the army's previous reports the enemy at Polotsk was behaving absolutely passively. They have just taken it into their heads.

"...If the Russians Get Cheeky"

The Russians are getting cheeky on the southern wing of the 2nd Army. They are attacking near Rogachev and Zhlobin. It gets even better, for the Gomel area is a bad-weather area and will remain so until the northern wing of Army Group Rundstedt comes forward. The Luftwaffe, which was instructed to keep a watch on this area, had previously been unable to locate anything of importance. The first major searchlight activity was reported there tonight. On the other hand forward progress through the swamps by my XXXV Corps is slow and laborious!

At 10:00 I called Brauchitsch, because I had to have confirmation that I was to carry through my battle and only then would be available for other tasks. I said:

"I have the impression that there is a fundamental difference in the assessment of the situation between the Army High Command and the army group. I continue to see the enemy situation in front of the army group as follows: near Rogachev and Zhlobin enemy forces equivalent to approximately two divisions in combat with the 255th Division. But the situation there is safe, because LIII Army Corps and other forces are standing behind it. But the enemy situation around Gomel is not absolutely clear, tonight's reconnaissance reports considerable activity there."

Brauchitsch interjected:

"I have always expected that the 'Gomel group,' which I estimate at ten divisions, would make its presence felt against the right shoulder of the army group."

I continued:

"The Russians are still in Mogilev, also to the north as far as Orsha enemy forces due east of the Dniepr. I suspect twelve to twenty Russian divisions in the Smolensk-Orsha-Vitebsk area. Another enemy group north of Gorodok, one to two Russian divisions in bunker positions around Polotsk; on the extreme northern wing attacks against the flank of the Kuntzen Group advancing toward Nevel. I have no serious concern for my right wing, especially not if XXXV Corps, which is still stuck in the swamps, arrives. On the other hand I must state that a battle is in progress at and east of the Dniepr, which began favorably with the break-in by the two panzer groups, but which is by no means decided. One must be careful not to take the overall situation there too lightly based on local impressions. A victory has not yet been won! Nevertheless I have established contact with *Generalfeldmarschall* von Leeb and in accordance with the Army High Command's directive I will assist him as far as it is in my power. For the present the requests conveyed by *Generalfeldmarschall* von Leeb's liaison officer have been completely fulfilled.

The Kuntzen Group – one motorized and one panzer division – has been deployed across the Nevel; 9th Army has instructions to have strong infantry forces follow in the same direction. If Polotsk is not taken quickly, I will instruct the 9th Army to leave only the most important forces there and carry on to the east with everything else.

Leeb is planning to carry out three 'pockets,' one west of Nevel, the second in the Kholm area and the third still farther north. As I said, the army group will immediately provide assistance at the 'pocket west of Nevel.' But wide-ranging encirclement movements by stronger elements of the Hoth Group in front of the 16th Army's front cannot be carried out until the Battle of Smolensk is over."

Brauchitsch replied:

"The battle of Smolensk first has to be brought to a conclusion while guarding the southeast flank, furthermore all preparations for assistance to the 16th Army have to be made in accordance with the directive issued by me. A continued drive to the east by the panzers after the capture of the area around Smolensk is out of the question. The Russians fight differently than the French, they are insensitive to their flanks. What matters therefore is not winning territory but destroying enemy forces. We must be clear that after taking the area around Smolensk a continued advance by the entire body of infantry is no longer possible for reasons of supply. We will have to make do with a sort of 'expeditionary corps,' which together with tanks will have to fulfill far-reaching missions."

In conclusion I reported:

"For the time being I cannot leave behind the garrison divisions as ordered by the Army High Command, because these forces are needed up front now for the battle. I have ordered that they move on."

Brauchitsch agreed with this and stated that, by and large, the views of the Army Group and of the Army High Command coincided!

Polotsk was taken in the afternoon. I spoke with Strauß about the army's subsequent tasks and told him that XX Army Corps [Materna] had to be inserted between V Corps [Ruoff], whose northern wing was moving on Vitebsk, and VI Corps [Förster], which today is near Polotsk. We are embroiled in a battle and it is very likely that the 9th Army will also become involved. It must prepare itself for this. Strauß reported to me that the 256th Division [Kaufmann] – a division of XX Corps – is, according to its commanding officer, at the end of its tether. I asked him to verify this report and said that I would have to recommend the division for relief if it can do no more. I know that the march performances and the associated demands are immense. But with the battle going on a "staying put" cannot be tolerated. [The division existed until 21 July 1944; the remnants to Corps Detachment "H" as the 256th Divisional Group.]

Weichs reminded me that the primary task of the 2nd Army – ahead to the northeast – remained the same, and that furthermore the army had to secure its right flank and thus that of the army group as well. This can best be achieved if the enemy attacking today in the area of Rogachev is thrown back across the Dniepr. Weichs is of the same opinion. I told him that the 4th Army had sent the 1st Cavalry Division to the attack from Stary Bykhov to the south on both sides of the Dniepr. Actually I should now subordinate it to Weichs, in order to assure the uniformity of the battle on his right wing. But Kluge, with whom I discussed the matter, so implored me to leave him the division temporarily, that I initially acceded to his request. I feel quite uncomfortable about it!

Canaris Fears the Worst

When, in the evening, I talked over the situation with Blumentritt, he poured out his heart to me about how difficult the command of the armored groups was, because the army never gave him a clear and complete picture of its situation and what it was planning!

The situation at Smolensk appears to be causing difficulties for Timoshenko; the following radio message to the Russian general in command at Smolensk was intercepted this morning:

"Your silence is disgraceful, when will you finally understand? They are concerned about your health. Give your assessment of the overall situation at once..."

This was immediately followed by a message that Smolensk was to be held at all costs!

Russian radio announced that the old position of commissar in the Red Army has been restored, that means that the command authority that was passed to the unit commanders a short time ago has been placed back in the hands of the commissars. The whole thing is an indication that they are seeking a stronger command and that the radical wing has prevailed.

In the evening I received a visit from *Admiral* Canaris, head of the intelligence group [Chief of the *Amt Ausland/Abwehr*, or Office of Foreign Intelligence]; he fears the worst.

18/7/41

Things look serious today on the southern wing of the 2nd Army. The enemy has raised his strength there to eight divisions, apparently with a tank corps in reserve. Weichs told me that he would probably also have to commit XIII Corps there. I declared that to be very unwelcome, to be considered only in the most extreme emergency. Now arriving behind LIII [Weisenberger] and XXXXIII [Heinrici] Army Corps' front are: the 260th Division [Schmidt, Hans; Army High Command Reserve] and the 167th Division [Vogl], which has concluded a lone battle lasting days far behind the general front. Weichs has to reach back for these two divisions first. But I also proposed that he move the 258th Division [Henrici] behind the right wing of XIII Corps, or more to the south, so that this division too might be within reach of the army's right wing in case of emergency.

The enemy appears to be sending additional forces down the highway from Moscow in the direction of Smolensk.

Drove to Headquarters, 4th Army, where I once again emphasized to Kluge the necessity of the Kuntzen Corps holding on at Nevel and the ultimate closing of the pocket near Yarzevo. Kluge agrees and will make every effort.

Then I drove to IX Corps. The Commanding General, Geyer, thinks all the reports on the enemy are exaggerated and doesn't believe that there are serious enemy forces near Mogilev or in the pocket around Smolensk. He could be right about Mogilev, but I disagree where Smolensk is concerned.

At the command post of the 137th Division [Bergmann] I learned that the division is unable to move forward because in front of it the 17th Panzer Division [Arnim] is stalled at a collapsed bridge. Awkward, because it is this division which was originally to have closed the pocket east of Smolensk.

When I returned home, Tresckow greeted me with the news that the 2nd Army was considering throwing XII and XIII Corps into the fighting on its right wing. I got the Chief of Staff on the phone; he confirmed the report and said:

"Nothing has happened with piecemeal attacks and the situation there can't be cleared up by fighting a defensive battle. Therefore the Commander-in-Chief wants to commit XII and XIII Corps to attack to the south."

I replied that that was not what I wanted done. I had already said many times that the army's primary mission lay in attacking across the Dniepr to the northeast. That's where the main forces belonged. Only the minimum possible forces must to be used to guard the flank. Shortly thereafter I issued a written order to the army to continue attacking northeast with its main force, move XIII Corps forward toward and across the Dniepr by the shortest route and also divert south from XII Corps only what is absolutely necessary. On orders from the Army Command, Headquarters, XXXXII Corps and the 96th Division are to be released to Army Group North.

"But That Can Change..."

19/7/41

I got the impression from the morning report that the 2nd Army was not acting as I wished and was moving XIII Corps too far to the south. So I sent my Chief of Staff there to set them straight and assert my view. It is high time that we get strong infantry forces across the Dniepr! So far the enemy has sent only scraped-together elements against the southern flank of Guderian's group. But that can change. I can only be certain of destroying the enemy near Smolensk if the 2nd Army finally gains ground to the east across the Dniepr and thus frees the armored forces necessary to close the pocket in the east and guard against the perceptible enemy pressure from the east. I consider the concern about the southern wing of the 2nd Army to be exaggerated, nevertheless the enemy continues to try and attack there. The two reinforced corps deployed there and the 31st Division, which today was sent to the attack to the south by the 2nd Army, have already won too many honors. It is regrettable that I wasn't able to get my way sooner, for 24 hours have been lost. In the morning I wanted to speak to Kluge. Instead Blumentritt came on the phone and claimed that Kluge was just driving away. I said to him:

"Please ask Guderian for me whether or not he is in a position to carry out the order of three days ago to link up with Panzer Group 3 near Yarzevo. If not, I have to commit other forces to do so."

I asked:

"Is everything alright with the command there? Why, for example, is the Infantry Regiment *Großdeutschland* still milling about far behind the front?"

At this point Kluge jumped in and said that he had overheard the conversation and had to defend the armored group against my accusation of poor command – which resulted in a brief argument. The enemy is trying to break out near Smolensk and on the northeastern and northwestern fronts of the pocket. The 7th Panzer Division [Funck] and the 20th Panzer Division [Stumpff] to its north are under attack from the east. The enemy is apparently moving up new forces through Vyazma.

20/7/41

Hell was let loose today! In the morning it was reported that the enemy had broken through the Kuntzen Corps at Nevel. Against my wishes, Kuntzen had sent his main fighting force, the 19th Panzer Division [Knobelsdorff], to Velikiye Luki, where it was tussling about uselessly. At Smolensk the enemy launched a strong attack during the night. Enemy elements also advanced on Smolensk from the south, but they ran into the 17th Panzer Division [Arnim] and were crushed. On the southern wing of the 4th Army the 10th Motorized Division [Loeper] was attacked from all sides and had to be rescued by the 4th Panzer Division [Freiherr von Langermann und Erlenkamp]. The gap between the two armored groups east of Smolensk has still not been closed!

I stepped in again and sent a general staff officer to Panzer Group 2, which characterized today's capture of Yelnya as a great success "which has to be exploited!"

I immediately replied that that was not what mattered, and that the only thing that did was the hermetic sealing of the Smolensk pocket while screening to the east. Greiffenberg spoke with Guderian by telephone at the same time and I now hope that he will be convinced.

No good continues to come from the insertion of Headquarters, 4th Army between the army group and the two armored groups! This battle is getting on my nerves – especially because Guderian is in fact right in his push to drive east! I also consider it a mistake that we don't immediately advance farther to the east until the last enemy reserves facing my front have been crushed.

Heusinger – Brauchitsch

Heusinger [Chief of the Operations Department] of the Army High Command telephoned this morning. I laid down the contents of our discussion in a following letter which I sent by courier to the Commander-in-Chief. Brauchitsch promised to come tomorrow and it will be good if he sees things more clearly before our meeting than previously appears to have been the case.

"(1) The breakthroughs at Nevel are attributable to the fact that, at the time, only elements of LVII Corps were available and could be reached for the secondary mission of maintaining a blocking position and that LVII Corps unnecessarily weakened itself further by sending the 19th Panzer Division off to Velikiye Luki.

(2) *Oberst* Heusinger expressed concern that something like what had happened to the pocket at Nevel might occur to the 'pocket at Mogilev.' No pocket exists at Mogilev, unless one views the many enemy groups and fragments still sitting in the large gaps between the advancing armored units to be 'encircled.' An 'encirclement' of the enemy elements at and east of Mogilev is out of the question until the safety of the elements of the army group fighting in the area around Smolensk is assured against the enemy forces attacking from the east and southeast. That is not yet the case as of today. At the moment there is only one pocket on the army group's front! And it has a hole! For so far we have unfortunately been unable to achieve the union of the inner wings of the two armored groups at and east of Smolensk which we have been striving for for many days; apart from several misunderstandings, this failure is due to the repeated attacks on the elements of Panzer Group 2 en route there by the enemy from the east, southeast and south. Panzer Group 3, too, has not only been attacked from inside the pocket, or from Smolensk and west, but from the east and northeast as well. The plan to close the pocket near the city of Smolensk itself through an attack from the northeast by the 7th Panzer Division failed because the division was itself repeatedly attacked from the east by strong forces with tank support. The enemy also attacked further north. The diversion of two divisions to Nevel by the Kuntzen Corps made itself unpleasantly felt here.

(3) The reasons for the delay in 2nd Army's advance across the Dniepr, as well as the army group's measures to overcome it, are well known. The army is now being urged forward strongly in its sector, while screening against the enemy facing its southern wing with approximately nine divisions.

The army group continues to see its objective as carrying through the battle near Smolensk and reaching its assigned area. The enemy, as evidenced by the radio messages intercepted daily and also by his behavior, wants to win back Smolensk at any cost and to this end is constantly moving in fresh forces. The assumption that is voiced here and there, that the enemy is not acting according to a plan, does not coincide with the facts. Given the energy he has shown in recent days, I think it doubtful that the enemy will allow the fighting here to cease when it suits us, even following the destruction of the forces almost encircled around Smolensk. If full freedom of action is to be won, then the forces which the enemy has brought up to the army group's front in recent days must also be destroyed."

The situation on the southern wing of the 2nd Army has cleared itself up, in that the enemy opposite the corps on the extreme right wing, XXXXIII Army Corps [Heinrici], has ceased his attacks and pulled back. It is also quieter in front of LIII Army Corps [Weisenberger].

Attacking south along the Dniepr, the 31st Division has advanced as far as Novy Bykhov and will hopefully cross the Dniepr there tomorrow. XIII Army Corps is crossing the river at and north of Stary Bykhov, XII Corps is attacking Mogilev, and the left wing of IX Corps is continuing to advance east down the highway.

More radio messages from the Russian high command of the western front have been intercepted, demanding in a threatening way the recapture of Smolensk.

The air fleets are to supposed attack Moscow tonight [Moscow was bombed on the night of 20-21 July; a total of 104 tonnes of bombs was dropped.] I would consider it more appropriate to commit the fighting strength of the Luftwaffe without any limitation to smash the enemy's reserves.

21/7/41

In the morning the report arrived that the gap at the eastern end of the Smolensk pocket had been closed – in the evening the opposite turned out to be true. Pilots report that strong enemy forces are marching out of the pocket to the east.

All day long heavy attacks against the southern flank and front of Panzer Group 2 [Guderian], against Panzer Group 3's [Hoth] eastern front, and on Smolensk. The situation facing XXIV Panzer Corps [Geyr von Schweppenburg] on the southern wing was so threatening that I had to order to the 2nd Army to restore it. In the army's view all of XIII Army Corps is necessary to do so, and with it IV Corps [Schwedler] is now being turned toward the enemy attacking the army group's southern flank.

Acknowledgement of the Enemy's Military Achievements

A quite remarkable success for such a badly-battered opponent! Pilot reports indicate that he is moving up additional forces against our southern flank.

Brauchitsch arrived in the morning. I described the situation to him and he approved my proposal that the army group advance east until the enemy sitting in front of its nose has been shaken off.

But a necessary precondition for this will be that clearing of the Smolensk pocket is assured. The army group's next task is to reach its assigned areas and there reorganize and bring up to strength its units, so that the advance can be resumed, to the southeast by elements of the southern wing and Panzer Group Guderian, and to the east or northeast by the main body and Panzer Group Hoth. Maximum preparations are to be completed by the beginning of August. If necessary, infantry divisions are to be disbanded to bring the panzer and infantry divisions up to strength. The big strategic idea is still unclear; we are supposed to receive a directive on it.

Kluge was present at the meeting. While I was outside he took the opportunity to complain to Brauchitsch about interference by me in his area of command! This claim is unfounded. Always, and now as well, I have scrupulously avoided any intermixing in Kluge's area of command, because of my awareness of his ego. But such was his eloquence that Brauchitsch fell for it and asked me to leave Kluge the necessary freedom. I replied that I was sorry if Brauchitsch was bothered with quarrels between generals at a serious time; but Kluge's action forced me to set things straight. I outlined in broad strokes Kluge's strange behavior from the time in Posen, his attacks on me then, his strange behavior on the telephone on the 19th [of July] etc. I told Brauchitsch that it was very hard not to wound his vanity.

"...That We...Give The Churches Back Their Vocations..."

22/7/41

In the morning the commander of my army rear area, Schenckendorff, arrived with the head of the military-economic staff [Military-Economic and Armaments Department, Thomas]. Schenckendorff described the cooperation of all the agencies operating in his area as very good. I told him that the last thing we needed was a hate-filled population in our rear and that we had to try to get the people to work with us willingly; in the country I am sure that this can be achieved either by giving the people a piece of land or by promising them a share of the harvest for their own use, in short, giving them a personal interest in seeing to it that something is harvested. We have also had good results with the reintroduction of Sunday, in that we gave the churches that had been converted into cinemas or market halls back their vocations. He was of the same opinion and said that he was already acting in this direction. The economic leader complained that the army had curiously taken agricultural machinery away with it, so that there was very little available for the harvest. But he hoped to be able to help himself, specifically if and when the promised farmers from home arrived to help out. A number of businesses, such as leather works, tanneries, bakeries, breweries, etc, some of which had considerable stockpiles put away, were already running again. There were difficulties at one tannery, because the SS had shot 60 of the business' workers as communists!

In general the day passed quietly, even on XXIV Panzer Corp's troubled front. The Russians are defending themselves doggedly at Mogilev, so that the attack by my two best divisions [the 23rd (Hellmich) and the 7th (Gablenz)] is making only slow progress.

Only reluctantly did I decide, following the urgings of the Army High Command, to subordinate the encircling front around Smolensk to Headquarters, 4th Army [Kluge]; it could no longer be avoided, because otherwise a mixup between the armored and infantry units becomes inevitable. The most obvious solution – technically and personally – would be to eliminate 4th Army Headquarters and couple the armored groups with the armies, as they were before.

In order to obtain information for planning our next steps, an inquiry was made of Kluge as to how much farther to the east we had to advance to shake off the enemy there and to achieve operational freedom, and whether and when the armored groups were in a position to carry out these tasks alone. The inquiry had just been sent when Brauchitsch called and said that the *Führer* had ordered that a further advance to the east by the panzers was out of the question!

I passed the order on to the 4th Army's Chief of Staff.

23/7/41

Strauß called in the morning and asked me to leave him his V Corps, which yesterday was subordinated to Headquarters, 4th Army, as part of the pocket front. I had to refuse for the moment. Blumentritt advised that all was proceeding well. Then, suddenly, everything changed again! Elements of VIII [Heitz] and XX Corps [Materna] must certainly still go into the pocket front. I therefore arrived at the solution of placing the now very strong elements of 9th Army deployed at the pocket back under that army's command and made them "subject to Kluge's directions for the pocket front." A jury-rigged structure!

On Panzer Group 2's southern flank the 10th Motorized Division [Loeper] is heavily engaged. XIII Corps' operation will bring it relief. VII Corps [Fahrmbacher] is attacking toward Mogilev from the west with two divisions, while the 78th Division [Gallenkamp] is advancing from the south on the east bank of the Dniepr.

We have still not succeeded in closing the hole at the east end of the Smolensk pocket.

24/7/41

Weichs telephoned in the morning and gave me a very pessimistic description of the situation on his southern wing. He suggested that Bobruisk would be threatened if further forces were taken away from his right wing. I told him that I didn't care about Bobruisk. He now had to move the forces to the other bank; I told him it was in his own interest, for he would have to attack on the east bank of the Dniepr later. I would accept the responsibility.

During the morning the advance notice for a new directive arrived, which divides my army group into three parts: according to the instructions, I am to divert one group of forces, including Panzer Group Guderian [PzGr 2], southeast to Army Group South, a group without tanks is to go towards Moscow, and Panzer Group Hoth [PzGr 3] is to be diverted north and subordinated to Army Group North [Leeb].

Opposition to Dispersal of His Forces

The army group commanders have been summoned by the Army High Command for tomorrow to discuss these new plans. I sent a report to Brauchitsch opposing the new operation and suggested that they remove the army group headquarters if they stick to the announced plan of action. Perhaps they will correctly construe from this suggestion that I am "piqued." That is rubbish! But if the army group is carved up into three parts there will be no need for the headquarters.

Mogilev, which is now under attack by three divisions supported by the artillery of a fourth, is in the process of collapsing but isn't dead yet. The Russians are unbelievably stubborn!

Toward evening I received a visit from Kesselring, who is unhappy about the new plan. He declared that he is in no position to effectively engage the Russian Air Force at Moscow from his present bases. I told him what I had just learned, that Göring had informed the *Führer* that large numbers of Russians were streaming out of the pocket at Smolensk to the east!

Then in the evening the *Führer*, too, called me and asked the status of the hole in the pocket. I briefed him on all the details, which he took in calmly. He suggested that perhaps we might try closing the pocket from the north. I replied that there were plans to do so, that at the moment the forces there were still too weak, and that I hoped to be able to carry it through in a few days.

Back from the front, Greiffenberg brought me a letter from Guderian in which he complained that Kluge had "revealed" to him that I was dissatisfied with his command and had made disparaging remarks to the Commander-in-Chief of the Army about his command. I was able to calm him and wrote to him that the latter did not correspond to the facts and that my momentary dissatisfaction was not to be taken seriously.

Small Pocket!

25/7/41

Generalfeldmarschall Keitel arrived in the morning for a briefing on the "hole at Smolensk." Then he related the *Führer*'s ideas on the subject, the gist of which was that for the moment we should encircle the Russians tactically wherever we meet them, rather than with strategic movements, and then destroy them in small pockets. This would be faster and more effective then the previously-used method. Unfortunately, I consider this to be a mistake and am convinced that it will take us longer to reach our objective this way! Keitel remarked that the *Führer* would like to see his proposed small pocket used on the 2nd Army's right wing and the elements of Panzer Group 2 situated there, or the XXIV (Motorized) Corps, take part. The *Führer*, too, is worried about this wing, because the forces defeated by Reichenau are retreating north in the direction of Mozyr and from there could fall upon my army group's southern wing. I told him that this conflicted with the directive given me yesterday by the Army High Command. According to it, the forces of my right wing, together with Panzer Group Guderian, are supposed to be sent against objectives far to the southeast, while Keitel's proposal calls for these elements to be turned southwest. Keitel is going to speak with the Army High Command about these matters, and I telephoned Greiffenberg, who is with the Army High Command, with the request that he do the same.

Keitel said that the occupation of Iceland by the Americans was not easy to take and that they had been forced to limit our submarines to attacking only vessels which are definitely hostile, so as not to give the Americans the excuse they are seeking to enter the war. They did exactly the same thing in the World War, and I fear that, just as then, now too the Americans will find another reason. The Japanese are taking the opportunity to establish themselves in Indochina, but in contrast they are lukewarm about the hoped-for attack on Russia! Neither one nor the other surprises me.

In the morning I learned that the 2nd Army wants to move VI Corps from Mogilev to the southeast, in order to free up XXIV Motorized Corps there. I put a stop to that and ordered that the corps' left wing be moved forward toward Choslavichi as soon as possible.

26/7/41

It turns out that the Russians have completed a new, concentrated buildup around my projecting front. In many places they have tried to go over to the attack. Astonishing for an opponent who is so beaten; they must have unbelievable masses of materiel, for even now the field units still complain about the powerful effect of the enemy artillery. The Russians are also becoming more aggressive in the air, which is not surprising, for we can't yet get at their air bases near Moscow. In the morning I reported to Brauchitsch the contents of yesterday's conversation with Keitel. I said that I couldn't reconciled myself to his proposed "smaller pockets." The small one around Rogachev is scarcely worthwhile. At the larger one around Gomel we will be missing the opposing pincer from the west. The only possible Dniepr crossing lies near Ryetschitza and will be very hard to take. Furthermore, both pockets face threats to their eastern flanks. If Guderian is turned south as sharply as planned, the gap between the later southern group and the elements of the army group going east will become ever larger. The attack by this group will get stuck with its right wing, for there are strong enemy forces at Rogachev. I continue to support a powerful, concentrated drive to the east by the entire army group, to destroy Timoshenko's badly-battered armies. Securing the attack's southern flank would, for the most part, be a matter for Army Group South. From all that I heard, however, I doubt that the Supreme Command will be talked into it.

27/7/41

The Smolensk pocket has finally been closed from the north. Our weak forces will hopefully contain the expected counter-pressure. Brauchitsch arrived in the morning with news that the *Führer* has ordered the attack to the south; Guderian [Panzer Group 2] is to advance east of the Sozh toward Gomel. I once again pointed out that the left flank of this attack will be threatened from Roslavl.

"Combat-Ready, If..."

Guderian arrived in the afternoon and reported that the answer to the Commander-in-Chief of the Army's question, whether the armored group could carry out the drive on Gomel before it was rested and brought up to strength, had to be no. The armored group would be combat-ready again on approximately the 5th [of August], provided replacement materiel and personnel had arrived by then. Concerning the planned attack to the south, Guderian declared the country into which he was to be deployed to be "impossible." He will have to swing out farther to the east, but not until the area surrounding Roslavl is in our hands. I briefed Brauchitsch on our conversation immediately and advised that I would order the attack on Roslavl. Available for the task are VII Corps [Fahrmbacher] and elements of IX Corps [Geyer]; but otherwise my front south of the Dniepr has become dangerously thin and there is only one division in reserve behind it. Out of this situation I am now supposed to head off in three different directions.

In the evening I ordered the withdrawal of both armored groups and subordinated Panzer Group Hoth to the 9th Army so as to put the relief movements and the final act of the Smolensk pocket in one hand. The southern boundary has been moved to the Dniepr. South of the river Headquarters, 4th Army has been withdrawn so that – as planned by the Army High Command – it can prepare for its new mission, the drive to the southeast, and be briefed by Headquarters, 2nd Army. Panzer Group Guderian, with IX Corps, which is already under its command, and VII Army Corps, which is coming from Mogilev, has been concentrated under Guderian's command with orders to take Roslavl. Whatever can be found in the rear army area is being scraped together for the coming missions, for the Army Group is much too thin, especially south of the Dniepr, to undertake anything serious. – Mogilev has fallen; 35,000 prisoners and 245 guns!

28/7/41

Reduction of the Smolensk pocket is proceeding slowly. Again today the enemy tried to burst the ring from within and without.

Strong enemy cavalry has appeared around the 2nd Army's southeast wing, making itself unpopular by carrying out ambushes and blowing up railroad tracks behind the front. Schenckendorff, commander of the rear army area, received orders to put things in order.

I once again discussed with Halder the difficulties associated with the new operations, which lie in the stripping of forces from the right flank of the elements of the army group deployed toward Moscow. He already knows that Guderian has rejected the push due east of the Sozh on account of the terrain and expects that his left wing will now be approximately at the Iput. If Guderian goes south instead of southeast, then he will provide no relief to the southern flank of the eastern group. Halder is in no doubt that under these circumstances a significant advance to the east by the weak forces left to the army group for the drive to the east will be impossible. He still hopes to change the *Führer*'s mind.

The commanders of the armies and armored groups arrived in the afternoon; Greiffenberg discussed with them the details of the relief of the armored groups and the insertion of the infantry divisions into the front line.

Then a summary of the new directive arrived: the army group is being scattered to the four winds.

The OKH's New Decisions Are Rejected

Kluge, who had dinner with me, is as opposed to the new decisions by the Army High Command as I am.

Schmundt arrived in the late evening and had the following to say about the *Führer*'s plans: the main thing is to eliminate the area of Leningrad, then the raw materials region of the Donets Basin. The *Führer* cares nothing about Moscow itself. The enemy at Gomel is to be wiped out to clear the way for larger operations.

That differs somewhat from what is said in the Army Command's directive!

29/7/41

I once again wrote to the Army Command, sorted out what limited forces are available for the individual operations to the south, east and northeast, and reported that the army group is too weak for a simultaneous attack in two directions. I proposed committing all the forces I could bring together to the mission chosen by the Army Command as the most important and putting aside the other missions.

Spoke by telephone with Strauß; I told him that the most urgent thing is to bring an end to the Smolensk pocket and free up the panzer corps so that it can rest and refit. I gave the army the task of establishing a bridgehead across the Dniepr, because reports by Panzer Group 3 [Hoth] indicated that elements were already across the Dniepr south of the highway. The objective – to capture bridgeheads over the Dniepr and the Vop and reach Beloye – can only be achieved if it is carried out easily and smoothly in the course of the advance.

Army Group North, whose southernmost corps, L Corps, is bogged down near Velikiye Luki, has proposed subordinating the corps to the 9th Army [Strauß] until things are moving there again. Strauß agrees with this subordination, therefore I issued the necessary orders.

"The Fact Is That Our Troops Are Tired..."

Powerful Russian attacks are in progress on almost the entire front of the 9th Army. Forty batteries [of artillery] have been counted at one place opposite its eastern front. In some cases the Russians have thrown scarcely-trained industrial workers from Moscow into the fight. The enemy achieved a penetration south of Beloye, the significance of which was at first overestimated by the 9th Army. The fact is that our troops are tired and also are not exhibiting the required steadiness because of heavy officer casualties. – In this situation orders arrived to release the Richthofen Air Corps [VIII *Fliegerkorps*]. When asked about this by Keitel, I had told him that it was highly undesirable at this moment and was, in the opinion of Kesselring, "impossible." The *Führer* was supposedly told the opposite, a misunderstanding which I asked Jodl to clear up and report to Brauchitsch.

In the evening a proposal arrived from Weichs [2nd Army]; he wants to create the much-debated small pocket at Rogachev with his own forces. I passed the proposal on to Halder, because it was to some degree inconsistent with the Army Command's plans concerning the "bigger pocket." The English are reporting: "The battle at Smolensk has ended with a Russian victory!"

30/7/41

I spoke to Weichs once again and asked whether he was still of the opinion that the proposed attack would succeed; he confirmed that he was.

Then I spoke to Brauchitsch. Because of the attack on Rogachev he reserved the decision to himself, agreed with Roslavl, and finally proposed encircling the enemy near Velikiye Luki – on the northern wing of the 9th Army – by having elements of the 9th Army advance on Toropets with tanks from the south, and elements of II Corps, which is south of Kholm, from the north.

I drove to the 9th Army, where they welcomed this proposal.

I telephoned Greiffenberg from 9th Army Headquarters and instructed him to inform Brauchitsch that a concentric attack on Toropets with the assistance of II Army Corps offered good prospects. Rogachev, Roslavl and Toropets – all three are "small" affairs, but they can't be avoided if we don't wish to be hindered by difficulties in the flanks as soon as we begin a new operation. However, I don't know yet if I will get panzer divisions for the attack at Rogachev and the one on Toropets, given the present state of the armored forces, and the going will be difficult without them.

When I returned, Greiffenberg greeted me with the news that the operation just ordered had been cancelled and that a new directive was coming.

In his Directive Number 34 of 30 July 1941, Hitler ordered Army Group Center to halt its offensive operations and go over to the defensive. This cardinal military-doctrinaire decision came as a reaction to the surprisingly strong Russian resistance, especially north and south of Smolensk.

The attack at Rogachev was approved by the Army High Command and orders were issued for the one at Velikiye Luki.

The 2nd Army wants to send its southern wing across the Dniepr at Rogachev but doesn't want to attack Zhlobin, farther to the south, because it is too strongly fortified. I disagree. If the main thrust by the right wing goes through Rogachev the operation will end in a frontal attack. They have to go as far as the Zhlobin area, have to leave the fortified city alone, and attack across the Dniepr to its right or left. The extreme southern wing of the army has to be sent ahead toward Ryetschitza. As well XXXXIII Corps has to attack now, also in order to make it easier for LIII Corps to advance. Greiffenberg spoke to the 2nd Army in this regard.

Hardenburg [Bock's adjutant] has become ill and has to be taken to Berlin.

Bock had had contact with the family of Count Hardenburg for many years before the Second World War. Renate Countess von Hardenburg wrote on 27 May 1931: " Our little Bock was also here for two days (Neuhardenburg Castle)..." From: Agde, Günther, Carl-Hans Graf von Hardenburg, Berlin 1994, PP 124.

31/7/41

The pocket at Smolensk is still not done, although four divisions have attacked there side to side on nearly normal frontages. Very regrettable, for the enemy's attacks on the army group's eastern front are growing ever stronger and I eventually have to release the divisions from the pocket in order to relieve Panzer Group 3 [Hoth].

The Chief of Staff of the 9th Army, Weckmann, is very downcast. He is also pessimistic about the situation on the northern wing. I told Strauß that it was imperative that the pocket be brought to a conclusion quickly and why.

Concerning the attack on the northern wing I said: orders for the attack have been issued; whether the 12th Division is coming from Army Group North I do not know. No matter what the circumstances the objective is to dislodge the enemy there. But he might examine the thing carefully and tell me whether, how and when the attack can be made without rushing. He must advise me if he comes to the conclusion that there is no chance of success.

A Russian courier pilot has landed behind our lines. The orders found in his possession have revealed the Russian distribution of forces opposite the army group's southern wing. I asked Weichs to have his Ic brief him on this. There is only one division facing his XXXXIII Corps, another far away from it at the Ptich. The opportunity is especially favorable for quick action by XXXXIII Corps to smash one, then the other Russian division with a two-fold superiority and in doing so also clear the way to the east for XXXV Corps.

"I wouldn't wait any longer."

Weichs said that he wanted to do it at the same time as the attack at Rogachev so as not to alert the enemy; but he was going to think it over again.

Kesselring is helping me as best he can, nevertheless his remaining forces are very weak after giving up VIII Air Corps [Richthofen]. He confirmed a prisoner's statement that the enemy is sending stronger forces against my front from Moscow. It is also not out of the question that the enemy is moving in forces from Leningrad.

I have almost no reserves left to meet the enemy massing of forces and the constant counterattacks. They took away my offensive air power and heavy artillery during the offensive and diverted some of the reserves originally destined for my front, the painful consequences of which are beginning to show. With the present state of the railroads I can't receive any help from home or through the shifting of forces. I have to fall back on the divisions of the army group deployed in the rear army area. It will take many days even for these to arrive. Only the 61st Division [Haenicke], which is marching in three widely-separated groups, is slowly nearing the fighting front. And the 9th Army is already urgently requesting that the first third of the division be positioned behind the Hoth Group [PzGr 3]. With a heavy heart I have to consent.

Greiffenberg briefed the Army High Command and asked that any units from home – replacement formations or whatever – be moved up into the rear area, because I urgently need those of my divisions still there at the front.

It is very nice of the Russians not to encode a large part of their radio transmissions. Today, for example, we heard the commander of the Russian cavalry operating behind my southern wing report that he had to withdraw because he was out of food, munitions and horses.

1/8/41

The business at Smolensk is still not in order. We don't appear to be impressing the Russians there much either, for an intercepted radio message said that there was "little activity" by the Germans. I once again spoke by telephone with Strauß and with the Commanding General of VIII Corps [Heitz], in order to once again point out the strategic importance of the rapid winding-up of the pocket. Since the afternoon report by the 9th Army suggests that it is already planning to withdraw three divisions from the pocket, I sent it a telex demanding "the total destruction of the enemy in the Smolensk pocket on 2 August."

Guderian's attack on Roslavl is going well.

Strauß has ordered the attack at Velikiye Luki for the 2nd [August] and has asked for strong support from the Luftwaffe, which was promised to him.

I once again spoke with Weichs as to whether it wasn't time to have XXXXIII Corps attack. His reasons against it didn't make sense to me. I may perhaps be able to free up a panzer unit for the attack on the east bank of the Dniepr by 9 August. Weichs is of the view that we should exploit the present favorable situation and should not wait for the panzer unit. From the Army High Command came a new directive which cancelled the previous instructions and ordered the army group to prepare for the drive to the southwest as well as a drive to the east. They have apparently given up on the attack to the northeast by the Hoth group.

2/8/41

The Russians built a bridge on the eastern front of the Smolensk pocket during the night and are "running off to the east," as one pilot report said! Panzer Group 3 is to try to take the bridge site by attacking from the north. I have made the commanders of the 17th Panzer [Arnim] and 20th Motorized [Zorn] Divisions responsible for seeing to it that everything is done to prevent the Russians from escaping the pocket. The situation became clearer in the afternoon; the 20th Motorized Division had lost the village of Ratschino, the site of the bridge, probably three days ago! I subsequently called the 9th Army, where I was only able to reach the Chief of Staff, to advise that the affair in the pocket had to be brought to an end now.

Things are going badly for the 293rd [Infantry] Division on the 2nd Army's extreme southern wing. It got its nose burned at the Ptich. That was to be expected, for I was unfortunately unable to prevent the bad luck through a timely attack by XXXXIII Corps. But now I have informed the army that I will have to order the attack if it doesn't do it itself. It subsequently advised that it had been ordered for the morning of the 4th [of August].

The attack by the 9th Army's left wing at Velikiye Luki has bogged down. An infantry division [the 251st, Kratzert until 6 August 41] appears to have dropped the ball.

The attack on Roslavl is still going well. The enemy troops there are poor, our losses are slight. It is a pity that we are at the end of our tether just now, and also that a thorough replenishing of the panzer divisions can no longer be postponed. It is bad that the nerves of those burdened with great responsibility are starting to waver; today there was an argument with Strauß, who took offence at something that never even happened. Unfortunately I also became angry.

3/8/41

Drove to VIII [Heitz] and V [Ruoff] Corps. Both have suffered considerable casualties, especially in officers, but are proud of their success. The fight in the Smolensk pocket is nearing its end. V Corps created a small extra pocket inside the big one, in which it took a large quantity of materiel and a few thousand prisoners. The number of prisoners at Roslavl is also encouraging.

Congratulations from Hitler on the "Unprecedented Successes"

4/8/41

In the morning the *Führer* arrived; he repeatedly congratulated me in a very friendly way on the "unprecedented successes."

I described the situation to him. From our subsequent discussion it appears that he is not yet clear on how the operations should now proceed. One of the possibilities he spoke of was an attack to the east; I happily agreed and said that in this way we would surely meet the Russian strength and that a decision against what was probably his last forces was to be hoped for there. Guderian [PzGr 2] and Hoth [PzGr 3] outlined the situation of the armored troops. The *Führer* immediately resigned himself to the fact that relief and repairs will take time. He will decide today to what extent he can help the panzer divisions replenish their equipment. When asked by the *Führer*, and on one later occasion, I was able to plead the cause of the friendly and helpful population. I expressed concern as to whether we had sufficient work forces in the country to bring in the harvest.

"This People Would Not Be Difficult To Lead!"

On the basis of rumors passed on to me, which later turned out to be exaggerated, I had Police General Nebel, who was responsible for my rear area but who was not under my command, issue instructions that within the limited bounds of my headquarters executions were only to be carried out if they involved armed bandits or criminals. Gersdorff reported that Nebel had promised to do so.

Yesterday a number of churches which the bolsheviks had converted, for the most part into cinemas or "godless exhibitions," were given back their vocation. The population had come, often from far away, cleaned the churches and decorated them with flowers. Many pictures of Christ and icons which had been hidden for decades were brought out. When the military services were over, the people – not just the old, but many young as well – streamed into the churches and kissed the holy objects – including the crosses around the necks of the armed forces chaplains – and often remained there praying until evening. – This people would not be difficult to lead!

The Smolensk pocket is coming to an end. Significant enemy elements have also been encircled at Roslavl. Near Yelnya the Russians have attacked and broken into our lines.

5/8/41

XXXXIII Corps finally attacked on the 2nd Army's right wing. It is advancing easily. The northern wing of XXXV Corps, which is to advance out of the swamps across the Ptich, has also slowly started to move. The penetration at Yelnya has been eliminated; otherwise it became quieter there today. I had hoped that would be the case, for the attacks there no longer make any sense for the Russians since they can no longer save the affair at Smolensk. The battle there is over, the take in prisoners and booty is very great! The Russians have also suffered badly at Roslavl. – On and behind the right wing of the 2nd Army the commander of the rear army area is still battling the Russian cavalry corps, of which hopefully not much will be left.

A precondition for any further operation is the defeat of the enemy on the army group's flanks, both of which are lagging far behind. I am not completely happy with the 2nd Army's attack plans on the southern wing and once again I tried through Greiffenberg to bring about a strengthening of both decisive attack wings. The situation would be better if XXXXIII Corps had attacked several days ago. But I hope that after their many futile attacks, the Russians there are tired and will not hold.

The attack on the northern wing, by 2nd Army, has to be repeated; it is no simple matter. Hopefully we will be able to refurbish at least one panzer division in time to take part in the attack. The Army Command has ordered that at least one division of Army Group North's II Corps [Brockdorff-Ahlefeldt] is to advance south from Kholm and thus support our attack. I don't believe it will happen, for Army Group North has its own work cut out for it.

In the evening I issued the following order of the day:

"With the destruction of the Russian divisions cut off at Smolensk, the three-week 'Battle at the Dniepr and Dvina and of Smolensk' has concluded in another brilliant victory for German arms and German fulfillment of duty.

Taken as booty were: 309,110 prisoners, 3,205 captured or destroyed tanks, 3,000 guns, 341 aircraft. The numbers are not yet complete. This deed of yours, too, has become part of history! It is with gratitude and pride that I look upon a force that is capable of such an accomplishment. Long live the Führer!"

Long Flanks!

6/8/41

A thorough study of the 2nd Army's proposal for the attack on its right wing, which is planned for the 7th [of August], revealed that just a single division is to attack on the entire Dniepr front and toward Zhlobin, at the most strongly-defended place. The attack on the right wing is thus doomed to fail. Everything will therefore have to come from the left. But there the divisions are holding fronts twelve kilometers wide and the only reserves behind them are one infantry regiment and the [1st] Cavalry Division. That won't do! With a heavy heart I gave the order to postpone the attack and asked Weichs to come and see me. By chance Halder arrived too. He agrees with my view. He was present when I discussed with Weichs my concept of how the attack was to be conducted; once again Halder was in complete agreement. The trend is simple:

Strengthen the two wings at the expense of the center by moving XXXXIII Corps into the area south of Zhlobin and taking a division from the center, and by moving the 162nd Division [Franke] to the eastern wing. A panzer division is to be deployed on the left wing if at all possible. Guderian protested against the handing over of a panzer division, even to the point of refusing an order. I can sympathize with him, as he wants to let his forces rest and bring them up to strength, but in this case he is carrying it too far! In Halder's opinion we can only cope with the Russian conduct of battle if we also deploy individual panzer divisions on the wings of the attack fronts, in order to prevent them being stopped.

If we don't succeed in doing so, in his opinion the result will be uncomfortably long flanks, as is the case with me at the moment.

Fighting Value of the Field Forces Drops

7/8/41

In the morning came the surprising report that at Roslavl the enemy has pulled back far to the south and especially to the southeast. I asked Guderian to immediately conduct reconnaissances in force in order to find out what is going on. Later in the day Guderian proposed taking advantage of the gap left by the enemy near Roslavl to overrun the enemy in front of his extreme right wing, or in front of the 7th [Infantry] Division, with the 3rd [Model] and 4th [Frhr. von Langermann und Erlenkamp] Panzer Divisions, in order to quiet the situation there. He requested that after completing this task, which he intends for the 9th, he might advance farther to the southwest toward Krasnopolye on the 10th, in order to roll up the enemy opposite the eastern wing of the 2nd Army. In this way the deployment of a panzer division on the left wing of the 2nd Army will become unnecessary! Since by evening the reports of the major enemy withdrawal had been confirmed, I gave Guderian free rein and by way of Greiffenberg pointed out that the attack on Krasnopolye was ordered for the 10th, if the situation at all allowed, and that after reaching Krasnopolye a further advance toward Chechersk could be of decisive importance.

In the course of the day I briefly discussed these plans with Halder, who agreed [See Halder War Diary, III, PP 159]. The 2nd Army was briefed and instructed to stand by to move out as soon as the attack by the tanks opposite the eastern wing became perceptible.

The extreme right wing continues to be a source of worry.

I tried to convince the 2nd Army how necessary it is to push ahead forcibly and thus provide the flanking cover that XXXXIII Corps needs to cross the Beresina and be able to attack across the Dniepr. Another day has been lost in spite of the fact that the leading division of XXXV Corps has as good as no enemy forces in front of it. As well there is the fact that the Beresina is 300 meters wide where XXXV Corps has to cross and the army's bridging equipment has not yet arrived.

On the rest of the army group's front small-scale attacks at the hot spots, otherwise quiet enough that the withdrawal of armored and motorized divisions from the front can continue.

The situation is nevertheless extremely tense. If I want to create a reserve and try to pull out a division to do so, it is declared "impossible," if a division deployed in the rear army area arrives at the front it is snatched from my hands! I therefore wrote to the commanders of the armies and armored groups, made them aware of the results of such a blinkered policy, and asked them to be reasonable on this point. – I don't exactly know how a new operation is to take place out of this situation and with the slowly sinking fighting strength of our constantly attacking forces – but things are undoubtedly even worse for the Russians!

A very friendly telegram from old Field Marshall von Mackensen came with today's Armed Forces communique.

8/8/41

VII Corps attacked south from Roslavl, encountered only weak enemy forces, and reached the area 30 km south and southeast of Roslavl. The enemy has in fact withdrawn or has been unable to plug the gap created by our surprise attack. If the attack to the southwest by XXIV Panzer Corps really gets going in the days to come, it can bring significant relief to the very tense situation. The tension was manifested today in two urgent requests from the 9th Army, one close on the heels of the other. The army requested the employment in the front of the last reserves stationed behind it, a shortening of its front line, and allocation of the 14th (Motorized) Division, which was just pulled out to rest and refit, as reserve. In the afternoon there came a telex from Panzer Group 3, which urgently asked that I refrain from allocating the 14th (Motorized) Division!

"...My Duty to Get Things Moving"

I first responded to the army with three questions:

"(1) Can the army hold its position at all without the armored group?

(2) Can the attack on Velikiye Luki be made in the present situation?

(3) Can the army begin a new operation in the foreseeable future or not?"

When, toward evening, a considered response arrived from the 9th Army, I released to it the last division for operations and the 14th Motorized Division to allocate as reserve. I left it to the army's discretion to order the withdrawal of the front from the projecting corner at Beloye, however I pointed out that the place would probably have to be taken again in the coming operation.

To the Guderian Group went orders to advance on Krasnopolye and to prepare for a further advance toward Chechersk after eliminating the enemy in front of the 7th Division. Guderian suggested carrying on to Gomel at once, which is the correct thing to do and which I would approve without hesitation if XXXXIII Corps on the extreme southern wing of the 2nd Army was not lagging so far behind that the counterattack lacked the pincer deployed toward Gomel. In spite of – or indeed on account of the great difficulties XXXXIII Corps is meeting in crossing the Beresina, I issued a detailed order to the 2nd Army calling for a capable mixed battalion from XXXXIII Corps to reach the Dniepr by the 10th [August]. I also gave a demanding order to XXXV Corps, even though I know what tremendous march difficulties the corps has to overcome on bottomless roads in pouring rain. I realize that this is an infringement on the army's powers; but it is my duty to get things moving.

"...Have the Feeling That the OKH Overestimates the Army's Forces"

9/8/41

Guderian launched his attack with XXIV Panzer Corps. The tanks are making slow progress over bottomless roads.

When Greiffenberg informed me that the Army High Command is taking an interest in our offensive plans on the northern wing, I called Halder and told him that I too was not happy with the direction of attack – from south to north – but that there was no other way to go about it, for we can't attack through the city of Velikiye Luki and going around to the north is out because, as 9th Army reports, there is impassable swamp there. Halder asked if we didn't want to commit tanks as well. I replied: if the Army High Command believes that the attack still has time, I would gladly wait until Hoth and his tanks are ready to attack again. Halder said that he would most like to develop the planned attack on the northern wing into a new large operation, for apparently the ideas of the Supreme Command are now developing in the direction we wish. I answered that the decisive factor in everything was when Hoth was ready to attack. – Furthermore I said to Halder that the 9th Army wasn't exactly eager to attack at the moment, for I have the feeling that the Army High Command has overestimated the army's forces. In the evening Hoth reported that he would be ready by the 20th [August]. I had that passed on to Halder and as well reported that we could attack on approximately the 23rd of August.

In the afternoon I received a visit from Weichs, who was offended by my constant pushing on his right wing. I tried to show him that it was the only way and we reached a mutual understanding in all cordiality.

He would like to make his attack [Rogachev] even if the panzer corps is unable to take part for whatever reason, but would like to wait for the participation of XXXXIII Corps, which should be possible from about the 14th [August]. He wonders whether in this case he should not – to avoid losing time – have his left wing attack on the 13th. I agree.

10/8/41

The attack by XXIV Panzer Corps has made good progress. But the corps does not appear to have gained nearly enough breathing room to continue in the direction of Chechersk. Yesterday evening came a proposal from Guderian, whose aim is to halt XXIV [Panzer] Corps' attack after the situation with the 7th Division is cleared up, make an about face, and exploit the gap at Roslavl for the entire Army Group Guderian to attack the enemy opposite its eastern front with a strong right wing and roll it up from south to north. Guderian justified this by saying that the Russians in front of the southern half of his front are worn down. A daring idea, but one that I can't approve without hesitation. The enemy at Yelnya is still not worn down – on the contrary! Powerful reserves have been identified behind his front. If he should be rolled up from south to north, our flank would be turned to these reserves. The attack could yield a brief tactical success, but then will result in a costly battle against the forces the enemy brings in from Moscow. Our previous experience suggests he will commit everything that he can scrape together. Army Group Guderian

[PzGr 2] is too weak to also defeat these forces on its own. 4th and 9th Armies are busy, Panzer Group Hoth [PzGr 3] will not be ready to attack until the 20th [August]. The whole thing becomes a partial blow which places the armored group at risk without promising a strategic success. We can risk more when the enemy in front of 2nd Army is defeated.

But in order to leave nothing undone, I authorized a brief advance by IX Army Corps toward – and at the bridge sites across – the Desna as suggested by Guderian. If it succeeds it will provide relief to the Yelnya salient, I can shorten my front, bring in reserves and as well create a good springboard for the later big operation, even if VII Corps is turned toward and over the Desna and links up with IX Corps at the Roslavl-Moscow road.

In order to be clear about the possibility of direct participation by XXIV Panzer Corps in the 2nd Army's attack, I telexed Guderian asking whether I can still expect the corps to make the advance on Chechersk. Answer:

"No, that would mean the end of the corps."

In view of the order to rest and refit the panzers I had to give in; I informed the 2nd Army that it could not now reckon on the direct participation of the corps in its attack and gave the army the go-ahead to begin its attack.

11/8/41

In the morning I spoke with Guderian about all outstanding matters. We are in agreement. He is in favor committing VII Corps to an advance across the Desna next to IX Corps, as I suggested.

2nd Army wishes to begin its attack on the 12th [August]. Its left wing division today joined XXIV Panzer Corps' attack. Not much will come of it, as the division frontage is 30 kilometers. XXIV Panzer Corps is battling in front of the 7th Division with the surrounded enemy, who is not giving up so easily, and is advancing rather weak battalions toward Krasnopolye and Kostyukovichi.

Greiffenberg drove to the Army High Command in order to discuss all unsettled matters and determine whether they have created a false impression of the fighting strength of the 9th Army there. The Army High Command rejected Guderian's proposal for a great offensive to the east, but considers the limited advance across the Desna ordered by me practical. The Commander-in-Chief of the Army [Brauchitsch] has now "ordered" that tanks are to be employed in the attack on the northern wing. I am very glad, for this order from the highest level relieves me of any further arguments with Hoth and the 9th Army. Finally, Brauchitsch "ordered" that elements of the Guderian Group [PzGr 2] are to advance on Chechersk and Gomel. If XXIV Panzer Corps is no longer in a position to do so, other panzer forces will just have to do it. With the poor equipment state of the panzer divisions, I have doubts whether they can force this order to be carried out.

12/8/41

The 2nd Army's attack, which unfortunately began east of the Dniepr only at first, is making good progress. XXXXIII Corps on the right wing will probably not be able to attack across the Dniepr until the day after tomorrow. Pity that it isn't possible to commit tanks to the south on the left wing of the attack west of the Sozh. I spoke with Weichs, who realizes that it is necessary to advance his right wing.

The enemy surrounded at Krichev by XXIV Panzer Corps and the 7th Division is still holding on. An advance by XXIV Panzer Corps on Gomel is thus ever more improbable, especially since the 4th Panzer Division has encountered strong opposition near Kostyukovichi and as well is being attacked on its eastern flank.

On the rest of the army group's front the Russians are attacking with small units. An attack yesterday near Yelnya led to a new, deep penetration; we have to bring about a change there somehow. 9th Army was also attacked; the day before yesterday the Russians broke through as far as the 5th Division's artillery positions.

I am racking my brains as to how to get some reserves. Promised are a Spanish division, the 12th [Seydlitz-Kurzbach], and the 183rd [Dippold], which is supposed to arrive in Grodno on the 18th [of August]. From Grodno to the front is 600 km! I must now take all my active divisions out of the rear army area and report this to the Army Command; I need every single man up front.

Army Group North is not advancing as quickly as expected.

Front 700 Kilometers Wide!

Army Group South [Rundstedt] is stuck at the Dniepr. And I, with 147 divisions, four of which are tied up far in the rear, and 2 armored groups, which will not be available for use until the 15th and 20th [August] and then only half so, am facing the main body of the Russian Army on a 700-kilometer front. In spite of his terrific losses in men and materiel the enemy attacks at several places daily, so that any regrouping, any withdrawal of reserves by the 9th Army has so far been impossible. If the Russians don't soon collapse somewhere, the objective of defeating them so badly that they are eliminated will be difficult to achieve before the winter.

13/8/41

The attack by the 2nd Army is progressing well. Guderian has brought in more than 16,000 prisoners and 76 guns at Krichev. Whether I will still be able to move the panzers from there toward Gomel is doubtful; material and human strengths will probably no longer be sufficient.

The Russians continue to attack at Yelnya. Otherwise only probing attacks on the entire front.

14/8/41

Another attack at Yelnya. 2nd Army's attack continues to make good progress.

In the morning I phoned Guderian for a briefing on the situation. It turns out that he intended to expand the planned attack over the Desna very much more than he was authorized. I told him that it was out of the question. He also informed me that the general in command of XX Corps [Materna] at Yelnya had reported that he had only one battalion left in reserve; thus Yelnya could not be held in the long run. He, Guderian, was of the opinion that it could only be held if:

(1) the attack proposed by him is carried out at least as far as the eastern end of the large forest east of the Desna,

(2) the flow of munitions is greatly increased and,

(3) strong Luftwaffe forces were once again committed at Yelnya.

If these conditions are not met the Yelnya salient will have to be abandoned.

"But the Reichsmarschall Has Ordered the Opposite"

After describing the army group's situation, I informed Brauchitsch that I had forbidden the attack with Guderian's desired long-range objectives, that on the other hand in view of the way the situation was developing at Yelnya I doubted whether an attack with a limited objective would bring relief in the long run. I could not promise a significant improvement in the delivery of ammunition, for the utmost was already being done in that regard. The matter of air support is different. I made it clear to the air fleet [*Luftflotte* 2, Kesselring] yesterday that the focus of its air attacks had to lie at Yelnya, not with 2nd Army as the air fleet assumed. But the *Reichsmarschall* has ordered the opposite. I asked that this matter be clarified, for rational command is impossible under conditions such as these.

Brauchitsch promised to do so and observed that we should also drop the limited attack in order to spare our resources for subsequent tasks. He would decide whether Yelnya was to be abandoned or not.

He still thinks it necessary to protect the army group's extreme right flank near Mozyr. I issued the necessary orders to the 2nd Army. Guderian was briefed on this discussion. The attack across the Desna has been called off.

I received the decision on the Yelnya salient in the evening; it contains many "ifs" and "buts" and turns responsibility over to me. The most interesting and encouraging thing about this message is that it talks of a possible later operation by the army group in an easterly direction!

Army Group North is making better progress. But at the same time Russian mobile forces have advanced northwest through the large gap between Lake Ilmen and Kholm. The Army Command inquired whether I can release elements of Panzer Group Hoth to the north. Since the motorized divisions have presently stripped their vehicles, it will probably take until the 18th before a division is ready to march.

15/8/41

Another inquiry to Guderian on account of the Yelnya salient; his reply: he hoped to be able to hold it if two divisions from IX Corps relieve the motorized divisions still deployed there and a further division is positioned behind the Yelnya salient as a reserve. That is possible and is being considered. It is difficult to decide whether holding the salient is right or wrong. If the Russians continue to attack, then holding is wrong; if they cease their attacks in the foreseeable future it is right, for Yelnya is a springboard for a further advance and also offers a certain protection for the road and rail junction of Smolensk.

The attack by the 2nd Army continues to progress well. There is no longer any point in deploying elements of XXIV Panzer Corps toward Gomel in order to approach it from the back side, for whatever the enemy is going to get out of the pocket is certainly already out. As well, Guderian reports that he doesn't have the fuel to reach Gomel, furthermore that the wear and tear on the equipment of the units advancing there would probably be such that repairs would be impossible in time for a later large operation. I spoke with Halder. After we had agreed not to deploy the corps toward Gomel Brauchitsch decided the opposite! Therefore the order just issued to the army is being changed again.

"...That It Is My Duty to State My Opinion"

The order arrived yesterday evening to release a motorized division to Army Group North, which is so threatened by the advance of Russian mobile forces from the southeast into its flank and rear that the continuation of its attack in the direction of Leningrad is said to be in jeopardy. Today the order was broadened, calling for the release of one panzer and two motorized divisions. I told Halder that after being so weakened a major offensive by the 9th Army and thus probably the army group as well would no longer be possible; at the same time I pointed out that going over to the defensive was no simple matter considering the large frontages held by my weak divisions; whether the line the armies are holding is really suitable for long-term defense also needs to be examined. Brauchitsch called me soon afterward, and I told him the same. He tried to persuade me, but I stuck to my position. When he said that everyone was screaming that something had to give, I replied formally that I was quite aware that sacrifices had to be made. But here the potential consequences were so serious that it was my duty to state my opinion. I cannot see the big picture, therefore I cannot understand why the panzer divisions which are now supposed to go to France were not employed first to reinforce Army Group North!?

OKH Position "That The Russians Are Simply 'Finished'!"

16/8/41

The Russian penetration against Army Group North appears to be causing quite a stir. Late yesterday evening I received the order to immediately dispatch elements of the panzer and motorized divisions I am to release without waiting for them to complete repairs. In the morning Brauchitsch called to satisfy himself that these elements were really on the move.

The attack by the 2nd Army has led to the encirclement of the enemy east of Zhlobin; naturally he is doing everything he can to break out. Forward of Gomel he is still offering resistance here and there.

Guderian has run into strong resistance on the right wing with the 4th Panzer Division, while his left wing is advancing well and has reached Mglin.

The inactivity of the Russians toward my front's break point south of Roslavl is curious. My own explanation is that the enemy has withdrawn the bulk of his forces into a position behind the Desna and that everything left in front of that position is just trying to buy time. The Army High Command's Foreign Armies Department has a different opinion. Their position is that the Russians are simply "finished!"

In the evening it was learned that the main body of the 2nd Army is all around the encircled enemy, but that Gomel has not been reached yet. I asked Weichs to send everything he could spare from the pocket front toward Gomel. I further said that pilot reports suggested that the enemy in front of his extreme right wing, in front of XXXV Corps, was retreating to the east. The corps must strike now, for we mustn't lose time. Weichs admitted that the enemy in front of XXXV Corps is weak.

17/8/41

Upon inquiry, 2nd Army advised that it had sent strong units toward Gomel. I underlined this once again by issuing an order which further demanded that a division at Chechersk be dispatched to the east, take a crossing southeast of Chechersk and repair the bridge there, in order to prepare the army's later route to the east; for the important thing now is to advance the army to the east as quickly and as far as possible, while guarding its right wing, in order to exploit the enemy's weakness resulting from the battles at Roslavl and Gomel. I therefore also agreed that the 1st Cavalry Division should go to the east bank of the Sozh. As the next line to be reached I named Klintsy-Kaimovichi.

Guderian is champing at the bit! Today he wants to advance toward Starodub with his left wing. I have approved that for reconnaissance units only, otherwise there will be no end to it. He is supposed to advance through Klintsy in the direction of Gomel and cover the thrust's left flank in the area of Unecha.

Strong Russian forces have attacked in 9th Army's sector and driven V Corps [Ruoff] back.

Oberstleutnant Christ, the general staff officer sent to XXXV Corps [Kaempfe] – at the eastern end of the Pripet Marshes – returned and reported that the outlook for this corps' attack on Mozyr is not rosy, primarily because it feels threatened on both flanks. I have the same impression. I don't know what the Army Command wants with the capture of Mozyr, on which it keeps insisting.

"The Attack Is Costing Unnecessary Blood..."

18/8/41

In a conversation with Brauchitsch, I said that Mozyr lies behind a broad marsh and river line and that the capture of the city would require the employment of two army corps. Brauchitsch said that he didn't care about the capture of the city, rather only that the crossing there was barred. I replied that nothing would be gained by that, for then the Russians would just go east of the barricade:

"The solution to the puzzle lies in the advance by the northern wing of Army Group South, the 6th Army [Reichenau]!"

I ordered the 2nd Army [Weichs] to push forward the 167th Division [Trierenberg] and the Behlendorff Group [34th Infantry Division] as far as the line Lake Vicholka-Kostyukovichi and take possession of crossings for a further advance. Shortly after the order went out, the army reported that resistance had collapsed in the pocket east of Zhlobin. I congratulated Weichs on this fine success and asked him to dispatch XXXXIII Corps toward Gomel and to sever communications between Rechitsa and Gomel as quickly as possible with advance detachments.

In the evening I received a report that the attack by the XXXV Corps had made only insignificant gains. The attack is costing unnecessary blood and I regret that my intention to forbid it was prevented by the Army Command's express order.

The enemy is attacking the 9th Army, namely the northern wing of VIII Corps and all of V Corps, with strong forces. It is relatively quiet at the Yelnya salient; there more than 500 Russians have been persuaded to desert by loudspeaker propaganda.

Army Group North is making good progress. Not only I, but also the Army High Command believe that we already have confirmation that taking the motorized forces from my front was a mistake. But from a strategic point of view the good progress by Army Group North is very favorable, for its turning toward Moscow and with it a closer cooperation between Army Groups North and Center appears to have moved into the realm of possibility.

19/8/41

The 2nd Army is pushing into Gomel; armed with shotguns, Russian industrial workers are taking part in the house fighting. Guderian is not making good progress in the direction of Gomel.

I ordered 2nd Army to advance to the general line Mglin-Yerschichi [south of Roslavl] "with no loss of time" and to arrange itself in depth on the right; XXXV Corps is to be moved up behind the southern wing by way of Rechitsa later. The army is to set aside two, later three divisions and place them at my disposal. Guderian and his armored group are to hold onto the towns they have captured and secure the advance by the 2nd Army and otherwise stand down and rest his units.

In the evening I once again made Weichs aware that no time must be lost! For now it might come to pass that, after 2nd Army's victory, and after the success of the planned attack on Velikiye Luki on 9th Army's northern wing, which is imminent, the entire army group can attack to the east!

9th Army reports that the enemy has broken into the left wing of VIII Corps. The 161st Division there is at the end of its tether. It almost looks as if the Russians noticed the departure of the motorized divisions behind 9th Army's front.

20/8/41

The break-in against the 161st Division is so serious that Hoth, who has assumed command of the 9th Army in place of the ailing Strauß, has called in his last available reserves – 7th Panzer and 14th (Motorized) Divisions. The 7th Panzer Division is to launch a counterattack this afternoon to relieve the 161st Division. I asked Hoth to commit the 14th (Motorized) Division as well; but Hoth reported that this division, held up by the approach of the 19th and 20th Panzer Divisions, did not arrive in time. The 19th and 20th Panzer Divisions are en route to the northern wing where they will assemble for an attack tomorrow.

I instructed Guderian to have the motorized SS Division start out for Smolensk and north; there it will be within reach, in case something happens with 9th Army – especially its VIII Army Corps, which has become very thin. Furthermore, after a lively struggle with my personal stays I moved the 87th Division forward from the rear army area, making use of the railway to Smolensk.

In the morning Guderian informed me that he was no longer able to take Novozybkov because XXIV Panzer Corps was at the end of its tether.

The 2nd Army has swept out the area between the Dniepr and the Sozh and has cleared Gomel of the enemy; the [1st] Cavalry Division is still engaged with the enemy east of Gomel.

The Battle of Gomel and Krichev has brought in more than 78,000 prisoners, about 700 guns of all types and approximately 144 destroyed tanks.

21/8/41

North of Mglin-Surazh-Klintsy and between Unecha and Surazh the spread-out Panzer Group Guderian, which "for reasons of materiel and fuel" can advance no farther toward Gomel, is in battle with Russian forces retreating in front of 2nd Army and trying to break through to the east. It is pressing for 2nd Army to speed up its advance, something I have been trying to achieve for a long time. Today the 2nd Army once again received a gentle nudge.

The 7th Panzer Division's counterattack in the hard-pressed 161st Division's sector had no success. It is bogged down; the division has lost a large number of tanks in the process. I should have persevered in my efforts to commit stronger forces to this attack. The attack at Velikiye Luki planned by 9th Army for today has been postponed due to bad weather.

The first results of the battle at Gomel are becoming evident: the enemy forces opposite XXXV Corps north of Mozyr and in front of the northern wing of Army Group South – or southeast of the Pripet Marshes – are withdrawing! Thus the specter of Mozyr is dead.

Guderian is still active. He is still attacking at Pochep. His VII Corps is also grappling with the Russians northeast of Roslavl. I called him in the evening and told him that annoying the Russians on their eastern front was not important now; it is more important that the armored group go over to rest status soon with the maximum forces possible. Unfortunately, I have to maintain its mission of intercepting the enemy retreating east before the 2nd Army as long as the enemy is there.

Consider the Operation to Be "Unfortunate"

22/8/41

The northern wing of the 9th Army has gone to the attack and is making good progress.

The first documents for the attack to the east by the entire army group were just completed and were about to go out to the armies, when the Army Command telephoned and informed me that on orders from the *Führer* strong elements of the 2nd Army and the Guderian Group were to be diverted south, in order to intercept the enemy retreating east in front of the inner wings of

Army Groups South and Center and ease the crossing of the Dniepr by Army Group South.

I called Brauchitsch and made clear to him the questionable wisdom of such an operation.

In the afternoon it turned out that Brauchitsch had apparently misunderstood me, for when someone else tried to talk him out of the operation, he is said to have replied:

"Bock isn't at all as unhappy about the affair."

I called Halder, cleared up the misunderstanding and stated to him that I considered the operation unfortunate, above all because it placed the attack to the east in question. All the directives say that taking Moscow isn't important! I want to smash the enemy army and the bulk of this army is opposite my front! Turning south is a secondary operation – even if just as big – which will jeopardize the execution of the main operation, namely the destruction of the Russian armed forces before winter.

It did no good! In the evening the order arrived for the "forces around Gomel" and if possible three mobile units to be diverted south. I therefore ordered that XIII Corps [Felber], with the 17th [Arnim], 260th [Police Division, Schmidt, Hans], 134th [Infantry Division, Cochenhausen] and the 1st Cavalry Division [Feldt] be sent south, that XXXV Corps [XXXV Senior Detachment, Kaempfe] at Mozyr follow with weak forces only as far as the Pripet, between Pripet and Dniepr, while the main body moved up through Rechitsa toward Gomel. Furthermore, 2nd Army was to go further to the east. Conferred with Guderian to determine which units could be released for the turn south. He flatly rejected the operation, first because XXIV Corps no longer had the strength, second because he couldn't dissipate his forces for a secondary operation, and third because the Mglin-Unecha-Starodub road specified for the advance to the south was nearly impassable. Halder is coming to see me tomorrow.

Schenckendorff [Commander Rear Army Area] visited me; he was, as always, understanding and reasonable.

On 21 August 1941 Hitler gave the Commander-in-Chief of the Army the following directive:

"The army's proposal for the continuation of the operations of 18 August does not correspond with my plans. I order the following:

1. The most important objective to be achieved before the onset of winter is not the occupation of Moscow, but the taking of the Crimea, the industrial and coal region on the Donets and the severing of Russian oil deliveries from the Caucasus area, in the north the encirclement of Leningrad and link-up with the Finns."

The Chief of the Army General Staff subsequently noted:

"Führer Directive of 21 August (WFST L Nr. 441412/41) arrived. It is decisive to the outcome of this campaign."

(Halder War Diary, Volume III, entry under 22/8/41. The Führer and Supreme Commander of the Armed Forces, WFST L Nr. 441412/42.)

Acts of brutality have occurred while prisoners of war are being shipped to the rear; I have objected strongly in a toughly-worded letter to the armies. With the exhausted state of the prisoners and the impossibility of feeding them properly on long marches through vast, uninhabited regions, their removal remains an especially difficult problem.

"The Bulk of the Russian Army Stands... Opposite my Eastern Front"

23/8/41

The attack at Velikiye Luki continues to proceed well.

Only yesterday I suggested to the Army Command that Army Group North prepare II Corps at Kholm to move out in a southeasterly direction as soon as the fighting at Velikiye Luki is over and my not insignificant forces deployed there can set out to the east. In this way the attack on the main Russian forces might yet get started, in spite of the "little infidelity" on my right wing.

Halder came in the afternoon. I summoned Guderian as well, because the topic of discussion was the diversion of forces for the attack to the south. Halder was beside himself. He showed me a memo from the *Führer* which justified the drive by saying that the most vital task was the elimination of the Crimea as an air base for attacking the Romanian oil fields and the cutting-off of the Russians from their own oil supply. To achieve this, Army Group Center, taking advantage of the unusually favorable situation on the inner wings of the army groups, had to initially advance south with its right wing to cut off the enemy forces standing between the inner wings of the army groups and make possible a crossing of the Dniepr by Army Group South. The memo went on to emphasize that it was necessary to smash the Russian Army. But the bulk of the Russian Army is standing opposite my eastern front and the opportunity to smash it is being taken away from me by the attack to the south! Added to that is the fact that Guderian has declared it impossible to initiate and sustain an operation to the south on the roads on which the exhausted XXIV Panzer Corps is hopelessly bogged down. He characterizes the attack, which on top of it leads along the southeast Dvina position with its left shoulder, as a "crime." A sweeping movement through Briansk, which he proposed, is out of the question. The only thing left to do is to bring the mobile forces around behind the front more than 200 kilometers and deploy them by way of Gomel! I can't assume responsibility for that. I therefore telephoned Schmundt and asked him to ask the *Führer* to listen to Guderian, in order to form a picture of the situation for himself. Further furious attacks against 9th Army's front by the Russians.

24/8/41

In the morning we heard from the Army High Command that Guderian told the *Führer* that an immediate southward advance by XXIV Panzer Corps and other armored forces was possible! He returned in the afternoon and said that Brauchitsch had greeted him with the words:

"It is all decided and there is no point in griping!"

Then when the *Führer*, to whom he had described the seriousness of the situation, stated to him how decisive to the war and urgent the advance to the south was, he finally [...] approved the deployment from the area of XXIV Panzer Corps!

Later in the morning it was learned that mobile forces of the 6th Army had taken a bridge over the Dniepr about 60 kilometers north of Kiev. But the existing orders stand. Seven divisions, as well as the [1st] Cavalry Division, and all elements of Panzer Group Guderian not absolutely vital for the fulfillment of my defensive mission, are being diverted south. Guderian is to lead his tanks, Headquarters, 2nd Army leads everything else. What is left of the 2nd Army is moving to the 4th Army; after relieving Panzer Group 2 its left wing will extend as far as Pochep.

The Army Command gave the following verbal briefing during the afternoon:

It is planned to advance the southern wing of Army Group North toward Ostashkov. My northern wing is to establish contact with Army Group at Lake Volga. As a result the army group's front will also be extended north by 60-70 km. My proposal is to move II Corps south of Lake Volga so as to achieve a concentric attack with my northern wing and in this way perhaps yet put into motion a general attack by the increasingly weakened army group.

But they apparently do not wish to exploit under any circumstances the opportunity to decisively defeat the Russians before winter!

"...The Objective To Which I Devoted All My Thought..."

The enemy is surrounded at Velikiye Luki. The 9th Army's First General Staff Officer [Weckmann] said:

"The battle is proceeding like a map exercise!"

This is the seventh or eighth time in this campaign that the army group has succeeded in encircling the enemy. But I'm not really happy about it, because the objective to which I devoted all my thought, the destruction of the main strength of the enemy army, has been dropped. It's going well on the northern wing at Velikiye Luki, the city has been taken, a small pocket has been eliminated, another is to be cleared tomorrow.

The directive from the Army Command announced yesterday arrived. After the preliminary briefing it contains nothing new. For me it conceals only one hope, but one to which there are few real clues;

it is that perhaps we will overrun the Russians in front of my northern wing and thus get things going to the point that at least the pressure on my eastern front is relieved. It can't hold much longer the way things look now. I am being forced to spread the reserves which I so laboriously scraped together for the hoped for attack behind my front just to have some degree of security that it will not be breached.

If, after all the successes, the campaign in the east now trickles away in dismal defensive fighting for my army group, it is not my fault.

The English and Russians have moved into Iran.

26/8/41

An order from the Army Command arrived during the night, calling for a tighter concentration of the Guderian Group to the west. It was passed on.

Army Group South's 6th Army has withdrawn from a bridgehead it won across the Desna and reports:

"The crisis on the northern wing will not be alleviated until Army Group center is in Chernigov!"

Hoth, current commander of 9th Army, submitted an assessment of the situation which points to the army's great expenditure of forces in the defense and suggests that in the long run this must lead to a difficult situation. I passed the assessment on to the Army Command and added that the situation looks the same on the northern wing, that I am committing all my reserves, but that this is no solution in the long run if the enemy has the forces to continue attacking. Withdrawing to a really suitable long-term position is out of the question, for there is none until behind the Dniepr. The only solution left is the one I keep suggesting: "Attack!" But then I pointed out that it is doubtful whether the opportunity to do so will come about. For after the diversion of the 2nd Army and major elements of Panzer Group Guderian, I am no longer in a position to carry out a big, concentrated attack as long as the enemy remains so strong opposite my front.

At noon I received Vietinghoff, Commanding General of XXXXVI Panzer Corps [Motorized Army Corps], Paulus of the Army High Command, and Kluge, who had acted as Mussolini's guide in Brest in my place. Vietinghoff consoled me about the conditions in the Yelnya salient. He, like his Chief of Staff Schleinitz, are of the opinion that offensive action is the way to clear up the situation there. Kluge listened to this and tomorrow, after taking over the army, will examine the entire question of the Yelnya salient, as well as the difficult problem of contact with the 9th Army. Paulus described how the or-

der to turn south was arrived at, saying that political and economic considerations tipped the balance.

The battle at Velikiye Luki is over: 34,000 prisoners and more than 300
guns. The numbers for my army group since the start of the eastern campaign
have thus risen to more than 800,000 prisoners, 6,870 tanks, about 6,500 guns
and 774 aircraft!

"Thus Nothing Came of the 'Destruction' of the Enemy"

27/8/41

Since I had the feeling that my northern wing was resting on the laurels of
Velikiye Luki, I telephoned Hoth. He confirmed my fears and told me that he
had stepped in and ordered the immediate deployment of XXXX (Motorized)
Corps and a panzer division towards Toropets. – Unfortunately the promised
cooperative action by Army Group North has not taken place. The deployment of I Corps, supposedly planned for today, was postponed for the second
time, by two days. Thus nothing came of the "destruction" of the enemy up
there ordered by the Army Command.

9th Army's eastern front subjected to heavy attacks, for which the Russians have concentrated their forces of late. Consequently they achieved a
deep penetration.

The 2nd Army is moving forward slowly but surely. Guderian, too, is
making good progress and his right wing has crossed the Desna at two places,
at Obolonye and at Novgorod-Severski. He called Greiffenberg several times
in the evening, very agitated, and berated his neighbor on the right, who was
advancing in the wrong direction, as a result of which his right and left flanks
were being attacked. As expected, this was followed by the demand for the
release of XXXXVI Panzer Corps, which is in reserve southeast of Smolensk!
I called Halder and told him that the situation on my defensive front was such
that a release of the SS-Division *Reich* was presently out of the question. I
also said that I felt it reckless to release the other two divisions of XXXXVI
(Motorized) Corps. Moreover, XXXXVI Corps with its two divisions was
lagging so far behind Guderian – 18th Panzer Division [Nehring] was still
south of Roslavl – that I had no idea whatsoever what Guderian was supposed

to undertake with XXXXVI Corps. But as Guderian's advance south sprang from an idea of the *Führer's*, I didn't want to decide the question on my own. Halder agreed. During the night Brauchitsch let me know that he was of the same opinion as I and that a release of the XXXXVI Corps could not be considered until the LIII Corps [Weisenberger] was so close to my defensive front that it was out of danger.

28/8/41

Army Group North informed me that it had once again postponed the deployment of II Corps, this time until the 30th. The reason was bad weather and poor roads. Neither is any better where I am. Furthermore, the army group advised that it intends to move II Corps forward to the northeast! During the night Halder informed Greiffenberg that the *Führer* considers a cooperative effort between the armored forces of my northern wing and the southern wing of Army Group North very promising. I therefore once again very seriously called Halder's attention to the situation on the 9th Army's defensive front: it cannot be held in the long run if the Russians continue to attack. Apart from the meager reserves there, it will be about five days before two divisions arrive at the threatened front. Under these conditions it is impossible for the army group, try as it might, to undertake major operations in a northeasterly direction. I have to halt on the upper Dvina, perhaps turn the panzer divisions south even sooner, in order to smash the enemy in front of the 26th Division and free the division – all this to obtain reserves for the defensive front as quickly as possible. If 9th Army fails to hold and Smolensk is lost, 4th Army, too, will have to pull back. – In a similar vein, but not so sharply, for I was still unaware of the new serious penetration of the defensive front, I reported on a petition by 9th Army to Army Command in yesterday's statement.

I briefed Hoth on this talk. He agrees with me on everything. The 2nd Army made virtually no progress today. I spoke with Weichs to spur him on. Guderian has won a small bridgehead over the Dvina at Korop and expanded the old bridgehead at Novgorod somewhat. His left panzer corps is crawling laboriously from Pochep toward the Desna; the 18th Panzer Division is still lagging far behind, south of Roslavl.

The Russians attacked the 9th Army again. The army's northern wing gained ground slowly over bad roads toward Toropets and the western flank of the enemy forces facing the 26th Division.

Paulus came to dinner in the evening. He had seen Guderian, whose Chief of Staff he had formerly been, and after his visit there was inclined to support Guderian's wishes, both concerning the speedy arrival of XXXXVI Panzer Corps and the closer proximity of the 1st Cavalry Division, thus the eastern wing of the 2nd Army, to the armored group.

Hardenberg was visited by Fritz-Dietlof Graf von der Schulenburg, who wrote:

"Visited Hardenberg, assessed the situation with him. We will take Leningrad, Moscow and the Donets Basin by mid-October. H. has doubts, but I firmly believe it."

Heinemann, Ulrich: "Ein konservativer Rebell, Fritz-Dietlof Graf von der Schulenburg und der 20. Juli", Berlin 1990, PP 221.

Also before the attack on Moscow, Hardenberg met the former Chief of the Army Command, Generaloberst von Hammerstein, at the Lietzen Head- quarters; Hammerstein gave him the following message to take back to Bock: "My dear Hardenberg, tell my friend Bock that if he doesn't wish to lose honor and reputation, that under the present circumstances he should return to his starting point as quickly as possible and wait there for what comes." (Hammerstein, Kunrat: "Spähtrupp", PP 241.)

"...Leave the Decision to Me"

29/8/41

Drove to Headquarters, 4th Army [Kluge] in Smolensk and then to the Headquarters of V [Ruoff] and VII [Heitz] Corps at the defensive front, re- turned by plane.

Everybody believes that after the recent measures the front can be held for a while longer, even if the Russians continue to attack. Discussed with Kluge the possibilities of an attack to resolve the situation in the Yelnya sa- lient. I can't decide yet, as I have to think the matter over.

Only very slow progress by the 2nd Army.

Panzer Group Guderian again asked for XXXXVI (Motorized) Corps. One of the reasons behind the request, the threat to the western flank of the panzer group, has been rendered invalid, because the panzer corps on the right wing carelessly informed 2nd Army that it did not feel threatened on its western flank. Nevertheless the decision is a hard one for me, because I still don't have a clear picture of the plans of the Supreme Command. I therefore had the Army High Command informed and told them:

"Should Guderian's advance go very deep, we cannot reckon on a return of the armored group in the near future; given the army group's tense situation, the matter has to be looked upon in a different way than if the armored group could be expected in the near future."

The Army High Command has left the decision to me! I therefore sent a telex to Panzer Group 2 to once again inquire as to its plans and I asked for a reply in writing.

Nothing special going on in 4th Army's sector. Limited offensive activity on 9th Army's defensive front; on the extreme northern wing Toropets was taken by us.

"...Its Chances of Success Are Very Slim"

30/8/41

Two orders with very far-reaching consequences from the Army High Command arrived in the morning: after crossing the Desna River, the elements of 2nd Army and Panzer Group 2 [Guderian] deployed there are to join Army Group South; the two divisions of my northern wing are to go to Army Group North, where a "crushing blow" is to be delivered against the enemy south of Lake Ilmen. As far as I can see its chances of success are very slim.

After carrying out this order Army Group Center is to take over the front from the bend in the Desna at Chernigov to approximately Lake Shedanye; measured roughly, that is a front of 800 kilometers. The idea of an offensive on my front thus appears to be dead.

I am now even more preoccupied than ever with the possibility of dealing with the enemy with limited attacks at least.

Guderian's reply to my inquiry of yesterday arrived this morning. I wish it were less angry and clearer instead. As the 18th Panzer Division is still lagging far behind, as I believe that it won't get its tanks through in the near future on the miserable supply roads, and further as a description of the situation by his former Ia [Bayerlein] leads me to believe that it is imperative that fresh forces be sent to the leading elements, I decided to place the Motorized Infantry Regiment *Großdeutschland* at Guderian's disposal. I can risk that now, because the 267th Division [Wachter], coming from 2nd Army, arrived in Roslavl today. The penalty was not long in coming! The enemy has broken into our lines south of the Yelnya salient. Kluge described the penetration as ten kilometers in depth with heavy tanks and asked that the 267th [Infantry Division] and elements of the 10th Panzer Division be placed at his disposal to clear up the affair. I gave him both divisions, in order to clear the table quickly and thoroughly. Here is proof that I cannot give more forces to Guderian without endangering my eastern front. The Russians also attacked again in the Yelnya salient and at various places on 9th Army's eastern front. The northern wing of the 9th Army is advancing slowly east through Toropets.

"Yet Attack in the Direction of Moscow!"

31/8/41

The day began with new demands from Guderian for the rest of XXXXVI (Motorized) Corps. Independent of this I ordered the 1st Cavalry Division subordinated to the armored group and sent to it from the 2nd Army. During the midmorning I received a lengthy radio message from Guderian, unpleasantly worded, in which he not only repeated his familiar wishes, but broadened them to include all of the army group's mobile units. My response was that I would decide if and when additional forces could be sent to him based on the overall situation on the army group's front. I rejected his request that the *Führer* decide.

Things continue to go very slowly with the 2nd Army. At midday I learned that of the four divisions of its southern front only one, the 134th [Cochenhausen], was attacking. The 260th [Schmidt, Hans] was waiting for the 134th's arrival and the 131st [Meyer-Bürdorf] could not attack because its left flank was under attack. At the Snova River line the enemy advanced, which effectively delayed the 1st Cavalry Division's departure and pinned down the 112th Division [Mieth] on the army's left wing.

The panzer group [Guderian] is being attacked on both flanks and is in a difficult situation.

4th Army launched a counterattack against the point of yesterday's penetration with the 10th Panzer Division [Fischer]. The Russians also attacked at the Yelnya salient.

9th Army made weak attacks only at the old places. Hoth proposed that, exploiting the success at Velikiye Luki, the army's northern wing continue to advance to the east edge of the great forest; an idea that I found very much to my liking in view of possible later operations, but which the Army Command rejected.

Kesselring visited me in the afternoon and revealed that the *Führer* intends to halt the advance by 2nd Army and the armored group at the Nezhin-Konotop railway line, in order to then attack in the direction of Moscow with all of Army Group Center and elements of Army Group North! A transfer of 2nd Army and the panzer group – as ordered yesterday by the Army High Command – is out of the question! I made an inquiry of the Army High Command as to whether this was true. Answer:

"Has not yet been decided, but it is being discussed!"

That was highly important to me, because now I could better tighten the reins on Guderian. I telegraphed him that – as per orders – his first objective was to reach the line Borzna-Bakhmach-Konotop and that a further, deeper advance to the southeast or south was out of the question. As the 255th Division from 2nd Army is arriving behind the 9th Army tonight, I can now place the SS Division [*Reich*, Hausser] at his disposal.

I fear that the Supreme Command's sudden change of opinion has come too late to force the decision against the main body of the Russian Army which I so desperately desired. Just concentrating my widely-scattered forces will be very difficult and time consuming.

1/9/41

The 2nd Army is slowly gaining ground toward the Desna. The enemy is gradually giving ground on its right wing, so that the formerly narrow attacking wedge is becoming somewhat wider. On its left wing the enemy continues to attack. Greiffenberg is flying to the army in order to once again convince it of the importance of a rapid advance and cause it to tightly concentrate its forces in its main direction of advance to the south.

No major changes with Guderian. – Scouting raids on the 4th Army's southern wing, further north, particularly in the Yelnya salient, powerful attacks, which prisoners claim are being carried out on Stalin's personal order. The enemy is answering the counterattack by the 10th Panzer Division and the infantry divisions there with repeated counterattacks. Nevertheless, our attack is gaining ground.

Against the 9th Army the enemy is attacking east of Smolensk and further north at his old favorite places. The extreme northern wing continues to push slowly toward the Dvina. I have once again had the question put to Hoth of what he thinks of an immediate advance through the forest country in front of the northern half of the 9th Army, taking into consideration the fact that we cannot begin the decisive attack to the east before the 20th or 25th of September, because the 2nd Army and Panzer Group Guderian cannot be ready sooner. He now proposes that we not do so, because he believes that taking Beloy and the eastern edges of the great forest would result in enemy counterattacks, which would cost us much blood before we could launch the decisive attack. After careful consideration he thinks it better to close ranks with his divisions behind the Dvina to let them rest and regain their strength, in order to be ready to attack later with full strength.

"My Attack Is Only Possible If..."

In the evening came the report that the 2nd Army's 260th Division had forced a crossing of the Desna east of Chernigov and had thrown two battalions across the river. I telephoned Weichs and asked him to see to it that the force on the opposite side was strengthened as quickly as possible and the crossing place widened, in order to split the enemy defense. Greiffenberg called

Guderian, Tresckow Army Group South, in order to convince both to advance quickly, before the weak forces of the 2nd Army flew back across the Desna.

2/9/41

The day began with Guderian again demanding more forces. The 10th (Motorized) Infantry Division has lost its bridgehead south of the Desna. Guderian's description of the situation was so pessimistic that I replied in writing that I had to decide if I should propose to the Commander-in-Chief of the Army that the armored group be pulled back across the Desna and employed on the right bank of the Desna to relieve the left flank of the 2nd Army, and I asked for his position. He answered that the armored group would fulfil the task that had been given it, and used the opportunity to make the "unusual" request for the assignment of additional forces!

The 2nd Army is advancing, but only slowly. But the bridgehead at the tip of the attacking wedge has held and was even expanded somewhat.

Today the enemy attacked the extreme southern wing of the 9th Army at Pochep and due north of it, there for the first time. If he keeps at it, we could end up in a fine mess! Our counterattack in VII Corps sector has achieved its objective; the 10th Panzer Division is being pulled out again. It is quieter in the Yelnya salient, but the Russians attacked 9th Army again. The army's northern wing is slowly nearing the Sp. Dvina. The two panzer divisions are making scarcely any progress on the muddy roads, so that the Army High Command's planned "shooting off" to Army group North is proceeding devilishly slowly.

Brauchitsch, who arrived with Halder, discussed the objectives of the attack to the east in broad outlines. Nothing is set, because it is still impossible to say when and where the attack by the 2nd Army and Panzer Group 2 can be ended. It is also not yet clear when strong elements of Army Group North will be ready to attack toward Moscow from the northwest. My attack is only possible if 2nd Army and Panzer Group Guderian are turned east again and if Army Group North provides all the assistance it can, for the center of my army group is so dispersed and so weakened by the tough defensive fighting that it is no longer capable of attacking on its own. The "intermezzo," as *General* Jodl of the Armed Forces High Command termed the turning of my right wing to the south, can cost us the victory. The attack to the east cannot begin until the last third of September at the earliest! Until then it is vital to preserve and save our strength, for only two fresh divisions, the 183rd [Dippold] and the Spanish [See: Munoz-Grandes; Gostztony, Peter: *Deutschlands Waffengefährten an der Ostfront 1941-1945*, Stuttgart, 1981, PP 241] are being sent to the army group from the rear. The question of giving up the Yelnya salient thus takes center stage. The divisions deployed there are being bled white as time passes. After several conversations with Kluge, I decided to order the salient abandoned. There is no long-term benefit, but I am gaining time and I can initially withdraw two divisions, which is very important, for there are only four divisions in reserve behind the 4th Army's more than 200-kilometer front, two of which already have one regiment in action.

Headquarters, XXXXVI Panzer Corps was placed at Guderian's disposal.

3/9/41

Heavy attacks against VIII Corps yesterday and today necessitated placing the 255th Division at the disposal of the 9th Army. In the evening the army, which only this morning declared itself able to get by with its own forces, urgently requested the commitment of the 162nd Division as well. I couldn't give it before I had other forces available to take its place in the dangerous Smolensk sector. Straightening the Yelnya salient will not free up any forces until the 6th; the leading elements of the 183rd Division, which I am having brought in from Nevel by train, may arrive at Smolensk the same day. The 162nd Division will therefore not be made available to the 9th Army until the 6th, but it will be moved nearer to VIII Corps' front.

On the southern wing of the 4th Army enemy forces with tanks broke through the overstretched front of the 34th Division [Behlendorff] in considerable depth. I put my sole reserve there, the 52nd Division [Rendulic], at the army's disposal, with the request that it be committed only if it is really necessary.

Reinforcement from Spain?

In the midst of all my worries the report by the German liaison officer with the slowly-approaching Spanish Division is refreshing. He says: "The Spanish view grooming the horses as a bother, feeding them unnecessary. Belts and suspenders are cut from new harnesses. Gas mask containers are often used as coffee pots. Dust and driving glasses are cut from the gas masks themselves. If a Spaniard has corns, he cuts appropriate holes in his shoes and boots to keep them from chafing. Rifles are often sold. New bicycles are thrown away as they find tire repair too boring. The MG 34 is often assembled with the help of a hammer. Parts left over during assembly are buried. They consider all women fair game. In Grodno there were orgies with jewesses, who were also taken along in the vehicles..." [See also 20/9/41]

4/9/41

Road conditions on the army group's north are indescribable. It turns out that LVII Panzer Corps [Motorized Army Corps, Kuntzen, later redesignated a panzer corps] cannot be moved northeast from the Toropets area. The Army High Command therefore ordered the corps sent through Toropets and Kholm, or around behind, to the 16th Army.

"...The *Führer* Is Dissatisfied..."

Generalfeldmarschall Keitel called twice in the course of the day. He said that the *Führer* is dissatisfied that Panzer Group Guderian is swinging out so far to the east across the Desna instead of concentrating its forces for the drive south. The *Führer* wants a report on the situation of the individual corps within the armored group and the subsequent intentions for them. If the army group and the Commander-in-Chief of the Army don't intervene with orders the *Führer* will do it.

In the evening Guderian responded to these questions with the same old answers. He took the opportunity to once again charge that in spite of all his requests too few forces had been given him, and these too late. I passed his response upstairs, adding that the Army High Command and I had already intervened with orders, that the army group was strained to the point of ripping apart (the divisions on the 4th Army's southern wing are manning fronts 40 km wide), that consequently a further release of forces to Guderian was out of the question, and that indeed it might even become necessary to turn the Guderian group around in response to a breakthrough on the 4th Army's southern wing. Guderian was so headstrong that I finally had to ask for his relief. Brauchitsch asked me to think things over again in the interest of the matter and give him my ultimate decision tomorrow.

The 2nd Army's right wing is bogged down in the face of strong enemy resistance. The center and the left wing are advancing slowly; the bridgehead over the Desna was reinforced.

Guderian made only limited progress; weak counterattacks against his eastern front here and there.

On the 4th Army's southern wing the enemy attacked again today; minor advances only at the Yelnya salient.

The heaviest attacks were against the 9th Army, on VIII Corps' front. The northern wing of the 9th Army is approaching the Sp. Dvina. LVII Panzer Corps [Motorized Army Corps] is preparing to depart.

5/9/41

Quieter day on the defensive fronts. The evacuation of the Yelnya salient is proceeding according to plan.

I have now placed the last reserve in its sector at the disposal of the 9th Army in order to relieve a battle-weary division. The army wanted to insert it into the line, which I could not approve because I have to have some sort of reserve behind the army's front. The grumbling over individual divisions is starting again, part of being on the defensive.

9th Army expanded its bridgehead at Chernigov and is advancing its left wing slowly toward the Desna; its right is still pinned down.

The armored group's only noteworthy progress was by its right wing, which took Sosnitsa. This freed the 1st Cavalry Division. I ordered the armored group to dispatch it in the direction of its northeast wing, or toward Pochep, where it is urgently needed, be it as a reserve behind the weakest sector of the army group's front, or to release elements of the armored group still deployed there.

Army Group South's northern wing has now succeeded in expanding its bridgehead across the Dniepr after time-consuming fighting; but there is no sign yet of attempts to cross the Desna; pressure by the 2nd Army by way of Chernigov remains one-sided.

Strauß is healthy again and has reassumed command of his army [9th Army].

"The Guderian Affair"

I informed Brauchitsch that I was agreeable to his settling the Guderian affair by talking to him, but I cannot hide my worries about new difficulties with this outstanding and brave commander.

6/9/41

In the morning I queried the armored group as to whether the cavalry division was moving as I had ordered. Answer: No, the enemy is still every-where here. I once again ordered the cavalry division halted, that it be set in march as ordered, and that I be informed of its march objectives. When Panzer Group 2 inquired whether it might withdraw its northeast wing behind the southeast [wing], I replied: "If forces are saved by doing so, yes!"

In the afternoon it was learned that the cavalry division still had no order to depart, nor had a warning order been issued. I called the Chief of Staff of the armored group, Liebenstein, on the phone and dictated to him personally my order to the cavalry division to depart; the order also placed the division under the direct command of the army group.

At the same time I requested that I be informed as soon as the order was passed on. When Liebenstein reported that the division had received the or-der, he added that Guderian, who he had reached en route, had added that the elements of the cavalry division south of Dolshok – parts of a brigade, the reconnaissance battalion and the bicycle battalion – did not have to leave with the rest of the division. Guderian declared that he would answer for this failure to follow my order in the history of the war.

I called the armored group at once and ordered the supplemental order deleted at once. I ordered the departure of the cavalry division without hesitation, because the left wing of the 2nd Army had contact with its reconnaissance battalion and the gap to the right wing of the SS Division *Reich* was only a few kilometers wide.

Apart from these battles with the armored group, the front was relatively peaceful, for which I am glad for my soldiers. The 2nd Army expanded its bridgehead and pushed forward slowly.

Chernigov is still being held by the enemy.

As enemy concentrations have been spotted opposite the weakest part of the front, near Briansk and Trubchevsk, since several days ago; I asked Kesselring to intervene there with his bombers, which he gladly promised to do. He told me that "above" was obsessed with the decision to commit an armored group from Army Group South's area near Kremenchug to the north, and Panzer group Guderian toward it to the south. Both armored groups would have to cover only 150 kilometers to join hands. Curious that I always get ny news from the air fleet first.

Ratio of Forces on the Eastern Front

A survey of the ratio of forces on the Eastern Front reveals the following picture:

Army Group South [Rundstedt]: 77 German divisions against 47 Russian divisions. Army Group North [Leeb]: 31 German against 25 Russian Divisions and my army group: 55 German against 86 1/2 Russian divisions!

7/9/41

Isolated attacks only on the right wing of the 4th Army, at Yelnya and on the army group's extreme northern wing. All going well with the 2nd Army, four divisions have won bridgeheads across the Desna. The armored group is making only mediocre progress. 6th Army is at last moving forward and has won bridgeheads across the Desna at several places.

Grolmann of the Army High Command came in the afternoon. He brought with him the new *Führer* directive, according to which the battle in front of the northern half of Army Group South is to be brought to a conclusion, with Army Group Center and Panzer Group 2 taking a decisive part. He did not yet bring binding orders from the Army Command. Further progress by the 6th Army will make it necessary for the 2nd Army to turn southeast to avoid getting mixed up with the 6th Army; the eastern wing of Panzer Group 2 is to be driven forward toward Romny-Lokhvitsa, in order to reach out towards the mobile forces of Army Group South advancing north from Kremenchug on approximately the 10th. When asked whether 2nd Army and the armored group should be subordinated to Army Group South, I said that I considered it to be correct in principle, but that Air Fleet 2 was against it for technical reasons. Moreover the subordination is hardly still worthwhile, the deciding orders have been issued, there's not much more left to say to Army Group South.

"...My Old Wish, The Attack on the Main Russian Forces..."

According to a directive from the *Führer*, my old wish, the attack on the main Russian forces, is yet to be fulfilled. If only the weather holds long enough, for the necessary reinforcements cannot arrive before the end of September! The overall situation for the attack is good, but not simple, especially not on the northern wing. I asked Grolmann to make it clear from the start that the planned tight turn by both of the attack's offensive wings does not correspond to my view in this case either. But this turn has to be screened to the east. It is also imperative that these screening forces be sent beyond the attack objective of Vyazma to the east. From experience in many battles I know that in the past this basic necessity was not fully appreciated "above."

Stumme, the Commanding General of XXXX Army Corps, came at noon; Kesselring in the afternoon.

8/9/41

The Russians continue to assail the defensive front with major and minor assaults. Their air superiority is especially uncomfortable; the bulk of our aircraft are deployed on the attack fronts.

2nd Army is making good forward progress. On the far right, between the Desna and the Dniepr, the right-wing division has established contact with the left wing division of the 6th Army.

An order arrived from Army Command during the night, according to which 2nd Army and Panzer Group Guderian remain subordinated to me; I am tied to the wishes of Army Group South. A corps headquarters and three divisions are to be withdrawn from the 6th and 2nd Armies for my eastern front as soon as possible.

The long-anticipated incident with the Americans has occurred. An American destroyer and a German submarine have been fired on. Each claims by the other.

9/9/41

2nd Army is making very good progress. Chernigov has been taken. Panzer Group 2 also made significant progress in the direction of Romny. Only weak enemy forces on its eastern flank.

The army commanders arrived in midmorning for the first conference on the new operation. Proposal to the Army Command, the main object of which is a strengthening of armored forces at the point of main effort of the coming attack, which is not difficult to do. As well I requested assistance from II Corps on my northern wing. The corps apparently doesn't want to; but it is desirable, since the heavy attack by the 9th Army, which will inevitably strike the strongest part of the enemy position frontally, can easily get bogged down if the enemy is left free to fall upon the attack's northern flank.

Chapter 5: 22 June 1941 to 5 January 1942

"...Not Getting All That Much Help"

10/9/41

2nd Army still doing well, except that the army is squeezing itself too much to the right. It received orders to pull out a division this morning, another and a corps headquarters shortly thereafter, in order to dispatch them to the army group's attack front.

Guderian making good progress; today a panzer division reached the assigned objective of Romny.

Army Group South doesn't want to commit its motorized units until tomorrow because it's raining there.

On the defensive fronts the same picture as in recent days.

I talked over details of the coming operation with Brauchitsch. Above all, I asked him once again to have the strongest possible forces from the 16th Army attack with us, to the southeast, on my northern wing, as otherwise 9th Army's attack will be too difficult and outflanking the enemy will be out of the question. Brauchitsch was evasive in his response.

Kesselring arrived in the afternoon. He was astonished by this attitude on the part of the Army High Command and claims to know for a fact that the *Führer* has ordered an attack by all available forces in support of my operation.

Army Group South is causing difficulties in the transfer of the 11th Panzer Division [Scheller as of 20/10/41], because the bridges built by the 6th Army are too weak for tanks. An engineer officer from Army Group Center is being sent with the necessary bridging equipment to bring the bridges in Army Group South's area up to the necessary strength. I'm not getting much help in quickly putting the new operation together, and yet everything depends on it!

11/9/41

The enemy is yielding in front of the 2nd Army. Union with the 6th Army was achieved. The army is pushing itself, even if very slowly, into its new sector to the east. Apart from the two divisions of the 2nd Army, on orders from the Army High Command one is also being moved in from the 6th Army for my later offensive.

Guderian is closing ranks. A shortage of fuel and bad weather is making any further movement difficult. At the request of Army Group South the armored group is to advance west in the direction of Priluki-Piryatin. The mobile units of Army Group South have not begun to attack yet!

Heavier Russian attacks on the 4th Army's defensive front.

They are calling our evacuation of the Yelnya salient, which came off very smoothly, a victory and are threatening further successes!

It is relatively quiet in front of the 9th Army, but there are indications of an attack.

The directive for the new operation arrived from the Army Command at noon. Nothing of what I recently said to the Commander-in-Chief of the Army was taken into consideration. Guderian is deployed toward Orel, too far to the east. Orders for assistance from the 16th Army are vaguely worded, it is to "maintain contact with the northern wing of the 9th Army" and is to "guard the 9th Army's flank." Finally concentration of the assault wing is to take place in the area of Vyazma, a town that lies in the middle of the enemy system of positions. In a clearly-worded letter I once again put my position before Brauchitsch. The Commander-in-Chief of the Army also received two other letters from me, one concerning the miserable propaganda and one aimed at improving the lot of the infantry in regard to replacements, equipment and propaganda.

12/9/41

On the defensive fronts the usual picture. The enemy is organized for attack opposite the familiar sectors of the 4th and 9th Armies and here and there attacks, sometimes with tanks.

Resistance has collapsed in front of the 2nd Army and Panzer Group 2. At the request of Army Group South, Panzer Group 2, which is stretched out over far more than 200 kilometers, was instructed to advance on Lokhvitsa as well as Priluki and Piryatin, in order to link up there with the tanks of Army Group South which early this morning set out toward the north from Kremenchug.

At noon came news that the enemy is streaming east out of the more than 200-kilometer-wide gap between Kremenchug and Romny in dense columns. Immediately afterward, three telephone calls were received from Army Group

South within a half hour, asking if Lokhvitsa had been reached yet! – At the request of South, this morning 2nd Army first received instructions to turn toward the line Nezhin-Priluki. I asked if it wouldn't be better to commit the army's right wing to the pursuit toward Priluki and "South" agreed.

Of course Guderian wants the 18th Panzer and 29th (Motorized) Divisions, which I'm still holding on to, so as to be able to carry out his missions in the Battle of Kiev. I am struggling with my conscience as to what to do. I can't let both divisions go. I could relieve one, the 18th Panzer Division, with the Cavalry Division, but the tanks could not reach the battlefield before the 17th [of September], which would be too late. Besides, the 18th Panzer Division is earmarked for the point of main effort in my upcoming attack. Halder, with whom I discussed this matter, supported my stand.

Roosevelt gave an outrageous speech in which he declared that the American fleet had orders to attack German submarines wherever it met them. This is not an offensive, but a defensive action!

13/9/41

2nd Army continues the pursuit. The three divisions designated for the coming operation have been pulled out and are headed northeast.

Panzer Group 2 took Lokhvitsa this morning; otherwise no significant changes.

At noon the army and some of the armored group commanders arrived to discuss the new operation.

Since no reply has yet arrived from the Army High Command to my written objections against the premature turn at Vyazma, I phoned Halder. We agreed that after a successful attack the inner wing of the panzers had to turn toward Vyazma; for the outer that meant a proceeding toward Gzhatsk. Consequently the screening operation to the east has to take place even further east.

14/9/41

In the morning I learned from Greiffenberg that we are to expect a letter from the Army High Command, which is now calling for an earlier turn. The outer wings of the attack are to head towards Vyazma! I called Heusinger [Chief of the Operations Section OKH] and told him that this meant that I would have to turn in front of the Russian anti-tank ditches with the bulk of the tanks. Apart from tactical considerations, my proposal, to first turn the bulk of the tanks toward the Vyazma-Gzhatsk road, was dictated by the system of roads. I said that we were happy to have succeeded in bringing five panzer divisions into the battle in the front lines simultaneously. But five roads were needed to move this mass of armor; it also follows that the "screening front" will have to lie, not at the Vorya – as demanded by the Army High Command – , but farther east. To spare further paperwork, we agreed to present the army group's intentions to the Army Command on a sketch map. But I requested a quick decision as there is no more time to lose.

The directive arrived at noon. I telephoned Halder and told him in general terms just what I had said to Heusinger. He told me that I mustn't take the order to head towards Vyazma with the outer wings too seriously. It was written that way primarily because my first proposal said to commit the outer wings there. I repeated what I had said to Heusinger in the morning, that that was a mistake and that I had of course meant the inner wings of the armored force.

As at Bialystok and Minsk and at Smolensk, those "above" are now once again showing a tendency toward very limited action and thus throwing away sweeping strategic effect.

After much drawing and erasing, by the afternoon a highly artistic map of the new operation had been created for the Army Command, on which I crammed together everything as tightly as possible to the west. But in reality the map left all doors open.

2nd Army continues the pursuit. I am pushing for advance detachments to reach Priluki as soon as possible, in order to close the ring around the enemy in front of the inner wings of the two army groups firmly and quickly, but also with an eye toward freeing up Panzer Group 2 as soon as possible.

Noticeably quiet on the remaining fronts. The Russians are digging in; it is not yet clear if they have given up on further attacks.

15/9/41

The ring has closed around the enemy in front of the inner wings of Army Groups South and Center. Leading elements of Panzer Group 1 [Kleist] have made contact with Panzer group Guderian south of Lokhvitsa.

The "Battle at Kiev" has thus become a dazzling success.

But the main Russian force stands unbroken before my front and – as before – the question is open as to whether we can smash it quickly and so exploit this victory before winter comes that Russia cannot rise again in this war.

Further elements of the 2nd Army are being freed up. It is also obvious that Panzer Group 2 will soon be squeezed out. I therefore suggested to Army Command removing two more divisions from 2nd Army, subordinating the remaining three divisions to 6th Army, thus to Army Group South, effective the 17th, and gradually freeing up Panzer Group 2.

The Army Command agrees.

Quiet on the army group's remaining fronts.

"Narrowmindedness Is Becoming an Art!"

The "battle of destruction" on the southern wing of Army Group North has come to nothing. My two panzer divisions are to return, but unfortunately their departure will be delayed by 24 hours.

Halder gave me a verbal response to the map of the new operation submitted to the Army High Command. The essence of it is that the battle is to be "even more limited" in scope! Narrowmindedness is becoming an art! And after the battle we will again be facing the enemy's reserves!

16/9/41

Quiet day. The Russians are pulling out forces. Kesselring came and was shocked that the gathering of forces for the attack is taking so long. I am too. In fact, of all the panzer divisions that Army Group North is to release to me, not one is yet on the march today.

17/9/41

The pursuit by 2nd Army and the armored group continues to proceed smoothly. Priluki has fallen. Otherwise quiet.

Letter to Halder

I wrote to Halder and complained that they were bothering me on the northern front with petty tasks and that the transfer of forces assigned to me from other army groups had not yet begun.

The most important part of the letter was the conclusion:

"I need not go into any more detail about what I think of the very narrow scope of attack imposed on me. But I think that one must ask himself the question, whether I am to lay down the law to the enemy or he to me!

If we make the timing of the turn by the tanks dependent on whether or not the infantry is stuck in the front lines, then the enemy is already dictating to us. And how is this eventual turn envisaged? If the tanks are advancing well, are they to be called back if the infantry gets bogged down somewhere, perhaps only temporarily – or are they to be deployed within a narrow scope from the start, thus giving away their advantages of speed and striking power and making them vulnerable to encirclement themselves? Or is it better to exploit the characteristics of the tanks, deploy them in depth [Vyazma-Gzhatsk] in order to sever the enemy's lifeline, smash his reserves and command appa-ratus there, and then, with full freedom of action, turn as far to the west as is necessary while screening to the east? My practical experiences as well as several pictures of the negative side I have seen leave for me no doubt which is the right one.

The bigger solution involves having to ride out crises, which is now part and parcel of big decisions."

18/9/41

The headquarters of the 2nd Army has become superfluous in the Battle of Kiev and has given up its command there.

Generaloberst Hoepner, who is to command the 4th Army's tanks, arrived this morning and was briefed.

Otherwise, with the exception of minor mischief-making, relatively calm! Serious uprisings under way in Serbia.

19/9/41

There will be further considerable delays in the arrival of the panzer and motorized divisions from Army Group North. As a result the date of the attack is pushed back ever further.

Stronger pressure from the east making itself felt against Panzer Group 2.

The commanding officer of the Spanish Division ["Blue Division"], General Munoz Grandes, reported to me for duty.

20/9/41

Today on the army group's northern wing, II Corps, together with the northernmost division of the 9th Army, was supposed to launch an attack to clear the forest and swamp terrain there of the enemy. The northern wing of the 9th Army has attacked – but not II Corps. Not until evening did we learn that the attack had been postponed to the 22nd. I made Brauchitsch aware in a polite way that that won't do. Further, I said that the buildup of infantry divisions was under way but that each day brought new delays in the transfer of forces from the neighboring army groups. The buildup in my front lines can't be concealed from the enemy in the long run. I must reach a decision: should I wait for the bulk of the promised forces or should I not? In spite of the difficulty of the attack, I am leaning toward "risking something" and attacking as soon as the most necessary units are in place.

Brauchitsch agrees.

Change in quarters [refers to the occupation of Army Group Center's new headquarters] in a day nursery west of Smolensk, where there are no children, but bugs.

"...An Unaccustomed Picture for German Soldiers' Eyes"

On the way I met the Spanish Division, an unaccustomed picture for German soldiers' eyes. Here and there one of them had procured a goose and tied it to his horse or bicycle, head down, alive, in order to keep it fresh. The division's horses are in a miserable state.

21/9/41

Drove to the 286th Division east of Smolensk and to a regimental command post, where the staff operates in a most primitive manner in foxholes. Morale is good even though the unit has some tough days behind it.

Still pressure from the east against Panzer Group 2.

At Novgorod-Severski the 29th (Motorized) Division is facing units of eight to ten Russian divisions. The enemy is trying to break out of the Kiev pocket against the southernmost elements of the armored group, in the Piryatin area.

22/9/41

Still quiet at the front, only Panzer Group 2 still engaged.

The enemy opposite the 4th and 9th Armies is organizing himself for defense and in places has pulled back his main line of resistance. He has apparently pulled out some artillery; difficult to ascertain whether tanks have disappeared too.

On the northern wing II Corps again failed to attack today, but will do so tomorrow; the 19th Panzer Division, which is to attack with it, will therefore not leave to join the army group tomorrow. The 8th Panzer Division probably isn't coming at all, so that Panzer Group Hoth [PzGr 3] will be significantly weaker for 9th Army's attack than expected.

At midmorning I drove over indescribable roads to the headquarters of XX Corps, where I chanced to meet the commanding officers of the 15th [Hell], 78th [Gallenkamp] and 268th [Straube] Divisions.

Kluge came in the afternoon and talked about his plans, with which I agree for the most part.

23/9/41

Once again II Corps did not attack. Delays in the transfer of the forces promised to me are beginning to become uncomfortable.

The Chiefs of Staff of the 2nd and 9th Armies, Witzleben [Witzleben, Hermann, Chief of Staff 2nd Army 1/11/40 – 26/10/41] and Weckmann [Chief of Staff 9th Army, 26/10/40 – 14/1/42] came to discuss their roles in the forth-coming attack. 2nd Army wants to stagger the timing of its attacks, which I cannot permit.

24/9/41

The Russians bombed our quarters during the night.

Kesselring arrived in the midmorning and informed me that VIII Air Corps is also being kept near Leningrad!

Then Brauchitsch arrived. I told him that I did not consider the attack by 9th Army feasible without the support of VIII Air Corps. Brauchitsch agreed and is going to intervene. He agrees with my plans. The meeting with all the army and armored group commanders, at which he was present, brought nothing new, except for the fact that Guderian and his armored group will be ready to attack on the 30th [September]. It suits me fine if he has a head start, for he is still so far from the right wing of the main attack that his advance cannot have a direct influence until four or five days later. The others can be ready on 2nd October, only Hoth proposes the 3rd.

Just when I think that I might be able to make a clear decision on the timing of the attack after all the chaos and delays of the last weeks, there comes a new cry for help from Army Group North: II Corps is itself being attacked by a superior force! The 19th Panzer Division cannot depart at all for the time being. The upshot is that I lose the 253rd Division, which is taken from the 9th Army and placed at the disposal of Army Group North, so that the 19th Panzer Division can finally be released. But the division is so bogged down in the mud that according to Army Group North it will take three days alone to assemble. Then in the evening came the bad news that the *Führer*, prompted by local difficulties at Leningrad, has halted the 36th (Motorized) Division which is en route to me. Under such circumstances our work is not simple.

The sum total of the day is that I, on the eve of the attack, have to do without the 8th Panzer Division, that the arrival of the 19th Panzer and 36th Motorized Divisions is unforeseeable, and that I must give up the 253rd Division to Army Group North. The arrival of VIII Air Corps is also questionable. Nevertheless, tomorrow I will give the final attack order, leaving open only the date and time of the attack, so that nothing is missed.

It is clear that the Russians are withdrawing forces from in front of my front to prop up their threatened northern and southern wings. It is time!

25/9/41

Army Group North's difficulties have so multiplied that I now have to give up the Spanish Division as well. I hold the view that the Russians must win a race to Leningrad; they have the far better rail system, while we have to carry out the bulk of our troop movements on foot.

If we are to prevent the Russians from withdrawing forces from in front of Army Group Center and moving them to Leningrad, Army Group Center has to attack; that is the best relief for Army Group North.

Various signs might indicate that the enemy is withdrawing. I instructed the armies to remain alert and stay on the enemy's heels wherever he gives ground.

26/9/41

As I had nothing to give 9th Army to replace the 253rd Division, Strauß reported that he must abandon the planned attack to capture the Jetkino-Beloy road, which is important for his supply, because he lacks the forces to do so.

Army Group North advised of further delays in transporting out the 19th Panzer Division. A decision as to whether and when I will be sent the 36th (Motorized) Division is still pending. I reported to the Army High Command that I would have to put back the date of the attack if the 36th Division did not march tomorrow and if the 19th Panzer Division did not come sooner.

I urged the air fleet to press with all the power it has for the timely arrival of Richthofen and his air corps.

The attack order was issued.

Midmorning drove to the 3rd (Motorized) Division.

27/9/41

The fear that the enemy might withdraw has not been confirmed; reconnaissances in force by the 4th Army reveal the opposite. The other armies have the same impression; the 9th Army even reckons on the possibility of an attack on its northern wing. As I need every last man for my attack, police and SS formations, including the Fegelein *Standarte* [*SS-Obersturmbannführer*, commander of the SS Cavalry Brigade], are being moved from the rear army area behind the left wing of the 9th Army as a reserve to meet any contingency.

The Army High Command has stepped in as a result of my report of yesterday: the 36th Division is on the march and the 19th Panzer Division is to be transferred sooner. After receiving Kesselring's promise that VIII Air Corps would arrive on time, I issued the attack date: the 30th of September for Guderian and the 2nd of October for the armies. Somewhat hurried, but we have no time to lose.

Midmorning drove to the 255th Division.

28/9/41

The last orders for the attack went out. Guderian's right wing is fighting its way slowly into its jump-off position for its attack.

The enemy is apparently pulling out more troops opposite my front, either to shore up the Budenny [Soviet Marshall, Deputy Minister of Defense, Commander-in-Chief of Army Group Southwest] army group or to relieve Leningrad.

29/9/41

A request went out to the air fleet to begin planned attacks on all important rail junctions opposite my front beginning today.

Drove to Headquarters, VII Corps [*General* Fahrmbacher], where every-thing has been prepared splendidly. Then to the 267th [Wachter] and 23rd [Hellmich] Divisions and to Panzer Group 4 [Hoepner]. The latter is still lack-ing in many areas. On the way I met the commander of the 5th Panzer Divi-sion, which is in good shape.

30/9/41

Guderian has attacked. His left wing is moving, his southern wing is still hung up and is being attacked from the east.

Drove to Headquarters, VIII Corps [Heitz], where much is still lacking for the attack.

1/10/41

In the course of an attempt to disengage Panzer Group Guderian's south-ern wing from the enemy, the 25th (Motorized) Division was attacked by tanks and escaped only at the cost of abandoning the vehicles of an entire regiment, which were stuck in the mud.

XXIV Panzer Corps [Geyr von Schweppenburg] is making good progress; but concern about Guderian's right flank will persist until Army Group South has relieved the elements of Panzer Group 2 still deployed in its sector, which is to begin this evening. A complete relief of the right flank will not happen until Guderian's infantry divisions arrive and that is still a long way off.

The unrest in Serbia is serious. There are also crises brewing in Holland, Norway and in the Protectorate. The English gnaw away with effective propa-ganda: "Work slower!"

2/10/41

The army group went to the attack according to plan. We advanced so easily everywhere that doubts arose as to whether the enemy had not in fact decamped. I drove to Panzer Group 4's command post, from where one has a smashing view of the 4th Army's battlefield, then to the Desna; in XXXXVI

(Motorized) Army Corps' sector, bridge building is taking longer than one would expect given thorough preparation.

3/10/41

On the left wing of the 4th Army, IX Corps [Geyer] attacked sooner than planned and discovered that the enemy opposite its front was as strong as before.

We are moving forward everywhere. Guderian's right wing has taken Orel. The performance of the infantry, namely that of XII [Schroth] and VII Corps, has been almost unbelievable. VIII Corps, part of 9th Army, won crossings over the Vop, V [Wetzel] and VI [Förster] Corps are also doing well. Already today Panzer Group Hoth reached the heights west of Kholm and received orders to turn toward the highway at and west of Vyazma. Kluge [4th Army] now wants to veer north west of the Kirov-Vyazma rail line with a panzer corps and two infantry corps, and continue straight ahead in the direction of Yukhnov with his right wing and the other panzer corps. The Kuntzen Panzer Corps [motorized army corps] is being readied to follow up on the right wing. As it is apparent that the enemy still has strong forces west of the mentioned rail line, I agree.

In the afternoon I drove to the 9th Army [Strauß], and released the 161st Division for use on its northern wing. In return I asked that the 86th Division [Witthöft], which starting today is being relieved from the front east of Smolensk and which is not taking part in the attack, be committed only after consulting with me, because I wish to have a say in seeing to it that everything is committed at the point of main effort. I placed two guard battalions belonging to the commander of the rear army area [Schenckendorff], which were at Toropets, at the disposal of the 9th Army for use in the front, in part to the 256th Division [Kauffmann] to clear the supply road through Jetkino, which might now perhaps yet be opened.

"...I Am Stepping In With Both Armies, To Push them Forward"

4/10/41

We are moving forward everywhere, in particular in the area of the infantry divisions, often in heavy fighting. So far the panzers have no outstanding accomplishments to show, I am stepping in with both armies to push them forward.

I am also worried about the armored group's [3 PzGr, Hoth] advance by way of Kholm, which was taken today. The 9th Army is keeping one eye on the front held by XXVII and VIII Corps, whose advance has no decisive importance, and the other on its left flank, where it sees ghosts, instead of placing everything on the card of breaking through from Kholm to Vyazma. Relief of Panzer Group 2's southern wing by advance detachments of Army Group South is progressing.

Just after informing Guderian that, according to a new decree by the Army Command this afternoon, he was to remain on the left bank of the Oka and that an advance on Tula was out of the question, Halder called and made the surprising statement that they were now considering sending the armored group in the direction of Tula! When I came out in favor of an advance toward Tula and Kaluga by the armored group from the very first moment, the idea was rejected by the Army High Command! I told Guderian that everything was probably going to change and instructed him to take possession of Mtsensk, and if possible also distance himself from Bolkhov and reconnoiter toward Tula in order to prepare for a possible turn toward Tula; for now, however, his main mission was to settle matters at Briansk.

5/10/41

Drove to the 7th [Gablenz], 197th [Meyer-Rabingen] and 252nd [Boehm-Bezing] Divisions; the latter, on the projecting northeast corner of the 4th Army, has scarcely any enemy forces before it. The left wing of the army's attack has broken through the enemy and is attacking north across the Ugra.

Elements of the 5th Panzer Division, which I saw, were apparently having difficulties advancing. I wished it to move faster in order to finally close the gap at Vyazma. En route I met Kluge, who is of the same opinion. Everywhere I went the units made a tremendous impression. But things are a mess on the big "Roslavl-Moscow highway." Four to five columns side by side, with unauthorized Luftwaffe elements wedged in between them, clog the road on which the entire supply effort, including deliveries of fuel for the tanks, depends.

When I returned home the picture was clear:

The enemy still has strong forces opposite my front. My main worry, getting the armored spearheads together at Vyazma, remains great, for Hoth's armored group has gained hardly any ground at Kholm in the face of stiff resistance. I understand the 9th Army's approach even less; it wants to commit elements of the 86th Division to a limited attack in XXVII Corps sector, thus on its defensive front, and it is opposed to me temporarily placing the 900th Brigade at the disposal of the armored group in order to free up those armored elements still lagging behind for the attack at Kholm. The army's justification for this is that the 900th Brigade is the only reserve behind its front! I sent it a telex, in which I once again pointed out that all depends on strengthening the attack at Kholm, everything else is secondary!

Hoth "Would Rather Stay"

At that movement orders came that Hoth [commander of Panzer Group 3 since 16 November 1940; succeeded by Reinhardt] was to take over an army [the 17th] in Army Group South? I am loathe to lose this outstanding armor commander; he, too, would rather stay.

6/10/40

In the morning I spoke with Kluge again about the need to push the panzer divisions forward and about the question of screening to the east. We agreed that XII Corps will have to alleviate the concern about the rear and flank from the army's right boundary to Yukhnov, including the tanks, as soon as possible.

The army had to leave behind weak forces from XII Corps at the southern end of the great swampy region of Bogoroditzk, which still hides all kinds of the enemy, to seal off the area.

I spoke to the Chief of Staff of the 2nd Army [Witzleben, Hermann; not Harteneck as in Mehner, Kurt: *Die geheimen Tagesberichte...*, Vol. 4, PP 367] and told him that the corps on the left wing was to advance as far as the line Sukhinichi-Zubovo and reconnoiter toward Kaluga. The weak forces of the army's right wing had to take part in the attack on Briansk planned tomorrow by the armored group [Guderian]. The middle corps had to act as a "rubber band" and maintain contact between the two wings.

Kesselring informed me that there were no indications at all of a threat to the northern flank of 9th Army's attack and that on the contrary the enemy was moving out troops south of Rzhev by train. A fresh telegram went out to the armies, urging them to drive the armored groups forward. I know that they have it tough, but there's nothing I can do.

In the evening came the report that the 7th Panzer Division had reached the highway west of Vyazma from the north! I used this happy result to urge Panzer Group 4 to now reach its own objective.

The difficult situation at Bryansk has been eased since the 17th Panzer Division surprisingly took the city and bridge this morning. The 2nd Army received orders to attack from the west with LIII Corps in order to free the Roslavl-Bryansk road and encircle the enemy south of the road. That is not an easy task , for LIII Corps is manning very broad fronts. But the road is needed to supply the armored group. The 2nd Army is not very happy, for it would like to create a larger "pocket," where, together with the armored group, it would encircle and destroy all of the enemy forces in front of it, including north of Bryansk. A fine idea in itself, but we don't have the required forces, for, just like the armored group, XIII Corps has to face its front toward the northeast and advance as quickly and as far as possible in that direction in order to begin exploiting the imminent victory at Vyazma and – if possible – drive into the last fortified position before Moscow [Kashira-Serpukhov-Borodino]. Unfortunately they will have to satisfy themselves with the small pocket south of Bryansk. I have ordered 2nd Army to reach the line Sukhinichi-Zubovo with its left wing and send reconnaissance forces ahead far as the line

Kosjolsk-Kaluga-Tawakowo. The 4th Army is subsequently to send its ground reconnaissance ahead as far as the line Medyn-Gzhatsk.

In the evening I had a bitter fight with Strauß [9th Army], who still wants to use the 86th Division in VIII Corps' front instead of sending it after the tanks by way of Kholm as I had ordered. He reported that the march and supply conditions through Kholm were so bad that movement on that road was impossible. Therefore the division is to advance east by way of Nejelowo and then north along the rail line through Kholm to the panzer corps. I can't confirm this report and unfortunately must reluctantly allow this action, but I told Strauß that under such conditions the requested move of the 19th Panzer Division behind Panzer Group 3 was also out of the question, whereupon Strauß replied that he also considered this impossible. I sent a telegram to the army, again reminding it that its most important task was to quickly send strong infantry forces after the tanks.

7/10/41

In the morning I spoke with Hoth, whose view differs from that of the army concerning the possibilities of advancing through Kholm. After his conversation with Strauß he had to assume that the latter had fought an unsuccessful battle with me over the employment of the 19th Panzer Division!? – I learned that the army is also pulling the 161st Division out of Beloy (a difficult to defend road junction) and that it intends to move the division farther to the north. That is inexplicable in view of the order to send strong infantry forces to follow up behind the tanks. I am intervening.

This morning the 10th Panzer Division reached Vyazma from the south; the 2nd Panzer Division also arrived, closing the ring around the main enemy forces. The attack is also progressing well on the other encirclement fronts.

Brauchitsch came at midmorning to discuss the next moves: immediate turn toward Tula by the 2nd Panzer Army [Guderian] – as it is called since yesterday; initiation of the pursuit in the general direction of Moscow by all forces that can be released from the encirclement front; on the northern wing northward advance by Panzer Group Hoth in order to bring about the collapse of the enemy front facing my left wing and the right wing of Army Group North [Leeb].

"...We Could Have Saved Blood and Time, If..."

Brauchitsch said that this time it was different than at Minsk and Smolensk, this time we could risk pursuing immediately. I am of the view that it was just as possible at Minsk and Smolensk and that we could have saved blood and time if they hadn't stayed the army group's hand back then. I am not in total agreement with the drive to the north by Panzer Group 3. Perhaps it will be spared me, for the heavy blow inflicted today may result in the enemy, contrary to previous Russian practice, yielding opposite my front as well; some signs point to that.

The armies were informed immediately in order to be able to begin the planned movements; the complete order followed in the evening. If the weather holds we may be able to make up for much of what was lost through Kiev.

In the evening I spoke with Strauß, who has now assembled three divisions close about Beloy and attacked to the northeast with one division. A lively argument developed when I suggested that my order to send strong infantry forces behind the armored group toward Vyazma, which was repeated daily, was not being followed and that the army was instead dancing another step.

8/10/41

In the morning I called Kluge and informed him that closure of the pocket's eastern front was complete.

Still lacking the impression of a solid conclusion with the 9th Army, I sent a general staff officer there by plane; but on his return he reassured me.

As it is not completely clear whether Kluge has really recognized the need for LVII Panzer Corps to begin its drive east immediately, I called his Chief of Staff and repeated that it was vital that we reach the position at Maloyaroslavets and Mozhaysk before the enemy. Haste is urgently required. Strong reconnaissance forces must be sent ahead as far as Moscow. Blumentritt [Chief of Staff 4th Army] agrees. By way of the Chief of Staff I suggested the army send strong infantry forces after the Kuntzen Corps as quickly as possible.

9th Army reports that Panzer Group 3 has driven through as far as the Vyazma-Sychevka road against negligible opposition. I issued orders for the army to take Sychevka tomorrow. To the question, when would the armored group be in the position to set out toward Kalinin and Rzhev, it answered that it would not be possible for three days for reasons of fuel. I can't wait that long with the enemy retreating in front of the 9th Army's northern wing. The armored group was therefore instructed to hurry up its preparations for the advance and was not to wait for the last elements to be released from the encirclement front.

Progress is slow at the Bryansk pocket; the 17th Panzer Division at bryansk and LIII Corps from the west are both gaining ground along the main road.

Orders came that the 2nd Panzer Army is to take Kursk.

Brauchitsch had already spoken about it. I had resisted the idea because the city lies far beyond my area, proposed in vain giving this mission to the 6th Army [Reichenau], and as well offered the two divisions of XXXIV Army Corps [means XXXXIV Senior Detachment] from my southern wing.

9/10/41

In the morning there came an order from the *Führer* that elements of Panzer Group 3, thus north of the highway, were to be relieved by elements of Panzer Group 4 from south of the highway for an advance to the north. That would take very much longer than a relief by infantry, involve unnecessary lateral movements over frightful roads, and open one hole in order to plug another.

The pocket at Vyazma is shrinking more and more. Numbers of prisoners and captured materiel growing.

To my regret, in the afternoon a special bulletin was issued which spoke of a second pocket at Bryansk. I called Halder and told him that I had deliberately never mentioned this "pocket," because its eastern front is more than shaky and because Guderian's weak forces are incapable of preventing some of the Russians from breaking out there. Then in the afternoon two breakout attempts there were contained, but only just. Guderian scraping everything together to prevent a large-scale escape. Bryansk and Trubchevsk were taken from the west.

During the night of 10 October, at 03:00, there arrived an order direct from the *Führer*, according to which the 19th Panzer Division and the Infantry Regiment *Großdeutschland* were to be sent to the Guderian group at once by way of Bryansk, in order to prevent the enemy south of Bryansk from breaking out to the east! I reported back that the 19th Panzer Division was at present southwest of Yukhnov and that an about face was impossible without threatening the supply of the 4th Army and the Luftwaffe, which was on the 19th Panzer Division's road. Moreover, according to information from the 2nd Army, the road to Bryansk will not be usable until the 10th at the earliest due to numerous demolitions; on the undamaged sections of the road are the fuel transport columns of the 2nd Panzer Army. Delivery of fuel by way of the previous route, a detour far to the south, had proved impossible in the long run in view of the awful road conditions. I requested orders as to which should have priority, the fuel or the Infantry Regiment *Großdeutschland*. I received the reply that they would do without the 19th Panzer Division; the fuel had priority, but the Infantry Regiment *Großdeutschland* was to be transferred to the 2nd Panzer Army by way of Bryansk as soon as practicable.

In an effort to clear up the situation around Bryansk I ordered that the surrounded enemy elements south of Bryansk were to be dealt with by the panzer army, those north of Bryansk by the 2nd Army, while the panzer army was also to prevent the last-mentioned enemy from escaping to the east.

LVII Panzer Corps [Kuntzen], which was supposed to advance through Maloyaroslavets, has been so held up by blown bridges that it has made scarcely any progress east across the Iswerja. On the highway the SS Division *Reich* [the SS Division *Reich* – Hausser – was assigned to Panzer Group Guderian] took Gzhatsk in heavy fighting.

9th Army received orders to quickly take possession of Zubtsov and Rzhev with whatever formations were available and thus pave the way for the planned advance on Kalinin by Panzer Group 3 [Reinhardt]. If we wish to still catch the enemy should he withdraw in front of Army Group North, it seems better to barricade the Volga crossings between Starytsa and Rzhev and first send Panzer Group 3 to Kalinin instead of north. If he doesn't withdraw, they can still advance north from Kalinin and Starytsa. Halder, with whom I discussed this, agrees with me.

In the evening 9th Army received notice of an order being issued tomorrow, which calls for Panzer Group 3, bolstered by an infantry corps, to be sent ahead as described above, but to attack with the army as soon as possible in an easterly direction, its right wing following the highway and the post road, its left wing roughly through Rzhev toward the southwestern tip of the Volga storage reservoir.

Guderian was advised that after reaching Tula he might be called upon to turn his army more sharply to the east than previously planned, roughly in the direction of Ryazan.

10/10/41

Drove to the 87th Division [Studnitz], which was advancing east across the Dniepr in order to reduce the pocket west of Vyazma. The division had lost contact with the enemy and those there refused to believe that there were still strong forces in the pocket and that 200,000 men had been captured already. The enemy is trying desperately to break out to the east and southeast.

The breakout attempts in the area south of Bryansk have apparently been contained; the unrest of the previous night was unnecessary. North of Bryansk the bulk of the enemy forces have probably already decamped to the east. Nevertheless, much remains to be taken there, especially in captured equipment.

Weichs [2nd Army] arrived in the evening. He received instructions to move the freed-up elements of his army northeast along the boundary with the 4th and sweep clean the area northwest of Bryansk.

The 4th Army's eastern front is fighting its way slowly across the Ugra and Iswerja to the northeast. Resistance is stiffening in front of the SS Division *Reich*.

In 9th Army's sector the reinforced Panzer Group 3 got moving and took Sychevka.

The weather is beginning to become unpleasant, snow and sleet with falling temperatures.

11/10/41

In the morning I received an inquiry from the Army Command as to how I envisaged the continuation of the operation. Set to work on the reply, but in the meantime a directive arrived from the Army High Command which specified a direction of attack of "Kalinin and west" for the 9th Army.

The pockets north and south of Bryansk and at Vyazma are being reduced; the enemy, in the latter pocket in particular, is making desperate attempts to break out. At one place he tried to break out in closed formations, artillery in the center.

Advancing in the direction of Moscow, the Kuntzen Corps has taken Medyn, Panzer Group Reinhardt Zubtsov. Reinhardt was informed that after reaching Starytsa and Kalinin the armored group will probably receive orders to continue its advance to Torzhok and reconnoiter from Kalinin north toward Rameshki.

As per orders, the Infantry Regiment *Großdeutschland* was sent to the 2nd Panzer Army by way of Bryansk. I have the impression that the regiment is more necessary on the northern wing of the army group, for strong forces will undoubtedly be needed there.

Starting soon, four infantry divisions and the 1st Cavalry Division will be withdrawn from the front and sent to the west. The 1st Cavalry Division is to be transformed into a panzer division [the 24th. Feldt remained as commander. The division was destroyed at Stalingrad in January 1943.] The story of the German cavalry is thus ended.

12/10/41

Guderian is not moving forward; just like Weichs [2nd Army] he is struggling with the Bryansk pockets.

The pocket at Vyazma has been reduced further, numbers of prisoners growing tremendously, the enemy's losses are enormous.

The right wing of the eastward-advancing 4th Army has taken Kaluga, the northernmost corps of the 9th has reached the enemy positions west and north of Rzhev and has broken through them with its right wing.

Panzer Group 3 has taken Starytsa. It was directly subordinated to the army group and now has received orders to advance on Torzhok, in order to make it impossible for the apparently faltering enemy in front of the inner wings of Army Group Center to retreat to the east, while occupying Kalinin and holding Starytsa and Zubtsov.

Weckmann [Chief of Staff 9th Army] arrived at midmorning and was briefed on the 9th Army's new missions, which call for an advance by the right wing toward the Klin-Kalinin road. The army's left wing is to take the enemy positions west of Rzhev. The center is to be moved up between the two so that it can – if necessary – swing north toward and across the Volga on either side of Starytsa.

In the evening I spoke to Brauchitsch, who approved my plans for the army group's further advance.

For the encirclement of Moscow he has in mind a line which lies about 45 kilometers from the city center. I pointed out that I do not have the troops for a wide encirclement and that such would also leave the enemy too much freedom and proposed a quite close sealing off of the city. The *Führer* has forbidden us to set foot in Moscow.

13/10/40

In the morning I spoke with Heusinger [Chief of the OKH Operations Department] of the Army High Command – Halder is ill – and learned that the *Führer* has ordered the sealing off of Moscow roughly in line with the railroad around the city. My other proposals for the army group's advance have been approved.

Kluge and Blumentritt [Chief of Staff 4th Army] were informed that the 4th Army's left boundary is being moved farther to the left roughly in the line Gzhatsk-Klin and that the later encirclement of Moscow will fall largely to the 4th Army.

The battle at Vyazma is coming to an end; at Bryansk it will last a few days longer. As a result of the fighting there and the awful road conditions, Guderian has not yet been able to continue to the northeast – a success for the Russians, whose stubbornness paid off.

Resistance has stiffened before the 4th Army's eastern front. The Russians threw newly-formed tank units against our attack. Nevertheless some progress was made.

Panzer Group 3 entered Kalinin in heavy fighting.

Discussed the situation with Weckmann, Chief of Staff of the 9th Army. I told him that with the enemy also retreating before the southern wing of Army Group North, a turn to the north by the 9th Army would scarcely be necessary, and that the army was to be moved up to the line Klin-Kalinin with a strong echelon behind the left wing.

Early this morning I received a "suggestion" from above that I turn elements of LVII (Motorized) Corps to the right, in order to open a crossing at Serpukhov for Guderian who is still 200 kilometers away. Then, in the afternoon, it was "proposed for consideration" whether elements of LVII Corps should not turn to the left to help the SS Division *Reich* forward at the highway. For now LVII Corps has enough to do on its own front.

14/10/41

A directive arrived this morning from the Army Command; it brought little that was new except that it toyed with the idea of deploying the extreme right wing of the army group toward Voronezh, and when it ordered all of the 9th Army, with the exception of Panzer Group 3, to assemble in the Kalinin-Starytsa-Torzhok area in preparation for a drive north through Vishni Volochek to bring about the collapse of the enemy front before the southern half of Army Group North. I briefed Weckmann on the unfortunate change of plan and the reason behind it. Like after Smolensk, once again the army group is to be scattered to the four winds and thus seriously weakened in its main direction of advance.

Preliminary orders went out to the armies and the armored group in the afternoon. Toward the ultimate objective it is planned that:

Driving past Moscow to the south, 2nd Panzer Army will encircle the city in the south and east, while the 4th Army is responsible for the encirclement in the southwest, west and north; 9th Army and Panzer Group 3 will veer north and are to drive through Torzhok toward Vishni Volochek. The right wing corps of the 9th Army will join the 4th, because otherwise this will be too weak to fulfill its missions. The 2nd Army is to cover the right flank of the operation and to this end initially reach the Don River line between Yelets and Stalinogorsk.

Enemy elements broke out of the southern pocket at Bryansk to the southeast and have been engaged by XXXIV Corps. There is still heavy fighting in the middle and northern Bryansk pockets – three have meanwhile formed there! The battle is over at Vyazma. Only limited progress on the 4th Army's eastern front in the face of bottomless roads and stiffening resistance.

The center of the 9th Army has put the run to enemy rear guards and is fighting in the Rzhev area against an enemy whose rear is already threatened by Panzer Group 3. More heavy fighting in Kalinin, but the road and rail bridges there have fallen into our hands.

The southern wing of Army Group North has only slowly begun to move. The enemy is still holding firm opposite the center and left wing of the 16th Army [Busch].

"What Will Become of Us in The Winter?"

15/10/41

Guderian informed me that because of stubborn enemy resistance the advance by his army to the northwest will not be possible until the Bryansk pocket is eliminated and his forces have regrouped. This will take some days. As well there are the indescribable road conditions, which make almost any movement by motorized vehicles impossible.

The change in the weather with its periods of snow, frost and rain, is wearing on the troops and is affecting morale. The question, "what will become of us in the winter?" is on everyone's mind.

The fighting at the Bryansk pockets is quite unpredictable; today, for example, a German regiment of the 134th Division was surrounded on all sides in the southernmost pocket.

Panzer Group 3 is fighting hard at Kalinin; the enemy is bringing in reinforcements from all sides, even from Moscow, in order to regain possession of this important point. Growing number of reports today that the Russians are retreating in front of the 16th Army's southern wing. The possibility of advancing Panzer Group 3 more to the northeast is drawing closer. For now it received the order already issued once, to reconnoiter in strength to Bezhetsk.

The 9th Army has gradually turned north, enemy rear guards were either forced back or were destroyed.

16/10/41

In the morning Greiffenberg telephoned Halder to inform him of the withdrawal in front of the 16th Army reported by the Luftwaffe and to tell him that the armored group's advance on Vishni-Volochek may not catch too much of the enemy. This was followed in the evening by a short telegram from the Army High Command, which talked about the "possibility" that Panzer Group 3 might be turned northeast after reaching Torzhok. The armored group's advance is slow on account of fuel and road difficulties. Further, since the 9th Army's infantry divisions are marching into the armored group and crossing with it, I found myself forced to subordinate the group to the 9th Army again to bring about a unified regulation of the marches. In the afternoon the 1st Panzer Division opened the way to Torzhok at Kalinin and set off toward the northwest. Enemy attacks at Kalinin were repulsed.

Nothing significant on the other army fronts. Guderian and the 2nd Army are still tied up at Bryansk.

The 4th Army, too, gained little ground on bottomless roads.

For the first time the Russian Army communique revealed that things are going badly on all fronts.

17/10/41

The northernmost of the three Bryansk pockets collapsed.

Otherwise the army group's front is as good as unchanged.

Enemy resistance is especially stubborn in front of the 4th Army.

Panzer Group 3 succeeded in gaining ground in the direction of Torzhok.

The Chief of Staff of the 9th Army [Weckmann] was ambushed on the road at Army Headquarters last night and has a concussion. In the evening a visit from Schenckendorff [commander of the rear army area]; he welcomed this news, because combatting the extensive, well-organized partisan movement is his primary mission at the moment. As an experiment, cossack squadrons are to be formed from the Russian prisoners of war for this purpose.

Visit by Minister Todt [Fritz Todt, Reich Minister for Armaments and Munitions from 1940 to 1942].

Snow and terrific roads.

18/10/41

The pocket south of Bryansk is finished. It's time, for the 2nd Panzer Army is moving forward toward Tula; the right wing of the 4th Army is now already hanging in the air.

4th Army reports that the Kuntzen Corps has reached Maloyaroslavets, XXXX Panzer Corps Mozhaysk. Whether we will be able to exploit these successes depends largely on the weather.

Panzer Group 3 has gained further ground in the direction of Torzhok.

Enemy resistance is stiffening opposite the 9th Army's left wing.

Disentangling the divisions squeezed close together in the Vyazma pocket is taking the 4th Army a very long time, especially since the few usable roads leading to the east are in heavy use by the armored groups. As yet virtually no infantry has been deployed between the highway and the 4th Army's northern boundary. In order to keep movement in the general direction of Moscow flowing as best I can, I ordered that once the road from the south to Kalinin has been cleared, the corps from the right wing of the 9th Army, which has already advanced far to the east, is to turn east in the direction of Volokolamsk and then join the 4th Army.

Plenty going on in world politics. In Japan a military cabinet has been formed which is said to be well-disposed towards us. Roosevelt claims that German submarines sank an American destroyer, which is being denied. The question is whether Roosevelt really wants war or whether they're just doing business over there.

19/10/41

Guderian assumed command of XXXXIII and LIII Corps, both released from the pocket east of Bryansk. Since in the evening he reported that he could not yet estimate the timing of his attack on account of the muddy roads and severe fuel problems, I had to temporarily take XXXXIII Corps away from him again and subordinate it to 4th Army, for the army's exposed right wing needed protection on its right flank. The 4th Army received orders to advance the corps in the direction of Aleksin and south.

Furthermore the army group is stuck fast in muck and mire. No fuel is reaching Panzer Group 3 either. Supply via Bryansk and on the highway is unbelievably difficult. The Bryansk road is in terrible shape; on the highway alone there are 33 demolitions, including 11 large bridges, to be repaired.

The elements of the 1st Panzer Division sent forward from Kalinin to Torzhok had to retire some way at the cost of men and materiel, since in the interim strong enemy forces had broken in between them and Torzhok.

I subsequently advised Strauß that Kalinin would long remain "the bleeding wound" of his army if strong infantry forces were not sent there very soon. Further I told him that in my opinion the point of main effort of his attack should lie in the area on either side of Starytsa. He expressed the view that "at least one panzer corps" should be sent north from Kalinin toward Bezhetsk. I replied that it wasn't time yet, but that – as per orders – he was to reconnoiter in strength there. It was too early to say whether the main assault would take place toward Bezhetsk or toward Torzhok. Since the enemy before the 16th Army was still holding fast, it was easily possible that it might remain Torzhok.

I issued the following order of the day:

"The battle at Vyazma and Bryansk has resulted in the collapse of the Russian front, which was fortified in depth. Eight Russian armies with 73 rifle and cavalry divisions, 13 tank divisions and brigades and strong army artillery were destroyed in the difficult struggle with a numerically far-superior foe.

The total booty: 673,098 prisoners, 1,277 tanks, 4,378 artillery pieces, 1,009 anti-tank and anti-aircraft guns, 87 aircraft and huge amounts of war material.

This difficult battle, too, you have come through with honor and in doing so completed the greatest feat of arms of the campaign!

I express my thanks and my appreciation to all command authorities and troops, in and behind the front, which contributed to this success."

20/10/41

Witzleben, Chief of Staff of the 2nd Army, has fallen ill. His successor, *Oberst* Harteneck, reported for duty this morning. I briefed him on the difficulty of the army's situation. It is to guard the army group's right flank and, on orders of the Army High Command, take Kursk – tasks which are made more difficult for the army by the condition of the badly strung out divisions, exhausted by punishing battles and marches over bottomless roads.

I drove up the highway to the front to see for myself the supply difficulties that had been reported there. The main reason that these difficulties are so great is because the detour roads around the blown bridges are deep in mud and nearly impassable.

The impression of the tens of thousands of Russian prisoners of war who, scarcely guarded, are marching toward Smolensk is dreadful. Dead-tired and half-starved, these unfortunate people stagger along. Many have fallen dead or collapsed from exhaustion on the road.

Guderian is still skirmishing with remnants of Russian units which broke out of the Bryansk pocket. The 4th Army is making only limited progress in a few places. Hopefully it will get better when the bulk of its infantry corps arrive.

9th Army is slowly closing ranks as it moves north. Panzer Group 3 has had to withdraw the elements sent forward in the direction of Torzhok even further, in order to fend off the enemy who is now attacking Kalinin from all sides.

21/10/41

The Russians are impeding us far less than the wet and the mud!

Limited progress by the 4th Army and the left wing of the 9th Army, 2nd Panzer Army and Panzer Group 3 are essentially at a standstill on the abysmal roads. At Dmitrov the panzer army mopped up the last of the enemy elements that broke out of the pocket. The Russians continue to attack at Kalinin.

In the evening Kluge [4th Army] spoke with me about the tremendous difficulty of any movement. He also informed me that pressure is being felt against his right wing from Tula by way of Aleksin and Tarusa. I called Guderian and asked him when he thought he would be ready to attack and told him that because of the weather the air fleet could not promise its support for the next three days. He reported that he intends to attack on the 23rd.

An order has been prepared, according to which the motorized units, which are paralyzed because of the road conditions, are temporarily to leave their vehicles and be put together as infantry units with limited artillery so that they don't sit about useless behind the front. Since I expect the same kind of resistance that my earlier order for the cavalry to fight on foot aroused, I sent an inquiry to the Army Command as to whether Brauchitsch agreed. The answer was "no!"

But this does not change the fact that sensible commanders take such actions on their own.

22/10/41

No significant progress anywhere.

The 9th Army's situation is unclear; we have been unable to find out what it intends to do. The weather foiled an attempt to send a general staff officer there.

In the morning I described the situation to Brauchitsch, especially the difficulty of movement. Then I took a stand against an order which calls for the only shell effective against the most powerful Russian tank – the T-34 – to be withdrawn from the front; we can't demand of the infantry that they stand fast in the face of enemy tank attacks if we take away their only effective means of defense.

Brauchitsch turned to Voronezh again; I was to give my opinion as to whether or not the deployment of the southernmost corps of the panzer army toward Voronezh was reasonable. In my written reply I rejected the idea, reasoning that the drive on Tula by the armored group was more important to me, and that I needed the entire 2nd Panzer Army, especially since the fighting strengths of the armored and motorized divisions were only those of regiments, and finally that the corps would become stuck in the mud east of Kursk just as it presently was west of the town.

The demands which combat, roads and weather are placing on the field units are enormous. Guderian reported that this is evident in the morale of individual divisions of XXXIV Corps.

Representatives of the press arrived from Germany in the evening; we are to show them the front.

23/10/41

I briefed Halder on my plan to order 9th Army to initially clear the enemy from the triangle between Kalinin, the Volga and the Volga storage reservoir, and then only attack to the north if all threats to the panzer corps' [LVI Corps] rear at Kalinin had been eliminated. Halder replied that this was entirely within the framework of my mission, whereupon I replied that my mission was to go to Torzhok; this advance could only be delayed by the new order to 9th Army. Halder replied that there was "absolutely no rush" for the advance on Torzhok.

This is new!

The order was sent to the 9th Army.

24/10/41

The 9th Army reported its plans regarding yesterday's order but did not express itself clearly, so I telephoned Strauß and once again made it clear that an advance north from Kalinin was out of the question until things had been cleared up behind the city and the crossings over the storage reservoir and the Volga had been closed to the enemy.

In the morning I received orders to deploy the right wing of the 2nd Army, which was to be bolstered with mobile forces – contrary to my proposal –, toward Voronezh. To this end I subordinated XXXXVIII (Motorized) Corps with one panzer and one motorized division to the 2nd Army, which tomorrow is assuming command of the army group's right wing. It received orders to first reach the general line Kursk-Maloarchangelsk, take possession of the Snov crossings for a further advance, and send mobile forces toward Voronezh "as soon as possible."

Given the condition of the army, the latter will undoubtedly not be possible in the immediate future.

Since there are indications that Kursk is only weakly held, I had Guderian, who is still in command there today, advised that by moving quickly from Fatezh, Kursk might perhaps still be taken at little cost.

Only very minor progress on the army group front. In some cases 24 horses are required to move a single artillery piece. 2nd Panzer Army, which today attacked in the direction of Tula, also gained little ground. The Russians attacked at Kalinin.

North of Starytsa, in front of VI Corps, whose attack has been delayed for several days, the enemy is withdrawing! I called Strauß and asked him to urge the Commanding General to be more aggressive.

Himmler came in the afternoon, in the evening the Swiss Colonel Bircher.

25/10/41

The 2nd Panzer Army has taken Chern. XXXXIII Corps [Heinrici] returned to the panzer army from 4th Army.

Resistance stiffening in front of the 4th Army. The enemy has moved in new forces from Siberia and from the Caucasus and has launched counterattacks on either side of the roads leading southwest from Moscow. The southern half of the 4th Army, with major elements of its artillery delayed by the muddy roads, has been forced onto the defensive. On the army's northern wing the left wing of the armored group and with it V Corps have made some progress in the direction of Volokolamsk. In order to ensure uniformity of action there, V Corps, as anticipated, has been subordinated to the 4th Army.

At Kalinin further heavy attacks by the Russians, who west of the city advanced southeast across the Volga.

VI Corps advancing in the direction of Torzhok. XXIII Corps also made some progress.

Seen on the whole, however, all that is nothing. The splitting apart of the army group together with the frightful weather has caused to us being bogged down. As a result the Russians are gaining time to bring their shattered divisions back up to strength and bolster their defense, especially since they have most of the rail lines and roads around Moscow. That is very bad!

26/10/41

Drove to my old 1st Cavalry Division [Feldt], which is going home for retraining; the cavalry brigade marched past me for the last time on its way to the entraining station.

Reports on the state of the 45th [Schlieper] and 134th [Cochenhausen] Divisions, which are hopelessly stuck in the mud of the heavy soil of the Ukraine, sound desperate.

In the evening Heusinger [Chief of the OKH Operations Department] informed me that consideration is being given to the idea of yet turning the 2nd Panzer Army toward Voronezh after it reaches Tula. Also under consideration is having the army group's northern wing take Bezhetsk with infantry only and combining Armored Groups 3 and 4 for a drive between Moscow and the Volga, direction Yaroslavl-Rybinsk. The army group is to advise whether both are possible in terms of supply, whether the supposition voiced at the highest level that 2nd Panzer Army lacks the necessary bridging equipment to cross the Oka is correct, etc.

I called Halder and said: I have no idea what the objective of the 2nd Panzer Army's departure for Voronezh is. It is essential at Tula and farther northeast. The situation is such that the southern half of the 4th Army between the Oka and the highway has been forced onto the defensive by the increasingly strong enemy, who today launched large-scale counterattacks. Kluge has been forced to commit his reserves, the 15th and 183rd Divisions, and has requested the release of my last reserve for the threatened front. It looks better north of the highway; for how much longer I cannot say. Relief for the 4th Army and a possible resumption of the attack can only come through a continuation of the panzer army's advance through Tula to the northeast. Turning this army is unjustifiable.

Halder replied that he agreed with me and that he thought turning the panzer army toward Voronezh was wrong. But he needed my position for further negotiations. I promised to examine the situation on the northern wing, but pointed out that at the moment an advance by motorized forces in the strategic sense was out of the question as they were all buried up to their axles in the mud. If I am to advance on Bezhetsk, whether with infantry or with tanks, I first have to have Torzhok and have to screen my left flank, as the right wing of the 16th Army, as he well knows, is not going to attack. I will examine whether it is possible to force two armored groups northeast between Moscow and the Volga and supply them. Halder replied that he didn't think it would work. But we have to reach the area of Rybinsk and Yaroslavl somehow, in order to eliminate the enemy northeast of this line for the continuation of the war in the coming year.

Some progress by the 2nd Panzer Army, by V and VI Army Corps.

Halt the Panzer Army?

27/10/41

Over bottomless roads, the 2nd Army is slowly pursuing the enemy retreating toward Kursk.

The panzer army advanced some distance toward Tula. Its infantry divisions are slowly struggling across the Oka against no serious resistance.

The enemy is moving in further reinforcements opposite the southern half of the 4th Army as far as the highway. On the northern wing brave V Corps has taken Volokolamsk.

Things don't look good at Kalinin. To the west the enemy has driven across the Volga and is trying to seal off the city from the south.

VI and XXIII Corps made limited progress to the north.

Toward evening an order arrived from the Army Command to halt the [2nd] panzer army [Guderian]! I immediately sent a response, saying that I could not carry out this order. Late in the evening I spoke with Heusinger once again as Halder could not be reached, and told him that diverting the panzer army south was impossible given the present road conditions. I had reported the supply difficulties to be expected in this event. As I said yesterday, a relief of the 4th Army can only be expected if the panzer army continues to advance. If this advance is halted, and if the bulk of the 4th Army has to remain on the defensive, in view of the anticipated attrition I will have to place my last reserves, the 23rd and 268th Divisions, at the disposal of the 4th Army. I would then have nothing with which to plug up the wide gap between the northern wing of the 4th Army and Kalinin and would be forced to take the necessary forces away from the 9th Army. This would also end this army's attack. In practical terms then, halting the panzer army means ceasing the attack on the entire army group front. It also happens that a turn to the south is impossible until we have possession of the Upa crossings at Tula. Not until there is a screening force there can we – under its protection – perhaps head south on the west side of the Upa – not before. For all these reasons I am not in a position to pass on the order to halt the panzer army. If the Army Command wants to do it, it will have to tell the army itself. The advance by the panzer army, including its infantry corps, has been started through unspeakable effort and after overcoming great difficulties. If I now order it to halt, they will think me mad. Heusinger said that this was also his view for the most part and that he would raise the matter up once again.

Two telegrams arrived during the night repeating the order to halt the panzer army!

Sent the army group's position in response to yesterday's inquiry from the Army High Command. It said: turn by 2nd Panzer Army toward Voronezh; as good as impossible at the moment as far as supply and roads are concerned, armored advance toward Rybinsk very difficult for the same reasons.

28/10/41

This morning I told Halder once again that I could not pass on the order in this form. I would order the panzer army to prepare for a possible turn. To do so it must – as reported yesterday – reach the Upa. Halder understands this.

The following order went to the panzer army:

"The possibility exists that the panzer army will be ordered to turn south. The army is to take steps to ensure that the turn can be carried out in case such an order is issued. It is the opinion of the army group, which agrees with the panzer army's report, that possession of the left bank of the Upa is a necessary condition for this."

An order from the Army High Command which arrived during the night says that the attack by the 9th Army is not to be continued north past the line Kalinin-Torzhok, and that an advance to the northeast between Moscow and the Volga toward Yaroslavl-Rybinsk and later toward Vologda is being planned by Panzer Group 3, which is to be bolstered by elements of Panzer Group 4. 9th Army received orders to halt its attack and only to push on to Torzhok if resistance lessened noticeably. Furthermore the order was repeated to bring order to the situation at and south of Kalinin and then to assemble Panzer Group 3 at and south of Kalinin for the planned advance.

A further order from the OKH arrived in the afternoon, according to which 2nd Panzer Army's drive on Tula was to be continued "so as not to lose time." An attempt was to be made to send mobile battalions up to the Oka in order to capture the bridges intact. Even if this should succeed, there is no certainty of securing the crossing, as the Russians work mainly with time fuses and remote detonation.

4th Army received orders to make preparations so that in the event of a freeze it can resume the attack at clear points of main effort north and south of the highway with no loss of time. Further it is to drive its northern wing sharply in the direction of Klin.

The question of the advance toward Voronezh has apparently led to differences among those at the top. In the afternoon a directive came from *Führer* Headquarters that Kluge was to go to the *Führer* as soon as possible...

I am to be informed, but not the Army High Command!

Schmundt arrived in the afternoon in the aircraft that was sent to meet Kluge in Smolensk; he confirmed my speculations.

Canaris joined me in the evening.

"I Assess the Situation Differently..."

29/10/41

Based on the morning reports it looks bad at Kalinin. When asked, Reinhardt, the commander of Panzer Group 3, reported that the enemy southwest of Kalinin was no longer a cause for concern; he has hopes that the attack by XXVII Corps, coming by way of Starytsa, will resolve the situation once and for all. He did not rate very highly the enemy force reported south of Kalinin; it consisted of small, fragmented parts of units, which – as he put it – had been milling about here from the beginning. I emphasized the compelling need to clear the area between Kalinin and the reservoir and asked if whether is not now possible, after the freeze, to finally bring up LVI (Motorized) Corps, which is lagging far behind. Reinhardt replied that he didn't need the corps

for the mopping-up mission south of Kalinin. Besides the corps was hopelessly bogged down with no fuel, which was strictly a question of supply
anyway:

"There is no difficulty with the enemy!"

I assess the situation differently: the gap between V Corps near
Volokolamsk and Kalinin is more than 70 km wide. For several days there
have been growing signs of enemy movements, even if by weak forces only at
first, into this gap. The enemy therefore knows our weak spot. If he still has
forces available, he will undoubtedly try to drive into the gap and thus take
possession of Kalinin. It is high time that this gap was closed. It should have
been up to 4th Army to extend itself to the reservoir. This has not happened
and now there is nothing left to do but hand this task over to the 9th Army, or
by committing the 86th Division of V Corps, push ahead the attack by the 4th
Army's northern wing to the northeast. The ultimate decision will depend on
consultations with the local commanders.

With a light frost and somewhat better weather, the 2nd Panzer Army,
well supported by the Luftwaffe, pushed its narrow attack spearhead to within
5 km of Tula. The army's infantry corps also gained ground slowly across the
Oka to the northeast.

Heavy Russian counterattacks at the highway. Apparently the enemy is
weakening in front of VI Corps – west of Kalinin – but not in front of XXIII
Corps on its left.

30/10/41

Guderian's weak spearhead reached the southern outskirts of Tula, which
is being defended by the enemy. Everything else is still lagging far behind on
the muddy roads. Otherwise no significant changes on the entire front – weather
filthy.

Infiltration by the enemy into the gap between 4th and 9th Armies growing. This is the source of my greatest worry at the moment.

This morning the order relayed by the Army High Command by phone on
the 28th October, to advance the 2nd Panzer Army through Tula, was confirmed by telegraph with the supplement that it was important to soon cut the
rail lines to Moscow from the south. In the afternoon there arrived a "directive

for the continuation of operations against the enemy between Volga Lake and Lake Ladoga."

The only change from the verbal announcement of 28th October is that now the entire Panzer Group 4 is to advance northeast with Panzer Group 3, bypassing Moscow to the north, and that the 253rd Division is to be moved from the right wing of the 16th Army to the 9th Army.

A summing-up directive for the next operation was sent by the army group to all armies. It contained nothing new for the 2nd, 2nd Panzer and 4th Armies; to secure its eastern flank, 9th Army was ordered to drive the enemy across the Lama and the Volga reservoir and pull a division out of its northern front. Subsequently the army is to prepare Panzer Group 3 for the specified advance.

My wish, to reinforce V Corps, which has broken through the enemy position and is already behind it, with the 86th Division, and then with this strong force roll up the enemy position south of Kalinin from behind and thus eliminate in the most effective manner the danger to the 9th Army's eastern flank, proved unfeasible. A thorough examination revealed that providing three divisions with supplies and ammunition in V Corps' area was impossible. As grotesque as it seems, I must therefore move the 86th Division along in front of the enemy position to the northeast so that the gap can be closed a all.

Hitler "Probably Didn't Believe" The Reports

31/10/41

I told Strauß that I was concerned that our views of the situation were diverging. The 9th Army's northern front had become little more than a secondary front, while its eastern flank between Yaropolets and Kalinin was of great significance. The enemy had realized this and was steadily bolstering his strength in this gap. Unless we at least seal off the gap for the time being, we will lose Kalinin. I asked him to send everything there that he could possibly make available. He must not be afraid to dismount LVI Panzer Corps and have it march on foot in order to ward off the impending danger until he is in a position to drive the enemy from the nook. I said that Reinhardt had expressed the view that the clearing of the army's eastern flank was to be linked with his attack to the northeast. I had stated and restated to him that we must lose no time in clearing the eastern flank, while Reinhardt's attack was out of the question until lasting cold arrived. Strauß agreed and asked I have at least elements of V Corps from the 4th Army's northern wing attack along the Lama to the northeast.

2nd Army has placed two reinforced battalions on the rails and is set on advancing from Orel to Kursk, led by an armored train. The first time the expedition was halted only 10 kilometers south of Orel by a blown track. – In spite of severe supply difficulties, 2nd Panzer Army is preparing to attack toward Tula. – In the 9th Army's area, the enemy force which had crossed the Volga southwest of Kalinin was thrown back across the river.

Status reports on the 95th [Infantry Division, Sixt von Arnim] and the 9th Panzer Division [Ritter von Hubicki] of the 2nd Army paint a sad picture; the head of the 95th is at Kursk, parts are in Kiev, elements are scattered over this 500-kilometer-long stretch.

Our losses have become quite considerable. In the army group's area more than twenty battalions are under the command of lieutenants.

Kluge returned from headquarters. The *Führer* asked for a detailed account of the battle conditions, but especially of the tremendous difficulties being caused 4th Army by the weather and the roads. He probably refused to believe the written reports, which is not surprising, for anyone who hasn't seen this filth doesn't think it possible.

1/11/41

The 2nd Army reached the northern outskirts of Kursk; limited local progress by the 9th Army's northern front.

Kluge spoke once again about the possibilities of attacking. He said that if he drove his forces forward now there might be a gain of a few kilometers then that would be it again because artillery and motorized weapons became stuck. I told him that we would gain nothing by that. Naturally we must stay alert to any weakening by the enemy and strike there immediately. But in general the army had to, as per orders, make thorough preparations for an attack as soon as the cold sets in. This time benefits the enemy but unfortunately there is no other solution.

The situation is enough to drive one to despair and filled with envy I look to the Crimea, where we are advancing vigorously in the sunshine over the dry ground of the steppe and the Russians are scattering to the four winds. It could be the same here if we weren't stuck up to our knees in the mud.

I had my Chief of Staff [Greiffenberg] propose to all the armies that they adopt a practice already in use elsewhere and form detachments equipped with *panye* ponies with single machine-guns mounted on *panye* wagons. The fighting strength of these detachments will be low; but there is no enemy at all in large parts of 2nd Army's area and that of the 2nd Panzer Army. There the emphasis now is less on fighting and more on moving forward to reach the desired objectives before the enemy does.

The Army High Command was again briefed on our desperate situation by Greiffenberg.

The foremost battalion of the French Volunteer Regiment [638th Infantry Regiment; regimental commander Colonel Roger Labonne, who initiated the formation of the first units of the French Volunteer Legion in Versailles] arrived at Smolensk. The regiment has been subordinated to the army group.

2/11/41

2nd Army took Kursk, which was defended only by rear guards.

A local attack along the highway by elements of 4th Army met fierce resistance. Limited progress on the 9th Army's northern front. The new Chief of Staff of the 9th Army – *Oberst* Hofmann – passed through. I briefed him at length along the lines my conversation with Strauß of 31st October.

In order to extend the railroads, on which everything depends, more quickly, the railroad construction engineers are being bolstered by auxiliary detachments from the field units.

Minister Goebbels, who was on his way to visit the army group at Brauchitsch's invitation, had to turn back en route because it was impossible to get through either by aircraft or car.

The notables of Smolensk have asked whether they might make a loyal address to the *Führer* and present me with a thank-you gift from the city. In my reply I informed them that German officers do not accept gifts, but that I would pass on the loyal address to the *Führer*.

3/11/41

Minor local penetration by the enemy on the right wing of the 4th Army. An attack along the highway by VII Corps was called off after middling success.

9th Army, whose nose is still too far to the north, reported that at one spot the enemy broke through to the road leading to Kalinin from the south. That's what happens!

The condition of the roads is becoming ever worse; even the highway has given way in various places, so that supplying the units is becoming increasingly difficult. Only in a few places can the superiors reach the front lines. The units are strained to the utmost.

There is still much of vital importance that can be gained if we get a few days of dry cold. I wish my railroads were finished.

I encountered an artillery regiment of the 5th Division on its way west. It is hard to recognize the men, horses and vehicles as a military column under their crust of dirt.

4/11/41

The penetration south of Kalinin has been cleared up.

Yesterday the 2nd Army's armored train reached a blown bridge about 30 km west of Kursk; its crew is standing guard over the important Orel-Kursk supply rail line, which at present is still in front of the army front.

Colonel Labonne, "A Great Idealist"

The commander of the French Volunteer Infantry Regiment and his adjutant dined with me this evening; an older man who has seen half the world, no old campaigner, no adventurer either, but apparently a great idealist; the adjutant was a reserve officer and a career politician.

The first transport carrying the French Volunteer Legion left for the Eastern Front in September 1941. The Legion was initially assembled at the troop training grounds at Deba, south of Warsaw, where it trained until the end of

1941. All three battalions of the infantry regiment were subsequently trans-ported to Smolensk. There the French Volunteer Legion was subordinated to VII Army Corps, which was part of the 4th Army.

5/11/41

It has begun to freeze, which makes movement easier. At the front only isolated advances by the Russians.

Flew to Orel to the 2nd Panzer Army, where all is in order. I am in com-plete agreement with Guderian's plans.

In the evening I informed Halder that the Luftwaffe was beginning to remove air as well as flak units. Apart from the fact that this means a very significant weakening with regard to our offensive intentions, the effect on the units which must remain here is not good.

Frenchmen in German Uniforms

6/11/41

Minor attacks against the 4th Army's front and also south of Kalinin. – A Russian division marched toward the right flank of the 2nd Panzer Army from the area of Yefremov, from the south, resulting in fighting there. – Moving over terrible roads, the tired 2nd Army advanced so slowly that it was unable to prevent this flanking march before its front, even though haste was urged on its northern wing.

Received an inquiry by the army, whether it might send elements forward to effectively cut the major north-south rail line opposite its front. I replied "Yes, apart from crossings with he east-west rail line."

On the 9th Army's left wing a local attack aimed at solidifying contact with the 16th Army made good progress.

A mine exploded on the highway at Jarzewo yesterday, four weeks after the German occupation.

Marshall Petain sent a message to the French Volunteer Regiment:

"On the eve of the battles that lie before you, I am happy to know that you do not forget that you carry part of our military honor with you... By taking part in this crusade, command of which has been assumed by Germany, you are earning justified claims to the world's gratitude and are helping deflect the bolshevik threat from us. It is your land that you are defending, while at the same time saving the hope of a reconciled Europe..."

As from all descriptions my impression is more of a free corps than that of a firmly-established unit, I ordered that the 7th Division, which the regiment is to join, should it send several officers and NCOs to act as "briefing personnel." On the one hand the detachment is to help the regiment, and on the other watch out that there are no cases of lack of discipline which might damage our reputation, for the French are wearing German uniforms [on the sleeve of their uniform they wore a blue-white-red badge with the legend "France."] In the evening it began to snow.

7/11/41

Oberstleutnant Christ, who was sent to fill in for the 9th Army's Ia, returned and outlined the plan for the attack to restore the situation south of Kalinin. Direction of the attack has been passed to Headquarters, XXVII Corps [Wäger]; in the main it is to be made by three infantry divisions, while the troops of the panzer group have only a minor role to play. The enemy has strengthened his forces southeast of Kalinin, is cocky and active, and almost daily advances up to and across the Latschino-Kalinin road. The attack is bound to fail if insufficient forces are committed against him. I therefore stepped in and sent a telex demanding that stronger forces from the panzer group be committed to the attack. Christ confirmed my suspicion that it is going to be very hard to get the panzer group to employ its motorized units – which cannot move on the hopeless roads – on foot. As well, a letter from the panzer group which arrived today held forth in detail and in generally negative terms about the use of motorized troops as foot soldiers. In my reply I made reference to Panzer Army Guderian, which is providing daily proof that motorized forces fighting on foot are capable of outstanding feats – they just have to want to!

2nd Army continues to advance slowly toward the east.

2nd Panzer Army has been forced to divert all of LIII Corps against an enemy force attacking its southern flank. This and a return to milder weather have further delayed the attack in the direction of Tula. – Only local attacks against 4th Army. – On the 9th Army's northern front a more serious attack against VI Corps. The left wing of the army continues to eat its way north through the enemy position in order to reach the southeast tip of Lake Seliger and thus solidify contact with Army Group North.

The Volga has frozen over at Kalinin; unfortunately, however, it is now starting to thaw.

8/11/41

Further fighting on the 2nd Panzer Army's southern flank, where the enemy was forced back only with difficulty. Substantial parts of the army's motorized forces are still strung out on the bottomless Tula-Orel-Karachev road; elements of one division are still at Sevsk. This means a depth of over 300 kilometers. Given the warm weather their arrival in the near future is doubtful. – On the 9th Army's left wing, the 253rd Division continues to fight its way bravely through the enemy's Volga position.

9/11/41

Guderian's situation doesn't look exactly rosy. Apparently the enemy has brought up stronger elements against the panzer army's flank and these are now attacking. – Through my Chief of Staff, I once again reminded the 2nd Army of the necessity of keeping together the forces of XXXV Corps and soon bringing them forward through Novosil. Unfortunately I know how hard that is given the road conditions. Since, in spite of everything, Guderian intends to attack tomorrow with his left-wing corps, which apparently is facing only weak opposition, I sent a request to 4th Army to provide whatever support it can for this attack in the area of Aleksin.

The 9th Army has chosen the 12th [of November] for its attack, but is worried that it won't be ready in time. I told the Ia, Blaurock, that I would be grateful if they were to push ahead with attack preparations, but that the day didn't matter; the 13th, the 14th or even the 15th was fine with me; the attack mustn't be rushed.

*33. At Army Group B Headquarters in Serrant;
Generalfeldmarschall Fedor von Bock (left), General
de Infanterie Hans von Salmuth (right).*

*34. Fedor von Bock (right) with his groom Walter
Jurkat seen preparing for a ride.*

35. Generalfeldmarschall Fedor von Bock (left) in front of Mont St. Michel (2 August 1940).

36. Generalfeldmarschall Fedor von Bock on horseback.

37. *Carl-Hans Graf von Hardenberg, Major of the Reserve (right), with Oberstleutnant Henning von Tresckow.*

38. *Generalfeldmarschall Fedor von Bock (2nd from left) and Generaloberst Heinz Guderian (right) on a hill overlooking the Neman (Memel) River, which formed the border with the Soviets, immediately prior to the start of Operation Barbarossa.*

39. Oberstleutnant Henning von Tresckow, Major Gericke, Generalfeldmarschall Fedor von Bock, and Major of the Reserve Carl-Hans Graf von Hardenberg (probably the summer of 1941).

40. Vitebsk, July 1941. Generalfeldmarschall Fedor von Bock (left) following a meeting with the Commander-in-Chief of the 9th Army, Generaloberst Strauß (to the right of Bock).

41. Generalfeldmarschall Fedor von Bock (left) with his adjutant Major of the Reserve Carl-Hans Graf von Hardenberg.

42. At the Soviet front: Generalfeldmarschall Fedor von Bock watches engineers erect a bridge (1941); with him is Major of the Reserve Carl-Hans Graf von Hardenberg.

43. Generalfeldmarschall Fedor von Bock with General der Infanterie Richard Ruoff and General der Artillerie Walter Heitz following a conference (30 August 1941).

44. While driving to the front (Nikolskoye), Generalfeld-marschall Fedor von Bock has met Generalleutnant Eccard Freiherr von Gablenz, the commanding officer of the 7th Infantry Division, who gives a report on the progress of operations (October 1941).

45. *Generalfeldmarschall Fedor von Bock has made his way to an infantry division during an offensive operation to check on the situation (Nikolskoye, October 1941).*

46. *Generalfeldmarschall Fedor von Bock and Generalleutnant Eccard Freiherr von Gablenz (October 1941).*

47. Another photo of Generalfeldmarschall Fedor von Bock taken during his visit to an infantry divison during offensive operations on the Nikolskoye front (October 1941).

48. Generalfeldmarschall Fedor von Bock (right) in conversation with the commanding officer of the 197th Division, Generalmajor Hermann Meyer-Rabingen (Nikolskoye, October 1941).

49. Generalfeldmarschall Fedor von Bock decorates members of a cavalry division with the Iron Cross (18 November 1941).

50. Oberleutnant Heinrich Graf von Lehndorff-Steinort (left, partly concealed) with Generalfeldmarschall Fedor von Bock (autumn 1941).

51. Generalfeldmarschall Fedor von Bock and General der Kavallerie Eberhard von Mackensen during a situation conference during the battle at the Donets (26 June 1941).

52. Advancing troops march past Generalfeldmarschall Fedor von Bock (east of the Donets, 26 June 1942)

Facing Page:
53. Adolf Hitler visits the Commander-in-Chief of Army Group South, Generalfeldmarschall Fedor von Bock, at his headquarters after the Battle of Kharkov (1 June 1942).

54. Situation conference in the headquarters of Army Group South (1 June 1942); Generalfeldmarschall Fedor von Bock (right).

55. *Pittsburg Sun-Telegraph of 12 August 1942: "General Fedor von Bock, veteran of many battles, leads the campaign against Russia. The son of a general, he served in Kaiser Wilhelm's army as a lieutenant."*

Facing Page:
56. Generalfeldmarschall Fedor von Bock (1943).

57. *Generalfeldmarschall Fedor von Bock (1943).*

58. *The manor house in Grodtken, Neidenburg District, East Prussia, where Generalfeldmarschall Fedor von Bock lived in 1943 and 1944; Wilhelmine von Bock, nee von Boddien, leased Grodtken back from the Reichsland in 1939.*

59. On the steps of the manor house in Grodtken: (from left to right) Fedor von Bock's wife Wilhelmine von Bock; Kurt-Adalbert von der Osten (Oberleutnant on leave from Russia); Generalfeldmarschall von Bock; Miss von Bergmann.

60. SS-Obersturmführer Felix Bartoll, Special Committee 20 July 1944, interrogated Renate Countess von Hardenberg after the attempt on Hitler's life on 20 July and questioned her about the possible participation in the plot of Generalfeldmarschall Fedor von Bock.

Marine-Lazarett Oldenburg i. H.

(Männlich) **Todesbescheinigung**

1. Vor- und Zuname: (Bei totgeborenen Kindern, Name des Vaters, bei unehelichen. Name der Mutter)	Fedor von B.o c k
2. Alter: (Bei totgeborenen Kindern das Alter des Kindes, bei Säuglingen ob ehelich oder unehelich)	Geburtsjahr unbekannt Monat unbek. Tag unbek.
3. Stand, Geschäft	Generalfeldmarschall
4. Wohnung, Straße, Nr. (evtl. Angabe des Stockwerkes, Hofes oder Kellers)	Oberkommando des Heeres
5. Tag u. Stunde d. Todes	4.5.45 04<u>20</u> Uhr
6. Ort, Wohnung, Straße, Haus-Nr. wo Tod erfolgt ist	Marinelazarett Oldenburg/Holstein
7. Krankheit: a. Grundkrankheit b. Begleitende Leiden c. unmittelbare Todesursache d. Selbstmord oder Unglücksfall	(Deutliche Schrift) siehe Rückseite

Oldenburg/Holstein, den 7. Mai 19 45

Falls der Verstorbene im Sterbeorte nicht wohnhaft gewesen und zur Kur der Krankheit hierher gekommen und hier verstorben ist, ist solches ausdrücklich in der Todesbescheinigung zu bemerken.

Flottenarzt u. Chefarzt

61. Fedor von Bock's death certificate.

62. The grave site of Generalfeldmarschall Fedor von Bock in Lensahn, Holstein. The wooden cross erected in 1945 was replaced by a stone cross in 1982 by the group which cares for the graves of the German war dead.

Against "Special Detachments" in the Prisoner of War Camps

Several days ago an order arrived concerning the use of "special detachments" in the prisoner of war camps in the rear army area; I stated my position on the matter in a subsequent telegram to the Commander-in-Chief of the Army:

"In my opinion the mission of the special detachments represents an infringement of the army's duties and rights. According to military convention and law the army is responsible for the life and security of its prisoners of war, no matter what type they may be, as long as they are under its power and protection. This responsibility is passed on to the camp commanders. It cannot be taken away from them and is – like any responsibility – indivisible. It is also inappropriate for members of the police to decide on the life and death of prisoners of war in military camps. The 'close cooperation with the camp commanders' does nothing to change the fact that he and with him the army are responsible for everything that goes on in the military camps.

If the separation of certain persons from the body of prisoners of war is necessary for political reasons, this can be done by the special detachments with the understanding of the camp commanders. Should the camp commander raise objections in individual cases, the decision rests with the military superior – the commander of the rear army area – after consultation his senior police officer.

Prisoners of war separated in this way should be transferred to the civilian administration's camp outside the army area. There, after all the documentation has been checked, they can be dealt with as the political necessities and the security of the Reich demand."

10/11/41

Further heavy fighting on the right wing of the panzer army south and southeast of Tula. The effect of the very slow approach by the northern wing of the 2nd Army has not yet made itself felt. Minor attacks against the 4th's front and heavier ones against the left wing of the 9th Army, where the enemy has achieved local success.

It has begun to freeze again.

11/11/41

As the forward movement of the 2nd Panzer Army has been placed in question by the fighting on its right flank, at the request of the 4th Army the 268th Division has been placed at its disposal so that it can protect its right flank itself as it advances.

The 2nd Army was ordered to bring its left wing forward as far as Yefremov-Volovo, the infantry divisions of its right wing to Livny. Further, the army is to advise whether it is in the position to put together a mobile force from XXXXVIII (Motorized) Corps for the advance on Voronezh.

The number of trains supplying the army group has been reduced to 23 per day. That is just enough for our daily needs. I have raised objections. When Greiffenberg reported to me that this protest had been rejected and that Halder had stated on this occasion that the Army Command did not think that the army group yet had the supplies necessary to attack now, I called Halder and said to him:

"In my opinion, the objectives you marked on the recently-delivered map as worthwhile surely cannot be reached before winter, because we no longer have the required forces and because it is impossible to supply these forces after reaching these objectives on account of the inadequate potential for supply by rail. Furthermore, I no longer consider the objectives designated 'worthwhile' by me in the army group order for the encirclement of Moscow, specifically the line Ryazan-Vladimir-Kalyazin, to be attainable. All that remains, therefore, is to strive to for a screening front in the general line Kolomna-Orekhovo-Zagorsk-Dmitrov, which is absolutely vital to the encirclement of Moscow. I will be happy if our forces are sufficient to obtain this line. The attack can be supplied to this point if the previous number of trains running to the army group is authorized.

Our planned interim objective is Moskva and the Moskva-Volga canal and the capture of its crossings. According to the report from the armies, this attack can be staged very soon. It is not impossible that the state of the attack force's units may force us to halt in this line. Conditions have thus forced the army group to work with very short-range objectives. But we will be unable to reach or hold even these if the flow of trains is not kept at its pervious level, at least for the immediate future. I will not obtain precise data until tomorrow afternoon, when I consult with the quartermasters.

Chapter 5: 22 June 1941 to 5 January 1942

No "Great Strategic Masterpiece"

The attack cannot become a great strategic masterpiece, because troop movements have so far largely been impossible and later will become impossible on account of the snow. The only thing that can matter, therefore, is to conduct the thrust in concentration at the tactically most favorable points. I cannot suggest waiting longer than is necessary to attack, because I fear that the weather conditions will then thwart our plans. If we get deep snow, all movement is finished."

Halder asked whether the attacks on the southern flank of Panzer Army Guderian had thwarted my plan to protect the right flank of 4th Army's attack with the panzer army. I answered:

"On the contrary. If the panzer army wasn't at Tula, the right wing of the 4th Army would have to deal with the powerful enemy forces with which the panzer army is now grappling. Whether Guderian is in the position to shake off the new enemy coming from the south I cannot say. I am trying to bring the northern wing of the 2nd Army forward to the northeast quickly, in order to relieve the pressure on Guderian and release him for a further advance to the northeast. Whether this will succeed given the state of the 2nd Army, I do not know."

In the course of an afternoon meeting with the supply officials, it turned out if the number of trains is kept at the reduced level of 23, stockpiling of the front, even for an attack with limited objectives, cannot be completed before 11th December; that means that in my opinion the attack will not take place! If the previous 30 trains can be maintained, the most necessary stockpiling – given suitable weather – is possible by the 18th of this month.

I reported the state of affairs to Brauchitsch and added:

If a rapid stockpiling by maintaining the higher number of trains is not feasible, I will have to give the order to dig in for the winter. It is impossible to let the units lie around for another four weeks, for this evening the temperature dropped to ten degrees below freezing. Brauchitsch said that we had to try to make use of the time by making preparations by sectors as the supply situation permitted. I replied that the first possible "sector" was that of the Moskva and the Moskva Canal, and that the calculations which had led to the 18th as the first attack date were based on this limited objective. I further informed him that according to word from Kesselring, the headquarters and noteworthy elements of Air Fleet 2 were to be taken away by the 18th at the latest and would therefore be lost to the attack.

Brauchitsch generally agreed with my views and promised a quick review of the railroad situation.

The following, initially verbal, orientations went out in the evening:

To 9th Army: Attack date the 15th. First objective the Lama and the Volga reservoir. If the attack progresses well, further objective: Teryayevo-Klin-Sawidowo. V Corps has orders to take the Teryayevo hills as soon as 9th Army attacks across the Lama.

4th Army was briefed and received the following message: for supply reasons attack unlikely before the 18th.

Both armies are to attack immediately wherever the enemy gives ground opposite the front.

East of Kursk 2nd Army's only contact was with enemy patrols; its northern wing reached the area west of Novosil with no resistance. The enemy is giving way on the right flank of 2nd Panzer Army; an enemy cavalry division was cut to pieces, far more than 2,000 prisoners and about 100 guns were brought in. Nothing of significance on the other fronts.

12/11/41

An advance detachment of the 2nd Army reached Novosil, but beyond that there was another stop in XXXV Corps' forward movement because the corps has to close ranks and bring up supplies. The 2nd Panzer Army closely pursued the beaten enemy on its southern flank. Local enemy attack against 4th Army north of the highway, which led to the loss of a village, otherwise nothing special.

I was informed verbally that the army group is to be guaranteed the minimum number of trains required for its attack preparations. But at almost the same time I received a report that several trains carrying Jews from Germany are being sent into the army group's rear area! I advised Halder that I would do everything I could to oppose this, because the arrival of these trains must result in the loss of an equal number of trains vital to supplying the attack.

In he evening I discussed the coming attack south of Kalinin with the Chief of Staff of 9th Army [Hofmann], who was passing through.

"15 to 20 Degrees Below Freezing"

13/11/41

Russian counterattacks on the left wing of the 2nd Panzer Army, which is slowly regrouping for the attack to the northeast. The engines of the tanks are beginning to fail as a result of the drop in temperatures to 15 to 20 degrees below freezing. Large numbers of trucks have broken down on the deeply-rutted, now hard-frozen roads.

14/11/41

2nd Army continues to close ranks slowly to the east.

The right wing of the 2nd Panzer Army advanced in the direction of Yefremov, formed up for the attack on Tula and repulsed attacks by the enemy on its left wing. 4th Army reported a concerted attack by a Russian division with numerous tanks against XII Corps' and parts of XIII Corps' front, which was generally repulsed; but in the process the advantage gained yesterday on the army's right wing was lost again. There were also small-scale attacks by the Russians on the remaining front of the 4th Army and the left wing of the 9th Army.

The field forces, especially the units of the 4th and 9th Armies, are suffering from an increase in activity by the enemy air force, which, in addition to attacks on the troops, sets their billets on fire with incendiaries. Through radio intercepts and statements by deserters we have identified English or American fliers operating over the army group's front.

The armies are all complaining about serious supply difficulties in all areas – rations, munitions, fuel and winter clothing. With the limited number of trains in use it is impossible to do anything about it. Naturally this has significantly complicated the attack preparations.

This morning I spoke with Strauß about the attack south of Kalinin planned for tomorrow. LVI Panzer Corps [Schaal; still a Motorized Army Corps, renamed LVI Panzer Corps on 1/3/42] has reported that it will not be ready to attack until the 16th or 17th. I demanded, however, that on the 15th the corps at least occupy the weak enemy forces facing it so that they cannot affect the attack's southern wing.

In the evening Kluge described the heavy fighting that took place while the Russian attack was being repulsed and said that the army's attack preparations would probably be further delayed as a result. He intends to attack with his northern wing, the Hoepner Group [PzGr 4] and V Corps, on the 17th with the limited objective of reaching the road to Istra on a broad front and capturing the high ground at Teryayevo. I can not grant his request, repeated since yesterday, for the transfer of my last reserve, the 23rd Division, as long as the situation on the 9th Army's right wing is uncertain.

Greiffenberg returned from a conference held by *Generaloberst* Halder with the Chiefs of Staff of the armies and army groups. All that remains of the recently propagated distant objectives opposed by the army group, is that the army groups are to do what they can.

In America a law has been passed allowing armed American merchant ships to sail into English ports. Control of the Mediterranean by the English and the absence of effective opposition by the Italian fleet and air force have allegedly led to the virtual severing of supply lines to our troops in North Africa and Crete. The British reported the loss of the aircraft carrier *Ark Royal*, "already sunk several times by the Germans," to torpedo hits.

15/11/41

2nd Army attacked south of Kalinin with the reinforced XXVII Corps and is making good progress. On the southern wing of the 4th Army, heavy Russian attacks with tanks against XIII Corps, which in places broke through to division headquarters. The corps had to be pulled back in a number of sectors. Smaller-scale attacks on the rest of 4th Army's front and on the northern front of the 9th Army.

In the evening a lengthy conversation with Kluge, who painted a black picture of XIII Corps' situation and declared that the corps cannot go over to the attack in the foreseeable future. He will be pleased if it holds its front. The attack by his left wing – the Hoepner Group and V Corps – is to unfold on the

17th as planned. The question arose whether VII, XX and parts of XII Corps should join the attack should it make good progress. I am in favor. But this will make supply very difficult, and I repeatedly told Kluge that only the army could oversee the details of this question and that his decision depended on it. The running of the trains is so irregular that I couldn't promise him an increase in deliveries. One can hope that the average of recent days can be maintained. I do not expect an improvement for several days.

The liaison officer to the French Legion reports that the regiment, which moved out from Smolensk on 9 November, is already almost worn out after four days on the march and two of rest, in spite of never having covered more than about 10 km a day over good roads.

It is said that the officers are ineffective and lack compassion and toughness. I issued instructions that the regiment should carry on in even shorter marches with necessary rest days. Even Colonel Labonne, the commanding officer, has expressed the wish to carry on.

Drove to Smolensk [HQ, Army Group Center], where I discovered all sorts of irregularities.

16/11/41

In the morning telephone conversations with the Commanding Generals of XII and XIII Corps [Schroth and Felber]. Schroth assessed the situation calmly, Felber, too, was reasonable but made no bones about the of difficulty of the struggle by his weak battalions, inadequately protected from the icy cold, against the numerically strong enemy in difficult wooded terrain.

Oberst Görltz, who is supposed to put the battered railroads back in order, arrived in the morning. The biggest problem is allegedly a terrific mixup in the Government General [Poland].

A telex was sent to the armies informing them that the army group has only a single division in reserve and that they therefore have to get by with their own forces. I further reminded them that the forces were to be held together and not jumbled up – as is the case with the 4th Army, which, admittedly, is fighting under very tough conditions.

The 2nd Army has moved only a little, will also be unable to move off to the east before the 20th. It was reminded once again that it is necessary to move forward in the direction of Yefremov soon; moreover, it is to dispatch small mobile formations to chase away the Russian detachments which are burning stores and crops under its very nose.

2nd Panzer Army has taken Bogoroditsk. The army is massing for an attack, point of main effort toward Stalinogorsk.

Guderian is full of confidence, the fuel situation is his only concern. 4th Army reported fresh, heavy attacks on XIII Corps, where yesterday's penetrations have not yet been cleared up. 9th Army reported that LVI Corps attacked today and has advanced as far as the Lama.

XXVII Corps has almost cleared the nook between the Volga reservoir and the Volga; the enemy is retreating across the Volga there.

When I sent an inquiry to the 4th Army, whether everything was ready for tomorrow's attack by Panzer Group Hoepner, I received the surprising reply that it isn't going to attack until the day after tomorrow! Only two regiments from V Corps' left wing are to attack tomorrow, following the 9th Army. I asked Kluge to explain the inconsistency with his statements of yesterday. He said, "the unclarity had arisen because the enemy has today attacked VII and XX Corps."

When I asked what he thought today of having his center join the attack if his northern wing made good progress, he said that he could not yet estimate whether XX Corps would be in a position to do so. He once again painted a very black picture of XIII Corps' situation. The units there certainly have it very hard, but the army has two complete divisions and much more behind the front.

17/11/41

Greiffenberg flew to 4th Army to get us a clear picture of what is going on. According to its daily report of 16th November, the army sees its situation as especially difficult and shifts part of the blame onto the 2nd Panzer Army's alleged failure to advance. I took the following position in this matter:

"As far as the number of divisions in relation to width of front is concerned, the 4th Army is better off than all the other armies of the army group. In spite of the extraordinary drop in strengths, on the whole the state of its forces is in no way worse than that of other fronts. Twenty infantry, six panzer, and two motorized divisions of the 4th Army are facing twenty-one Russian infantry divisions, ten to eleven armored brigades and one cavalry division. In terms of numbers, the 2nd Panzer Army's ratio of forces is significantly less favorable. The fact is that the enemy opposite the 4th Army is building up its defensive and offensive strength by moving in fresh and particularly good forces; the army group, too, hopes for a relief of the 4th Army as a result of the 2nd Panzer Army's advance. As I informed the 4th Army, the panzer army continues to attack successfully in spite of supply difficulties. A continuation of this attack to the northeast has been planned and initiated. I am equally justified in expecting relief from the attack by Panzer Group Hoepner in conjunction with the 9th Army. Hoepner's attack scheduled for the 17th was postponed until the 18th at the last moment, which in view of its association with the attack by 9th Army already under way is not without risk. In the daily report for the 16th it states that the resumption of the attack south of the Moskva is not possible at present, while the Commander-in-Chief informed me on the evening of the 16th that VII Army Corps is supposed to attack with a limited objective, as far as the Mura. Request clarification."

I informed Halder of my position by telephone and had it conveyed to 4th Army by Greiffenberg. Greiffenberg was forced to remain at Maloyaroslavets due to mechanical trouble with the aircraft. At about 18:00 he reported that the attack planned for tomorrow by the Hoepner group, including VII Corps, is still on. But a quarter of an hour later the Ia of the 4th Army [Stieff] reported that only V Corps and elements of XXXXVI (Motorized) Corps are attacking tomorrow with limited objectives, while XXXX (Motorized), IX and VII Corps are not to attack until the 19th. The reason is said to be a suggestion by the Hoepner Group. I briefed Halder on the army's wavering intentions and added that I consider a piecemeal attack to be a mistake but unfortunately can't intervene because amending orders did not get through. The situation on the right wing of the 4th Army is serious and difficult; the 260th, 137th and 17th Divisions are exhausted, the enemy continues to attack. On the other hand the 268th and elements of the 263rd Divisions are on the way and the 258th Division has been moved farther to the south. My hope is that the enemy does not have the forces to repeat the attack for a long time. Halder asked for my assessment of the chances for 2nd Panzer Army's attack; in Guderian's view they are favorable. The conversation ended with Halder asking me to put pressure on the 4th Army, in order to, if possible, convince it to have its center attack as well.

Today the enemy continued to attack XIII Corps; small-scale attacks on the rest of the front. Heavy attacks as well as charges by three Siberian cavalry regiments were bloodily repulsed by V Corps. LVI (Motorized) Corps of the 9th Army has fought its way slowly across the Lama; its left wing broke through to the northeast south of the reservoir and has gained considerable ground. The Volga has been reached everywhere between the reservoir and Kalinin. Small-scale Russian attacks on the 9th Army's northern front.

18/11/41

Halder is contemplating proposing an order to Brauchitsch which would have the 4th Army attack with the bulk of its forces. I warned against this and told him that XIII Corps' situation is so serious that the army was even considering a withdrawal behind the Protva. XII Corps has also been affected by the fighting and the reserve formerly behind XX Corps has been sent south, so that I don't know if XX Corps is capable of attacking. The attack by all the other corps has been ordered for tomorrow. Halder said that we must understand that things are going much worse for the enemy than for us and that these battles are less a question of strategic command than a question of energy. That may be. Only one mustn't forget that the Russians have brought in 34 fresh divisions from Siberia since Smolensk and that 21 of these are positioned opposite the army group's front.

Today the main body of the 2nd Panzer Army, its right flank on the attack against enemy forces at Yefremov, launched an attack to the northeast and moved forward slowly. Its left wing remains on the defensive because it is too weak. Further heavy attacks on the right wing of the 4th Army against XIII Army Corps, which the army fought off only with difficulty. Small-scale attacks on the rest of its front. On the extreme left wing the attack initiated today by XXXXVI (Motorized) and V Corps gained ground slowly in the face of stubborn resistance.

LVI (Motorized) Army Corps of the 9th Army won the crossing over the Lama. The armored group wants infantry to follow: "That will happen as soon as the armored group can show significant progress."

Strauß will relieve further elements of the armored group – the 36th Motorized Division, 900th Brigade and elements of the 1st Panzer Division – at Kalinin and send them to the armored group for the attack.

19/11/41

9th Army was directed to repair one of the crossings over the Volga reservoir, quickly and if necessary in an ad hoc fashion, and send screening forces across to the south to free up the 6th Panzer Division.

To a suggestion by the *Führer*, relayed by the Army High Command, to encircle the enemy northwest of Moscow by turning the northern wing of the attack south, I replied to Halder that the suggestion is welcomed and that we are considering the idea here too. It is doubtful whether my forces are sufficient to carry it out. I have only one division behind the front; one motorized and one panzer division are in the process of being relieved at Kalinin. Whether these forces will be sufficient to carry the thrust from the reservoir to the south and at the same time screen its eastern flank will depend on the enemy's power of resistance and whether the two motorized units arrive in time. Their earlier release was not possible, because the nook south of Kalinin had to be cleared first. A further hindrance is supply. In spite of all our efforts, it may turn out that we are halted in the middle of the attack for reasons of supply. Nevertheless, I have not waited to attack, because the present period of good weather, also with regard to the Luftwaffe, has to be exploited.

2nd Army set off to the east with advance detachments; resistance very weak. 2nd Panzer Army attacking toward Yefremov and, in the front, advancing slowly through Dedilovo to the east. The attacks on the right wing of the 4th Army have abated; the five corps of the army's left wing have all now gone to the attack and have made progress against stubborn resistance, which is especially pleasing on the left wing, by V Corps. Panzer Group 3 has also made good progress. With Strauß's agreement the panzer group was directly subordinated to the army group. It is first to reach Klin and the Klin-Kalinin road and extend screening forces toward the Moskva Canal and the reservoir; the panzer group was reminded of the importance of a rapid occupation of the Solnechnogorsk narrows. Whether the narrows can be reached quickly depends in large part on the fuel situation. Unfortunately the operation by the 1st

Panzer and the 36th Motorized Divisions to bolster and get moving the attack by LVI Corps, initially so promising, is impossible for many days on account of lack of fuel. All available fuel is being brought forward.

20/11/41

In the morning I was just about to leave by car for Panzer Group 4, when a directive from the Army High Command arrived; it spoke of destroying the enemy in the Moscow front in two operations, first north, then south of the highway. There is also talk of a later advance on Yaroslavl. I stated my position by telephone, as follows:

"The guidelines given in the Army High Command's directive are in line – as far as the northern operation is concerned – with the army group's view and the orders already issued in the course of the operation. But the army group must point out that all movements are to a large extent contingent on the poor supply situation. For example, reports from Panzer Group 3 state that the forces relieved at Kalinin will not have the fuel to make them operational until the 24th and 28th November. Screening of the planned operation to the east will therefore be scanty at best.

The directive for the second, the southern part of the operation: 'to eject the enemy grouping astride the highway through cooperation between both wings', is based on inaccurate assumptions concerning the state of the army group's forces. The army group must once again report that the right wing of the 4th Army is incapable of effective attacks for the foreseeable future. According to a report by the army, the forces of the 17th and 137th Divisions, which were involved in the heavy defensive fighting, are spent, the remaining divisions badly battered. XII and XX Corps are also too weak to break through the enemy positions. After the success of the first part of the operation, it might perhaps be possible to force the enemy in front of 4th Army's right wing to withdraw by applying sharp pressure from the north in conjunction with a frontal attack by XIII Corps and XX Corps at tactically favorable points. After giving up four divisions, the army group's forces will not nearly suffice to destroy the enemy, especially since it must be assumed that the enemy will bring in further reserves from Moscow. It is still impossible to estimate when sufficient fuel will be available for an advance in the direction of Yaroslavl. At the present rate of fuel delivery it will be many weeks yet. The army group feels it most unlikely that weather and the state of its forces will then still allow such an advance."

In the afternoon a meeting with Hoepner in my train, which I had sent ahead to Gzhatsk. Objective of the attack currently under way: crush the enemy opposite his front, if possible by a double-sided envelopment, as we discussed. The local objective of the overall operation the Moskva Canal-western outskirts of Moscow and then – if possible – farther down the Moskva. The army group can go no farther.

The attack has made progress, especially by IX Corps north of the Moskva.

In the evening came news that Guderian wants to place his main direction of advance through Mikhailov toward Ryazan. I was about to discuss this with Greiffenberg on the phone, when he interrupted

me with the news that Guderian had reported that he could no longer reach his assigned objective! I instructed Greiffenberg to ask again whether I can report this sudden reversal of opinion to the Army Command.

"...Divisions Whose Strength is Spent"

21/11/41

Guderian has driven to the front to once again see the situation for himself. The panzer army requested the deployment of the 296th Division, which was just placed in reserve at Orel, "in order to close a gap at the front."

In the afternoon, when asked by Greiffenberg, the army was still of the opinion that it would not reach its objective. Under these conditions subordinating the 296th Division is out of the question. But during the night a telegram arrived from the 2nd Panzer Army, stating that the 296th Division had to be placed at its disposal "to exploit the success achieved today."

Drove from Gzhatsk to VII Corps. The Commanding General has been visibly affected by the heavy fighting and described the pitiful state of his divisions, whose strength is spent.

Losses among the officer, in particular, are making themselves felt. Many second lieutenants are leading battalions, one first lieutenant leads a regiment, regimental combat strengths of 250 men, also the cold and inadequate shelter, in short: in his opinion the corps can do no more. I gave him a word of encouragement and said that I wasn't demanding major combat operations from him at present, but that he must give pursuit if the enemy withdrew and that he must not lose contact with IX Corps advancing beside him on his left. I got the same impression from the 197th Division, which suffered a setback this evening. Then I drove to IX Corps, which is making good forward progress and whose sole concern is the increasing length of its right flank to the VII Corps. At XXXX (Motorized Army) Corps, the Commanding General described to me the severity of the fighting and the great demands being made on the units:

"We'll still get to the Moskva Canal, but then we're finished!"

The corps on the left wing of the 4th Army has again made very good progress. I therefore sent my only reserve, the 23rd Division, to this corps in closed formation.

Panzer Group 3 is slowly gaining ground in the direction of Klin. The group was authorized to move up the entire 1st Panzer Division and, if necessary, elements of the 36th (Motorized) Division.

I had Kluge informed that, according to my personal impressions, lengthening IX Corps' right flank on account of the inability of VII Corps to move might endanger the attack. I asked him to examine whether we should move the 258th Division, which he still has behind his front, north and send it to IX Corps, or whether he thinks it better to insert the division into XX Corps, where it is at present, and attack northeast with this corps and perhaps also elements of XII Army Corps as soon as possible. The latter solution is the bigger one; but I don't know if it is possible. Late in the evening Kluge decided for this solution.

The whole attack is too thin and has no depth. Based on the number of divisions, as seen from the green table, the ratio of forces is no more unfavorable than before. In practice the reduced combat strengths – some companies have only 20 and 30 men left – the heavy officer losses and the overexertion of the units in conjunction with the cold give a quite different picture. Still, in spite of everything we might succeed in cutting off several enemy divisions west of the Istra reservoir. But it is doubtful if we can go any farther. The enemy can move everything he has to Moscow. But my forces are not up to a concentrated, powerful counterattack. I am moving up the 255th Division, which is in the rear, although the commander of the rear army area considers this denuding of further areas dangerous.

22/11/41

This morning I viewed the "winter course" instituted by *Major* von Schlebrügge at Gzhatsk. It is being held in an extremely well built winter camp set up the Russians prior to the Vyazma battle. By the afternoon I was back in Smolensk.

The 2nd Army continues to advance. Tomorrow its left wing will make contact with the panzer army's right wing at Yefremov.

The latter broke through to the northeast between Stalinogorsk and Tula yesterday and today took Stalinogorsk. The attack by Hoepner's group [4th Panzer Army] and Reinhardt [Panzer Group 3] has made only limited progress. The enemy pulled out forces from in front of the 4th Army's right wing and threw them against the attack.

In Libya strong English forces have been on the offensive for several days.

23/11/41

2nd Army was attacked from the south and southeast at Tim; the 6th Army has not moved.

2nd Panzer Army has extended its breakthrough toward Venev and expanded it to the east. The enemy is withdrawing forces in front of its left wing. He has also gone over to the defensive in front of the 4th Army's right wing.

While southwest of Istra resistance is undiminished, in front of VII and IX Corps and the two panzer corps [refers to XXXX and XXXXVI Motorized Army Corps], the reinforced V Corps was able to continue its advance and, with the 2nd Panzer Division, took Solnechnogorsk. Panzer Group 3 took Klin. Since there are still significant enemy forces west of Istra Lake, which will make further progress by the panzer corps and V Corps difficult, the 23rd Division was placed at their disposal. 4th Army received orders to push the left wing of its attack through Solnechnogorsk to the south and southeast. Panzer Group 3 is to screen the attack's eastern flank. I spoke with Kluge about the planned attack by XX Corps. It turns out that he will have to be satisfied with crushing the enemy west of the Istra and call a halt to any further advance by the reinforced Panzer Group 4. The attack by XX Corps thus loses its sense and purpose and must be called off.

Guderian came in the afternoon and reported that he can reach his assigned objective, even though the strengths of his panzer and infantry divisions have fallen alarmingly. If the army really does reach the Oka between Ryazan and Kolomna, it will be left hanging there in an exposed position – unless this drive also causes the enemy to withdraw in front of 4th Army. All that is available to cover the 2nd Panzer Army's southern flank is the forces of the 2nd Army, meaning seven quite weak divisions manning about 350 km of front – the distance to the immovably fixed northern wing of Army Group South. All this won't work in the long run. But as long as there is a chance that the enemy in front of 4th Army might give ground in the face of 2nd Panzer Army's attack, Guderian's drive must be continued, even if the panzer army has to be pulled back again after reaching the Oka and after thoroughly destroying the railroad between Ryazan and Kolomna.

"The Eleventh Hour"

I first briefed Brauchitsch, then Halder, on my opinion and made it very clear that the state of our forces must not, "for heaven's sake," be overestimated in future and that they must be clear that as far as this attack is concerned it is "the eleventh hour."

Brauchitsch, like Halder, nevertheless advocated a continuation of the panzer army's attack, even at the risk that it might be pulled back later. Both stressed once again that the important thing was to inflict as much damage as possible on the enemy. When I said to Halder that I am doing what I can, he replied:

"Yes, we are very pleased about that."

I asked if the order to go toward Voronezh with the army group's right wing still stood, even if the 6th Army continued to remain stationary – the answer was yes. I nevertheless pointed out that the only panzer division available for this advance, the 9th, currently had no serviceable tanks!

2nd Army received orders to halt its right wing at the Tim for now and to send reconnaissance forces ahead to Voronezh; the army is to reach Yelets with one group and the Don between Dankov and Yepifan with another and send an advance detachment ahead to Gorlovo-Mikhailov. 2nd Panzer Army is to continue to attack; Kashira is to be taken.

In the evening I sent an inquiry to Halder asking what was to take place after operations have ceased and whether the Army Command would specify the lines to be held and the position and extent of a rear position. The answer said that the course of the front lines is up to the army group, the question of a position in the rear is being examined!

24/11/41

Resistance is mounting in front of 2nd Army.

2nd Panzer Army, whose right wing is still engaged at Yefremov, took Mikhailov and broke through to Venev and across the Osetr. In response the enemy is moving in fresh forces from Moscow. At the request of the panzer army I placed a third of the 296th Division at its disposal. All quiet on the 4th Army's defensive front; its attack wing continues to gain ground slowly; XXXXVI Panzer Corps has reached the Istra reservoir. Fierce resistance south of Solnechnogorsk. After repulsing weak enemy forces north and northeast of Klin, Panzer Group 3 made preparations to advance to the southeast. 9th Army reports nothing out of the ordinary.

25/11/41

Contact with the enemy by all spearheads of the 2nd Army.

"Armored Group Eberbach" of the 2nd Panzer Army broke through to just south of Kashira, where it met resistance from enemy tanks.

On the right flank, the army sent reconnaissance and demolition teams forward to the Ryazhsk-Ryazan rail line. Fighting for Stalinogorsk with nearly-encircled, fiercely-defending enemy forces. If possible, the army is to advance north across the Oka at Kashira. But its primary mission is the destruction of the enemy around Tula. The attack by XXXXIII Corps, or the left wing of the panzer army, is planned for the 27th. The 4th Army is to support this attack by sending a regiment across the frozen Oka at Boldyrew and through pressure from XIII Corps in the direction of Serpukhov.

The attacking wing of the 4th Army has crossed the Istra at two places. The 11th Panzer Division crossed the dry reservoir over a corduroy road. 2nd Panzer Division of V Corps has advanced about 12 kilometers to the southeast. Panzer Group 3 has gained ground in the direction of Rogachev in heavy fighting.

In the evening *General* Schmidt [Rudolf] ate dinner with me; he is to assume command of 2nd Army for the duration of Weich's illness.

Good news from Africa; the English are apparently taking a beating there.

26/11/41

The 2nd Army is slowly fighting its way forward. 2nd Panzer Army reports attempts by the enemy forces encircled at Stalinogorsk to break out; the Russians are moving in forces from all sides against the Eberbach Brigade driving toward Kashira. Only limited progress on the attack front of the reinforced Panzer Group 4. Panzer Group 3 made very good progress.

In the evening I issued orders that as soon as it reaches the Moskva Canal, Panzer Group 3 is to turn south with the strongest possible forces and advance towards Krasnaya Polyana in order to facilitate 4th Army's advance. Bridgeheads are to be established across the Moskva Canal.

27/11/41

Black day for the 2nd Panzer Army! First a rather gentle pressure made itself felt against its right flank. Then the enemy pushed very hard from the north through Kashira against the spearhead of Panzer Brigade Eberbach; he also moved forces through Serpukhov south across the Oka. At the cost of abandoning their vehicles and weapons, the Russians surrounded at Stalinogorsk broke out to the northeast. The attack by XXXXIII Corps on the panzer army's left wing has gained only a little ground. The supporting drive by the right wing of the 4th Army across the Oka had to be called off after limited initial success. In the evening Guderian, who was himself at the front, had his Chief of Staff inform me that in view of the great enemy superiority and on account of the shortage of fuel, the panzer army would have to call off the operation if the right wing of the 4th Army did not attack across the Oka "without delay." Furthermore, the army asked for the 296th Division in order to at least defeat the enemy at Tula. I told Liebenstein that an advance by 4th Army "without delay" was out of the question and that if I sent the 296th Division the army would have to forego a relief of its elements at and south of Yepifan by the 2nd Army, because it would then lack the forces to do so. The panzer army is to see through the battle for Tula and as well screen to the east and north. The order to advance its screening forces northeast as far as the Oka and north through Kashira was rescinded.

4th Army reports nothing out of the ordinary. IX Corps, which was actually supposed to attack today, closed ranks. Progress by XXXX [Motorized Army] Corps and XXXXVI Panzer Corps [Motorized Army Corps] was limited. V Corps turned south toward Solnechnogorsk. On the extreme eastern wing, in a bold advance the 2nd Panzer Division reached the area of Kluschino, 30 km north of Moscow. Panzer Group 3's right wing is within 3 km of Yakhroma on the Moskva Canal.

The enemy is very active in front of the 9th Army and has staged numerous counterattacks.

In the evening I spoke with Kluge, who feels the time has come for XX Corps to attack and wishes to commit it on the 29th. I wasn't sure if that was right and asked him to think it over one more time. Furthermore, I discussed the notion of withdrawing the 11th Panzer Division, which after its advance across the Istra reservoir between XXXXVI and V Corps is wedged in uselessly, and moving it to the extreme left wing. At the moment Kluge advises against it. He also initially rejected the idea of subordinating V Corps to Panzer Group 3 because command of the corps would be simpler from there.

I subsequently informed Panzer Group 3 that it was less important to move very strong forces toward Moscow than to do it quickly.

28/11/41

The 2nd Panzer Army received the order discussed with Liebenstein yesterday. The 296th Division was subordinated to it. Since an advance by 2nd

Panzer Army northeast to the Oka is now out of the question, 2nd Army received orders not to advance its northern wing beyond Yefremov and to reconnoiter as far as the Don.

From a discussion with Blumentritt it became clear that the corps on the right wing of 4th Army's attack, IX Corps, has not "closed ranks" as I was previously told, but is waiting for XX Corps' attack. That is shocking news to me! Now everything will depend on whether XXXX, XXXXVI and V Corps win enough ground to make continuation of the attack worthwhile. The gains by today's attack were not all that great. Nevertheless, the northern wing of 4th Army's attack made some progress and the 2nd Panzer Division was able to hold its exposed position.

Reinhardt called in the afternoon. The 7th Panzer Division has won the crossing over the Moskva Canal at Yakhroma and has established a bridgehead. Reinhardt proposed that he continue the advance across the canal to the east with the panzer group. His divisions are pushing for this and the drive's supply is assured. I had been preoccupied with the idea for days; its execution might bring about the collapse of Moscow's entire northeastern front provided we simultaneously kept the advance by 4th Army's northern wing going. But that is not yet assured. I was given further cause to consider when toward evening Panzer Group 3 reported heavy attacks against the bridgehead at Yakhroma while asking whether the bridgehead had to be held "at all costs." I sent the following reply:

"Yes and no, no unnecessary casualties!"

I therefore let the first order to the armored group stand, to also reach the canal at Dmitrov and move forces west of the Moskva Canal to the south as fast as possible.

In the evening spoke with Kluge, who now is leaning toward another postponement of the attack by XX Corps planned for tomorrow.

I also do not think that the moment has come.

No Second Verdun

29/11/41

Fighting by the 2nd Army and 2nd Panzer Army, numerous small-scale Russian attacks against 9th Army. The attack by XXXX, XXXXVI and in part V Corps is making good progress. Panzer Group 3 has given up the bridgehead at Yakhroma, but unfortunately has not yet set off to the south and is battling the enemy who, already outflanked by V Corps, is still on the right flank of the 7th Panzer Division.

In a conversation with Halder I described the overall situation as such that if we do not succeed in bringing about the collapse of Moscow's northwestern front in a few days, the attack will have to be called off; it would only lead to a soulless head-on clash with an opponent who apparently commands very large reserves of men and material; but I don't want to provoke a second Verdun.

Panzer Group 4 complains that the enemy is constantly marshalling fresh forces opposite its front and urges that 4th Army also go to the attack south of the highway. Kluge subsequently decided to order the attack for the 1st, "provided that he wasn't forbidden to do so."

He is aware of the dangers a failed attack brings with it given our reduced combat strengths, but he would nevertheless like to try it. I replied that I also think the time has come to attack; "I would not forbid it."

Kluge called again late in the evening and asked what the status of the attack was, as he had to issue orders to his troops now. I replied that I saw no reason not to attack.

In the evening I had Greiffenberg brief Halder as follows:

"Headquarters, 4th Army intends to go to the attack on 1/12 with LVII Panzer and XX Corps to relieve the attack front north of the Moskva. I have given my consent, because it is certain that the enemy is shifting forces north from the central and southern fronts of the 4th Army and because the army group believes that the Supreme Command is very keen that the Russian continues to be attacked even at the risk of the units burning themselves out."

Halder replied:

"This assessment agrees in every point with the view of the Army High Command."

30/11/41

The 2nd Army, which in spite of repeated reminders continues to press on to the east, received orders that it is now less important to capture territory than it is to close ranks and bring forward the elements of the army lagging far behind, in order to be strong in case the enemy attacks from Voronezh, where large concentrations have been reported.

Panzer Group 3 has still gained no ground to the south. A radio message was set, again reminding it of the importance of a rapid advance in a southerly direction. Toward evening I got in touch with Reinhardt by telephone; it was surprisingly difficult to convince him of this necessity.

I sent a telex to Guderian in which I tried to make clear to him that his constant requests for reinforcement – which were repeated again today – must remain futile and why. Certain qualities seem to be organically linked with the position of commander of a panzer group!

Heusinger informed Greiffenberg that the forces committed to the attack by the 2nd Panzer Army appear to the *Führer* to be too weak and that VII Corps should not advance as part of 4th Army's attack because the enemy is supposed to be "encircled." Moreover Heusinger said that the present attack was only supposed to be the prelude to attacks on Voronezh and Yaroslavl! I telephoned Brauchitsch and told him that I had already instructed Guderian to concentrate his forces but that I was unsettled by his opinion concerning the 4th Army's attack. I had pointed out verbally and in writing that the army was exhausted and that the best that it might do would be to somehow get the attack south of the highway going by exploiting tactically-favorable opportunities, in order to relieve the attack north of the highway. An "encirclement" of the enemy would require forces that I no longer have. And an attack by VII Corps is totally out of the question, for the corps would be too weak. Its extreme wing only is to take part in the attack by XX and IX Corps, so as to stay in contact with them. I repeatedly have the impression of a false assessment of my fighting strength. Several times I had to ask if Brauchitsch was even still listening and only at the end did he pose the surprising question of whether the attack had been ordered and for when. Something isn't right there.

The attack by XXXX and XXXXVI Corps has made passable progress. V Corps moved forward and closed ranks. Far behind its left wing Panzer

Group 3 broke through the enemy west of Yakhroma and hopefully tomorrow it will finally carry on to the south.

Army Group South has lost Rostov to an attack by superior enemy forces. Much of the population took part in the fight against the retreating German troops. Army Group South will have to withdraw some distance to establish a tenable front there. Unfortunately the headquarters of Air Fleet 2 has left me to go to the Mediterranean. It is the end of a marriage that has lasted almost without a break since the start of the war. *General* von Richthofen [VIII Air Corps] has assumed command of the air force units working with the army group.

Summary of the defensive battles fought by Army Group Center in front of Moscow beginning in December 1941:

1. Defense of Yaropolets-Kely	*20/12/41 - 15/1/42*
2. Defensive fighting for Sukhinichi	*20/12/41 - 28/1/42*
3. Defensive battle at Kursk	*21/12/41 - 4/2/41*
4. Defensive fighting northwest of Livny	*21/12/41 - 2/1/42*

"Attack...Without Sense and Objective!"

1/12/41

Since I have the impression that Brauchitsch didn't understand me yesterday, and in spite of everything those at the highest levels of command still overestimate my forces, I sent the following telex to the Army Command:

"In spite of the repeated inquiries and reports sent to the Army High Command by the army group calling attention to the alarming state of its forces, it was decided that the attack should be continued, even at the risk of the units being completely burned out. But the attack currently under way is for the most part being conducted frontally, taking advantage of every tactical opportunity. As reported, I lack the strength for large-scale encirclement movements and now also the opportunity to shift troops to any large degree. The attack will, after further bloody combat, result in modest gains and will also defeat elements of the enemy forces, but it will scarcely have a strategic effect. The fighting of the past 14 days has shown that the notion that the enemy in front of the army group had 'collapsed' was a fantasy. Halting at the gates of Moscow, where the road and rail net of almost all of Eastern Russia converge, is tantamount to heavy defensive fighting against a numerically far superior foe. The forces of the army group are not equal to this, even for a limited time. And even if the improbable should become possible, to gain further territory at first, my forces would not nearly be sufficient to encircle Moscow and seal it off to the southeast, east and northeast. The attack thus appears to be without sense or purpose, especially since the time is approaching when the strength of the units will be exhausted. A decision is required now as to what will happen then. At present the army group is extended over 1,000 kilometers with a single weak division in reserve behind the front. In this state, with the heavy losses in officers and the reduced combat strengths, it could not withstand even a relatively well-organized attack. In view of the failure of the railroads there is also no possibility of preparing this extended front for a defensive battle or supplying it during such a battle.

I am unaware of the command's intentions. But if the army group is to ride out the winter on the defensive, it will only be possible in the general course of its present dispositions if sufficiently strong reserves are brought in to allow it to deal with incursions and permit the temporary relief of the exhausted divisions of the fighting front to rest and recuperate. 12 divisions will be needed for this. I don't know if they are available and can be brought in in the foreseeable future. Another essential condition is order and dependability in the running of the trains and with it the possibility for well-regulated supply and stockpiling. If both conditions cannot be completely met, an abbreviated position in the rear suitable for defense will have to be chosen for the eastern army without delay and all suitable personnel assigned to set up quarters, supply dumps and defensive positions, so that the order to move into it can be issued without delay."

2nd Army continues to slowly push the enemy to the east. 2nd Panzer Army captured the jump-off position for tomorrow's attack.

4th Army has gone to the attack with XX and LVII (Motorized) Corps and has achieved good initial success in heavy fighting in the icy cold. North of the highway the only significant progress was by IX Corps; on the left wing, V Corps will resume the attack tomorrow after completing its buildup. Behind V Corps the 23rd Division and part of Panzer Group 3 are battling enemy forces still offering resistance in the area northwest of Iksha.

"Confirmation of a Completely False Appreciation of 4th Army's Forces..."

In the evening the Army High Command forwarded an inquiry from the *Führer* as to why, south of the highway, the 4th Army is attacking northeast and not north; the *Führer* thinks it better to first go east then turn north later to destroy the enemy – fresh confirmation of a completely false appreciation of the 4th Army's forces.

After I had spoken with Kluge, I briefed Halder and told him that it was astounding how little the highest levels of command were informed of my reports. The attack by the weak LVII and XX Corps had inevitably been launched at right angles to the front. We are pleased by any success, whether to the northeast or east. As I have reported a hundred times, I lack the forces to encircle the enemy. According to a report from Kluge, XII and XIII Corps are incapable of attacking. I subsequently instructed Kluge that if Guderian's attack succeeds and the attack by LVII and XX Corps goes forward, XII and XIII Corps will have to attack too. But I can't fight a battle of annihilation with these forces. Halder replied: this briefing corresponds with the reports I have been making almost daily for some time on the state of the field forces, for which the Army Command is grateful. My letter of today is a clear line of reasoning. The Army Command is now going to present its position to the Army High Command again in writing.

2/12/41

The 2nd Panzer Army has launched an outflanking attack at Tula and initial progress is good. The attacking troops are terribly weak; to bolster the attack we have to make do with weak screening forces on the northern and eastern flanks.

Elements of a division of XX Corps of the 4th Army drove deep into the enemy south of the highway but were unable to hold there, for elements of the same division were encircled by the enemy when they attacked and will have to be broken out tomorrow.

Only limited progress north of the highway. The advance road being used by Panzer Group 3 leads through swampy terrain and is heavily mined, consequently it, too, is advancing slowly. The enemy moves his divisions here and there opposite the attack front. But he has once again succeeded in bringing forward fresh – even if initially weak – reserves against the flank of the 3rd Panzer Division at Yakhroma. He sees exactly where danger would threaten – if I had the necessary forces! In the evening a telex was sent to all the corps headquarters telling them that the undoubtedly serious moment of crisis that the Russian defenders are facing must be exploited wherever the opportunity presents itself; I have my doubts whether the exhausted units are still capable of doing so.

The fiasco at Rostov is stupid. A deep withdrawal by the 1st Panzer Army appears to be necessary there.

The city of Smolensk presented me with a document thanking me for liberating it from bolshevism.

3/12/41

In the morning Kluge briefed me on the situation and informed me that he had ordered the withdrawal of the attack spearhead at Troitskoye. When I asked if he was sure that the forces themselves wouldn't prefer to remain in their forward position, he replied that that would be totally impossible.

My concern as to whether the *Führer* is getting the unvarnished truth about my situation gave me no peace. I therefore called *General* Jodl of the Armed Forces High Command and said to him:

"Though I don't want to go over the heads of the Army High Command, I am calling you because I don't know if the view of the attack with respect to the state of the forces which I have been putting forward for some time is really clear to the highest level of command. The situation today is such that south of the highway the attack spearhead of the 258th Division, which had advanced as far as Troitskoye, had to be withdrawn as it was under attack from all sides and found itself in a most difficult situation. To the right rear of this attack spearhead, elements of the 258th Division are encircled and have to be broken out. A report from 4th Army says that the obvious solution, namely to advance right and left of the highway to the level of the attack spearhead and thus relieve the pressure on it, is out of the question as its forces are too weak to face strong Russian counterattacks. Yesterday Panzer Group 4 reported only minor progress.

Panzer Group 3's advance is being delayed by enemy resistance west of Yakhroma, but to a greater extent by its heavily-mined advance road which leads through as yet unfrozen swamp.

Nevertheless, I am not giving up hope that pressure by Panzer Group 3 will yet result in V Corps' flank being relieved so that this corps can advance south and carry the attack even further. But I cannot promise this. The attack is still ordered for the entire front, but, as I have been doing for days, so today I am pointing out that the hour is in sight when the troops will be exhausted. If the attack is called off then, going over to the defensive will be very difficult. This thought and the possible consequences of going over to the defensive with our weak forces have, save for my mission, contributed to my sticking with this attack so far."

I briefed Halder on our conversation.

Toward midday Kluge reported that he had to propose withdrawing the attacking troops of LVII and XX Corps behind the Nara, as the situation at the front was untenable. I reserved decision until 17:00, because I wanted to wait for the northern attack group's daily report. But at 16:00 Kluge reported that an attack from the north against the left wing of XX Corps had made the situation so threatening that he had ordered the withdrawal on his own. After only limited progress, Panzer Group 4 also reported that its offensive strength "was largely at an end."

The enemy has grown stronger in front of Panzer Group 3's southern wing at Dmitrov and Yakhroma by moving in additional forces and has gone to the attack. But Panzer Group 3 believes it can deal with him, especially if the 23rd Division lends its support in attacking this enemy. Since Panzer Group 4 is of the view that the attack by its left wing cannot be continued until Panzer Group 3 is almost abreast this wing, I "temporarily" subordinated the 23rd

Division, which today fought in very close contact with 1st Panzer Division anyway, to Panzer Group 3.

The results were urgent protests by Panzer Group 4 which, however, had no impact.

2nd Army met stubborn resistance at Yelets. Since the army is again talking about reaching the Don line, I called Schmidt and explained to him once more the reasons for not doing this. He has to realize that taking and holding Yelets means extending his line far to the east. Schmidt is of the view that it is "impossible" to leave this important junction undestroyed in front of his front. He wants to take it, destroy the railroad and then withdraw.

2nd Panzer Army's attack toward Tula is making progress. Russian attacks were repulsed by the forces sent ahead to screen the northern flank.

9th Army reports quiet.

At noon a telegram arrived from the *Führer* wishing me a happy birthday.

4/12/41

On the 2nd Army's southern wing, the 16th Motorized Division was pulled back a distance near Tim in the face of superior pressure.

XXIV (Motorized) Corps broke into Yelets amid heavy fighting. The ring around Tula is not yet closed. I am worried whether it will be, for the enemy is moving fresh forces – including a division from the interior of Russia – to the south and southwest by way of Kashira.

Withdrawal of the 4th Army's attack spearheads behind the Nara came off without a hitch. Localized fighting only on the army's northern wing – pressure from the enemy has increasing considerably at the Moskva Canal and southwest of Yakhroma. Here, too, the enemy has moved in additional forces – a division from central Russia and a mixed brigade – with the result that we are being forced onto the defensive there.

As Panzer Group 3 has no reserve left, I inserted the 900th Brigade (with the strength of a reinforced battalion), which had formerly been behind the 9th Army, at Klin.

Icy cold.

5/12/41

2nd Army took Yelets. 2nd Panzer Army reported heavy counterattacks by the Russians, which were for the most part repulsed, though the 29th Motorized Division lost a great deal of equipment. Again today movements around Tula did not make the desired forward progress.

Relatively quiet in front of the 4th Army. Enemy forces massing opposite IX Corps. Very heavy fighting by Panzer Group 3 at the Moskva Canal, where the enemy continues to feed fresh forces into the battle. On the 9th Army's right wing, southeast of Kalinin, the Russians advanced across the Volga and penetrated 10 km against the 162nd Division. Details still lacking.

Panzer Group 3 reported that its offensive strength is gone and that it can only hold its positions if the 23rd Division remains subordinated. I discussed with Kluge whether, given the situation, the attack by Panzer Group 4 planned for tomorrow should go ahead; he said that it should not. Panzer Group 3 received orders to go over to the defensive. 23rd Division remains subordinated to it. Moreover, it and 4th Army were ordered to make preparations for a withdrawal to the general line Nara-Moskva to Karymskoye-Istra reservoir-Ssenseskoje Lake-east of Klin when the order is given. Orders for the linking up of Armored Groups 3 and 4 will be issued by the army group as soon as the intentions of both armored groups concerning the manner of the withdrawal are known.

Late in the evening Guderian reported that he had to call off the operation because XXIV (Motorized) Corps was being threatened from all sides in its exposed forward position; as well the unbearable cold of more than 30 degrees below freezing was making moving and fighting by the tired, thinned-out units extremely difficult. Our own tanks are breaking down, while those of the Russians are better suited to winter conditions. After several digs by Guderian, whose Chief of Staff [von Kurowski] only yesterday evening gave a very optimistic assessment of the operation's chances, I concluded the conversation by agreeing to his suggestion that we gradually pull the army back behind the Don and the Schat River lines. I stressed that at all events the army must try to create reserves in the course of this turning back. Guderian raised objections that I could not accept, especially since his army is better off than all the others as far as forces are concerned.

6/12/41

2nd Army has not come to rest; once again it was exhorted not to go farther east than absolutely necessary. The withdrawal by the 2nd Panzer Army is largely proceeding as planned. But inevitably, since motors frequently fail in the icy cold – as much as 38 degrees below freezing – some vehicles and guns have had to be abandoned. A quiet day for 4th Army apart from enemy attacks on V Corps. Heavy attacks by superior forces against the eastern front and especially the northeastern front of Panzer Group 3; the penetrations were for the most part eliminated by committing the last of its reserves.

The armored group reported that, beginning tonight, it has to pull back to the designated line in three movements. This withdrawal was hurriedly coordinated with the left wing of the 4th Army, whereby Kluge expressed the wish that the bulk of Panzer Group 4 delay its withdrawal for as long as possible, on the one hand to permit careful preparation of the evacuation, but also to demonstrate to the enemy that the withdrawal was not as a result of his pressure. When I asked if the army could hold its forward position "indefinitely," Kluge replied that the "winter position" had to lay to the rear, or on either side of the Istra reservoir. That is how we had discussed it between us. I subsequently left it to the army's discretion to time its withdrawal as it saw fit, as long as it ensured that contact was maintained with Panzer Group 3.

Kluge offered to try to free some sort of a reserve – even if only a battalion – from Panzer Group 4 in order to help Panzer Group 3; I gratefully accepted, for so far we have been unable to throw the enemy back across the Volga on the 9th Army's right wing; the 9th Army therefore needs its weak reserves itself.

The Army Command was informed that the withdrawal of Panzer Group 3 and with it the northern wing of the 4th Army is unavoidable.

Growing complaints by the units about the enemy's air superiority. The matter of winter clothing, too, is far from satisfactory. First it was too late coming, so that even today not all units have their winter things, and now it is inadequate in quantity as well as quality.

After the first battle in Africa was apparently decided in our favor, renewed, heavy fighting is in progress.

7/12/41

Difficult day. The right wing of Panzer Group 3 began withdrawing during the night. The penetrations on the panzer group's northern wing are unpleasant. The enemy has also significantly expanded his penetration on the 9th Army's right wing. I dispatched whatever I could lay my hands on to Panzer Group 3: a regiment of the 255th Division is being sent in trucks one battalion at a time to Klin, where the first elements arrived this morning; the only support Panzer Group 4 has been able to come up with so far is a reinforced company; the motorized Engineer Instruction Battalion, which was supposed to be going to Germany, was halted and likewise sent in the direction of Panzer Group 3. 9th Army will and must help itself.

The enemy is also more active in front of the 4th Army, especially opposite Panzer Group 4. The remnants of the 255th Division were therefore assembled in the Rusa area.

2nd Panzer Army suffered a setback at Mikhailov, which had to be abandoned by a forward battalion of the 10th Motorized Division at the cost of much equipment. Otherwise the withdrawal by the panzer army proceeded according to plan.

The 2nd Army, which in spite of all my urgings, pushed farther to the east, became involved in costly fighting with strong enemy forces. The cold is also causing casualties; one regiment reported that 318 men fell out due to frostbite.

Causes For The Serious Crisis

Three things have led to the present serious crisis:

(1) The onset of the autumn muddy period.

Troop movements and supply were almost completely paralyzed by the deeply mud-clogged roads.

Exploitation of the victory at Vyazma was not possible.

(2) The failure of the railroads. Inadequate service, insufficient numbers of wagons, locomotives and trained personnel – inability of locomotives and operating installations to withstand the Russian winter.

(3) Underestimation of the enemy's ability to resist and his reserves of men and materiel.

The Russians realized that by destroying nearly all the man-made structures on the main lines and roads they could so increase our transportation difficulties that the front would lack the most vital things needed to live and fight. Munitions, fuel, rations and winter clothing did not arrive. The performance of our motor vehicle assets, overburdened by the failure of the railroads and a 1,500-kilometer advance, is dropping noticeably. As a result, today we have been robbed of any possibility of significant troop movements and with failing supply face an opponent who has gone over to the counterattack by ruthlessly employing his inexhaustible masses of people. The Russians have put shattered divisions back on their feet in a surprisingly short time, brought new ones to the threatened front from Siberia, from Iraq and the Caucasus, and made an effort to replace their lost artillery with large numbers of rocket launchers. Today there are 24 more – for the most part full strength – divisions facing the army group's front than on the 15th of November. On the other side the strength of the German divisions has been reduced to less than half by the constant fighting and by the forceful onset of winter; the fighting strength of the armored troops is far less. Casualties among officers and non-commissioned officers are shockingly high and at present can be made good even less than those of the enlisted men.

The orders for the ruthless pursuit of the enemy were justified as long as the Supreme Command believed that he was fighting for his life with the very last of his forces; the effort to decisively defeat him in one short push was worth "the ultimate sacrifice" – as the Army High Command demanded. But that was a mistake and the army group is now forced to go over to the defensive under the most difficult conditions. Only today we received a message from the *Führer* with the wish that the Stary Oskol-Yelets-Yefremov railroad be placed behind our front as an important cross-connection.

Japan has attacked American and English territory.

8/12/41

Schmidt [2nd Army] informed me that after destroying the militarily important installations at Yelets, he was going to begin the army's withdrawal to the "winter position" tonight. He feels two to three more divisions are necessary if he is to hold this position against serious attacks. In the afternoon I learned that enemy cavalry have broken through in the direction of Livny in considerable strength. With the broad disposition of the 2nd Army, this is difficult to parry. A motorized SS brigade, which was supposed to head south on orders from the *Führer*, was placed at the disposal of the 2nd Army, but cannot arrive for several days. Stronger enemy forces pressing the eastern front of 2nd Panzer Army. Small-scale attacks against 4th Army north of the highway. As planned, its left wing is pulling back while maintaining contact with Panzer Group 3. But the enemy broke through its center and advanced as far as the rail line west of the Klin-Kalinin road. Headquarters companies, construction troops and flak formations – whatever they could lay their hands on – were thrown against the enemy. The limited reinforcements from the 255th Division and Panzer Group 4 have not arrived yet as the roads are icy and clogged with traffic. Tomorrow morning an attempt is to be made to fly about 500 men with machine-guns to Klin. 9th Army reports that the enemy has made only limited progress at the point of penetration north of the reservoir; the army is bringing forward everything that is available, but it will take time.

Crisis of Confidence?

Guderian called in the evening; he described his situation in the blackest terms and in doing so used said that he could not conceal from me that, as he put it, a crisis of confidence was taking hold. He asked for the hundredth time if those at the very top were aware of this situation. I asked him to say against whom the crisis of confidence was directed and left it up to him to fly to the Army Command himself; he left both unanswered. The conversation ended with me telling him that complaints were useless here, I could not give him reinforcements, either one held out or let himself be killed. There were no other choices. Thus the only important thing was to see to it that everyone stubbornly held onto whatever he had to hold.

4th Army suggested giving Hoepner command of Panzer Group 3, in order to put the actions there in one hand. Hoepner himself had expressed this wish. I jumped at the opportunity, for now Hoepner will be more interested in helping Panzer Group 3. I issued orders for the subordination, with instructions to halt the enemy as soon as possible, but at the latest in the line: northern tip of the Istra reservoir-southwest tip of the Volga reservoir.

I described the situation to Halder and said that nowhere was the army group capable of withstanding a strong attack by the Russians. Halder tried to mitigate this, which I could not allow. Again and again I stressed how necessary the delivery of reinforcements was if I was to hold. Halder replied that the Army Command had no say in the sending of reinforcements from the west.

9/12/41

This morning I spoke with Halder again and as a supplement to my report of yesterday briefed him on my strange conversation with Guderian.

The enemy has been able to expand his three points of penetration against the 2nd Army, Panzer Group 3, and on the right wing of the 9th Army. The SS brigade cannot intervene with 2nd Army before the 14th. The reinforcements which were supposed to have been flown to Panzer Group 3 were grounded because the weather was too bad to take off. The battalion sent ahead in trucks failed to get through on the icy, traffic-clogged roads. One regiment has just reached the point of penetration against 9th Army.

By chance I learned that far more than 1,000 men of the divisions of Panzer Group 3 are being held back in Vitebsk. Incomprehensible, for it is this armored group which is complaining the loudest about reduced combat strengths. An inquiry received a vague response. I therefore gave orders that every man who is trained and can carry a weapon is to go to the front by train tomorrow.

Referring to the map, we selected a rear position on the shortest line Kursk-Orel-Gzhatsk-Rzhev-Volga Lake; the armies are to scout this line and provide detailed assessments. It is time we got busy with it.

10/12/41

This morning I discussed the question of the withdrawal with Kluge. He is all in favor of attempting to manage with local adjustments and in general putting off the withdrawal for as long as possible.

I subsequently sent the following telegram to Brauchitsch:

"I am repeating the report I have made many times, that the army group's front cannot be held over the long term with the available forces. Even if we succeeded in somehow and somewhere parrying the existing penetrations, it would mean the exhaustion of the last of my forces. This view coincides with that of every army commander. In spite of the unfavorable weather and difficult roads the army group's front is in constant movement, because all forces which can be released from the quieter fronts are being pulled out and thrown into the breaches. Apart from in a few sectors of the 4th and 9th Armies, no work has been done on positions and winter quarters. Due to the icy, snow-covered roads, the state of the tanks, tractors and trucks, and the exhaustion of the field forces, a large-scale withdrawal by the army group to a shorter line, roughly Kursk-Orel-Gzhatsk-Rzhev-Volga Lake, will inevitably result in quite heavy losses in guns and equipment. The limited withdrawals of recent days have proved this. As well, a withdrawal of this kind will lead the units into unprepared conditions in the middle of winter; its thorough preparation would require weeks. Therefore there is no other choice but to stubbornly defend every foot and only withdraw locally when there is no other choice. But this carries with it the danger that somewhere a unit will collapse completely before the offensive power of the Russians weakens. Intercepted radio messages confirm that the enemy intends to continue attacking.

I am therefore repeating the request that I have been making for a long time, to accelerate the delivery of reinforcements and thus enable the battle to continue with some chance of success and not leave the fate of the army group to chance."

Just as this was about to be sent, word arrived that the Army Command is going to send three to four divisions from the west, which will of course be very slow and late in coming. The telegram was therefore not sent. I did have Greiffenberg read it to *General* Halder, who agreed completely with its contents.

During the day Kluge again briefed me on the critical situation on the 4th Army's northern wing. At Hoepner's suggestion, if the enemy pressure continues he apparently wants to withdraw his northern wing behind the Lama and then around in a broad arc to the northern wing of the 197th Division, thereby placing his pivot almost on the highway. This contradicts his statements of this morning and I demanded that he initially withdraw no further than the line Istra reservoir-southwest corner of the Volga reservoir. In order to enable this and not give up the right wing of the 9th Army, the 36th Motorized Division will have to hold as long as it possibly can and keep its left wing on the Volga reservoir. I placed the entire 255th Division at his disposal and repeatedly stressed that it was important that we oppose the enemy with something from the west. There is already much too much at Klin and the Volokolamsk to Klin road is clogged with vehicles.

The attacks against 9th Army have abated somewhat.

The situation is bad for the 2nd Army, where the enemy has overrun elements of the 95th Division and broken through with a cavalry and an infantry division. The army has no reserve, the units are dead tired; apparently elements of the 95th Division were completely smashed in today's fighting, resulting in a serious crisis there. A security division and an infantry regiment were brought forward from the rear area; Guderian is to help with whatever he can; the SS brigade was urged to pick up its pace as much as possible. At that moment all the lines were destroyed by a snowstorm, therefore I radioed the Army Command. Not until the night did I reach Halder by telephone; he had not yet received the radio message. He too is unable to help and also does not know if aircraft are available to fly in the airborne division. I asked him to have the 6th Army at least take over garrisoning Kursk from me, so that the 2nd Army's front can be made somewhat narrower.

In response to Guderian's suggestion of a "crisis of confidence," Brauchitsch telegraphed all the Commanders-in-Chief of the armies, informing them that he, like the *Führer*, was completely informed about the situation but that the utmost had to be demanded of the forces in the field.

"By Constantly Withdrawing..."

11/12/41

The breakthrough against the 2nd Army is due less to the employment of powerful forces by the Russians than it is to a breakdown by our totally exhausted troops. The 45th Division was supposed to stage a counterattack but was unable to do so because of shortages of ammunition and men; the fighting strength of the 134th Division has also fallen alarmingly.

Two regiments from Army Group South and a division headquarters which will be arriving in Kursk in the next few days have been subordinated to Army Group Center, also an SS cavalry brigade on the northern wing. The force in Kursk is being put at the disposal of the 2nd Army, the SS the 9th Army. The 2nd Army received orders to commit the newly-acquired reserves in such a way as to halt the enemy penetration east of the Kursk-Orel railroad.

Toward evening Strauß reported that had to gradually withdraw his right wing to the southwest tip of the Volga reservoir, on the one hand to prevent the 86th Division from being wiped out, but also because the northern wing of Panzer Group 3 is withdrawing south of the Volga reservoir. I gave my consent and spoke once again with Kluge, reminding him that contact between the 9th Army and the left wing of Panzer Group 3 at the southwest tip of the Volga reservoir absolutely has to be assured. In battle the forces may only pull back where it is really necessary. By constantly withdrawing we will never halt the Russians and a large-scale withdrawal under pressure from the enemy could have unforeseeable consequences.

4th [Kluge] and 9th [Strauß] Armies received orders to scout, and as far as possible prepare, a blocking position in the general line Narski Bog-Tarjajew-northeast of Starytsa.

"My Last Reserve..."

12/12/41

For the time being, the Russians at the point of penetration north of Livny apparently have only cavalry behind our front. Perhaps we may yet succeed in bringing the remnants of the exhausted 45th and 134th Divisions back to a covering position. To the right the enemy is attacking the 9th Panzer Division. At Yefremov the left wing of the 2nd Army is also engaged in heavy fighting. Everything going according to plan with 2nd Panzer Army, only in a 20-km-wide gap northwest of Tula, which has been a source of worry for days and which Guderian allegedly cannot close, are there Russians. On the left wing of the panzer army XXXXIII Corps has no forces with which to eject the enemy. An advance battalion of the 137th Division, which is located behind 4th Army's front, was therefore dispatched to Aleksin.

North of the highway the enemy yesterday advanced across the Moskva against VII Corps. So far they have failed to throw him out again. The withdrawal on the left wing of the 4th Army has apparently succeeded, although brave V Corps had to withstand heavy attacks at Solnechnogorsk. The sparse reports from the breach north of Klin sound somewhat more favorable. My last reserve, a combat engineer battalion, was placed at the disposal of the 4th Army; it is to be deployed as a screening force at the Lama. 9th Army was instructed to place a battalion of the 86th Division behind its right wing at the Lama crossing at Nikolskoye. On the whole, Russian attacks on either side of Kalinin today were repulsed.

The Chief of Staff of the 2nd Army [Harteneck] today proposed that we place command between Kursk and Tula in one hand.

I told Halder that, in spite of many doubts, I was toying with the idea of subordinating 2nd Army to Guderian. He thinks the solution a good one. The order was given. Immediately afterward I spoke with Schmidt, the Commander-in-Chief of the 2nd Army, to inform him of my decision; he was of the opinion that I had misunderstood his Chief of Staff's suggestion. Nevertheless the order stands.

"...That I Have No More Suggestions To Make"

13/12/41

The 2nd Army's situation remains highly critical. The meager reinforcements are slow in coming and between Novosil and XXXIV Corps [?, probably XXIV Mot. Army Corps or XXXV Senior Detachment] sits the enemy. It is questionable if the corps will succeed in fighting its way through.

The 2nd Panzer Army's fighting withdrawal is going according to plan. After the enemy broke into the 296th Division south of Tula, the army ordered the division to withdraw further and at the same time gave up the Tula-Odoyevo road to the enemy by turning back its left wing. Therein lies a very great danger! In the evening I tried to get the army to at least somehow occupy the point where this road crosses the Upa.

Relatively weak enemy attacks against 4th Army at Naro-Fominsk. North of the highway the enemy was able to expand his penetration against VII Corps because a counterattack by a regiment of the 255th Division failed and led to a counterstroke. The situation is to be restored tomorrow. On the army's left wing, Panzer Group 3, somewhat less desperate fighting. The establishment of a tenable screening force on the Lama has not yet been achieved; a lack of fuel is supposedly to blame.

The 251st Division's counterattack south of Kalinin made progress but did not lead to a smashing success.

I spoke with Strauß and told him that he had to make the most thorough possible preparations for the evacuation of Kalinin.

As always in such situations, everything went wrong. At Pochep, where I removed the security division to prop up the 2nd Army, a railroad bridge was blown up by partisans; near Vyazma two trains collided and blocked the tracks to traffic, which was inadequate to start with; a train carrying fuel to Panzer Group 4 supposedly arrived empty; VII Corps suddenly reported a shortage of ammunition and so on.

Brauchitsch arrived. I discussed the situation with him. He has an accurate picture of what is happening and shares my opinion. I told him "I have no more suggestions to make; I made them earlier. The question that has to be decided now goes beyond the military. The *Führer* has to decide whether the army group has to fight where it stands, at the risk of being wrecked in the process, or whether it should withdraw, which entails the same risk. If he decides for withdrawal, he must realize that it is doubtful whether sufficient forces will reach the rear to hold a new, unprepared and significantly shorter position. The few reinforcements promised me are so slow in coming that they can play no decisive role in this decision."

Kluge, who on the 10th was in favor of "holding," is leaning toward withdrawal today; as well Reinhardt, commander of Panzer Group 3, wrote that we must "finally disengage"; he forgets that for days he has had the freedom to withdraw, but that it is not easy to disentangle and "disengage" his mass of troops at Klin on the single road leading to the rear.

Bringing fuel from the railroad terminuses to the units on the icy roads is endlessly difficult, and yet all movement depends on it.

Unfortunately my physical state has gone so downhill that I had to ask Brauchitsch to think about finding a replacement for me, as I don't know how long I can hold out after my serious illness of the previous year.

14/12/41

In the morning Strauß reported that the situation southeast of Kalinin had forced him to shorten his front again. Since this places Kalinin at risk, he asked to be allowed to issue the order to evacuate Kalinin if it becomes necessary. I agreed.

Panzer Group 3 once again requested immediate disengagement, but also reported that this is not possible without a heavy loss of materiel and also that it will not be able to hold unless it is covered by infantry in a position in the rear. Panzer Group 4, which has failed to eliminate the penetration against VII Corps, reported that it has to withdraw, in fact withdraw behind the Rusa; the originally planned position farther forward cannot be held. Together with Reinhardt's report, this conceals the danger that the inner wings of the 4th and 9th Armies might tear apart.

As Kluge was on the road and could not be reached, I called Hoepner and told him that he had to hold fast to the 9th Army at the Narski Bog with his right wing and the Volga reservoir with his left, and that in between he might retire in stages where it was unavoidable. In the 2nd Panzer Army's area the gap west of Tula continues to be highly dangerous. In the south in 2nd Army's area, it looks as if the 134th Division can fight its way out, while it remains doubtful for the remnants of the 45th Division. Of the reinforcements, so far approximately five battalions have arrived at Novosil.

Toward evening Brauchitsch arrived after having spoken with Kluge and Guderian. He has come to the view that the gradual withdrawal into a rearward position, as charted on the map by the army group, is unavoidable. Even the center, which means the bulk of the 4th Army, will not be able to hold its position if the forces on its left and right are forced to fall back. Schmundt, who was also there and who listened in on these discussions, called Jodl to get a decision from the *Führer*. He decided, verbally at first, that he had nothing against a straightening of the projecting salients at Klin and Kalinin, also that a withdrawal by Army Group Guderian was inevitable. Otherwise, however, nothing must be given up and no retreat made as long as the most necessary preparations had not been made in the rearward lines. In the evening an order was sent out to coordinate, and as far as possible prepare, the withdrawals by the armies.

In my talks with Brauchitsch and Schmundt I declared that apart from the attempt to find a way out for the moment, it is now vital that we select a position and use everything – construction units, residents and police – to prepare and equip it, and that it be manned on a timely basis by a screening force brought in from the rear and fortified at least well enough so that it can halt the Russians in case they should succeed in breaking through the army group.

15/12/41

Difficult conversation with Guderian about the gap west of Tula; he refuses to acknowledge any possibility of closing it from the south. I then placed the rest of the 137th Division from the 4th Army at his disposal and stressed the necessity of sending something, no matter how weak, by sleigh or some other method to Odoyevo. The last battalion of the security division which was sent to 2nd Army was diverted and subordinated to the panzer army with the proviso that the battalion was to be used to block the Oka crossings at Lichwin. Kluge dispatched weak rear-area elements of some sort to Kaluga for the same purpose. The latter informed me that he had ordered the withdrawal by Panzer Groups 3 and 4 as it had become unavoidable. Against VII and also IX Corps the Russians are infiltrating through our thin lines in the forests and it has become necessary for us to put some space between us and the enemy. He hopes that the extreme northern wing is in the position to maintain contact with the 9th Army. But the right wing of the 9th Army has to be pulled back, which has in any case – according to a report by 9th Army –

become necessary. This evening Kalinin was evacuated after the bridges were blown.

If today the situation of the withdrawing Panzer Group 3 appeared somewhat tense, there came a new cry for help from Panzer Group 4. Behind IX Corps' front are Russian cavalry, which were attacked by elements of the corps, their front facing west. Panzer Group 4's Chief of Staff [Beaulieu] was given the job of stiffening the backbone of the group's commander [Geyer] and Chief of Staff [Linstow]. I gave Schmundt, who was still here, the opportunity to speak at length with all the army Chiefs of Staff by telephone.

2nd Panzer Army continues to withdraw according to plan.

In 2nd Army's area the reserves which were committed succeeded in forcing back the Russians southwest of Novosil and restored contact with the 134th Division; in the process it turned out that the division's bloody losses were bearable! The army hopes that the same thing will work with the remains of the 45th Division.

Hitler "So Far Not Properly Informed of The Seriousness of the Situation..."

16/12/41

2nd Army reported that elements of the 45th Division fought their way through to the rear. But the enemy has moved in fresh forces there. He is also beginning to exert pressure opposite the northern wing of Army Group South. The gap west of Tula is still wide open and the enemy is channelling additional forces into it. On the left wing of the panzer army XXXXIII Corps was forced to fall back even farther. Kluge is seriously concerned about his right wing, where the enemy's initial weak attacks were repulsed. Things look bad on the right wing of Panzer Group 4, where the 267th Division's line was breached and it lost its artillery and where the 78th Division is apparently cut off. The enemy is deep in Panzer Group 3's rear at Terjajewa and it was only with great difficulty that it was able to regain possession of its line of retirement.

When I briefed Halder on the situation, he read to me an order from the *Führer* in which he demanded that the 4th Army "withdraw not one step farther," but authorized limited withdrawals by Army Group Guderian [2nd Panzer Army], Panzer Groups 3 and 4, and the 9th Army where unavoidable. The gaps at Lichwin and Tula are to be closed by reserves. I could only report that I have no reserves left!

In the afternoon Greiffenberg informed me that he had been told by Schmundt that the *Führer* had booted out the Commander-in-Chief of the Army during today's situation briefing and that for now Schmundt was to maintain direct communication with Army Group Center.

I telephoned Schmundt in the evening, briefed him on the latest aggravation of the situation and asked him whether Brauchitsch had described the true seriousness of the situation to the *Führer* and given him my report that the destruction of the army group cannot be ruled out if it is required to fight in its present forward position. Schmundt replied that he knew nothing of such a report to the *Führer*. I then dictated to him word for word the report I had submitted to the Commander-in-Chief of the Army on 13th December and added:

"The reason why it is questionable whether the units can hold in a new, but unprepared line is clear: I will not get my motorized units back on account of the fuel shortage and the icy roads, but also my horse-drawn guns, because the horses can't do it. Typical is the 267th Division, which today left behind its artillery when it fell back. The danger that we will arrive in the rear without artillery if we retire further is therefore great. On the other hand the order to hold causes me to concern that the units will possibly pull back without orders."

Schmundt then elaborated on the *Führer*'s ideas which had led to the order to hold. Army Groups North and South are sitting firm in their holes and can hold at present; so can Army Group Center. The *Führer* had said:

"I can't send everything into the winter because Army Group Center has had its lines breached in several places."

He had taken charge of everything and everything possible would be done to send people to the front. It is regrettable that it turns out that the *Führer* was not properly informed of the seriousness of the situation. I replied that my conscience was clear in this matter, whereupon Schmundt declared that he was well aware of that, having convinced himself during his visit here.

Hitler Puts All His Eggs In One Basket

I went on: "The *Führer* must know that he is putting all his eggs in one basket here. In his order he says that I am to commit all my reserves in order to close the gaps. Even though we have had bad experiences with taking security troops from the rear areas, today I pulled out two more police battalions there. These are my sole reserves!

Schmundt replied that he had reported all this to the *Führer*. He said that the dangers involved in withdrawing were probably the same, which I affirmed, while adding that weighing the pros and cons was very difficult at the present time. In truth counting one's buttons is the only way to determine which is the right thing to do. Schmundt promised to report to the *Führer* immediately.

In closing I said:

"You know that my health is hanging by a silk thread. If the *Führer* thinks that a fresh force belongs here, which I understand fully, under no circumstances is he to concern himself about me. What is at stake here is not individuals, but the whole. I ask that you tell him this. Understand me correctly: this is not a threat but merely the statement of a fact."

At 12:30 the *Führer* called and said that he had received my report from Schmundt. I replied that it was a repetition of the report I had made to Brauchitsch on the 13th December. The *Führer* then explained, quoting my reasons almost word for word, the pros and cons of staying or retreating, and came to the conclusion that under the prevailing conditions it made no sense to withdraw to an unprepared position, leaving behind artillery and equipment. In several days we would be facing the same situation again, but now without heavy weapons and without artillery. There was only one decision and that was not to take a single step back, to plug the holes and hold on. He had personally set everything in motion to help. The Luftwaffe will be reinforced to the extent possible and infantry will be brought in. Everything is being harnessed. He repeated that he was convinced that there is only one decision, namely to hold. I said that I had already issued an order to this effect but that it was my duty to report that in this situation the army group's front could give way somewhere – whereupon the *Führer* replied:

"That has to be accepted."

17/12/41

Two strict orders went out, one to hold at all costs, another to ruthlessly mobilize all those still swarming about behind the front.

The situation continues to be extraordinarily tense. The 2nd Army urgently requested reinforcements. The 4th Army, where the enemy has made several penetrations against the right wing, has helped itself temporarily by pulling out the weak 17th Division. Some elements at least of the 78th Division, cut off yesterday, have rejoined the 4th Panzer Division, but morale there is very solid.

Panzer Group 3, too, has been forced back. The enemy is pursuing the withdrawal by the right wing of the 9th Army closely and there is significant fighting in places there. There are reports of enemy forces massing in the Torzhok area.

The two motorized police battalions released in the rear army area will set out for the 4th Army tomorrow.

"Desertion?"

Brauchitsch called in the afternoon and said:

"You spoke about your health recently. After conferring with the *Führer* I am suggest to you that you apply for the leave you mentioned to restore your health."

As Brauchitsch asked me on the 14th to hold on if possible, this strikes me as "rather sudden." I asked whether they would not interpret this as desertion on my part. Brauchitsch answered with a decisive "no." The conversation, which was on the friendliest terms, concluded with a brief discussion of the question of my replacement. Right afterward I called Schmundt and told him to tell me openly if the *Führer* wouldn't also interpret this as walking out in a difficult situation; I would very much rather collapse at my post than bear the consequences of the accusation of "desertion." Schmundt answered immediately:

"In no way whatsoever."

When I then asked him if the *Führer* felt that he had to reproach me for any reason, Schmundt answered very decisively:

"No, on the contrary, in yesterday's discussion about this very topic he emphasized your great services and said: after the serious illness of last year, combined with the demands of this campaign, he could completely understand your sick report. I can assure you unequivocally that you can set your mind at rest about this."

18/12/41

In the morning a new order from the *Führer* calling on the troops to hold at all costs; I passed it on to the armies. Bombers and reinforcements are to be flown to the army group.

At midmorning I spoke with Hoepner in an effort to stiffen his backbone.

2nd Army's situation relatively quiet. 2nd Panzer Army continues its fighting withdrawal. In the gap west of Tula serious attacks against XXXXIII Corps, which managed to hold.

The several day old threat of new pressure on the right wing of the 4th Army is uncomfortable. The enemy has crossed the frozen Oka and forced back the very weak forces there. The Russians also attacked 4th Army's other fronts, largely without result. Panzer Groups 3 and 4 retired further. At the army group's request, the 9th Army moved the 162nd Division to Latschino to support the withdrawing Panzer Group 3 if needed.

Kluge, who is to take over for me, arrived in the afternoon. We discussed the necessity of transferring the chief responsibility for defending the gap west of Tula to the 4th Army, since XXXXIII Corps is being pushed across the Oka and the danger exists that contact might be broken with Panzer Army Guderian. Guderian has been reporting for days that he can't send any forces there, thus the 4th Army has to try to free additional forces from its front. The 17th Division, which was pulled out there yesterday, is on the march south. The necessary subordination of Panzer Group 3 to the 9th Army was also discussed. Finally I pointed out to Kluge that enemy groupings opposite 9th Army's northern front suggest that an attack against the army group's northern flank might be possible. For the present the Army Command, which I had informed of this by Greiffenberg, does not share my concern.

Handover of Army Group Center

Toward evening Brauchitsch called and informed me that the *Führer* had approved my requested leave until "the complete restoration of my health."

19/12/41

At 11:00 I took leave of my staff. I asked them to remain firm and confident, because I believe that the end of the present "dirty period" is in sight. The Russians can scarcely have all that many forces left; a report just came that a division has just surfaced opposite the 4th Army's right wing which had previously attacked in front of Panzer Group 4.

Kluge assumed command at 11:00.

20/12/41

In the morning, before my departure, Greiffenberg told me that the *Führer* had himself assumed command of the army. Brauchitsch, who hinted this to me yesterday on the telephone, has gone home "sick."

Drove by car to Wilna. Hardenberg came with me.

21/12/41

Continued to Steinort [*Führer* Headquarters].

Meeting with the *Führer* – New Discoveries

22/12/41

At midday I reported to the *Führer* in *Führer* Headquarters; he was very cordial. He spoke at length on the situation, the seriousness of which he appreciates, and said that my reports had not been passed on to him in the form in which they had been submitted! Once again I took the opportunity to call his attention to the compelling need for a radical improvement of the transportation system. I also repeated my proposal of 1st December, to build a defensive position, just in case, which is far enough removed from the front that it would not be affected by the present fighting.

As I was leaving I said briefly: "The 'Russian illness,' together with a certain overexertion so brought me down that I had to fear that I might fail in command. Might I report as soon as I am back in shape again?"

The *Führer* answered, "yes."

Schmundt told me once again that I had only been placed "on leave" and that no reproach was being made against me.

Continued on to Berlin.

25/12/41

From Berlin I sent telexes to Halder and Schmundt, advising them that I was expected to recover in three to four weeks.

In the course of a telephone conversation, Greiffenberg confirmed the rumor that Guderian, who had again been causing difficulties, was sent home. He went on to say that Kluge had exchanged the army group's 1st Adjutant, Below, for one of his own adjutants from the 4th Army [Kübler]. When I expressed my astonishment, Greiffenberg stated that they had as yet received no order as to whether Kluge was to "stand in" for me or was supposed to "replace" me, but that a clarification was necessary, for Kluge holds the view that he is keeping the army group! I called Halder and asked him to see to it that this matter was cleared up.

The situation on the army group's front remains serious; the railroad situation appears especially bad.

"Transferred to the Officer Reserve"

1/1/42

Keitel, chief of the Personnel Office, came and informed me "that the *Führer* considers another change in the command of the army group inadvisable in the present difficult situation." He asked me to be understanding. I am being transferred to the officer reserve.

When I asked whether in these circumstances I should even bother reporting fit for duty again, Keitel replied, "But of course! You remain available and another command is possible at any time."

Here again my question as to whether any sort of reproach was being raised against me was answered with a clear no. When I interjected that it appeared that an investigation was being carried out in some quarters into a connection between my case and the departure of Brauchitsch, Keitel declared that that was out of the question and that such rumors were unwarranted.

5/1/42

Schmundt sent me a letter which, written in a very friendly way, was intended to alleviate my personal concerns and assured me that the *Führer* trusted me as in the past. I wrote back that my recovery would probably take until the beginning of February: "But I am available if I am needed sooner."

CHAPTER SIX

16 JANUARY 1942 to 15 JULY 1942

(EASTERN FRONT)

Commander-in-Chief Army Group South/B

Summary of the military actions under Bock's command as Commander-in-Chief of Army Group South

1. Securing of the Crimea (coastal defense)	17/11/41 - 4/7/42
2. Retreat to the Kerch Peninsula and battles around and northwest of Feodosiya	28/12/41 - 18/1/42
3. Siege battles for Fortress Sevastopol	1/1/42 - 1/6/42
4. Defensive battles at the Parpatsch Position	19/1/42 - 7/5/42
5. Battle on the Kerch Peninsula and the capture of Kerch	8/5/42 - 21/5/42
6. Attack and capture of Fortress Sevastopol	2/6/42 - 4/7/42

Battles on the upper Donets and on the Don at Ssemina

1. Battles at Oboyan and Rshawa	1/1/42 - 16/1/42
2. Defensive battles north of Kharkov	17/1/42 - 11/5/42

Defensive Battles in the Donets Region

1. Defense of the Donets Basin	22/11/42 - 10/7/42
2. Defensive of the Mius Position	2/12/41 - 21/7/42

Defense of Kursk	5/2/42 - 27/6/42
Spring Battles near Kharkov	12/5/42 - 26/6/42
1. Defensive battle near Kharkov	12/5/42 - 21/5/42
2. Battle of annihilation at Barvenkovo	17/5/42 - 27/5/42
3. Battle of encirclement southwest of Kharkov	22/5/42 - 27/5/42
4. Defensive battle at the Donets	8/5/42 - 21/6/42
5. Battle at Volchansk	10/5/42 - 16/6/42
6. Battle of Izyum-Kupyansk	22/6/42 - 26/6/42

16/1/42

General von Drabich [Drabich-Waechter; Chief of the P.1 group of the Army Personnel Office] called and asked whether I was ready to immediately take over Army Group South. Since, at the urging of the doctors, I had made the decision to go to Semmering to recuperate for several weeks and as everything was ready there, I asked for a quarter of an hour to think it over. When I then said yes, Drabich brought the order for me to report to the *Führer* as soon as possible. Reichenau [Commander-in-Chief since 1 December 1941] had suffered a stroke, which he would probably not survive.

They had sent Hoepner [formerly of 4th Panzer Army, retired on 8 January 1942] home; Strauß and several commanding generals from my old army group had fallen ill.

17/1/42

Travelled in an unheated sleeper car to Insterburg. On the train were numerous Spanish officers. I was ashamed of our railroad, for the car was dirty and we were late too!

Hitler: The "Strategic Threat" Is "Eliminated!"

18/1/42

In Jägerhöhe near Angerburg I learned that Reichenau had died [17 January 1942]. Reported to the *Führer*; he brought me up to date on the situation, especially as it concerns Army Group South. He sees the strategic threat as eliminated, although there is still plenty to be ironed out! The question of Army Group South he considers "taken care of." The army group has first to hold; in spring it is to attack. The *Führer* knows how bad the railroad situation is and that it is a source of great difficulties. I could only encourage his position in this regard. He has now combined the direction of all the railroads, even in the occupied territories, in the hands of the Minister of Railroads [Dorpmüller].

The *Führer* spoke optimistically about the world situation. He views the threat that England will lose her primary sources of oil as obvious and decisive. – Apart from the *Führer*, only soldiers were present at the subsequent breakfast. – Leeb, Commander-in-Chief of Army Group North, has gone home at his request. Schmundt said that he [Leeb] doesn't believe he can deal with the crises which his next assignments will bring. Schmundt knows that the numerous changes in the senior command positions are giving cause for gossip at home and abroad. They are going to try to control it. Thus the newspapers are to include a friendly telegram from the *Führer* with the news of Brauchitsch's operations, Rundstedt is to represent the *Führer* at Reichenau's funeral, the *Führer* has been photographed in conversation with me for the papers, and so on.

19/1/42

In three hours and twenty minutes I overflew the 1,050 kilometers from Rastenburg to Poltava [HQ Army Group South]. Hoth [17th Army], who is leading the army group at the moment, fetched me from the airport. He is very worried. Yesterday powerful enemy forces took the offensive opposite the inner wings of the 17th and 6th Armies and drove deep into the German lines in several places. The enemy also attacked 2nd Army. At present the only available reserves are two-thirds of the 73rd Division [Bünau] behind the south wing of 1st Panzer Army and elements of the 88th Division [Gollwitzer], which is arriving in Kursk in a very slow succession of trains. The heavy mixing of units is apparent in almost all the armies. In the Crimea the 11th Army [Manstein] recaptured Feodosiya, which was lost in December.

20/1/42

I assumed command of Army Group South, which was promptly reported by English radio.

The situation is serious. The most critical places are north of Artemovsk and west and northwest of Izyum, where the enemy has broken through with tanks. The penetration at Artemovsk is to be headed off by committing the last reserves of the 17th Army and a reserve of the 1st Panzer Army [Kleist]. At present there are no forces available for Izyum. A third dangerous penetration followed against 2nd Army northeast of Schtschigry, where a cavalry corps reinforced by infantry smashed a deep breach and is feeling its way toward Kursk. There, too, there are only very weak reserves; the 88th Division is arriving in only one train per day! The main pressure lies on the 17th Army's front, against which fifteen attacking divisions and four armored units have so far been identified. Such a powerful drive cannot be stopped by the army group's existing forces for long. The 1st Romanian Division coming from Romania and the 113th Division [Zickwolff] destined for the Crimea will have to be deployed in the threatened front in a defensive role. But with the terrible state of the railroads that will take weeks! As well the Russians have strong reserves and thus are in a position not only to keep their attack going, but to broaden it. Indications of this are to be seen opposite the Italians on the north wing of 1st Panzer Army. I spoke with Kleist, who at my request has pulled a division out of the line and is readying it to leave for the 17th Army, and asked him to create new reserves and put them behind his north wing. The Army Command was informed and asked to send at least one further division as quickly as possible.

I spoke with Paulus, who today took over the 6th Army; I suggested that he position the strongest possible reserves behind his south wing in order to check the dangerous penetration northwest of Izyum through an attack from the north.

An attempt by the 11th Army to make an about face northeast of Feodosiya then pursue and overrun the Russians was unsuccessful.

21/1/42

This morning columns of enemy armor and vehicles supposedly broke through far to the west from the breach in the front at Izyum. I committed all available air forces against them. It turns out that the vehicles that "broke through" were German! Nevertheless the situation remains serious enough. Numerous attacks against the army group's front were repulsed. 17th Army intends to eliminate the breach at Artemovsk by counterattacking; for now it must let the penetration at Izyum run, for it lacks the forces to deal with both simultaneously. The enemy cavalry in 2nd Army's [Weichs] bulge is pushing farther southwest. The army will have to help itself, for I have no more reserves.

I called the *Führer* and outlined the situation and my intentions. Concerning the Crimea, I reported that the enemy has once again occupied a strong position northeast of Feodosiya. Our divisions there are tired. Since I have also had to take air forces away from the Crimea to support the front under attack, I cannot at present support the continuation of 11th Army's attack to Kerch, although prompt action there would be the right thing. The *Führer* agreed with everything.

1st Panzer Army was instructed to energetically take up the battle against the concentrations discovered opposite its north wing, especially with the artillery. As discussed yesterday, the 100th Light Division [Sanne] was pulled out of the line, because it could do so most quickly, and was dispatched to the 17th Army. For the time being the 73rd Division is remaining behind the front.

Now The Russians Are "The Faster"

22/1/42

The enemy is maintaining pressure on the 17th Army. Heavy attacks from all sides against the southern cornerpost of the breach front around Slavyansk. In spite of attempts to supply them from the air, the garrisons of several strongpoints on 17th Army's northern front have run out of ammunition and have been surrounded or overrun. To their west enemy cavalry and tanks are advancing toward Barvenkovo. The 298th Division [Zehler], which was overrun and severely mauled on the 18th, has assembled in the more than 40-km-wide gap to the north. At the north end of the gap the enemy is attacking the south wing of the 6th Army. 17th Army has requested the withdrawal of the 257th [Sachs] and 68th [Meissner] Divisions 5 to 6 km to the south, because relief of the surrounded strongpoints is impossible due to insufficient forces and the complete destruction of their garrisons must be expected. I briefed Heusinger of the Army High Command and said that the intended withdrawal would not improve the situation but that a retreat would have to be authorized there, as a result of which holding on would become senseless because of the fall of the adjacent strongpoints. The two outermost strongpoints on the right and left must be held. The *Führer*, who has expressly reserved to himself the decision on giving up front-line sectors, ordered that only those strongpoints which are out of ammunition or have no rations are to be abandoned.

The Russian cavalry corps which penetrated the 2nd Army's front has moved little today; isolated attempts to attack north and south from the breach were repulsed.

On the map it appears a simple matter to assemble an assault group from the 1st Romanian Division coming by way of Dnepropetrovsk, the remains of the 298th Division in the gap west of Izyum, and the reserves gathering behind the 6th Army's south wing, and with it restore the situation at the boundary between the 17th and 6th Armies. But things look very much different with temperatures of 30 to 40 degrees below freezing, icy roads and failing railroads, with the terrible state of the inadequately-fed horses and that of the vehicles, which is even worse, because all movements require a tremendous amount of time which cannot be predicted in advance.

It is characteristic of our situation that in the army group's area alone twenty-one batteries with serviceable guns, full crews and adequate ammunition have been sitting idle because their tractors and vehicles have become unusable!

Everyone who can carry a weapon has been scraped together to plug the worst gaps; Luftwaffe formations, rear area services, armored trains, etc, have been committed. One can no longer call this muddling along with tiny formations "command," and for the reserves approaching painfully slowly on foot and by rail – 100th Light, 1st Romanian and now as well the 113th Division released by the Army High Command – their direction of action is determined by the course and availability of the railroads. The Russians, on the other hand, have large masses of cavalry and thoroughly capable railroads, which they skillfully use to expand the successes they have achieved. Now they are the faster!

23/1/42

Several more strongpoints which expended all their ammunition have been abandoned on the south side of the Izyum penetration. On the north side, near Balakleya, heavy fighting by the south wing of the 6th Army. In the center the enemy is pursuing hard the remnants of the shattered 298th Division. In the southern penetration north of Artemovsk, too, the enemy pressure is still so strong that our counterattack gained no ground. – Again today the 17th Army stressed the seriousness of its situation, especially the threat to the Dnepropetrovsk-Stalino supply rail line. It wanted to evacuate Barvenkovo; I forbade that, because holding the town is of far-reaching significance. But its concerns are not unfounded, especially since the Russians are feeding additional reserves in the direction of the breakthrough gap by rail.

1st Panzer Army has pulled Headquarters, XI Corps [Kortzfleisch] out of the line and moved it behind the center of the penetration at Izyum. The units sent to the breach are to be concentrated under its command and if possible used in a coordinated counterattack. To what extent this succeeds depends upon the speed of the enemy advance, against which the entire air force has been committed in an effort to slow it down. It is bad that the 298th Division has only two artillery pieces left and that the artillery of the 1st Romanian Division is still with the 1st Panzer Army on the coast. Everything possible is being tried to help out. Formations have been set up using security troops from the rear army area to guard the Dniepr bridges against a breakthrough by Russian tanks.

Today the Russian cavalry advanced only hesitantly in the breach against 2nd Army. Our own counterattack from the south made some progress.

A telegram from the Army High Command arranged the unified command at the breach already planned by me and mentioned above. It further ordered that attempts were to continue to clear the Kerch Peninsula so as to subsequently free forces for the attack on Sevastopol, which is still far in the future.

Generaloberst Löhr, commander of Air Fleet 4, with which I have to work, came at noon. In the afternoon Lehndorff [*Oberleutnant* of the Reserve] arrived; he is to stand in for Hardenberg [*Major* of the Reserve, Bock's personal adjutant since autumn 1940].

24/1/42

The enemy continues to drive west in the Izyum bulge; at the same time he again tried to crush the remaining cornerposts of the 17th and 6th Armies and outflank their bent-back wings. In the south Barvenkovo has now been lost, in the north fighting is particularly heavy at Balakleya. My Chief of Staff, *General* von Sodenstern, briefed Halder; yesterday's very serious assessment by the 17th Army [Hoth] also went to the Army High Command. I described the situation to the *Führer* by telephone and pointed to the threat to the sole remaining supply railroad for the 17th Army and the 1st Panzer Army. I asked for a decision on whether it was really still right to continue the attack ordered on Kerch or whether the 60th Panzer Battalion [Eberhardt; actually the 60th Motorized Infantry Division, subsequently referred to as the 60th Panzer Battalion], which is vital to this attack, should not be committed at the break-in front. I am in favor of this solution, for it's life or death at the break-in front. In the afternoon the Army High Command released the panzer battalion for the 17th Army. The 2nd Romanian Division, which is still far west of the Dniepr, was also placed at the army group's disposal.

In the afternoon an order was issued which coordinates the assembly of all the reserves en route to the breach and instructed the 1st Panzer Army to make further reserves available for the 17th Army by ruthlessly weakening its front. To this end the 14th Panzer Division was also moved in. Unfortunately a regiment of the 73rd Division had to be sent as well, so that all that is left of this division behind the panzer army's front is a reinforced regiment. The counterattack by the 2nd Army has so far had no significant success. Dangerous, for there are signs of new pressure north of the point of penetration of the Russian guards cavalry corps and the enemy is apparently feeding additional forces into the area west of Kursk by rail.

My loyal followers have finally arrived, my clerk Jüngling and the cook by air, my driver Wolf by car; with several breakdowns, it took them 6 days to get here from Berlin and Angerburg respectively!

"In Reichenau's Personal Possessions..."

Reichenau's personal possessions included a draft proposal to the *Führer* whose objective was to secure the positive cooperation of the Ukrainian population through appropriate measures and thus make them into allies against bolshevism. The basic concepts behind the proposal coincide with the view I presented to one of Rosenberg's colleagues in Smolensk. I therefore presented Reichenau's proposal to the Army High Command so that it might be brought to the attention of the *Führer*.

25/1/42

17th Army repulsed attacks in the south bulge; in the northern one the enemy took several more strongpoints and attacked south and southwest through Barvenkovo around the west wing of the 17th Army with cavalry and tanks. On the other side the 100th Light Divison, initially without heavy weapons, is arriving slowly. Enemy advances toward Lozovaya, in the bulge's front, were repulsed by the 298th Division. At the northwest tip of the penetration the 6th Army's "Friedrich Group," which was supposed to stage an attack today, was itself attacked by superior forces and fell back some distance to the north "so as not to be drawn into battle before preparations are completed."

Heavy attacks were repulsed at Balakleya. The cavalry which broke through against 2nd Army advanced to Schtschigry but was thrown out again. The army's counterattack to close the breach in the front is gaining ground slowly. The enemy also attacked north of this breach. The 2nd Army is toying with the idea of retreating from the deep, projecting salient in its center. The Army High Command was informed; after a detailed assessment of the situation I requested that a division be moved behind the boundary between the 6th and 2nd Armies and – after a discussion with Manstein – the transfer of air forces to the Crimea, where we have had to passively watch the enemy's landing and attack preparations because our air forces are too weak. I directed the same request to Jeschonnek, the chief of the Luftwaffe General Staff.

In the evening a lengthy conversation with Paulus, who is moving whatever reserves he can find behind his right wing.

Offensive Solution to the Crisis?

26/1/42

Further attack preparations by the enemy in the Crimea. 1st Panzer Army repulsed an attack on its north wing. Somewhat quieter on the 17th Army's eastern and northern fronts. Arriving on the west wing, the 100th Light Division, which was supposed to take Alexandrovka, was attacked by the 5th Russian Cavalry Corps near Stepanovka and temporarily put in a bad situation. It was learned from an intercepted order that this corps' mission was to first gain our supply railroad to Stalino and then turn east. It is especially uncomfortable that on the western front of the breach the remnants of the 298th Division had to give up Lozovaya under pressure from two enemy infantry divisions. In the 6th Army's area the Russians have ceased their attacks on Balakleya but are attacking to its west. 2nd Army reports heavy, back and forth fighting against the cavalry corps which breached its front. So far it has been unable to close the front behind the enemy.

Hoth and I discussed the idea that the only way out of this crisis is an offensive one. But he is so under the influence of events that during the night he made the quite unfeasible proposal for the 17th Army to make an about face and fight its way through to the west. The Commanding General of the corps which has suffered worst in 17th Army's battles has reported sick; when I discussed the situation with him, he asked me which was more important to save – replaceable equipment or the irreplaceable veteran unit leaders, who are now being sacrificed by rigidly holding onto the front. He does not realize that the equipment cannot be replaced in the foreseeable future and that without equipment we will have even less of a chance of holding farther to the rear.

What "Retreat Means"

27/1/42

In the morning I called Hoth, rejected his proposal and told him that the army had to hold no matter what; retreat not only means abandoning guns and equipment, but also our wounded in hospitals and we know that the Russians do not spare them. I further pointed out to him that we must only use what is absolutely necessary from the slowly-arriving reserves to prop up the front. Everything else has to be strictly husbanded so that we may solve this crisis offensively as soon as sufficient forces have arrived. That will take days yet; until then everyone has to hold where he stands.

In the Crimea the enemy made small-scale assaults at Sevastopol and on the eastern front and was repulsed. The Russian forces which landed near Sudak a few days ago were driven back into the sea apart from a small remnant. On 1st Panzer Army's front small-scale attacks were repulsed. 17th Army also reported small-scale attacks only. On its west wing the enemy cavalry is slowly advancing further south; for now the enemy infantry at Lozovaya has not yet attacked again. In 6th Army's area the Russians attacked west of Balakleya and were repulsed. The weak forces of the 2nd Army are slowly succeeding in confining the Russian guards cavalry corps in the bulge; otherwise only small-scale attacks there too.

An order was issued, again focussing on the 17th and 6th Armies, that the penetration had to be eliminated by attacking and which laid down the general directions of attack.

Heavy snowfall complicates movement much more for us than for the Russians, who with their lighter vehicles are better able to cope. The slower the reserves arrive, the more difficult the crisis is to overcome; if it becomes too late to attack and the forces must be thrown into the battle individually, they will not be sufficient to seal off the penetration. This assessment was reported to the Army Command and once again the transfer of forces was requested.

28/1/42

Several more strongpoints were abandoned on the 17th Army's left wing. Croatian troops have let themselves be overrun by Russian cavalry at the south tip of the bulge. I have the feeling that the 17th Army headquarters is overtired as a result of the demands of recent days and have decided to transfer command to the very enterprising Headquarters, 1st Panzer Army on the most threatened front. After consulting with Kleist, the simplest way to achieve this turned out to be to temporarily subordinate the 17th Army to "Army Group Kleist." The new command structure took effect at 11:00. I called the *Führer* and reported to him:

"Three Russian cavalry corps entered through the bulge near Izyum; one turned north against the west wing of the 6th Army and toward Krasnograd, while two corps are advancing south toward the supply railroad of both southern armies and are outflanking the west wing of the 17th Army. The two Russian infantry divisions at Lozovaya advanced no farther yesterday, indicating that perhaps they have a defensive mission at first, to cover the operation by the cavalry corps to the west. I do not know whether the enemy is bringing forward additional forces. A continuation of his attacks, primarily against the two remaining cornerposts of the breach, is to be expected. The direction of advance of the two southern cavalry corps, toward my supply railroad, is especially disquieting. The planned counterattacks against them will only be made if a particularly effective leader is in charge there. Headquarters, 17th Army is understandably tired. The troops assembled there for the counterattack come for the most part from the 1st Panzer Army. I have therefore subordinated the 17th Army to the 1st Panzer Army and request your approval retroactively."

The *Führer* agreed.

The enemy carried out small-scale attacks at numerous places on the front, against 1st Panzer Army, on the right wing of the 6th Army, and north of the big breach against the 2nd Army, where he gained little ground.

At noon an order was sent to all the armies by radio, according to which the voluntary abandonment of strongpoints requires approval from me. In another order I urged the offensive exploitation of any opportunity that presents itself, because in this we are superior to the Russians and because only in this way can the situation be mastered.

Kleist reported that if things go relatively smoothly he will be ready to attack with the 14th Panzer Division [Kühn] on the 31st. Plenty late, but I will have to be pleased if he can meet this deadline in spite of all the snowdrifts and supply problems.

In response to my requests for reinforcements, the Army Command has ordered the transfer of two Hungarian security brigades, which are to be followed by a third, from the west Ukraine to Kharkov.

29/1/42

According to the morning reports yesterday there were encouraging counterattacks at various places, for example north of Artemovsk and by the 100th Light Division. On the other hand the 17th Army reported that it had to evacuate several towns west of Slavyansk before yesterday's order concerning the abandonment of strongpoints arrived. That amounts to an invitation to the enemy to make a concentric attack against XXXXIV Corps [Angelis; since 26 January 1942]! Hoth explained that the evacuation had been unavoidable but that he had no more doubts that we now absolutely had to hold. Today the enemy staged local attacks at many places on the army group's front; the heaviest was the one southwest of Slavyansk! On the extreme right wing of the 6th Army Russian attacks were repulsed with heavy losses. In the 2nd Army's area heavy fighting in the bulge; the enemy also continues to press to its north. Since strong security units have had to be moved from the rear areas to the front, partisan activity has revived in the rear.

According to a report by the 11th Army, Russian attack preparations in the Crimea continue. Of all the army's requests, the only one I could at least partly grant is for air support; I transferred the main effort of the Luftwaffe, which today could not operate over the breach sites because of weather, to the Crimea for one day. The Army High Command has promised to send a squadron of torpedo bombers.

The Army Command announced the following future changes: the 28th Light Division [Sinnhuber], which will leave the west at the beginning of February, three Italian divisions for April and three for May.

30/1/42

In 1st Panzer Army's sector the enemy attacked the Italian Corps and was repulsed; otherwise only minor attacks. In 17th Army's area efforts by the enemy to break through toward Slavyansk from all sides; a village was lost southwest of Slavyansk, otherwise the attacks were beaten off. In the bulge near Petropavlovka, where initially there was only a German construction battalion, strong cavalry pushed southwest. Weaker attacks were repulsed on the bulge's western front. Heavy fighting on 6th Army's entire south front, where strong Russian attacks broke down. The assault group assembled by 1st Panzer Army in the area of Postischewo and elements of the 14th Panzer Division are to launch a counterattack in a northerly direction tomorrow. Assembly of the attack group on the 6th Army's right wing encountered delays due to the snow, and it will be unable to attack as a body. I urged Paulus to hurry as much as possible so that this group is not drawn into the defensive fighting at the southeast corner of the army and thus lost to the counterattack. Massing of the 1st Romanian and 113th Divisions, the 60th Panzer Battalion [Eberhardt] and especially the 454th Security Division [Koch] around Pavlograd and Krasnograd is proceeding slowly.

The only new forces shown by the enemy at the breach today was a division which he moved in from Rostov.

Development's in 2nd Army's sector are encouraging; the Russians are increasingly being forced out of the bulge in our lines with visibly heavy losses. In the afternoon I called the *Führer* and requested that he order the immediate transfer of 50 tanks from Germany, since under the present weather conditions it is likely that the counterattacks by the 14th Panzer Division and the 60th Panzer Battalion will cost many tanks. A request through channels would take too long. I also requested the Knight's Cross for an especially deserving officer, which he authorized.

The Army High Command informed me of a statement by the Hungarian General Staff, according to which the skill and armament of the Hungarian security brigades makes them suitable only for use in rear areas. That is especially unpleasant because these brigades are our only support from the Hungarians at the present time.

On 20 January 1942 in Budapest, Generalfeldmarschall Keitel and Colonel-General Szombathelyi discussed arrangements for Hungary's participation in the summer campaign of 1942. Whereas Keitel requested 23 divisions, the ultimate result was the formation of the Hungarian 2nd Army with approximately 200,000 men. Its commander in chief was the 59-year-old Colonel-General Gustav von Jany. The army was organized into nine "light" infantry divisions and one armored division. The decision to employ Hungarian forces outside the country's borders was not debated as the constitution required. Keitel's promise to equip the Hungarians with additional weapons and equipment according to existing "possibilities" was, to a very large degree, also not kept.

"Blowing Snow and Heavy Drifting"

31/1/42

Once again I instructed the armies that the crisis was to be solved by offensive means and that every unit leader had to be convinced of this necessity. The army group's plan was given as a concentric attack on the Barvenkovo-Bliznetsy-Metschelowa area by the 1st Panzer Army [Assault Group Hube, 60th Panzer Battalion and XI Corps] and the 6th Army [Assault Group Dostler] with the objective of destroying the enemy.

The Russians launched heavy attacks east of Artemovsk and around Slavyansk in blowing snow and heavy drifting. East of Artemovsk they penetrated to a depth of four kilometers; otherwise they were repelled. Minor attacks against XI Corps and 6th Army's southern front. Radio intercepts suggest that the enemy is moving tanks in behind his southwards-advancing cavalry in the bulge. In spite of its weakness and in spite of all the snow, "Assault Group Hube" attacked, scattered enemy outposts and recaptured the village lost by the Croats on the 28th. Elements of the 60th Panzer Battalion which have so far arrived also attacked and drove the enemy out of Petropavlovka.

1/2/42

Once again I reminded the Army Command of the enemy's preparations for an attack in the Crimea and repeated my request for the speedy transfer of air forces.

It has been confirmed that the enemy is pulling forces out of the breach front and is shifting them west into the bulge. As a result of the snow conditions the forward movements of our attack forces are very slow. I repeatedly urged the 6th Army to speed things up.

The Russians again directed heavy attacks against Slavyansk from the east, but mainly from the west.

The Russians also attacked on the 6th Army's southern front. They were repulsed everywhere. Near Lozovaya the Romanians repelled another assault. From the map it appears that our counterattack should not be committed as ordered, rather more extensively from the northeast corner of the 17th Army and the southeast corner of the 6th Army. With the difficulty of movement, it is important that we immediately safeguard the sole, seriously-threatened supply railroad in the south and in the north prevent the 6th Army's southwest wing from being further outflanked. This is only still possible if the troops are sent to the threatened positions by the fastest means.

2nd Army received orders to assemble strong reserves in the Kursk area after restoring the situation at Schtschigry.

2/2/42

My request for air forces for the Crimea was repeated in writing.

1st Panzer Army received instructions to go to the attack with XI Corps [Kortzfleisch] as soon as the bulk of the Romanian infantry and a regimental group from the 113th Division reached a position in line with the 298th Division. The main weight of the attack is to be placed on the north wing.

Relatively quiet on the army group's eastern front. Successful counterattacks west of Slavyansk by 17th Army; in spite of deep snow and difficult terrain, Assault Group Hube and the 60th Panzer Battalion have fought their way forward. Enemy cavalry advanced south into a gap on the assault group's right. 1st Panzer Army was instructed to seal off the cavalry penetration by committing local reserves and render it ineffective by promptly sending the

Hube Group on toward its former objective of Alexandrovka. On the 6th Army's southern front heavy attacks were repulsed with grievous losses to the enemy. Paulus reported that after restoring the situation in the front, which is to take place tonight, tomorrow night he intends to attack southeast with the Dostler Group [57th Infantry Division]. I encouraged him in this.

Railroad tie-ups in the rear have delayed the departure of the 113th Division.

The same day Hardenberg, still staying in Neuhardenberg, wrote to Ingeborg Geisendörfer, former private tutor at Neuhardenberg: "Fedi [familiar name for Fedor von Bock] is always extremely happy to receive your faithful correspondence. He is back in the field again, but more to the south, as replacement for one who died. Happily I can stay here another eight days, then I am to join him in his new command. It's a great pity that our old command and our good comrades won't be there." (In: Agde, Günter, "Carl-Hans Graf von Hardenberg...", Berlin, 1994, PP 144).

3/2/42

Limited combat due to heavy snowstorms and icy cold.

Elements of the 100th Light Divison have engaged enemy forces which broke through between it and the Hube Group [16th Panzer Division]. Because of the snowdrifts, the attack groups of Army Group Kleist made only limited progress; those of 6th Army also scarcely moved forward. Small-scale attacks by the Russians on the bulge's western front. Preparations for a new attack opposite the southeast corner of the 6th Army. Air reconnaissance also indicates that the enemy is moving additional forces into the breach north and south of Izyum.

Unfortunately the 1st Panzer Army independently committed the last regiment of the 73rd Division at the Mius Front; consequently there are no reserves there worthy of note.

4/2/42

English radio says that Timoshenko wants to retake Kharkov and Dnepropetrovsk, in order to deny the Germans the most important jump-off points for their planned spring offensive toward the Caucasus!

Russian attack preparations in the Crimea are apparently almost complete.

On the rest of the army group front heavy snowstorms continue to make any sort of movement difficult. Delivery of fuel to the Hube attack group and to the 60th Panzer Battalion possible only with sleighs on the drifted roads. Both therefore unable to move. The enemy attacked west of Slavyansk and was repulsed. The Russians which had penetrated between the 100th Light Division and the Hube Group were forced back. The 60th Panzer Battalion is engaged in heavy fighting with a Russian infantry division. Enemy infantry took a village from the Romanian 1st Division on the western front of the bulge. Especially heavy attacks on the southern front and now also on the south part of 6th Army's eastern front were for the most part beaten off. "Assault Group Dostler" on the left wing of the 6th Army still has not yet attacked. Once again I urged action. Paulus, who is on the spot, will get things moving.

In 2nd Army's area, counterattacks have succeeded in completely closing the breach of 18th January. Outstanding achievement!

Fight Until the Blood Freezes!

5/2/42

Snowstorms prevented any large-scale movements. The Russians, too, limited to small-scale attacks; east of Kharkov they infiltrated with patrols.

We are as good as cut off from the outside world. For eight days no courier aircraft have taken off or landed.

6/2/42

Manstein sent another telegram on account of the imminent attack in the Crimea; it contained nothing new, apart from a letter from the navy, which, due to a shortage of forces, cannot provide any help in defending the Crimea.

Paulus called from Kharkov. He reported that the 208th Regiment, whose attack we have been waiting for since the 29th [January], has 700 casualties from freezing and exhaustion; nevertheless, he will launch the attack to take the hills near Alexeyevskoye as soon as possible. I repeatedly reminded him that every lost hour is to the enemy's advantage.

The day was very unsettled in spite of severe cold and continuing storm. Small-scale Russian attacks on the eastern and northwestern fronts of the 17th Army were repulsed. The Hube Group's attack collided with the attack of a Russian infantry division; by evening the situation was still unclear; however the battle there does not appear to be going badly. Weak Russian detachments advanced into the rear through the gap between XI Corps and the 6th Army; in several villages they rounded up all the men of fighting age and then withdrew, taking the men and all the food they could find. The enemy attacked on the 6th Army's right wing and was for the most part beaten off. The day before yesterday the enemy achieved a minor penetration against the southeast corner of the 6th Army south of Wolochow Jar and today was able to expand it; patrols continue to infiltrate our lines in the wooded country east of Kharkov. I pointed out to the Chief of Staff of the 6th Army, *General* Heim, the need for a unified command opposite the point of penetration and reminded him that no village might be surrendered voluntarily.

The Army Command ordered the removal of the 3rd Panzer Division [Breith] from the 2nd Army; it is to be rested in the rear.

Great difficulties in the railroad situation as before. Yesterday received a situation report from Weichs [2nd Army]; Paulus also characterizes things as untenable. I have made my transport officer dictator over the small military domain of railroads in the army group's area. That can only help a little. However he promises an improvement from the intensified regauging program and the hoped for abatement in the cold.

7/2/42

A stronger enemy attack was repulsed east of Slavyansk at the Bakhmut. Troitskoye was lost in heavy fighting west of Slavyansk, the adjoining fronts were held with difficulty. The attack by the Hube Group and the accompanying 100th Light Division gained five to six kilometers of ground to the north against superior enemy forces while fending off further counterattacks. The 60th Panzer Battalion is still fighting at Alexandropolye. XI Corps reported back and forth fighting on the front held by the Romanians. On the left wing a regimental group of the 113th Division closed ranks but has not yet advanced. For the first time Russian patrols were found wearing German uniforms. 6th Army repulsed further heavy attacks on either side of the southeast corner of its front. The Dostler Group still has not attacked! Once again I spoke with Paulus, who had just come back from the front, and told him that I would have to take other steps if he did not force the attack. I can't allow forces as strong as the Dostler Group to sit there uselessly while other sectors of the front are ablaze.

Intercepted radio communications indicate the possibility of major enemy preparations east of Belgorod; that is a sector of the front that has been seriously weakened in order to obtain forces with which to parry the attack at the breach. I have an uncanny feeling about the gap at the boundary between Army Group Kleist and the 6th Army; I instructed both to employ "strong mobile patrols" to keep an eye on it.

8/2/42

Especially restive day. The Russians staged unsuccessful attacks with tanks on both sides of the Bakhmut. Fresh armored attacks also broke down west of Slavyansk. The heavy fighting by the 100th Light Division and the Hube Group continues to go well, even though not much ground was gained fighting off the continuing enemy attacks. The Kohlermann Group [129th Corps Artillery] took Alexandropolye. Small-scale enemy attacks were repulsed by XI Corps. The Dostler Group has finally gone to the attack and progress has been quite good, especially by its right wing. Fresh enemy attacks around the southeast corner of the 6th Army collapsed.

"The Railroad Situation Remains Difficult"

9/2/42

Again today the enemy repeated his futile attacks. East and west of Slavyansk. Army Group Kleist's attack groups fought their way forward against stubborn resistance and persistent counterattacks. Small-scale attacks were repulsed on the army group's left wing.

The right wing of the 6th Army progressed very slowly, best of all was the Romanian ski unit! Quiet on the southeast corner of the army group; the enemy was forced back out of the bulge at Wolochow Jar.

I asked Paulus to deploy offensive patrols to clarify the situation east of Belgorod.

The railroad situation remains unbelievably difficult. We must move troops by rail to parry the penetration. These trains are lost for the movement of supplies, so that the necessary stockpiling for the muddy period is hardly possible.

The partisans are becoming bolder, in places they are turning up with artillery pieces.

10/2/42

Heavier enemy attacks east of Slavyansk; only minor attacks west of the city. With the rain and ice the Hube and Kohlermann attack groups gained only a little ground. The 6th Army's right wing – the 610th Security Regiment, which is inadequately equipped with heavy weapons – is stuck fast. Dostler [57th Infantry Division], too, made little progress. Quiet on the rest of the front. Suspicion of enemy massings northeast of Belgorod intensifying.

11/2/42

After consulting with Kleist I gave an order intended to drive XI Corps forward. A copy was sent with the same purpose to 6th Army, for the gap between the two can only be closed by moving forward.

Kortzfleisch, the Commanding General of XI Corps, expressed all sorts of misgivings about the attack in a conversation with my chief of staff

[Sodenstern]. I therefore telephoned him and told him that we all had to grapple with deficiencies, that I was aware of his weakness in artillery and the state of the 298th Division, but that I nevertheless had to call for the attack because the strategic situation demands it.

The enemy's attacks at the Bakhmut are growing weaker. The enemy was repulsed west of Slavyansk, where he continues to attack with powerful forces. Things going well on the 1st Panzer Army's attack front as well as for the 100th Light Division, the Hube Group and the Kohlermann Group. Alexandrovka was taken. The extreme right wing of the 6th Army is still stuck fast and is being attacked from the south. But aside from that the Dostler Group reported some progress, especially by the Romanian ski unit. A strong Russian tank attack led to a local penetration at the southeast corner of the 6th Army. On the rest of the front only reconnaissance probes by the enemy, one of which was carried out over the ice of the Sea of Azov against 1st Panzer Army.

Following its failure against the 2nd Army, the Russian 3rd Guards Cavalry Corps is apparently being transported to the site of the breach at Izyum. It is to early to say whether the long motorized column reported by a pilot to be nearing Barvenkovo from the east is the leading edge of this corps.

Intercepted orders suggest that the enemy probably does not intend to attack soon on the Kerch Peninsula. I passed a report from 2nd Army which describes its hopeless vehicle situation to the Army High Command, adding that conditions in the other armies are about the same and that this fact has to be taken into consideration in plans for the future.

Warmer weather.

12/2/42

The enemy continues to attack with strong forces west of Slavyansk; groupings were also spotted east of the city; stubborn resistance in front of the attack groups of the 1st Panzer Army. XI Corps, whose point of main effort is actually supposed to be on its north wing, attacked on its south wing and gained little advantage. The north wing was not yet capable of attacking as a result of tremendous difficulties in assembling the 113th Division. The enemy attacked the south flank of the 600th Security Regiment from the gap on the

6th Army's right wing, at first with weak forces. In three different conversations I drew Paulus' attention to the danger looming there and tried to get him to put even stronger pressure behind the attack by the Dostler Group, which again today got as good as nowhere. Isolated attacks were repulsed at the southeast corner of the 6th Army. A limited Russian attack against the extreme north wing of the 2nd Army also collapsed.

Today the intercept service identified the massings located around Izyum yesterday as elements of the guards cavalry corps and as the headquarters of the Russian 12th Army. I had Army Group Kleist move additional forces from its southern front and transfer them to the breach front. The army group had already contemplated withdrawing the 1st Mountain Infantry Division [Lanz] for this purpose.

The president of the State Railroad Administration in Poltava, Ganzenmüller, visited me. He placed the blame for the failure of the railroads on inadequate peacetime preparations, especially on the failure to acquire additional equipment in time.

13/2/42

This morning the 6th Army reported a strong enemy attack by the Red 21st Army on a front of about 50 km northeast of Belgorod! 2nd Army was immediately ordered to dispatch the reserves at Kursk – two weak battalions and two batteries – to the 6th Army at Oboyan. As well the army is to assemble the strongest possible reserves at Kursk.

On the rest of the army group's front only minor attacks, which were repulsed. On the 6th Army's right wing the enemy pushed the 610th Security Regiment back some distance and is now pressing from the south against the attack group.

In the evening the 6th Army reported that the attack northeast of Belgorod by six Russian divisions, some with tanks, had been beaten back; however, unrest at and behind the front led him to expect that it would be resumed.

Today aerial reconnaissance, which has been almost totally absent for some time, again achieved poor results; it reported enemy forces detraining southeast of Izyum.

Continued warm weather. The muddy period has apparently begun in the Crimea.

14/2/42

Halder discussed with Sodenstern – in a thoroughly positive way –an assessment of the situation submitted yesterday by us, which said that the danger of a Russian attack in the Crimea is not acute at the moment, that the main threat on the army group's eastern front is the bulge at Izyum, that the new attack by the 6th Army might be linked to it strategically, and that consequently the point of main effort, including that of the Luftwaffe, must lie on the army group's eastern front.

Army Group Kleist reported quiet apart from isolated counterattacks against the attack groups; in XI Corps' area remnants of the 298th Division took two villages from the Russians. The 6th Army's weak attack group again failed today to break the enemy resistance, the fighting went back and forth. Enemy attacks were repulsed north of Balakleya at the southeast tip of the 6th Army. At XXIX Corps' [Obstfelder] front northeast of Belgorod numerous uncoordinated attacks by the enemy broke down with heavy casualties.

5,000 Horses Starved

15/2/42

With temperatures once again dropping, the Russians attacked east of Slavyansk with strong forces and tanks and were repulsed. The attack groups of Army Group Kleist made further progress despite stubborn resistance and repeated counterattacks. XI Corp's attack also achieved local success. The extreme right wing of the 6th Army pushed slowly across the Orjol river line to the east; the attack group there again failed to make any progress. The emphasis of the enemy attack northeast of Belgorod today lay near Prokhorovka and south, which was also obviously a point of main effort for their air forces and artillery. The attacks were repulsed. Nevertheless I ordered another battalion transferred from 2nd Army to Oboyan.

17th Army reported that to date 5,000 of its horses have starved to death! This, too, is due to the failure of the railroads. The feed is there, but we don't receive it at the front.

A directive from the Army Command contains instructions on how to act during the muddy period. It holds nothing that was not in an order issued by the army group on the 9th. But it also regulates the planned sequence for resting the units and, without specifying an objective, speaks in broad terms of operations planned for spring.

A decree was finally issued allowing the limited assignment of land to Ukrainian farmers to begin. At least a beginning has been made.

The English in Singapore have surrendered!

16/2/42

Heavy Russian attacks were again repulsed east of Slavyansk, near Berestowaja and at the Bakhmut. Resistance has stiffened in front of the tireless attack groups of Army Group Kleist and expressed itself again today in heavy counterattacks. XI Corps continues to fight its way slowly forward. Minor attacks were repulsed on the right wing of the 6th Army. It is noticeably quiet in front of the army's southeast corner near Balakleya. The Russians also failed today to pull themselves together for concentrated attacks on the new attack front northeast of Belgorod; minor attacks collapsed in close-quarters fighting.

The Russian 3rd Guards Cavalry Corps located near Izyum on the 12th could not be found again. Its whereabouts are of great interest in assessing the enemy's intentions.

17/2/42

11th Army expecting enemy attacks again, in particular from Kerch. After his heavy losses of the previous day the enemy did not renew his attacks on Army Group Kleist's northeast front. Mackensen [III Panzer Corps] fought his way forward bravely again today. The progress made by XI Corps' 1st Romanian Division and the 113th Division was pleasing; Orelika Station was taken. Attack Group Dostler reported that the fighting surged back and forth and little progress was made. North of Balakleya an old breach in the front was cleaned up. Near Laski southeast of Oboyan the enemy attacked with heavy artillery support but only in regimental strength and was beaten off. Conspicuous is the intense aerial activity by the enemy in the area of Slavyansk and northeast of Belgorod. Different signs suggest that the Russian guards cavalry corps is in reserve in the area of Izyum.

The Hungarian liaison officer delivered a letter in which the Chief of the Hungarian General Staff once again "filed a protest" against any use at the front of the Hungarian security brigades which were moved forward into the Kharkov area. The effect of this is especially unpleasant, because German construction battalions, staffs, column personnel and the like, which are neither equipped nor trained for combat, have been employed in the front lines for some time.

"Victory or Defeat"

18/2/42

Quiet on Army Group Kleist's eastern front. An attack to clear the old breach east of Slavyansk is making progress. The enemy has launched heavy, concentrated counterattacks against Attack Group Mackensen; two villages were lost, but in the main the attacks were repulsed. Russian attacks against XI Corps also broke down; in bitter fighting the corps reached the rail line in several places at and east of Lozovaya. On the right wing of the 6th Army the Dostler attack group did not continue to attack. Heavy attacks by the Russians northeast of Belgorod led to limited penetrations but were otherwise repulsed. 2nd Army reported a successful attack of local significance.

The development on the right wing of the 6th Army unfortunately made it necessary to bring the 2nd Romanian Division, which is slowly arriving at Novo-Moskovsk, forward to the left wing of Army Group Kleist, for the hope of closing the gap through a concentric attack by XI Corps and the right wing of the 6th Army has to be abandoned for the time being. But at the present time we cannot endure gaps in the front, as the enemy has pulled several cavalry divisions out of the line in the bulge and thus has strong mobile reserves at his disposal.

The railroad situation continues to be so bad that any significant stockpiling for the muddy period is out of the question. I reported that to the Army High Command and added:

"If we do not succeed in fundamentally changing things, the outcome of the muddy period will decide victory or defeat."

19/2/42

The Minister of Railroads [Dorpmüller] visited me at midmorning. He hopes that there will be an improvement in the railroad situation in the spring...?

I briefed the *Führer* on the situation and told him that the enemy had pulled a cavalry corps out of the line; together with the guards cavalry corps still behind the front, this gives the enemy strong mobile reserves with which to sustain his attacks, whether at the Izyum bulge, against Kharkov, or at Oboyan.

A prisoner was taken from a formation of the guards cavalry corps near Oboyan yesterday. The army group, in contrast, has no reserves on the entire Kharkov front. The last regimental group of the 88th Division, which is planned for this role, has been delayed 24 hours by the miserable railroad situation. But holding the area around Kharkov is not just of decisive importance now, but for the spring as well. I therefore requested that consideration be given to the possibility of transferring the 3rd Panzer Division, which is now assembled near Kursk, to Kharkov and have it rest and refit there. The *Führer* promised to look into it.

Our own attack in the bulge east of Slavyansk ran into superior forces and has been halted. The Mackensen attack group [III Panzer Corps] and XI Corps repulsed enemy attacks; again today XI Corps made limited progress, but increased counter-pressure by the enemy on its north wing is becoming apparent. Enemy attacks collapsed on the 6th Army's right wing and at the old hot spot northeast of Belgorod. One of the incursions of yesterday was eliminated by counterattack. But 6th Army reported further enemy concentrations behind the attack front.

2nd Army repulsed local, small-scale attacks.

Toward evening Army Command advised that we might move elements of the 3rd Panzer Division behind the threatened sector of the front on the 6th

Army's left wing, but that they were to be returned to Kursk once the fighting is over. Orders were subsequently issued for a reinforced regimental unit of the 3rd Panzer Division to move into the area of Belgorod at the disposal of the army group.

20/2/42

Night aerial reconnaissance and prisoner statements revealed that the enemy is moving fresh forces behind his attack front northeast and also southeast of Belgorod. I ordered that all available units of the 3rd Panzer Division and the 88th Division are to be moved to the Belgorod-Oboyan area as reserves for the 2nd Army.

Army Group Kleist reported heavy fighting. The Russians launched small-scale attacks on either side of Slavyansk, but attacked the entire front of the Mackensen attack group and XI Corps with much superior forces, in some cases newly arrived units and tanks. They succeeded in breaking through the Hube Group [16th Panzer Division] in the direction of Alexandrov in two places and overran XI Corps' 1st Romanian Division with tanks and threw it back 10 to 12 km. On the 6th Army's extreme south wing a Russian attack scattered a balloon battery being used in the defense as infantry. The Dostler Group withstood heavy attacks northeast of Belgorod; a village was lost northeast of Belgorod, however. 2nd Army reported successful small-scale advances.

A telegram arrived from the Army Command concerning the railroad situation; they assured that everything possible was being done to improve the situation. The criticism which Halder made verbally to Sodenstern, that we are moving to many troops by train resulting in shortfalls in supply, is unjustified, for not a man was moved by train who wasn't desperately needed at the front.

"Regain the Initiative"

A memo was presented to the Army High Command about the expected situation in the spring and, at Halder's suggestion, a proposal for the conduct of operations. It discussed the tremendous difficulties involved in preparing for an attack given the present state of the railroads and the resulting probability that the enemy would steal a march on us with his attack. In any case I consider the gathering of strong reserves around Kharkov to be necessary if we are to regain the initiative.

Manstein [11th Army] sent a telegram concerning the threat posed to the Crimea and the inadequacy of his forces; Hoth [17th Army] complained about the insufficient number of trains; Paulus [6th Army] described the ineffectiveness of the scraped-together units which were sent to his right wing as a stopgap measure; these are all known to me, unfortunately constantly repeating them changes nothing.

21/2/42

Before noon I briefed the *Führer* and said:

"Yesterday's attack against the Mackensen Group was conducted with 6 divisions and 4 armored brigades and forced the group back into the area north of Alexandrovka. The enemy has attacked strongly there again today, and also, though on a narrower front, against the 13th Panzer Division and the Celere Division. Offensive preparations have been identified on either side of the projecting salient held by the 76th Division [Rodenburg] southeast of Slavyansk. At the urging of Army Group Kleist, I propose that we withdraw these divisions to a shorter line in order to spare them and conserve forces."

The *Führer* agreed. I continued:

"It is a calamity that the 1st Romanian Division has let itself be overrun by tanks; the result is a gap between it and the Mackensen Group. By tomorrow we will be able to assemble three, later five scraped-together battalions behind this gap. In 6th Army's sector there are growing indications of an attack between Volchansk and Laski, or east of Belgorod. A senior headquarters was identified there today; I cannot yet say whether this is the guards cavalry corps we have been looking for. As far as reserves, I can bring together two reinforced infantry regiments from the 3rd Panzer Division and the 88th Division behind this front."

In response to concern expressed by the *Führer* about the gap between the Mackensen Group and XI Corps, I could only reply by referring to the planned employment there of five "emergency" battalions, for the 1st Mountain Infantry Division is needed by the Mackensen Group and the 2nd Romanian Division has to go to the north wing of XI Corps to finally place something behind the gaping hole between it and the 6th Army. According to the evening reports the enemy has penetrated four kilometers against the 76th Division. Repeated heavy attacks were made against the Mackensen Group and were, except for one place east of Alexandrovka, beaten off. According to a report by the Commanding General of XI Corps, with whom I spoke personally, "don't count on the infantry of the 1st Romanian Division any longer; it is completely torn to shreds!" Tomorrow, after pulling together German reserves, Kortzfleisch wants to counterattack against the enemy forces, apparently still weak, which broke through to the south and west. Limited activity on the 6th Army's southern front. Isolated attacks by the enemy northeast of Belgorod were repulsed, in places in heavy fighting.

I asked Paulus to consider if and how the Dostler Group can be got moving again, in order to close the gap to XI Corps and prevent the enemy from inserting additional forces. The 2nd Army again received orders to assemble everything that it can scrape together in the way of reserves near Kursk.

22/2/42

Localized fighting in the Crimea. The 11th Army expects the attack there to come on the 23rd or 24th. On Army Group Kleist's northern front the enemy continues to attack the 76th Division with strong forces. Fighting was still going on as darkness fell. Very heavy attacks were again directed at the Mackensen Group; they were repulsed. On the south wing of XI Corps our own counterattack met with only limited success; the enemy also continues to attack. Our weak battalions assembled behind the gap between Samara and Ternovka are pushing slowly toward the north. The infantry of the 1st Romanian Division were rounded up again. Strong enemy attacks were repulsed near Lozovaya. In the 6th Army's sector the Russians staged minor assaults east of Kharkov and northeast of Belgorod; the fighting surged back and forth but the attacks were repulsed. In 2nd Army's sector, too, unsuccessful counterattacks by the enemy against a section of a position taken by us yesterday.

Though the Russian 2nd Cavalry Corps, which until a short time ago was still opposite the right wing of the 6th Army, has now been identified opposite the west wing of Army Group Kleist, the 6th Army does not think itself strong enough to advance its right wing to link up with Kleist's left wing.

The 8th [Light] Division [Hoehne] originally destined for the Crimea was transferred to Army Group North by the Army High Command. The Army Command is demanding that the 28th Light Division, whose leading motorized elements are already in Kharkov but the bulk of which is still en route far west of the Dniepr, be diverted to the Crimea in its place. Risky business at a moment when the enemy is on the offensive with far superior forces north and south of Kharkov. At the same time the Army Command arranged the transfer of the 19th Romanian Division and the 22nd Panzer Division [Apell] to the 11th Army and requested a report as to how we plan to make our attack in the Crimea. – Partisan troubles continue to make themselves felt in an uncomfortable way in the 2nd Army's rear area.

23/2/42

In the morning I learned that XI Corps has abandoned Lozovaya and Pamjutin and has withdrawn to the west. Otherwise "Red Army Day" passed much more quietly than anticipated. The attack expected by Manstein in the Crimea also failed to materialize.

Lively patrol activity by both sides on the ice of the Sea of Azov. Minor attacks were repulsed near Slavyansk. After his heavy losses of yesterday, the enemy facing the Mackensen Group did not attack again, but definitely against XI Corps, where fighting was still going on in the evening. Minor attacks against 6th Army's southern front, stronger attacks northeast of Belgorod, where a village was lost. 2nd Army's sector generally quiet.

I spoke with Paulus, told him that he must now drive forward with his right wing in order to finally close the gap to XI Corps. I had to reject as hopeless his suggestion of resuming the advance where he attacked before. The army received orders to regroup in such a way as to link up with XI Corps when it advances. I asked Kleist, who happily is already thinking offensively again, to commit XI Corps' attack so that it advances due east rather than southeast as he had planned, in order to prevent the gap to the 6th Army from opening again.

24/2/42

Minor attacks west of the Bakhmut (east of Slavyansk), in XI Corps' sector, northeast of Belgorod and also against 2nd Army were beaten off.

25/2/42

A quiet day with warmer weather. Weak, small-scale attack on the eastern front of the Crimea, against XI Corps and 2nd Army. Kleist believes that the Russians, who took tremendous casualties in their attacks, are exhausted. But he lacks the strength for an immediate riposte. Before they can attack, Mackensen [III Panzer Corps], XI Corps and the 6th Army must all regroup, which will take several days. Hopefully the muddy period will be that long in coming.

After much argument, proposals and counter-proposals, I assented to the majority of the trains carrying supplies until the middle of March, so as to ensure at least the most critical stocks of food for men and horses for the muddy period; replacement and troop transports must be put back until the second half of March; the railroads can't handle both at the same time.

.

26/2/42

Stronger local attacks in the Crimea, especially near Sevastopol, were repulsed. 11th Army reports massing of aircraft and tanks on the Kerch Peninsula. Warships fired on the coast without inflicting any damage. – In Army Group Kleist's sector the enemy attacked XI Corps and was repulsed. They believe the enemy has brought fresh forces into action there. 6th and 2nd Armies reported nothing of significance.

27/2/42

The anticipated attack in the Crimea broke out on both fronts. At Sevastopol it was repulsed apart from a local penetration. On the eastern front, however, the Romanian 1st Division was overrun; in the process two German artillery battalions and an anti-tank unit were lost. The attack was parried after 4 to 5 km; German reserves are on the way. As well as minor attacks on the eastern front, the enemy attacked Army Group Kleist at the Bakhmut, east of Slavyansk, with large numbers of tanks. After hard fighting the attack broke down. The suspected reinforcement opposite XI Corps was confirmed. The enemy attacked with several armored brigades there. One village was lost. With the limited steadfastness of the Romanians and the weakness of the German troops there, the situation is not without risk. 6th Army repulsed weak, 2nd Army stronger local attacks.

"A Swedish Newspaper Article"

A Swedish newspaper article on the situation on the Eastern Front says "the German Army accomplished everything humanly possible in Russia in 1941." It is less satisfied with the political front. It says that the Germans have done nothing to split apart the Russian internal front, nothing to rally the anti-bolshevik population of the occupied territories behind them, as a result of which Germany today faces a united national-Russian front under Stalin's command.

28/2/42

Yesterday's penetration at Sevastopol has been reduced. In the east on the isthmus the Romanian division was pushed back farther before the two German regiments approaching over muddy roads were able to counterattack; as a result the penetration became twelve kilometers deep and the defenders faced the threat of being separated from the water. The army has taken what measures it could to win through. The 28th (Light) Division is still far off, an acceleration of its approach is impossible. As well, the leading elements of the 22nd Panzer Division are not expected in the Crimea for five days. Heavy attacks on numerous sectors of Army Group Kleist's front; the enemy achieved a deep penetration due east of the Bakhmut. The Mackensen Group was attacked by 6 divisions; 2 villages were lost; otherwise the attack there collapsed. In the weakly-guarded gap between the Mackensen Group and XI Corps, or between Samara and Ternovka, enemy cavalry and tanks broke through at various places. They also made deep breakthroughs on the left, against XI Corps' right flank. 6th and 2nd Armies reported insignificant fighting. After the heavy attacks of today Army Group Kleist will not be able to carry out the joint attack by the Mackensen Group and XI Corps planned for tomorrow; it will have to limit itself to local counterattacks to clean up the worst penetrations. The right wing of the 6th Army is to attack as planned to reduce the gap between XI Corps and the 6th Army. Kleist wants to pull the 60th Motorized Division out of the line northeast of Taganrog and transfer it to the front which has been breached. I am very much in agreement.

1/3/42

In the Crimea the enemy continued his attacks on the eastern front only; a hill was lost. Massing of enemy artillery, of aircraft, tanks and reserves indicate further attacks. The 11th Army has dispatched its last reserves to the eastern front. Minor attacks were repulsed near Sevastopol. The bombardment by enemy warships of various points on the coast continues.

Heavy, confused fighting in Army Group Kleist's sector. The enemy penetration east of the Bakhmut has not yet been eliminated, the fighting there sways back and forth. The enemy also continues to attack with strong forces and tanks west of the Bakhmut, northwest of Slavyansk, on the left wing of the 17th Army, the Mackensen Group, especially between Samara and Ternovka, and on the right wing of XI Corps. In most cases where he has broken through he has pulled back again. On the whole the front is being held, even if only with difficulty.

An attack by two regiments on the right wing of the 6th Army gained some ground. In 2nd Army's sector small-scale attacks at the old hot spot, with one village lost.

The Army Command finally ordered that the 3rd Panzer Division is to refit not in Kursk, but in Kharkov. In my memo of 20th February I had said that the enemy could beat us to the punch in staging an offensive. Today I pointed out that remarks by their radio indicate that the enemy no longer has any doubts as to the location and objective of the German spring offensive, so that surprise is out of the question. It is also likely that he will continue his proven tactic, which is to deplete our forces before spring by attacking constantly and draw our gradually-arriving reserves into the fight immediately. It is to be assumed that he has the necessary forces to do so, for there are still strong reserves behind his front. There is much to suggest that he also has the means – in personnel and equipment – to raise new armies in the rear. I conclude that we will only be capable of far-reaching offensive operations against such a tactic if we succeed in making good the heavy loss of forces expected in the continued defense through the timely transfer of replacements and correspondingly stronger offensive units.

2/3/42

Today in the Crimea the enemy attacked on both fronts, he was repulsed. At Sevastopol the penetration of the 27th was cleared up. Quiet reigned on the eastern front of Army Group Kleist and of the 6th Army. Also no significant fighting in 2nd Army's sector. But the enemy attacked almost the entire northern front of Army Group Kleist with strong forces. One village was lost on 17th Army's left wing. The heaviest pressure lay between Mackensen and XI Corps, between Samara and Ternovka. The Russians tried to break through with heavy armored assaults; masses of cavalry were positioned behind the tanks in a narrow area and were caught by repeated attacks by the Luftwaffe. Russian forces which broke through yesterday were destroyed behind our front. The leading elements of the 60th Motorized Division are supposed to reach the threatened front at the Samara tomorrow. The last units of the Romanian 2nd Division, the leading elements of a *bersaglieri* (sniper) regiment and the last regiment of the 113th Division are also approaching the breached front slowly from the west. The situation there will remain very serious until they arrive.

A minor attack on the left wing of XI Corps was beaten off.

Our attack group on the right wing of the 6th Army continues to fight its way slowly across the Orjol river line to the east.

"Totally at Odds" with the "Foreign Armies" Department

3/3/42

Weak, small-scale attacks by the Russians at Sevastopol. On the northern front of Army Group Kleist the enemy pressure continues at the same places. Local penetrations on both sides of the Bakhmut and at the boundary between 17th Army and the Mackensen Group were for the most part eliminated by counterattacks. 17th Army requested permission to abandon two villages at this boundary. With Kleist's agreement I turned down the request. Between Samara and Ternovka the much fought-over village of Ossatschij was retaken with support from the Luftwaffe. Several villages were also taken by the attack group on the south wing of the 6th Army, a counterattack by two Russian regiments was repulsed. A Romanian ski unit deployed there retreated and was taken in by German reserves. Quiet on the 6th Army's eastern front. The Russians again attacked 2nd Army today at the old hot spot, west of Livny, with tank support and were beaten off. Detraining reported around Yelets and Livny.

The Americans are making a lot of noise to the effect that the war now has to be taken to the enemy!

4/3/42

Quiet in the Crimea. Local attacks up to division strength against the northern front of Army Group Kleist were repulsed on both sides of the Bakhmut west of Slavyansk and on the right wing of the Mackensen Group. XI Corps took several villages. The attack group on the right wing of 6th Army was attacked and forced back in places. The "Foreign Armies" Department of the Army High Command said in its situation report of 2nd March that the attacks south of Izyum and in the Crimea "do not constitute a large-scale offensive with unified objectives and a centralized command" but are only "minor actions"! Twenty infantry divisions, 5 rifle brigades, 10 cavalry divisions, 10 armored brigades, followed by 4 cavalry divisions with 2 armored brigades, have been attacking south of Izyum on a total frontal width of 120 km, concentrated in points of main effort, for weeks! Since 9 divisions with cavalry and tanks attacked simultaneously on the Kerch Peninsula and on the opposite side strong forces from Sevastopol, both supported by the fleet, I don't know where a centralized command is lacking there! The Army Command was informed that the assessment by the "Foreign Armies" Department is totally at odds with my own.

In the intervening report the Army Command was informed that the constant Russian attacks in the bulge had resulted in such a rate of attrition among our troops that the planned offensive solution of the break-in before the muddy period is no longer possible with the forces available.

5/3/42

No significant fighting in the Crimea. Enemy submarines probed the south coast. – Enemy assaults against Army Group Kleist limited to both sides of the Bakhmut and were repulsed; our line moved forward insignificantly between Samara and Ternovka; XI Corps repulsed small-scale attacks. On the right wing of the 6th Army a village lost yesterday was retaken. Advances by the Russians there were repulsed. Enemy pressure noticeable from the south from the gap to XI Corps. The rest of the army group's front quiet. The movements spotted in front of the 2nd Army's north wing near Yelets and Livny continue. – A "native" cossack squadron has distinguished itself in the fighting against the partisans in the 2nd Army's rear area. Sodenstern informed Heusinger by phone that local "experts" are saying that the abnormal weather might be a harbinger of a short muddy period which would have little effect on Russian operations. He asked whether it was advisable that I tell the *Führer* about it. Heusinger answered that a talk between the *Führer* and me was always welcome. Immediately afterward Halder called Sodenstern and said that the *Führer* had read my assessment of 1st March. He also received the memo of 20th February.

But he now has so little time to examine far-reaching operations that he couldn't have looked them over!

For this reason it is questionable whether my call concerning the matter discussed with Heusinger achieved its purpose at the moment. The Army Command has nothing at all to go on as far as formation of strategic reserves in the Russian hinterland is concerned. I put them at about 25 divisions in the

Caucasus; but otherwise they have received no intelligence whatever from abroad of new formations. Rather it is said that there is visible disorganization in many areas in the Russian hinterland. Halder declared the wording of the "Foreign Armies" Department situation report which I complained about yesterday to be "unfortunate" – which ended the matter.

A liaison officer in the service of Rosenberg, the Minister for Occupied Territories, reported to me and asked what wishes of a political nature the military command had in regard to the Ukraine. I said to him:

"I have an interest in seeing to it that the civilian population in the army's rear is quiet. Even now I don't think achieving this will be easy. However we must give the population clear objectives and keep our promises. I welcome the allocation of land begun in conjunction with the agrarian reform and I will see to it that this promise is kept quickly and without ulterior motives in my area of command." When the liaison officer touched upon the religious question I declared that "the same rules must apply here. If we promise the population religious freedom, then this promise too has to be kept. Politicized clergymen will obviously have to be removed; but we should leave the rest alone. In this way the population will be quiet and cooperative. We might even succeed in making them 'accomplices against the bolshevik system and interest them in seeing to it that the Russians don't return. But wherever the population opposes us we must take drastic measures."

The liaison officer said "that these are also Rosenberg's thoughts."

Next he wanted to hear about a disagreement between the military commands and the Reich Commissar for the Ukraine, *Gauleiter* Koch. I couldn't do him this favor because the army group has no point of contact with Koch.

6/3/42

Strong enemy attacks collapsed in front of Sevastopol. Weaker advances were repulsed on the northern and eastern fronts of Army Group Kleist and on the right wing of the 6th Army. In the Crimea rain. On the rest of the army group's front frost and snow, making the prediction of a short muddy period probably somewhat premature.

7/3/42

Increasing cold and snow showers in the Crimea as well. 11th Army and Army Group Kleist both reported limited combat activity as a result. With better weather the enemy made local attacks against the 6th Army at numerous places. On the right wing a regiment was driven back 3 kilometers and at the north end of the Izyum bulge the enemy broke through to such a depth between the strongpoints that Glazunovka was entirely and Shebelinka largely cut off. The 2nd Army repulsed minor attacks. In the evening Paulus requested permission to abandon Glazunovka; the town was occupied by a regimental headquarters and two battalions which were supposedly almost out of ammunition. He asked for the release of the elements of the 3rd Panzer Division located near Kharkov and the units of the 299th Division [Moser] destined for the 2nd Army. I did not believe that Glazunovka had expended all its ammunition in one day of attack; I therefore turned down his request. I requested of the Army Command the release of the Kharkov elements of the 3rd Panzer Division with the division's veteran commander *Generalmajor* Breith as leader. The order for the departure of units to the 2nd Army remains in force.

8/3/42

Nothing of significance in the Crimea. 11th Army expects further attacks. On the right wing of the 1st Panzer Army, several enemy divisions attacked XIV Panzer Corps [Motorized Army Corps, Wietersheim; renamed XIV Panzer Corps on 21st June] on a narrow front at the spot where the 60th Motorized Infantry Division was removed a few days ago; the attack was repulsed. Heavy attacks against the left wing of the 17th Army also broke down. The enemy continued his attacks against the 6th Army on the northern front of the Izyum bulge. Glazunovka held, Shebelinka was overrun. Our forces just succeeded in heading off the enemy driving toward the Donets short of the river. The Russians also attacked northeast of Kharkov. While on the 6th Army's southern front he formed his point of main effort by concentrating front-line divisions, here he again deployed two divisions which had been held in reserve for a short time. In addition to several minor penetrations, in this way he succeeded in breaking through 12 km to the Volchansk-Kharkov road and encircled two strongpoints on this road. Minor attacks were repulsed at many other places on the army group's front.

As my request of yesterday for the release of the Beaulieu Regiment [394th Regiment] of the 3rd Panzer Division had not been answered, I telephoned the *Führer*, described the situation to him and got from him a decision that in an emergency I was justified in using the regiment and the motorcycle battalion of the 3rd Panzer Division. In the morning I placed all the reserves behind its front at the disposal of the 6th Army. Paulus called in the evening and once again requested the Beaulieu Regiment, in order to retake Shebelinka with its help. Nevertheless I did not give it to him, because I cannot predict how the situation northeast of Kharkov is going to develop. But late in the evening, when the army reported that pressure by the enemy from the south toward the Donets was becoming dangerous and that the bridgehead south of Borisoglebsk was being held only with difficulty, I gave the Beaulieu Regiment orders to set out for Borisoglebsk in the morning. The motorcycle battalion is being sent to the 6th Army to bolster the defense west of Volchansk.

The penetrations against the 6th Army are not surprising. Its divisions are holding sectors of front 20 to 30 kilometers wide. Wherever the enemy concentrates its forces against them, he simply walks through. The most important thing then is to head him off before he achieves a penetration of greater significance.

9/3/42

In the morning Paulus reported that on his southern front the enemy had crossed the Donets and reached Liman with infantry. Glazunovka has fallen. At the Volchansk penetration our strongpoints are still holding at the road, the enemy is in the forest to the south of it. All the reserves the army could raise have been dispatched to the penetration points, with the emphasis on the south wing. I put the Headquarters of the 3rd Panzer Division and the Beaulieu Regiment at the disposal of the army and demanded that command be placed in one hand at the southern penetration point. Further, the army received orders to barricade the Donets river line in the rear between Smijew and Chuguyev and the road leading to Kharkov from the east with scraped-together security forces as well as anti-tank and anti-aircraft guns and see that the local defense of Kharkov is assured.

It is to be assumed that the enemy will continue to sustain the attacks against the 6th Army. The enemy still has two divisions and the 3rd Guards Cavalry Corps behind the front there. Radio traffic by the 6th Guards Cavalry Corps opposite Army Group Kleist's left wing was overheard; it suggests it is to be transferred – perhaps to the 6th Army's southern front. Night reconnaissance has found movements from the east in the general direction of Kharkov.

I briefed the *Führer* on the situation and the latest measures; he agreed. In the Crimea the Russians have become more active. Kleist reports that they attacked again at the site of yesterday's attack. In the south, in XIV Panzer Corps' sector, they were repulsed; on the left wing of the 17th Army they entered two villages, but for the most part their attacks collapsed there too. Toward evening it was learned that the enemy, contrary to 6th Army's report, had not yet reached Liman; apparently only weak forces have so far crossed the Donets. All day long the Russians tried in vain to overrun our strongpoints still holding on south of the Donets. At the Volchansk penetration a counterattack succeeded in restoring contact with the surrounded Starytsa strongpoint. Pressure from the enemy in the forests against the road has increased. 2nd Army reported quiet. A regiment of the 2nd Army near Kursk was made army group reserve in order to transfer it to the 6th Army as soon as transport space is available.

Big Spring Operation?

10/3/42

The expected attack in the Crimea has not begun yet. Today the enemy attacked Army Group Kleist again at the old places. While he was repulsed by XIV Panzer Corps, he did succeed in capturing three strongpoints from the 17th Army, including the much fought over Tscherkeskaja. The army group moved its reserve, the 60th Motorized Division nearer to the left wing of the 17th Army. On the 6th Army's southern front, the Beaulieu Regiment [394th] advanced through Diman and threw the enemy back across the Donets. Russian attacks against strongpoints south of the river were beaten back. West of

Kharkov the enemy has infiltrated stronger forces into the wooded country north of Petschenesch. On the road to Volchansk a second surrounded strongpoint was relieved and a village lost yesterday was retaken. But the enemy in the wooded terrain south of the road has grown stronger and attacked the north wing of the 294th Division [Gabke] situated there from the north. One strongpoint was lost. By stretching to the utmost, 6th Army can move another three battalions to the breach point, of which two will arrive tomorrow. Beginning tomorrow, the 429th Infantry Regiment from Kursk will be moved by truck and railroad from Belgorod to Kharkov as army group reserve. As soon as it can be spared at Liman, the Beaulieu Regiment will be moved back to Kharkov as well. 2nd Army reported all quiet.

Railroad movements from the Caucasus in the direction of Rostov and via Voronezh to Valuyki show that the enemy is bringing in fresh reserves; spy reports also suggest a continuation of the attacks. Movements from the east toward Kursk are thought to be feints; 2nd Army attributes only local significance to the detrainings spotted in Yelets and Livny.

An assessment of the situation was presented to the Army High Command; it culminated by stating that the Izyum bulge must be eliminated by offensive means immediately after muddy period. Our forces are insufficient to defend the tightly-stretched front of the bulge. I therefore requested the transfer of two fresh divisions to the 17th Army by the middle of April, two to the 6th Army, and the provision of forces with which to relieve the 9th Panzer Division in the 2nd Army's front. In this case no new forces whatsoever have been deployed to defend against the attack in the Kharkov area expected immediately after the muddy period. My original intent, to carry out the elimination of the Izyum bulge in conjunction with the big operation planned for the spring, has been rendered invalid, because it was not possible to reduce the pocket before the muddy period to the point where it posed no acute threat. But it now looks as if the enemy will not give us the time that is necessary to prepare for a major operation in peace.

11/3/42

Minor attacks were beaten back in front of Sevastopol. The same in XIV Panzer Corps' sector and on the left wing of the 17th Army. On the 6th Army's right wing a village was lost to a small-scale Russian attack. On the army's southern front the enemy severed the sole link with the strongpoints still holding south of the Donets. Not until dusk was it restored by the Beaulieu Regiment, again on the offensive. The infiltration of the forest north of Petschenesch by the Russians is assuming menacing proportions; weak screening forces at the Babka have so far been able to fend off the enemy advancing through the forest. The enemy continues to press ahead in the Volchansk bulge. The planned counterattack by three battalions made no headway, but the penetration was stemmed for the time being.

There are four obvious pressure points:

The one in XIV Panzer Corps' sector is no cause for concern at the present time.

The one on the left wing of the 17th Army must be considered serious, because all that is facing the enemy's very strong point of main effort there is the 97th Light Division, which has been in heavy action for weeks and whose fighting strength has dropped alarmingly. Kleist will bring relief in that tomorrow the 60th Motorized Division, bolstered by tanks from all of the Mackensen Group, will advance north from the left wing of the 17th Army to smash the enemy's assembly areas in front of the 97th Light Division and so bring peace for a while. Unfortunately, as a result the attack between Samara and Ternovka planned by the army becomes invalid.

The third pressure point lies on the 6th Army's southern front. As well the loss of Shebelinka has created an uncomfortable "thin" spot at the bend of the Donets between (Lower) Bishkin and (Upper) Bishkin. I gave my consent to withdrawing a Hungarian hussar squadron from one of the security brigades and employing it there.

The fourth, at present most sensitive spot, lies in the bulge at Volchansk and in the forests to its south. The 429th Regiment and elements of the 3rd Panzer Division of the 2nd Army begin arriving in Kharkov tonight and are intended for use against the bulge.

Toward evening I verbally briefed the *Führer* on the situation and my plans. I advised him that the leader of the Hungarian 108th Security Brigade, Major-General Abt, had reported that he is ashamed that he and his brigade are sitting behind the front while German construction battalions and transport column personnel are in the heaviest fighting at the front; he has asked that his unit be sent into action. Abt was directed to report this to the Honvéd Ministry [Honvéd – "Home Defense"; the Hungarian National Army organized by Kossuth in 1848 to defend Hungary against Austrian intervention troops; later designation for the entire Hungarian Army]. Given the menacing situation, I asked the *Führer* to do what he could from his end to bring about the release of the brigade. When the *Führer* objected that the brigade had no anti-tank weapons, I made a commitment to provide them and thus assumed responsibility for their deployment. – I released the brigade to the 6th Army.

Army High Command announced the arrival of one panzer and three infantry divisions by rail at Kharkov and Stalino beginning on 23rd March.

12/3/42

In the Crimea uncoordinated advances by the enemy. No attacks in Army Group Kleist's sector. Reinforced by tanks, the 60th Motorized Division went to the attack and advanced as far as the hills south of Schawrowo. The attack is to continue tomorrow until Schawrowo is taken. On the 6th Army's southern front, yesterday's attack by the Beaulieu Regiment hit the enemy so severely that he launched no serious attacks today. North of Petschenesch the Russians pushed toward the Babka River line; southwest of Volchansk, too, they moved up to the Babka after taking Star Saltow; to the north they pushed forward out of the forests to the west and southwest; our strongpoints on the Kharkov-Volchansk road are still holding.

Conversations with the 6th Army revealed that it is toying with the idea of withdrawing the 44th Division [Siebert]. It is clear that a breakthrough near Chuguyev by the enemy would put this division in a difficult position. But I could not authorize the tempting withdrawal behind the Donets, because it would mean the loss of an important springboard for later attacks, because a considerable part of the artillery would have to be left behind, and because there is concern that the Russians might pursue immediately and arrive at the Donets at the same time as the 44th Division. I therefore had to take it upon myself to leave the 44th Division up front. I instructed the 6th Army "that not a single foot of ground is to be surrendered unless absolutely necessary. The defense of Kharkov rests upon the fighting front east of the city and not until the very last at the outskirts of the city itself. All soldiers in Kharkov capable of fighting are to be sent to the front. Security forces are to be placed in Smijew and Chuguyev. I agree with the plan to counterattack with the units of the 3rd Panzer Division under the command of *General* Breith and two to three battalions. It is to be deployed so that it leads to the destruction of the enemy."

The 6th Army moved the Hungarian 108th Security Brigade [Battalion] forward in the direction of Smijew.

Apart from the movement of replacement transports to the 17th Army, which finally began today, also beginning today 7 to 8 replacement battalions are being transported to the 6th Army.

13/3/42

In the morning I discussed the subsequent conduct of battle with Paulus: it is important that we keep our nerve until *General* Breith's counterattack can be carried out with sufficient forces. XVII Corps [Hollidt] must hold on the south wing of the breach; as well the corps has to move the strongest possible reserves behind this wing. On the north wing it is important that our strongpoints on the Volchansk-Kharkov road continue to hold. The breach front must essentially be held by the units that are deployed there; I don't see much point in throwing lone fresh battalions into this front. Paulus stated that all this fully corresponds to his intentions.

Two hours later 6th Army reported that enemy tanks had broken through at the road from Star Saltow to the west and that a frontal action against this foe by the Beaulieu Regiment had thus become necessary, "because there is nothing left between the enemy and Kharkov!"

I called Paulus and expressed misgivings about deviating from the decision, which had just been recognized to be correct, to stage a concentrated counterattack by the Breith group from the northwest, just because a few tanks were driving in the direction of Kharkov. It would be different if the tanks were being closely followed by large masses of infantry, making it a serious breakthrough. Paulus stated that that was the case! The forces at the Babka had been overrun, the division commander was gathering a handful of stragglers at Nepokrytaja in order to hold it. I answered:

"If you are convinced of the accuracy of this report and that there is no other way of stopping the drive, I can't talk you out of it. You just have to be clear that such a use of the Beaulieu Regiment is highly undesirable, for with it the cohesive offensive use of the Breith Group is smashed.

You must at least try to pull the regiment out again after a brief blow."

Reports which arrived by seven in the evening said that the enemy had not seriously attacked the Kharkov front north of Petschenesch. Nepokrytaja is still in German hands! Our weak lines are also still holding southwest of Andrenka. – Air reconnaissance reported the movement of strong enemy motorized forces through Volchansk to the breach point.

In the Crimea the enemy attacked on the eastern front with about 100 tanks and was rewarded with only an insignificant local success on the extreme north wing. Army Group Kleist has spotted enemy forces massing west of Slavyansk; isolated advances were beaten back. The attack by the 60th Motorized Division was called off in the face of strong countermeasures; the division is to be pulled out of the line again. On the 6th Army's southern front, enemy attacks were repulsed near (Upper) Bishkin.

Between the two conversations with Paulus I briefed the *Führer* on the situation. At the urgent request of Army Group Kleist, I tried to have the order for the withdrawal of the parachute regiment from the 1st Panzer Army put off. But the *Führer* needs the regiment for other purposes, which was predictable. Regarding the events at Kharkov, he stressed that it is important for later tasks that we hold onto the 44th Division's position forward of the Donets. That has already been ordered.

14/3/42

The enemy continues to attack on the eastern front in the Crimea. He succeeded in taking one village; otherwise he was repulsed. In Army Group Kleist's sector a major (500 to 600 men) assault across the ice of the Sea of Azov on a 30-km-wide front was beaten off at the mouth of the Mius. Soon afterward an attack by two divisions with tanks began against XIV Panzer Corps, which also collapsed. Heavy local attacks on the left wing of the 17th Army and the right wing of the Mackensen Group. In spite of this the 60th Motorized Division was successfully withdrawn. 6th Army reported that renewed attacks on (Upper) Bishkin were beaten off. To the north, at the "thin spot," enemy cavalry entered the forest and skirmished with the Hungarian hussar squadron. On the army's southern front the enemy launched repeated attacks and took another strongpoint. This in itself unimportant loss will unfortunately entail abandoning further strongpoints south of the Donets. North of Petschenesch the enemy attacked two strongpoints at the Babka in vain. Subsequent to this, in XVII Corps' sector, the Russians advanced across the Babka but were thrown back again; a Russian sleigh battalion is gadding about behind our front there. The strongpoints on the Volchansk road were held against repeated attacks. To the south as well the enemy's advance appears to have been stopped for the time being by the Beaulieu Regiment's counterattack and the intervention there of all the air force's at the army group's disposal. Return to icy cold on the entire front.

The Romanian 19th and 20th Divisions are being sent to the army group and will arrive in Odessa between 17th March and 4th April.

15/3/42

In the Crimea the enemy attacked on the eastern front, but only in strong but uncoordinated assaults; one hill was lost. Losses and the strain of combat are beginning to show on the divisions there. At Sevastopol strong attacks were beaten off. Kleist reported fresh preparations by the enemy opposite XIV Panzer Corps. The enemy is also preparing new attacks on the left wing of the 17th Army and on the right wing of the Mackensen Group; weak isolated attacks were beaten back. In 6th Army's sector the Russians are apparently moving additional cavalry into the wooded country north of (Upper) Bishkin. The Hungarian security brigade is approaching slowly to counter this, hindered by cold weather and heavy drifting. The enemy several times attacked Bishkin itself, but to no avail. Unfortunately the last strongpoint south of the Donets, Melowaja, was lost, apparently for lack of supplies. Enemy assaults southeast of Petschenesch were repulsed. At the breach southwest of Volchansk the enemy crossed the Babka in the south sector and attacked our strongpoints at the river and to the west of it. In the north of the breach our strongpoints continued to hold. The attack by the Beaulieu Regiment has gained ground in the direction of Andrenka. Except for a battalion and a handful of freshly-manned tanks from Kharkov, the army has committed all its reserves.

Two battalions en route from 2nd Army by train will not arrive until 17th March. The army will be in a difficult situation if the enemy advances in the direction of Kharkov tomorrow, which is entirely possible given the gaps that exist. Its idea to turn the Beaulieu Regiment around after Andrenka is taken and then having it attack south will not be feasible before the 17th or 18th March, if at all. – Paulus came in the evening; his briefing on the situation contained nothing new.

Concerning the Personnel Makeup of the 6th Army

16/3/42

I called Halder and said that "in this context" the command of the 6th Army was not equal to the difficult situation in the long run. It is difficult to advise and help the army because it tends to see the worst in everything and underestimate its own forces. It comes up with a "but" for every proposal; in short, it lacks "the holy fire." Add to this that I have repeatedly had to instruct the army to be more precise in its reports. Paulus is a good man, but if he stays the Chief of Staff will have to change. Halder replied that Heim was probably somewhat "eccentric"; Heim's reports also struck him in such a way as to give the impression that they were written for a purpose. – I ended by asking that he give consideration to a change in the position of Chief of Staff of the 6th Army; I will make the ultimate request as soon as things prove to be no longer bearable.

A rather weak landing attempt by the enemy between the Crimea and the mouth of the Dniepr supported by warships failed. Minor attacks at Sevastopol. On the eastern front in the Crimea heavy attacks again collapsed. Army Group Kleist reported local attacks beaten back by XIV Panzer Corps [Motorized Army Corps]; enemy continues to mass forces there. The enemy also pursuing attack preparations at the boundary between the 17th Army and the Mackensen Group. In 6th Army's sector attacks were again repulsed at Bishkin! In the wooded country to the north of it, Hungarians and German reserves sent there have skirmished with weak enemy forces. Numerous heavy attacks were repulsed at the breach east of Kharkov, often through counterattacks;

today the six attacking divisions there were joined by the motorized rifle brigade of the 3rd Guards Cavalry Corps.

The last reinforced regiment of the 11th Division [Thomaschki] is nearing Dnepropetrovsk from the west. I have issued orders for the regiment to be sent to Krasnograd by truck and readied there at my disposal. It will stand by there, ready to be committed at Kharkov or at the dangerously-thin boundary between Army Group Kleist and the 6th Army in case the enemy begins to bore through there. But secretly I hope that I won't need the regiment now, in order to be able to ready the entire 113th Division [Zickwolff] for other use later.

28th Light [Sinnhuber] and 22nd Panzer [Apell] are arriving slowly in the Crimea. Hopefully, in spite of the great losses suffered by the hard-fighting front, I will be able to keep the divisions out until we can go to the attack.

Eastern Front: "...Become Thin"

The commander of one of the divisions on the quiet eastern front of the 17th Army, a man known to me as considerate and reasonable, described the overstrain affecting his unit. The division, which has seen heavy fighting and which has so far received replacements for only the smallest part of its losses, has had to give up forces to the army's threatened western front. As a result the eastern front has become so thin that relief or rest has been out of the question for weeks. The overstrain has led to total apathy among the men, added to that the high officer casualties, so that any attack by the enemy must be cause for concern. Training is out of the question under these conditions. – And the situation is even more serious at the fronts engaged in combat.

17/3/42

Local attacks only at Sevastopol. In the afternoon an attack by strong Russian forces collapsed in front of 11th Army's eastern front. Heavy localized fighting at the boundary between the 17th Army and the Mackensen Group without significant results for one side or the other. The 6th Army repulsed fresh attacks at (Upper) Bishkin. Again today localized attacks only at the breach east of Kharkov, which were beaten back.

18/3/42

On the eastern front in the Crimea and in Kleist's sector localized attacks only at the old hot spots. An advance carried out by five Russian battalions between Samara and Ternovka was also beaten back. Fighting developed in the wooded country northwest of (Upper) Bishkin, with the objective of driving out the enemy forces that had infiltrated there. Localized attacks were repulsed at the Volchansk breach. An attack restored contact with the cut-off strongpoint at Bol Babka. A new Russian division was identified in action southwest of Volchansk. The enemy has thus now committed seven and a half divisions in the approximately 30-km-wide breach.

19/3/42

At midmorning I briefed the *Führer* on a limited attack planned for tomorrow by Manstein in the Crimea, in which he intends to use –in addition to the static divisions – the 22nd Panzer and weak elements of the 28th Light Division. Further I advised him that I expected the attack east of Kharkov, including by the armored group, to continue if it remained generally quiet today. I said that an attack at the southwest corner of the Izyum bulge reported today was scarcely anything to take to heart.

Attacks with strong armor and artillery support broke down in front of the eastern front in the Crimea. Kleist reported further attacks at the boundary between the 17th Army and the Mackensen Group. An attack by enemy tanks between Samara and Ternovka was repulsed. In the 6th Army's sector the Hungarians saw combat in the wooded country northwest of [Upper] Bishkin, where the enemy has grown stronger. Southwest of Volchansk the enemy showed little desire to attack today; isolated attacks broke down. The 2nd Army repelled scouting raids, inflicting heavy losses on the enemy.

Heim, Chief of Staff of the 6th Army, expressed his intention to assemble as strong as possible an attack force near Ternovaya to take Rubezhnoye and the Donets bridge there and thus sever the lifeline to the Russians in the breach.

The attack can take place on the 24th at the earliest; hopefully the Russians will give us that much time. I have placed the elements of the battalions of the 530th Infantry Regiment, which will not be arriving until tomorrow on account of the snowdrifts, at the disposal of the 6th Army for the attack. Headquarters, VIII Corps [Heitz], which has arrived at Poltava, was also subordinated to the army for use on its right wing.

20/3/42

After limited initial success, the attack by the 11th Army on the Crimean eastern front encountered superior enemy forces and ground to a halt. Bad weather made air support impossible. In Army Group Kleist's sector the enemy launched numerous local attacks between the Bakhmut and the right wing of the Mackensen Group. Two battalions which broke through to Slavyansk from the northwest were destroyed; the remaining attacks were beaten off. A counterattack smashed a later, stronger assault between Samara and Ternovka. In 6th Army's sector our own attack in the wooded country north of [Upper] Bishkin still has not been a striking success. Russian tank attacks collapsed on 6th Army's southern front. In the bulge at Volchansk heavy fighting at Bol Babka and Pechanaya, which was lost temporarily, but ultimately remained in German hands. At Nepokrytaja, too, the enemy was beaten back. Insignificant scouting raids against 2nd Army's front.

Lessons From the Fighting in the Crimea

21/3/42

After receiving the first reports from the 11th Army I called the *Führer* and reported: the attack in the Crimea had failed, on the one hand because the unexpected onset of bad weather, which did not start until preparations were under way, made operations by the Luftwaffe impossible. According to the army, by then it was too late to cancel. The lesson that must be drawn for the Crimea, with its unpredictable weather, is that a way has to be found to stop the attacks even at the last minute. The *Führer* interrupted me and said that if orders could be given to call off an attack already under way (– which in fact was not the case –), it could also have been called off sooner. The universally valid lesson was that we must not attack without strong air support. I replied that every last one of the air fleet's machines had been readied for this attack, and went on: the second reason for the failure lay in the fact that the attack ran into strong enemy forces massing for an attack. This is confirmed by the fact that after the German attack was beaten off the enemy himself went over to the attack with strong forces and heavy tanks. The army sees as the final reason for the failure the still inadequate unit training of the new panzer division. At the moment I cannot yet say what conclusions must be drawn from yesterday's events for the attack to clear the entire Crimea. But I have to point out one: Manstein is of the opinion that the air forces in the Crimea and over the Black Sea must be strengthened. I am asking that no order be issued tying down Air Fleet 4 for the duration, for I must retain the ability to commit the main weight of the Luftwaffe at the focus of the ground fighting; otherwise we cannot see these battles through. The *Führer* agreed. – Fortunately the division's losses were less than first feared: 12 tanks are total writeoffs, 60 have to be repaired. The division had to leave 38 tanks behind en route to the Crimea, hopefully they will arrive soon; thus the division will probably be at full combat readiness again in the near future. I cannot yet estimate the personnel losses. – The rest of the army group's front has been quiet so far today. The enemy has continued to get stronger at the old hot spots. He has inserted two new divisions opposite the 17th Army [Hoth], one from his reserve, one from the eastern front, and probably positioned a further cavalry division behind them. He has also grown stronger southwest of Volchansk by committing a new tank brigade. Further concentrations have been discovered between Samara and Ternovka, so that a resumption of the attacks is expected on all three sectors of the front.

On the eastern front in the Crimea local attacks collapsed. In Army Group Kleist's sector, as yesterday, heavy but uncoordinated attacks around Slavyansk as far as the right wing of the Mackensen Group, which, after deep breakthroughs by tanks in places, were all beaten back. In the 6th Army's sector the Russians launched futile attacks against [Upper] Bishkin and the bridgehead south of Novo-Borisoglebsk. At the breach at Volchansk he succeeded in entering Pechanaya.

22/3/42

In the Crimea only weak localized advances by the enemy. Army Group Kleist reported repeated futile attacks at the same old places. The enemy wants to knock down the corner post of Slavyansk, perhaps to also take possession of the railroad leading into the Izyum pocket before the muddy period. Enemy attacks were repulsed between Samara and Ternovka, in 6th Army's area the Russians were pushed slowly toward the Donets in the wooded country north of [Upper] Bishkin; south of the Donets the strongpoint at Kopanskoje was lost; in the breach southwest of Volchansk heavy fighting for our strongpoints, which in the main proceeded favorably. The 294th Division's commander and 1st General Staff Officer [Plock] were killed by an aerial bomb.

A statement on the possibilities of clearing the Izyum penetration was presented to the Army High Command: since an attack before the muddy period is impossible, it will have to be staged immediately afterward, otherwise the Russians will beat us to it. I reject the idea of staging the attack from the north on the east bank of the Donets, which is in itself correct, because the forces needed for the attack proper and to screen its left flank cannot be brought together in time. All that is left is to make the attack from the northwest and south on the west bank, following the flooding Donets. Even then it will be no simple matter to muster the attack forces, because at present the enemy's daily attacks on the bulge's southern front make any shifting of troops impossible. We are so thin on the northern front that movements are out of the question. The difficulties involved in resting and refitting the units under these conditions are clear. As far as I can tell today, the following can probably be raised for the attack: in the south – one panzer division, one motorized division and three infantry divisions; in the north – two panzer divisions and one infantry division, dangerously few!

There is scarcely any doubt that the Russians will return to the attack east of Slavyansk and east of Kharkov very soon after the muddy period, at the latest as soon as our attack in the bulge begins. These fronts must therefore be made as strong as possible so that they will hold.

A telex was sent to the Army High Command, in which I once again listed the reasons why Headquarters, 11th Army had chosen not to postpone the attack of the 20th in spite of bad weather. Learning something from this debacle seems more important to me than looking for someone to blame. In fact it now turns out that the attack did not fail on account of the absence of air support, but because the terrain had not been scouted well enough, because the newly-formed panzer division was insufficiently trained and because it still lacked inner stability. I telegraphed the army's commander-in-chief and asked him forcefully to take special care in the education and training of the replacements and the newly-arriving divisions.

23/3/42

In the Crimea scouting raids on the eastern front. In Kleist's sector heavy attacks concentrated west of Slavyansk, which for the most part were beaten back. The army expects especially heavy attacks tomorrow. The Russians succeeded in taking a village from the Romanians between Samara and Ternovka. A trouble spot at the boundary with 6th Army was eliminated by a brief advance by the left wing of XI Corps and the extreme right wing of the 6th Army. The strongpoint south of Novo-Borisoglebsk lost yesterday was recovered. In the north part of the breach at Volchansk the enemy attacked unsuccessfully with strong forces.

The last reinforced regiment of the 113th Division, assembled near Krasnograd as army group reserve, was placed at Army Group Kleist's disposal, with the proviso that the regiment was to be deployed by XI Corps in such a way as to allow the corps to organize its units.

A strict order from the *Führer* has decreed that no attacks are to be made without air support, and that a way must be found to call off a planned attack if the weather makes air support impossible. This order led to difficulties. For the counterattack at Volchansk planned by 6th Army tomorrow morning, the infantry have to depart at 02:00, because they have to move into their open readiness positions while it is still dark. The army says that pulling them out of these positions by day is impossible – the same situation, therefore, as the 11th Army on the 20th. I ordered the Luftwaffe weather report brought in at 01:30; if it is favorable the move into the readiness positions is to begin and the attack go ahead; I will bear the responsibility. – I briefed Halder on this course of events and told him that "dubious and cautious" officers could hide behind this order at any time and thus the willingness to accept responsibility and attack is not raised. What had made the army great was the fundamental rule better to make a mistake than do nothing at all! I warned against destroying that. Halder shared my opinion and said that he would bring it up with the *Führer*.

"It Is Beginning to Thaw"

24/3/42

On the eastern front in the Crimea the enemy attacked with strong forces and was beaten back. – In Army Group Kleist's sector the attacks, especially west of Slavyansk, are growing stronger; the Russians have used heavy artillery up to 210mm there; these attacks also broke down. – In 6th Army's sector the Hungarians continue to push back the enemy in the forest country northwest of [Upper] Bishkin. The enemy is growing stronger opposite the army's southern front. – The counterattack by the reinforced 3rd Panzer Division led to gratifying initial successes; several villages were taken. But the crossing at Rubezhnoye was held by the Russians with heavy tanks. – It is beginning to thaw.

25/3/42

The attacks have weakened on the eastern front in the Crimea. Army Group Kleist reported more heavy but uncoordinated attacks against the Slavyansk point, which were repulsed. – In 6th Army's sector the forest area north of [Upper] Bishkin has been cleared of the enemy. The counterattack at the Volchansk breach by the 3rd Panzer Division has failed. Heavy tanks and a newly-committed division of the 3rd Guards Cavalry Corps brought it to a halt and forced the attack force back. It is my impression that the attack was not carried out in a logical manner; added to that is the fact that the offensive strength of our infantry has dropped, in particular because of the heavy officer casualties during the winter, and that our anti-tank weapons are still inadequate to deal with the Russian heavy tanks. – Enemy scouting raids against the 2nd Army. – In the rear army area fighting with partisans, which unfortunately resulting in considerable losses to us as well.

48 hours late, the initial elements of the 23rd Panzer Division [Boineburg-Lengsfeld], which is coming from the west in a slow succession of trains, arrived in Kharkov.

According to a report by the "Foreign Armies" Department of 20th March, "based on all available intelligence" it reckons "with certainty" on new Russian formations on a level of about 50 to 60 divisions! This is in total contradiction to the statements made to Sodenstern by the Chief of Staff of the field forces on 5th March in response to my assessment of the situation.

26/3/42

A powerful, concentrated attack supported by tanks and aircraft collapsed in front of the 11th Army's eastern front. XIV Panzer Corps repulsed a strong, local attack then counterattacked and drove the enemy back. On the rest of the army group's front only weaker local attacks. – 6th Army reported further powerful counterattacks by the enemy in the north part of the Volchansk bulge, where now apparently all three divisions of the 3rd Guards Cavalry Corps are committed. – Scouting raids continue on the 2nd Army's front.

Two divisions are being transferred to the army group as OKH reserve. Beginning in early April, they will detrain near Grodno and Rovno and from there are to march 900 and 700 km respectively to the front!

In the afternoon I was visited my Herr von H., who is presently the Foreign Office's liaison officer with 11th Army. This experienced, apparently rational man considers the collapse of the British Empire to be inevitable.

27/3/42

In the Crimea it is relatively quiet. – Army Group Kleist reported relatively weak local attacks in the sectors held by XIV Panzer Corps, the mountain infantry corps, the Italians, and west of Slavyansk. A heavier attack was beaten back on the right wing of XI Corps.

In 6th Army's sector the enemy attacked in the north part of the bulge at Volchansk, where there are now ten Russian divisions in action, with heavy tanks and was repulsed in heavy fighting. Nevertheless an order was sent to 6th Army that the 3rd Panzer Division is to be pulled out of the line and rested, and moreover that the battalions belonging to 2nd Army are to be sent back as soon as possible. To facilitate the relief and to familiarize the 23rd Panzer Division, the army was authorized to deploy two of the division's rifle battalions in the front in brief rotation.

The severity of the fighting against the irregulars in the 2nd Army's rear is illustrated by the following numbers: in the period from 25th February to 25th March 1,936 partisans were shot, two artillery pieces, 4 anti-tank guns, 15 machine-guns and much equipment captured. Our own losses were 95 men killed, 143 men wounded, including the losses of three Cossack squadrons which distinguished themselves in this fighting.

"...Because It Suits His Plans Better"

28/3/42

No major combat by the 11th Army and Army Group Kleist except for an attack against the right wing of XI Corps, which was repulsed by the Romanians. The many scouting raids which the army group has carried out with good success in recent days has had a favorable effect on fighting morale. The 6th Army reported heavy fighting at the scene of the previous attacks, which near Andrenka led to an insignificant loss of terrain. Otherwise, as with 2nd Army, only limited fighting.

As there are indications that the Army Command is reckoning on an earlier beginning of the attack to clear the Izyum bulge than are we; I briefed Halder on the following considerations:

In the Volchansk bulge the enemy is still attacking with powerful forces. The withdrawal of the 3rd Panzer Division ordered by me is not yet possible. Today planned air attacks succeeded in destroying two bridges over the Donets in the Russian rear. It is extremely questionable whether the imminent flood will really cause them to abandon their bridgehead southwest of Volchansk. The Russian bridgehead poses a threat to the planned attack to clear the Izyum bulge. I am therefore faced with the decision whether Volchansk has to be cleared first or whether we can take the risk of letting this canker remain. If we clear Volchansk first, it will take about 14 days, calculated from the buildup for the attack, until the same forces are ready again to attack the Izyum bulge.

Therefore it would be hard for me to decide for the Volchansk attack, for the Izyum attack is based on the Donets being in flood; it must thus be carried out as soon as the ground allows. Halder asked if bolstering the defensive strength of the front west of Kharkov, perhaps through the use of the Hungarian brigade and artillery, so that it could hold if need be, might suffice. Also being debated is the question of how the Russians will react to the Izyum attack. Will they attack Kharkov or will they move their forces down from there to deal with the Izyum attack? Halder leans toward accepting the latter, probably because it suits his plans better. His question as to the duration of the muddy period I answered by saying that I believe that it will last about 4 weeks from the beginning, which hasn't fully set in yet.

The Army High Command have already established rates of expenditure for artillery ammunition for March and now also for April which will undoubtedly be exceeded if the muddy period does not bring the fighting to a standstill. A year ago consideration was given to converting some ammunition factories to other commodities because of heavy over-production!

29/3/42

Quiet day for 11th Army and Army Group Kleist following repeated nocturnal assaults by the Russians. In 6th Army's sector the enemy again attacked in the Volchansk bulge with heavy tanks and was repulsed; to the south a village was cleared of the enemy.

On the right wing of the 2nd Army, where it is still freezing, a limited attack by us led to local success.

Comments by a Soviet General Staff Officer

According to the *Exchange Telegraph*, a senior Russian General Staff Officer said the following:

"We have 60 days left in which everything has to be done to weaken the attack preparations of the Germans and prevent them from massing their forces in an orderly way!!"

30/3/42

At the front around Slavyansk the enemy attacked with powerful artillery support and tanks and was repulsed. On all the rest of the army group's front only limited fighting of local significance.

Return to lower nighttime temperatures since yesterday.

31/3/42

Activity in the Crimea limited to scouting raids. Near Slavyansk a relatively strong local attack and further heavy attacks were beaten back by XIV Panzer Corps. An arriving replacement battalion was caught in an air raid while detraining and lost 22 dead and 91 wounded. – On the 6th Army's southern front the enemy attacked with stronger forces, drove across the Donets with two to three battalions and was thrown back across the river again. Also heavy fighting in the bridgehead south of Novo-Borisoglebsk. In the Volchansk bulge small local operations slowly forced the enemy out of the forest and back across the Donets; in the north Russian attacks again failed. On the south wing of the 2nd Army a local attack was beaten back.

Paulus came at midmorning. He requested the release of a reinforced rifle regiment and a tank battalion of the 23rd Panzer Division to make another attempt to clear the Volchansk bulge. Based on the experience of the first attack I consider these forces to be too weak. Employment of the entire 23rd Panzer Division, which would promise success, is out of the question because the entire division will not be here until mid-April and by then the muddy period will have arrived. I turned down his request. Despite all of Paulus' objections I demanded that the 3rd Panzer Division be pulled out of the line and rested and temporarily placed another battalion from the 23rd Panzer Division at his disposal to ease the relief.

"Fridericus" In The Direction of The Izyum Bulge

In the afternoon I told Halder of Paulus' request and my decision to turn it down. Halder was "grateful" for my decision.

The attack proposals for "Fridericus" – the attack to clear the Izyum bulge – have arrived. In my reply I tried to get Kleist to concentrate his forces tightly on the right wing instead of – as he proposes – conducting the attack from three different directions and thus frittering away his offensive strength. The important thing for him is to advance quickly with his right wing in order to bar the Donets and go as far as he can toward the 6th Army's very weak assault group. Simultaneously I ordered the attack placed under a unified command. – Nothing of fundamental importance to say about 6th Army's proposal.

In the evening came the surprising announcement from the Army High Command that "'Fridericus' has to be made from the area south of Chuguyev!" All sorts of assumptions were given to justify this demand but no facts. I have not answered for now.

1/4/42

Attacks were beaten off on Slavyansk's northwestern front. On the 6th Army's southern front, Kopanskoje south of the Donets was lost, further attacks were repulsed in the bridgehead south of Novo-Borisoglebsk; to its right and left weak enemy forces again crossed the Donets. Repeated Russian attacks in the north tip of the Volchansk breach broke down.

2/4/42

Further attacks near Slavyansk, where a strongpoint was lost. The enemy continued to attack the 6th Army's southern front and tried to get new forces across the Donets southwest of Novo-Borisoglebsk using very hastily erected bridges. A town was lost in the north part of the Volchansk bulge; to the north of the bulge weak enemy battalions felt their way across the Donets. On the south wing of the 2nd Army the Russians have attacked the village recently taken by the army several times in the past few days and again today things were noticeably unsettled there.

Warmer weather on the army group's entire front.

A report by the 11th Army which sheds light on the disproportion of the forces in the Crimea was submitted to Army High Command. I nevertheless took the position that the attack on Kerch should be carried out as soon as possible so as not to give the enemy time to continue his attacks and bring up reinforcements, which would make the disproportion of forces in the Crimea even greater. I therefore consider postponing the attack until the second half of May, or until the time when two fresh divisions can "perhaps" be transferred to the 11th Army, to be undesirable, especially since it is quite uncertain whether the overall situation on the Eastern Front in May will permit the transfer of forces to the 11th Army.

3/4/42

By and large the day passed quietly in the Crimea and for Army Group Kleist. In the 6th Army's sector an enemy attack in the bridgehead south of Novo-Borisoglebsk led to local penetrations. Just north of the Volchansk breach the enemy moved reinforcements across the Donets. 2nd Army reported no significant fighting.

A telegram arrived from the Army Command, according to which the attack on Kerch is to wait for the arrival of 12 anti-tank guns and 32 tanks for the 22nd Panzer Division. That could mean postponing the attack for 14 days!

4/4/42

On the Crimean eastern front the enemy attacked at night with two regiments; the attack was beaten off. – Futile assaults by Russian tanks at and south of Slavyansk. Counterattacks by the 6th Army eliminated yesterday's breach south of the Donets. The enemy forces which crossed the Donets north of the Volchansk breach, about a regiment strong, attacked the strongpoint at Ogurzewa from all sides and were beaten back for the most part.

2nd Army reported quiet.

The muddy period has begun. It is therefore questionable whether the Romanian 4th Division, the leading elements of which arrived today at Dnepropetrovsk, can reach the fighting front to relieve the 113th Division before the roads become impassable.

5/4/42

At Slavyansk, Russian attacks supported by tanks again collapsed in heavy fighting. On the 6th Army's front all quiet after the recent, costly – for the Russians – battles. The enemy attacked in division strength at the south end of the Volchansk breach and was repulsed. At the north end of the bulge only scouting raids. Gatherings of tanks there and near Ogurzewa suggest that further attacks are likely.

6/4/42

On the entire army group front localized attacks only, all of which were repulsed. The Donets is slowly starting to overflow its banks. A planned campaign of air attacks against the Donets bridges behind the breaches at Izyum and Volchansk has begun.

Kleist's new proposal for the "Fridericus" attack was submitted with my backing; it says that the attack is out of the question before 4th May.

7/4/42

In 6th Army's sector weak enemy forces were driven back across the Donets near Ogurzewa.

Generally a quiet day. I pressed Paulus to pull out the 3rd Panzer Division so that it can be rested for "Fridericus." The picture brought back by an officer dispatched to this division was sad.

8/4/42

Quiet day. – Offensive preparations by the enemy on the Crimean eastern front.

9/4/42

The enemy attacked on the entire Crimean eastern front with strong forces and over 100 tanks and was repulsed with the loss of half his tanks. – In the

6th Army's sector, in the Volchansk bulge the enemy was driven out of a town in our main line of resistance, parts of which he had occupied.

Paulus' Division "Exhausted"

Paulus described the deplorable state of the 294th Division, which lies opposite the breach at Volchansk; the division is exhausted; Paulus doesn't believe that it will ever regain its full fighting strength. The withdrawal of the 3rd Panzer Division, which began today, is therefore a "big gamble."

Manstein is to visit the *Führer* next week to discuss his attacks in the Crimea. Since Halder wants to brief Sodenstern on plans for the spring, I suggested combining the two trips so that the army group can, if necessary, take part in the discussion concerning the Crimea.

10/4/42 to 22/4/42

On the 10th flew to Berlin on leave. Return on the 22nd. Only on the 12th did the Russians attack again – in vain – on the Kerch Peninsula; it was quiet for the rest of the period due to the muddy conditions.

The enemy has withdrawn his cavalry and guards divisions except one from the front and replaced them with infantry divisions. There are no indications that the divisions taken from the Izyum bulge have been withdrawn across the Donets. A new group of forces – the 48th Army – is assembling around Yelets, where motorized columns have been seen moving south.

Sodenstern and Manstein together made a presentation to the *Führer* concerning the attacks in the Crimea, with which the *Führer* agreed. The question of the attack to clear the Izyum and Volchansk bulges is not yet clear. The Army Command still insists that "Fridericus" be conducted with its north wing northeast of the Donets. – The general order for the big operations has arrived. Preparations are slowly getting under way. The essential aspects of the directive correspond to the army group's proposal of the 20th February, only they have broken the total operation into three periods – in keeping with the belated arrival of the attack units.

23/4/42

A telex was sent to Army High Command in which I again requested that "Fridericus" be carried out with all forces on this side, or southwest of, the Donets, because seven divisions will be needed for 6th Army's attack northeast of the river and these will not be available in the foreseeable future. Further I requested approval for the elimination of the Volchansk bulge as soon as the weather permits. It is a precondition for the defense of Kharkov as well as for the orderly conduct of operations and can probably be carried out in a few days.

24/4/42

Limited increase in combat as the ground slowly begins to dry and the high water recedes.

From the Army High Command came the reply that the *Führer* does not want to "forbid" the attack at Volchansk, but he can only approve it if "there are assurances of a smashing success with minimal personnel and material losses!"

We must also be clear that losses before the big operations cannot be replaced; although no man can guarantee the "certain success of the attack with minimal casualties," I gave the order for it to go ahead because it is necessary.

The *Führer* stuck to his position in the "Fridericus" matter.

25/4/42

Sodenstern reported that the Army High Command advised him verbally that during the night the *Führer* had decreed that the Volchansk attack was not to go forward until after the attack at Kerch. I called Halder and said something like the following:

"I am considering the attack at Volchansk now because the Donets is still in flood and the enemy in the bulge at present has only one usable bridge behind him. Therefore he cannot bring significant reserves across from the other side and will, if the attack succeeds at all, be destroyed. Later everything will be harder.

Just as in the first failed counterattack, after the high water recedes the enemy can be reinforced from the other side of the Donets at any time. Then I will need double the forces for the attack, which will then not offer nearly the same chances of success. I am not recommending the attack for my own amusement. I just think it necessary, as well as a basis for the operations to come and for securing Kharkov. – Doesn't the *Führer* think the enemy will attack us at Kharkov?"

Halder answered:

"No; such strong German forces are assembling near Kharkov that the enemy undoubtedly knows about it and will take care not to attack us there."

"...Forbidden the Attack"

I am of a different opinion and referred to my assessment of the situation of 1st March. Halder believes that he [Hitler] is against the Volchansk attack primarily because he fears it will take air forces away from our coming attack in the Crimea. I asked Halder to inform the *Führer*, who is in Berlin at present, that this is not the case. – After Sodenstern once again pleaded the case for the attack with Heusinger, in the evening I was informed by telephone "that the *Führer* has forbidden the attack!"

A telex from the Army High Command contained a lengthy explanation of the order to conduct the north part of "Fridericus" left of the Donets. The north part of the attack is to be made narrower and, in order to allow the cooperation of the entire Luftwaffe, is not to be carried out until after the attack in the Crimea is finished. Sodenstern spoke to Heusinger and asked with which forces the Army Command proposed to carry out this attack; he replied that they were planning on two divisions and a panzer division!! Such a powerful thrust undoubtedly contains the seed of failure. I cannot warm to it.

The 2nd Army smashed local attacks by the enemy, some while still in preparation. Otherwise, as far as I can tell from the events of today, the enemy is quieter.

26/4/42

Minor attacks by the enemy in the Crimea and against the 6th Army.

At Halder's request an assessment of the situation was sent to the Army Command. It culminates by saying that there are no indications of an enemy attack with strategic objectives, rather that the Russians will fight this year to gain time. It is unlikely that they will wait completely passively for the German attack, instead their dispositions and previous behavior suggest that they will continue to try to harass our buildup and draw the massing German divisions into the battle prematurely.

The assessment is therefore essentially the same as on 1st March.

27/4/42

Generally quiet day. The 1st Panzer Army [Kleist] reports offensive preparations by the enemy opposite its right wing.

28/4/42

Flew to Simferopol and drove from there to the Kerch front, where I visited the headquarters of XXX Corps [Fretter-Pico], the 50th [Schmidt, Friedrich], 28th [Light, Sinnhuber] and 132nd [Lindemann, F.] Divisions and the 22nd Panzer Division [Apell]; I also saw Richthofen [VIII Air Corps], who is preparing his operations in the Crimea, as well as the Commanding Generals of the Romanian mountain infantry corps and the Romanian 4th Mountain Infantry Division.

In spite of the most careful preparations, this attack remains especially risky on account of the ratio of forces. – Brief visit to ancient Feodosiya, which looks desolate; the jetty has been blown up to make enemy landings difficult, sunken Russian ships lie in the harbor. Returned to Headquarters, 11th Army at Ssarabu near Simferopol before dark, as the road is "partisan-threatened" later on.

Quiet at the front. In fighting with partisans behind the 2nd Army the Hungarian security units committed there initially came out on the losing end!

29/4/42

Drove from Headquarters, 11th Army through the lovely mountainous region of the southwest Crimea where the trees are beginning to blossom while the peaks of the Yaila Mountains are still snow covered. Visited the 24th Division [Tettau] then drove to a heavy artillery battalion's observation post with a view of Sevastopol and large parts of the attack zone. Subsequently flew back from Simferopol.

At the urging of the Army High Command, in the evening we hastily worked out the initial drafts of our directives for the spring offensive, throwing them together on the green table with no scouting of the terrain or input from the army; after some changes are made they will be sent to the Army Command the day after tomorrow.

The front has become more active. The enemy was especially restive opposite the right wing of Army Group Kleist.

30/4/42

The order for "Fridericus" was the result of a painful birth. With much effort the attack forces of the 6th Army north of the Donets were raised by a about a third; as well the 113th Division, at the cost of largely denuding the east front of the Izyum bulge, was positioned so that it could take part in 6th Army's attack right or left of the Donets. The Romanian 20th Division was placed at the disposal of Army Group Kleist in order to release the 1st Mountain Infantry Division for the attack. – The whole thing isn't pretty, but it can't be changed as long as the *Führer* sticks to his demand. At the front things are the same as yesterday. The 6th Army fears a tank attack at [Upper] Bishkin.

1/5/42 to 2/5/42

Insignificant fighting. – The partisans in the 2nd Army's rear are uncomfortable. They slip into the swampy terrain east and south of Trubchevsk, which is almost inaccessible to our troops, and are hard to catch even though an entire Hungarian combat division as well as a Hungarian security division and weak regional defense units have been sent against them.

Two Hungarian divisions from the units arriving on the 2nd Army's south wing from Germany are to relieve elements of the 88th and 16th (Motorized) Divisions as soon as possible so that they might finally be able to rest and refit somewhat.

The attack on Kerch originally planned for the 5th May has had to be postponed by two days because the air force is not ready.

3/5/42 to 4/5/42

Numerous scouting raids by the Russians, including one with boats, across the Sea of Azov. – The enemy opposite the 11th Army has gone over to the defensive with dispositions in depth; no wonder, for the massed operations by the Luftwaffe could not be kept hidden from him. – Fighting continues in the partisan area behind the 2nd Army.

5/5/42

In the Crimea the enemy has put out signs bearing the challenge:
"Come on! We're waiting!"

I asked Manstein whether, in spite of all that, he can carry out the attack in its originally planned form. After the forward lines in the south sector have been breached, it calls for the bulk of the attacking troops to turn sharply north and then west against the rear of the north part of the Russian front, leaving only weak forces to screen to the east. If the enemy really is arrayed strongly in depth, we should consider whether it would not be better to drive east with all forces once breakthrough has been achieved. Manstein believes that he has to stick to the old plan. – Since the Luftwaffe still isn't ready, the attack had to be postponed by another day. A telex was sent to the Army High Command with a note that aerial reconnaissance photos from April show that large parts of the stream running along the 6th Army's attack front in flood, making it a serious tank obstacle! If this picture is confirmed by new aerial photos it will place the 6th Army's attack left of the Donets in question.

The movements opposite the 1st Panzer Army's south sector have continued. – Numerous reports of troop movements opposite the 6th Army's southern front into the Izyum bulge were supplemented by statements made by deserters, who claim that three divisions and a tank brigade are preparing to attack there. At Volchansk, too, the enemy also appears to be moving in fresh forces. Complying with a request from 6th Army, the 71st Division assembled near Kharkov was placed at its disposal for use in its future attack sector. It is in the wrong place there if the Russians attack in the northwest corner of the Izyum bulge and at Volchansk or if for any reason we do not attack to the left of the Donets. Nevertheless everything is to stay as it is for now, in order to prepare "Fridericus" as instructed and avoid arguments.

Halder was briefed over the proceedings involving the 11th and 6th Armies. He apparently isn't taking the difficulties opposite the 6th Army's attack to heart. He argues against the notions that the Russians might beat us to it and attack on both sides of Kharkov, but not with as much conviction as before.

6/5/42

At the Army High Command they're racking their brains over whether the enemy has withdrawn in the Crimea. The *Führer* has let it be known that a "reconnaissance attack" might possibly be necessary to clarify the situation. I spoke with Manstein who confirmed the earlier picture, according to which the enemy by and large has not "withdrawn," but more likely arranged himself in great depth. The "reconnaissance attack" is unnecessary, for scouting raids have today revealed that the Russians still have seven divisions in the front.

7/5/42

The enemy, probably provoked by our own raids, attacked north of Slavyansk in regimental strength with tanks and was for the most part beaten back. – Stronger scouting raids against the Romanian divisions in XI Corps' sector. – In 2nd Army's rear area partisans succeeded in blowing up tracks near Woroshba, which interrupted traffic for 48 hours.

Lengthy meeting with the Chief of the Personnel Officer [Keitel, Bodewin – Chief of the Army Personnel Office], who arrived here.

Operation "Bustard Hunt"

8/5/42

11th Army went to the attack on its east front. The location and timing of the attack appeared to surprise the enemy and it gained up to 12 kilometers in the initial onslaught. 80 Russian aircraft were shot down. At Sevastopol the Russians remained quiet. Brief conversation with Manstein produced total unanimity as to how the operation [refers to Operation "Bustard Hunt," whose goal was to retake the Kerch Peninsula] should proceed. – At Slavyansk the Russians continued to attack without success. Much restlessness and movement opposite the rest of the front, especially southeast of Slavyansk, in the Volchansk bulge and in front of the 2nd Army's left wing.

Kleist's Chief of Staff Faeckenstedt [army group, consisting of the 1st Panzer Army and the 17th Army] came at midmorning and spoke about "Fridericus" [Operations "Fridericus" I and II were aimed at straightening the front]. In my opinion the army group is too weak in its direction of attack and too strong in its secondary mission, the advance on Barvenkovo. Faeckenstedt admitted that but justified his solution by referring to decisive terrain difficulties which I cannot check in detail; I therefore had to give in.

6th Army requested the employment of the 113th Division with VIII Corps and a regiment of the 305th Division just arriving at Kharkov in the Volchansk bulge, because it is expecting the Russians to attack at both places. The army justified this with the strange claim that "Fridericus" would not be adversely affected by these measures. My great worry that the Russians will beat us to it with their attack has not diminished. Nevertheless, I must do everything to at least safeguard the possible success of "Fridericus," which in spite of all my protestations has been ordered in this form. I therefore denied the army's requests and once again pointed out that it had to do all it could to expedite preparations for the attack and push ahead with consolidating its positions.

9/5/42

At midmorning I briefed the *Führer* on the gratifying development in the Crimea. Concerning the rest of the army group's front, I reported that brisk movements had been seen southeast and east of Slavyansk for several days. Whether they were connected with the attacks taking place at Slavyansk I could not yet say. The enemy is also restive in the northwest corner of the Izyum bulge and at Volchansk. At the first-named place he has bolstered his forces by at least one, perhaps by three divisions with tanks. I cannot yet tell whether this is to be taken as a sign of offensive intent. The *Führer* said that perhaps in time the Luftwaffe in the Crimea will be free to be committed against enemy attacks. I replied that I had no fear of the attacks themselves, they would be stopped. The uncomfortable thing is that as a result of such attacks the enemy might seriously endanger our own plans.

Things continue to go extremely well in the Crimea; a composite motorized unit has broken through to a depth of 50 km. In the evening, when the previously held-back 22nd Panzer Division was to attack, it began to rain, bringing all movement to a standstill!

The enemy attacked north of Slavyansk again today and was repulsed by counterattack. Two powerful scouting raids in the Volchansk bulge were also beaten back. – Further fighting with partisans in the 2nd Army's rear area.

"...The Enemy's Power of Judgement Not To Be Underestimated"

An article in the *New Zurich Times* dated 30th April discussed the Russian plans concerning the expected German offensive. The article is very insightful both in regard to the Russian plans and the enemy's power of judgement, which is not to be underestimated.

The news is bad concerning the prospects for the harvest. In large areas of Germany the winter corn has frozen; Hungary and Romania, as I am told from Budapest, are facing a total crop failure.

10/5/42

The rain in the Crimea, which lasted until morning, has paralyzed the tanks for the time being and kept the Luftwaffe on the ground. Not until noon did we go forward again. The [22nd] Panzer Division encountered enemy tank battalions, smashed them and fought its way north in the direction of the coast against stubborn resistance. The Groddeck Motorized Battalion [244th Inf.Rgt.], which was sent ahead to the east, reached and crossed the Tatar Trench. There have also been signs of rearward movements by the enemy since midday in the north sector of the front, which has not yet been attacked. Manstein intends to drive to the coast with the tanks to surround the enemy still in the north sector, but drive the right wing of his attack farther to the east and northeast. – Correct!

At Slavyansk isolated advances in up to battalion strength. Same thing in the Volchansk bulge, also weaker attacks against 2nd Army.

Paulus spoke about "Fridericus"; I agree apart from a few details.

11/5/42

All is going well in the Crimea. The ring around the enemy in the north part of the Parpatsch position was closed by the 22nd Panzer Division advancing along the coast and reduced by the attack from the left wing of the 11th Army. The units deployed to pursue the enemy to the east, the Groddeck Battalion and the 132nd and 170th Divisions, are advancing again after fighting off enemy counterattacks. The Romanian 8th Cavalry Division, which was deployed on the extreme left wing, has been pulled out of there and joined the pursuit toward Kerch. The number of prisoners taken is high. At Sevastopol it is quiet. – In the afternoon I briefed the *Führer*.

The enemy again attacked with tanks north of Slavyansk and after temporary penetrations was thrown back. Numerous scouting raids on the rest of the Kleist Group's front and against 6th Army. It is apparent from the "daily reports," which arrived during the night, that the situation in the northwest tip of the Izyum bulge and at Volchansk is coming to a head, suggesting that an attack is imminent.

Partisans blew up another section of track in the 2nd Army's rear. The fighting is assuming an increasingly serious character; today the enemy attacked there with 800 men and numerous tanks. His aim appears to be to break through to the Kiev-Kursk railroad, which we are using for our buildup, and perhaps also the Orel-Kursk road.

The Army High Command agrees for the most part with our proposals for the big operation. An idea that was touched on before appears in its statement, to possibly have Army Group List, which is to command the armies on the right in the third operation directed to the south, participate in the second part of the operation as well, perhaps to the extent of subordinating the 1st Panzer Army to it. That would mean that I would command in the north part of the operation and List in the south – an unnecessary complication! [Directive No. 41 of 5 April 1942 called for the German summer offensive to take place in four steps:

1. Breakthrough toward Voronezh

2. Destruction of the enemy facing the 6th Army west of the Don

3. Division of Army Group South into Army Group B, Bock, and Army Group A, List, and a pincer operation by both army groups to capture Stalingrad

4. Conquest of the Caucasus.]

The justification, that if the operation goes favorably an attack by the north wing of the 17th Army, now under List, might also be considered, is more than feeble.

Fighting "For Our Very Existence"

12/5/42

The destruction of the encircled enemy elements in the Crimea is complete. The pursuit in the direction of Kerch continues against disorganized opposition. – In the 6th Army's sector the enemy has attacked with powerful forces and many tanks in the northwest tip of the Izyum bulge and at Volchansk. By midmorning it was obvious that he had achieved significant penetrations at both places. There were also two, apparently unimportant penetrations farther north, against the 79th Division. I asked Army Command for the release of the 23rd Panzer Division and informed them that the 71st and 113th Divisions also had to be committed to parry the Russian drive. The request was granted; but the army group was made responsible for seeing to it that the 23rd Panzer Division is used only to the extent necessary and that this division is ready for employment in "Fridericus" "on the originally planned date!" In the afternoon it was found that the penetration against VIII Corps had assumed a serious form, so that the employment of the 113th Division had already become unavoidable. Things were apparently even worse in the Volchansk bulge; the breach is much more than 20 km wide, two villages in the center of the breach were lost and in the evening enemy tanks were within 20 kilometers of Kharkov!

The commitment of all available reserves, including the usable elements of the 3rd Panzer Division, was now necessary to restore order. I called Halder and told him that executing "'Fridericus' on the originally planned date" was now out of the question. Halder replied that he did not have the *Führer*'s order in front of him, but he understood that as far as possible we were to stick to our primary mission, our own attack, and that troops were not to be committed to fix blemishes. I replied.

"What we've got here is no blemish, rather our very existence is at stake."

My efforts were aimed at getting the reserves into action together in an offensive role and not frittering them away. My orders to the 6th Army were worded appropriately. I asked Paulus, who came over later in the evening [from HQ 6th Army in Kharkov to army group headquarters in Poltava], not to attack prematurely and in no case without the Luftwaffe. Fortunately it is now possible to release elements of the Luftwaffe in the Crimea and transfer them to the 6th Army.

On the rest of the front only scouting raids. Movements east of Slavyansk, on both sides of the Bakhmut, may possibly be attack preparations. 2nd Army also suspects the enemy is making offensive preparations on its south, but especially its north wing. In the 2nd Army's partisan area the Hungarian 6th Light Division began its attack. – During the night a telegram arrived from the Army High Command, which toned down significantly the conditions for the employment of the 23rd Panzer Division.

"It's Going Well in the Crimea"

13/5/42

It's going well in the Crimea. Isolated resistance at the Tatar Trench was broken by the Groddeck Battalion. The battalion is in pursuit toward Kamysh-Burun and Kerch.

Localized Russian attacks collapsed near Slavyansk. Quiet on 2nd Army's front.

At midmorning I briefed the *Führer* on the 6th Army's situation, which is serious enough. The enemy has broken through far to the west against VIII Corps, the corps' entire front is under heavy pressure. The penetration near Volchansk is more extensive to the north than it appeared yesterday. The premature attack by the 23rd and 3rd Panzer Divisions has been under way since 09:30; I first learned of it after they had already attacked. – The Luftwaffe is slow in complying with the order to transfer forces from the Crimea to the 6th Army's threatened fronts. – All I have left in reserve is the 355th Division [Kraiß] which is still approaching slowly, and the question arises whether the breakthrough on VIII Corps' right wing can be stopped by the prepared attack by Army Group Kleist northwest from the Slavyansk-Alexandrovka area, or whether due to lack of forces – on the ground and in the air – I must limit myself to the suggestion that I assemble the limited available forces behind Kleist's left wing for a local counterattack against the enemy's flank and rear in front of VIII Corps. At the moment the 6th Army is tied down by the Russian attack, but Kleist appears too weak to completely close the Donets front behind the Russian penetration, which would entail breaking through from Slavyansk to Balakleya and simultaneously screening this drive to the east, alone. The enemy can still throw at him elements of 16 divisions, 9 cavalry divisions and 7 armored brigades from the Izyum bulge without touching his attack forces. It is therefore extremely questionable if this attack will force the Russians to abandon their attack. Added to that, Kleist won't be ready for the bigger counterattack before the 18th; but the smaller will scarcely lead to the complete elimination of the Izyum bulge, which cannot help but be of significance to the planned big operations. If the supreme command does not place the divisions en route to my front at my disposal, then I cannot relieve it of the decision whether to choose the big or the small solution. For the time being it is up to the *Führer* to make the divisions which are required for the smaller solution ready to march.

14/5/42

In the Crimea we have reached Kerch, where the Russians are still putting up resistance. To the east as well, powerful units whose retreat to the sea is cut off are still defending themselves. – Localized attacks at Slavyansk; nothing of significance in 2nd Army's sector.

Big Attack or Half Solution?

By morning the situation in 6th Army's sector had cleared up enough to reveal that the enemy had broken through on the right wing of VIII Corps and was feeling his way toward Krasnograd with cavalry. The 454th Security Division has given ground and is still holding in only a few places. Our own tank attack in the Volchansk bulge has not produced decisive results and, after regrouping, is to be continued during the evening. It can scarcely be expected to break through then. But with it the possibility of an advance from the 6th Army's south front, toward Army Group Kleist attacking north from Slavyansk, becomes ever less. I called Halder and said that after these events Kleist's attack with the available forces could scarcely produce the desired success. Kleist, with whom I had just spoken, thinks the attack feasible only if the enemy does not attack first. He believes he can reach the general line mouth of the Bereka-Aleksandrovsk, "not more?" If Kleist gets stuck half way, his attack will become a failure whose repercussions must weigh on all further plans for the eastern campaign. I cannot accept the responsibility for that on my own. The supreme command must decide whether it will make available the reinforcements on the ground and in the air necessary to maintain the bigger attack or whether it must content itself for now with the smaller, therefore partial solution. Thus I have arrived – with a heavy heart, from the army group's point of view – at the proposal that we send everything that Kleist can scrape together, approximately three to four divisions including a panzer division, to the left wing of XI Corps and from there use it to attack the south flank of the breakthrough. I ended my discussion with Sodenstern about these matters with the comment: "Now the *Führer* will order the 'big' solution. The laurels for the 'big' decision will thus fall to the supreme command and we have to be satisfied with that."

In the afternoon the *Führer* called and ordered the bigger solution! He has called for the transfer of all the air forces that can be let go from the Crimea and elsewhere. With their help the enemy is to be held up in the break-through front until Kleist attacks. The start of the attack is to be accelerated as much as possible. A great weight fell from my shoulders and I cheerfully approached this solution, especially as strong air support is assured.

By evening it had become clear that there is a gap more than 20 km wide between the right wing of VIII Corps and the 454th Security Division, through which Russian cavalry and tanks are feeling their way west. 6th Army received orders to barricade the Berestowaja, at least at the crossings, with whatever forces it can scrape up. The elements of the 454th Security Division which veered south were subordinated to Kleist; he is to place his reserves, provided that they are not involved in the attack, behind his left wing.

By evening the attack by our tanks at Volchansk had gained little ground. Altogether the 6th Army has lost 16 batteries! In return Kleist advised that he can attack on the 17th.

"It's All or Nothing Here Now!"

15/5/42

The *Führer*'s verbal orders of yesterday were confirmed by telex. The army group's requests for the transfer to the battlefield of the 24th Panzer and another division rolling toward Kursk were partly denied, partly deferred. I moved in everything for the battle that could be moved in: two thirds of the 22nd Panzer Division, as well assault gun and anti-tank battalions from the Crimea were transferred to Kleist as quickly as possible. Kleist received orders to free additional reserves from his eastern front. To begin with the approaching 305th Division is to assemble on a broad front between Poltava and Kharkov, 2nd Army is to free strong elements of the 88th Division and transfer them to the 6th Army.

The city and port of Kerch have been taken by the 11th Army. Some enemy elements are still defending themselves desperately on the peninsula northeast of Kerch. The quantities of captured material are growing rapidly.

Near Slavyansk small-scale attacks with tanks were repulsed. In the forest to the north much activity was seen around tanks. The enemy has become more restive in front of XI Corps and on the left wing of Army Group Kleist; tanks were seen there too.

In the breakthrough bulge the enemy is feeling his way toward Krasnograd. To the north he made several attacks against the 113th Division which has withdrawn behind the Berestowaja; he was beaten back for the most part with the help of the Luftwaffe. To the left, the situation of the Hungarian security divison is uncertain. The enemy also staged unsuccessful attacks in the south sector and center of the Volchansk bulge. Again today the counterattacks by our panzer divisions gained little ground but they have checked the enemy's offensive strength. Here, too, the air fleet was of great help. In the north part of the bulge, directly opposite a wide gap in our front, the enemy remains passive. Far ahead of the front the strongpoint at Ternowaja is still holding out. To the left of it and in the Belgorod bridgehead Russian attacks were repulsed. In the 2nd Army's sector scouting raids and the slowly progressing attack against the partisans in the rear area.

At the request of the Army High Command, it was sent an assessment of the situation, the gist of which could be summed up as:

"It's all or nothing here now!"

16/5/42

The Russians are still defending themselves in the extreme north tip of the Crimea. – Localized attacks on the Romanian-held front of XI Corps were repulsed. In the breach, the enemy attacked across the river north of Krasnograd, which was held by weak forces of the 454th Security Division. The lead battalion of the 305th Division coming from Poltava marched off on hearing the sound of battle and arrived just in time to prevent a disaster there. – The enemy broke into the positions of VIII Corps at different places. In the Volchansk bulge heavy Russian attacks were beaten back at Bol Babka and in the north end of the bulge. Our armored attack has made good progress and established contact with Ternowaja. Unfortunately it will not be possible to continue the attack to the north tomorrow and thus smash once and for all the Russian breakthrough east of Kharkov, because the enemy has grown so strong on the panzers' east flank that turning the 23rd Panzer Division to the east has become unavoidable. So here, too, there is a yawning gap in the front that cannot be closed at present. The foremost elements of the Gollwitz Group brought in from the 2nd Army cannot reach Oboyan until the 19th.

At noon I drove to Krasnograd to stiffen the backbone of the weak units fighting there. As always in such situations, the air was filled with rumors of catastrophe. – On my return in the evening I learned that several penetrations against VIII Corps and the retreat of the Hungarians on its left wing had led the Commanding General to withdraw the corps by about ten kilometers. I was unable to rescind the order, for according to Paulus' report the movement was unavoidable and already under way. Very bad, for now there is not only a broad gap on the VIII Corps' left extending to the 44th Division, but the breach north of Krasnograd has been widened even more. I issued a strict order that any withdrawal by a divisional unit was subject to my approval. A regiment of the 305th Division, which detrained near Kharkov, was positioned behind the northwest corner of the gap; at the southwest corner the panzer army scraped together a regiment from every possible unit. It is difficult to see how the attack by Army Group Kleist beginning tomorrow will be sustained. Continued Russian resistance in the Crimea is delaying the departure of the 22nd Panzer Division; Kleist maintains that he cannot take any further elements from his eastern front unless at least one regiment from the 73rd Division, which is still in combat in the Crimea and even later will be difficult to let go there, is transferred to him. I do not know yet how to solve the problem. But it has to be solved, for a far-reaching decision lies in the battle at Kharkov.

17/5/42

Still fighting northeast of Kerch. – Army Group Kleist went to the attack and made good progress on the entire attack front. Attacks by Russian cavalry near Krasnograd, heavy tank attacks against VIII Corps and also in the Volchansk bulge were repulsed, in many cases by the last forces available.

A new assessment was sent to the *Führer* in which I stated that the battle cannot be brought to a successful conclusion with the forces available and asked for an answer to my requests to the Army High Command in this regard.

Generaloberst Löhr, Air Fleet 4's Chief of Staff, arrived to discuss operational matters. – The commander of the Hungarian army [2nd], which is to join the army group, Colonel-General von Jany, reported for duty.

18/5/42

The end is approaching in the northeast of the Kerch Peninsula amid heavy fighting.

The attack by Army Group Kleist [1st Panzer Army and 17th Army] continues to go very well [in action were 4 infantry divisions, 3 light divisions, 2 panzer divisions and 1 motorized division with 166 tanks and 17 assault guns]; it has reached the hills south of Izyum and the lower course of the Bereka and passed Barvenkovo. Night reconnaissance reported long columns of vehicles headed northwest from Barvenkovo in the direction of VIII Corps, where the enemy attacked in vain with many tanks. In the Volchansk bulge, too, he had no success in spite of the lavish use of tanks. Enemy movements were reported from Voroshilovsk to the northwest in the direction of the Donets between Krasny Liman and Izyum. It is too soon to say whether these are linked to defensive or offensive intentions on the part of the enemy. If he intends to attack with these forces, it would be simpler if he started from Voroshilovsk to the west. – On 2nd Army's north wing stronger, artillery-supported attacks were repulsed.

Flew to the panzer army [1st]; Kleist's views and mine in total agreement.

In the evening I spoke with Halder. I said that I had to keep bothering the Army Command with the same reports because I am worried that they underestimate the importance and severity of this battle. The enemy is attacking VIII Corps with eight to nine armored brigades, at Volchansk with seven to eight armored brigades in addition to powerful infantry. VIII Corps is all in. When Halder said that Kleist's attack should swing west, I declared: I consider turning the army group impossible while the Bereka crossings are not in our hands. In my opinion, in addition to quickly relieving VIII Corps, the attack's objective must now be the destruction of the enemy in the Izyum bulge.

During the night Halder called Sodenstern and asked: "Hasn't your Commander-in-Chief also stated his position too strongly?", which Sodenstern denied with gratifying clarity.

Kerch Peninsula "Mopped Up"

19/5/42

The Kerch Peninsula has been almost completely mopped up. The booty from the battle has climbed to 149,000 prisoners and 1,100 guns. Our total personnel losses are approximately 7,000 men. – The 22nd Panzer Division has begun preparations for departure.

The right wing of Army Group Kleist pushed across the Bereka and took the heights west of Petrovskaya, where enemy resistance stiffened. South of the Bereka, III Corps attacked west and reached the general line Novopolye-Gavrilovka. To its west a Russian attack group is said to be in formation. Tomorrow it is to be attacked concentrically by III Corps and the right wing of XI Corps. On the western front of the Russian breach, at and on either side of Krasnograd, where two cavalry divisions were reported yesterday, it is quiet. The attacks directed against VIII Corps have lessened in fury and cohesion; pilots report tanks and trucks leaving in a southeasterly direction. The enemy attacks in the Volchansk bulge continue to be strong but are now uncoordinated and produced only limited partial successes. However the counterattack by our tanks has not yet restored contact with surrounded Ternowaja. – The offensive preparations on the north wing of the 2nd Army are no longer being viewed with certainty as signs of an imminent attack; it is even thought that the enemy might be moving troops near Yelets.

In the evening I briefed the *Führer* on the present situation and the success at Kerch. I informed him that after today the crisis of the defense in the Kharkov battle had hopefully been overcome. Contrary to the position the Army High Command had so far taken, the *Führer* raised for consideration whether it wasn't advisable to advance farther up the Donets with Kleist's right wing! That is precisely my view! The gap to the southeast corner of the 6th Army is only 25 km wide and I would be very happy if my weak forces were able to close it against the growing enemy defense. Moreover I want to set out from the 6th Army's southern front toward Army Group Kleist, even with such weak forces as there are there, as soon as possible. Kleist's Chief of Staff, Faeckenstedt, was briefed on my conversation with the *Führer*; in any event the army group is to take Potopopovka, the next Donets crossing north of Petrovskaya, as soon as possible. Again today no signs of major offensive plans by the enemy against Kleist's east flank. Notably heavy rail traffic, probably also unloadings, reported at Kupyansk.

Deployment of the first approaching division, the 336th [Light], as requested by me was finally authorized; all my other requests remain undecided.

"Blue" – The Big Summer Offensive

20/5/42

During the night an order came from the *Führer* that the specified deadline for "Blue" is to be kept and that the attack on Sevastopol is to begin on 5th June if at all possible. Preparations are to be the job mainly of the Luftwaffe and heavy artillery, so that the loss of a German attack division which has to remain on the Kerch Peninsula is not all that serious. Further the *Führer* ordered the withdrawal of the *Leibstandarte*, which Kleist had previously reckoned was impossible.

The mopping-up action near Kerch is almost over. Weak remnants of the enemy are trying to escape across the Black Sea on rafts. – The right wing of the panzer army's attack group has advanced north through Potopopovka. On the 17th Army's Donets front the enemy has gone over to counterattacks, particularly in the area of Izyum. Attacking west, III Corps took Mechebilovo and destroyed two Russian divisions. The attack by the Romanians of XI Corps has achieved little. The enemy has further weakened opposite 6th Army's right wing and in front of VIII Corps; however, advances from VIII Corps' front still met tough resistance.

In the Volchansk bulge fresh attacks by the enemy. In the south half he was repulsed. The counterattack by the 23rd Panzer Division gained ground in the direction of Ternowaja. In the north part of the bulge the fighting went back and forth; in the sector of the 79th Division Grafowka and a village to its north remain in Russian hands. Kleist reported his intent to cease the attack to the west and continue the drive north employing all available mobile units. The 6th Army intends to bring the strongest possible forces into the area of Balakleya and Andrejewka in order to attack southward from there. Ternowaja – in the Volchansk bulge – is to be abandoned as soon as it has been relieved and evacuated according to plan. The armored forces thus freed up are to be transferred to the southward attack. I agree with these plans, which have been discussed many times, and in the evening issued a corresponding order, whose objective is the total severing of the Izyum bulge. So everything will turn out well after all!

21/5/42

11th Army is regrouping for the attack on Sevastopol.

On the Donets front enemy attacks were repulsed at Izyum. On the right wing of Army Group Kleist, the 14th Panzer Division pushed ahead as far as the heights west of Chepel' for tomorrow's attack to the north. The attack by the Romanians and the 298th Division gained some ground. The enemy has ceased his attacks opposite VIII Corps; the right wing, the 305th Division, pushed southeast toward the Berekowaja. Troop movements from the south part of the Izyum bulge to the northeast were spotted, as well as further withdrawals to the east and southeast opposite VIII Corps. The Luftwaffe attacked heavy enemy concentrations south of Andrejewka and around Savintsy on the Donets, where columns streamed toward the bridge from the east and west. The enemy attack is also faltering in the Volchansk bulge; Ternowaja was relieved. – On the north wing of the 2nd Army an attack by three enemy battalions was repulsed.

In the evening I reminded the armies by telex that bringing the battle to a rapid conclusion is of decisive importance and that therefore VIII and XI Corps must also advance energetically.

22/5/42

Drove through Krasnograd to the front, but the trip was a waste of time due to getting lost and other difficulties.

The attack by the Mackensen Corps [III Corps] of Army Group Kleist broke through to the Donets south of Balakleya and to within 6 km of the 6th Army's bridgehead at Andrejewka. The ring has thus been closed, even if very loosely for now, around the enemy in the Izyum bulge! On its western front, too, III Corps pushed the enemy back further, compressed him to the west and thus aided the progress of the attack by the XI Corps' right wing. Tonight one division can be pulled out of III Corps' western front and another tomorrow and transferred to the very thin north wing of the assault. The 22nd Panzer Division is coming slowly. Since the enemy has halted his attacks altogether at Volchansk and the forces released there are reported on their way to Kupyansk, it is to be expected that the breakout attempt by the encircled enemy, whose main pressure will probably lie between Petrovskaya and Balakleya, will be seconded from the outside by an attack from the forces moved in by way of Kupyansk. To counter this it is important to strengthen and take the pressure off Kleist's weak right wing, and to drive into the pocket from all sides to bring about its quick collapse. The latter was begun today when the 355th Division on VIII Corps' right wing advanced to the Berestowaja against weakening resistance. However direct relief for the attack's right wing will have to wait for the attack ordered for tomorrow morning from the Andrejewka bridgehead by hastily scraped together forces and tanks of the 6th Army. Weak relief attacks opposite the 6th Army's north wing broke down. In the 2nd Army's rear partisans succeeded in demolishing another track.

In the evening I briefed the *Führer* on the situation. He was very pleased about the success and agreed with my plans. He expressed concern about a possible relief attack against the thin front held by the 44th and 297th Divisions north of Balakleya. I was able to inform him that measures had been initiated to support them. The operations department had doubts about the planned advance out of the Andrejewka bridgehead and had urged that the forces deployed for it advance north of the Donets toward Savintsy in keeping with the old "Fridericus." I had to reject the idea, because the forces are much to weak for that, especially since they would run into the midst of approaching enemy reinforcements and because the important thing now is to hermetically seal the pocket and bring about its collapse.

The Army High Command was informed that the attack on Sevastopol cannot take place before 10th June and that for this and many other reasons a postponement of the start of the big operation until about 21st June is unavoidable.

OKH "...Informed That This Operation is a Half Measure"

23/5/42

Defending fanatically, weak enemy groups continue to hold out in holes in the rocks north of Kerch.

In the Kharkov battle the enemy made desperate attempts to burst the ring from within and without. Right and left of Izyum he attacked across the Donets and was repulsed. Particularly heavy attacks with tanks from the loop in the Donets near Savintsy; they broke down as did strong breakout attempts against III Corps. The left wing of Army Group Kleist took Lozovaya and reached the Orel River line from the southwest. As the divisions are pressing ever closer together there, the withdrawal of the 298th Division can be started.

The right wing of the 6th Army also made good progress and neared the Upper Orel. The advance through Andrejewka was a success and contact was established with the leading elements of III Corps of Army Group Kleist attacking from the south.

The Hungarian 6th Light Division will have to be taken out of the struggle against the partisans behind the 2nd Army in order for it to reach its assembly area in the front for the coming operations in time. But since the fighting there is in no way over, it will flare up again as soon as the division turns its back. The Army High Command was informed that this operation is a half measure.

24/5/42

In the Crimea more than 3,000 prisoners were brought out of the quarries and holes in the rocks near Kerch. The number of prisoners has thus grown to more than 170,000.

Continued attempts by the enemy to burst the ring around the Izyum pocket. Attacks from inside the pocket with numerous tanks from Izyum and from the loop in the Donets near Savintsy; these were repulsed everywhere. The left wing of Army Group Kleist and the right of the 6th Army gained further ground against weakening resistance. The Breith Group, elements of the 3rd [Breith] and 23rd [Boineburg-Lengsfeld] Panzer Divisions and the 44th Division [Deboi], which attacked from the Andrejewka bridgehead, drove south into the pocket and thus took the pressure off the western front of the hard-fighting III Corps. In the Volchansk bulge a diversionary attack by the enemy south of Ternovaya led to a local penetration. Further enemy forces have been sighted decamping for the south from there. Minor attacks on the rest of the front held by the 6th and 2nd Armies. My concern about the revival of the partisans behind the 2nd Army was confirmed today.

25/5/42

At the battle front the pocket was further reduced in size. While resistance against the Breith Group and III Corps is still stiff in places, it has visibly decreased opposite the weak attack forces of the 6th Army. Relief attempts by the enemy in the Donets loop near Savintsy failed again. Further enemy forces are en route there from Kupyansk. The 389th Division was squeezed out and sent north. The idea of eliminating the enemy attacks through Savintsy by means of an advance from Balakleya, or north of the Donets, has been the topic of discussion for days. But the very enterprising new Chief of Staff of the 6th Army [Schmidt, Arthur; relieved Heim] rejects the attack completely. If they wish to achieve a reasonably tenable line they cannot be satisfied with taking the isolated village of Savintsy, but must advance as far as the river line north of Izyum. This will cost time and forces, especially tanks; but the latter desperately require time to rest and make repairs so as to be ready again in time for the big operation. Preparations by the Luftwaffe for Sevastopol and then again for the new operation would also be disturbed. For now, therefore, I cannot decide in favor of the attack. A verbal inquiry by the Army High Command was answered in this vein.

According to a telex from the Army High Command, in spite of all objections the *Führer* is insisting that the deadline for the start of the operation of

15th June be adhered to; he further ordered that the attack on Sevastopol begin on 7th June.

26/5/42

On arriving in Kharkov by train in the morning, I learned that the 1st Mountain Infantry Division [Lanz], which last night had been committed to an attack through the 60th Motorized Division's sector, had been overrun by a counterattack by concentrated masses of Russians and that powerful enemy forces had broken through in and north of the Bereka Valley toward the east in the direction of Petrovskaya. These enemy forces were stopped west of Petrovskaya in the morning hours and were encircled again by elements of the 13th and 22nd Panzer Divisions and the 298th and 389th Divisions. I drove by way of the Breith Group, the 44th Division and the 23rd and 16th Panzer Divisions to the 60th Motorized Division and the 1st Mountain Infantry Division. The picture was the same everywhere; being squeezed ever harder, the enemy still made attempts to break out here and there but was on the verge of collapse. I could see from a hill southeast of Lozovaya that the pounding the smoking pocket was taking from our batteries on all sides was being answered only weakly by the Russians. Masses of prisoners streamed to the rear, while our panzers and elements of the 1st Mountain Infantry Division passed them as they advanced to attack – an overwhelming scene. – Again today the enemy at the Donets front staged uncoordinated attacks in an effort to relieve the surrounded units. Movements by road and rail toward the Izyum-Volchansk front continue. But new divisions are being released daily from the shrinking encircling ring in the Bereka Valley to support the eastern front; as a result I no longer have any worry about new relief attacks by the enemy.

27/5/42

The battle is nearing its end. Already today the booty exceeded 150,000 men and 1,000 guns. Weak relief attempts at the Donets front failed.

Late in the evening an order came stating that the *Führer* had now decided to attack the enemy between Izyum and Savintsy – and in the Volchansk pocket(!!). Taking advantage of the success achieved in this battle, he wants to destroy as much of the enemy forces as possible as quickly as possible before we begin our own main operation.

28/5/42

This morning I sent a proposal to the Army High Command concerning the conduct of the attacks ordered yesterday, pointing out to them the exhaustion of the troops, especially those of III Panzer Corps [Mackensen], and the difficulty of resting and refitting them for the big operations. When asked which attack was to be made first, I decided in favor of Izyum, because it is quicker. Discussions as to what affect the new decisions will have on the starting date of the big operation went back and forth.

On the battlefield only fragments of the enemy continue to resist. No significant relief attempts today. – The rest of the army group's front was quiet. The "spring battle of Kharkov and at the Donets" is over. 22 Russian rifle divisions, 7 cavalry divisions and 15 armored brigades were beaten, surrounded and wiped out by a far lesser number of German, Romanian and Hungarian units. Only a few of the enemy divisions fighting in the Izyum breach escaped destruction.

29/5/42

During the night the order arrived that Volchansk is to be taken care of first, because stronger enemy elements have supposedly been caught there than at Izyum and because the attack will have a direct impact on the coming big operations. The latter reason is correct; it had led me to propose the attack on the 23rd April, at a time when it would have been easier and more effective. But at that time it had been forbidden.

No significant fighting at the front. The haul from the battle has grown to 239,306 prisoners, 2,026 guns and 1,249 tanks; about 540 aircraft were shot down. – Our own losses were about 20,000 men.

"They Are Attributing an Objective to Me That I Don't Have..."

30/5/42

Futile attacks by Russian tanks in the bend of the Donets near Savintsy. The enemy captured a strongpoint from the Hungarians on the 2nd Army's southern wing; a stronger local attack which followed soon after was repulsed.

The attack aimed at the relief of the 6th Army for the attack at Volchansk deployed too many forces frontally and too little on the wings; the army was instructed to concentrate more forces on both wings – point of main effort on the southern wing.

The enemy news service is claiming that the battle near Kharkov is still going on with undiminished intensity and that I made futile attempts to cross the Donets! The are attributing an objective to me that I don't have, so that afterward they can prove that I failed to reach it!

31/5/42

The Russians attacked the Hungarians unsuccessfully with 5 battalions.

1/6/42

Minor attacks against the Hungarians again today, also on the 6th Army's northern wing and the 2nd Army. At the Donets patrol activity only.

The *Führer* arrived; the commanders of the armies were present except for Manstein. He [Hitler] listened to briefings on the Kharkov battle and our subsequent plans. In order to ensure the availability of the strongest possible air forces for all the imminent attacks – Sevastopol, Volchansk, Izyum and the big operation – he agreed to a postponement of the start of the latter, which is most necessary. – The *Führer* sees the overall situation as favorable, placing an especially high value on the growing numbers of ships sunk – in May alone Germany sank more than 900,000 tonnes. He considers the aim of the upcoming operation to be decisive.

Reorganization of Army Group South

2/6/42

The planned artillery bombardment of Sevastopol has begun.

The enemy is restive in front of the 2nd Army; preparations in front of the Hungarians, brisk firing before the XXXXVIII Panzer Corps [Kempf – former XXXXVIII Motorized Army Corps, renamed on 21 June 1942], and an attack by two regiments against LV Corps on the army group's extreme wing, which was repelled by counterattack, point to an increasing nervousness on the part of the enemy, who as everybody knows is expecting our attack on Voronezh.

Army Group Kleist is being disbanded on 8th June, on which date the following organization of the army group will take effect: in the Crimea the 11th Army [Manstein], north of Taganrog the reinforced XIV Army Corps [Wietersheim], which comes under direct control of the army group, then the 17th Army [Salmuth], the 1st Panzer Army [Kleist], 6th Army [Paulus], and the 2nd Army [Weichs] with the subordinated 2nd Hungarian [Jany] and 4th Panzer [Hoth] Armies. The organization is to pave the way for future development.

3/6/42

In the Donets bend near Savintsy the 1st Mountain Infantry Division took a village from the Russians. The enemy is shoring up his positions in the Donets front on either side of Izyum. In the past few days he has weakened his forces in the Volchansk bulge by at least two divisions. Preparations for fresh local attacks are apparently being made opposite the Hungarian front. Submitted 6th Army's attack proposal for Volchansk. The demand for the formation of a better-defined point of main effort was met for the south wing, on the north wing not as clear as is needed.

Visited by Marshall Antonescu [Head of the Romanian government], who made a good and soldierly impression.

4/6/42

52 Russians deserted during an attack by an enemy battalion southeast of Kharkov! Several battalions attacked the Hungarians at two places; they broke into the lines but were counterattacked and driven out again; but the situation is not entirely clear. There is no cause for concern, however, as the enemy is too weak there for larger operations.

Headquarters, 2nd Hungarian Army, to which until now the Hungarian units were subordinated for administrative functions only, today assumed tactical command. For now, only the III Hungarian Corps is under its command. In order to ensure coherence of the attack in the coming operation, the Hungarian Army and the 4th Panzer Army have been combined with the 2nd Army under the command of Headquarters, 2nd Army as "Army Group Weichs."

5/6/42

Attempts by the Russians to recapture the village in the bend of the Donets taken on the 3rd were beaten back.

The enemy has grown restive opposite 6th Army's front, either side of Volchansk, his artillery fire has increased. He also appears to be planning new local attacks on the 2nd Army's right wing, against the Hungarians.

The "Wilhelm" Attack

6/6/42

Scouting raids at the Donets, against 6th Army and the Hungarians were repulsed.

Toward evening I informed the *Führer* that I had to postpone the "Wilhelm" attack by 24 hours on account of the reduced ability to employ tanks and aircraft caused by the heavy rains of recent days. The start of the big operation within the time frame allowed us would probably not be affected. On the other hand a lengthier postponement might force us to put off the attack at Izyum, with regard to the Luftwaffe, until after the start of the big operation. The weather in the Crimea is better, and the infantry attack begins tomorrow. The *Führer* agreed with everything.

7/6/42

The attack on the northern front of Sevastopol met stubborn enemy resistance everywhere and has gained little ground so far. On the extreme south wing the 28th [Light] Division [Sinnhuber], which attacked without air support, made a limited advance but by evening was forced to retire. Otherwise only local attacks and scouting raids against the Hungarians and to their north.

The weather is such that the attack at Volchansk is out of the question tomorrow, probably also the day after tomorrow. At the army's request I ordered a 48 hour postponement so as not to have the troops lying about in the wet unnecessarily. It is enough to make the start of the "big" operation independent of the attack at Volchansk – time wise as well – if I have two divisions of the 1st Panzer Army march to the 6th Army to replace the two divisions there which are to take part in the Volchansk attack and the "big operation." But this measure will result in the panzer army lacking two divisions for the attack at Izyum, therefore it will have to be delayed until the Volchansk attack is concluded and the situation there consolidated to the point that in addition to the panzers two divisions can be sent from there to the 1st Panzer Army. Also the Izyum attack cannot be made until the necessary air forces are freed from the "big" operation. That could take a long time; but the time is not lost as it will be to the advantage of the tank and motorized divisions employed at Volchansk, which desperately need to rest and refit. A corresponding proposal was sent to the Army High Command.

8/6/42

Stubborn resistance at Sevastopol again today. Nevertheless the attack on the north front made better progress. No attack in the south sector. A request by the 11th Army to transfer the 46th Division [Haccius], which remained at Kerch on the *Führer*'s orders, to Sevastopol to sustain the attack, was rejected by the Army High Command.

1st Panzer Army reported repeated counterattacks against the village taken by the 1st Mountain Infantry Division on the 3rd. the enemy is digging in in front of the 6th Army, numerous scouting raids in battalion strength and greater against 2nd Army, also the laying of mines by the enemy.

Heusinger (Army High Command) advised verbally that our requests, namely postponing of the attack at Izyum and the transfer of two divisions from 1st Panzer Army to 6th Army, have been approved. They seem to have changed their minds about the beginning of the big operation, for Heusinger said that the *Führer* has decided to continue the attack on Sevastopol as long as it offers a chance of success, which means leaving the Luftwaffe there that long as well. That might result in a lengthier postponement of Operation "Blue!"

9/6/42

Progress was made on the northern front at Sevastopol in spite of heavy Russian counterattacks. – Intensified artillery fire near Taganrog, scouting raids against the 2nd Army.

Heusinger's statements of yesterday were confirmed by a telex, in which 18th June was confirmed, as we requested, as the earliest attack date for the big operation. The wish was expressed to extend the Volchansk attack as far as Olkhovatka. Not new and also not bad, but only possible if the linking-up of the two attack groups near Bely Kolodes is assured, because if we swing out too far there is a danger that our weak attack groups will become stuck. – I turned down a request by 6th Army to postpone the attack until the 11th.

10/6/42

On Sevastopol's northern front further progress in bitter fighting.

The attack by 6th Army led to gratifying initial successes. On the right wing, by late morning tanks had crossed the Burluk River line 10 kilometers beyond the front; a bridge fell into our hands intact. In the afternoon the 16th Panzer Division [Hube] advanced more than 20 kilometers to the northeast. Near Pechenegi the 297th Division [Pfeffer] succeeded in establishing a bridgehead across the Donets. The north group also took the enemy completely by surprise; three bridges over the Donets were taken intact. Only on the extreme north wing did the enemy offer stubborn resistance.

The *Führer* is in Bavaria. I therefore asked Halder for permission to bring the north wing of the attack forward so that it can be inserted now in its future attack sector for the "big" operation. This will result in the 336th Division

[Lucht] being relieved of a twenty-kilometer screening front; the division will thus be free for the continuation of the advance to the east. I would also like to position a battalion of the 23rd Panzer Division behind the north wing of the attack in order to have it ready there as army group reserve for any eventuality. Halder agreed.

According to intercepted radio communications, the Russians are planning a counterattack against our southern attack wing.

In the evening travelled by train to Kharkov.

11/6/42

Yesterday Russian counterattacks with tanks against the 44th Division on the southern wing of the attack led to the loss of a hill, but otherwise they were brought to a standstill with the support of the Luftwaffe.

Drove from Kharkov to III Corps [Mackensen], to the Pflugbeil Air Corps [IV *Fliegerkorps*], to the 44th [Deboi] and 71st [Hartmann] Divisions and to LI Corps [Seydlitz-Kurzbach]. The 16th Panzer Division, which had advanced farthest to the north, was attacked from all sides by superior numbers of enemy tanks and went no farther. The advance by the 14th [Kühn] and 22nd [Apell] Panzer Divisions has been hindered by difficulties with the bridges, as well heavy rain began falling in the afternoon which very quickly transformed everything into deep mud. The amount of ground gained by the 14th and 22nd Panzer Divisions was therefore limited. But today the north group of the attack, the VIII Corps [Heitz], once again made good progress; the 305th Division [Oppenländer] advanced to and beyond Bely Kolodes. Enemy counterattacks with tanks against the north flank of the attack, the 336th Division [Lucht], were repulsed.

In the evening I learned from Headquarters, 6th Army that the enemy was falling back across the Donets before the center of the attack front. Our weak troops deployed in the front are giving chase.

At Sevastopol very little progress in the north; in the south, where today we were supposed to attack with the support of the entire air force, as good as none. The decision as to what is to happen here has to be made very soon, since previous opinion says that the "big operation" is scarcely feasible without the removal of air forces from Sevastopol.

At the front I ran into my old batman of many years, Wachholtz, who is now an *Oberleutnant* in command of a company.

12/6/42

At noon I spoke with Paulus about yesterday, when the Luftwaffe was employed too long in front of the 44th Division's defensive front instead of in front of the armored spearheads. I asked him to drive the tanks to the north today, disregarding the east flank, and put the main effort of the Luftwaffe in front of the tanks. This was followed by a telex containing the same message. But the day did not yet bring decisive successes. The 16th Panzer Division faced a superior foe with almost 100 tanks; the 14th and 22nd had to deal with difficult terrain, so that closure of the ring around the retreating enemy has not yet been achieved, even though VIII Corps' right wing gained further ground to the southeast. Counterattacks were beaten back by the 44th Division and the north wing of the VIII Corps.

Little progress at Sevastopol. In an assessment of the situation requested by the army group, Manstein declared that a continuation of the attack promised success, provided he is sent reinforcements for the air force and 3 infantry regiments and if deliveries of ammunition continue as before. The assessment was sent to the Army High Command along with my position, which is that without the requested infantry reinforcements the attack no longer has a chance of success, but that I assigned no great importance to a further strengthening of the Luftwaffe in dealing with the fortifications built into the rock. But I went on to say that I had to ask for a decision on the starting date for the big operation so that the attacking divisions don't end up waiting day after day with their vehicles packed, but instead are put in a position where they can make use of the wait for training.

The Dream of the "Big Operation"

13/6/42

Vigorous advances by the 22nd Panzer Division from the south attack group and the 305th Division from the north group have closed the ring around the enemy southeast of Volchansk. Elements escaped, nevertheless by evening the reported booty was 20,000 prisoners, more than 100 guns and about 150 tanks. Surrounded weak enemy elements continue to resist.

At noon I spoke with Schmidt [Arthur], Chief of Staff of the 6th Army, who suggested that we follow up now and take the commanding hills near Olkhovatka, where the enemy is giving ground. With the main mission of encircling the enemy now accomplished, I was in full agreement; the III Panzer Corps remained subordinated to the 6th Army for this task. I think it even more important that VIII Corps drive the enemy across the Neshegol with its left wing in order to capture the widest possible and most advantageous jump-off position for the "big operation." Schmidt shares this view.

At Sevastopol several groups of defensive works were taken; our losses there are heavy. – On the rest of the front only scouting raids, especially against 2nd Army. Discussions with the Army High Command went back and forth about the effect in the long run of Sevastopol and the Volchansk attack on the planned "big operation." Apart from the fact that the Volchansk will force the enemy to send reserves there, the starting situation for the first part of the operation ("Blue" 1) will be significantly improved by the attack. If need be, the Luftwaffe will be able to fulfill its mission in "Blue 1" even without the units which must now remain at Sevastopol and thus, as I see it, any further postponement of "Blue 1" is unnecessary. For some time there have been new ideas about "Blue 2" floating about aimed at making the planned encircle-ment even more effective. The delay at Sevastopol complicates the buildup to "Blue 2," because divisions which are supposed to take part in the operation are presently still fighting at Sevastopol.

14/6/42

The advance continues at Sevastopol in heavy fighting. In addition to the 3 regiments requested on the 12th, Manstein has asked for a further reinforce-ment of 4 infantry regiments, as well as assault guns and replacements.

Near Mariopol and Yalta a weak landing attempt by the Russians was repulsed.

Things continue to go well for the 6th Army; the commanding hills due west of Olkhovatka were reached. The attack on the north wing of VIII Corps is not to be resumed until tomorrow. The booty has risen to more than 24,000 prisoners, over 200 guns and 266 tanks; our total losses are about 3,000 men.

"Army Group Weichs" reported scouting raids one to two battalions strong, which opposite the panzer army were repeated up to seven times. Especially heavy air attacks on Kharkov have unfortunately claimed numerous victims.

At noon "Fridericus" reappeared! I took the following position: "Fridericus" will probably lead to a tactical success if the enemy thinks it is the attack he is expecting. The attack will result in a further delay in refurbishing the armored units of the 1st Panzer Army. Since the entire air force is required for "Fridericus" and for "Blue," the former will mean another postponement of the "big operation."

But every day that "Blue" is delayed is a loss and means foregoing exploitation of the success at Volchansk, which was greater than expected. – By way of reply an order – not altogether clear in its details – arrived during the night, according to which "Fridericus" is to be carried out and "Blue 1" is to follow as soon as the bulk of the Luftwaffe employed in "Fridericus" is free again. Several Luftwaffe units are to be transferred from the Crimea for "Blue 1," so that the 11th Army must reckon on getting along without these units from about the 20th. The Army High Command advised verbally that the earliest possible date for the "Blue 1" attack is now the 23rd.

"Laborious and Costly Struggle to Advance"

15/6/42

Further laborious and costly struggle to advance at Sevastopol. In 1st Panzer Army's sector a Russian scouting raid crossed the Donets north of Slavyansk. 6th Army repulsed several weak counterattacks against its newly-won front. The north wing of VIII Corps gained fifteen kilometers to the east and reached the line which was its objective.

16/6/42

The attack has moved forward in the southern sector at Sevastopol. But the shortage of infantry is making itself felt. The first of the three infantry regiments readied by the army group for the Crimea departed today. An enemy assault detachment which landed north of Kerch was wiped out.

At Olkhovatka an attack by several Russian battalions with tanks was beaten back. Nothing of significance on the remaining fronts.

17/6/42

Decisive successes were achieved in front of Sevastopol; five large defensive works in the old and new lines of the northern front were taken; but in the south sector only limited progress; the gains the Romanians made there were lost again.

Fresh small-scale attacks are apparently imminent at Olkhovatka and south.

The "Fridericus" attack should have begun today, tomorrow at the latest. But the daily downpours make any movement so difficult that attacking before the 20th is out of the question. As a result the attack date for the big operation is again uncertain.

18/6/42

Sevastopol's northern front has collapsed, Severnaya Bay was reached in several places. On the southern front an attack on the vital Sapun Heights misfired; limited progress by the Romanians. Manstein pointed out that a pause in the attack is inevitable as a result of the regrouping of the artillery and infantry, which unfortunately will benefit the enemy. He once again requested reinforcements for the infantry.

The enemy is restive opposite the 6th Army's newly-won front; many tanks were sighted near Kupyansk.

After renewed heavy rains, "Fridericus" had to be postponed by a further two days. The Army High Command thinks it possible that the *Führer*, who is still on the Obersalzburg, may now let "Fridericus" drop in order to avoid postponing the beginning of "Blue 1" any farther. This makes everything uncertain, for both the timing of the beginning of "Blue 1" and the starting situation for "Blue 2" depend on the execution of "Fridericus"! It makes a great difference whether the right wing of this attack is deployed from the present position of the 1st Panzer and the 6th Armies or, after the success of

"Fridericus", from the Oskol. At the present time the Army Command has three different proposals from the army group for the conduct of this operation; so far none has received a reply.

Rumors are intensifying that the Army High Command wants to conduct Operation "Blue 2" itself and for this reason wants to commit Army Group List as well. We, as well as List's Greiffenberg [Chief of Staff Army Group South], consider this wrong and Sodenstern again warned Heusinger of the mistake of tearing this operation, which requires a unified command like no other, in two by inserting a new army group.

"Blue 2" will be decisively influenced by the employment of many mobile units. Controlling them will require quick decisions and very rapid execution; I doubt that inserting another army group will make this any easier.

General Gariboldi, commander of the Italian Army arriving in the army group's area, reported to me for duty.

19/6/42

Sevastopol's northern front has been taken care of except for the "Lenin" and "North" forts. I passed Manstein's assessment of the situation, which culminated in the request for the delivery of new forces, on to the Army High Command and suggested diverting the infantry of the approaching 371st Division [Stempel] to the Crimea. This would mean the loss of the division for "Blue 2", which I feel is bearable. Army High Command decided that the 371st Division will relieve a battle-tested front-line division and this will then go to the Crimea. – North of Kerch a fresh, weak, futile landing attempt by the enemy.

Static divisions of the 6th Army took a projecting section of the enemy position north of Volchansk surprisingly quickly; about 500 prisoners were brought in. Our position was so shortened as to spare a division which we can very well use for "Blue 1."

Needless exchange of telexes with the Army High Command as to why the northern wing of "Fridericus" is attacking the way we want and not otherwise.

Heavy rainfalls will probably delay "Fridericus" even farther and have repeatedly prevented my planned flight to Army Group Weichs.

20/6/42

Fort "Lenin" was taken on Sevastopol's northern front; on the southern front the Romanians made some progress. – For several days traffic on the railroad north from Rostov, in front of the Wietersheim Group, has been noticeably heavy. Inclement weather has made accurate determinations on detrainings impossible. – The enemy is continuing to mass tanks east of Olkhovatka, opposite the 6th Army's front, which projects farthest east. The army group's intelligence officer estimates the enemy force assembled there at 22 armored divisions, of which about half can be supposed to be "war weary." Combined with yesterday's scouting raids on this front and the strengthened anti-aircraft defense, we must be prepared for the possibility that the enemy is going to attack here. These facts were reported to the Army High Command with the addition that quick action is now called for! It is too early to say whether the enemy will attack before we do and if "Fridericus" will still be feasible afterward.

But "Blue 2" should be ordered without delay so that the enemy does not regain the initiative. The weather at last appears to be improving.

To be ready for any eventuality at Olkhovatka, I ordered the 3rd and 23rd Panzer Divisions, which are standing by for "Blue" near Kharkov, to move up in the direction of Volchansk. There they will be in position for the buildup to "Blue 1" and will also be at hand to be committed against an enemy attack at Olkhovatka.

"Fell into the Enemy's Hands"

The General Staff Officer of the 23rd Panzer Division [Reichel, 1a 23rd Panzer Division] flew to the front in a *Storch* with all the orders for "Blue 1" and crash-landed or was shot down 4 km beyond our front. The aircraft was identified by a German patrol, a hole was found in the gas tank but no blood or traces of fire, so that it appears likely that all the orders fell into enemy hands. This situation also speaks in favor of the immediate launching of "Blue 1," especially since now, at the end of June, we have no more time to lose.

21/6/42

In the morning I told Halder that I was ordering "Fridericus" to begin tomorrow and that in view of the enemy buildup at Olkhovatka it was important to launch "Blue 1" quickly. I asked him to tell this to the *Führer*, who is still in Bavaria. Halder had doubts whether he could reach him today. In reply I once again stressed the urgency of my request. I went on to tell him that I had moved the 3rd and 23rd Panzer Divisions from Kharkov in the direction of Volchansk in order to be ready for any eventuality.

The last permanent fortifications on Sevastopol's northern front have fallen; on the eastern front, opposite the Romanians, the Russians are apparently withdrawing. The right wing of the southern front also made encouraging progress. Since I don't yet believe in a collapse of resistance, I suppose that the enemy, after his doubtless heavy losses, is shortening his front to gain forces for the defense of the fortress' southern front. – The day passed quietly on the rest of the army group's front. The conspicuous movements opposite the Wietersheim Group's right wing continue and new are 5 bridges across the Donets east of Slavyansk. – The 6th Army's easily-gained success of the day before yesterday brought in 946 prisoners and 20 guns.

22/6/42

On Sevastopol's northern front the main effort was shifted to the east wing in preparation for an attack on the commanding Gaitani Hills tomorrow. On the eastern front and the north part of the southern front the Romanians and the right wing of the German attack made progress, especially in a northerly direction, with the objective of forcing the enemy out of his salient projecting to the east or cutting him off there in conjunction with the attack by the north group.

A weak scouting raid against the north coast of the Sea of Azov was repulsed.

The 1st Panzer Army launched the "Fridericus" attack. The Donets was crossed quickly at and northwest of Izyum, Savintsy was taken. Things went more slowly for the tanks, which only got halfway to Kupyansk against stubborn resistance. The lack of mobility of III Panzer Corps' rifle units made itself felt.

Initial reports of large-scale withdrawals by the enemy have not been confirmed. in the course of the day the enemy counterattacked on the right wing at Savintsy and the north wing of the attack, resulting in a setback in the north. The day's overall result was thus not overwhelming. Rain which began falling during the night at first brought all movement by the tanks to a complete halt. According to pilot reports, elements of the enemy force massed at Olkhovatka appear to be leaving for the north, perhaps the result of the orders ["Blue 1"] found on the downed general staff officer [Reichel]. The bodies of this officer and his pilot were recovered by a German patrol; no indications were found that the papers he was carrying had been destroyed.

Heavy enemy rail traffic at Rostov continues. My first instinct is that this is a defensive measure, for the Russians must hold the Rostov area for as long as possible if they wish to defend the Caucasus.

The enemy appears to be organizing in depth opposite the 2nd Army.

Orders came to arrange the buildup for "Blue 1" so that the attack can begin on 26th June if the order is given.

23/6/42

On Sevastopol's northern front the north shore of Severnaya Bay has largely been cleared of the enemy. The north group's left wing and the south group's right wing are making slow progress.

The attack by 1st Panzer Army is going well; on the right wing, east of Izyum, the going is hard, but the enemy is beginning to yield on the rest of the front. The right wing of the panzer corps drove far to the south into the retreating enemy columns, while its left advanced as far as Kupyansk. By evening the enemy was in retreat on the entire front.

Movement of vehicles from Olkhovatka in a northwesterly direction toward Korocha have been reported for several days. If the enemy is in fact in possession of our attack orders, this movement is difficult to explain.

Who Is Responsible?

The matter of the loss of the secret orders by the general staff officer shot down on the 19th is assuming serious proportions. Halder tried to get me to travel to see the *Führer* tomorrow. I called Schmundt [Hitler's Chief Army Adjutant] in Berlin and told him that I didn't expect anything to come of it as long as the *Führer* did not have the results of the ongoing interrogations. I asked that, if after reading them the *Führer* still believed that he has to take serious action against somebody, that I be heard first, for I can see no serious guilt in any of the participants other than the general staff officer who was killed [Bock was thus judging the facts that the general staff officer in question had taken orders of a strategic nature with him in an aircraft whose route of flight led over enemy territory without a pressing need.] During the night Schmundt advised that the *Führer* would not be arriving in East Prussia until tomorrow afternoon and therefore could not meet with me tomorrow; everything else would be decided tomorrow.

General von Rabenau, Chief of the Army Archive, confirmed the rumor that many war files, including almost all the war diaries of my army groups from Poland and the Western Campaign had been destroyed by fire – "outside his office."

24/6/42

I briefed Halder on the success of the 1st Panzer Army. Only yesterday I pointed out to him that, in contrast to his previous fighting style, the enemy was seeking to retreat, there as well as at Volchansk. I can imagine that in larger terms he intends to avoid any major defeats now in order gain time for the Americans to intervene. So far, however, there are no signs of a withdrawal in front of the 2nd Army; there the enemy is apparently in the process of organizing an in-depth defense. But I once again asked that the orders be issued for the start of "Blue" at the earliest possible date, meaning the 27th, which followed in the evening. No significant progress at Sevastopol.

22nd Panzer and 10th Light Divisions linked up at Goroschowatka, the southern part of the 1st Panzer Army's pocket is thus closed. 16th Panzer

Division reached the Oskol at Kupyansk and drove south to close the north part as well. The entire attack front is on the advance, the enemy has now yielded in front of the north wing of the attack and has retreated beyond the stream line northwest of Dwuretschnaja.

Orders arrived that the *Führer* will see me tomorrow.

25/6/42

Progress on the left wing of the northern sector and in Sevastopol's eastern sector, the Romanians took "Bastion II."

The fighting by 1st Panzer Army has largely been brought to a conclusion. More than 21,000 prisoners, about 100 tanks and 250 guns were captured.

Flew to *Führer* Headquarters. The interrogations of the officers concerning the loss of the secret orders sent to Halder yesterday have not yet been given to the *Führer*; as was said to me, doesn't that say something!? – *Feldmarschall* Keitel received me first. Visibly nervous, he painted a dark picture of the situation. The *Führer* was insisting on setting a warning example. It is his view that the generals are disobedient and he obligated him, Keitel, to tell me that I must not make an attempt to dissuade the *Führer* from his plan of drastic punishment! Keitel then read to me a list of the supposed punishable offenses he had compiled. The list had been drawn up with no knowledge of the statements of the participants and contained mistakes, and I pleaded with keitel not to make use of this paper. The *Führer* received me an extraordinarily depressed mood. Schmundt was present. I described the facts as I saw them from all the reports and interrogations. Only seldom did the *Führer* interrupt me to ask a question. I was able to state my opinion calmly, the gist of which was that a scarcely-imaginable degree of guilt lay on the shoulders of the dead general staff officer, but that apart from that no conscious breach of discipline was found anywhere, just as little any punishable sloppiness; however, the commanding general of the XXXX Panzer Corps [XXXX Mot. Army Corps, renamed XXXX Panzer Corps June 1942, Stumme] could well be accused of having gone too far in his memorandum to his division commanders concerning their neighbor, specifically the missions of the 4th Panzer Army. In my eyes this was a clumsy error with perhaps serious consequences. It had to be punished as such – as an error [this would have prevented Stumme from being relieved of his position as well as avoided a court martial!]. In conclusion I was able to tell the *Führer* that I knew how concerned he was about the notion that obedience in the army, especially among the senior officers, has been lost. I said that I could take the burden from his shoulders, for as an old, experienced soldier I knew that his concern was unfounded. He could be assured that I and certainly every other senior officer would act without mercy whenever and wherever disobedience showed itself. The *Führer* also listened to these statements attentively and calmly. As was to be expected, he made no decision yet, but after a lengthy discussion of the situation he bade me farewell very cordially, obviously in a different frame of mind than when the conversation began.

26/6/42

Flew back to Poltava [HQ Army Group South].

At Sevastopol the enemy is gradually being forced back across the Tschornaja River line from the east and northeast. The capture of the commanding heights around Gaitani has not yet succeeded. – New weak landing attempt near Kerch. – Mopping-up action by the 1st Panzer Army on the left bank of the Oskol. – Downpours, which make all movement impossible, forced a postponement of the attack until 28th June.

27/6/42

The heights around gaitani were taken. – Lively enemy shipping traffic at the Taman Peninsula.

Numerous scouting raids, in some cases in greater than regimental strength, on nearly every army front. 6th Army reported that fresh downpours make it impossible for it to attack on the 28th. After securing the agreement of the supreme command, I ordered that the 6th Army is to attack the day after tomorrow. The timing is all the more critical, as the earlier attack by 2nd Army may perhaps entice the enemy to remove elements of his powerful armored forces located opposite the right wing of the 6th Army's attack, in order to throw them against the attack by Army Group Weichs.

At 18:00 a telegram arrived from *Feldmarschall* Keitel, saying that the *Führer* has ordered the Commanding General of XXXX Panzer Corps [Stumme], his Chief of Staff [Franz], and the commander of the 23rd Panzer Division [Boineburg-Lensfeld] relieved of their posts in the affair of the lost secret orders! I am to decide the exact time of the dismissal. The generals chosen to replace them have already arrived. Quite apart from the matter itself, removal of these two excellent armor commanders who are well-acquainted with the area is especially regrettable just now, because XXXX Panzer Corps is to spearhead the attack in the 6th Army's point of main effort. Conversations with Halder and Schmundt confirmed that my impression of the calm attitude of the *Führer* after my presentation on the 25th was correct. But while studying the files he discovered that a clerk of the 23rd Panzer Division was to be court martialled. This gave him the impression that they were trying to shift the blame onto a subordinate!

I had already told him during my talk on the 25th that proceedings against the clerk were out of the question; I said that I too felt that initiating proceedings against this NCO was unnecessary, but that I did not intervene because perhaps there was the possibility that the trial might shed more light on the matter. But in fact the proceedings against the NCO were stopped on the 23rd, because there was no incriminating evidence against him. Upsetting the supreme commander with all its consequences was thus unnecessary. I called the *Führer*, informed him of this fact, and said that I would find it a heavy burden if, as a result of unclear statements, I was held responsible for the serious consequences that followed. The *Führer* refused to accept this and admitted that the intended proceedings against a subordinate had incensed him. I replied that the notion of shifting guilt onto the NCO had already been refuted, since the commanding general of the panzer corps [Stumme] had ordered the cancellation of the court martial. When I asked whether the orders given were to remain in force the *Führer* answered "*ja*."

28/6/42

On Sevastopol's eastern front the enemy has been forced back toward the Sapun Heights and onto the hills near Inkermann, thus capturing the jump-off positions for the decisive attack. Enemy shipping traffic at Taman continues to be heavy; landing attempts near Kerch and on the north coast of the Sea of Azov were frustrated. The enemy staged further uncoordinated and for him, costly, tank attacks against the south wing of the 6th Army. The roads are so badly softened that the army will not be able to attack tomorrow. In contrast to other delays I don't mind this one, because it gives the enemy time to retire – a decision which he might make under the pressure of today's initial success by 2nd Army. Army Group Weichs broke through the enemy positions on a broad front, crossed the Tim and in several places the Kshen on the entire attack front, and drove through to a depth of 50 km with its tanks! If the army had the impression at the start that the enemy "was gone," it turned out in the course of the day that this was not the case. In several sectors, namely right and left of the breakthrough point, he fought back hard and staged heavy coun-terattacks, as a result of which the attack by the Hungarians on the right wing and by elements of XXX Corps [XXXI Corps in original; Fretter-Pico] did not make much headway. I subsequently advised Weichs [2nd Army] that even if the Hungarians remained stuck where they were, the 4th Panzer Army must not turn inward before their front, but must break through with all forces toward Voronezh. – Unfortunately it began to rain in the army group's area during the night.

The enemy is very active in the air; numerous bombing raids are making themselves felt in an uncomfortable way.

When I heard that the Commander-in-Chief of the 6th Army, Paulus, was considering requesting a court martial against himself in the matter of the lost secret orders, I said to him: "That is totally out of the question; concern your-self with the business at hand!"

29/6/42

At Sevastopol, elements of the north group made a surprise crossing of Severnaya Bay during the night and dug in on the heights on the south shore. The "old fort" west of Inkermann and the north part of the commanding Sapun Heights were taken.

17th Army repulsed a powerful local attack by the Russians.

After the ground dried out the attack by Army Group Weichs again made good progress on the entire front.

30/6/42

The capture of the Sapun Heights had the following consequences:

The north wing of the attack south of Severnaya Bay pierced another system of positions on a broad front and neared the outskirts of the city, reaching it in places. The south wing also made good progress.

The 6th Army has gone to the attack. Its main force encountered heavy resistance between Volchansk and Neshegol including numerous dug-in tanks; the 3rd Panzer Division was pulled out to the right in order to drive through the attack zone of the 113th Division, which is advancing well, and reach the defenders' rear. Very nice tactical move, but I am worried about frittering away the tanks, all the more so because the 3rd Panzer Division might easily be deflected from its direction of attack as it swings south. When I spoke to the Chief of Staff of 6th Army I learned that the movement was already under way. I then reminded him that it was important that the Oskol be crossed south of Novy Oskol quickly, as ordered, and that the tanks reach the high ground southeast of Chernyanka and Stary Oskol quickly. To this end the army's weak armored forces must return to the advance together. VIII Corps has to be kept close to XXXX Corps on the right so that the army's point of main effort remains sufficiently strong. These instructions were repeated in a telegrammed order.

The weak XXIX Corps [Obstfelder; in original XIX Corps], which in fact was only supposed to escort the attack, has made surprising progress; by today it was already at Korocha.

In Army Group Weichs' sector the Hungarians again failed today to overcome the Russian rear guards. Fresh thundershowers held up the tanks, especially their supplies, as a result of which gains were minimal. So far there is no sign of the expected buildup of strong Russian forces against the attack's north flank; only a few new armored divisions have turned up there and attacked the left wing of Army Group Weichs.

In the evening I asked Halder for permission to bring forward the Army Command's reserve behind Army Group Weichs, the 340th [Butze] and 323rd [Bergen] Divisions, in an easterly direction instead of to the southeast as he wants. In this way they will be on hand to promote the advance by or guard the left flank of Panzer Army Hoth [4th] and, if neither is necessary, to turn to the south.

1/7/42

Flew to Schtschigry; there I met Hoth [4th Panzer Army]. We agreed that the panzer army has to drive through to Voronezh in a compact mass without looking left or right. I could not get to the units as fresh downpours have made the roads almost impassable. I drove to the headquarters of the Hungarian 2nd Army. They realize that they are facing only rear guards, nevertheless they have so far failed to eject them from their well-built positions. I requested that the Commander-in-Chief leave weak forces only opposite the enemy's front and concentrate everything else on the left and resume the advance to the southeast with the strongest possible forces following the panzer army. I believe that the Hungarians [2nd Army, Jany] are brave; but their command apparatus is clumsy and slow.

The leading elements of the 3rd Panzer Division have crossed the Oskol south of Volokonovka. The VIII Corps infantry also reached the river at Chernyanka – an outstanding feat! To its left elements of static divisions are advancing on Skorodnoye from the south.

In Army Group Weichs' sector the 387th Division [Jahr] reached a village 20 km northwest of Stary Oskol. The most forward elements of the panzer army fought off an attack by fresh Russian armored forces which were thrown against it and drove on to Kulewka. The infantry divisions of the panzer army's left wing reached the Kshen. Opposite the left-wing corps powerful attacks by enemy tanks broke down after temporary limited successes.

The Army Command is urging that I encircle the enemy forces holding in the bend of the Oskol west of Valuyki with the static divisions there. The 6th Army thinks that possible. The orders were issued with the reminder to bring elements of XVII Corps toward the east side of the Oskol between the 3rd Panzer Division and Valuyki as quickly as possible in order to make it difficult for the enemy to retreat across the river there.

I briefed the *Führer* on the situation and said that I was sending the 6th Army's mobile forces north instead of northeast, in order to cut off those enemy forces not already cut off and at the same time relieve Panzer Army Hoth of any worry about its right flank as it advances on Voronezh. The close encirclement of the enemy forces still west of the Oskol by closing the door at Stary Oskol was to be achieved mainly by infantry forces. The *Führer* agreed.

Immediately after this conversation came the report that the enemy was retreating before the 6th Army. I issued the following order: 6th Army to initiate pursuit on the entire front, mobile forces in the lead toward Istobnoje and Siniye-Lipyagi. Screening of right flank by infantry divisions in line Valuyki-Nikolajewka-Korotoyak. Army Group Weichs continue to attack with the Hungarians and Panzer Army Hoth, panzer army toward Voronezh, 16th Motorized Division is to be sent to the panzer army after the crossing at Stary Oskol has been barricaded. Left wing of the army to screen the northern flank of the attack.

Sevastopol has fallen! A success which is first and foremost due to Manstein's command.

"Attack by the 6th Army"

2/7/42

The remnants of the Russian Sevastopol army, squeezed together in a tiny area on the outer fringes of the Khersonyes Peninsula west of Sevastopol, face destruction.

Localized assaults by the enemy against the Wietersheim Group and, 5 battalions strong, against the 17th Army, were beaten back.

The attack by 6th Army to clear the bulge west of Valuyki made good progress on the right wing; however the left wing was pinned down by enemy tank attacks until the afternoon. The 3rd Panzer Division helped fight off the attacks; today the division is still clinging to its bridgehead at Volokonovka! That is the curse of the evil deed of 30th June!

All the remaining army front pushed toward the Oskol against weak resistance.

In Weichs' sector the Hungarians slowly began to move. The enemy has probably withdrawn. The vanguard of the 387th Division and the attack spearheads of the 4th Panzer Army were attacked by enemy armored forces, which were defeated. The Olym was crossed at a number of places against heavy resistance. The infantry divisions of the panzer army's left wing gained some ground to the east. The extreme left wing of the panzer army and LV Corps [Vierow] attacked the enemy and were repulsed. Transport movements have been sighted from the east toward Voronezh and from the northeast toward Yelets.

In the evening I spoke with Halder about the situation, especially about the deployment to the northeast of XXXX Panzer Corps I had ordered. I am having a hard time getting the 6th Army to do so, and it wants to send the tanks to Korotoyak. There they will get bogged down in a bend in the river and do no good. They belong on the battlefield so as to smash the enemy elements still east of the Oskol retreating east and to relieve the 4th Panzer Army of any worry about its right flank. Halder agreed. I learned that the supreme command no longer places any decisive importance on the capture of Voronezh. That is new! At the moment I must follow the existing orders, for wheeling south with the panzer army is out of the question until after we reach the Don.

3/7/42

The *Führer* arrived at 07:00; even though he had to have left *Führer* Headquarters at about 04:00, he was in an especially receptive, friendly mood. He confirmed what Halder had said yesterday and gave me freedom to deviate from the objective of Voronezh if excessively heavy fighting was required to reach it. All that matters to him is that the large aircraft factories and, if possible, the railroad installations are rendered unusable; it is all the same to him whether the 4th Panzer Army reaches the Don somewhat more or less south of it.

Discussed the Army High Command's thoughts on the future conduct of the entire operation, which arrived during the night. The idea was raised of launching "Blue" with infantry forces only to avoid losing time. I pointed out that this would make it impossible to encircle the enemy, who has gradually learned from past experience. The enemy will withdraw in time, as he has tried to do, though so far not altogether successfully, in all the battles this year. It is therefore important that we attack as soon as possible with the mobile forces and in doing so strike just behind the Aidar, beyond which the enemy will probably withdraw as soon as he recognizes the threat of being outflanked on both sides. The *Führer* agreed. The question was then discussed whether it was advisable to send forces from the Crimea across to the Taman Peninsula in conjunction with "Blue 3," in order to bring about a rapid collapse of the enemy defense on the lower Don. Sodenstern proposed reexamining this idea to the Army High Command yesterday; I also spoke in favor of it and received orders to begin preparations for the operation. Finally Halder raised the question of the division of command for "Blue 2."

I stuck to my previous refusal, because all planning, preparation, readying of forces, and so on was in my hands and the participation of a second army group will only complicate command. Decisions are often required which must be made and put into action very quickly. I doubt if this would be possible with two army groups in command. The matter remained undecided.

In the discussion the *Führer* made fun of the English for sacking every general for whom something went wrong and thus undermining the freedom of decision in their army.

In the Crimea the fighting is nearing its end.

In the army group's southern sector scouting raids and continued activity in the air by the enemy.

The enemy in front of 6th Army is beaten; the bulk of his forces have escaped from the bulge west of Valuyki; the army wheeled its two right-wing corps toward the line Valuyki-Nikolajewka-Korotoyak. The inner wings of the 6th Army and Army Group Weichs joined hands at Stary Oskol. The enemy elements still west of the Oskol were cut off. Northeast of Stary Oskol the right wing of the 4th Panzer Army drove into fleeing Red columns. The panzer army is advancing fast toward the east on the entire front and its leading elements are within a few kilometers of the Don. South of Livny enemy tanks continue to attack in vain; the focus of the enemy's attacks has shifted to the area between Kshen and Olym; to the left of that today he attacked weakly or not at all. I instructed Army Group Weichs to send the 340th and 323rd Divisions toward Voronezh and north as quickly as possible, the 387th and the Hungarian 6th [Light] toward Voronezh and south, in order to have infantry forces in hand for the protection of the panzer army's northern flank and for the rapid relief of this army after reaching the Don, so that after achieving their mission the tanks are free for "Blue 2" with no loss of time.

The 6th Army is pressing to be let loose toward Korotoyak with its mobile forces. It is also thoroughly desirable to catch elements of the enemy retreating through Korotoyak and in the confusion of the moment quickly and easily take possession of bridgeheads across the Tichaja Sosna. But I must also see to it that the 4th Panzer Army can fix its eyes on Voronezh and on guarding its northern flank. Only then will it be possible to take Voronezh quickly and easily and hold onto it until the required demolitions are carried out there. I therefore instructed the 6th Army to dispatch mobile forces toward Ostrogozhsk and Korotoyak and take over the job of screening the 4th Panzer Army's southern flank at the Don between Korotoyak and the army boundary.

The Commander-in-Chief of the Romanian army to be formed on my right wing, General Dimitrescu, reported for duty and had breakfast with me.

4/7/42

In the morning came the news that the 24th Panzer Division and the Infantry Regiment *Großdeutschland* had reached the Don, elements of the former have crossed over a burning bridge southwest of Voronezh and have established a bridgehead. Weichs is worried because the panzer army has been attacked on its northern flank and now major elements are pinned down there. I therefore gave authorization for the Hungarian armored division, the final elements of which will arrive tomorrow, to be moved forward in an easterly direction. For now the division remains in the army group reserve.

When I learned that the 6th Army had committed the entire XXXX Panzer Corps toward Korotoyak but sent only reconnaissance units to the northeast, I gave orders that an entire division was to be diverted there – again with the thought in mind that the 4th Panzer Army must be freed of any worry about its right flank at least. In the course of the day it was learned that there were still enemy tank forces between the Don and the Oskol and that these were engaged with the eastward-advancing 16th Motorized Division. The 6th Army's XXXX Panzer Corps made little progress today, supposedly it was held up by mines. When the army kept nagging about whether an entire motorized division had to be sent to the northeast, I decreed that the 23rd Panzer Division was to be sent there. To the question what should be done first, capture the bridgeheads at the Tichaja Sosna or guard the 4th Panzer Army's southern flank, I answered: "both!"

The first task is to be dealt with by two mobile and one infantry divisions, the second by the 23rd Panzer Division.

The right wing of the 6th Army pushed ahead through the forests north of Valuyki against weakening resistance.

VIII Corps [Heitz] has also wheeled east, together with the right wing of Army Group Weichs, XXIX Corps is participating in the destruction of the surrounded enemy south of Stary Oskol.

The 4th Panzer Army succeeded in establishing 3 bridgeheads across the Don west of Voronezh; elements of its left panzer corps are in combat with the enemy streaming back toward Voronezh. On the panzer army's left wing the 11th Panzer Division is in heavy fighting with enemy forces attacking from the north. The enemy's attacks west of Olym have grown weaker, in some cases petered out altogether. But since I have deployed infantry to guard the northern flank between the Don and the Olym, and the 4th Panzer Army must also free itself there after ending its mission at Voronezh, I placed Headquarters, XXIX Corps [Obstfelder; in original XIX Corps] at the disposal of Army Group Weichs along with two divisions which today were still fighting at Stary Oskol as part of the 6th Army.

Air reconnaissance found columns streaming back from the northwest toward Korotoyak, from there to the east and north, and from the northwest toward Voronezh and from there to the south, as well as motorized forces approaching Yelets from the north.

5/7/42

The morning picture showed that the southward removal of the 3rd Panzer Division during the initial assault on 30th June is still having an effect today. The division is lagging far behind. Orders were sent to 6th Army by telegram, demanding that XXXX Corps pull together the 3rd Panzer and 29th Motorized Divisions and reach the assigned objective of Ostrogozhsk-Korotoyak before the day is over. I demanded the same of the 23rd Panzer Division, which tactically is subordinate to the 4th Panzer Army. The boundary between Army Group Weichs and the 6th Army was moved south to the Potodan.

During the afternoon Halder informed Sodenstern that the *Führer* is annoyed at the slow progress by the right wing. The 6th Army should have had bridgeheads across the Tichaja Sosna long ago! He also doesn't know what the 23rd Panzer Division is supposed to be doing "up there!" The 2nd Army should be pulling divisions from its left wing and transferring them to the right instead of attacking unnecessarily. I advised Halder that the slow progress by the panzer corps had been addressed; moreover I had objected in vain to the removal of the corps' most important and best commanders shortly before the attack. I reminded him that part of the reason for the lagging behind of the 3rd Panzer Division was that it had been diverted along the Oskol the day before yesterday as a result of an intervention on the part of the supreme command. As for the 23rd Panzer Division, it is engaged in heavy fighting at Repiewka. Thus we have proof that there are still significant enemy forces on the 4th Panzer Army's right flank and that the division thus belongs there. The bridgeheads desired by the *Führer* have already been established at Budjonny, Nikolajewka and Ostrogozhsk. The 2nd Army's missions are all clear. But the army is engaged on almost the entire front. As well there exists a written directive from the Army High Command stating that it is desirable to place the Livny-Voronezh road behind the front. Halder replied that this had only been a "working theory" – a change which I opposed strongly.

Toward evening, when it became clear that resistance was weakening, I instructed 6th Army to pursue and gave as its initial objective the line Liman (that is the southernmost bridgehead across the Oskol) – Veidelevka-Varvarovka-Kamenka. I reported this to the Army Command with the addition that I had ordered the railroad bridge over the Don at Svoboda blown. At the same time I reported that the relief of the mobile divisions at Voronezh depended on the arrival of the infantry, and their deployment to the south on the timely provision of fuel. The answer came that the right wing of the 6th Army can only attack when the enemy is gone! The strengthened left wing can advance and wheel about. Pivot point at Budjonny. They want to set a trap for the enemy and they believe he will fall for it if we don't attack him in the front! The bridge at Svoboda is not to be blown, rather one which lies twenty kilometers northeast of it.

Enemy resistance has stiffened at Voronezh, however at present the enemy is weak in artillery but is moving in reinforcements from all sides. Hoth's old aversion against the attack was expressed in an intercepted radio communication by the Army High Command's liaison officer with him. But Weichs definitely wants to make the attempt to take Voronezh tomorrow morning as long as the enemy is weak, in particular in artillery. The Army High Command was advised that Weichs only considers holding the bridgehead possible if the city of Voronezh is incorporated; he believes that the railroad traffic at Voronezh from the west bank of the Don cannot be cut if the bridgehead is abandoned.

I agree with Weich's position. The supreme command decided otherwise: the attack might "perhaps" take place at a later time.

24th Panzer Division and *Großdeutschland* are to be relieved in the bridgeheads in front of Voronezh by the nearest motorized divisions.

The enemy attacks against the left wing of Army Group Weichs are becoming ever weaker. A powerful Russian attack group at Uriskoje was attacked concentrically, including with tanks, and destroyed.

The booty from Sevastopol has climbed to more than 95,000 prisoners and vast amounts of equipment.

Orders came that List is to assume command over the 11th, 1st Panzer and 17th Armies on the 7th [July]. Thus the battle will be cut into two parts; it would be correct to have the two last-named armies attack as quickly as possible.

6/7/42

Conversation with Heusinger in the morning. An advance detachment of the 29th Motorized Division [Fremerey] has reached the railroad 25 km southeast of Ostrogozhsk. A further bridgehead across the Tichaja was established southeast of Ostrogozhsk by the 3rd Panzer Division. I intend to order the 6th Army to break through to the Kalitva with its eastern wing and armored forces while screening its left flank. I had to request confirmation of my plan, since it would be uncomfortable for me to have to withdraw orders already given as yesterday. I consider keeping the pivot point at Budjonny to be a mistake, for the enemy there is decidedly weak and in my impression consists of nothing more than rear guards. Equally unchanged is my view that an attack by the entire 6th Army is the right thing to do in this situation.

Weichs requested that the 2nd Army be moved forward to the line Don-Snov-Sosna-Trudy. With the enemy weak, this position can be reached easily now and would spare far more forces than the shorter position since there is a river obstacle in front of almost the entire front. Even if the salient projecting far to the northeast causes me no discomfort, I think it advisable to give in to the army's request, because its further advance to the north will serve to relieve Army Group Center and deceive the enemy as to our true direction of attack. I also asked for a decision on this matter.

At midmorning the situation was as follows: on the northern wing the 4th Panzer Division attacked and totally destroyed two enemy armored brigades. The enemy is falling back on Army Group Weichs' entire northern front, in places he is reported to be in "flight." Almost simultaneously came the news that the enemy had apparently evacuated Voronezh and that during the night a squadron of the 24th Panzer Division had broken through the south part of Voronezh to the Voronezh River.

I called Halder and told him pointedly that the enemy was totally defeated, that all of the 6th Army must attack, with the main effort on the left wing of course, but on the entire front. Angered by the whining of the past days, I requested permission to occupy Voronezh and asked whether, after the Army Command had forbidden the 2nd Army to advance any farther, the 9th Panzer Division was now to be ordered to withdraw after its victory. This argument also failed to change the Army Command's mind about forbidding the 6th Army's northern wing from advancing into its desired line. The planned movement of the 6th Army's right wing is a mistake, its left wing was turned loose. In the course of the day this wing gained a great deal of ground to the south.

The Don bridge at Korotoyak fell into our hands intact. Voronezh and one Don bridge were occupied unopposed.

The Army High Command subsequently pressed me to turn the panzer army loose at and north of Voronezh and have it head south. That is undoubtedly the right thing to do, but it depends on how quickly the relieving units arrive.

Overrun and scattered enemy units are running around everywhere in the rear of the 6th Army and Army Group Weichs, making it difficult to calculate the number of prisoners and amount of booty.

Near kerch 100 Russians were captured while trying to break out of a mine in which they had been hiding since mid-May.

7/7/42

Yesterday evening the 3rd Panzer Division, part of the 6th Army's left wing, reached the Kalitva at Rossosh. The 305th Division is also closing in on the river. Toward noon 6th Army reported that the bulk of the enemy had – as expected – withdrawn before LI Corps. VIII Corps, which is advancing south by way of Nikolajewka, reports that the retreat lacks any unified command, only here and there are jumbled-together groups putting up a fight, the enemy is abandoning guns, all in all the signs of a local collapse are mounting. I reported this to *General* Jodl of the Armed Forces High Command and said that I had ordered an attack on the entire front. Weich, too, reported that the enemy was retreating in front of his northern flank and asked whether he might not move into the line toward which he was striving. I decided that his right wing had to stay with the line Olkhovatka-Gorki which was ordered yesterday, but that west of that he might move forward as far as the Sosna and the Trudy under the condition that a division was pulled out of the front in connection with this movement. In the evening the order was broadened, calling for a division to be pulled out of the left wing and sent east in any case. Further the army group received two urgent orders aimed at speeding up the departure south of its motorized units. In the course of the day it was learned that yesterday's reported "flight" by the enemy opposite the northern front was only true locally, for today the enemy went over to the attack in various places there.

By evening the 6th Army had crossed the Kalitva on the entire front of VIII Corps and the XXXX Panzer Corps. LI and XVII Corps advanced up to 18 kilometers through the abandoned enemy positions. In the evening the army received orders to advance with XXXX Panzer Corps as far as the hill south of Mikhailovka, initially screening toward Pavlovsk, close ranks there, capture bridgeheads across the Boguchar and scout to all sides. Strong infantry forces are to be sent in behind XXXX Panzer Corps. Furthermore, I advised that *Großdeutschland* and the 24th Panzer Division were to attack south tomorrow and at first would be subordinated to XXXX Panzer Corps.

A directive from the Army High Command says that Army Group List, my old 1st Panzer Army and the 17th Army, is to attack on the 9th with its main weight through Sissitschansk, in order to reach the hills near Wyssotschinoff. On the rest of the front Army Group List is to attack only if the enemy decamps. Wyssotschinoff is the old objective of the "Blue 2" attack; the Army High Command is thus still hanging onto "Blue 2" and would like to encircle a foe who is no longer there.

8/7/42

The leading elements of the 23rd Panzer Division released in the north have reached XXXX Panzer Corps. The *Großdeutschland* Division, which was relieved at Voronezh is also marching south, while the 24th Panzer Division, held up by blown bridges and thundershowers, cannot set off until tomorrow. In the morning attacks from the north toward Voronezh were repulsed. In the northern part of the city several nests which probably missed the general evacuation are still holding on.

At noon I submitted a telex to Halder, in which I said that the enemy was without any doubt retreating in front of the 6th Army's entire front and also south of it and that as presently deployed by the Army Command the double-sided envelopment will probably hit nothing, that in my opinion Operation "Blue 2" is dead and the Army Command must consider with what intent and to where the panzer forces of my left wing should now be sent. The enemy in front of the 6th Army's right wing continues to retreat. The two corps on the right wing advanced well over 30 kilometers against almost no resistance. VIII Army Corps met somewhat stronger resistance, which was broken; this corps, too, gained 30 kilometers and is already beyond the Aidar River line. XXXX Panzer Corps encountered enemy forces north of Mikhailovka; by evening still no final reports from there. Elements of the corps captured an intact bridge over the Don at Belogorye northwest of Pavlovsk. At Svoboda there are still enemy troops on the south bank of the Don. They attacked our small bridgehead at Korotoyak. To the north there are still elements on the west bank of the Don, which will have to be cleared out by the slowly-approaching Hungarians tomorrow or the day after.

The 2nd Army's northern front is going over to the defensive. The enemy, who was not pursued, has made an about face and has staged local attacks, particularly between the Don and the Olym. The army expects stronger attacks.

Faced with all these facts, by well into the night the Army Command still had not decided on an order concerning the continuation of the operation. In a conversation between *General* Heusinger and Sodenstern, the former said that both army groups had to come to an agreement over the subsequent command of the two panzer armies! Is that better than both panzer armies under the strict control of one army group?

9/7/42

The 6th Army's right wing continued toward the Aidar, the center turned left to establish contact with the XXXX Panzer Corps, the divisions of the left wing are approaching the Don. The center of XXXX Panzer Corps encountered strong enemy forces, which were thrown back; by evening the corps was southwest and southeast of Mikhailovka and had established a bridgehead across the Boguchar. The Russians in front of 6th Army are retreating to the east in dense columns. Again today attacks against the Korotoyak bridgehead were repulsed.

In the early afternoon XXXXVIII Panzer Corps reached the Tichaja Sosna with the *Großdeutschland* [Division] and the 24th Panzer Division. The river was crossed in places and the units had to refuel.

In Army Group Weichs' sector the arrival of the Hungarians at the Don is taking a very long time; its eastern front is generally quiet. On the northern front the enemy attacked on both sides of the Olym with strong forces, achieved several insignificant penetrations but was beaten back for the most part.

When no order for the continuation of the operation had arrived by 19:30, I placed a call to the Army High Command and proposed that they name the area around N. Astachoff as the next objective for my panzers. By advancing quickly over the commanding high ground we might reach the last roads before my front over which the enemy is retreating and so perhaps yet catch a part of him. Late in the evening I was informed that the *Führer* had ordered the XXXX Panzer Corps to advance along the railroad to Millerovo with its main force and toward Meshkov with its left wing, in order to quickly take possession of the rail line and "cut off the enemy's retreat"; a later further advance toward Kamensk on the Donets is possible.

A bridgehead is to be established across the Don at Boguchar, in order to enable an eventual advance by the panzer army east of the Don toward Stalingrad! When I asked if I should consider this an order, I was told: no, only as a preparatory measure. My objection that the units had to have their orders for tomorrow morning now also failed to change anything. I instructed the XXXX Panzer Corps to send its strong right wing toward Millerovo, the left toward Meshkov, and screen its left flank – we won't get much of the enemy this way!

10/7/42

A telegram from the Army High Command which arrived during the night confirmed yesterday's verbal directive and added that after crossing the Donets, Army Group A [List] was to capture crossings over the Aidar at and south of Starobelsk and then advance toward the line Kamensk-Millerovo. Furthermore, an order arrived that the 9th [Baesler] and 11th [Balck] Panzer Divisions, which were just starting to be relieved northwest of Voronezh, are to be placed at the disposal of the Army High Command ready for travel and transport. Hopefully they won't take away both divisions, for there exists no doubt that we can expect the attacks against Weichs' northern flank to continue for some time.

On an order from the army group the Hungarian army corps arriving in the second line has been diverted to the southeast and through the 6th Army's area to the Pavlovsk-Korotoyak sector of the Don, in the expectation that the bulk of the 4th Panzer Army will have crossed over the Tichaja Sosna bridges when the leading elements of the Hungarians arrive.

In Army Group A's sector the 1st Panzer Army [Kleist] crossed the Donets at Lisichansk. On its left the Romanians are also on the advance. The right wing of the 6th Army reached the Aidar on the entire front and following brief skirmishes with rear guards took possession of the crossings. The divisions of the center drove across the Belaya to the southeast and sought to link up with the panzer corps, the leading elements of which reached the area of Nikolskoye and east in the evening. VIII Corps pushed left in order to release the tanks near Boguchar and established the required bridgehead there. The divisions of the left wing are approaching the Don. At Svoboda the enemy was driven back across the river. On Weichs' southern wing the Hungarians have taken over screening at the Don, except for the most important sector due north of the mouth of the Rossosh, where the Russians are still on the west bank. relief of the motorized division at Voronezh is proceeding slowly; bridge conditions are difficult and the enemy is attacking Voronezh from the north. The enemy has also staged heavy attacks with tanks on the northern front between the Don and the Kshen, but they are uncoordinated. Various local penetrations have to be eliminated. Especially difficult is the situation of the green 340th Division [Butze], which was struck by a heavy armored attack while relieving the panzers. Today alone 50 Russian tanks were destroyed on this front.

Again there are no directives for the coming day. I sent a proposal to the Army Command that XXXXVIII Panzer Corps [Kempf], which today is still stuck back at the Tichaja Sosna with fuel problems, be moved forward along-side the XXXX Panzer Corps; they agreed with this.

11/7/42

The Russians have blown the Don bridge at Boguchar. The Army Command will now have to do without the bridgehead it had demanded there.

Our pilots have attacked dense columns which had become backed up at the Don bridges as they retreated; large elements of the enemy have thus got away.

In the morning came the news that the enemy is also withdrawing east in front of the north half of Army Group A. A conversation with the Army High Command revealed that it will be proposed to the *Führer* that the panzer army be sent toward the Donets with its right wing toward Kamensk and east. I issued the following order to the 4th Panzer Army: Objective of the XXXX Panzer Corps with the 23rd and 3rd Panzer Divisions: Donets at Kamensk and southeast, all remaining forces into the area Kashary-high ground around Bokovskaya.

By evening the 6th Army's right wing had gained further ground to the southeast. XXXX Panzer Corps was also moving south again with light fighting. XXXXVIII Panzer Corps, which is moving forward to join it, was held up by fuel and bridge difficulties. The left wing of the 6th Army reached the Don.

In Army Group Weichs area the Hungarians still have no contact with the enemy, who is still on the west side of the Don at Jaryw. The relief of the motorized division at Voronezh is in progress. On the northern flank the enemy launched particularly heavy attacks north of Zemlyansk and achieved a deep penetration. In response to a request the Army High Command made available the 9th [Baeßler] and 11th [Balck] Panzer Divisions in order to launch a quick, sharp blow to completely restore the situation there.

12/7/42

During the night a directive arrived from the Army High Command for the continuation of operations:

"Army Group B [Bock] is to proceed in the general direction of the mouth of the Donets, sending all available forces ahead in the direction of Kamensk, with the objective of engaging the enemy north of the Don and destroying him by attacking his rear. The remaining forces are to cover this movement to the east and create the conditions for the advance in the direction of Stalingrad."

Apart from being unclear, this directive scatters my weak armored units to the four winds.

Sending all available forces ahead in the direction of Kamensk is impossible on account of the road conditions. Each motorized unit now needs its own road.

Six tributaries run from the north and northeast to the south into the Donets in front of the 4th Panzer Army's front. It will be possible to send the leading element, XXXX Panzer Corps, forward along two land ridges between these rivers toward the Donets between Kamensk and Forschtadt. The following XXXXVIII Panzer Corps will be sent forward toward the commanding plateau which extends south from Bokovskaya through Morosovskaya. If the area of Morosovskaya is reached, the corps can be sent to the right and straight across the Don toward the Donets, or left toward enemy forces threatening the entire operation from the east. I brought up these thoughts with *Oberst* von Grolman of the Army High Command yesterday when the Army Command was considering deploying my panzer forces in the country cut by rivers south of Millerovo. They were probably not understood, for during the night a telegram came from the Chief of the General Staff to Sodenstern with the request to "oppose any unnecessary broadening of the deployment of the mobile forces to the east. The army's next mission lies in the south. Turning of the units to the south against the rear of the enemy holding north of Rostov must be possible at any time. Deployment of mobile forces in a southeasterly or easterly direction is justifiable only as required to provide the necessary flanking cover."

Meanwhile the left wing of Army Group A as well as my right wing were nearing the town of Millerovo. Strong armored forces and infantry divisions will conglomerate in a small area there, in the center of the operation, while the wings are too weak!

Flew to 4th Panzer Army in Olkhovatka, where I discussed the continuation of the operation with Hoth and saw elements of *Großdeutschland* and the 24th Panzer Division. Despite the burning heat and frightful dust the troops are in outstanding spirits. It is regrettable that both divisions are still immobilized without fuel.

On the remainder of the front everything is going according to plan. The Hungarians on Weichs' right wing finally came to grips with the Russians still on this side of the Don and after brief success – retreated! The Russians attacked Voronezh's northern front and were repulsed. The counterattack against the enemy armor which drove into the northern flank staged by the 9th and 11th Panzer Divisions, which were made available by the Army High Command for that purpose, went well, even if it did not lead to a total encirclement as was hoped for. In any case the Russians were so battered that they withdrew. That is significant, for among the units identified opposite von Weich's northern front between Voronezh and the left wing are 33 armored brigades.

13/7/42

At midmorning I telegraphed Halder:

"The enemy opposite the 4th Panzer Army and the northern wing of Army Group A is withdrawing, with elements to the east and southeast and strong elements to the south. I believe that the destruction of significant enemy forces will not be achieved in an operation which is strong in the center and weak on the wings and whose main direction of advance leads through Millerovo into the midst of the enemy. Instead the main thrust by the 4th Panzer Army should be directed through the Morosovskaya area into the area of the mouth of the Donets and east while guarding its rear and its eastern flank."

In the afternoon *Feldmarschall* Keitel informed me by telephone that by order of the *Führer* the 4th Panzer Army was to join Army Group A, as had been envisaged by the supreme command. Further he took me completely by surprise by passing on to me the order that *Generaloberst* von Weichs was to take over command of Army Group B and that I was being placed at the disposal of the *Führer*!

14/7/42

Midmorning I briefed Weichs on the situation and state of the army group.

In the afternoon an order arrived which deployed the 4th Panzer Army in the manner I proposed yesterday.

15/7/42

Weichs assumed command at 06:00, at 07:00 I flew to Berlin.

POSTSCRIPT
15 JULY 1942 TO 2 MAY 1945

**Feldmarschall von Bock's Struggle For His Honor
As a Soldier and Against Hitler's Intrigues**

*On **14/7/42** Bock spoke by telephone with Schmundt, Hitler's chief army adjutant. In the course of their conversation "the latter confirmed the alleged delay in the departure of the 24th Panzer Division and the 'Großdeutschland' Division from Voronezh to the south as the reason behind the decision made about me. I do not believe that, because it cannot stand up to even the most casual scrutiny. Schmundt suggested that I ask to meet with the Führer. I thought it better if he inform me when the Führer is in Berlin and wants to see me. Schmundt promised to do so." Thus Bock decided against an immediate correction of Hitler's decision to relieve him and instead placed his hopes on rehabilitation!*

15/7/42

The following telex was passed on to me from the army group [Army Group B]: "Effective 13th July *Generalfeldmarschall* von Bock resigned his position as Commander-in-Chief of Army Group B and has been placed at the disposal of the *Führer* and Supreme Commander of the Armed Forces."

20/7/42

Before I left Poltava I asked Sodenstern to have a summary prepared from the war diary of everything involving the relief and departure of the two divisions from Voronezh. This summary must show if there was any oversight on the part of the army group. The need to speed up the departure to the south was always clear to me; everything possible was done toward that end. But I need evidence to be able to prove the unfounded nature of the accusation.

Sodenstern wrote today that the summary is complete, but that – in agreement with List and Weichs – he strongly advises that I not take any steps. Since the reasons named by Keitel "could not be sufficient or even substantial," they would just look for others which would be harder to refute. Schmundt also advised "especially forcefully" that I leave things alone for the time being and said, "that the *Führer* fully intends to speak with you as soon as the running of the current operation no longer takes up as much of his time."

22/7/42

I replied to Sodenstern that I would heed his advice, and in this letter I once again turned against the unfounded nature of Keitel's reasons as well as an "expanded" reason that has meanwhile seeped through, which seeks to trace the ill-feeling back to the history behind the Kharkov battle.

31/7/42

Sodenstern wrote that new, strict regulations prevent him from sending the war diary extracts without the permission of the OKH; but he has no doubt that authorization will be forthcoming. Then he went into the matter of the turn to the south and wrote:

"The conversation with *Generaloberst* Halder took place on 5th July at 14:40 and had the following content:

The *Generaloberst* described the *Führer*'s train of thought, which he had expressed in the course of that day's noon briefing. He was following the development of the operation with great impatience. In particular he complained that the XXXX Panzer Corps had not yet been turned southeast in the general direction of Starobelsk and that the headquarters commanding the northern flank was apparently unclear about the basic concept of the operation, to release the strongest possible forces to the southeast. Our forces in the area south of Livny were still much too strong.

I subsequently advised the *Generaloberst* that the basic trend of the operation was absolutely clear to both the headquarters of the army group and that of Army Group Weichs and that everything was being done to carry it out. However, there was some concern about the southern flank of 4th Panzer Army, whose rapid advance toward Voronezh appeared threatened should enemy forces show up there, which is certainly to be expected. This consideration caused the Commander-in-Chief of the army group to stick to his decision to move at least some elements of XXXX Panzer Corps (23rd Panzer Division) into the area around Krasno Lipje... As far as turning the XXXX Panzer Corps south, I can say that: On 5th July at 11:30 orders were issued that the XXXX Panzer Corps (without the 23rd Panzer Division) was to break through toward Ostrogozhsk and Korotoyak before the day was over.

That evening (20:20) the *Feldmarschall* advised the *Führer* by telex that the 6th Army had captured bridgeheads at Liman, Budjonny, Nikolajewka and Ostrogozhsk and that orders had been issued for the follow-up to the south, at first to the line Topoli Station-Veidelevka-Varvarovka-Kamenka-Nikolskoye (south of Svoboda). On 6th July the 6th Army's plan to advance the XXXX Panzer Corps as far to the southeast as fuel allowed, meaning roughly as far as the Kalitva, was approved..."

I consider Halder's statements in the above-mentioned conversation to be a not unusual product of the supreme commander's impatience. I called Halder to point out the unjustified nature of the charges and to show how every reason for impatience had been overtaken by events. If this resulted in sharp words on my part, they were the natural frictions associated with moments of high tension. There was no question of a lack of clarity about the conduct of the operation, which was also stressed by Sodenstern; and I had never even thought about a serious disagreement.

It is strange that they made Weichs Commander-in-Chief of the army group [B] after thinking on the 5th that he didn't grasp the sense of the operation!

I replied to Sodenstern that I would do without the war diary extract, because I didn't want to expose myself to what would my using it would entail. I also know that I didn't overlook anything in the matter of the turn to the south. In my letter I again stated that our order to turn was issued at least 24 hours before Halder's call arrived on the 5th. Further, I wrote:

"Everybody knows that the idea that the three planned operations would run together came from us! It was we who feared that the supreme commander was not completely clear about the scale of the success and thus about the measures to be taken. This concern was confirmed by the fact that the supreme commander did not believe that the enemy was retreating before our right wing until 24 hours too late!..."

6/8/42

Sodenstern wrote that Schmundt had seen him and had stated that the *Führer* would "with certainty" himself arrange to talk with me.

The former commander of XXXX Panzer Corps, General der Panzertruppe Stumme, visited von Bock in the first half of August. In a letter to Paulus on 14 August 1942 he wrote: "...After a brief stop in Poltava and a very comradely farewell evening with G.FM. von Bock, who told me of his great efforts with the Führer to avoid blowing the matter out of proportion and to change his opinion to not guilty, the three of us flew home to Germany."

5/9/42

At the front and at home they are being told that I am ill. As well there are rumors circulating about my departure, some of them of absurd. On 9th August *Das Reich* published a large photo of me in the field and treated my command – among other things – in a kindly fashion. Other domestic and foreign papers continue to print my name and until well into September continued to speak of "Army Group Bock."

October 1942

Only gradually is the truth seeping through; English radio calls me a "scapegoat!"

List and Halder have been sent home. Schmundt has taken over the Army Personnel Office instead of the junior Keitel, while keeping his post as the *Führer*'s adjutant.

In September Foreign Minister Ribbentrop gave a speech in which he celebrated the *Führer*'s generalship and said that the plans for all the campaigns and battles originated from him alone. On 4th October Göring underscored these statements in a major public speech and substantiated them with a series of comments which had to have had a depressing effect on every officer sent home.

I took exception to these comments in a letter to Schmundt; in doing so I touched on the unfounded nature of the reasons given by Keitel in July for my retirement. When Hardenberg delivered this letter on 10th October, he declared that the reasons given at the time by Keitel for my relief "were as stupid as could be!" He was told that the true reasons lay deeper. During the 1941 campaign I had opposed the *Führer*'s plan to pursue the attack east of the Dniepr to the south and north instead of to the east. Brauchitsch had failed to get his way in the face of my "strong personality," otherwise the war would probably already be over...!? The *Führer* has a great deal of respect for me; it is not out of the question that he might use me again somewhere else; but in the present situation he can only work with people who act according to his wishes.

This argument is also contradicted by the facts. My opposing stand in the summer of 1941 [see 20 July 1941] had not interfered with the turn to the north or the south, much less prevented it. After their transfer to Army Group North, the bulk of the armored units given up by Army Group Center were stuck in the mud there! And in the south, at the Battle of Kiev, after my objections had been rejected again I wheeled south with powerful forces, which was due to Halder's plan! And Guderian's panzer army had already reached its objective in the enemy's rear when the tanks of Army Group South hadn't even set off across the Dniepr. And nevertheless the war is far from over! This new argument also fails to agree with a letter written to me by Schmundt on 4 January 1942, or after these events. In it he said:

"As I was able to ascertain again today, I can only repeat that the former state of trust in which the *Führer* held you has not been affected in the least. The *Führer* is very happy at the thought of having in reserve a general who, after your complete recovery and convalescence, will be ready at any time for new assignments..."

Schmundt replied to my complaint about Göring's speech [4/10/42] on 12th October. His answer did not address the core of the matter. It based itself on the point of view that the highest-ranking officers are not included in such public statements.

The letter ended with the words:

"I will do everything I can to bring about the promised meeting with the *Führer*. In recent days I have had no time to do so..."

They are still dragging me into the public. In mid-October German radio polemized against the English intelligence service's lies and said that according to English reports I had been shot, another time locked up in a concentration camp, then I went walking on the *Unter den Linden*, then again the *Führer* wanted to speak to me, and now – I am in Japan! In response the English radio drew a parallel between Ludendorff's departure in 1918 and my retirement – a very lame comparison!

Reasons for the Changes in Command

Beginning of November 1942

The *Neue Zürcher Zeitung* of 1st November contained an article about the changes in senior German officer and general staff positions. Several possible reasons were given for Halder's as well as my retirement:

Differences of opinion over future conduct of operations, opposing views in the burning question of the treatment of prisoners of war and the Geneva Convention, and finally differing opinions on the extreme measures allegedly planned by the supreme commander in the occupied territories. However, it was suggested that the deepest reason for all the changes is that the *Führer* alone leads and as well he wishes to turn the younger generation into willing tools. The paper supported its case by examining Göring's speech of 4th October, in which he said that the general staff will have to be content with the role of a faithful clerk...

On 26 November 1942 Hardenberg received a letter from Sodenstern. Also see 22 March 1943.

End of November 1942

Conversations with people who ought to know how things are going brought some light into the darkness of my dismissal. According to what I was told, the *Führer*'s impatience over the supposed and slow turn to the south – which Halder also mentioned in his conversation with Sodenstern on 5th July – grew and grew and finally reached the point where the strain on his nerves demanded a solution, which he thought he could achieve only through a change in command.

3/12/42

And today a congratulatory telegram arrived from the *Führer*.

Further Defense Attempts

4/12/42

While going through the appendices of the diary I found a dangerous discrepancy in the record of a telephone conversation with the *Führer* on 13 May 42 – the most critical day of the Russian attack at Kharkov. It said:

"Only two possibilities remain to clear up the situation of the VIII Army Corps:

(1) ...

(2) Transfer using units of Army Group von Kleist..."

This obvious copying error could be interpreted to mean that I had intended to transfer some of Kleist's forces directly to VIII Corps and stuff them in there to solve the crisis defensively. This plan never existed! On the contrary, from January [1942] on I was of the view that the Russian offensive could only be parried by offensive means. Numerous orders and telexes reveal that I had never left any doubt about that. The telephone conversation of 13th May concerned itself only with whether the "Fridericus" attack, which had been prepared for a long time, could be justified at that moment from the point of view of forces and the situation, or whether we ought to content ourselves with the proposal for a less ambitious counterattack – the attack from the Pavlograd area against the rear and flank of the enemy in front of VIII Corps. There can be no doubt about anything after a close examination of the telephone conversation as well as the situation report submitted to the OKH on 14th May. Nevertheless, I consider it necessary to clear up this discrepancy. Therefore Hardenberg wrote Sodenstern on my behalf and informed him of the error. On 26th November the latter replied that "there is no doubt" that I never had any idea of transferring units from von Kleist to the VIII Corps, rather I had only spoken about assembling an attack group at Pavlograd. Both he and the Ia – *Oberst* Winter – are ready to confirm this in writing.

On 4th December Hardenberg delivered a letter to the director of the Potsdam Army Archive, Dr. Strutz, in which I clarified these things and asked that the clarification be added to the Army Group South war diary, which was readily promised.

9/12/42

After completing all this writing, while examining the telephone conversation of 13 May 1942 I found a second damaging section. It read:

"The *Führer* instructs that the forces of Army Group Kleist whose withdrawal to VIII Corps is being considered are to be made ready to march."

This is undoubtedly an error on the part of the officer in charge of the war diary. I don't believe that the *Führer* expressed himself that way, because Sodenstern or I or one of the other officers listening in would undoubtedly have picked up on the considerable misunderstanding that would have resulted from such an answer on the part of the *Führer*. I also informed Sodenstern of this error.

Contacts with Paulus and Salmuth

2/2/43

A few days ago a letter came from Paulus from Stalingrad dated 23rd December [Paulus ceased military resistance on 31 January 1943], in which he wrote:

"My brave army is presently fighting under the most difficult conditions. But we are confident that we will master the situation." ? - ? *These two question marks document Bock's more realistic assessment of the military situation than that of Paulus, who was fighting in Stalingrad in December 1942!*

My former Chief of Staff Salmuth, who in July of last year took over command of the 2nd Army as von Weichs' successor, or over my corpse, is in Berlin. Disagreements with the army group led to his removal from this position. It is his contention that permission to evacuate the Voronezh salient, which was seriously endangered after the Hungarian collapse, was given too late and it was this that was responsible for the serious setback suffered by his army. His comparison with Stalingrad, where the 6th Army was denied the timely approval to break out, is a fair one.

Salmuth just saw Schmundt, who thinks it certain that he will be used again. Concerning my situation, Schmundt told him that the *Führer* has raised the subject several times recently and expressed a wish for my return to duty!

Inactivity and Desire for Reinstatement

The implementing regulations for the law announced on 30th January, whose purpose is to harness the entire strength of the people for "total war," are gradually being made public. All younger women and all men up to 65 years of age are to report for duty. – I continue to sit around doing nothing!

22/2/43

In view of the threatening situation at the front, misgivings over the removal of many military leaders are growing louder. Perhaps that is why the Berlin newspapers today gave such prominence to Guderian's return to duty;

after more than a year of waiting he has been named Inspector of Armored Forces, but this still doesn't mean a command at the front. Fresh rumors about me are swirling through the air. It is alleged that I have refrained from speaking out because I was paid 250,000 Marks to keep silent! Then I was named Commander-in-Chief of the entire Eastern Front. The most radical solution is a rumor which I received in writing, which says that they are intentionally covering up my death under mysterious circumstances, which occurred months ago.

Lessons in Military Doctrine and Bitter Experiences

1/3/43

The headquarters of my old army group was pulled out of the front and is in reserve at the Dniepr. The former Ia, Winter, visited me and in broad outlines described the developments leading up to the catastrophe of Stalingrad and the subsequent fighting. From all the various descriptions it became clear to me that – as in the winter months of 1941 – the supreme command reckoned that the collapse of the Russians was imminent, in overestimating its success split its forces to pursue, and ultimately was too weak everywhere. Then came the Russian counterattack with the failure of the Romanians, the Italians and finally the Hungarians, which was so complete that the few German divisions interspersed among them were unable to avert the disaster. The 6th Army's request to abandon Stalingrad and fight its way out, which was supported by all the commanders, was rejected by the supreme command. – Only now, under the force of events, have they brought themselves to decide to finally evacuate the projecting positions in the central and northern sectors of the Eastern Front. In Winters' opinion it must be assumed that we will successfully bridge the period until the onset of the muddy period without further mishaps. What is planned then, he does not know.

I do not know the details. But one thing is certain: the war cannot be waged without reserves! They must be created, and in all areas. Only when we have succeeded, with the inevitable loss of space and time, can we hope to be equal to the tasks which lie before us. Until then we must keep our nerve and the supreme command must not attempt a third time, following deceitful temptation and based on inadequate information, to fulfill great, decisive missions with insufficient forces.

Air Raid on Berlin

22/3/43

On 21st March the celebration of Heroes Memorial Day in Berlin; in the course of this the *Führer* was shown an exhibit by Army Group North in the arsenal, which among other things included a pictorial representation of the seven offensive battles of 1941 which were fought under my command. I had let Schmundt know that I would be present, so that they didn't run into me unprepared. But the *Führer* made do with a brief handshake as he came and went and thus avoided any discussion and disagreement.

Toward the end of the celebration I spoke with Schmundt, who gave a new reason for my being put out of action:

I had telegraphed the *Führer* proposing a purely frontal solution to overcome the crisis at Kharkov and as well requested all of the Eastern Front's reserves, so that consequently any major offensive became impossible! Sodenstern expressly confirmed that my general staff had been excluded from this telegraphed proposal! I rejected this unheard-of twisting of the facts and said: "If Sodenstern really said that I have to obtain a clarification, for that is not true!"

In the afternoon I sought out Halder and asked him whether he knew anything about the alleged exclusion of my general staff. He said that he had heard at the time that Sodenstern and Winter had been in favor of the "bigger" solution, that I had instead decided in favor of the "smaller" one, but that he had heard nothing about any exclusion of my officers. Winter stated by telephone that the claim was untrue, that Sodenstern had suggested the "big" solution but that I, following lengthy discussions with the chief of staff, for which he was only partly present, had decided based on the reports from the armies in favor of the smaller solution. Sodenstern then drafted the telex to the Army High Command based on my proposal.

On 22nd March Salmuth told me that the story is being spread that I had – without informing my chief of staff or the Ia – called the *Führer* late in the evening or even during the night and proposed to him a frontal solution to the crisis at Kharkov!

On the 21st, after my conversation with Schmundt, I asked Field Marshall Keitel to set aside a little time for me on the 22nd. The meeting took place this morning. I stressed that I was aware that what I had to say would change little about my situation; but I could not let go unchallenged the untrue claim that I had excluded my staff in order to propose a timid solution to the *Führer* which I, in the opinion of the denouncers, was probably too cowardly to say in front of their faces. The truth is – as I said – that after an extensive exchange of opinions with me, Sodenstern had himself drafted the telex to the Army High Command with my proposal. Keitel said that he didn't know how Schmundt had reached this conclusion. He had only heard that the chief of staff and the Ia had favored the big solution and that I had decided on the small one. Whether Sodenstern was still advocating the big solution on the 13th and 14th I don't remember: Winter said that that's how it was. But it makes little difference, for I alone bear the responsibility one way or the other! But there can be no talk of an exclusion!

As proof of this, as well as evidence against the accusation that I advocated a frontal solution, I gave Keitel Sodenstern's letter to Hardenberg of 26 November 1942.

When the conversation again turned to the events leading up to the Kharkov battle, I said: the Luftwaffe was not subordinate to me; in spite of all my requests I was unable to obtain the necessary resources from the Crimea. The OKH had reserved to itself the use of the approaching reserves. Under these conditions the 17th Army had doubts; even Kleist reported:

"We can no longer reach the line Bereka-Alexandrovka!"

With the weak forces available to me, with inadequate air support, the probability of getting stuck halfway was great. Associated with this was the danger that my forces, which would be needed for the coming big offensive, would be frittered away uselessly in the unavoidable back and forth fighting that would follow. The idea that the military commander must often accept the uncertainty of success is certainly nothing new to me. But here the commander of the army group could not do so alone, because a failure would endanger the later plans of the supreme command. But with hands tied he could only decide in favor of the suggestion for the small solution. This, an attack from Pavlograd to the north – which was in no way frontal – was a stopgap measure. It led through a confined area to an at first limited objective which could be reached with the means at hand and thus left open all possibilities for the later big offensive. At the time I said to my chief of staff that this proposal meant abandoning the laurels of the big solution which we had hoped for and prepared for so long. – When the *Führer* then ordered the big solution, bringing in stronger air forces, no one welcomed it more than I! Keitel declared: at first the *Führer* was unhappy about your proposal. But as the attack progressed he looked at things more calmly, until finally joy over the brilliant success outweighed everything else.

But now Voronezh [!] – continued Keitel. – At the start of the operation Halder and I had doubts whether the capture of Voronezh wouldn't tie up the attacking mobile forces there longer than was consistent with the desire to advance down the Don as quickly as possible. After rereading the differently-worded written directive for the operations, I proposed to the *Führer* flying to you to tell you that the capture of Voronezh as contained in the orders was not necessary. But after the discussion in Poltava on 3rd July I gained the impression that this view had not been expressed clearly enough. Therefore as we were leaving, on the steps I reminded Sodenstern of the significance of Voronezh.

I stated: "Talk of Voronezh ended with me saying to the *Führer*: 'I understand what was just said to mean that I am to take Voronezh if I can get it easily or without fighting, but that I am not to allow myself to become engaged in a major battle to capture the city'." The *Führer* confirmed this with a nod of his head. As things went on there arose a complication. The OKH liaison officer with the 4th Panzer Army radioed his superiors that Voronezh could probably only be taken after heavy fighting. Weichs was of the opposite opinion, I agreed with him and while discussions with the OKH on this theme went back and forth, on 6th July a squadron of the 24th Panzer Division passed through Voronezh with almost no fighting and after the OKH was advised the city was occupied...

Keitel said: "Long afterward during the subsequent course of the operations the *Führer* often referred to the '48 hours lost at Voronezh' as a serious loss of time."

I replied: "But one should not forget that the entire operation demonstrably proceeded very much faster than was planned. Several times, including during the meeting with the *Führer* on 3rd July, I referred to the danger that the Russians were withdrawing. It is obvious and also apparent from the war files that I did everything I could under the circumstances to wheel south quickly. When Halder called *General* von Sodenstern on 5th July and told him that the *Führer* was impatient and had said that the army group should have had bridgeheads across the Tichaja Sosna long ago, I was able to reply that these bridgeheads had in fact been established."

I didn't go into further details which better illustrated how the army group pushed south and the resistance that was met, so as not to drag out the conversation unnecessarily. I also didn't bring up the fact that it had been the army group, not the supreme command, which had pointed out the likelihood that the operations would proceed more quickly and that one would slide into the other, and of the need to attack quickly with the southern wing of the army and as well leave the entire operation in one hand at the start.

Finally Keitel remarked that the *Führer* had also expressed doubts back then as to whether my health was adequate to see me through the operations currently in progress (!), a statement that could hardly have been meant seriously.

When the conversation ended I asked Keitel to set Schmundt straight concerning the false charge that I had "excluded" my general staff. Keitel expressly promised to do so. I didn't touch on the question of a talk with the *Führer* again; but Keitel brought it up himself: "I can't promise that I will find the opportunity to inform the *Führer* of all these connections and the actual course of events. That could only happen in a – I would like to say – semi-official way and I have no opportunity for that. The *Führer* only sees me in the presence of two stenographers, in whose presence I can't discuss such delicate matters!"

...When I asked what they thought about the subsequent conduct of the war, Keitel answered: "The others are collapsing! Even the Russians!"

26/4/43

...Anonymous virulent letters, with which I was bothered for a long time, and whose more or less confused line of reasoning called for an internal revolt, have stopped. Instead today I received a letter from a woman in Bremen; she wrote that things cannot go on as they are, that we must have a sovereign again and that she – very kindly – has chosen me. I even have enough time to take note of such nonsense...

Further Cardinal Doubts

...As I have no factual information I cannot assess the situation. I don't know where the supreme command wishes the main effort to be, don't know whether the battle in the east can be avoided at all, and know equally little as to whether the plan to wear down the Russians with limited blows is based on positive intelligence on the state of the Russian defensive strength. If this is in fact waning, then the German attack is justified. But if it isn't, if the supreme command is again basing everything on just wishful thinking, then the "battle of attrition" at Orel will be nothing but a repeat of the Battle of Verdun [1916], which as everybody knows led to the bleeding white of the German Army. But we need our forces in order to so smash the coming Anglo-American attack that the enemy gives up its repetition as hopeless. I don't know whether our wealth of forces is so great that we can also capable of major actions in the east.

"...With Bound Hands"

End of August 43

...The English dropped inflammatory leaflets over Berlin in which my name was again mentioned as an "uncomfortable warner." As was the case in the years 41 and 42 the English propaganda is helping the business of my enemies.

Beginning of September 43

...Heavy air raid on Berlin during the night of 4th September, in which my house was damaged for the fifth time. The air terror is making itself felt in the mood of the people, foremost however is the desire for the revenge which we are so often loudly promised.

10/9/43

...The war is nearing its climax and I watch like a criminal with bound hands!

22/10/43

Some time ago my nephew L. [Lehndorff] had the opportunity to speak with *General* Schmundt on a train about my situation. When L. asked why they were treating me so badly after all I had done, Schmundt answered: "Frederick the Great also treated prince Heinrich badly!" [Louis Ferdinand Prince of Prussia. *Im Strom der Geschichte*: Munich 1993, PP 24.] As to the "real reason" for my removal from command Schmundt said that "after Voronezh I had stared like a rabbit at a snake instead of acting as the *Führer* wished!" It is absolutely certain – even Keitel said so himself – that I was never made aware of the true nature of the *Führer*'s wishes, a mistake that could have been cleared up by a single question to me.

On 24/1/44 Renate Countess von Hardenberg wrote to Ingeborg Geisendörfer: "Uncle Fedi [Bock] and wife here to look after their apartment which is pretty much kaput." (Agde, Günter. "Carl-Hans von Hardenberg...": Berlin 1994, PP 147.)

On 26/3/44 Bock wrote to Dr. Werkmeister: "I follow everything that is going on from my 'dungheap' here with the same interest as if I were standing on a 'general's hill' and as well continue to try to be of the most use I can possibly be to my fatherland as a farmer." (Bock to Werkmeister in: BA-MA, Werkmeister bequest N 492/2.)

End of April 44

...Today I received a very cordial letter from a former subordinate, Rittmeister of the Reserve Hoesch, an industrialist from the Ruhr, which concluded with the words:

"In you fate – even if it is against your will – will preserve for posterity the picture of the distinguished, intelligent, great soldier – the undefeated general."

Mid-July 44

The war is approaching a crisis with giant strides – and I continue to be sentenced to watch idly...

The first "revenge weapon" – the V 1 – has been used against England. The morale effect of this long-range rocket weapon is surely great. But it seems unlikely to me whether the weapon's accuracy is good enough to strike the bases for the invasion, the English sea and air bases and the production facilities in southern England really effectively. Further revenge weapons have been promised publicly and are to appear in the near future.

Rundstedt, former CIC West, returned home with great honors. His successor is Kluge! Recent months have brought many other changes in the senior command posts of the army (Manstein, Kleist, Küchler, Busch).

On the "Seydlitz Case"

For the first time since my departure from the front I was officially informed of drastic proceedings and measures in the army. I received a letter dated 30th may from Schmundt in his capacity of Chief of the Personnel Office with a summary of educational and organizational decrees for the army, "which will interest you, highly-respected *Herr Generalfeldmarschall.*" In connection with this I was informed of the "Seydlitz Case." *General* von Seydlitz, who was taken prisoner at Stalingrad, had gathered round him an apparently quite considerable part of the German officer and soldier POWs against the national-socialist German government and was now also trying to promote the same thing within the German Army, asking surrounded units to

543

surrender and so on. This is probably the first time in Prussian history that a general became a blatant traitor! I always took Seydlitz to be a simple, very direct and decent man and the only explanation I can find for the unbelievable is that under the tremendous mental strain of the fighting at Stalingrad he succumbed to sophisticated bolshevik influence.

The most significant of the measures revealed to me is a decree creating a "Chief of the National-Socialist Army Operations Staff." He is to be responsible for the creation of political will and for political activism in the army by providing unified political and ideological leadership.

Daily Life at the Grodtken Estate

9/7/44

...We are sitting on our leased farm at Grodtken in East Prussia, close to the old border with Russia; for days there had been no radio, no lights and at times no telephone; the lines were wrecked by a lightning strike.

The newspapers come irregularly and very late, so that one must guard against falling into the many rumors that are swirling about. By order of the party 27 men from the estate are to leave head over heels tomorrow morning to work on entrenchments on the eastern frontier. Hopefully their employment was prepared together with the military so that it will be of some real use, for the loss or people right before the start of the harvest is uncomfortable.

On the 20th of July 1944

On 10 July 1944 in Grodtken, Hardenberg informed his superior von Bock about the planned assassination attempt against Hitler. In his report of New Year's Eve 1945 Hardenberg wrote:

"Ten days earlier I drove to see him and told him that action was going to be taken against this system in the very near future. He knew my position, I had to tell him that I was involved; his, the field marshall's person, was of course not incriminated in any way. I owed him this confession, for although he in no way shared my political views he always allowed me to state my opinion frankly. Indeed I often had the feeling that he was directly seeking an opposing view – but couldn't bring himself to do so." [Gerbet, Klaus. *Carl-Hans Graf von Hardenberg, 1891-1951, Ein preußischer Konservativer in Deutschland*: Edition Hentrich, Berlin 1993, PP 140.]

According to Hardenberg's account [New Year's Eve 1945], Bock called him from Grodtken on the evening of 20 July 1944 "and complained [to him] in the strongest terms that he had been forbidden to leave his residence by the district commander in East Prussia acting on orders from Keitel. The conversation was certainly monitored and later it was also reviewed."

21/7/44

Yesterday an assassination attempt was made against the *Führer* by an *Oberst* Stauffenberg! The *Führer* escaped almost unhurt, several people around him were more or less seriously injured.

The government stated that the ringleaders – a very small circle of mostly retired officers – were shot or have shot themselves.

They wish to change the course of history with such means? Apart from everything else, it is of benefit only to the enemy!

Göring and Goebbels have been given extensive powers to obtain the utmost effort from the homeland. Himmler has been named commander of the Home Army, Guderian "transferred to the general staff."

23/7/44

This evening the acting commanding general, *General* Wodrig, called from Königsberg and said that the deputy chief of the Personnel Office, *General* Burgdorf, had informed him on Keitel's behalf that the Gestapo has reported that I am about to leave East Prussia. I might be considering whether this was the right moment and whether it might not make a bad impression on the population. – I replied that this talk was probably due to the fact that a few days ago I had sent my wife's youngest daughter, who was here with pneumonia, to her father in Pomerania in the company of one of my employees after she became able to travel. At the same time my wife had sent a few boxes of children's things and other superfluous items to Pomerania. But my wife and I were here. I said that I would soon telegraph Keitel...

In this time Renate Countess von Hardenberg, the wife of Claus-Hans Count von Hardenberg, who had been in Sachsenhausen concentration camp since 25 July 1944, was interrogated several times by the Gestapo. Naturally the Gestapo was also interested in Hardenberg's superior, Generalfeld-marschall von Bock. So there appeared on 27 July 1944 "a new Gestapo man..., who then worked exclusively on our case: Commissar Bartoll, a me-dium-size man in SS uniform, about 28 years of age [Bartoll was born on 11/ 4/1911], blonde and pale. He had a very changeable expression, a narrow cruel mouth and small shrewd eyes... When he came to the question of why H. wanted to take his life, I answered furiously: 'Would you let yourself be led off like a criminal?' This visibly enlightened him. 'Then why was he expecting to be arrested?' 'Because he heard that Field Marshall von Bock had been ar-rested too.' English radio had in fact erroneously reported this. Then he asked about Field Marshall von Bock. Now I became more confiding and spoke at greater length about this harmless topic, for I knew that Bock wasn't a part of it. I spoke of his very interesting accounts of his campaigns, which even for a lay person like me were extremely gripping. He also knew how to make the current army reports and operations easy to understand. Furthermore he was a passionate hunter and was always happy to join our hunts.' 'What was his attitude toward the Führer?' He always spoke of him with the greatest re-spect." (The fellow didn't need to know how embittered and sick he was after his dismissal.) (Hardenberg, Renate Countess von. Letter to Wilfried von Hardenberg summer 1946 in: Gerbet, Klaus. "Carl-Hans Graf von Hardenberg...": Berlin 1993, PP 167 and Agde, Günter. "Carl-Hans Graf von Hardenberg. "Ein deutsches Schicksal im Widerstand." Aufbau Taschenbuch Verlag, Berlin 1994, PP 77.)

1/8/44

I received the following shocking news from Countess Hardenberg, the wife of my adjutant: "My husband tried to escape arrest yesterday [25th July]... God refused to accept his sacrifice, two shots just missed his heart."

Hardenberg is apparently linked to the assassination attempt in some way. Shocking and dreadful! What will become of the countess and the children, who cling lovingly to their father, what of their beautiful, so well maintained estate?

New heavy attacks in east and west.

It is now unavoidable that I must find somewhere for us to live in Schötzow, in case we really do have to leave here...

5/8/44

The names of 23 of the officers who took part in the assassination attempt were announced on the radio; Witzleben is at the top of the list! An honor court led by Keitel and Rundstedt has applied for the ejection of the participants from the army and their delivery to the people's court. As before, nothing is said of Hardenberg...

6/8/44

Acting on behalf of the Chief of the Personnel Office [Schmundt], the military commander of Allenstein brought me a list of those sentenced to death for taking part in the attempt to assassinate the *Führer* on 20th July, as well as the officers who were kicked out of the armed forces for being involved in it but have not been brought to trial yet. A shocking document – and the first official news that I have received about the arrest at the end of July of my adjutant Hardenberg, who is said "to be looking forward to his trial."

8/8/44

...During the night it was reported on the radio that Witzleben, Hoepner, von Hase and several other of the officers involved in the conspiracy were convicted and hanged by the people's court!

12/8/44

In recent days the papers have published lengthy accounts of the interrogation and conviction of the main participants in the conspiracy – frightful! The De*utsche Allgemeine Zeitung* wrote quite correctly: "It was a political crime and all that matters now is to put this event into the service of the politics of the nation, into the service of the war effort."

...Luckily my wife's young son was found not to have scarlet fever; instead news came yesterday that he has been drafted into the auxiliary service and has to report on the 14th [August]. This morning my wife drove to Pomerania to see him before he leaves.

19/9/44

I have meanwhile learned that Lehndorff was also mixed up in the assassination affair of 20th July and arrested. – Kluge has shot himself!?

On Schmundt

Beginning of October 44

...Schmundt died of the injuries he suffered in the assassination attempt of 20th July. Earlier, until well into the war, he was very nice to me. Even after my meeting with the *Führer* in June 42, in which I spoke up for Generals Stumme and von Boineburg, he had such effusive words for my behavior that it seemed too much of a good thing to me. Then quite suddenly there came – I don't know why – the volte-face. First it was a game of hide and seek in the manner of my retirement, then came blatant insincerities in the same matter, and finally such unrestricted maliciousness broke through that I can find no other explanation for it than a guilty conscience!

Schmundt did not have his own opinion in operational matters; he was therefore influenced. But using his influence to give a less insulting, bearable form to the decision made about me without any explanation and with no chance of vindication – he apparently never thought of that! On the contrary! By his behavior in the Lehndorff case in the fall of 43 he had insulted me in an extremely damaging way which was unprecedented to the Prussian way of thinking. His death has spared us the confrontation that would have been unavoidable after the war.

Mid-October 44

...On the 19th [October] the mayor announced the first measures to be taken for an evacuation of Southeast Prussia – the area where we are living at the present time. Population, cattle and important inventory are not to be evacuated to the west, but to the north!?

Volkssturm

18/10/44

By way of *Oberst* von der Groeben of Army Group Center I enquired of the Army High Command how the field marshalls at the disposal of the *Führer* were supposed to formally behave toward the call-up of the *Volkssturm*. On 20th October Groeben, after speaking to the Chief of the Army General Staff, replied that "a general regulation was intended." I then asked Groeben to get in touch with Field Marshall von Küchler, who is also in East Prussia and therefore in a similar situation, in order to discover what he thinks of the matter. It turned out that Küchler "hadn't given the matter any thought."

On the 23rd [October] I telephoned my clerk in Berlin and gave him the order to inform *Oberstleutnant* Brink of the personnel office in Berlin, who is responsible for the field marshalls, of my query to the OKH and its response, and as well to tell him the following verbatim:

"Obviously I am available when and where I am needed. It is in itself superfluous to say, for according to my appointment I am 'at the disposal of the *Führer*.' But I would like to know how I am to behave if it comes to discussions in the question of the *Volkssturm* with party offices, in whose hands the organization was placed. The subordination of a field marshall to anyone holding a lower military rank is out of the question." I added emphatically that my inquiry was not to be construed as if I were pursuing any position. On the 26th my clerk reported that Brink shared my view and that in his opinion the OKH's answer was inadequate; he wants to bring about a clarification. I replied that a verbal confirmation of the correctness of my view was good enough.

31/10/44

Following a meeting with the Chief of the Personnel Office came the answer, "that I am over the age limit for the *Volkssturm*. If I nevertheless want to make myself available, it would be appropriate to turn to *Reichsführer* Himmler."

The matter is thus over for me. If they wanted to use me, they knew from my inquiry of the 23rd that I was ready and could obtain the *Führer*'s decision. I am not about to expose myself to a rejection by Himmler.

25/11/44

...The evacuation preparations for our district initiated by the party bear the stamp of inexperience and will scarcely be able to stand up to reality. If it comes to evacuation we shall have to try to help ourselves as best we can. Numerous evacuation trains from collecting camps and districts near the front depress the morale of the people but are unavoidable. My driver, Kallinich, who tried in vain to make several purchases in Neidenburg, said: "They are all acting there as if they were no longer there!" We continue to keep our people working and as far as planning and ordering act as if there was no danger.

3/12/44

The *Führer* wished me a happy birthday.

Solms' Arrest

...My former adjutant Solms was arrested some time ago. The reason is said to lie in the administration of the house of Baruth, which he ran for his brother the prince, who is also under arrest. My clerk, former secretary in Baruth, was interrogated in connection with the case, as a result of which I abandoned my original plan to seek fallback quarters with Solms. Under interrogation he said that I had dropped the plan when I learned of he investigation surrounding Solms [there were also contacts between Hardenberg and Solms]. He was also asked if it was true that a large limousine sitting in Casel was a gift from me to Solms! My clerk correctly characterized this charge as "trumped up and false." Investigation revealed that the car had been legally requisitioned by the army some time ago.

These are surely minor details, but they are part of my situation.

Beginning of January 45

...Interest in my private life is still apparently not entirely extinguished. A policeman has made inquiries at a neighboring farm, on which I have never set foot, as to whether I visit there.

18/1/45

...In the early afternoon it was reported that Russian tanks have broken through to Soldau (10 km east of Grodtken).

...Since my presence in Grodtken was of no more use and further instructions were no longer possible, at about 22:00 I left with my wife for Pomerania.

2/4/45

...On 1st April the radio announced that the *Werewolf* has been called up in the enemy-occupied areas. That means a call to the civilian population to take part in the fighting! I don't know if I would have proposed this measure in our present situation.

23/4/45

...The drive to Petersdorf near Lensahn was uneventful; the number of vehicles lying burnt-out at the side of the road after being shot up by enemy aircraft is considerable...

24/4/45

...Manstein, who has also found accommodation in the area, sought me out.

Sense of Responsibility and "Lackey's Soul"

25/4/45

...If the supreme command in Berlin is eliminated it is planned to place military and political in the separated regions of northern and southern Germany in military hands! In Busch's [CIC Army Group Northwest until 23/3/45] opinion Himmler is out of the question because he is said to have lost the trust of the upper echelon because of his actions, including the failure of his SS units in Hungary. The realization that the soldier is the surest and most dependable support of the nation finally appears to be sinking in. Hopefully not too late! Guilt for the shaking of trust in military leaders, which began long before the war, does not lie alone with the people who deliberately pursued this plan, but most of all with the leading soldiers who tolerated it and whose lackey's soul hastily and eagerly gave way to any pressure in this direction. In doing so they inflicted immeasurable and irreparable damage on the country.

Manstein – Dönitz

28/4/45

Together with Manstein drove to see Dönitz, who is supposed to have assumed military and political control in Northern Germany. That turned out to be an error. Dönitz has full authority only in the event that the *Führer* goes to "Southern Germany." Dönitz answered my objection that in the catastrophic state of affairs Hitler was already as good as out of the picture, and in any case could and probably would be completely eliminated at any minute, by saying that as far as he was concerned he would not assume command as long as Hitler was alive; he supposed that H[itler] had a directive or "a political testament" for this event. I replied that if anything was still to be salvaged it would only be possible through very tightly-controlled leadership from up here. "Who is in control here now?"

Dönitz replied: "The *Führer* through a staff of *General* Jodl's, which is situated in the area of Wismar." We all agreed that it was now vital to take the troops firmly in hand and lead them in such a way that the largest possible part of the population and of the army would be saved from being cut off by the Russians. Dönitz is quite sure that the English will take possession of the Trave-Elbe line but thinks it likely that out of loyalty to the Russians they will not allow the population striving to reach the west to cross this line. A strong bridgehead established yesterday by the English at Lauenburg suggests that an English advance on Lübeck is imminent.

I got the impression from this conversation that Dönitz isn't telling the whole story.

We subsequently visited the General Staff liaison staff located with Dönitz. The latest reports there from all the fronts were shocking.

...Keitel is, as we learned here, also in Mecklenburg, is therefore Jodl's superior. Neither his character nor his skill make him one to look to for salvation! – But intervene? - ? I hardly believe that that is possible in this situation; as well it is probably too late. Yesterday was the very latest date at which orders to disentangle the situation should have been given...

1/5/45

Großadmiral Dönitz's adjutant called and asked whether I could reach manstein to tell him the following: "The *Führer* has named Dönitz his deputy and successor. Dönitz requests that Manstein go to him before the day is over."

I was able to pass the message on to Manstein at 16:00.

Clear Refusal to Dönitz

During the night Manstein's adjutant called and informed me that the *Führer* is dead. He has named Dönitz to succeed him. D[önitz] had intended to make Manstein Commander-in-Chief of the Army. But after a conference with Himmler, Ribbentrop and Keitel has had to change his mind!!! – Dönitz thus appears to be planning to go on working with the leaders who are responsible for Germany's bad fortune! I don't know what's causing him to do that.

Dönitz announced on the radio that the only purpose for continuing the fight is to save the largest possible part of the German population from the clutches of the bolsheviks. Fighting against the Anglo-saxons only if they seek to interfere with this plan.

2/5/45

...Goebbels has sent Dönitz a list of new ministers, allegedly drawn up by the *Führer*, which names him and Bormann, together with others, as ministers!!! Dönitz has rejected the list...

APPENDICES
Appendix A
GENEALOGICAL INFORMATION

Moritz Albert Franz Friedrich Fedor von Bock, *Generalfeldmarschall*

Born 3/12/1880 Küstrin
Died 4/5/1945 Oldenburg, Holstein from injuries and burns sustained in a strafing attack 2 km north of Lensahn, Holstein on 3/5/1945. Was buried in Lensahn cemetery.

I 9/10/1905 Mally von Reichenbach (Died 10/12/1910)

II 20/10/1936 Wilhelmine Gottliebe Jenny, nee von Boddien
Born 14/11/1893 Strasbourg, Alsace
Died 3/5/1945 in strafing attack

Father: Moritz Karl Albert von Bock, *Generalmajor*
Born 15/1/1828 Koblenz
Died 16/4/1897 Berlin Charlottenburg

Was raised to the nobility on 19/1/1873, because on 19/1/1871 while serving as a *Major* and commander of Infantry Regiment No. 44 during the Battle of St. Quentin he refused to surrender command though severely wounded and instead remained with his regiment until the battle was over. He was recommended for the award of the Order *Pour le Mérite*; however, Kaiser Wilhelm I instead decided in favor of the award of the title of nobility.

Mother: Olga Helene Franziska von Falkenhayn
Born 4/3/1851 Burg Belchau, Graudenz District
Married 19/10/1873 Graudenz
Died 14/12/1919 Berlin-Wilmersdorf

Henning Bernhard von der Goltz (1681-1734)

Johanna Ulrike (Unika) (1720-1772)

Married 1739 August Gebhardt von der Marwitz (1695-1753)

Heinrich Ludwig Leopold August von der Marwitz

Wilhelmine
Married Felix von Gentzkow

Laura
Married Freiherr von Rosenberg

Franziska
Married Fedor Tassilo von Falkenhayn
Erich von Falkenhayn Olga von falkenhayn
Married *Generalmajor* von Bock

Grandfather: Friedrich Wilhelm Bock, Major and second in Command of Magdeburg
Born 25/5/1780 Ohlau
Died 1/2/1838 Magdeburg

Grandmother: Albertine von Hautcharmoy
Born 16/6/1800 Ratibor
Died 11/1/1876 Teplitz

Appendix B
MILITARY CAREER

Attended school in Wiesbaden and Berlin;
1888 Royal Prussian Cadet Institute Groß- Lichterfelde (7th Company)
Senior Non-Commissioned Officer

15 March 1898 Service entry; effective 15 March 1989 as Second-Lieutenant in 5th Guards Regiment Berlin-Spandau.
Commission: 15 March 1898 (Mm)

1 June 1902 attached to Pioneer battalion 3 (until 28 June 1902)

1 October 1903 attached to Military Gymnastics Institute (until 29 February 1904)

1 March 1904 attached to Military Gymnastics Institute as assistant instructor

12 July 1904 Adjutant (I Battalion) in the 5th Guards Foot Regiment

28 January 1906 Adjutant 5th Guards Foot Regiment

10 September 1908 *Oberleutnant* (5th Guards Foot Regiment)
Commission: 10 September 1908 (Z2z)

22 March 1910 Grand General Staff (attached as of 1 April 1910)

22 March 1912 *Hauptmann*
(left with Grand General Staff transferred to the General Staff of the Guards Corps)
Commission: 22 March 1912 (R2r)

1 October 1913 at first 2nd (Ib), as of September 1914 1st (Ia) General Staff Officer of the Guard Corps 1914. In this function at outbreak of the First World War.

21 January 1915 Ia in general Staff of the Guards Corps

May 1915 transferred to the General Staff of the 11th Army.

28 January 1916 transferred to 4th Foot Guards Regiment as battalion commander (until 10 February 1916)

6 August 1916 Ia of the 200th Infantry Division

30 December 1916 *Major*
Commission: 28 December 1916 (Uu)

24 March 1917 Ia in the General Staff of the Guards Corps

11 April 1917 Ib in the General Staff of Army Group "German Crown Prince"

27 July 1917 Ia in the General Staff of Army Group "German Crown Prince"

April 1918 Award of the Order *Pour le Mérite*

November 1918 Assigned to Reichswehr Army Group Headquarters I as First General Staff Officer

10 January 1919 Placed at the disposal of Headquarters, III Army Corps and the Army Peace Committee

22 February 1919 Transferred to the Grand General Staff

14 March 1919 Member of the military representation of the German Peace Delegation

25 May 1919 Transferred to the 5th Foot Guards Regiment and Reichswehr Army Group Headquarters I for special duties

26 September 1919 Relieved from the command of Reichswehr Army Group Headquarters I (until 3 January 1920)

12 December 1919 Attached to the General Staff of Reichswehr Army Group Headquarters I

16 May 1920 Chief of Staff Military Area Headquarters III

18 December 1920 *Oberstleutnant* effective 1/10/1920 – no commission

1 October 1920 Chief of Staff of the 3rd Division and of Military Area Headquarters II (Berlin)

1 February 1922 Received RDA from 1 October 1920

1 April 1924 Commander of the Light Infantry Battalion (II) of the 4th Infantry Regiment (Kolberg)

1 May 1925 *Oberst*
RDA: 1 May 1925 (1)

5 October 1925 Assigned to artillery course at Jüterbog (until 31 October 1925)

1 February 1926 Transferred to staff of the 4th Infantry Regiment

1 June 1926 Named commander of the 4th (Prussian) Infantry Regiment

5 November 1926 Assigned to combat school course (Döberitz)

1 February 1929 *Generalmajor*
RDA: 1 February 1929 (8)

1 November 1929 Transferred to staff of Army Group Headquarters 1, named commander of the 1st Cavalry Division (Frankfurt/Oder)

1 February 1931 *Generalleutnant*
RDA: 1 February 1931 (2)

1 October 1931 named commander of the 2nd Infantry Division and commander in Military Area Headquarters II (Stettin)

1 March 1935 *General der Infanterie*
RDA: 1 March 1935

1 April 1935 Named commander of the Army Command Headquarters (Dresden)

20 May 1935 Assigned to command Group Headquarters 3

15 October 1935 Commander-in-Chief Group Headquarters 3
(renamed Army Group Headquarters 3 on 4 February 1938)

12 March 1938 While Commander-in-Chief of the 8th Army also assigned to the commander of the Austrian Federal Army (until 3 April 1938)

15 March 1938 *Generaloberst*
RDA: 1 March 1938 (2)

10 November 1938 Named Commander-in-Chief of Army Group Headquarters 1 (Berlin)

Appendices

26 August 1939 Named Commander-in-Chief of Army Group North (Polish Campaign) consisting of two armies; subsequently Army Group B (West) transferred east in September 1940; designated Army Group North with the start of the war against the Soviet Union.

10 October 1939 Named Commander-in-Chief Army Group B

19 July 1940 *Generalfeldmarschall*
RDA: 19 July 1940 (4)

22 June 1941 Commander-in-Chief of Army Group Center in the war against the Soviet Union; main battles in this function: Bialystok, Minsk, Roslavl, Smolensk, Gomel, Kiev, Vyazma and Bryansk

19 December 1941 Officer Reserve OKH (Berlin)

16 January 1942 Named Commander-in-Chief of Army Group South (Eastern Front)

9 July 1942 Assumed command of newly-formed Army Group B after the division of Army Group South
15 July 1942 Taken ill – no subsequent command until the end of the war

3 May 1945 Seriously injured in strafing attack near Lensahn, Holstein

4 May 1945 Died as result of injuries

Appendix C
DECORATIONS

First World War:

25 October 1916 Knight's Cross of the Royal House Order of Hohenzollern with Swords

1 April 1918 *Pour le Mérite*

Second World War:

22 September 1939 Bar to the Iron Crosses, First and Second Class

30 September 1939 Knight's Cross of the Iron Cross

1 June 1939 Order of the Yugoslavian Crown, First Class

27 August 1940 Grand Cross of the Order of the Crown of Italy

27 November 1942 Order "Michael the Brave" IIIrd and IInd Class

1 December 1942 Order "Michael the Brave" Ist Class

6 January 1943 Grand Cross of the Hungarian Order of Merit

Appendix D
DOCUMENTS

Document 1: From the order by *Generaloberst* Fedor von Bock, Commander-in-Chief of Army Group 3, of 1 October 1938 concerning the assumption of executive power in the Czech border regions.
(BA Potsdam, Film No. 13773)

Document 2: Appeal to the citizens of Paris of 14/6/1940
(In: Lottmann, Herbert R. *Der Fall von Paris 1940*: Piper, Munich 1994, PP 438)

Document 3: Army Group order for Operation "Typhoon" of 26/9/1941
(BA-MA Freiburg: 13715/4, PP 307)

Document 4: Army Group order for the "Continuation of Operations in the Direction of Moscow" of 7/10/1941
(War Diary Army Group Center, PP 129-131)

Document 5: Army Group order for the "Continuation of Operations" of 30/10/1941
(War Diary Army Group Center, PP 192-202)

Document 1

A

With the entry of German troops into the Sudeten-German area I have assumed executive authority in the areas to be occupied in the sector
Right boundary: Elbe
Left boundary: Grulich-Schildberg (town exclusively).
Mission and objective of the executive authority are:
(a) Establishment and maintenance of peace and order in the occupied area and its protection
(b) Protection of the population
(c) Preparation for the transfer of authority in the occupied area to the Reich.
Only the planned organs are summoned to carry out the assigned mission ...

B

1. The activities of the Sudeten-German internal government are unaffected. The decision of the head of the civilian administration is to be sought where there are disagreements or the filling of an administrative officer is required.
2. Special courts are responsible for all offenses against posted orders; special regulations will follow concerning the setting-up of these courts. Otherwise the jurisdiction of the Sudeten-German local and military courts remain in effect for now, in so far as the case is not handled by a special court.
3. Active or passive resistance against our forces is to be broken. Acts of passive resistance include sabotage of public or military installations and strikes. Unreliable elements are to be placed in protective custody by the Secret Military Police and Secret State Police.

This is to operate on the principle that the secret Military Police is responsible for anti-sabotage and counter-espionage, the Secret State Police all other enemies of the state. Persons placed in protective custody who are guilty of a punishable offence are to be transferred to the local police or court jail.

The Secret State Police is exclusively responsible for supervision of all other persons placed in protective custody ...

Document 2

Citizens of Paris

German troops have occupied Paris.

The city is under the control of a military government.

The Military Governor of the Paris Region will take the necessary measures to ensure the safety of the soldiers and the maintenance of order.

The orders of the military authorities must be obeyed unconditionally.

Avoid all irresponsible actions.

Any form of sabotage, whether active or passive, will be severely punished.

It is left to the circumspection and judgement of the population to bring about the advantages of the privileges entitled an open city.

The German soldiers have orders to respect the population and its property provided that the population remains quiet.

Everyone must remain in their apartments or at their place of work and resume their normal activities.

This is the best way for everyone to serve the city, the population and himself.

The Commander-in-Chief of the Army Group

H. Lottman wrote of this: "Only a few of those who read the text of the poster could know that it was signed by General Fedor von Bock, whose divisions had nothing to do with Operation Sickle Cut and the breakthrough at Sedan but instead had advanced south, east and west of Paris – and then directly into the city."

Document 3

Headquarters of Army Group Center H.Q., 26/9/41
Ia No. 1620/41 CO Secret Command Matter 35 copies
2nd copy

Secret Command Matter!
Command Matter!
For officers' eyes only!

Army Group order for the attack

1. After a difficult period of waiting the *Army Group* is taking the offensive again.
2. *4th Army* with subordinate *Panzer Group 4* will attack with point of main effort either side of the Roslavl-Moscow road. Following the successful break-through powerful elements of the army will turn toward the Smolensk-Moscow highway on either side of Vyazma while screening toward the east.
3. *9th Army* with subordinate *Panzer Group 3* will break through the enemy positions between the highway and the area around Beloye and drive through to the Vyazma-Rzhev railroad. The main assault by the mobile forces, which are always to be supported by strong infantry, is to be carried out in the direction of Kholm; it is planned that it will turn east of the Upper Dniepr toward the highway at and west of Vyazma while screening to the east. The northern flank of the army's attack is to be guarded.
The road through Yetkino to Beloye is to be captured for our own supply.
4. Prepared measures are to be taken to simulate the attack on the *inner wings of the 4th and 9th Armies* between the area of Yelnya and the highway, as long as there can be no attack on these fronts, and the enemy is to be tied down if possible through concentrated individual advances with limited objectives.
5. *2nd Army* will cover the southern flank of the 4th Army. To this end it will break through the Desna Position with main effort on its northern wing and drive through in the direction of Sukhinichi-Meschtschowsk. The army is to screen toward the municipal and industrial area of Bryansk-Ordzhonikidzegrad.

The possibility of seizing the municipal and industrial area – especially the railroad installations and bridges – is to be exploited, notwithstanding the boundary with Panzer Group 2.

6. P*anzer Group 2* will advance – presumably attacking two days before the start of the armies' attack – across the line Orel-Bryansk. The right wing is to follow the Swopa and Oka River line. Its left wing will roll up the Desna Position from the south and defeat the enemy in the southeast bend of the Desna in cooperation with 2nd Army.

The municipal and industrial area of Bryansk-Ordzhonikidzegrad is to be taken by a mobile unit if it succeeds in the first attempt. Otherwise it is to be cut off for the time being and taken later by forces of the XXXV Army Corps in conjunction with the Luftwaffe.

7. B*oundaries:*

(a) Between *Army Group South* and *Army Group Center.*

(to be ordered by the OKH)

(b) Between *Panzer Group 2* and *2nd Army.*

Rail line from Gomel to Pochep (2nd Army) – Panikovka (Pz.Gr. 2) – Piljscheno (Pz.Gr. 2) – municipal and industrial area Ordzhonikidzegrad (Pz.Gr. 2) – Darkowitschi (2nd Army) – Ogor (2nd Army), then Ustye-Sukhinichi rail line (2nd Army). After the capture of Bryansk by Panzer Group 2 the Gomel-Bryansk-Sukhinichi (2nd Army) rail line will be established as the general boundary.

(c) Between 2nd and 4th A*rmy.*

Krichev (2nd) – Miloslavichi (4th) – Yerschichi (4th) –Ssesslaw (2nd) – Ssnopol (4th) – Pesochnya Station (Kirov) (4th) – Wolaja (2nd) – Szerpejsk (4th).

(d) Between 4th and *9th Army.*

Senno (9th) – highway intersection 25 km west of Smolensk (9th) –Smolensk (4th) – Dniepr to Rachino – Kusino – Wosma bend at Kondratowa (villages from rachino to 9th Army).

Extensions will be ordered in keeping with the development of the situation.

(e) Between Army *Group Center (9th Army)* and *Army Group North (16th Army).* To Luschnicha as before, from there through northern edge of Lake Gorodno – southwest tip of Lake Shedanye – Starytsa (North).

8. Ar*my Group South* will bring its northern wing (6th Army) forward in a generally easterly direction past Kharkov to the north.

Army Group North will screen with 16th Army in general line:

Lake region north of Lake Shedanye-Lake Ilmen.

9. The *reinforced Air Fleet 2* will smash the Russian Air Force in front of the Army Group and support the attack by the armies and panzer groups with all means.

Attacks against industry in the Moscow area take second place to these missions and will be carried out only when the situation on the ground permits. Railroads leading east from the line Bryansk-Vyazma-Rzhev are to be kept under attack in order to make it difficult for the enemy to bring in supplies and fresh forces.

10. I will specify the *day and hour of the attack* in keeping with the directives issued by me to commanders-in-chief and commanders on 24/9.

Signed von Bock

Document 4

Headquarters of Army Group Center H.Q., 7/10/1941
Ia No. 1870/41 Secret Command Matter CO 27th Copy

Secret Command Matter!
Commanders only!
For officers' eyes only!

Order for the continuation of operations direction Moscow

1. The enemy armies encircled west of Vyazma face destruction. To this end the entire encirclement front continues to attack. All non-essential forces are to begin pursuit immediately of enemy forces which have escaped in the direction of Moscow, in order to leave the enemy no opportunity to build up a new defensive front.

2. *2nd Panzer Army* will break through to Tula as early as possible and capture the bridges there for further advance in the direction of Kolomna and Kashira-Serpukhov.

The municipal and industrial area of Bryansk-Ordzhonikidzegrad and the bridges there are to be held securely until relief by forces of the 2nd Army. Sufficient forces are to guard the Bryansk-Orel supply road and railroad.

3. *4th* and *9th Army* are to destroy the enemy armies surrounded in the Dorogobush-Vyazma area, employing infantry corps to relieve the mobile units for the new missions.

4. *4th Army* will advance without delay:

(a) with the newly-subordinated XIII and the XII Army Corps toward and across the line Kaluga-Medyn,

(b) with the LVII Army Corps (20th Pz.Div., 19th Pz.Div., which is to be pulled out of the line, and the 3rd Inf.Div.), which for the time being is directly subordinated to the army, via Medyn toward the Protva crossings at Maloyaroslavets and Borovsk. Advance forces are to take the fortified river line there. A powerful detachment is to quickly take possession of the crossings at Kaluga and hold until the arrival of the XIII Army Corps,

(c) with all available forces of *Panzer Group 4* generally following the path of the highway from Vyazma to Mozhaysk, quickly taking the fortifications there.

5. *9th Army* is to win the line Gzhatsk-south of Szytschowka in order to shield the battle of encirclement to the northeast. All elements of the panzer group which become free are to assemble in and behind this line for an early advance in the direction of Kalinin or Rzhev. Ground reconnaissance is to be carried out toward the Volokolamsk-Rzhev rail line.

6. *2nd Army* is to destroy the enemy groupings in the Trubchevsk-Shisdra area in cooperation with 2nd Panzer Army (see number 2) quickly clearing the vital Roslavl-Bryansk supply road.

Later it will be the mission of the 2nd Army to advance in the direction of Tula-Kaluga. Following the destruction of the enemy forces south of the Roslavl-Bryansk road, the 1st Cav.Div. and the fittest infantry division are to be sent to the 2nd Panzer Army in the direction of Orel.

7. *Boundaries.*

(a) between 2nd Panzer Army and 2nd Army:

Will be specified later.

Demarcation for security etc. In the rear army areas by direct agreement.

(b) between 2nd Army and 4th Army:

To Yerschichi as before, then Lyudinovo (2nd) – Kosjolsk (4th), then for reconnaissance and security between 2nd Panzer Army and 4th Army Kosjolsk (4th) – course of the Shisdra to where it meets the Oka-road from Ferzikovo to Serpukhov (4th).

(c) between 4th Army and 9th Army:

Highway to Vyazma as before, then Vyazma (4th) – highway as far as Gzhatsk (highway for 4th, town of Gzhatsk for 9th) – Ruza (4th). After infantry divisions move out the highway to Vyazma will also be ordered as boundary for 9th Army.

8. Changes in former disposition of forces.

(a) XXXV Senior Detachment with 1st Cav.Div., 95th, 262nd, 293rd, and 296th Divisions from 2nd Panzer Army to 2nd Army at 12:00 on 10/10/1941.

(b) XIII Army Corps with 17th, 52nd and 260th Divisions from 2nd Army to 4th Army at 12:00 on 8/10/1941. For the time being the reinforced 163rd

Inf.Rgt. presently standing guard on the Shisdra will remain tactically subordinated to the 2nd Army.

9. 4th Army is to assemble Inf.*Rgt.* *"Groß-Deutschland"* around Roslavl as army group reserve.

Signed von Bock

Document 5

Headquarters of Army Group Center H.Q., 30/10/41
Ia No. 2250/41 Secret Command Matter 27th Copy

Secret Command Matter!
Commanders only!
For officers' eyes only!

Order for the continuation of operations

1. In order to attain the objective of the encirclement of Moscow set in Army Group Order Ia No. 1960/41 Secret Command Matter of 14/10/1941, it is first necessary to defeat the enemy between the mouth of the Moskva and Kalinin. All preparations for the new operations are to be made so that the probably short period of snow-free cold can be exploited without delay and to its full extent.

2. The mission of the *2nd Army* remains unchanged; it is to first take possession of the general line Kursk-Maloarkhangelsk and north and send mobile forces ahead toward Voronezh as soon as possible.

3. *2nd Panzer Army* will advance between Ryazan and the Kashira area across the Oka. Insofar as road conditions permit, small, highly mobile detachments well provided with fuel are to be sent forward to effectively cut the railroads from the south to Moscow and take the Oka crossings by surprise; combat engineers must be provided to disarm time-fused devices. Whether the bulk of the panzer army subsequently has to be brought forward east or west of the mouth of the Moskva depends on the crossing possibilities and on the situation after the capture of Tula.

A reminder is made of the importance of capturing the industrial area of Stalinogorsk and Kashira.

4. *4th Army* is to make preparations to resume the attack at clearly defined points of main effort south and north of the highway with no loss of time as soon as the weather and the necessary movements of forces and stockpiling of ammunition at the front permit.

Intended points of main effort are to be reported.

The army is to go on driving its northern wing hard in the general direction of Klin. Advance in the direction of Yaroslavl-Rybinsk by Panzer Groups 3 and 4 reinforced by infantry is planned later, as soon as weather and supply situation permits.

5. *9th Army* is to clean up the situation around Kalinin in its deep eastern flank north of Yaropolets. It will drive the enemy back across the Lama River line and take possession of the crossings over the western tip of the Volga reservoir. Afterward it will ready Panzer Group 3 as ordered for the later advance south of the Volga reservoir to the northeast.

On its northern front the army will assume a defensive posture in a general line Kalinin-south of Torzhok-B. Koscha. The left wing of the army is to be driven forward from the Szjelisharowo area sufficiently far to the northeast that the Szjelisharowo (planned end point of railroad)-Sztaritza road can be used as a supply road. Follow-up as far as the general line Kalinin-Torzhok and west is to be made where enemy resistance is found to be weakening.

253rd Division is placed under the command of 9th Army effective immediately, for the time being its supply will continue to be provided by 16th Army. As soon as possible, a division is to be taken from the northern front and assembled in the general area of Starytsa. *Army Group North* is to tie up the enemy south of Lake Ilmen through local attacks and follow up immediately in case of a withdrawal.

6. *Boundaries:*

(a) between Army Group South (6th Army) and Army Group Center (2nd Army) as before:

Romny (A.Grp.South) – Kursk (A.Grp.Center) – Gorschetschnoje (A.Gr.Center) – Voronezh (A.Gr.Center) – Mutschka (A.Gr.Center).

(b) between 2nd Army and 2nd Panzer Army as before:

Unecha (40 km southwest of Trubchevsk) – Trubchevsk (2nd Pz.) –Orel (2nd Pz.) – Bogoroditsk (2nd) – Mikhailov (2nd Pz.) –Ryazan (2nd Pz.).

(c) between 2nd Panzer Army and 4th Army:

Yerschichi (4th) – Lyudinovo (2nd Pz.) – Kosjolsk (4th) – course of the Shisdra to Serpukhov (4th).

(d) between 4th and 9th Army:

"Highway" to Vyazma, town of Vyazma for 9th Army, then highway to south of Gzhatsk for 4th Army (may be used by 9th Army with direct agreement) – Gzhatsk (9th).

(e) between Army Group Center (9th Army) and Army Group North (16th Army):

Grodno Lake – Peno – Ragosa – north road from Ostashkov to Vishni Volochek (via Tolpino) – Owinischtscho (road and town to North).

7. French 638th Inf.*Rgt.* will be placed under the command of Army Group Center in all respects when it arrives in Smolensk. After assembling around Smolensk the regiment will be sent at first to Vyazma in easy marches by 9th Army.

signed von Bock

SOURCES

Sources

1. Bundesarchiv-Militärarchiv (BA-MA), Freiburg
BA-MA 13715/4, PP 307
BA-MA NF 1/20
BA-MA WF 03/16719, PP 247
BA-MA WF 03/16719, PP 252
War Diary Army Group Center, C, PP 129-131
War Diary Army Group Center, C, PP 192-202

2. Private Sources
War Diary of *Generalfeldmarschall* Fedor von Bock (in possession of Kurt-Adalbert und Dinnies von der Osten)

3. Other Sources
Television film *Zwischen Pflicht und Verweigerung – Generalfeldmarschall Fedor von Bock*. Author: Dr. Klaus Gerbet, broadcast by Fernsehsender IA (Berlin, Land Brandenburg) on 28 April 1995.

Books

Bazan, Heinrich Banniza von/Müller, Richard. *Deutsche Geschichte in Ahnentafeln*: Berlin, 1939.

Bazan, Heinrich Banniza von. *Familie, Sippe, Volk*: Vol. 5, 1939, PP 126.

Borchert, Klaus. *Die Generalfeldmarschälle und Großadmiräle der Wehrmacht*: Podzun-Pallas, Wölfersheim-Berstadt, 1994.

Bücheler, Heinrich. *Carl-Heinrich von Stülpnagel. Soldat –Philosoph – Verschwörer:* Ullstein, Berlin; Frankfurt an Main, 1989.

Fest, Joachim. *Staatstreich – Der lange Weg zum 20. Juli:* Siedler, Berlin, 1994.

Gerbet, Klaus. *Soldatenpflicht oder Widerstand, Generalfeldmarschall Fedor von Bock und sein Adjutant Carl-Hans Graf von Hardenberg:* in Buchwald, Werner/Simon, Hermann. *Gerhard Hentrich – Der Verleger. Eine Festschrift zum 70. Geburtstag für Gerhard Hentrich.* Edition Hentrich, Berlin, 1994.

Görlitz, Walter. *Paulus. "Ich stehe hier auf Befehl!" Lebensweg des Generalfeldmarschalls Friedrich Paulus:* Frankfurt am Main, 1960.

Guderian, Heinz. *Erinnerungen eines Soldaten:* Motorbuch Verlag Stuttgart, Stuttgart, 1994 (13th edition).

Halder, Franz. *Kriegstagebuch. Tägliche Aufzeichnungen des Chefs des Generalstabes des Heeres 1939-1942:* Stuttgart, 1962-1964.

Heuer, Gerd F. *Die deutschen Generalfeldmarschälle und Großadmirale:* Rastatt, 1978.

Heusinger, Adolf. *Befehl im Widerstreit. Schicksalstunden der deutschen Armee 1923-1945:* Tübingen, 1950.

Hoffmann, Joachim. *Stalins Vernichtungskrieg:* Verlag für Wehrwissenschaften, Munich, 1995.

Jacobsen, Hans-Adolf. *Fall Gelb. Der Kampf um den deutschen Operations-plan zur Westoffensive 1940*: Wiesbaden, 1957.

Jacobsen, Hans-Adolf/Rohwer, Jürgen. *Entscheidungsschlachten des Zweiten Weltkrieges*: Frankfurt am Main, 1960.

Keilig, Wolf. *Das deutsche Heer 1939-1945. Gliederung, Einsatz, Stellenbesetzung*: Bad Nauheim, 1956.

Lottmann, Herbert R. *Der Fall von Paris 1940*: Piper, Munich, 1994.

Manstein, Rüdiger von/Fuchs, Theodor. *Erich von Manstein – Soldat im 20. Jahrhundert, Militärisch-politische Nachlese:* Bernard & Graefe Verlag, Bonn, 1994.

Erich von Manstein. *Aus einem Soldatenleben 1887-1939*: Bonn, 1958.

Erich von Manstein. *Verlorene Siege*: Munich, 1955, 1976.

Mehner, Kurt. *Die geheimen Tagesberichte der deutschen Wehrmachtführung im Zweiten Weltkrieg 1939-1945*: Biblio Verlag, Osnabrück, 1992, Vols 2-4.

Meyer, Georg. *Generalfeldmarschall Ritter von Leeb. Tagebuchaufzeichnungen und Lagebeurteilungen aus zwei Weltkriegen*: Stuttgart, 1976.

Moll, Otto E. *Die deutschen Generalfeldmarschälle 1939-1945*: edited by W. Marek, Rastatt, 1962.

Müller, Klaus-Jürgen. *Das Heer und Hitler. Armee und nationalsozialistisches Regime 1933-1940*: Stuttgart, 1969.

Neue Deutsche Biographie, Vol. 2, *Bock*, by Fritz von Siegler, Berlin, 1955.

Osten, Kurt-Adalbert. *Herrenhaus Knauten, Kreis Preußisch Eylau, East*

Prussia und seine Geschichte in Deutsches Adelblatt, 15 May 1985.

Ottmer, Hans-Martin. *"Weserübung" – Der deutsche Angriff auf Dänemark und Norwegen im April 1940, Operationen des Zweiten Weltkrieges:* produced by Militärgeschichtlichen Forschungsamt, Vol. 1, R. Oldenbourg Verlag, Munich, 1994.

Piekalkiewicz, Janusz. *Die Schlacht um Moskau. Die erfrorene Offensive*: Pawlak, Gustav Lübbe Verlag, Bergisch Gladbach, 1981.

Piekalkiewicz, Janusz. *Der Zweite Weltkrieg*: Econ Verlag, Düsseldorf, 1985.

Reinhardt, Klaus. *Die Wende vor Moskau – Das Scheitern der Strategie Hitlers im Winter 1941/42:* produced by Militärgeschichtlichen Forschungsamt, Vol. 13, Deutsche Verlags-Anstalt, Stuttgart, 1972.

Schall-Riaucour, Countess H. *Aufstand und Gehorsam, Offizierstum und Generalstab im Umbruch – Leben und Wirken von Generaloberst Franz Halder, Generalstabschef 1938-1942:* Limes, Wiesbaden, 1972 (with foreword by General Rtd. Adolf Heusinger).

Stahl, Friedrich-Christian. *Fedor von Bock (Zum 50. Todestag).* In: *Ostdeutsche Gedenktage 1995, Persönlichkeiten und historische Ereignisse.* Kulturstiftung der deutschen Vertriebenen, 1995.

Turney, Alfred W. *Die Katastrophe vor Moskau. Die Feldzüge von Bocks 1941-1942*: New Mexico, 1946.

"Unser Heer", magazine, 4/8/42, Headquarters in the East, Army Group von Bock.

GLOSSARY

Ia	1. Generalstabsoffizier (Ltr der Führungsabteilung)	Kdo	Kommando
		Kdr	Kommandeur
Ic	3. Generalstabsoffizier (Feindbild)	KG.	Kommandierender General
		LaSK	Landstreitkräfte
Abt.	Abteilung	lei	leichte
Adjutant	Adj.	Ltr	Leiter
A.H.A.	Allgemeines Heeresamt	Lw	Landwehr
AK	Armeekorps	MG	Maschinengewehr
AOK	Armeeoberkommando	MBefh	Militärbefehlshaber
Art	Artillerie	m.d.F.b.	mit der Führung beauftragt
Befh.	Befehlshaber	mot	motorisiert
Brig.	Brigade	OB	Oberbefehlshaber
Btl.	Bataillon	OBE	Oberbefehlshaber des Ersatzheeres
Char.	Charakter als ...	OBH	Oberbefehlshaber des Heeres
d.G.	des Generalstabes		
Div.	Division	OBL	Oberbefehlshaber der Luftwaffe
erh.	erhalten		
ErsTr	Ersatztruppen	Obstlt	Oberstleutnant
FaR	Fußartillerieregiment	OKdo	Oberkommando
Fhnr.	Fähnrich	OKH	Oberkommando des Heeres
Fhr.	Führer	OKW	Oberkommando der Wehrmacht
Fjk.	Fahnenjunker		
FüRes	Führerreserve	OpA	Operationsabteilung
Gen	General	OQu	Oberquartiermeister
GenArt	General der Artillerie	Pz	Panzer
GenInf	General der Infanterie	PzA	Panzerarmee
GenKdo	Generalkommando	PBrg	Panzerbrigade
GenPzTr	General der Panzertruppen	PzD	Panzerdivision
GFM	Generalfeldmarschall	PzTr	Panzertruppen
GenOberst	Generaloberst	PGr	Panzergruppe
GenLt	Generalleutnant	PzK	Panzerkorps
GenMaj	Generalmajor	PzRgt	Panzerregiment
GenSt	Generalstab	RRgt	Reiterregiment
HGr	Heeresgruppe	Rgt	Regiment
HPA	Heerespersonalamt	RH	Reichsheer
HQu	Hauptquartier	RM	Reichsministerium
ID	Infanteriedivision	RW	Reichswehr
i.G.	... im Generalstab	RWM	Reichswehrministerium
Insp.	Inspekteur	WE	Wehrersatz
IR	Infanterieregiment	WKr	Wehrkreis
Kav.	Kavallerie	WKrKdo	Wehrkreiskommando
KavDiv	Kavalleriedivision		

579

INDEX OF NAMES

Dönitz, Karl Lebensabriß, 28.4.45, 1.5.45, 2.5.45
Dorpmüller, Julius-Heinrich 18.1.42, 19.2.42
Dostler, Anton 31.1.42, 2.2.42, 4.2.42, 7.2.42, 8.2.42, 10.2. bis 12.2.42, 17.2.42, 18.2.42, 20.2.42, 21.2.42
von Drabich-Waechter, Viktor 16.1.42

E

Eberbach, Heinrich 25.11. bis 27.11.41
Eberhardt, Friedrich-Georg 16.9.39, 3.10.39, 16.9.41, 24.1.42, 30.1.42, 31.1.42, 2.2.42, 4.2.42, 7.2.42, 28.2.42, 2.3.42, 10.3. bis 14.3.42

F

Faeckenstedt, Ernst Felix 8.5.42, 19.5.42
Fahrmbacher, Wilhelm 14.5. bis 16.5.41, 27.5. bis 30.5.41, 26.6.41, 30.6.41, 23.7.41, 27.7.41, 8.8.41, 10.8.41, 11.8.41, 21.8.41, 2.9.41, 29.9.41, 3.10.41, 3.11.41, 15.11. bis 17.11.41, 21.11.41, 23.11.41, 30.11.41, 12.12. bis 15.12.41
Faidherbe, Louis Léon César Lebensabriß
von Falkenhausen, Alexander 16.5.40, 17.5.40
von Falkenhayn, Erich Lebensabriß
von Falkenhayn, Olga Helene Franziska Lebensabriß, Kurzbiogr.
von Falkenhorst, Nikolaus 17.8.39, 3.9.39, 5.9.39, 7.9.39, 12.9.39, 15.11.39, 27.4.40
Fegelein, Hermann 27.9.41, 11.12.41
Fehn, Gustav 29.9.41, 5.10.41
Felber, Hans 23.10.39, 23.4.41, 14.5. bis 16.5.41, 26.6.41, 18.7.41, 19.7.41, 22.8.41, 6.10.41, 14.11. bis 18.11.41, 20.11.41, 25.11.41, 1.12.41
Feldt, Kurt 13.3.40, 21.3.40, 11.5.40, 25.2.41, 14.5. bis 16.5.41, 28.6.41, 29.6.41, 15.7.41, 6.8.41, 17.8.41, 20.8.41, 24.8.41, 28.8.41, 31.8.41, 5.9.41, 6.9.41, 12.9.41, 11.10.41, 26.10.41

Feßmann, Ernst 8.1.40
Filatow 10.7.41
Fischer von Weikersthal, Walther 27.5. bis 30.5.41
Fischer, Wolfgang 30.8. bis 2.9.41, 7.10.41
Foertsch, Hermann 2.5.41
Förster, Otto-Wilhelm 27.5. bis 30.5.41, 27.6.41, 11.7.41, 15.7.41, 25.7.41, 3.10.41, 24.10. bis 27.10.41, 29.10.41, 7.11.41
Franco, F. Bahamonde 3.12.40, 14.6.41
Franke, Hermann 6.8.41, 3.9.41, 5.9.41, 5.12.41, 18.12.41
Franz 27.6.42
Fremerey, Max 12.9.41, 21.9.41, 5.12.41, 5.7.42, 6.7.42
Fretter-Pico, Maximilian 28.4.42, 28.6.42
Friedrich der Große (II.) 21.12.40, 22.10.43
Friedrich, Rudolf 25.1.42
Freiherr von Fritsch, Werner Lebensabriß
Fromm, Fritz 30.10.39
Fuchs, Thedor Lebensabriß
von Funk, Hans 19.7.41, 20.7.41, 20.8.41, 21.8.41, 6.10.41, 28.11.41, 29.11.41

G

Gabcke, Otto 10.3.42, 22.3.42
Freiherr von Gablenz, Eccard 25.8.39, 13.9.39, 12.11.39, 17.11.39, 8.4.40, 18.5.40, 14.5. bis 16.5.41, 22.7.41, 7.8.41, 8.8.41, 10.8. bis 12.8.41, 5.10.41, 6.11.41
Gallenkamp, Curt 23.7.41, 22.9.41, 16.12.41, 17.12.41
Ganzenmüller, Albert 12.2.42
de Gaulle, Charles 12.12.40, 7.6. bis 9.6.41
Geber 1.7.41
Geisendörfer, Ingeborg 2.2.42, 24.1.44
Georg II. 23.4.41
Gercke, Rudolf 3.7.41
Freiherr von Gersdorff, Rudolf-Christoph 4.8.41
Geyer, Hermann 25.8.39, 13.3.40, 28.3.40, 11.5.40, 23.5.40, 25.5.40,

1345678

26.5.40, 31.5.40, 14.5. bis 16.5.41,
27.6.41, 1.7.41, 5.7.41, 18.7.41,
20.7.41, 27.7.41, 10.8.41, 11.8.41,
15.8.41, 3.10.41, 17.11.41, 20.11.41,
21.11.41, 23.11.41, 27.11.41,
28.11.41, 30.11.41, 1.12.41, 5.12.41,
15.12.41

Freiherr Geyr von Schweppenburg,
Leo 25.8.39, 1.9.39, 2.9.39, 10.9.39,
10.7.41, 21.7.41, 22.7.41, 25.7.41,
8.8. bis 12.8.41, 15.8.41, 20.8.41,
22.8. bis 24.8.41, 1.10.41, 4.12.41,
5.12.41

Freiherr von Gienanth, Curt Ludwig
10.2.41, 1.4.41, 24.6.41

Giraud, Henri 8.6.40

Goebbels, Joseph Lebensabriß, 6.12.39,
18.3.41, 2.11.41, 21.7.44, 2.5.45

von Goeben Lebensabriß

Gollnick, Hans 24.9.41, 26.9.41,
27.9.41, 18.11.41, 19.11.41, 21.11.41,
10.12.41

Gollwitzer, Friedrich 19.1.42, 20.1.42,
19.2 bis 21.2.42, 1.5.42, 2.5.42,
15.5.42, 16.5.42

Göring, Hermann Lebensabriß 8.1.40,
4.3.40, 19.7.40, 24.7.41, 14.8.41, Okt.
42, A Nov. 42, 21.7.44

Görlitz, Walter Bemerkg. zur Edition
Görltz 16.11.41

Gostztony, Peter 2.9.41

von Greiffenberg, Hans 26.9.39, 8.4.40,
2.5.41, 13.5.41, 17.5. bis 19.5.41,
21.5.41, 4.6.41, 6.6.41, 23.6.41,
24.6.41, 26.6.41, 2.7.41, 7.7.41,
11.7.41, 13.7.41, 15.7.41, 20.7.41,
24.7.41, 25.7.41, 28.7.41, 30.7.41,
31.7.41, 5.8.41, 7.8.41, 11.8.41,
9.8.41, 27.8.41, 28.8.41, 1.9.41,
14.9.41, 16.10.41, 1.11.41, 9.11.41,
11.11.41, 14.11.41, 17.11.41,
20.11.41, 21.11.41, 29.11.41,
30.11.41, 10.12.41, 16.12.41,
18.12.41, 20.12.41, 25.12.41, 18.6.42

Greiner, H. Bermerkg. zur Edition

Greisser 6.2.41, 1.4.41, 5.6.41

Groddeck, Karl Albrecht 10.5.42,
11.5.42, 13.5.42

von der Groeben, Peter Geleitwort,
25.1.40, 24.5.40, 2.5.41, 9.5.41,
18.10.44

Grohé 6.12.39

von Grolmann, Helmuth 7.7.41, 7.9.41,
12.7.42

Freiherr von Grote, Woldemar 13.9.39

Guderian, Heinz Lebensabriß, 25.8.39,
9.9.39, 10.9.39, 14.9.39, 15.9.39,
17.9.39, 13.2.41, 25.2. bis 27.2.41,
9.4. bis 10.4.41, 1.5.41, 14.5. bis
16.5.41, 4.6.41, 7.6.41, 12.6.41, 22.6.
bis 29.6.41, 3.7. bis 10.7.41, 13.7.41,
14.7.41, 19.7. bis 21.7.41, 23.7. bis
28.7.41, 1.8.41, 4.8.41, 6.8. bis
11.8.41, 13.8. bis 17.8.41, 19.8. bis
2.9.41, 4.9. bis 15.9.41, 19.9.41,
21.9.41, 22.9.41, 24.9.41, 27.9.41,
28.9.41, 30.9.41, 1.10.41, 3.10.41,
4.10.41, 6.10. bis 9.10.41, 11.10. bis
16.10.41, 18.10. bis 22.10.41, 24.10.
bis 1.11.41, 5.11. bis 9.11.41, 11.11.
bis 14.11.41, 16.11. bis 21.11.41,
23.11. bis 3.12.41, 5.12. bis 10.12.41,
12.12. bis 16.12.41, 18.12.41,
25.12.41, Okt. 42, 22.2.43, 21.7.44

Güntzel, Ernst 17.11.41, 20.11.41,
17.12.41, 18.12.41

H

Haase, Curt 30.8.39, 11.9.39, 13.9.39,
19.10.39

Haccius, Ernst 8.6.42

Haeckel, Ernst 17.11.41

Haenicke, Siegfried 9.9.39, 10.11.39,
31.7.41

Halder, Franz Lebensabriß, 14.6.39,
E Juli 39, 19.8.39, 21.8.39, 22.8.39,
25.8.39, 29.8.39, 30.8.39, 5.9.39,
7.9.39, 11.9.39, 12.9.39, 16.9.39,
20.9.39, 24.9.39, 26.9.39, 27.9.39,
30.9.39, 17.10.39, 25.10.39, 6.11.39,
12.11.39, 15.11.39, 18.11.39,
22.12.39, 6.1.40, 8.1.40, 9.1.40,
16.1.40, 17.1.40, 25.1.40, 7.2.40,
25.2.40, 14.3.40, 15.5. bis 17.5.40,
21.5.40, 22.5.40, 2.6.40, 7.6.40,
8.6.40, 10.6.40, 12.6.40, 16.6.40,
17.6.40, 26.6.40, 4.7.40, 7.7.40,
21.10.40, 2.1.41, 31.1.41, 24.2.41,
30.3.41, 1.4.41, 2.5.41, 4.5.41, 4.6.41,
23.6.41, 25.6.41, 2.7.41, 6.7.41,
10.7.41, 13.7.41, 14.7.41, 20.7.41,
28.7.41, 29.7.41, 6.8.41, 7.8.41,

9.8.41, 15.8.41, 22.8.41, 23.8.41,
27.8.41, 28.8.41, 2.9.41, 12.9. bis
15.9.41, 17.9.41, 4.10.41, 9.10.41,
13.10.41, 16.10.41, 23.10.41, 26.10.
bis 28.10.41, 1.11.41, 5.11.41,
11.11.41, 12.11.41, 14.11.41, 17.11.
bis 19.11.41, 23.11.41, 29.11.41,
1.12.41, 3.12.41, 8.12. bis 10.12.41,
12.12.41, 16.12.41, 25.12.41, 24.1.42,
14.2.42, 20.2.42, 5.3.42, 16.3.42,
23.3.42, 25.3.42, 28.3.42, 31.3.42,
9.4.42, 25.4.42, 26.4.42, 5.5.42,
12.5.42, 14.5.42, 18.5.42, 10.6.42,
21.6.42, 23.6. bis 25.6.42, 27.6.42,
30.6.42, 2.7.42, 3.7.42, 5.7.42, 6.7.42,
8.7.42, 13.7.42, 31.7.42, Okt. 42,
A Nov. 42, E Nov. 42, 22.3.43

Freiherr von Hammerstein-Equord,
Kunrat 28.8.41

Freiherr von Hammerstein-Equord, Kurt
28.8.41

Hansen, Christian 11.11.39, 16.11.39,
10.1.40, 13.3.40, 11.5.40, 30.5.40,
31.5.40, 2.6.40, 13.6.40

Graf von Hardenberg, Carl-Hans
Lebensabriß, 30.7.41, 28.8.41,
20.12.41, 23.12.41, 23.1.42, Okt. 42,
A Nov. 42, 4.12.42, 22.3.43, 10.7.44,
23.7.43, 1.8.44, 5.8.44, 6.8.44,
3.12.44

Gräfin von Hardenberg, Renate 24.1.44,
23.7.44, 1.8.44

Harpe, Josef 1.4.41, 4.7.41

Harteneck, Gustav 6.10.41, 20.10.41

von Hartmann, Alexander 5.5.42,
12.5.42, 11.6.42

von Hase, Paul 8.8.44

Hasse, Wilhelm 30.8.39, 26.9.39,
16.12.39, 23.1.40, 24.4.40, 22.4.40,
11.5.40, 26.5.40, 27.5.40, 11.6.40,
10.12.40

Ritter von Hauenschild, Bruno 15.5.42,
4.7. bis 9.7.42, 12.7.42

Hausser, Paul 13.3.40, 11.5.40, 27.8.41,
31.8.41, 6.9.41, 9.10.41, 10.10.41

von Hautcharmoy, Albertine
Lebensabriß, Kurzbiogr.

Heim, Ferdinand 6.2.42, 16.3.42,
19.3.42, 25.5.42

Heinemann, Erich 25.4.41

Heinemann, Ulrich 28.8.41

Heinrici, Gotthard 27.6.41, 18.7.41,

30.7.41, 31.7.41, 1.8.41, 2.8.41, 5.8.
bis 9.8.41, 12.8.41, 18.8.41, 19.10.41,
25.10.41, 25.11.41, 27.11.41,
12.12.41, 16.12.41, 18.12.41

Heitz, Walter 21.5. bis 23.5.40, 28.5.40,
6.6.40, 13.6.40, 25.4.41, 22.6.41,
24.6.41, 25.6.41, 23.7.41, 1.8.41,
3.8.41, 18.8. bis 20.8.41, 29.8.41,
3.9.41, 4.9.41, 30.9.41, 3.10.41,
4.10.41, 6.10.41, 19.3.42, 8.5.42,
12.5. bis 14.5.42, 16.5. bis 22.5.42,
11.6. bis 15.6.42, 30.6.42, 1.7.42,
4.7.42, 7.7.42, 8.7.42, 10.7.42,
4.12.42, 9.12.42

Hell, Ernst-Eberhard 10.11.39, 7.4.40,
11.5.40, 26.5.40, 22.9.41, 26.10.41

Hellmich, Heinz 30.6.41, 22.7.41,
29.9.41, 27.10.41, 14.11.41, 21.11.41,
23.11.41, 1.12.41, 3.12.41, 5.12.41

Henderson, Sir Nevile Meyrick 27.8.39

Henrici, Sigfrid 4.12.41, 1.7.42

Dr. Henrici, Waldemar 13.2.41, 14.5.
bis 16.5.41, 18.7.41

Herr, Traugott 21.2.42, 26.5.42

Heß, Rudolf 30.4.40, 30.5.40, 10.5. bis
12.5.41, 17.5. bis 19.5.41

Hesse 6.2.40

Heusinger, Adolf 25.1.40, 20.7.41,
14.9.41, 13.10.41, 26.10.41, 27.10.41,
30.11.41, 22.1.42, 25.4.42, 5.3.42,
8.6.42, 9.6.42, 18.6.42, 6.7.42, 8.7.42

Himmler, Heinrich 10.9.39, 13.3.40,
17.5.40, 5.6.41, 24.10.41, 21.7.44,
31.10.44, 25.4.45, 1.5.45

Hitler, Adolf Mai/Juni 39, 14.6.39,
22.8.39, 3.9.39, 4.9.39, 8.9.39,
21.9.39, 26.9.39, 27.9.39, 29.9.39,
30.9.39, 2.10.39, 17.10.39, 21.10.39,
22.10.39, 25.10.39, 26.10.39,
31.10.39, 1.11.39, 4.11.39, 6.11.39,
9.11.39, 11.11.39, 12.11.39, 18.11.39,
21.11.39, 23.11.39, 30.11.39, 7.1.40,
16.1.40, 25.1.40, 4.3.40, 13.3.40,
16.3.40, 18.3.40, 21.3.40, 30.4.40,
7.5.40, 15.5. bis 17.5.40, 20.5.40,
21.5.40, 24.5.40, 29.5.40, 31.5.40,
1.6.40, 2.6.40, 17.6.40, 18.6.40,
25.6.40, 28.6.40, 14.7.40, 19.7.40,
14.8.40, 11.11.40, 3.12.40, 1.2.41,
27.2.41, 18.3.41, 28.3.41, 30.3.41,
9.4.41, 10.4.41, 4.5.41, 10.5. bis
12.5.41, 27.5. bis 30.5.41, 14.6.41,

3.10.39, 6.11.39, 12.11.39, 30.11.39,
22.12.39, 8.1.40, 13.5.40, 16.5.40,
19.5.40, 22.5.40, 23.5.40, 2.6.40,
6.6.40, 9.6.40, 13.6.40, 15.6.40,
26.6.40, 22.7.40, 2.1.41, 28.2.41,
2.5.41, 9.5.41, 11.5.42, 20.5.42,
2.6.42, 29.6.42, 2.2.43, 22.3.43
Sander, Erwin 11.5.42
Sanne, Werner 21.1.42, 22.1.42,
25.1.42, 26.1.42, 29.1.42, 3.2.42,
4.2.42, 7.2.42, 8.2.42, 11.2.42
Schaal, Ferdinand 31.8.39, 2.9.39,
5.9.39, 7.9.39, 9.9.39, 10.9.39,
28.6.41, 29.6.41, 23.10.41, 29.10.41,
31.10.41, 14.11.41, 16.11. bis
19.11.41, 29.6.42, 2.2.43, 22.3.43
Schall, Riaucour H. 25.1.40
Schaumburg, Ernst 10.11.39, 10.5.40
Schede, Wolf 18.7.41
Scheller, Walter 10.9.41, 25.11.41,
27.11.41
Schellert, Otto 24.9.41, 26.9.41,
30.10.41, 8.11.41
von Schenckendorff, Max Lebensabriß,
1.7.41, 22.7.41, 28.7.41, 5.8.41,
22.8.41, 3.10.41, 17.10.41
von Schlebrügge 22.11.41
Freiherr von Schleinitz, Wolf-Dietrich
26.8.41
Dipl.-Ing. Schlemmer, Hans 14.12.41,
15.12.41
Graf von Schlieffen, Alfred 8.9.39
Schlieper, Fritz 5.7.41, 26.10.41,
11.12.41, 12.12.41, 14.12. bis
16.12.41
Schmidt, Arthur 13.5.40, 25.5.42,
13.6.42, 30.6.42
Schmidt, Friedrich 28.4.42
Schmidt, Hans 18.7.41, 22.8.41,
31.8.41, 1.9.41, 17.11.41
Schmidt, Rudolf 13.5.40, 25.11. bis
1.12.41, 3.12. bis 18.12.41
Schmundt, Rudolf 16.3.40, 25.6.41,
13.7.41, 28.7.41, 23.8.41, 28.10.41,
14.12. bis 17.12.41, 22.12.41,
25.12.41, 5.1.42, 18.1.42, 23.6.42,
25.6.42, 27.6.42, 14.7.42, 15.7.42,
20.7.42, 6.8.42, Okt. 42, 2.2.43,
22.3.43, 22.10.43, 6.8.44, M Juli 44,
A Okt. 44
Schramm, P.E. Bemerkg. zur Edition
Schroeck, Erich 10.6.40

Schröter, Bernhard Lebensabriß
Schroth, Walter 14.5. bis 16.5.41,
22.6.41, 27.6.41, 29.6.41, 1.7.41,
5.7.41, 18.7.41, 20.7.41, 3.10.41,
6.10.41, 14.11. bis 16.11.41,
18.11.41, 20.11.41, 21.11.41, 1.12.41
Schukow, Georgij Konstaninowitsch
26.3.41
Schubert, Albrecht 8.7.41, 9.7.41,
10.7.41, 25.10.41, 27.10.41, 29.10.41
Graf von der Schulenburg, Fritz-Dietlof
28.8.41
Schulze-Wegner, Guntram 26.3.41
Schuster, Karlgeorg 24.6.40, 28.6.40
Schwantes, Günther 30.1.40
von Schwedler, Viktor 17.1.40, 9.3.40,
6.4.40, 9.5. bis 11.5.40, 18.5.40,
19.5.40, 22.5.40, 23.5.40, 25.5. bis
27.5.40, 8.7.41, 21.7.41
von Schwerin, Richard 12.5.42, 20.5.42
Seidemann, Hans 9.7.41
Freiherr von Senfft zu Pilsach,
Wolfgang 24.8.41
von Seydlitz-Kurzbach, Walter 31.7.41,
12.8.41, 11.6.42, 7.7.42, M Juli 44
Dr. Seyß-Inquart, Arthur 16.5.40,
19.5.40
Siebert, Friedrich 28.7.40, 12.3.42,
13.3.42
Sinnhuber, Johann 14.6.40, 27.5. bis
30.5.41, 27.6.41, 29.1.42, 22.2.42,
28.2.42, 16.3.42, 19.3.42, 28.4.42,
7.6.42
Sintzenich, Rudolf 16.6.40, 18.6.40
Sixt von Arnim, Hans-Heinrich
31.10.41, 10.12.41, 12.5.42, 15.5.42,
30.6.42
von Sodenstern, Georg 10.10.39,
24.1.42, 11.2.42, 14.2.42, 20.2.42,
5.3.42, 25.3.42, 9.4. bis 22.4.42,
25.4.42, 14.5.42, 18.5.42, 18.6.42,
3.7.42, 5.7.42, 8.7.42, 12.7.42,
20.7.42, 22.7.42, 31.7.42, 6.8.42,
A Nov. 42, E Nov. 42, 4.12.42,
9.12.42, 22.3.43
Solms 3.12.44
Sorsche, Konrad 17.8.39, 25.8.39,
30.8.39, Mai/Juni 39, 13.9.39
Ritter von Speck, Hermann 11.6.40,
12.6.40, 18.6.40
Dr. Speidel, Hans, 14.6.40
Speidel, Wilhelm 7.1.40, 8.1.40,

W

Wachholtz 11.6.42
von Wachter, Karl-Friedrich 11.5.40,
  30.8.41, 29.9.41, 16.12.41
Wäger, Alfred 21.3.40, 1.4.40, 7.4.40,
  11.5.40, 14.5.40, 19.5.40, 21.5.40,
  22.5.40, 31.5.40, 4.10.41, 5.10.41,
  29.10.41, 7.11.41, 15.11.41, 16.11.41
Weckmann, Kurt 27.2.41, 21.5.41,
  28.6.41, 8.7.41, 15.7.41, 31.7.41,
  2.8.41, 24.8.41, 23.9.41, 12.10. bis
  14.10.41, 17.10.41
von Wedel 28.8.39
von Wedel, Hasso 3.10.39
Freiherr von Weichs, Maximilian
  21.10.39, 23.10.39, 25.10.39,
  31.10.39, 29.11.39, 5.1.40, 9.2.40,
  2.3.40, 26.6.41, 27.6.41, 1.7.41, 4.7.
  bis 7.7.41, 11.7.41, 14.7.41, 15.7.41,
  18.7. bis 21.7.41, 24.7.41, 25.7.41,
  27.7. bis 2.8.41, 5.8. bis 22.8.41,
  24.8. bis 2.9.41, 4.9. bis 15.9.41,
  17.9.41, 18.9.41, 23.9.41, 6.10.41,
  9.10.41, 10.10.41, 12.10.41, 14.10.41,
  16.10.41, 24.10.41, 27.10.41, 30.10.
  bis 2.11.41, 4.11.41, 6.11.41, 7.11.41,
  9.11. bis 12.11.41, 14.11. bis
  16.11.41, 19.11.41, 22.11. bis
  25.11.41, 20.1. bis 1.2.42, 4.2.42,
  6.2.42, 11.2. bis 13.2.42, 15.2.42,
  19.2. bis 3.3.42, 5.3.42, 7.3.42, 9.3.
  bis 11.3.42, 15.3.42, 19.3.42, 20.3.42,
  25.3. bis 29.3.42, 31.3.42, 2.4. bis
  4.4.42, 25.4.42, 28.4.42, 1.5. bis
  4.5.42, 7.5. bis 16.5.42, 18.5.42,
  19.5.42, 21.5. bis 24.5.42, 30.5.42,
  1.6.42, 2.6.42, 4.6.42, 5.6.42, 8.6.42,
  9.6.42, 13.6.42, 14.6.42, 19.6.42,
  22.6.42, 24.6.42, 27.6. bis 15.7.42,
  20.7.42, 31.7.42, 2.2.43, 22.3.43
Weisenberger, Karl 18.7.41, 20.7.41,
  30.7.41, 27.8.41, 6.10.41, 8.10.41,
  19.10.41, 7.11.41
Weiß, Walter 27.5. bis 30.5.41, 28.8.41
Dr. Werkmeister, Karl 26.3.44
Werth 17.2.42
Wetzel, Wilhelm 10.4.40, 27.5.40,
  28.8.40, 15.7.41, 31.8.41, 3.9.41,
  27.9.41, 3.10.41, 25.10. bis 27.10.41,
  29.10. bis 31.10.41, 11.11.41, 14.11.

bis 19.11.41, 21.11.41, 23.11.41,
  25.11.41, 27.11. bis 1.12.41, 3.12.41,
  6.12. bis 8.12.41, 10.12.41, 13.12.41
Weyer, Peter 30.1.40, 9.4.40
Weygand, Maxime 31.1.41, 1.2.41
von Wietersheim, Gustav 28.11.39,
  30.5.40, 5.6.40, 6.6.40, 9.6.40, 10.6.
  bis 12.6.40, 8.3. bis 11.3.42, 14.3. bis
  16.3.42, 26.3.42, 27.3.42, 31.3.42,
  2.6.42, 20.6.42, 21.6.42, 2.7.42
(von) Wiktorin, Mauritz 17.8.39,
  27.8.39, 9.9.39, 31.3.40, 9.5. bis
  12.5.40
Wilhelm (Kronprinz) Lebensabriß,
  19.7.40
Wilhelm I. Lebensabriß, Kurzbiogr.
Wilhelm II. 15.5.40
Wilhelmina 15.5.40
Wilck, Hermann 27.5. bis 30.5.41,
  27.6.41, 19.8. bis 21.8.41
Winkelmann 14.5.40, 15.5.40
Winter, August 4.12.42, 1.3.43,
  22.3.43
Witthöft, Joachim 21.9.41, 3.10.41,
  5.10.41, 6.10.41, 29.10.41, 30.10.41,
  11.12.41, 12.12.41
von Witzleben, Erwin 31.1.41, 5.8.44,
  8.8.44
von Witzleben, Hermann 27.6.41,
  23.9.41, 6.10.41, 20.10.41
Wodrig, Albert 12.9.39, 15.9.39,
  16.9.39, 1.3.40, 19.3.40, 11.5.40,
  13.5.40, 23.7.44
Wolf 24.1.42
Wolff, Werner 30.8.41
Woroschilow, Kliment Efremonwitsch
  2.7.41
Wosch, Heinrich 8.8.41, 20.8.41, 1.5.42,
  2.5.42

Z

Zehler, Albert 22.1.42, 23.1.42, 25.1.42,
  26.1.42
Zickwolff, Friedrich 13.3.40, 21.3.40,
  20.1.42, 22.1.42, 30.1.42, 2.2.42,
  7.2.42, 12.2.42, 17.2.42, 2.3.42,
  16.3.42, 23.3.42, 4.4.42, 30.4.42,
  8.5.42
Zorn, Hans 5.2.40, 17.4.41, 2.8.41

INDEX OF PLACES

A

Aachen Einltg. Vorbereitg. Westfeldzug, 13.12.39, 27.3.40, 1.4.40, 16.5.40
Aandalsnes 20.4.40
Abessinien 6.2.41
Abbeville 21.5.40, 24.5.40, 2.6. bis 4.6.40, 15.6.40
Afrika 12.12.40, 31.1.41, 1.2.41, 30.3.41, 9.4.41, 10.4.41, 6.6.41, 14.11.41, 25.11.41, 6.12.41
Ägypten 12.12.40
Aidar 3.7.42, 8.7. bis 10.7.42
Aire 24.5.40
Aisne 7.6. bis 10.6.40, 12.6.40
Albanien 18.3.41, 30.3.41
Albertkanal 24.2.40, 10.5.40, 11.5.40
Aleksin 19.10.41, 21.10, 41, 9.11.41, 12.12.41
Alexandropolje 7.2.42, 8.2.42
Alexandrowka 26.1.42, 2.2.42, 11.2.42, 21.2.42, 13.5.42, 22.3.42
Alexandrowsk 20.2.42, 21.2.42, 14.5.42
Alexejewskoje 6.2.42
Allenstein 25.8.39, 30.8.39, 6.9.39, 1.10.39, 6.8.44
Amerika 21.9.39, 16.11.39, 5.1.40, 14.8.40, 3.12.40, 1.2.41, 12.3.41, 30.3.41, 27.5. bis 30.5.41, 6.6.41, 14.6.41, 14.11.41, 24.6.42
Amiens 24.5.40, 3.6.40, 5.6.40, 6.6.40
Amsterdam 13.5.40
Andelys 10.6.40
Andrejewka 20.5. bis 24.5.42
Andrenka 13.3.42, 15.3.42, 28.3.42
Angerburg 18.1.42, 24.1.42
Angers 22.7.40
Angulème 23.6.40
Antwerpen Einltg. Vorbereitg. Westfeldzug, 25.10.39, 26.10.39, 29.11.39, 2.12.39, 12.1.40, 16.1.40, 23.1.40, 25.1.40, 6.2.40, 24.2.40, 27.2.40, 3.3.40, 11.5. bis 13.5.40, 16.5. bis 21.5.40
Ardennen Milit. Vorbereitg. auf den Westfeldzug, 20.12.39, 22.12.39, 28.12.39, 12.1.40, Einltg. Offensive Westfeldzug
Ärmelkanal Milit. Vorbereitung auf den Westfeldzug, 21.5.41
Arras Lebensabriß, 21.5.40, 22.5.40
Artemowsk 20.1. bis 23.1.42, 29.1.42, 31.1.42
Arys 10.9.39
Asowsches Meer 11.2.42, 23.2.42, 14.3.42, 3.5.42, 4.5.42, 22.6.42, 28.6.42
Atlantik 18.12.39, 20.6.40, 28.6.40, 21.5.41, 6.6.41
Augustow 25.4.41

B

Babka 11.3. bis 15.3.42
Bachmatsch 31.8.41
Bachmut 7.2.42, 8.2.42, 11.2.42, 16.2.42, 24.2.42, 27.2. bis 1.3.42, 3.3. bis 5.3.42, 20.3.42, 12.5.42
Bad Godesberg 28.10.39
Bad Salzbrunn 14.6.39, 25.8.39
Bajewo 14.7.41
Balakleja 23.1. bis 27.1.42, 14.2.42, 16.2.42, 17.2.42, 13.5.42, 20.5.42, 22.5.42, 25.5.42
Balkan 3.12.40, 19.12.40, 27.3.41, 4.5.41, 17.5. bis 19.5.41
Baltikum Einltg. Rußlandfeldzug, 11.3.41, 30.3.41
Baranowicze 10.9.39, 25.6. bis 27.6.41, 3.7.41, 4.7.41
Baruth 3.12.44
Barwenkowo Überblick der Kriegshandlg. HGrS, 22.1. bis 25.1.42, 31.1.42, 11.2.42, 8.5.42, 18.5.42
Basel Milit. Vorbereitg. Westfeldzug
Bayern 10.6.42, 21.6.42
Beaumont 9.6.40
Beauvais 7.6.40, 8.6.40
Belaja 10.7.42

Belchau 1.10.39
Belchau, Burg Lebensabriß, Kurzbiogr.
Belgien 27.8.39, 3.10.39, Einltg. Vorbe-
reitg. Westfeldzug, 9.10.39, 11.10.39,
25.10.39, 6.11.39, 10.11.39, 16.11.39,
14.1.40, 1.2.40, 24.2.40, 8.4.40,
12.4.40, Einltg. Offensive Westfeld-
zug, 19.5.40, 27.5.40, 31.5.40,
14.12.40
Belgorod 7.2.42, 9.2.42, 10.2.42, 13.2.
bis 24.2.42, 10.3.42, 15.5.42
Belgrad 27.3.41
Belogorje 8.7.42
Belorußland Einltg. Rußlandfeldzug
Beloy 1.9.41, 26.9.41, 7.10.41
Bely Kolodes 9.6.42, 11.6.42
Bengasi 6.2.41
Bereka 14.5.42, 18.5.42, 19.5.42,
26.5.42, 22.3.43
Berekowaja 21.5.42
Beresina 27.6.41, 29.6.41, 1.7.41,
3.7.41, 4.7.41, 6.7.41, 7.8.41, 8.8.41
Beresinasümpfe 27.3.41, 14.5. bis
16.5.41
Berestowaja 16.2.42, 14.5.42, 15.5.42,
22.5.42
Bergues 30.5.40, 2.6.40
Berlin Lebensabriß, 17.8.39, 24.8.39,
27.8.39, 30.8.39, 23.9.39, 28.9. bis
30.9.39, 3.10.39, 4.10.39, 21.10.39,
24.10.39, 28.10.39, 31.10.39,
1.11.39, 4.11.39, 6.11.39, 18.11. bis
22.11.39, 30.11.39, 8.12.39, 15.12.39,
16.12.39, 23.12.39, 7.1.40, 15.1.40,
23.1.40, 11.2.40, 23.2.40, 12.3.40,
15.3.40, 27.3.40, 27.4.40, 2.5.40,
9.7.40, 12.8.40, 13.8.40, 11.9.40,
20.9.40, 11.11.40, 3.12.40, 21.12.40,
24.2.41, 7.3. bis 10.3.41, 15.3. bis
18.3.41, 26.3.41, 27.3.41, 9.4. bis
15.4.41, 18.4.41, 17.5. bis 19.5.41,
24.5. bis 26.5.41, 31.5. bis 3.6.41,
7.6. bis 9.6.41, 20.6.41, 30.7.41,
22.12.41, 25.12.41, 24.1.42, 10.4. bis
22.4.42, 25.4.42, 23.6.42, 14.7.42,
15.7.42, 2.2.43, 22.2.43, 2.3.43,
22.3.43, E Aug. 43, A Sept. 43,
22.10.43, 24.1.44, 18.10.44, 25.4.45,
Kurzbiogr.
Berlin-Dahlem Lebensabriß
Berlin-Spandau Lebensabriß, Kurzbiogr.
Berlin-Wilmersdorf Kurzbiogr.

Beshezk 15.10.41, 19.10.41, 26.10.41
Bessarabien 28.6.40
Bethune 24.5.40, 9.6.40, 10.6.40,
12.6.40
Bialowicer Heide 16.9.39, 27.6.41,
1.7.41
Bialystok Lebensabriß, Überblick
Kriegshandlg. HGrN, 10.9.39,
12.9.39, 20.9.39, 2.10.39, 25.6.41,
28.6. bis 30.6.41, 8.7.41, 14.9.41,
Kurzbiogr.
Biarritz 9.8. bis 11.8.40
Bielsk 23.4.41
Bischkin 11.3.42, 13.3. bis 22.3.42,
24.3.42, 25.3.42, 30.4.42
Bjeloj 29.7.41, Anlagen
Bjely 14.7.41, 8.8.41
B. Koscha Anlagen
Blisnezy 31.1.42
Blois 15.6.40
Bobr 4.5.41, 17.5. bis 19.5.41
Bobruisk 27.6.41, 29.6.41, 4.7.41,
20.7.41, 24.7.41
Böhmen Lebensabriß
Bogorodizk 16.11.41
Bogorodizkaja 6.10.41
Bogutschar 7.7.42, 9.7. bis 11.7.42
Bokowskaja 11.7.42, 12.7.42
Bol Babka 18.3.42, 20.3.42, 16.5.42
Bolchow 4.10.41
Boldyrew 25.11.41
Bordeaux 26.6.40, 9.8. bis 11.8.40
Borissoglebsk 8.3.42
Borissow 25.6.41, 29.6.41, 7.7.41,
11.7.42
Borodino 6.10.41
Borowsk Anlagen
Borsna 31.8.41
Bourg et Comin 2.6.40
Boutschar 9.7.42
Brahe Überblick Kriegshandlg. HGrN,
2.9.39
Brandenburg, Provinz Lebensabriß
Breda 21.11.39, 27.11.39, 2.12.39,
16.1.40, 6.2.40, 13.5.40
Bremen 26.4.43
Bresle 7.6. bis 9.6.40
Brest Überblick Kriegshandlg. HGrN,
10.9. bis 12.9.39, 14.9. bis
17.9.39, 2.10.39, 17.6.40, 18.6.40,
20.6.40, 28.6.40, 22.6 bis 27.6.41,
26.8.41

Kritschew 12.8.41, 13.8.41, 20.8.41,
  Anlagen
Krojanke 26.8.39
Krone 4.9.39
Kronstadt Einltg. Rußlandfeldzug
Kschen 28.6.42, 1.7.42, 3.7.42, 10.7.42
Kulewka 1.7.42
Kulm 3.9.39, 4.9.39, 6.9.39
Kulmer Land Mai/Juni 39, E Juli 39,
  4.9.39
Kupjansk Überblick Kriegshandlg.
  HGrS, 19.5.42, 22.5.42, 25.5.42,
  18.6.42, 22.6.42, 23.6.42, 27.6.42
Kursk 8.10.41, 20.10.41, 22.10.41,
  24.10.41, 27.10.41, 31.10. bis
  2.11.41, 4.11.41, 11.11.41, Überblick
  Kriegshandlg. v. Moskau HGrM,
  9.12. bis 12.12.41, Überblick Kriegs-
  handlg. HGrS, 19.1.42, 20.1.42,
  24.1.42, 1.2.42, 13.2.42, 19.2.42,
  21.2.42, 1.3.42, 9.3.42, 10.3.42,
  11.5.42, 15.5.42, 14.6.42
Kusino Anlagen
Küstrin Lebensabriß, Mai/Juni 39,
  25.8.39, Kurzbiogr.
Kutno 12.9.39, 16.9.39, 27.9.39

L

La Baule 30.7.40, 1.9.40
Ladogasee 30.10.41
Laeken 28.5. bis 30.5.40
La Fére 6.6.40
Lama 30.10.41, 31.10.41, 11.11.41,
  16.11. bis 18.11.41, 10.12.41,
  12.12.41, 13.12.41, Anlagen
Langemarck 31.5.40
La Rochelle 28.7.40
Laski 17.2.42, 21.2.42
Latschino 18.12.41
Lauenburg 28.4.45
Le Bourget 13.6.40, 14.6.40
Le Havre 8.6.40
Le Mans 10.6.40, 15.6.40
Lemberg 10.9.39, 20.9.39
Leningrad Einltg. Rußlandfeldzug,
  1.2.41, 30.3.41, 6.7.41, 28.7.41,
  31.7.41, 15.8.41, 22.8.41, 28.8.41,
  24.9.41, 25.9.41, 28.9.41
Lensahn Lebensabriß, 23.4.45,
  Kurzbiogr.

Lepel 8.7.41
Les Bouleaux 30.5.40
Le Touquet 4.6.40
Libyen 12.12.40, 5.1.41, 31.1.41,
  26.2.41, 18.3.41, 21.5.41, 6.6.41,
  14.6.41, 22.11.41
Lichwin 15.12.41, 16.12.41
Lida 27.6. bis 29.6.41
Lietzen 28.8.41
Lille 27.10.39, 21.5.40, 23.5.40,
  26.5.40, 28.5.40, 31.5.40, 2.6.40,
  3.6.40
Liman 9.3.42, 10.3.42, 5.7.42, 31.7.42
Lipjagi 1.7.42
Lipsk 25.4.41, 21.5.41
Lissitschansk 10.7.42
Litauen 11.3.41, 14.6.41
Liwny 11.11.41, Überblick Kriegs-
  handlg. v. Moskau HGrM, 8.12.41,
  12.12.41, 3.3.42, 5.3.42, 10.3.42,
  3.7.42, 5.7.42, 31.7.42
Lochwiza 7.9.41, 12.9.41, 13.9.41,
  15.9.41
Loire 14.6. bis 19.7.40, 21.6.40, 7.7.40
Lötzen 25.8.39, 10.9. bis 12.9.39,
  29.9.39
Lomza Überblick Kriegshandlg. HGrN,
  4.9.39, 5.9.39, 9.9.39, 11.9.39
Lorient 21.6.40
Losowaja 25.1. bis 28.1.42, 1.2.42,
  18.2.42, 22.2.42, 23.2.42, 23.5.42
Losowenka 26.5.42
Löwen 11.5. bis 13.5.40
Lübeck 28.4.45
Lublin 11.9.39
Ludwigslust Lebensabriß
Lukow 15.9.39
Luschnicha Anlagen
Lüttich 25.10.39, 29.11.39, 5.1.40,
  6.1.40, 9.2.40, 2.3.40, 13.3.40,
  21.3.40, 1.4.40, 7.4.40, 10.5.40,
  11.5.40, 13.5.40, 14.5.40, 17.5.40,
  18.5.40, 20.5.40
Luxemburg 21.10.39
Luzarches 9.6.40, 10.6.40
Lys 23.5.40, 25.5.40

M

Maas 25.10.39, 1.11.39, 11.11.39,
  21.11.39, 7.1.40, 9.1.40, 12.1.40,

Ratibor Kurzbiogr.
Ratschino 2.8.41, Anlagen
Rembertow 21.6.41
Repiewka 5.7.42
Retschinza 18.8.41, 19.8.41, 22.8.41
Rhein 21.10.39, 25.10.39, 28.12.39,
 23.1.40, 13.3.40, 30.4.40, 16.6.40,
 28.6.40
Rheinberg 13.1.40
Rjasan 9.10.41, 11.11.41, 20.11.41, An-
 lagen
Rjashsk 25.11.41
Rjetschitza 26.7.41, 30.7.41
Rochefort 17.6.40
Roermund 6.2.40
Rogatschew 3.7. bis 5.7.41, 8.7.41,
 15.7.41, 26.7.41, 29.7. bis 31.7.41,
 9.8.41, 25.11.41
Romilly 12.6.40
Romny 7.9.41, 9.9.41, 10.9.41, 12.9.41,
 Anlagen
Roslawl Lebensabriß, 10.7.41, 14.7.41,
 16.7.41, 27.7.41, 30.7.41, 1.8. bis
 5.8.41, 7.8.41, 8.8.41, 17.8.41,
 19.8.41, 21.8.41, 27.8.41, 28.8.41,
 30.8.41, 5.10.41, 6.10.41, Kurzbiogr.,
 Anlagen
Rossosch 7.7.42, 10.7.42
Rostow 30.11.41, 2.12.41, 30.1.42,
 10.3.42, 10.6.42, 20.6.42, 22.6.42,
 12.7.42
Rotterdam 16.1.40, 24.2.40, 12.5.40,
 15.5.40
Rouen 7.6. bis 10.6.40
Rowno 26.3.42
Rozan Überblick Kriegshandlg. HGrN,
 3.9.39, 23.6.40
Rschew 6.10.41, 8.10.41, 9.10.41,
 12.10.41, 14.10.41, 9.12.41, 10.12.41,
 Anlagen
Rshawa Überblick Kriegshandlg. HGrS
Rubeshnoje 19.3.42, 24.3.42
Ruhrgebiet 9.10.39, 25.10.39, 23.11.39,
 E April 44
Rumänien 14.8.40, 3.12.40, 26.3.41,
 30.3.41, 20.1.42
Rusa 7.12.41, 14.12.41, Anlagen
Rußland Geleitwort, 22.8.39, 29.9.39,
 30.11.39, 13.3.40, 28.6.40, 14.8.40,
 3.12.40, 2.1.41, 31.1.41, 1.2.41,
 10.2.41, 27.3.41, 30.3.41, 27.5 bis
 30.5.41, 5.6.41, 14.6.41, 20.6.41,

25.7.41, 15.9.41, 4.12.41, 27.2.42,
 9.7.44
Ryasan 23.11.41, 25.11.41
Rybinsk 26.10. bis 28.10.41, Anlagen

S

Saarbrücken 16.6.40
Sachsenhausen 23.7.44
Sagorsk 11.11.41
Saloniki 11.11.40
Samara 22.2.42, 28.2. bis 3.3.42, 5.3.42,
 11.3.42, 18.3. bis 23.3.42
Sambre 17.5.40
San 19.9.39, 20.9.39
Sapunhöhen 18.6.42, 28.6. bis 30.6.42
Sawidowo 11.11.41
Sawinzy 21.5. bis 25.5.42, 27.5.42,
 30.5.42, 3.6.42, 22.6.42
Schara 29.6. bis 1.7.41
Schat 5.12.41
Schawrowo 12.3.42
Schebelinka 7.3.42, 8.3.42, 11.3.42
Schelde 10.5.40, 19.5. bis 22.5.40
Schildberg Anlagen
Schklow 7.7.41, 9.7.41
Schlesien Einltg. Polenfeldzug
Schötzow Lebensabriß, 1.8.44
Schtschigry 20.1.42, 25.1.42, 1.2.42,
 1.7.42
Schwarzes Meer 14.6.41, 21.3.42,
 20.5.42
Schweden 14.6.41
Schwetz 2.9.39, 4.9.39, 6.9.39
Sedan 16.1.40, 13.5.40, Anlagen
Seligersee 7.11.41
Seine 7.6. bis 12.6.40, 13.6.40, 15.6.40,
 7.7.40
Selency Lebensabriß
Semljansk 11.7.42
Semmering 16.1.42
Senne 19.4.40
Sennelager 27.3.40
Senno Anlagen
Serbien 9.4. bis 10.4.41, 17.4.41,
 18.9.40, 1.10.40
Serpuschow 6.10.41, 13.10.41, 25.11.41,
 27.11.41, Anlagen
Serrant 17.8. bis 18.8.40, Bild
Sewastopol Überblick Kriegshandlg.
 HGrS, 23.1.42, 27.1.42, 26.2. bis